Morocco Handbook

Julius Honnor

Come to Morocco for its elusive magic and exotic mystery and you will probably leave with more prosaic, yet intimate, human memories: kids playing football in a dusty square, a blind man selling bunches of fresh mint, or some good-natured banter with a *babouche* seller in the local souk. The romantic image is real enough, but this is also a viscerally lived-in place, a seething mass of humanity and inhumanity, of sounds and colour and pungent smells.

Morocco is rewarding and remarkably good value as a destination for walking, surfing and yoga; for aimless exploring or for focused lazing. But whatever you're doing here, it's the nature of the place itself that gets deepest into the pores of your skin. So close to Europe, yet so very different, it has dark, dank alleys as well as magnificent desert sand dunes, dirty tanneries as well as soaring mountains and secret valleys.

The depth of experience in the detail is part of the extraordinary attraction of the country. Once you leave the sumptuous luxury and the dazzling intricacy of your riad behind, no guidebook can ever tell you about the mass of life around every medina corner, or the views from every bend in the road. And the near impossibility of knowing it all just adds to the seduction of trying.

THIS PAGE Looking out from the Medersa Bou Inania, Fès
PREVIOUS PAGE Stock up on Moroccan crafts, like *babouches* (slippers), at a Marrakech souk

Don't miss...

Atlantic Ocean

Casablanca

El Jadida

Oualidia

Safi

Essaouira ②

Marrakech ①

Jbel
Toubkal ▲
(4167m)

Tiz

Oua

Agadir

Anti-Atlas

⑦ Tafraoute

Mirleft

Sidi Ifni ⑧

T

N

50 km

50 miles

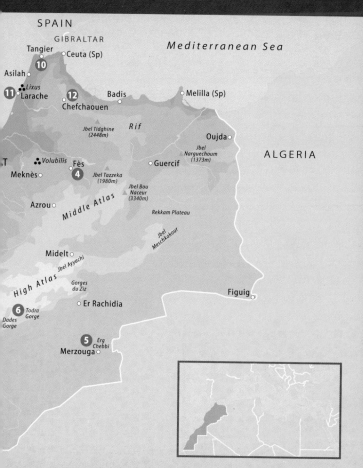

Try some snails at a food stall in Jemaâ el Fna square, Marrakech

Itineraries for Morocco

There's a lot of Morocco and trying to do too much in too short a time is a recipe for an unsatisfying trip. Also bear in mind that journeys that appear relatively quick on a map can take far longer than you might imagine. This is especially true of routes that cross the Atlas mountains, where precariously perched switchbacks, wandering goats, fossil sellers and locals carrying absurd loads on decrepit bikes with no brakes or lights will inevitably slow you down. History and geography have created enormous variety in the country. It's possible to sample cities, mountains, coast, desert, Arabic and Berber cultures, and French and Spanish colonial influences, as well as surfing, skiing, trekking and whitewater rafting. Just make sure you've left enough time to sip mint tea and watch the sun set.

ITINERARY ONE: 1 week
Marrakech, Atlantic coast, High Atlas and imperial cities

If you have a week, you could discover Marrakech, with a side trip to the coast, or into the Atlas Mountains. Alternatively, you could head to Fès and Meknès, the main imperial cities, and see something of the Middle Atlas.

You'll need at least three nights to soak up the sights, sounds and smells of Marrakech. Essaouira, on the coast, is a relatively easy side trip, the calm of the Atlantic contrasting well with the rush of the Red City.

Intricate *zellige* tiles decorate Morocco's ancient walls

Morocco's rugged Atlantic coast has some superb surfing spots

Or you could spend the rest of your week n the High Atlas. Day trips from Marrakech re possible or there are plenty of sleeping ptions if you want to do some short walks n the hills. Three suggested routes include: o to the Ourika Valley; the Taroudant road a Tin Mal and Tizi-n-Test; or to the Tizi-n-ichka Pass and Telouet.

The imperial cities of Fès and Meknès are good alternative to Marrakech. They are ss visited but offer an increasing array of sitor comforts such as riad accommodation.

RAVEL TIP

medinas, don't fight the inevitability getting lost; instead use the position the sun to roughly orientate yourself.

TRAVEL TIP

Riads will usually send someone to meet you at the airport – a good reason to spend your first night in one.

You could also use Fès as a base to visit the ancient Roman city of Volubilis and the cedar forests of the Middle Atlas.

Some flights arrive in Agadir, which is not a special destination in itself but a good base for a surfing or driving holiday in southwest Morocco. In a week you could cover Taroudant, the prehistoric rock carvings of the Akka area, Sidi Ifni and Mirleft and the Anti-Atlas around Tafraoute. There would be plenty of time for the beach, too.

Flying or sailing into Tangier, there are some attractive options in the north of

Fishing boats moored in the harbour at Essaouira

Morocco. Tangier itself warrants a couple of days, though after that you may want to get away to the calm prettiness of Asilah, or the rather more rugged Larache on the Atlantic coast. Alternatively, Tetouan's labyrinthine medina would make a good stop en route to Chefchaouen, from where there are good walks.

ITINERARY TWO: 2 weeks
Cities and mountains

With two weeks, you could do a circuit of the major cities, and a week either trekking in the mountains or taking in some of the places on the southern side of the Atlas – the Draâ and Dadès valleys, or maybe Taroudant and Tafraoute, close to Agadir.

TRAVEL TIP
Consider spending double for both front spaces in a shared taxi for the most comfortable ride.

A complete circuit around the Atlas could take you from Marrakech to Fès by train and then back via the Dadès and Todra gorges, stopping for a camel trek in the sand dunes, either in Merzouga or Zagora. It's just about possible to do this by public transport, but a car makes it much easier. If you're in a hurry and have your own transport you could travel from Fès to Marrakech in four days, although a week would make it a more pleasant experi-

Rich green vegetation sparkles against the bare pink rocks of the Dadès and Todra gorges

TRAVEL TIP

ring an old mobile and buy a Moroc-
an sim card for it. Make more than
couple of Moroccan calls and it will
robably save you money.

nce. Alternatively, it's possible to visit the
ighlights south of the Atlas as part of an
rganized trip from Marrakech.

You could also do a circuit that combines
Rabat, El Jadida, Essaouira and Marrakech
with walking in the High Atlas. Or you
could visit Tangier and the northwest along
with Rabat, Fès and Meknès, with time to
visit some more out-of-the-way places,
such as the small spa town of Moulay
Yacoub, as well as Larache and Asilah.

ITINERARY THREE: 3-4 weeks
Walking tours and coastal resorts

A three- or four-week trip will enable you
to get to know parts of Morocco really
thoroughly, and maybe take a one- or
two-week organized walking tour up in the
High or Anti-Atlas.

For the hardy, the highlight of a three-
week trip might be five or more days
walking in the Vallée des Aït Bougmez,
south of Azilal. This could be combined
with time at one of the coastal resorts
(Essaouira or maybe Oualidia), or along
the southern valleys and gorges as far as
Merzouga. And you would still have time
to do some urban sightseeing in Marrakech, Fès or Casablanca.

The Hassan II Mosque in Casablanca is the third largest in the world after those at Mecca and Medina

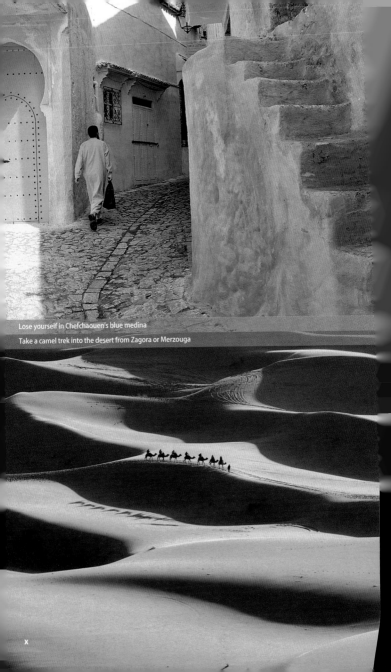

Lose yourself in Chefchaouen's blue medina

Take a camel trek into the desert from Zagora or Merzouga

x

Contents

Contents

Essentials

Planning your trip

Best time to visit Morocco

Morocco is a good destination all year round, although January and February can be a bit cold and miserable in the north; Tangier and Fès are not much fun in heavy rain. However, after a wet winter, spring is green and sprinkled with flowers in northern and central Morocco. Routes from Tangier are busy in summer with returning migrant workers from Europe in overloaded cars and are best avoided. Urban sightseeing is fine all year round, although in Marrakech and Fès the heat can be oppressive during the day from July to late September. If you are going to do the southern routes, such as the Dadès and Draâ valleys, February and March are magnificent. Blossom fills the valleys, the days are bright and you won't suffer too much on public transport or driving.

Summer and autumn are good for walking and climbing in the High Atlas; spring can be too, though lingering snow often makes higher routes difficult unless you have good equipment. The Jbel Saghro, south of the High Atlas, is a winter walking destination, as are the Anti-Atlas. Windsurfers and surfers will find winds on the Atlantic coast are stronger in summer, but the swell is bigger in winter.

Desert and pre-desert areas are mostly dry and hot but, from December to February, are also extremely cold at night. On the other hand, mountain areas can get quite hot during the summer days. Occasional but heavy showers occur, turning dry riverbeds into dangerous flash floods, while snow blocks the passes of the High Atlas in winter.

Some of the major cities, in particular Casablanca, have high pollution levels, which can make life unpleasant, especially in summer.

What to do in Morocco

Ballooning

Drifting over the Haouz plain near Marrakech, with the Atlas Mountains rising out of the red earth, is a great way to get a sense of the importance of the Red City to the surrounding area. Marrakech-based Ciel d'Afrique (www.cieldafrique.info) organize hot-air balloon flights. Basic excursions involve leaving Marrakech around 0530 for a flight over the Jebilet, the hills north of Marrakech. A flight shared with other people will cost around €185.

Birdwatching

Home to 460 species, Morocco has the greatest diversity of birdlife north of the Sahara. There are coastal marsh and lagoon sites, and top destinations for birdwatchers include **Kariet Arkmane** and the **Oued Moulouya** (Nador), the lagoon of **Moulay Bousselham** north of Rabat, **Oualidia** and **Essaouira**. The reserve at **Tidzi**, south of Essaouira and the **Oued Massa National Park** (Agadir) are home to Morocco's rarest resident bird, the bald ibis. Once widespread in Central Europe, this bird nests alongside the gulls and lanner falcons at Oued Massa.

UK operators **Nature Trek**, T01962-733051, www.naturetrek.co.uk, and **Sunbird Tours**, T01767-262522, www.sunbirdtours.co.uk, offer several birding holidays to Morocco.

Camel trekking

Most of the hotels around **Erg Chebbi** will arrange treks, or there's **Désert et Montagne Maroc**, contactable via Dar Daïf guesthouse in Ouarzazate, or on T0524-854949, www. desert-montagne.ma. **Zagora** is another good place to arrange a trek. Apart from the quick camel ride into the dunes (especially popular at Merzouga), there are 2 options: the *méharée* and the *randonnée chamelière*. The *méharée* actually involves you riding the camel, the *randonnée chamelière* (camel hike) means you walk alongside the camels, which are essentially used as pack animals. In the former option, you can cover a lot more ground, riding for 4-5 hrs a day. A good organizer will lay on everything apart from sleeping bags, although blankets are generally available. The best time of year for treks in the south is Oct to Apr (although sandstorms are a possibility between Nov and Feb). On a 6-night camel hike out of Zagora you see a combination of dunes and plains, palm groves and villages, taking you from Zagora down to the dunes of Chigaga, with an average of 5 hrs walking a day.

Horse riding

The horse is the object of a veritable cult in Morocco. *Fantasias* – spectacular ceremonies where large numbers of traditionally dressed horsemen charge down a parade ground to discharge their muskets a few metres away from tents full of banqueting guests – are a great occasion to see Moroccan riding skills. The late King Hassan II assembled one of the world's finest collections of rare black thoroughbred Arab horses, and wealthy Moroccans are often keen for their offspring to learn to ride. Many towns have riding clubs, and national show-jumping events are shown on TV. If you'd like time in the saddle, see www.ridingtours.com. Also try the following: **La Roseraie** at Ouirgane, on the Taroudant road, T0544-439128, www.laroseraiehotel.com; **Palmeraie**

Golf Palace, Marrakech, www.pgp.co.ma; **Cavaliers d'Essaouira**, 14 km inland from Essaouira on the Marrakech road, next to restaurant **Dar Lamine**, T0665-074889 (mob).

Mountain biking

Areas popular with mountain bikers include **Tafraoute** in the Anti-Atlas and the region between the **Dadès Gorge** and **Toundoute**, north of Skoura. Clay washed onto the tracks by rain dries out to form a good surface for bikes. Most towns will have bike hire companies. **Unique Trails**, www.unique trails.com, and **Wildcat Adventures**, www. wildcat-bike-tours.co.uk, are UK-based operators running cycling trips to Morocco.

Skiing

Oukaïmeden (2600 m), an hour's drive up in the High Atlas south of Marrakech, is Morocco's premier ski resort. However, irregular snowfall dents Morocco's reputation as a ski destination. Falls of snow rarely exceed 20 cm and often melt quickly in the bright sun, only to refreeze, leaving a brittle surface. On the occasions when there is good snow, it can become busy, with Moroccans rushing down from Casablanca or Rabat.

The summit above the plateau is **Jbel Oukaïmeden** (3270 m). There is a ski-lift, and pistes range from black to green. Further east, in the High Atlas of Imilchil, the **Jbel Ayyachi** (3747 m) has some descents; good terrain for wilderness skiers.

Refuge of the Club Alpin Français, in Oukaïmeden, T0524-319036, www.ffcam.fr, hires out ski gear and should be able to advise on skiing conditions. **Royal Moroccan Federation of Skiing and Mountaineering**, Parc de la Ligue Arabe, Casablanca, T0522-203798, is another useful source of information. **Auberge Timnay**, T0555-583434, timnay@iam.net.ma, at Aït Ayyachi near Midelt, should also be able to provide information.

Packing for Morocco

A good rule of thumb is to take half the clothes you think you'll need and double the money. A backpack or travel pack (a hybrid backpack/suitcase), rather than a rigid suitcase, covers most eventualities and survives the rigours of a variety of modes of travel well. A lock for your luggage is strongly advised. Light cotton clothing is best, with a fleece or woollen jumper for evenings. Hikers will need comfortable walking boots that have been worn in. During the day you will need a hat, sunglasses and high-factor sun cream.

Surfing

Morocco is beginning to develop a serious surf industry, mainly led by Europeans who have set up surf camps, especially around Taghazout, north of Agadir. Away from the hotspots, there are also plenty of largely untapped surfing opportunities along the country's long Atlantic coastline.

In general, **northern Morocco** consists of a series of beach breaks interspersed with a few rocky points and reefs and, around the larger cities and towns, man-made jetties and groynes that marshal the sand. This region is generally overlooked by travelling surfers as it is colder and wetter than breaks further south, but it does hold a few gems. From Tangier down to Bouznika, huge stretches of sand see few surfers until the urban breaks of **Rabat**, home to one of Morocco's largest surf clubs as well as a river mouth left that can reel on and on. At **Mohammedia**, the points and reefs are popular with local body-boarders and surfers, with only the occasional traveller stopping for a few waves. **Casablanca** is a huge urban sprawl with some polluted breaks but, once past the shanty towns, the countryside opens up again and the undulating rocky coastline offers incredible opportunities. There are many unknown breaks between the points at **El Jadida**, **Safi** and **Immessouane**. From the now-busy line-ups at Immessouane, the landscape changes. The rugged coastline here is home to Morocco's most famous waves – spots like **Anchor Point** and **Killer Point** (see box, page 233). Below Agadir the desert south

beckons. Beaches expand, temperatures rise and the number of surfers drops off to virtually zero. Tracks lead to isolated, dried-up river mouths, while long expanses of beach breaks, some backed by cliffs, are only broken by the occasional points and reefs. Here a couple of Morocco's premium points exist. You won't find them listed in this guide, but they are out there for the adventurous to discover.

Trekking

There are considerable opportunities for walking in Morocco. The most popular area is the **Toubkal National Park** in the High Atlas. However, as roads improve and inveterate trekkers return for further holidays, new areas are becoming popular. Starting in the west, to the south of the High Atlas, the **Jbel Siroua**, page 244, east of Taroudant, is a plateau with pleasant spring walking. The **Western High Atlas**, page 104, is best from late Apr to Oct, with various loops up into the mountains. You will probably want to climb North Africa's highest peak, Jbel Toubkal (4167 m); the only problem is that the mountain has become almost too popular. South of Azilal, the beautiful **Vallée des Aït Bougmez**, page 118, is also becoming popular. For weekend trekkers, there are gentle walks along the flat valley bottom but the Aït Bougmez also makes a good departure point for tougher treks, including the north–south crossing of the west-central High Atlas to Bou Thraghar, near Boumalne and El Kelaâ

Hammams

A ritual purification of the body is essential before Muslims can perform prayers and, in the days before bathrooms, the 'major ablutions' were generally done at the hammam (bath). Segregation of the sexes is, of course, the rule at the hammam. Some establishments are only open for women, others are only for men, most have a shift system (mornings and evenings for the men, all afternoon for women). In the old days, the hammam, along with the local *zaouïa* or saint's shrine, was an important place for women to gather and socialize, and even pick out a potential wife for a son.

Very often there are separate hammams for men and women next to each other on the ground floor of an apartment building. A passage leads into a large changing room/post-bath area, equipped with masonry benches for lounging on and (sometimes) small wooden lockers. Here you undress under a towel. Hammam gear today is usually shorts for men and knickers for women. If you're going to have a massage/scrub down, you take a token at the cash desk where shampoo can also be bought.

The next step is to proceed to the hot room: five to 10 minutes with your feet in a bucket of hot water will have you sweating nicely and you can then move back to the raised area where the masseurs are at work. After the expert removal of large quantities of dead skin, you go into one of the small cabins or *mathara* to finish washing. (Before doing this, find the person bringing in dry towels so that they can bring yours to you when you're in the *mathara*.) For women, in addition to a scrub and a wash there may be the pleasures of epilation with *sokar*, a mix of caramelized sugar and lemon. Men can undergo a *taksira*, which involves much pulling and stretching of the limbs. And remember, allow plenty of time to cool down, reclining in the changing area.

Hotel hammams include **Riad El Fenn**, see page 65, with a *gommage* treatment that ends with two halves of a fresh orange being squeezed over your body and a jar of wonderful-smelling rosewater being poured over your head and face. The hammam at the funky **Riad El Cadi**, see page 67, has a small solar-heated pool and a jacuzzi you can dip into afterwards. Richard Branson's **Kasbah Tamadot**, see page 112, in Asni, has a hammam a few steps away from a lovely dark blue swimming pool.

des Mgouna. On this route, you have the chance to climb the region's second highest peak, **Irhil Mgoun** (4071 m).

The **Middle Atlas** is much less well known to walkers. Certain parts are quite a Hobbit land, especially between Azrou, page 173, and the source of the Oum er Rabi river, where there is beautiful walking in the cedar forests. Despite its proximity to the rich farmlands of Meknès and the Saïs Plain, this is an extremely poor region that would benefit from increased ecologically friendly tourism.

The best time of year for walking is Apr to Oct; in the high summer keep to the high valleys, which are cooler and where water can be obtained. Views are not as good in the High Atlas at the height of summer because of the haze. Camping or bivouacking is fine in summer but in autumn indoor accommodation is necessary, in refuges, shepherds' huts or local homes. The use of mules or donkeys to carry the heavy packs is common.

To organize your trip, you can either book through a specialist trekking operator in your home country or hope to find a guide available when you arrive. In popular trekking areas, such as Toubkal, guides can fairly easily be found in trailhead settlements.

Specialist maps and walking guides are useful but can be hard to find in Morocco. You may be able to buy some at the **Hotel Ali** in Marrakech. Classified guest rooms in rural areas now have the **GTAM** (Grande Traversée des Atlas Marocains) label of approval. Places where trekking guides can be arranged include: **Hotel Ali** in Marrakech (High Atlas); **Auberge Timnay** near Midelt (Middle Atlas and Jbel Ayyachi); and **Auberge Souktana**, Taliouine, near Taroudant (for Jbel Siroua).

If you are setting up a trek yourself, note that a good mule can carry up to 100 kg (approximately 3 rucksacks). A mule with a muleteer costs around 120dh per day; a good guide should be paid 250dh per day, a cook around 150dh. When buying food for the trek with your guide, you will have to buy enough for the muleteers, too. Generally, trekkers will consume about 100dh worth of food and soft drinks a day. If you do a linear trek rather than a loop, you will generally have to pay for the 'mule-days' it takes to get the pack animals back to their home village.

In order to fully appreciate the beauty of the Atlas, trekkers need to ensure that the walking is as comfortable as possible, and this includes finding ways to deal with dehydration and fatigue. As on any hill trek, a steady, regular pace should be maintained. A good trip leader will ensure you make an early start, to enjoy walking in the cool mornings. Vehicle pistes look alluring to walk on but are in fact hard on the feet. Keep to the softer edges or go for footpaths when possible. Gorges are not the easiest places to walk in, so your local guide should know of the higher routes, if there is one that is safe. Pay particular attention if your route involves some scree running; you don't want to leave the mountains on a mule because of a sprained ankle. If you are not used to walking at altitude, try to avoid high routes in the early stages of your trip. Ensure you pause if a dizzy feeling sets in. In villages that see a lot of tourists children will be on the lookout, ready to scrounge a dirham or a 'bonbon'. They may be useful in showing you the way through to the footpath on the other side of the settlement.

There are a few books on trek routes in English. Alan Palmer's *Moroccan Atlas* trekking guide (Trailblazer, 2010) has 44 trail maps; Des Clark's *Mountaineering in the Moroccan High Atlas* (Cicerone, 2011) concentrates on winter walking for the experienced mountaineer, covering 40 peaks over 3000 m. Experienced Atlas walker Hamish M Brown's new *The High Atlas* (Cicerone, 2012), covers 48 routes, details the area's culture and offers practical guidance.

You can also contact the **Royal Moroccan Federation of Skiing and Mountaineering**, Parc de la Ligue Arabe, Casablanca, T0522-203798.

Responsible travel

The tourism industry in Morocco is very important for the country's economy, and creates thousands of jobs. Many national parks, valuable archaeological sites and museums are funded by visitor entry fees, which in turn promote their protection. Additionally, some tour operators fund conservation and community projects. By earning from tourism, the poorer people who rely on the land for their livelihoods are more likely to protect their environments for the benefit of tourism, and these projects are well worth supporting.

10 ways to be a responsible traveller
There are some aspects of travel that you have to accept are going to have an impact, but try to balance the negatives with positives by following these guidelines to responsible travel.

• **Cut your emissions** Plan an itinerary that minimizes carbon emissions whenever possible. This might involve travelling by train, hiring a bike or booking a walking or canoeing tour rather than one that relies on vehicle transport. See opposite page for details of carbon offset programmes. Visit www.seat61.com for worldwide train travel.

• **Check the small print** Choose travel operators that abide by a responsible travel policy (if they have one it will usually be posted on their website). Visit www.responsibletravel.com.

• **Keep it local** If travelling independently, try to use public transport, stay in locally owned accommodation, eat in local restaurants, buy local produce and hire local guides.

• **Cut out waste** Take biodegradable soap and shampoo and leave excess packaging, particularly plastics, at home. The countries you are visiting may not have the waste collection or recycling facilities to deal with it.

• **Get in touch** Find out if there are any local schools, charities or voluntary conservation organizations that you could include in your itinerary. If appropriate, take along some useful gifts or supplies; www.stuffyourrucksack.com has a list of projects that could benefit from your support.

• **Learn the lingo** Practise some local words, even if it's just to say 'hello', 'thank you' and 'goodbye'. Respect local customs and dress codes and always ask permission before photographing people – including your tour guide. Once you get home, remember to honour any promises you've made to send photographs.

• **Avoid the crowds** Consider travelling out of season to relieve pressure on popular destinations, or visit a lesser-known alternative.

• **Take only photos** Resist the temptation to buy souvenirs made from animals or plants. Not only is it illegal to import or export many wildlife souvenirs, but their uncontrolled collection supports poaching and can have a devastating impact on local populations, upsetting the natural balance of entire ecosystems.
CITES, the Convention on International Trade in Endangered Species (www.cites.org) bans international trade in

around 900 animal and plant species, and controls trade in a further 33,000 species. Several organizations, including WWF, TRAFFIC and the Smithsonian Institution have formed the Coalition Against Wildlife Trafficking (www.cawtglobal.org).

• **Use water wisely** Water is a precious commodity in many countries. Treating your own water avoids the need to buy bottled water which can contribute to the build-up of litter.

• **Don't interfere** Avoid disturbing wildlife, damaging habitats or interfering with natural behaviour by feeding wild animals, getting too close or being too noisy. Leave plants and shells where you find them.

Code green for hikers
• Take biodegradable soap, shampoo and toilet paper, long-lasting lithium batteries and plastic bags for packing out all rubbish.
• Use a water filter instead of buying bottled water and save fuel at remote lodges by ordering the same food at the same time. Only take a hot shower if the water has been heated by solar power.
• If no toilet facilities are available, make sure you are at least 30 m from any water source.
• Keep to trails to avoid erosion and trampling vegetation. Don't take short cuts, especially at high altitude where plants may take years to recover.

Code green for surfers
• Help conserve underwater environments by joining local clean-ups or collecting data for Project AWARE (www.projectaware.org).

• Choose resorts that properly treat sewage and wastewater and support marine protected areas.
• Avoid handling, feeding or riding on marine life.
• Never purchase marine souvenirs.
• Don't order seafood caught using destructive or unsustainable practices such as dynamite fishing.

How should I offset my carbon emissions?
Carbon offsetting schemes allow you to offset greenhouse gas emissions by donating to various projects, from tree planting to renewable energy schemes. Although some conservation groups are concerned that carbon offsetting is being used as a smoke-screen to delay the urgent action needed to cut emissions and develop alternative energy solutions, it remains an important way of counterbalancing your carbon footprint.

For every tonne of CO_2 you generate through a fossil fuel-burning activity, such as flying, you pay for an equivalent tonne to be removed elsewhere through a 'green' initiative. There are numerous online carbon footprint calculators (such as www.carbonfootprint.com). Alternatively, book with a travel operator that supports a carbon offset provider like TICOS (www.ticos.co.uk) or Reduce my Footprint (www.reducemyfootprint.travel).

It's not all about tree-planting schemes. Support now goes to a far wider range of climate-friendly technology projects, ranging from the provision of energy-efficient light bulbs and cookers in the developing world to large-scale renewable energy schemes such as wind farms.

Getting to Morocco

Air

The main international airports in Morocco are **Aéroport Marrakech Menara**, page 46; **Aéroport Casablanca Mohammed V**, page 305, **Aéroport Agadir Al Massira**, page 228 and **Aéroport Tangier Ibn Battouta**, page 342. There are also some international flights to **Aéroport Les Angads**, 15 km from Oujda; **Aéroport Charif Al Idrissi**, Al Hoceïma; **Aéroport Fès Saïss**, Fès; **Aéroport Hassan I**, Laayoune; **Aéroport Taourirt**, Ouarzazate, and **Aéroport Rabat-Salé**, 10 km from Rabat. All these airports are well connected by buses or *grands taxis*.

Major European airlines run frequent scheduled flights to Morocco's main airports at Casablanca-Mohammed V, Marrakech and Agadir, with most flights operating from France and Spain. National carrier **Royal Air Maroc (RAM)** (www.royalairmaroc.com) is reliable. Prices are similar to Air France and British Airways. The cheapest flights are usually with budget airlines EasyJet, Ryanair and Atlas Blue. Charter flights are another possible cheap option; run by package holiday companies, they fly mainly to Agadir.

From the UK and the rest of Europe
EasyJet (www.easyjet.com) flies daily from London Gatwick to Marrakech. **Ryanair** (www.ryanair.com) flies a few times a week from London Luton, also to Marrakech, and to Fès from London Stansted on Thursdays and Sundays.

Budget airlines aside, options from the UK to Morocco include **Royal Air Maroc** (www.royalairmaroc.com), which flies daily from Heathrow to Casablanca. RAM also flies out of main western European airports. **Air France** (www.airfrance.com) flies out of Paris to Casablanca and Rabat.

Fly-boat It is possible to get a flight to Gibraltar, Almería or Málaga, and then continue by boat to Ceuta or Tangier in northwest Morocco, or Melilla or Nador further east (see Ferry, below).

From North America
RAM flies to Casablanca from Montreal and New York. (Flight time New York to Casablanca, six hours 40 minutes).

From Africa and the Middle East
RAM runs regular services between Casablanca and many African cities. From the Canary Islands (Las Palmas) there are direct flights to Agadir and Laayoune. Middle Eastern RAM destinations include Dubai, Jeddah and Riyadh.

Ferry

Shortest ferry crossings from Europe to Morocco are from Tarifa, Algeciras or Gibraltar to Tangier or Ceuta. Longer crossings run from Almería and Sète, France, to Melilla and Nador. Ceuta and Melilla are Spanish enclaves so you cross a land border in Africa. Algeciras to Ceuta is fast but the advantage is lost at the Fnideq land border crossing into Morocco. Algeciras to Tangier is the most convenient crossing, Tangier being the northernmost

Taking your car to Morocco

Foreigners are allowed temporary import of a private vehicle for up to six months in total (be it one or several visits) per calendar year. Documents required are car registration documents and a Green Card from your insurance company, valid in Morocco, which will be inspected at the border along with your International Driving Licence (or national licence). The car will be entered in the driver's passport and checked on leaving the country to ensure that it has not been sold without full taxes being paid. It should be noted that some car hire companies do not allow customers to take cars into Morocco from Europe. The minimum age of driving is 21. Car entry is not possible from Mauritania.

On arrival, complete customs form D 16 bis, called 'Declaration d'importation temporaire', and specify the intended duration of stay. Visitors arriving at the border without valid recognized insurance cover may take out a short-term policy available at any frontier post. A customs carnet is required for a trailer caravan but not for motor caravans. If using a vehicle or caravan of which you are not the owner, carry with you a letter of authorization signed by the owner. Customs officials may require a detailed inventory in duplicate of all valuable items but routine items such as camping equipment need not be listed.

point on the Moroccan rail network and (almost) the starting point of the autoroute down to Casa-Rabat. In the summer months, those with cars will find ferries booked solid months in advance, as Moroccans working in Europe return home to visit family.

When you leave Spain for Morocco, your passport is checked by the Spanish authorities before boarding. Moroccan border formalities are undertaken on board: you fill in a disembarkation form and have your passport stamped at a *guichet*, generally as you get on board. Leaving Morocco, you fill in an embarkation form and departure card, which are stamped by the port police before getting on the boat. (Various people will offer to sell you the police *fiches* but they can be found free when you check in.) When you travel from Spain to Spanish enclaves Ceuta and Melilla, this does not apply.

Websites providing details of services (boats and hydrofoils) include **www.tras mediterranea.es** and **www.frs.es**.

Algeciras to Tangier

The main ferry route between Spain and Morocco is the Algeciras–Tangier passenger and car service (note that it is booked solid for cars in summer and around Muslim feast days). Algeciras has regular bus services from Gibraltar and Málaga, both towns with cheap flights from the UK, and a train service from Madrid. The ferry terminal, near the town centre, has a ticket office and money-changing facilities. There are similar facilities in the Tangier terminal. The ferry takes two to three hours, the catamaran 30 minutes, and there are normally between six and 10 services a day, either way, with some seasonal variation. Be early for your ferry, allowing at least an hour to clear the police and customs, particularly in Tangier. Be cautious about scheduling onward journeys on the same day, in view of the delays. Check the Moroccan railways (ONCF) website, www.oncf.ma, for the latest train times.

One-way passenger fares including car are around €100, children from four to 12 years old are half price and under four-year-olds are free. It is cheaper to buy a return in Tangier than two singles, if applicable. Tickets can be bought at either terminal or at numerous agents in both towns. The ferries have adequate facilities for the short crossing, including bars, restaurants, lounges, as well as a bureau de change. Food and drinks are on the expensive side and can be paid for in dirhams or euros.

Arrival in Tangier Arriving by ferry in Tangier, generally from Algeciras, can be a pain in the neck. Getting off the boat and going through customs can take ages, and various hustlers will be on hand to misinform innocents abroad as they emerge from the ferry terminal. For a woman travelling alone, arrival by ferry in Tangier can be intimidating.

Passport formalities are accomplished on board. Once off the boat, there are various exchange facilities but ATMs are only available at banks in the city centre.

Onward transport options from Tangier are train (ONCF) or bus. Trains run from the Tangier-Moughougha station (also spelt Morora), out beyond the old bull ring and the city limits, 10 km away. Take a sky-blue *petit taxi*, or a Mercedes share taxi. Generally, there are four train departures a day from Tangier-Moughougha to Casa-Voyageurs in Casablanca. The night departure, around 2130, goes through to Marrakech, arrival 0800, and has couchettes.

Inter-city CTM buses for main northern Moroccan towns run from outside the port gates. If there is no departure to suit you, take a *petit taxi* (15dh) to the main bus station (*gare routière*), which is 2 km away. There are six-passenger Mercedes taxis here for Tetouan (20dh) and other destinations.

Algeciras to Ceuta

The Algeciras to Ceuta connection is cheaper and quicker than Algeciras to Tangier, but should you need to overnight, accommodation in Ceuta is more expensive than in Morocco. (Ferries for Ceuta are run by the same companies from the same terminal in Algeciras.) The crossing takes 55 minutes, with slightly fewer services on Sunday. Passenger fares one way are from €102 including car. It is possible to buy tickets at either terminal or from numerous agents.

Arrival in Ceuta Ceuta is a popular port. Once off the ferry, you take a bus to the border from Plaza de la Constitución in the town centre. Spanish customs is generally quick; the Moroccan customs can be slow for those with their own car. From Fnideq on the Moroccan side of the frontier, Mercedes taxis to Tetouan cost 20dh a head. Moroccan banks have exchange facilities near the frontier.

Gibraltar to Tangier

Direct services from Gibraltar run daily and take 2½ hours. Fares start at about €99. Day-tour travellers take precedence over booked return tickets, so be warned. There are now high-speed **hydrofoil** services, crossing time 1½ hours, from Gibraltar to Tangier, see www.frs.es.

Almería (and Málaga) to Melilla and Nador

Almería to Melilla is an eight-hour crossing, run almost every day by Transmediterranea. The service is much used by migrant workers originating from the eastern Rif. One-way passenger fares start around €174 including car. The Almería to Nador service is broadly similar, there being almost daily sailings in winter, up to 18 sailings a week in summer. A further service does the Málaga to Melilla run, generally leaving in the early afternoon and taking 7½ hours.

Arrival in Nador Buses and Mercedes taxis leave from a terminal at the end of the Avenue des FAR, close to the waterfront (buses for Melilla from here). There is another bus terminal (CTM and others) in the town centre, close to the Municipality.

Arrival in Melilla The Spanish-Moroccan border is best reached by bus from the central Plaza de España, 10 minutes' walk from the ferry terminus. The border can be crossed in five minutes on a good day. At peak times of year (Easter Week, end of August), the process can be much slower. You need to fill out a Moroccan entry card before getting to the passport window. Various people will try to sell you these, otherwise ask for one at the window and return to your place in the queue at the window. Once over on the Moroccan side at Beni Enzar, there are Mercedes taxis and a bus to Nador.

Sète to Nador or Tangier

Comanav runs car and passenger ferry services from Sète in the South of France to Nador and to Tangier. Book via www.southernferries.co.uk. Single fares including car from Sète to Tangier start at €200 but are more expensive in summer. These are relatively luxurious services, running daily between Tangier (leaving 1800) and Sète (leaving 1900), a journey of 36 hours. Return passenger fares from Sète to Nador start at €180, again depending on the time of year. The service runs every four days at the height of the season (June to September).

Train

Train travel to Morocco is a relatively cheap option and a convenient way to tie in a visit to Morocco with a short stay in Europe, though Interrail tickets are no longer valid in the country. **ONCF** Moroccan rail services can be checked on www.oncf.ma.

Transport in Morocco

When planning a trip in Morocco, remember that the distances are great and that long trips on buses can be tiring. Bus journeys are often excruciatingly slow, even over relatively short distances. To make maximum use of your time, especially if you don't mind dozing on a bus, take night buses to cover the longer distances. If you have sufficient funds, then there is always the option of internal flights – although these may not always fit in with your schedule. Public transport is reasonably priced, and the train network is good and being heavily invested in, although it doesn't cover the whole country. Car hire can be expensive; although you may be able to get a small car for 1800-2500dh a week, you still have petrol or diesel costs on top of this. In many places, however, a car enables you to reach places which are otherwise inaccessible.

Air

Royal Air Maroc (www.royalairmaroc.com) operates domestic flights, most routed via Casablanca and requiring waits in the airport. Cities served include Tangier, Marrakech, Agadir, Ouarzazate, Laâyoune and Dakhla. There are limited direct flights between Marrakech and Fès. There are flights to and from Laâyoune on most days. A flight from Oujda to Casblanca (one a week) cuts out a 10-hour train journey.

For **RAM** enquiries, call T089-000 0800. All major towns have RAM agencies, generally on the main boulevard.

Road

Bicycles and motorcyles
Mountain bikes, mopeds and sometimes small motorcycles can be hired in tourist towns. There is no shortage of mechanics to fix bikes and mopeds. Trains, buses and even *grands taxis* will take bikes for a small fee. Some European companies now run cycling holidays, with bikes being carried on vans on the longer stretches. Off-road biking is popular near Tafraoute in the Anti-Atlas and the Gorges du Dadès.

If you go touring with a bike or motorcycle, beware of the sun. Wear gloves and cover those bits of exposed skin between helmet and T-shirt. For motorcyclists, helmets are complusory, and *gendarmes* will be happy to remind you of the fact.

Riding a motorbike in Morocco is even more testing than driving a car. Watch out for stray pedestrians and note that vehicle drivers will not show you much respect. Where flocks of animals are straying across the road, try not to drive between a single animal and the rest of the flock, as it may well try to charge back to join the rest. Use your horn. If you are going to go off-road, wear boots and make sure your tyres are in tiptop condition.

Theft from bicycle paniers is a problem. Anything loosely attached to your bike will disappear when you are being besieged by a horde of children in an isolated village.

Bus
Domestic bus services are plentiful. Price variations are small, while the quality of service varies enormously. Broadly speaking, if the train, a **Supratours** bus or a *grand taxi* run to your destination, don't bother with the small bus companies. For early morning services it's worth getting your ticket in advance, also at peak times when many Moroccans are

No rules of the road

Driving in Morocco is hazardous. *Grands taxis*, buses and lorries thunder along, forcing oncoming lesser vehicles on to the hard shoulder, if it exists. Sometimes there is a tyre-splitting gap between tarmac and dusty edge. Pedestrians wander out into the road and cyclists stray into the fast lane. On poor roads, you may see Moroccan drivers holding a palm up to their windscreens. This is to reduce the risk of shattering due to stones shooting up from the wheels of oncoming cars.

People also seem to overtake in the most suicidal of places. You can effectively buy yourself a driving licence in Morocco, and the accident figures are appalling:

25.6 deaths per 1000 accidents per year in Morocco, as against 2.6 deaths per 1000 accidents in France. The Gendarmerie royale is having a crackdown, however, especially on speed limits, and 400dh fines may be levied on the spot.

Do not rush, go with the flow and take your time. Apart from Casablanca, Morocco's cities are not large, and you will soon be out on the calmer country roads. Here you will share the roads with numerous animal-drawn carts and pack animals. This makes for slow driving but can also be dangerous at night. Most roads lack catseyes and most agricultural vehicles and mule carts drive without lights.

travelling, like the end of Ramadan and around Aïd el Kebir (two months after the end of Ramadan). You will find that there is a man who helps stow luggage on the roof or in the hold, so have a couple of dirham coins handy for him.

In southern Morocco, the safest and most comfortable service is also with Supratours. Next best is the **CTM**, Compagnie de transport marocain (white buses with blue and red stripes). Often (but not always) their services run from stations away from the main *gare routière* (inter-city bus station). This is the case in Casablanca, Fès and Marrakech, for example. For Tangier, the CTM station is just outside the port zone gates. For information (*renseignements*) on CTM services, try T0522-458881 or www.ctm.ma. Both Supratours and CTM buses usually run on time. As an example of prices, a single Marrakech to Essaouira costs 65dh with Supratours.

Local bus companies Other private bus companies are generally much slower, apart from a few *rapide* services – try **Trans-Ghazala**. There are regional companies, like the **SATAS**, which serves much of the south, and all sorts of minor companies with names like **Pullman du Sud**. While such buses get to parts that the CTM cannot reach, they are often slow. Bus terminals have a range of ticket windows (*guichets*), displaying destinations and times of departure. Several companies may serve the same destination and, as you head into the bus station, you may be approached by touts who will urge you to prefer one company over another. The main Casablanca bus station functions on this basis, to the extent that the ticket windows are practically out of business.

Safety Vehicles used by many private bus companies do not conform to high safety standards. Drivers are severely underpaid and, to make up for their low wages, may leave half-full, aiming to pick up extra passengers (whom they won't have to declare to their employers) en route. This makes for a slow, stop/go service. On routes worked by several companies, drivers race each other to be first to pick up passengers in the next settlement. Given the poor condition of the vehicles and the often narrow roads, accidents are inevitable.

City buses Most towns have city buses which provide great opportunities for local pickpockets when crowded. Casablanca buses are terrible, so have 20dh notes ready for short red-taxi runs. The orange **Alsa** buses in Marrakech are fine.

Car hire → *See also box, page 17.*

As distances are great, having a car makes a huge difference to the amount of ground you can cover. All the main hire car companies are represented and there are numerous small companies, which vary hugely in reliability. The Peugeot 205 is felt to be a more reliable small car, with slightly higher clearance and better road holding. A good deal would give you a Uno for 500dh a day, unlimited mileage, although some Marrakech agencies can be cheaper. 4WDs available in Morocco include the Suzuki Gemini (two people) and the Vitara (four people), at around 800dh per day; long-base Mitsubishi Pajeros (six people) are hired at 900-1000dh per day. Toyotas are said to be the best desert 4WDs. Landrovers are very uncomfortable for long cross-country runs on road, especially in summer without air conditioning. There is huge demand for hire cars during the Christmas and Easter breaks. Always try to have the mobile phone number of an agency representative in case of emergency. Many cars do not as yet use unleaded petrol – if you have one that does, you will find that not all petrol stations have unleaded, especially in the south. Always drive more slowly than you would in Europe.

Remember that you are responsible for damage if you take a car unsuited to the piste into areas suitable only for 4WDs. Regarding insurance, the best agencies will provide all risk insurance. Check for scratches and especially tyre condition (this includes spare tyre), presence of jack and warning triangle, working lights and safety belts. When hiring an all-terrain vehicle, try to ascertain that the agency you are hiring from has a reliable, well-maintained fleet. Make sure that the vehicle will go into four-wheel drive easily.

In general, you will need dirhams to pay, as only the larger agencies take credit cards. They will take an imprint of your credit card as a guarantee. See individual city and town listings for details of companies.

Car insurance A good agency will have agreements with garages across Morocco for repairs. The garage will talk to the agency about the nature of the repairs, and the matter will be handled. If the damage is your fault (eg because you have taken the car onto rough tracks in breach of contract), you will be responsible for covering the cost of repairs. In the case of accidents, you have to get a *constat de police* (a police report), which is a document drawn up by the police, stating whose fault the accident is. Depending on the type of insurance, the client pays a percentage of the cost of repairs. You can have a *sans franchise* (rental contract), which means that you will have nothing to pay, or with a franchise set at a certain level, that is a 50% franchise means that you pay 50% more than rental cost, so that in a case of an accident, you pay only 50% cost of repairs.

Petrol and other costs You may have to pay for the petrol already in the tank of your hire car. Usually, the car will be almost empty, and you fill up yourself. At the time of writing, diesel in Morocco is around 7.5dh per litre, petrol 10.5dh. Hire cars in Morocco generally run on petrol (*super*) rather than diesel. Lead-free petrol is *sans plomb*. A fill-up (*le plein*) for a Fiat Uno or a Clio costs around 400dh. In such a car, 250dh does the four-hour trip on winding mountain roads from Marrakech to Ouarzazate. A fill-up with diesel for a Pajero 4WD costs around 600dh, and on this the vehicle will do the 800-km trip from Marrakech to Zagora and back.

In remote areas, remember to fill up whenever possible, preferably at one of the larger petrol stations (Shell, Mobil, CMH, in most cities, Ziz in the South). There have been cases of petrol being watered down, with unfortunate results, in certain places. New-looking service stations in towns are best.

Should you need tyre repairs, prices vary. Expect to pay upwards of 50dh as a foreigner in a hurry in a small town, rather less if you have time to wait in some rural outpost.

Risky roads There are a number of dangerous stretches of road which you may have to deal with in your hire car. Much concentration is needed on the four-hour drive on the winding, mountainous N9, Marrakech to Ouarzazate, via the Tizi-n-Tichka. Fog and icy surfaces are possible in winter. There are roads which seem excellent, you drive fast and then meet sudden dips and turns, such as Ouarzazate to Skoura, Agdz to Nekob. The new N11, the Casablanca to Marrakech motorway, has much improved road transport between the two cities but care must be taken on the Rabat to Fès N1, especially as there are few crash barriers. In the Middle and High Atlas barriers are put across the road on routes to Azrou, Ifrane, Midelt and over the Tizi-n-Tichka and Tizi-n-Test when snow blocks roads.

Road accidents cost the State about US$1.2 billion a year, according to official figures. In 2009 nearly 4000 people were killed in Morocco on the roads.

Highway code The Moroccan highway code follows the international model. Speeds are limited to 120 kph on the autoroute, 100 kph on main roads, 60 kph on approaches to urban areas and 40 kph in urban areas. Speed restriction signs do not always follow a logical sequence. There are two types of police to be met on the roads: the blue-uniformed urban police and the grey-uniformed gendarmes in rural areas. The latter are generally stationed outside large villages, at busy junctions, or under shady eucalyptus trees near bends with no-overtaking marks.

The wearing of seat belts is compulsory outside the cities, and the gendarmes will be watching to see you're wearing them. It is traditional to slow down for the gendarmes, although as a foreigner driving a hire car you will generally be waved through. They will not, on the whole, ask for 'coffee money' from you. Note, however, that the police are empowered to levy on-the-spot fines for contravention of traffic regulations. Fines are now quite severe in response to the high number of fatal accidents due to careless driving.

Other highway code tips: red and white curb markings mean no parking; warning triangles are not compulsory – but highly useful; in the case of an accident, report to nearest gendarmerie or police post to obtain a written report, otherwise the insurance will be invalid.

Off-road driving In addition to well over 10,000 km of surfaced road, Morocco has several thousand kilometres of unsurfaced tracks, generally referred to as pistes. Some of these can be negotiated with care by an ordinary car with high clearance. Most cannot, however, and 4WD vehicles are increasingly popular for exploring the remote corners of Morocco.

Fans of 4WDs should plan their trips carefully, noting that bad weather can impede travel. Snow blocks mountain tracks in winter, rain and melt-water can make them impassable. Ask locals about conditions. In many areas, pistes are being upgraded – or are no longer well maintained, as they have been made superfluous thanks to the presence of a new tarmac road. However, not all road improvement works are of very high quality. A hard winter can leave mountain tarmac partly destroyed, or wash large quantities of rubble and clay on to the road surface.

If you are driving into remote areas, always travel with two vehicles. In the hostile desert environment, if things go wrong, there is nobody to get you out if you are by yourself. If you are unused to off-road vehicles, employ the services of a driver (around 300dh a day). He will know the routes well and be able to chat to locals and other drivers about the state of the tracks. If you don't have a driver and get a bit lost, you can always pick up a local hitchhiker who will show you the way. Outside the main tourist towns, he is unlikely to be a 'fake' guide. When out in wild country, never take an unknown piste if a storm is on its way or as night is falling. Check before you leave the names of villages on the way and remember that some tracks lead to abandoned mining operations rather than helpful hamlets. Do not go full tilt into a ford without checking the depth of the water first by wading in. You do not want to be stranded in an *oued* in full flood. Remember that progress will be slow, and that, after wet weather, you may have to dig/pull vehicles out. Distances tend to be measured in hours rather than in kilometres.

Car parking In towns, parking is fairly easy. Parking meters rarely function, and instead a sort of watchman, identified by blue overalls and a metal badge will pop up. Give him some spare change, say 10dh, when you return to your undamaged vehicle. At night, it is essential to leave your vehicle in a place where there is a night watchman (*le gardien de nuit*). All good hotels and streets with restaurants will have such a figure who will keep an eye out.

Hitchhiking
It is possible to hitchhike in Morocco. There are lorries which go to and from Europe, and drivers can sometimes be persuaded to take a passenger. In remote areas, vans and lorries may pick up passengers for a bargained price. However, don't count on hitching, as vehicles out in the sticks are generally packed with locals. Landrover taxis (jeeps) and Mercedes Transit are not run for hitchers – they are public transport with a price. Hitching is inadvisable for women travelling on their own.

Taxi
Long distance *grands taxis*, generally Mercedes 200 saloon cars, run over fixed routes between cities, or within urban areas between the centre and outlying suburbs. There is a fixed price for each route and passengers pay for a place, six in a Mercedes, nine in a Peugeot 504 estate car. Taxis wait until they are full. You may, however, feel rich enough to pay for two places in order to be comfortable at the front (and be able to wear a safety belt). In a Peugeot estate, the best places are undoubtedly at the front, or, if you are quite small, right at the back. The middle place in the middle row is probably the worst.

Between towns, *grands taxis* are quicker than trains or buses and, normally, only a little more expensive. Each town has a rank for *grands taxis*, generally, although not always, next to the main bus station. The drivers cry out the name of their destination and, as you near the taxi station, you may be approached by touts eager to help you find a taxi.

In mountain areas, the same system applies, although the vehicles are Mercedes transit vans (where there is tarmac) or Landrovers, which have two people next to the driver and 10 in the back.

Petits taxis are used within towns and are generally Fiat Unos and Palios. They are colour-coded by town (blue for Rabat, red for Casa, khaki for Marrakech, tasteful pistachio green in Mohammedia). Officially they are metered, with an initial minimum fare, followed by increments of time and distance. There is a 50% surcharge after 2100. A *petit taxi* may take up to three passengers. In Marrakech, Rabat and Casablanca, drivers generally use the meters; in Tangier they try to charge what they like. In some cities (notably Rabat and Casablanca, where taxis are in short supply) drivers allow themselves to pick up other passengers en route if they are going the same way, thus earning a double fee for part of the route. Taxi drivers welcome a tip – many of them are not driving their own vehicles and make little more than 100dh a day. In terms of price, a short run between old and new town in Marrakech will set you back 12dh. Casa Port station to Casa Voyageurs is about 12dh too.

Train

The **ONCF** (Office national des chemins de fer) runs an efficient though generally slowish service between major cities. There is 1900 km of railway line, the central node being at the railway town of Sidi Kacem, some 46 km north of Meknès. Coming into Casablanca airport, you can take the blue Bidhaoui shuttle train to Casa-Voyageurs station on the main north–south line. This line runs from Tangier to Marrakech, with significant stations being Kénitra, Sidi Kacem, Salé, Rabat, Casa-Voyageurs, Settat, and Benguerir. The ONCF's main west–east route does Casa-Voyageurs to Oujda, the main stations on this route being Rabat, Sidi Kacem, Meknès and Fès. A new fast double-decker service connects Casablanca with Fès in three hours 20 minutes. There are also frequent trains from Marrakech to Fès. ONCF timetables are available at all main stations and can be accessed at www.oncf.ma.

Prices and journey times
Prices are reasonable. A first-class single ticket, Marrakech to Fès, is 276dh, or 180dh in second class. Services between Casablanca and Rabat, depending on station and class, range form 32dh to 55dh. Casa-Voyageurs to Tangier is 175dh first class. In terms of time, Casablanca to Marrakech generally takes three hours; Casablanca to Rabat just under one hour; Rabat to Fès nearly four hours; Fès to Oujda is 5½ hours; Rabat to Tangier is 4¾ hours; Marrakech to Fès is around seven hours.

Train-bus link
Supratours run buses to connect with trains from a number of stations. Routes covered include Tnine Sidi el Yamami, just south of Asilah, to Tetoutan; Taourirt to Nador and Khouribga to Beni Mellal. From outside Marrakech station, Supratours has connecting buses to Ouarzazate, Essaouira, Agadir, Laâyoune and Dakhla. Sample prices as follows: Marrakech to Agadir 95dh, Agadir to Laâyoune 210dh, Marrakech to Ouarzazate 80dh.

Train classes
On the trains, first-class compartments are spacious and generally quieter than second class. Second-class rail fares are slightly more expensive than the CTM buses. You gain, however, in time saved, reliability and safety. Trains normally have a snack trolley.

Where to stay in Morocco

Morocco has a good range of accommodation to suit all budgets. There are several well-appointed business hotels in the main cities, luxurious places for the discerning visitor and clean basic hotels to suit those with limited funds. Independent travellers appreciate the growing number of *maisons d'hôte* or guesthouses (generally referred to as riads, see box, page 68), some very swish indeed, while, in the mountain areas, walkers and climbers will find rooms available in local people's homes. Modern self-catering accommodation is also sometimes available.

There is an official star rating system, although few hotels will boast about their membership of the one-, two- or even three-star categories. There does not appear to be very tight central control on how prices reflect facilities on offer. There are considerable variations in standards, and surprises are possible. Note, too, that breakfast is often not included in the room price – except in riads.

Cheap

At the budget end of the market are simple hotels, often close to bus or train stations. There may be a washbasin, sometimes a bidet. Loos and showers will usually be shared and you may have to pay for a hot shower. The worst of this sort of accommodation will be little better than a concrete cell, stifling in summer. The best is often quite pleasant outside summer, with helpful staff and lots of clean, bright tiling. Rooms often open on to a central courtyard, limiting privacy and meaning you have to leave your room closed when out. Outside the big tourist cities, such hotels have almost exclusively Moroccan customers. Although such hotels are generally clean, it may be best to bring a sheet with you if you're planning to use them a lot. Water, especially in the southern desert towns, can be a problem. Generally, there will be a public bath (hammam) close by for you to take a shower after a long bus journey.

Mid-range

More expensive one-star type hotels are generally in the new part of town (*ville nouvelle* neighbourhoods). Showers may be en suite, breakfast (coffee, bread and jam, a croissant, orange juice) should be available, possibly at the café on the ground floor, for around 20dh. Next up are the two- and three-star places. Most will be in the *ville nouvelle* areas of towns. Rooms will have high ceilings and en suite shower and toilet. Light sleepers need to watch out for noisy, street-facing rooms. Some of these hotels are being revamped, not always very effectively. In this price bracket are a number of establishments with a personal, family-run feel.

Expensive

Top hotels are generally run by international groups, such as Accor and Le Méridien. Upmarket hotels in Morocco can either be vast and brash, revamped and nouveau riche, or solid but tasteful and even discreet with a touch of old-fashioned elegance. The main cities also have large business hotels.

Riads and guesthouses

The big phenomenon of the late 1990s and 2000s in the Moroccan tourist industry has been the development of the guesthouse. Wealthy Europeans have bought old property in the medinas of Marrakech, Fès and Essaouira as second homes. Rather than leave the property closed for much of the year, the solution was to rent it out. See box, page 68.

Accommodation price codes

€€€€ over €140   €€€ €71-140
€€   €35-70   €   under €35

Prices are for double rooms. Singles are marginally cheaper. See page 36 for exchange rates.

Youth hostels (Auberges de jeunesse)

There are 11 hostels in all affiliated to HI, located in the cities (Casablanca, Rabat, Fès, Meknès and Marrakech, Oujda and Laâyoune) as well as Azrou (Middle Atlas) and Asni (High Atlas). Overnight charges are 20-40dh, with use of the kitchen 2dh. There is a maximum stay of three nights and priority is given to the under-30s. For information try the **Moroccan Youth Hostel Federation**, Parc de la Ligue arabe, Casablanca, T0522-220551. It is often better to go for cheap hotels, more conveniently located and with better toilets and showers. The Casablanca hostel was improved in 2002, the Fès hostel has had good reviews but is in the *ville nouvelle*, as is the Marrakech hostel. Both are convenient for the train station, but a long way from sights and old-town atmosphere.

Mountain accommodation

In the mountains, you can easily bivouac out in summer or, in the high mountains, sleep in a stone *azib* (shepherd's shelter). There are three main options for paid accommodation: floor space in someone's home, a gîte of some kind, or a refuge run by the **CAF** (Club Alpin Français). The refuges are shelters with basic dormitory and kitchen facilities. Rates depend on category and season but about 15-50dh per night per person is usual. The CAF can also be contacted via BP 6178, Casablanca, T0522-270090, and BP 4437, Rabat, T0537-734442.

In remote villages, there are *gîtes d'étape*, simple dormitory accommodation, marked with the colourful **GTAM** (Grande traversée de l'Atlas marocain) logo. The warden generally lives in the house next door. Prices here are set by the **ONMT** (tourist board), and the gîte will be clean if spartan. The board also publishes an annual guide listing people authorized to provide gîte type accommodation.

In mountain villages where there is no gîte, you will usually find space in people's homes, provided you have a sleeping bag. Many houses have large living rooms with room for people to bed down on thin foam mattresses. It is the custom to leave a small sum in payment for this sort of service. On the whole, you will be made very welcome.

Camping

There are campsites all over Morocco – the **ONMT** quotes 87 sites in well-chosen locations. Few sites, however, respect basic international standards. Security is a problem close to large towns, even if the site is surrounded by a wall with broken glass on top. Never leave anything valuable in your tent. Many campsites also lack shade, can be noisy and the ground tends to be hard and stony, requiring tough tent pegs. As campsites are really not much cheaper than basic hotels and, as even simple things like clean toilets and running water can be problematic, hotel accommodation is usually preferable. There are some notable exceptions however (see listings throughout the book).

Food and drink in Morocco

Moroccan cuisine → See page 472, for a glossary of food terms.

The finest of the Moroccan arts is possibly its cuisine. There are the basics: harira and bessera soups, kebabs, couscous, tagine and the famous *pastilla*: pigeon, egg and almonds in layers of filo pastry. And there are other dishes, less well known: gazelle's horns, coiling m'hencha and other fabulous pastries. The Moroccans consider their traditional cooking to be on a par with Indian, Chinese and French cuisine – though the finest dishes are probably to be found in private homes. Today, however, upmarket restaurants, notably in Marrakech, will give you an idea of how good fine Moroccan food can be. Moroccan cuisine is beginning to get the international respect it deserves, with new restaurants opening in European capitals. However, the spices and vegetables, meat and fish, fresh from the markets of Morocco, give the edge to cooks in old medina houses.

The climate and soils of Morocco mean that magnificent vegetables can be produced all year round, thanks to assiduous irrigation. Although there is industrial chicken production, in many smaller restaurants, the chicken you eat is as likely to have been reared by a small-holder. Beef and lamb come straight from the local farms.

In addition to the basic products, Moroccan cooking gets its characteristic flavours from a range of spices and minor ingredients. Saffron (*zaâfrane*), though expensive, is widely used, turmeric (*kurkum*) is also much in evidence. Other widely used condiments include a mixed all spice, referred to as *ra's el hanout* ('head of the shop'), cumin (*kamoun*), black pepper, oregano and rosemary (*yazir*). Prominent greens in use include broad-leaved parsley (*ma'dnous*), coriander (*kuzbur*) and, in some variations of couscous, a sort of celery called *klefs*. Preserved lemons (modestly called *bousera*, 'navels', despite their breast-like shape) can be found in fish and chicken tagines. Bay leaves (*warqa Sidna Moussa*, 'the leaf of our lord Moses') are also commonly employed. Almonds, much used in pâtisserie, are used in tagines too, while powdered cinnamon (Arabic *karfa*, *cannelle* in French) provides the finishing touch for *pastilla*. In pâtisserie, orange-flower water and rose water (*ma ouarda*) are essential to achieve a refined taste.

Eating times vary widely in Morocco. Marrakech gets up early – and goes to bed early, too, so people tend to sit down to dine around about 2000. Tangier takes a Spanish line, rising late, taking a siesta and eating late. Across the country, the big meal of the week is Friday lunch, a time for people to gather in their families. The main meal of the day tends to be lunch, although this varies according to work and lifestyle. As anywhere, eating out in plush eateries is a popular upper-income occupation. Locals will tend to favour restaurants with French or southern European cuisine, while Moroccan 'palace' restaurants are patronized almost exclusively by tourists.

Starters

Harira is a basic Moroccan soup; ingredients vary but include chick peas, lentils, veg and a little meat. Often eaten accompanied with hard-boiled eggs. *Bissara* is a pea soup, a cheap and filling winter breakfast. *Brivat* are tiny envelopes of filo pastry, akin to the Indian samosa, with a variety of savoury fillings. They also come with an almond filling for dessert.

Snacks

Cheaper restaurants serve kebabs (aka *brochettes*), with tiny pieces of beef, lamb and fat. Also popular is *kefta*, mince-meat brochettes, served in sandwiches with chips, mustard and *harissa* (red-pepper spicy sauce). Tiny bowls of finely chopped tomato and onion are another popular accompaniment. On Jemaâ el Fna in Marrakech, strong stomachs may want to snack on the local *babouche* (snails).

Main dishes

Seksou (couscous) is the great North African speciality. Granules of semolina are steamed over a pot filled with a rich meat and vegetable stew. Unlike Tunisian couscous, which tends to be flavoured with a tomato sauce, Moroccan couscous is pale yellow. In some families, couscous is the big Friday lunch.

Tagines are stews, the basic Moroccan dish. It is actually the term for the two-part terracotta dish (base and conical lid) in which meat or fish are cooked with a variety of vegetables, essentially, carrots, potato, onion and turnip. Tagine is everywhere in Morocco. Simmered in front of you on a *brasero* at a roadside café, it is always good and safe to eat. Out trekking and in the South, it is the staple of life. For tagines, there are four main sauce preparations: *m'qalli*, a yellow sauce created using olive oil, ginger and saffron; *m'hammer*, a red sauce which includes butter, paprika (*felfla hlwa*) and cumin; *qudra*, another yellow sauce, slightly lighter than *m'qalli*, made using butter, onions, pepper and saffron, and finally *m'chermel*, made using ingredients from the other sauces. Variations on these base sauces are obtained using a range of ingredients, including parsley and coriander, garlic and lemon juice, *boussera*, eggs, sugar, honey and cinnamon (*karfa*).

In the better restaurants, look out for *djaj bil-hamid* (chicken with preserved lemons and olives), sweet and sour *tajine barkouk* (lamb with plums), *djaj qudra* (chicken with almonds and caramelized onion) and *tajine maqfoul*. Another tasty dish is *tajine kefta*, basically fried minced meat balls cooked with eggs and chopped parsley. In eateries next to food markets, delicacies such as *ra's embekhar* (steamed sheep's head) and *kourayn* (animal feet) are popular.

A dish rarely prepared in restaurants is *djaj souiri*, aka *djaj mqeddem*, the only *plat gratiné* in Moroccan cuisine. Here, at the very last minute, a sauce of beaten eggs and chopped parsley is added to the chicken, already slow-cooked in olives, diced preserved lemon, olive oil and various spices.

All over Morocco, lamb is much appreciated, and connoisseurs reckon they can tell what the sheep has been eating (rosemary, mountain pasture, straw, or mixed rubbish at the vast Mediouna tip near Casablanca). Lamb is cheaper in drought years, when farmers have to reduce their flocks, expensive when the grazing is good, and is often best eaten at roadside restaurants where the lorry drivers pull in for a feed.

Desserts

A limited selection of desserts is served in Moroccan restaurants. In the palace restaurants, there will be a choice between *orange à la cannelle* (slices of orange with cinnamon) or some sort of marzipan pâtisserie like *cornes de gazelle* or *ghrayeb*, rather like round short-cake. *El jaouhar*, also onomatopoeically known as *tchak-tchouka*, is served as a pile of crunchy, fried filo pastry discs topped with a sweet custardy sauce with almonds. Also on offer you may find *m'hencha*, coils of almond paste wrapped in filo pastry, served crisp from the oven and sprinkled with icing sugar and cinnamon, and *bechkito*, little crackly biscuits.

Most large towns will have a couple of large pâtisseries, providing French pastries and the petits fours essential for proper entertaining. See **Pâtisserie Hilton**, Rue de Yougoslavie, Marrakech. Here you will find *slilou* (aka *masfouf*), a richly flavoured nutty powder served in tiny saucers to accompany tea but you won't find *maâjoun*, the Moroccan equivalent of hash brownies, made to liven up dull guests at wedding parties.

In local *laiteries*, try a glass of yoghurt. Oranges (*limoun*) and mandarins (*tchina*) are cheap, as are prickly pears, sold off barrows. In winter, in the mountains, look out for kids selling tiny red arbutus berries (*sasnou*) carefully packaged in little wicker cones. Fresh hazelnuts are charmingly known as *tigerguist*.

Dishes for Ramadan

At sunset the fast is broken with a rich and savoury *harira* (see above), *beghrira* (little honeycombed pancakes served with melted butter and honey) and *shebbakia* (lace-work pastry basted in oil and covered in honey). Distinctive too are the sticky pastry whorls with sesame seeds on top.

Cafés and restaurants

Cafés offer croissants, petit-pain and cake (Madeleine), occasionally soup and basic snacks. Restaurants basically divide into four types: snack eateries, in the medina and *ville nouvelle*, are generally cheap and basic. Some are modelled on international themed fast-food restaurants (**Taki Chicken** in Rabat). Then you have the *laiteries*, which sell yoghurt, fruit juices and will make up sandwiches with processed cheese, salad and *kacher* (processed meat). Full-blown restaurants are generally found only in larger towns, and some are very good indeed. And, finally, in cities like Fès and Meknès, Marrakech and Rabat, you have the great palaces of Moroccan cuisine, restaurants set in old, often beautifully restored private homes. These can set you back 500dh or even more. Some of these restaurants allow you to eat à la carte (**El Fassia** in Marrakech, **La Zitouna** in Meknès), rather than giving you the full banquet menu (and late-night indigestion).

Eating out cheaply

If you're on a very tight budget, try the ubiquitous food stalls and open-air restaurants serving various types of soup, normally the standard broth (*harira*), snacks and grilled meat. The best place for the adventurous open-air eater is the Jemaâ el Fna square in Marrakech. Another good place is the fish market in the centre of Essaouira. There is a greater risk of food poisoning at street eateries, so go for food that is cooked as you wait, or that is on the boil. Avoid fried fish that is already cooked and is reheated when you order it.

Vegetarian food

Moroccan food is not terribly interesting for vegetarians, and in many places 'vegetarian cuisine' means taking the meat off the top of the couscous or tagine. The concept is really quite alien to most Moroccans, as receiving someone well for dinner means serving them a tagine with good chunk of meat. There are some excellent salads, however. Be prepared to eat lots of processed cheese and omelettes.

Food markets

Each city has a colourful central market, generally dating back to the early years of the 20th century, stuffed with high-quality fresh produce. Try the one off Avenue Mohammed V in Casablanca (which has some good basketwork stalls), the markets on the Avenue Hassan II in Rabat (to your left off the Avenue Mohammed V as you enter the medina) and the Guéliz market in Marrakech, again, on the Avenue Mohammed V, on your left after the intersection with Rue de la Liberté as you head for the town centre.

Eating in people's homes

Moroccan families may eat from a communal dish, often with spoons, sometimes with the hands. If invited to a home, you may well be something of a guest of honour. Depending on your hosts, it's a good idea to take some fruit or pâtisseries along. If spoons or cutlery are not provided, you eat using bread, using your right hand, not the left hand since it is ritually unclean. If the dishes with the food are placed at floor level, keep your feet tucked under your body away from the food. In a poorer home, there will only be a small amount of meat, so wait until a share is offered. Basically, good manners are the same anywhere. Let common sense guide you.

Drink

Tea

All over Morocco the main drink apart from water is mint tea (*thé à la menthe/attay*) a cheap, refreshing drink which is made with green tea, fresh mint and masses of white sugar. The latter two ingredients predominate in the taste. If you want a reduced sugar tea, ask for *attay msous* or *bila sukar/sans sucre*). In cafés, tea is served in mini-metal tea pots, poured from high above the glass to generate a froth (*attay bi-rizatou*, 'tea with a turban') to use the local expression. Generally, tradition has it that you drink three glasses. To avoid burning your fingers, hold the glass with thumb under the base and index finger on rim. In some homes, various other herbs are added to make a more interesting brew, including *flayou* (peppermint), *louiza* (verbena) and even *sheeba* (absinthe). If you want a herb tea, ask for a *verveine* or *louiza*, which may be with either hot water or hot milk (*bil-halib*).

Coffee

Coffee is commonly drunk black and strong (*kahwa kahla/un exprès*). For a weak milky coffee, ask for a *café au lait/kahwa halib*. A stronger milky coffee is called a *café cassé/kahwa mherza*.

Other soft drinks

All the usual soft drinks are available in Morocco. If you want still mineral water (*eau plate*) ask for Sidi Harazem, Sidi Ali or Ciel. The main brands of fizzy mineral water (*eau pétillante*), are Oulmès and Bonacqua, a water produced by Coca Cola.

The better cafés and local *laiteries* (milk-product shops) do milkshakes, combinations of avocado, banana, apple and orange, made to measure. Ask for a *jus d'avocat* or a *jus de banane*, for example, or for a usually excellent lucky dip, a *jus mixte*.

Wines and spirits

For a Muslim country, Morocco is fairly relaxed about alcohol. In the top hotels, imported spirits are available, although at a price. The main locally made lager **beers** are Flag, Flag Spécial, Stork, Castel and Heineken. In the spring, look out for the extremely good Bière de Mars, made only in March with Fès spring water.

Morocco produces **wine**, the main growing areas being Guerrouane and Meknès. Reds tend to prevail. **Celliers de Meknès** (CdM) and **Sincomar** are the main producers. At the top of the scale (off-licence prices in brackets), are Médaillon (90dh) and Beau Vallon (CdM, 90dh, anything up to 185dh in a restaurant). A CdM Merlot will set you back 45dh. Another reliable red is Domaine de Sahari, Aït Yazem, a pleasant claret, best drunk chilled in summer (30dh). The whites include Coquillages and Sémillant, probably the best (40dh). At the very bottom of the scale is rough and ready Rabbi Jacob, or, cheaper and still cheerful, Chaud Soleil. The local fig firewater is Mahia la Gazelle.

If you want to buy alcohol outside a restaurant, every major town will have a few licensed sales points. Often they are very well stocked with local and imported wines. The **Marjane** hypermarket chain, in all the major cities, also has an off-licence section. **Asouak Essalam**, the main competitor, does not stock alcohol, however. In Ramadan, alcohol is on sale to non-Muslim foreigners only and many of the off-licences shut down for the month. At Marjane, towards the end of Ramadan, you may well be asked by locals to buy a few bottles for their end of fasting party.

Festivals in Morocco

Morocco has a number of regional and local festivals, often focusing around a local saint or the harvest time of a particular product, and are fairly recent in origin. The *moussems*, or traditional local festivals, have on occasion been banned in recent years, the authorities giving as a reason the health risks created by gatherings of large numbers of people in places with only rudimentary sanitary facilities. The main Moroccan festivals come in 3 categories: firstly, the more religious festivals, the timing of which relates to the lunar Islamic year, see page 37; secondly the annual semi-commercial regional or town festivals with relatively fixed dates; and thirdly, the new generation of arts and film festivals.

Regional or town festivals
Feb Festival of the Almond Blossom, Tafraoute, see page 30.
Apr Honey Festival, Immouzer des Ida Outanane.
May Rose Festival, El Kelaâ des Mgouna, Dadès Valley.
Moussem de Sid Ahmed Ben Mansour, Moulay Bousselham, north of Kenitra.
Jun Cherry Festival, Sefrou.
Festival of Folk Art and Music, Marrakech.
Moussem de Moulay Abdeslam ben M'chich, Larache.
Moussem de Sidi Mohammed Ma El Ainin, Tan Tan.
Jul Festival of Sea Produce, Al Hoceïma.
Aug Moussem of Moulay Abdallah, El Jadida.
Festival des Pommes, Immouzer du Kandar.
Moussem of Moulay Idris Zerhoun, Moulay Idriss.
Moussem of Setti Fatma, Setti Fatma, Ourika Valley near Marrakech.
Moussem of Sidi Ahmed ou Moussa, Tiznit.
Sep Marriage Festival, see page 30.

Horse Festival, Tissa near Fès.
Moussem of Moulay Idris al Azhar, Fès.
Oct Date Festival, Erfoud.

Arts festivals
Feb Salon du livre, Casablanca. Morocco's biggest annual bookfair. Prix du Grand Atlas, literary events.
May Les Alizés, Essaouira. Small classical music festival in early May, www.alizes festival.com.
Festival des Musiques Sacrées, Fès – generally late May running into Jun, see page 30. Attracts a strange mixture of the spiritual, the hippy and the wealthy. Accompanied by popular music concerts open to all. See www.fesfestival.com.
Mawazine Festival, Rabat. The capital comes alive with world music and pop concerts held in various venues. Whitney Houston closed the 2008 festival.
Jun L'Boulevard, Casablanca. Annual urban music (hip-hop, electro, fusion, rock etc) festival, www.boulevard.ma.
Festival Gnaoua, see page 30, Essaouira. One of Morocco's most successful music festivals, www.festival-gnaoua.co.ma.
Festival Rawafid des créateurs marocains de l'étranger, Casablanca. Late Jul. Focusing on work by Moroccan creative artists abroad. Music and film.
Aug Arts Festival, Asilah. Paintings of the medina, festival now in its 30th year.
Sep Festival international du film méditerranéen, Tetouan. Long-established but slightly erratic small film festival.
Tanjazz Tangier jazz festival, mixture of free and paying concerts, www.tanjazz.org, see page 30.
Dec Festival international du film de Marrakech, Marrakech, see page 30. Established annual film fest, www.festivalmarrakech.info.

Six of the best festivals

Morocco has some popular festivals focusing on music and film, as well as some more low-key celebrations away from the main urban centres. For a full list of festivals in Morocco, see page 29.

Fête des Amandiers (Almond Blossom Festival), Tafraoute

Every January and February the festivities in this beautiful Anti-Atlas location are overshadowed by the natural display given by the trees, as they light up the red rocky mountainsides with dazzling white and pink flowers. See page 250.

L'Boulevard, Casablanca

Casablanca's music festival is a rare Moroccan celebration of contemporary urban style: electronica, hip hop and rock. For four days in spring the soothing restaurant strummers are forgotten as a competition is held between Moroccan bands and international gigs are held in the Stade de l'Étoile. See www.boulevard.ma.

Festival des Musiques Sacrées du Monde, Fès

The World Sacred Music Festival is a huge celebration of the tunes of spiritual tradition. Every June Morocco's holy city is completely taken over for the two weeks of the festival, with vast concerts in squares around the city. From sufi to gospel, classical to flamenco, it features music from around the globe, with the aim of breaking down cultural and musical boundaries. See www.fesfestival.com and page 154.

Gnaoua World Music Festival, Essaouira

Also in June, the pretty streets of Essaouira sway to the sounds of Gnaoua, the so-called Moroccan blues, a melding of sub-Saharan, Arabic and Berber styles and traditionally the music of black Moroccan slaves. Acrobatic dance accompanies the music, and tens of thousands of visitors flood the town. The festival is often a place of exciting musical experimentation, as the age-old spiritual traditions of the music are combined with international jazz, reggae, blues and hip-hop influences. See www.festival-gnaoua.net.

Moussem des Fiançailles, Allamghou, near Imilchil

More than 2500 m up in the Atlas, isolated Imilchil's wedding festival in September is a chance, at the end of summer, for thousands of locals to dress up in their jewellery and finest clothes and find a partner. Music, dancing, sheep and cows accompany the party. See box, page 118.

Tanjazz, Tangier

In September street concerts and processions, free be bop dancing lessons and film showings at the Cinémathèque de Tanger accompany five days and nights of performances on two stages at the Italian Palace and all-night jams in the city's bars. See www.tanjazz.org and page 356.

Festival International du Film de Marrakech

A celebration of the best of Moroccan and international film, Marrakech's film festival in December, chaired by Morocco's Prince Moulay Rachid, awards the Golden Star to the best film of the past year and provides a chance to see the best of North African arthouse cinema. See www.festivalmarrakech.info.

Shopping in Morocco

Morocco is a shopper's paradise. The famous souks in Marrakech, in particular, are a great place to buy souvenirs as well as experiencing the cut and thrust of haggling with the experts. Good items to buy in Marrakech include thuya wood boxes, painted wood mirrors, ceramics, leather bags and *babouches* (shoes/slippers) and wrought-iron mirror frames. The fashionable coastal town of Essaouira is also a good place to shop; objects made in fragrant, honey-brown thuya wood are everywhere, from small boxes inlaid with lemon-wood to chunky, rounded sculptures. Fès, too, is a good place to find typical Moroccan goods; the souks, *kissaria* and boutiques offer a splendid selection for visitors, though the best buy is probably the blue-and-white painted, rustic pottery once typical of the city. See under each destination for more details and the best places to find these items.

Essentials A-Z

Accident and emergency

Police: T19. Fire brigade: T15. Larger towns will have an **SOS Médecins** (private doctor on-call service) and almost all towns of any size have a pharmacy on duty at night, the *pharmacie de garde*. Any large hotel should be able to give you the telephone/address of these. For most ailments, a *médecin généraliste* (GP) will be sufficient.

Children

Moroccans love children. This trait of the culture is particularly understandable when you realize how difficult life is for many families and how many children die in childbirth or infancy in the rural areas, due quite simply to a lack of basic health education in the Amazigh languages and Moroccan Arabic.

If you hire a car via an international agency, specify the sort of child seats you require and do not be surprised if your requirements get lost somewhere along the way. Most local car hire agencies will be unlikely to have children's seats.

If you will be doing a lot of driving, make sure you have things in the car to entertain kids. Try and stay in hotels with pools.

On the health and safety front, make sure your kids are up to date with all their vaccinations (see page 33). Tap water in major cities is safe to drink, but some children may still react to drinking different water. In rural areas, give children bottled drinks or mineral water. And, on busy streets and squares, keep a tight hold, as the traffic is often hectic.

Customs and duty free

Visitors may take in, free of duty, 400 g of tobacco, 200 cigarettes or 50 cigars and personal items. You may also take your pet to Morocco. It will need a health certificate no more than 10 days old and an anti-rabies certificate less than 6 months old. Foreign currency may be imported freely.

Prohibited items

There are severe penalties for possession of or trade in narcotic **drugs**: 3 months to 5 years imprisonment plus fines (see also drugs below). Be aware that **wild animal pelts** and some other items openly on sale in Morocco cannot be legally imported into the EU. This also includes products made of animal pelts. Live wild animals may not be exported from Morocco and their import into EU is in most cases illegal.

Disabled travellers

Morocco really cannot be said to be well adapted to the needs of the disabled traveller. However, don't let this deter you. Some travel companies are beginning to specialize in exciting holidays, tailor-made for individuals depending on their level of disability. *Nothing Ventured* edited by Alison Walsh (Harper Collins) gives personal accounts of worldwide journeys by disabled travellers, plus advice and listings.

Dress

In coastal resorts, you can wear shorts and expose arms and shoulders. However, when wandering round medinas and going to city centres, both men and women should cover shoulders. Sandals are fine but shorts should be baggy not skimpy. Expect lots of remarks and attention if you do go wandering round the souks in your running shorts. Have some smart but cool tops with you for summer travelling. Inland, winter is cold. Night temperatures in the desert and at altitude are low all the year – a fleece is handy, even as a pillow.

Drugs

Kif or marijuana represents a good source of income for small farmers in the Rif. However, the European Union has put pressure on Morocco to stop production. There is no serious attempt to stop those Moroccans who so wish from having a gentle smoke, and kif is also consumed in the form of maâjoun cakes, a local variant of hash brownies, which have been known to lead to much merriment at otherwise staid occasions. However, as a tourist, under no circumstances do you want to be caught by the police in the possession of drugs of any kind. And anyone caught exporting the stuff will be made an example of.

Electricity

Morocco has a fairly reliable electricity supply of 220V, using continental European round 2-pin plugs. In some more remote areas, however, there is no mains electricity.

Embassies and consulates

For all Moroccan embassies and consulates abroad and for all foreign embassies and consulates in Morocco, see http://embassy.goabroad.com.

Gay and lesbian travellers

Foreign gay men have long been a feature of life in towns like Marrakech and Tangier. The latter may be long past its heyday of the 1950s and 1960s, but Marrakech continues to attract wealthy gay men. According to the penal code, 'shameless or unnatural acts' between persons of the same sex can lead to short prison sentences or fines, though this has never seemed to put anyone off. Note also that body language is very different in Morocco. Physical closeness

between men in the street does not necessarily indicate a gay relationship. For the corruption of minors, the penalties are extremely severe.

In Marrakech, gay travellers (or rather their friends) have run into problems with the *brigade touristique*, set up to ensure that visitors – of whatever persuasion – go unhassled.

Health

No vaccinations are required unless you're travelling from a country where yellow fever and/or cholera frequently occurs. You should be up to date with **polio**, **tetanus**, and **typhoid** protection. If you are going to be travelling in rural areas where hygiene is often a bit rough and ready, then having a **hepatitis B** shot is a good thing. You could also have a **cholera** shot, although there is no agreement among medics on how effective this is.

Major health risks include acute **mountain sickness**, which can strike from about 3000 m upwards and, in general, is more likely to affect those who ascend rapidly (for example by plane) and those who over-exert themselves. Acute mountain sickness takes a few hours or days to come on and presents with headache, lassitude, dizziness, loss of appetite, nausea and vomiting. When trekking to high altitude, some time spent walking at medium altitude, getting fit and acclimatizing is beneficial.

Some form of **diarrhoea** or intestinal upset is almost inevitable; the standard advice is to be careful with drinking water and ice; if you have any doubts about the water then boil it or filter and treat it. In a restaurant, buy bottled water or ask where the water has come from. Food can also pose a problem; be wary of salads if you don't know whether they have been washed or not. In major cities, tap water should be fine to drink, though many visitors stick to bottled water to make sure.

Out in the sticks you should definitely only drink the bottled variety.

There is a very minimal risk of **malaria** in Morocco and usually prophylaxis is not advised but check before you go. If you are going to be travelling in remote parts of the Saharan provinces, then a course of malaria tablets may be recommended.

A **rabies** vaccination before travel can be considered but, if bitten, always seek urgent medical attention – whether or not you have been previously vaccinated – after first cleaning the wound and treating with an iodine-base disinfectant or alcohol.

Further information
Foreign and Commonwealth Office (FCO) (UK), www.fco.gov.uk
National Travel Health Network and Centre (NaTHNaC), www.nathnac.org.
World Health Organisation, www.who.int.
Fit for Travel (UK), www.fitfortravel.nhs.uk.
A-Z of vaccine and travel health advice requirements for each country.

Insurance

Before departure, it is vital to take out full travel insurance. There is a wide variety of policies to choose from, so shop around. At the very least, the policy should cover personal effects and medical expenses, including the possibility of medical evacuation by air ambulance to your own country. Make sure that it also covers all activities that you might do while away: trekking or surfing, for example. There is no substitute for suitable precautions against petty crime, but if you do have something stolen while in Morocco, report the incident to the nearest police station and ensure you get a police report and case number. You will need these to make any claim from your insurance company.

Internet

Internet cafés can be found in city centres and even quite out-of-the-way places. Areas of cheap hotels attracting budget travellers will have several cybercafés. The better private guesthouses have Wi-Fi and internet connections.

Language

Arabic is the official language of Morocco, but nearly all Moroccans with a secondary education have enough French to communicate with, and a smattering of English. In the North, Spanish maintains a presence thanks to TV and radio. Outside education, however, Moroccan Arabic in the cities and Amazigh in the mountains are the languages of everyday life, and attempts to use a few words and phrases, no matter how stumblingly, will be appreciated. Those with some Arabic learned elsewhere often find Moroccan Arabic difficult. It is characterized by a clipped quality (the vowels just seem to disappear), and the words taken from classical Arabic are often very different from those used in the Middle East. In addition, there is the influence of the Berber languages and a mixture of French and Spanish terms, often heavily 'Moroccanized'. In many situations French is more or less understood. However, you will come across plenty of people who have had little opportunity to go to school and whose French may be limited to a very small number of phrases.

If you wish to learn Arabic, **ALIF** (Arabic Language Institute in Fès, T0535-624850, www.alif-fes.com), an offshoot of the American Language Centre, has a very good reputation. They organize a range of long and short courses in both classical and Moroccan Arabic. Courses in Amazigh languages can be set up, too.

See Footnotes, page 462, for lists of useful words and phrases.

Media

Press

Moroccan newspapers are produced in Arabic, French and Spanish. The main political parties all have their newspapers. From the mid-1990s, the general tone of the press became increasingly critical, dealing with issues once taboo. Of the daily newspapers, *Le Matin du Sahara* and *Maroc Soir* give the official line. The party press includes *L'Opinion*, *Libération* and *Al Bayane*. These newspapers are cheap and give an insight into Morocco and its politics. Coverage of overseas news is limited, but sheds interesting light on attitudes to major international issues. The daily *L'Economiste* is essential reading for some insight into the general economic climate.

More interesting, and generally better written, are the weekly newspapers, which include *Maroc-Hebdo* and *La Vie économique*. The best discussion of contemporary issues is provided by *Le Journal*, which also provides major economic and business coverage. Morocco's best news magazine is *Tel Quel*, see www.telquel-online.com. *Téléplus* has some cultural events coverage. Aimed at a sophisticated urban audience, the glossy monthlies, *La Citadine* and *FDM* (*Femmes du Maroc*), have articles on issues concerning Moroccan women alongside the fashion features.

The main foreign newspapers are available in town centre news kiosks, generally on the evening of publication. As these are expensive for most Moroccans, some kiosks run a 'rent-a-magazine' service for loyal customers. Occasionally, an issue of a foreign news publication with a very critical article on Morocco will fail to be distributed.

Television and radio

Radio Télévision Marocaine (RTM) is the state service, predominantly in Arabic and French. The news is given in Arabic, French and Spanish, with early afternoon summaries in the 3 main Berber languages.

All agree that the RTM provides humdrum fare – hence the huge popularity of satellite television and the second channel **2M**, pronounced 'deux-em', which started life as a pay station, broadcasting North American and European feature films and some local current affairs programmes. **2M**'s news broadcasts are generally more lively than those on the **RTM**.

The most popular radio stations are **RTM-Inter** and the Tangier-based commercial radio station **Médi 1**, which gives news and music in Arabic and French and is also available on the web. Northern areas can pick up broadcasts from Spain, Portugal, and Gibraltar.

Money

Currency

The major unit of currency in Morocco is the dirham (dh). In 1 dirham there are 100 centimes. There are coins for 1 centime (very rare), 5, 10, 20 and 50 centimes, and for 1, 2, 5 and 10 dirhams, as well as notes for 20, 50, 100 and 200 dirhams. The coins can be a little confusing. There are 2 sorts of 5 dirham coin: the older and larger cupro-nickel ('silver coloured' version), being phased out, and the new bi-metal version, brass colour on the inside. There is a brownish 20 dirham note, easily confused with the 100 dirham note. The 50 dirham note is green, the 100 dirham is brown and sand colour, and the 200 dirham note is in shades of blue and turquoise. Currency is labelled in Arabic and French.

You can sometimes buy Moroccan dirhams at bureaux de change at the London airports but dirhams may not be taken out of Morocco. If you have excess dirhams, you can exchange them back into euros at a bank on production of exchange receipts. However, as European cash and Visa cards function in Moroccan ATMs (*guichets automatiques*), in major towns it is possible to withdraw more or less exactly the amount you need on a daily basis. At weekends and during big public holidays, airport and city-centre ATMs can be temperamental. The most reliable ATMs are those of the **Wafa Bank** (green and yellow livery) and the **BMCI**.

Moroccans among themselves sometimes count in older currency units. To the confusion of travellers, many Moroccans refer to francs, which equal 1 centime, and reals, though both these units only exist in speech. Even more confusingly, the value of a real varies from region to region. A dirham equals 20 reals in most regions. However, around Tangier and in most of the North, 1 dirham equals 2 reals. Alf franc (1000 francs) is 10 dirhams. Unless you are good at calculations, it's easiest to stick to dirhams.

**Exchange rate → ** *US$1 = 8.5dh,*
UK £1 = 13.5dh, €1 = 11.1dh (Feb 2012).
There is a fixed rate for changing notes and no commission ought to be charged for this.

Credit cards
Credit cards are widely accepted at banks, top hotels, restaurants and big tourist shops. For restaurants, check first before splashing out. Remember to keep all credit card receipts – and, before you sign, check where the decimal marker (a comma in Morocco rather than a dot) has been placed, and that there isn't a zero too many. You don't want to be paying thousands rather than hundreds of dirhams. To reduce problems with card fraud, it makes sense to use a credit card for payments of large items like carpets and hotel bills. If a payment is not legitimate, it is a lot less painful if the transaction is on the credit card rather than drawn from your current account.

Traveller's cheques
Although somewhat time-consuming to change, traveller's cheques (TCs) are still useful (though a small commission will be charged for changing them). Take TCs from a well-known bank or company, preferably in euros. Some hotels and shops will exchange TCs.

Banks
Main banks include the **BMCE**, **Crédit du Maroc**, **Wafabank** and **Banque Populaire**; all are widespread. The **BMCE** and the **Crédit du Maroc** seem to have the best change facilities, while the **Banque Populaire** is often the only bank in southern towns. Banking in Morocco can be a slow, tortuous process. The easiest way to get money is thus to use your credit or debit card at a cash dispenser. See Opening hours, below, for banking hours.

Cost of travelling
As a budget traveller, it is possible to get by in Morocco for £30-35/US$60-70 a day. Your costs can be reduced by having yoghurt and bread and cheese for lunch and staying in an 80dh a night hotel (you can often find even cheaper options in small towns).

Accommodation, food and transport are all relatively cheap compared to Europe and America, and there is a lot to see and do for free. However, this budget does not allow much room for unexpected costs like the frequent small tips expected for minor services. If you start buying imported goods, notably cosmetics and toiletries, foods and electrical goods, things can get expensive. Allowing £40/US$80 is more realistic.

In top-quality hotels, restaurants, nightclubs and bars, prices are similar to Europe. Rabat, Casablanca and Agadir are the most expensive places, while manufactured goods in remote rural areas tend to cost more. Around the 200dh mark, you can get a much better meal in a restaurant than you can in western Europe. Shoppers will be more than satisfied with the gifts on sale (prices negotiable). Prices for food and drink are non-negotiable.

Cost of living
Although prices for many basics can seem very low indeed to those used to prices in European capitals, the cost of living is high for most Moroccans. At one end of the scale, in the mountainous rural areas, there is Morocco's fourth world, still on

the margins of the cash economy. In these regions, families produce much of their own food and are badly hit in drought years when there is nothing to sell in the souk to generate cash to buy oil, extra flour and sugar. This precariousness means much 'hidden' malnutrition.

Conditions are improving for the city shanty-town dwellers. Here, families will be getting by on 2000dh a month, sometimes much less. The urban middle classes, those with salaried jobs in the public and private sectors, are doing fairly well. A primary school teacher may be on 3000dh a month; a private company employee at the start of their career will make around 3000dh a month, too. This category has access to loans and is seeing a general improvement in living standards. Morocco's top-flight IT technicians, doctors and business people have a plush lifestyle, with villas and servants, available to few Europeans. And, finally, a very small group of plutocrats has long been doing very, very well, thank you.

To put the contrasts in perspective, there are parents for whom the best option is to place their pre-adolescent girls as maids with city families in exchange for 300dh a month. The Amazigh-speaking boy who serves you in the corner shop may be given 50dh a week, plus food and lodging (of a sort). His horizons will be limited to the shop; there will be a trip back to the home village once a year; he may never learn to read. At the other, distant end of the scale, there are couples who can easily spend 40,000dh a semester to purchase an English-language higher education for one of their offspring at the private Al Akhawayn University in Ifrane.

Opening hours

The working week for businesses is Mon to Fri, with half-day working Sat. On Fri, the lunch break tends to be longer, as the main weekly prayers with sermon are on that day. Official business takes considerably longer in Ramadan.

Banks: 0830-1130 and 1430-1600 in winter; afternoons 1500-1700 in summer; 0930-1400 during Ramadan.
Museums: Most close on a Tue. Hours generally 0900-1200 and 1500-1700, although this can vary considerably.
Post offices: 0830-1230 and 1430-1830, shorter hours in Ramadan.
Shops: Generally 0900-1200 and 1500-1900, although this varies in the big towns.

Post

Posting letters is relatively easy, with the **PTT centrale** of each town selling the appropriate stamps. Postage costs to Europe are 6dh for a letter and 6.5dh for a postcard. It is best to post the letter in the box inside or just outside this building as these are emptied most frequently. Each **PTT Centrale** will have a poste restante section, where letters are kept for a number of weeks. There is a small charge on collection. **American Express** post restante is handled by Voyages Schwartz. Letters to or from Europe can take up to a week.

Public holidays

1 Jan New Year's Day.
1 May Fête du Travail (Labour Day).
9 Jul Fête de la Jeunesse.
30 Jul Fête du Trône. Commemorates the present king Mohammed VI's accession.
20 Aug Anniversaire de la Révolution.
6 Nov Marche Verte/El Massira el Khadhra. Commemorates a march by Moroccan civilians to retake the Spanish-held Saharan territories of Río de Oro and Saguiet El Hamra.
18 Nov Independence Day. Commemorates independence and Mohammed V's return from exile.

Religious holidays

Religious holidays are scheduled according to the Hijna calendar, a lunar-based calendar. The lunar year is shorter than the solar year, so the Muslim year moves forward by 11 days every Christian year.

1 Muharram First day of the Muslim year.

Mouloud Celebration of the Prophet Mohammed's birthday.

Ramadan A month of fasting and sexual abstinence during daylight hours.

Aïd el Fitr (the Lesser Aïd) A 2-day holiday ending the month of Ramadan.

Aïd el Kebir (the Great Aïd) A 1-day holiday that comes 70 days after Aïd el Fitr. Commemorates how God rewarded Ibrahim's faith by sending down a lamb for him to sacrifice instead of his son. When possible, every family sacrifices a sheep on this occasion.

During **Ramadan**, the whole country switches to a different rhythm. Public offices open part time, and the general pace slows down during the daytime. No Moroccan would be caught eating in public during the day, and the vast majority of cafés and restaurants, except those frequented by resident Europeans and tourists, are closed. At night, the ambience is almost palpable. There is a sense of collective effort, shared with millions of other Muslims worldwide. People who never go out all year are out visiting friends and family, strolling the streets in Ramadan. Shops stay open late, especially during the second half of the month. Ramadan is an interesting and frustrating time to visit Morocco as a tourist, but probably to be avoided if possible if you need to do business.

Safety

Morocco is basically a very safe country, although there is occasional violent street crime in Casablanca and (very rarely) Marrakech. Travelling on public transport, you need to watch your pockets. Do not carry all your money and cards, etc, in the same place. A money belt is a good idea. Never have more money than you can afford to lose in the pockets of your jeans. Thieves operate best in crowds, getting on

and off trains and at bus and taxi stations where they can quickly disappear into an anonymous mass of people.

Be aware of the various skilled con-artists in operation in certain places. Hasslers of various kinds are active at the gates of Tangier port and, to a lesser extent, in Tetouan. There are all sorts of ruses used by hasslers to extract a little money from tourists: 'the sick relative story', 'the *grand taxi* fare to Rabat to start university story', 'the supplement for the onward reservation to Chaouen story'. You need to be polite and confident, distant and sceptical and even a little bored by the whole thing. Learn the values of the banknotes quickly (the yellow-brown 100dh and the blue 200dh are the big ones, a red 10dh is no great loss). Keep your wits about you. Remember, you are especially vulnerable stumbling bleary-eyed off that overnight bus.

Should you be robbed, reporting it to the police will take time – but may alert them to the fact that there are thieves operating in a given place. For safety matters with regard to women travelling alone, see page 41.

Security and terrorism

On the night of 14 May 2003, Casablanca was shaken by co-ordinated suicide bomb attacks targeting a Jewish social club and a major hotel. Over 40 Moroccans were murdered. Salafiya-Jihadiya fundamentalist groups organized these murders and the national security forces reacted with a wave of arrests. Summer 2003 saw the men responsible, including some of the suicide-bombers who survived, on trial. Nine of those found guilty escaped from prison in Kénitra in 2008.

After 2003, Morocco had seen little urban terrorism and violence until the Marrakech bombing of 2011, see page 431.

The Moroccan government claims to have broken up 55 terrorist cells since 2003, and there are around 1000 Islamists in the country's jails on terrorist charges. There is tight monitoring of all fundamentalist activity and zero tolerance of anything which might lead to violence. As anything Jewish is an obvious target, there are police outside most synagogues.

Student travellers

Morocco is a good place for the budget traveller, as food and accommodation costs are reasonable. Public transport is also very cheap for the distances covered, but often slow for getting to out-of-the-way places. Note that there are few student discounts of the sort available in Europe. The youth hostels have been upgraded and most are now well run.

Telephone

Lots of Moroccans have mobile phones but there are also phone shops or *téléboutiques*, clearly marked in distinctive blue and white livery. They stay open late in summer, are always supervised, have change available and (generally) telephone directories (*annuaires téléphoniques*). The machines are sometimes old French coin phones, and international calls are no problem. For internal calls, put in several 1dh coins and dial the region code (even if you are in the region), followed by the number (a total of 10 digits beginning 0). For overseas calls, put in at least 3 coins of 5dh, dial 00 and wait for a musical sequence before proceeding. Calls can also be made from the *cabines téléphoniques* at the PTT Centrale. Give the number to the telephonist who dials it and then calls out a cabin number where the call is waiting. Note, it is significantly more expensive to phone from a hotel. When calling Morocco from abroad the code is 212 and you then drop the first zero.

Mobile phone coverage in Morocco is reasonably good, though international roaming prices are expensive. It might be worth getting a sim card from www. sim4travel.net, which allows free incoming calls and cheaper international calls, or buying a local Moroccan sim card on arrival.

Time

Morocco follows the UK all year round, with GMT in winter and GMT+1 in summer. Ceuta and Melilla work on Spanish time.

Tipping

This can be a bit of a 'hidden cost' during your stay in Morocco. Tipping is expected in restaurants and cafés, by guides, porters and car park attendants and others who render small services. Make sure you have small change at the ready. Tipping taxi drivers is optional. Do not tip for journeys when the meter has not been used, because the negotiated price will be generous anyway. For porters in hotels, tip around 3dh, on buses 3dh-5dh, and 5dh on trains and in airports.

Tour operators

There are a number of companies that specialize in Morocco. Some of the trekking companies have many years of experience.

UK and Ireland
Acacia Adventure Holidays, LGF, 23A Craven Terr, London, T020-7706 4700, www.acacia-africa.com. Leading African travel specialists, offer a comprehensive selection of adventure holidays, overland safaris and tented and lodge safaris. Good value for money.
Africa Explored, Rose Cottage, Summerleaze, Magor, Newport NP6 3DE, www.africaexplored.net. Overland camping expeditions and safaris, including a 3-week comprehensive circular journey from Tangier, called 'Morocco Encountered', visiting the main cities and main sites, and a shorter 2-week Morocco Encountered with a flight back from Marrakech. Their 22-week Trans-African expedition begins in Morocco and goes on through Mauritania to Nairobi.
Atlas Mountain Information Service (AMIS), 26 Kircaldy Rd, Burntisland, Fife, KY3 9HQ T01592-873546. Small agency run

by the very knowledgeable Hamish Brown, who organizes treks and climbing trips.
The Best of Morocco, Delta Pl, 27 Bath Rd, Cheltenham, Gloucestershire, Gl53 7TH, T0800-171-2151 (UK only), T+44 1242-77-6500 (outside UK), www.morocco-travel.com. Offer unlimited flexibility using quality hotels.
Exodus Travels, T0845-805-0348, www.exodus.co.uk. Well-established worldwide operator.
Explore Worldwide, 1 Frederick St, Aldershot, Hants GU11 1LQ, T0845-013-1537, www.exploreworldwide.com. Offers small exploratory accompanied travels. On offer are eight days in the Jbel Siroua including Taroudant; 15 days trekking in the High Atlas attempting an ascent of Mount Toubkal; 15 days in the sparsely populated Jbel Saghro; 15 days exploring the mountains, desert and coasts in winter; 15 days visiting the imperial cities of Marrakech, Rabat, Fès and Meknès then moving on into the great sand sea. This group attempts to make the impact of tourism positive – by taking small groups, dealing with local suppliers for transport and food, and controlling litter and waste disposal.
Guerba Adventure & Discovery Holidays, Wessex House, 40 Station Rd, Westbury, Wiltshire BA13 3JN, T020-3147 7777, www.guerba.co.uk. Tours and treks.
Imaginative Traveller, Camp Green, Debenham, Suffolk, IP14 6LA, T0845-287 2962, www.imaginative-traveller.com. Has well-trained, motivated ground-staff who have worked in lots of countries. As you would expect, an imaginative choice of hotels. Main clients are experienced travellers with professional jobs who do not have the time to set up holidays for themselves. Lots of free time built into schedules.
Naturally Morocco, T01239-710814, www.naturallymorocco.com. Recommended, environmentally responsible company with lots of Moroccan experience and expertise.
Prospect Music and Art Tours, 79 William Street, Herne Bay, Kent, CT6 5NR, T01227-743307, www.prospecttours.com.

Accompanied tours with experts in art and art history, archaeology and architecture.

North America
Cross Cultural Adventures, PO Box 3285, Arlington, VA 22203, T1-703-237 0100, www.crossculturaladventures.com. Custom-crafted adventures for independent travellers and special-interest groups, from private Atlas treks to soft adventures by Mercedes cars.
Heritage Tours, 121 West 27th St, Suite 1201, New York 10001, T1-800-378 4555, www.htprivatetravel.com. Custom-designed in-depth itineraries. Specialize in cultural and historic tours, sahara encampments, crafts and architecture.
Sahara Trek, T1-727-421 0218, www.sahara trek.com. Offers weekly inclusive adventure and sightseeing tours. Package to custom-designed. Desert trekking, imperial cities, golf, whitewater rafting, beach resorts, skiing.

Tourist information

Moroccan tourist boards abroad
For **Moroccan National Tourist Board (ONMT)** locations worldwide, see www.visitmorocco.org.

Morocco on the web
Background
www.emarrakech.info News of the Red City, regularly updated but in French only.
www.lexicorient.com/morocco Information on cities with photographs.
www.north-africa.com Weekly analysis on economics, politics and business. Subscriber service.
www.riadzany.blogspot.com Titled 'The View From Fez', this blog is actually a great round-up of what's going on in Morocco as a whole.

Crafts and culture
www.alif-fes.com For those wanting to study Arabic and Amazigh languages.

www.kelma.org French-based site with news and views from the gay community in the Maghreb, Belgium and France. **www.maroque.co.uk** For design inspiration.

Visas

No visas are required for full passport holders of the UK, USA, Canada, Australia, New Zealand/Aotearoa, Canada, Ireland and most EU countries. Benelux passport holders require visas at the present time. On the aeroplane or boat, or at the border, travellers will be required to fill in a form with standard personal and passport details, an exercise to be repeated in almost all hotels and guesthouses throughout the country. From the point of entry, travellers can stay in Morocco for 3 months.

Visa extensions

These require a visit to the Immigration or Bureau des Etrangers department at the police station of a larger town, as well as considerable patience. An easier option is to leave Morocco for a few days, preferably to Spain or the Canary Islands, or to one of the two Spanish enclaves, either Ceuta, close to Tangier, or Melilla, rather more remote in northeastern Morocco. People coming into Morocco from either of these Spanish enclaves for a second or third time have on occasion run into problems with the Moroccan customs. With numerous foreigners resident in Agadir and Marrakech, it may be easiest to arrange visa extensions in these cities. Approval of the extension has to come from Rabat and may take a few days.

Weights and measures

Morocco uses the metric system.

Women travellers

Young women travelling with a male friend report few difficulties – and couples with small children will find that the little ones attract a great deal of kindly attention. However, a woman going out on her own from the hotel without male escort will soon notice the difference. For women travelling alone, the hassle and stares can be extremely tiring after a while. So what do you do? In towns, dress fairly smartly, look confident, busy and as though you know where you're going. (Depending on your age, this may make hustlers think twice; is this person with an official delegation, do they have a Moroccan husband?) Observe what smart Moroccan women are wearing, how they walk in public. Women from fairly traditional families will be wearing headscarves, others may be wearing expensive dark sunglasses.

Women students waiting (say) for a *grand taxi* or in your train compartment will probably be delighted to have a chance to chat with an English speaker – as long as you don't look too outlandish by their modest standards of dress. Remember, a lot of importance is given to looking smart and respectable in Morocco. Many Moroccans lack the means to do this, and the unkempt European is really a bit of an extraterrestrial to them, the object of all sorts of prejudices and not worthy of much respect.

One way to deal with hassle from men is to develop a schoolmarmish manner. Modestly dressed, you are interested in Roman ruins, architecture, birds, women's issues (but probably not local politics), you are a serious person. This may put your hassler off – or lead to some intelligent conversation. And, if you do decide you want someone to show you around, then agree on the fee beforehand. This can save you time and prove entertaining too, if the person is genuine.

The plain clothes *Brigade touristique* are in action in a number of the main holiday destinations stamping down on hassle. For a local observed giving a tourist a hard time, this can mean big problems, namely 1000dh fine and/or a month in prison. Apart from Casablanca, Moroccan cities are really quite provincial places where faces get known quickly. This is true even of Marrakech. The problem is then what happens if you are with a genuine Moroccan friend? You will have to convince the plainclothes policeman that you know the person you are with well and that there is no problem.

Working in the country

Morocco has a major unemployment problem. University educated young adults find it hard to get work, especially those with degrees in subjects like Islamic studies and literature. At the same time, industry and business are desperately short of qualified technicians and IT-literate staff. Low salary levels mean that the qualified are tempted to emigrate – and many do, fuelling a brain-drain that has reached worrying levels. In cities, adults with a low level of skills find it hard to get work, basically as many simple jobs in small companies are done by badly paid, exploited adolescents. For the foreigner, this means that there are few opportunities for work, although international companies setting up in Morocco do employ foreign managerial staff, generally recruited abroad. Basically, the only opening if you want to spend time in Morocco is through teaching English, which is badly paid even with organizations like the British Council or the American Language Centres. It is your employer who will help you deal with the formalities of getting a *carte de séjour* (residence permit). For you to be able to work, your employer has to be able to satisfy the relevant authorities in Rabat that you are doing a job in an area in which Morocco has a skills shortage.

Europeans can obtain residence relatively easily, providing they can prove that they have a regular source of income and that regular transfers of funds are being made into their Moroccan bank account. Towns where the police are used to processing the official paperwork for this sort of foreign resident include Agadir, Essaouira, Marrakech, Fès, Rabat and Tangier.

Contents

Footprint features

At a glance

⊖ **Getting around** Marrakech is quite spread out. There are plenty of *petits taxis* or buses though. Essaouira is easily explored on foot.

⊗ **Time required** Allow at least 3 days for Marrakech and, perhaps, a further three to relax on the coast in Essaouira.

☽ **Weather** Winters can be cold, but often sunny, and summers extremely hot. Spring and autumn are the best times to be here. It is generally dry, though occasional winter rain can make the medina muddy and slippery.

⊗ **When not to go** Both Marrakech and Essaouira get very busy over Christmas, New Year and Easter. Summer in Marrakech can be unbearably hot, though out on the coast it's cooler. Essaouira fills up for the annual Gnaoua Festival in Jun.

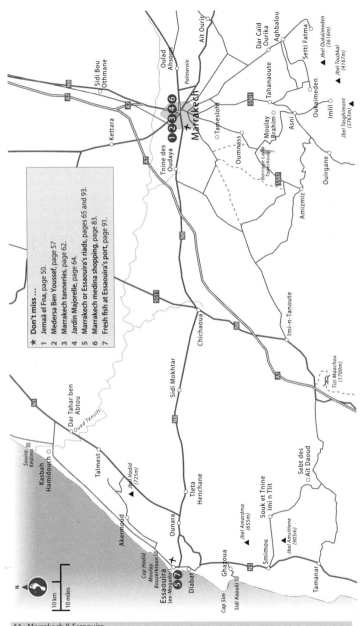

★ Don't miss...
1. Jemaâ el Fna, page 50.
2. Medersa Ben Youssef, page 57
3. Marrakech tanneries, page 62.
4. Jardin Majorelle, page 64.
5. Marrakech or Essaouira's riads, pages 65 and 93.
6. Marrakech medina shopping, page 83.
7. Fresh fish at Essaouira's port, page 91.

The Red City, so called because of the terracotta wash used on its buildings, lies within reach of both the cool High Atlas valleys and, beyond arid plains to the west, the coast. Marrakech has attracted European visitors since at least the 1920s and is one of the great historic cities of North Africa. Focus points are the elegant 12th-century Koutoubia Mosque and the Jemaâ el Fna 'square', famed for its seething mass of entertainments and open-air restaurants. Around them stretches the medina, a place of narrow streets, flat-roofed houses and minarets. The souks are thronged with handicrafts of every shape and size, from silken caftans and pottery drums to carved wooden chests and the orange-woollen expanses of Chichaoua carpets.

West of Marrakech, the photogenic fishing port of Essaouira is an isolated but popular side-trip from Marrakech. The town has been an important port for centuries and its high walls have been battered by various sea powers, as well as Atlantic waves. Its fishing industry survives, though the focus is increasingly tourism, and the surrounding beaches are popular with windsurfers. Beautiful and relaxed, it is the perfect antidote to Marrakech's more frenetic attraction.

Marrakech

Marrakech is Morocco's main point of entry for tourists, many of whom never venture far beyond its red walls, despite the enticing and dramatic backdrop of the High Atlas mountains, snow-capped until April or May and a venue for numerous excursions (see page 104). The city has a memorable beauty, with its palm-lined streets and red earth walls, surrounding a huge medina of flat-roofed houses. Above all, Marrakech is worth visiting to experience the vibrant mass of food stalls, musicians and snake charmers in the seething Jemaâ el Fna square, and for its souks – a labyrinthine network of markets, where people come to buy and sell from all over the surrounding plains, the High Atlas and the Sahara. ▸▸ *For listings, see pages 65-88.*

Arriving in Marrakech → *Colour map 2, B4.*

Getting there

Accessible by air, road and rail, the city makes an excellent central point of arrival in Morocco, situated at the meeting point of routes for Essaouira (Atlantic coast), Ouarzazate (key to the gorges south of the Atlas and Sahara desert), and the northern imperial cities. **Airport Marrakech Menara** ⓘ *T0524-447910, www.marrakech.airport-authority.com*, is 6 km west of the city, by the Menara Gardens. The number of passengers the airport handles has tripled over the past decade, and an award-winning new terminal building was completed in 2008. There are further extensions planned for 2012. The **BMCE** and the **Banque Populaire** have bureaux de change, closed outside office hours, and there are ATMs. Euros may be acceptable to taxi drivers. A *petit taxi* (three passengers) or *grand taxi* (six passengers) from the airport should cost 100-150dh (more after 2000) to the medina or Guéliz, and takes 15 minutes. Although fares are fixed price, published on an airport noticeboard, taxi drivers still try to charge more. Agree the price first. Alternatively, there's a handy airport shuttle bus, No 19, which runs every 30 minutes to Jemaâ el Fna and stops at most hotels in Guéliz, Hivernage and the Palmeraie; 20dh single, 30dh return. For the quickest connection to the train or bus station, your best bet is to take a 15-minute taxi ride and agree the fare. If you're staying in a riad, it's normal practice to arrange a meeting point at the edge of the medina, from where someone will escort you; finding a riad on your own is difficult. You can also ask your riad to arrange airport transfer for about 200dh, which saves a lot of hassle.

From the **railway station** to the heart of the *ville nouvelle* is a 15-minute walk; Jemaâ el Fna and the old city is a further 20-minute walk. A taxi into the city from the station is around 15dh; alternatively, take bus No 3 or 8 from outside the station along Avenue Hassan II and Avenue Mohammed V, to the medina.

Inter-city public **buses** arrive at Bab Doukkala bus station or *gare routière*, a 15-minute walk from Jemaâ el Fna. Bus companies **CTM** and **Supratours** also stop at Bab Doukkala but have their main termini in Guéliz near the train station. ▸▸ *See Transport, page 87, for further details.*

Getting around

Marrakech is a spread-out city, built on a plain – hence the large number of mopeds and bicycles; rental of a two-wheeler is an option, though not without risk in the chaotic traffic. Short taxi journeys in Marrakech should not be more than 10 or 15dh – try to have change and insist on using the meter even though you may be told that it is broken. The most

48 hours in the city

The highlights of the city are less its museums and historic sites than the streets and souks of its medina, and you should allow plenty of time for wandering, stopping for mint tea and getting inevitably lost. **Jemaâ el Fna** makes a good place to start with a fresh orange juice. **Rue Riad Zitoun el Jedid**, to the southeast of the square, is an easily navigated introduction to the medina that takes you down to the impressive riad/palace museums of **Dar Si Said** and **Palais La Bahia**, hopefully before the bus tours arrive. The **Saâdian Tombs** are also a must-do, but can get very crowded. Get some lunch around here before heading north again to the **Koutoubia Mosque** – non-Muslims are not allowed in but the **Jardin de la Koutoubia** is a good spot for a post-prandial wander, and has views of the minaret. Shopping in the souks can be overwhelming – it's a good idea to restrict yourself to perusing on day one, perhaps up Rue Mouassine or Rue Semarine. Then grab a drink on one of the café terraces overlooking Jemaâ el Fna as it comes to life at sundown. If you're feeling brave, you could then descend to eat at one of its stalls, or, for something a little smarter, catch a *petit taxi* to one of the excellent restaurants in the *ville nouvelle*.

On day two, catch the **souks** at their best early in the morning and grab a bargain or two before heading to the **Medersa Ben Youssef**, the city's architectural jewel. **Café des Épices**, or its sibling **Terraces des Épices** make great lunch spots, after which you could head east out to the **tanneries**, or north to **Sidi Bel Abbes**, taking in plenty of street life en route. Catch a taxi to the calming and colourful **Jardin Majorelle** for a wander among the greenery and glimpses of electric blue, before changing into something smart for dinner at one of the medina's atmospheric riad restaurants.

---

picturesque way to drive around is in a calèche, a horse-drawn carriage, but it is perfectly possible to explore the centre on foot.

Hassle The 'hassle' which deterred some visitors in the past is reduced a little thanks to the unseen but ever-vigilant **Brigade Touristique** and the predominant atmosphere is relaxed. If you are robbed or hassled, the Brigade Touristique is based on the Mamounia side of the Koutoubia, near the CMH petrol station (look for the blue and yellow livery), in a small building on a public square with a few trees.

Tourist information **Office du Tourisme** ⓘ *Pl Abd el Moumen Ben Ali (on Av Mohammed V opposite Café Negoçiants), T0524-436131, Mon-Fri 0830-1830.* **Conseil Régional du Tourisme** ⓘ *Pl Youssef Ibn Tachfine, opposite Koutoubia, T0524-385261, Mon-Fri 0830-1830.*

Background

The city

In some early European maps Marrakech appears as 'Morocco city', although 'Maraksh' is the Arabic name. The origins of the name are obscure: some see it as a corruption of 'aghmat-urika', the name of an early town. The city is surrounded by extensive palm groves, into which suburbs are gradually spreading. Yet there are also sandy, arid areas near and, even, within the city which give it a semi-Saharan character.

And then, there are the mountains. Arriving from Fès or Meknès you run alongside the bald arid Jebilet: 'the little mountains', or cross them at Sidi Bou Othmane as you come from Casablanca or Rabat. Perhaps the most beautiful approach to Marrakech is on the N7, from Casablanca and Sidi Bennour, which crosses the Plateau des Gantours and the end of the Jebilet. However, from most points in Marrakech, cloud and heat haze allowing, it is the High Atlas, the Adrar (literally 'the mountains'), which dominate. At times the optical illusion is such that the snow-covered mountain wall appears to rise from just behind the city.

Marrakech is Morocco's fourth largest city. The population is around 1.5 million, although nearer two million including the suburbs. Its people are a mix of Arab and Amazigh; many are recent migrants from surrounding rural regions and further south. For centuries an important regional market place, Marrakech now has a booming service economy and there is still a wide range of handicraft production and small-scale industry, particularly in the medina. Out in the western suburbs are new factories.

Increasingly, tourism is seen as the mainstay of the city's economy. Marrakech is one of the major tourist attractions of Morocco and many of the city's large number of unemployed or under-employed supplement their incomes by casual work with tourists.

Almoravid origins and role
Marrakech was first founded in 1062 by Youssef Ibn Tachfine, the Almoravid leader, as a base from which to control the High Atlas mountains. A kasbah, Dar al Hajar, was built close to the site of the Koutoubia Mosque. Under Youssef Ben Tachfine, Marrakech became the region's first major urban settlement. Within the walls were mosques, palaces and extensive orchards and market gardens, made possible by an elaborate water transfer and irrigation system. The population was probably a mixture of people of black-African descent from the Oued Draâ, Imazighen from the Souss Valley and the nearby Atlas, and Amazigh Jews. The city attracted leading medieval thinkers from outside Marrakech.

Marrakech was taken by the Almohads in 1147, who almost totally destroyed and then rebuilt the city, making it the capital of their extensive empire. Under the Almohad Sultan Abd el Moumen, the Koutoubia Mosque was built on the site of Almoravid buildings, with the minaret added by Ya'qub al Mansour. Under the latter, Marrakech gained palaces, gardens and irrigation works, and again became a centre for musicians, writers and academics, but on his death it declined and fell into disarray.

Merinid neglect and Saâdian revival
While the Merinids added several *medersas* to Marrakech, Fès received much more of their attention and was preferred as the capital, although from 1374 to 1386 Marrakech was the centre of a separate principality. Marrakech was revitalized by the Saâdians from 1524, with the rebuilding of the Ben Youssef Mosque and the construction by Ahmed al Mansour Ad Dahbi of the El Badi Palace and the Saâdian Tombs. Marrakech also became an important trading post, due to its location between the Sahara and the Atlantic.

Alaouite Marrakech
The Alaouites took control of Marrakech in 1668. In the early 18th century the city suffered from Moulay Ismaïl's love of Meknès, with many of the major buildings, notably the El Badi Palace, stripped to glorify the new capital. The destructive effects of this period were compounded by the civil strife following his death. However, from 1873, under Alaouite Sultan Moulay Hassan I and his son, the city's prestige was re-established. A number of the city's fine palaces date from this time and are still open to visitors.

Early 20th century: Glaoui rule

From 1898 until independence, Marrakech was the nerve-centre of southern Morocco, ruled practically as a personal fiefdom by the Glaoui family from the central High Atlas. The French took control of Marrakech and its region in 1912, crushing an insurrection by a claimant to the Sultanate. Their policy in the vast and rugged southern territories was to govern through local rulers, rather as the British worked with the Rajahs of India.

With French support, Pacha T'hami el Glaoui extended his control over all areas of the south. His autonomy from central authority was considerable, his cruelty notorious. And, of course, there were great advantages in this system, in the form of profits from the new French-developed mines. In the 1930s, Marrakech saw the development of a fine *ville nouvelle*, Guéliz, all wide avenues of jacarandas and simple, elegant bungalow houses and, on acquiring a railway line terminus, Marrakech reaffirmed its status as capital of the south. It was at this time, when travel for pleasure was still the preserve of the privileged of Europe, that Marrakech began to acquire its reputation as a retreat for the wealthy.

Capital of the south

In recent decades Marrakech has grown enormously, its population swelled by civil servants and armed forces personnel. Migrants are attracted by the city's reputation as 'city of the poor', where even the least qualified can find work of some kind. For many rural people, the urban struggle is hard and, as the Tachelhit pun puts it, Marrakech is ma-ra-kish, 'the place where they'll eat you if they can'.

North of the medina, new neighbourhoods like Daoudiate and Issil have grown up next to the Université Cadi Ayyad and the mining school. South of the medina, Sidi Youssef Ben Ali, referred to as SYBA, is an extension of the old town and has a reputation for rebellion. West of Guéliz, north of the Essaouira road, are the vast new housing areas of Massira, part low-rise social housing, part villa developments. The most upmarket area is on the Circuit de la Palmeraie. Little by little, the original farmers are being bought out, and desirable homes with lawns and pools behind high walls are taking over from vegetable plots under the palm trees. East of the medina is the vast Amelkis development, a gated community complete with golf course and the discrete Amenjana 'resort'. Here the money and privilege are accommodated in an area equal to one third of the crowded medina.

Future of Marrakech

The early 21st century saw Marrakech in an upbeat mood. The Brigade Touristique, set up to reduce the hassling of tourists, has been reasonably successful. Tourist activity, property development and riad businesses were booming during the first decade of the new millennium, but, with the global economic recession post-2008, this progress has reached a plateau. The ongoing problem for the city is how to deal with the influx of visitors. Certain monuments have reached saturation point: the exquisite Saâdian tombs, for example, are home to a semi-permanent people jam. And, while being packed with people is an important part of the attraction of Jemaâ el Fna, there is the danger that the magic of the place will eventually be diluted by the massive numbers of visitors. The square is now closed to traffic for some of the time, but the roads around the edge of the medina are hellishly busy.

In April 2011 an explosion rocked the famed Café Argana in the main square of Jemaâ el Fna (see page 431). Though the **Café Argana** is being rebuilt at time of writing, and after a short hiatus where travellers avoided Marrakech, the city has fully recovered.

The 'Venice of Morocco'?

Marrakech continues to draw the visitors in and to maintain its hold on the Western imagination. The setting is undeniably exotic, eccentricities are tolerated and (rather less honourably) domestic help is cheap. Features in international decoration magazines fuel the demand for property; major monuments are being restored. One-time resident the late Yves St Laurent even dubbed Marrakech 'the Venice of Morocco' – which might seem an appropriate description on a February day with torrential rain on Jemaâ el Fna.

Still, the Red City retains a sense of rawness, despite the creeping gentrification, and remains the closest Orient one can find within a few hours, flight of the grey north European winter. Provided city authorities can keep vehicle pollution in check, it looks set to maintain its popularity.

Places in Marrakech

Central Marrakech is clearly divided into two parts: the large historic city, the **medina**, and the *ville nouvelle*, **Guéliz**. The focal point of the medina, and indeed of the whole city, is the **Jemaâ el Fna**, an open place full of street entertainers and food sellers, adjacent to which are the most important souks. Handily for the tourist, it is located in the middle of the main areas of historic sights. North of Jemaâ el Fna are the **souks** and the **Sidi Ben Youssef Mosque**, the city's main mosque after the Koutoubia. On a walk in this neighbourhood, you can visit the **Almoravid Koubba**, the **Medersa Ben Youssef**, and the **Museum of Marrakech**. South of Jemaâ el Fna, down Riad Zitoun el Kedim, is an area of **palaces**, the **Saâdian Tombs** and a small ethnographic museum, the **Maison Tiskiwine**.

If you are staying in a riad, you may well be in the **Bab Doukkala** or **Leksour/ Mouassine** neighbourhoods, the former on the Guéliz side of the medina. The latter is very central, just north of Jemaâ el Fna, and is one of the most chic enclaves, home to bijou gallery places like the **Dar Cherifa** *café littéraire*. Bab Doukkala is handier for the bus station. For visitors with more time, the Thursday flea market at **Bab el Khemis** is ideal for those seeking gems amongst junk and second-hand treasures. Another point of interest are the **tanneries** at Bab Debbagh.

A popular feature of a visit to Marrakech is a tour of the gardens. This will include the **Jardin Majorelle**, quite close to Bab Doukkala, the **Menara**, a large square pool set in a vast olive grove south of Guéliz, and the **Agdal**, another olive grove close to the Sidi Youssef Ben Ali neighbourhood. To the east and north of Marrakech, across the Oued Issil, is the **Palmeraie**. Close to the Medina, the gardens between Koutoubia and Mamounia have been totally replanted with roses. Even once scruffy Arset Moulay Slimane, opposite the Municipality on your way to Jemaâ el Fna, has been spruced up.

Most visitors will spend some time in Guéliz, the suburb laid out by the French in the 1920s. Despite all the new apartment buildings and traffic, it is worth a wander for its cafés, upmarket boutiques and art galleries, and it has many of the city's best restaurants. The main thoroughfare is Avenue Mohammed V and the evening promenade here is popular.

Jemaâ el Fna

The Jemaâ el Fna, unique in Morocco, is both the greatest pull for tourists and still a genuine social area for Marrakchi and those flooding in from the surrounding regions. 'La Place' is full of people hawking their goods or talents and others watching, walking, talking and arguing. It is particularly memorable during Ramadan when the day's fast ends. Whatever

Jemaâ el Juice

Ask people about their impressions of Jemaâ el Fna and they'll mention the snake charmers, the food, the acrobats, the swarming mass of humanity, but also the orange juice. Around the edges of the square, from dawn to dusk and beyond, are stalls piled high with immaculately stacked oranges; a 4dh glass of refreshing juice from the army of drink vendors is an important part of the Jemaâ el Fna experience. Depending on which stall you get it from, it may come slightly watered down with squash, and the locals complain when there's no sugar added, but it's invariably delicious and absurdly cheap. Expect to pay 10dh if it's freshly squeezed (and therefore entirely unadulterated) in front of you, or for grapefruit.

the time of day or year, Jemaâ el Fna is somewhere that visitors return to again and again, responding to the magnetic pull that affects locals as much as tourists, to mingle with the crowd or watch from the terrace of the **Café de France** or **Les Terrasses de L'Alhambra**.

Background

Jemaâ el Fna means 'assembly of the dead' and may refer to the traditional display of the heads of criminals executed here until the 19th century. In 1956, the government attempted to close down the square by converting it into a corn market and car park, but it soon reverted to its traditional role. In the late 1980s, the bus station was moved out to Bab Doukkala. In 1994, the square was fully tarmacked for the GATT meeting. The food stands were reorganized and the orange juice sellers issued with smart red fezzes and white gloves. Pickpockets are occasionally a problem on Jemaâ el Fna, and visitors should beware when standing in crowds around the buskers. Keep plenty of small change handy for the various entertainments and orange juice, and keep wallets or handbags out of view.

At 'La Place'

During the day you can explore the stalls and collections of goods: fruit, herbs and spices, clothes, shoes, alarm clocks and radios, as well as handicrafts. There are snake charmers and monkey tamers, watersellers and wildly grinning Gnaoua musicians with giant metal castanets, all too ready to pose for photographs. Sheltering from the sun under their umbrellas, the fortune tellers and public scribes await their clients. In the evening, the crowd changes again, a mix of students and people pausing on the way home from work, smart tourists strolling to restaurants in the medina – and backpackers ready for hot tagine or harira soup at one of the foodstalls. You may see Ouled el Moussa tumblers or a storyteller enthralling the crowd. Sometimes there are boxers, and usually there are groups of musicians: after much effort to extract a few dirhams from the crowd, an acoustic band will get some Berbers dancing, while around a hissing gas lamp a group will perform a song by Jil Jilala, an activist group popular in the 1970s.

More recent attractions include the *nakkachat*, women with syringes full of henna, ready to pipe a design onto your hands. 'Hook the ring over the coke bottle' is popular, or you can try bowling a football between two impossibly narrow goal posts for a dirham or two. You may find an astrologer-soothsayer tracing out his diagram of the future on the tarmac with a stubby piece of chalk. A modern variation on the traditional *halka* or storyteller's circle touches harsh social reality: local people listen to a true tale told with dignity by the relatives of a victim of poverty or injustice. And should you need an aphrodisiac, there are

① Marrakech

Where to stay 🛏

Bab **2** *B1*
Dar Hanane **8** *B6*
Dar Les Cigognes **9** *E6*
Dar Rhizlane **22** *D2*
Diwane **23** *A1*
du Pacha **6** *A2*
Fashion **1** *B1*
La Maison Arabe **18** *B4*
La Mamounia **11** *D3*
La Sultana **19** *E5*
Le Nid **16** *D5*

Les Jardins de la Médina **20** *E5*
Les Jardins Mandaline **14** *A5*
Moroccan House **26** *A2*
Riad 72 **7** *B4*
Riad Charaï **3** *A4*
Riad El Fenn **4** *C4*
Riad el Ouarda **5** *A5*
Riad Kaiss **17** *D5*
Riad Malika **12** *B4*
Riad Marianis **15** *B5*
Riad Tizwa **13** *B4*
Riad Tlaatawa-Sitteen **25** *B5*

Ryad Mogador Opera **24** *B1*
Toulousain **10** *A2*
Villa des Orangers **21** *D4*

Restaurants 🍴

Al Bahriya **3** *B1*
Al Fassia **1** *B2*
Bistro Thai **9** *B2*
Café du Livre **13** *A2*
Café Les Négociants **14** *A1*
Catanzaro **15** *A1*
Dar Zellij **2** *A4*

Essaoussan **5** *C4*
Grand Café de la Poste **10** *B2*
Kaowa **11** *A3*
Kechmara **8** *A1*
La Trattoria **16** *B1*
Le 16 **12** *B2*
Le Bagatelle **17** *B1*
Le Carioca **18** *B1*
Le Foundouk **4** *B5*
Nid'Cigogne **6** *E5*
Rotisserie de la Paix **19** *B1*
Vlème Ave **21** *A1*

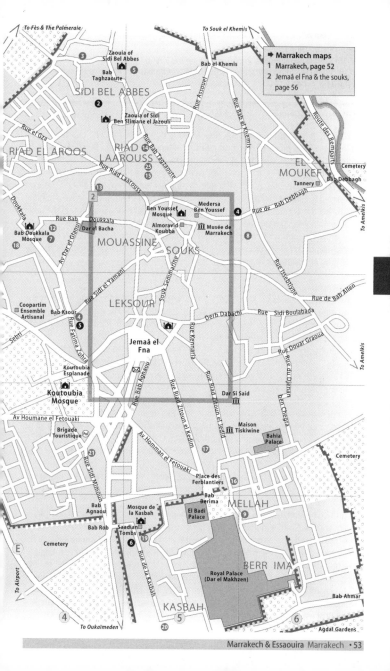

To Fès & The Palmeraie
To Souk el Khemis

Zaouia of Sidi Bel Abbes ❸ ❺
Bab Taghzaoute

Bab el Khemis

SIDI BEL ABBES ❷

Zaouia of Sidi Ben Slimane el Jazouli

Rue el Gza

RIAD EL AROOS

RIAD LAAROUSS ⑭

❷⑤
Rue Riad Laarouss ⑮

Rue Riad Laarousse ❶❸

Medersa Ben Youssef ④

Ben Youssef Mosque

Rue Bab Doukkala
Dar el Bacha

Almoravid Koubba

Musée de Marrakech ⑧

EL MOUKEF

Cemetery
Bab Debbagh

Rue de Bab Debbagh

Tannery ▪

Av Dar el Glaoui

Bab Doukkala Mosque ❼ ⑫

❶❽

MOUASSINE

SOUKS

Souk Semmarine

Rue Issebtiyne

Rue de Bab Allen

LEKSOUR

Coopartim Ensemble Artisanal ▪

Bab Ksour ④
❺

Rue Fatima Zohra

Rue Sidi el Yamani

Derb Dabachi

Rue Kennaria

Rue Sidi Boutabada

Rue Douar Graoua

Jemaâ el Fna

Koutoubia Esplanade

Koutoubia Mosque

Rue Bab Agnaou

Av Houmane el Fetouaki

Brigade Touristique ❷①

Rue Sidi Mimoun

Rue Riad Zitoun el Kedim

Av Homman el Fetouaki

Rue Riad Zitoun el Jedid

Dar Si Said ▪

Maison Tiskiwine ▪

⑰

Place des Ferblantiers ⑯

Bahia Palace

Cemetery

ben Chegra

To Amelkis

To Amelkis

Bab Agnaou

Mosque de la Kasbah

Bab Rob

Saadian Tombs ⑲ ❻

Bab Berima

El Badi Palace

MELLAH ❾

Cemetery

E

Cemetery

To Airport

Rue de la Kasbah

⑳

KASBAH ❺

BERR IMA

Royal Palace (Dar el Makhzen)

Bab Ahmar

Agdal Gardens

To Oukaïmeden

➜ Marrakech maps
1 Marrakech, page 52
2 Jemaâ el Fna & the souks, page 56

Route des Remparts

Rue Bab el Khemis

Rue Assouel

stalls with tea urns selling cinnamon and ginseng tea and little dishes of black, powdery *slilou*, a spicey sweet paste.

Thanks to campaigning by a team led by Spanish writer and Marrakech resident Juan Goytisolo, Jemaâ el Fna has received UNESCO recognition for its place in humankind's oral tradition.

Koutoubia Mosque

The 65-m high minaret of the Koutoubia Mosque dominates the whole of Marrakech. Visible from afar, it provided the focal point for urban planner Henri Prost when he laid out the modern neighbourhood of Guéliz. The Koutoubia is clearly visible as, unlike the Qarawiyin Mosque in Fès, it is set apart from the dense building of the old town. An unlikely legend goes that as this structure overlooked the harem, only a blind muezzin was allowed to climb it to call the faithful to prayer. The name 'Koutoubia' derives from the Arabic *kutub* (books) and means the 'Booksellers' Mosque', reflecting the fact that the trade of selling manuscripts was conducted in a souk close to the mosque. As this is a place of prayer, and in every way the most important mosque in the city, dress decently if you are going to approach the site to view it at length. Behind the mosque are gardens and some good photo opportunities.

Background

Unusually, the Koutoubia is a double mosque, both parts dating from the reign of the second Almohad ruler, Abd el Mumin (1130-1163). Standing on the esplanade facing the minaret, the ruins of the first Koutoubia are behind railings to your right (first excavated in the late 1940s, and re-explored recently). The bases of the prayer hall's columns, and the cisterns under the courtyard are clearly visible. The ground plan of the second Koutoubia, still standing, is the same as that of the ruined one (17 naves). The Almohad mosque at Tin Mal (see page 106), open for visits by non-Muslims, has a similar plan.

The site of the mosque is itself historic and was originally occupied by a late 11th-century kasbah, the Almoravid Dar al Hajar. The successful Almohads destroyed much of the Almoravid city and, in 1147, built a large mosque, close to the fortress. In all likelihood they had to do this because, puritan as they were and considering the Almoravids to be heretics, they could not pray in a tainted building. Unfortunately, the orientation of the new Almohad mosque was not quite right – the focus point in a mosque is the direction of Mecca and should be indicated by the mihrab, or prayer niche. The solution was to build a second mosque – the present Koutoubia – even though the faithful at prayer can correct this directional problem themselves, under the direction of the imam, once the right direction has been worked out.

Thus two mosques existed for some time side by side, the first probably functioning as a sort of annexe. Given Almohad religious fervour, the congregations were no doubt large. Today, the bricked-up spaces on the northwest wall of the Koutoubia Mosque indicate the doors which connected them. However, the older structure fell into disrepair and eventual ruin. The excavations of 1948 also revealed a *maqsura*, or screen, in front of the mihrab, which could be wound up through the floor to protect the Sultan, and a *minbar*, or pulpit, which was moved into position on wooden rollers. The two cisterns in the centre may have been from a previous Almoravid structure. On the eastern flank of this mosque was an arcade of which a niche and the remains of one arch remain.

Kids in Marrakech

There's plenty to entertain children in Marrakech, from the Jemaâ el Fna snake charmers to acrobats that will come somersaulting your way the moment you sit outside at a restaurant. But there's little that's specifically designed for kids. A day out at a pool outside the city (see box, page 86) is a good bet, and a trip to the mountains provides some needed space. A horse-drawn calèche tour of the city walls is a good way to see something without the scrum of street level, and places such as the Menara gardens sometimes have camels that can be ridden through the palm groves. For real wide-eyed excitement go for an early morning balloon ride over the nearby countryside (page 85).

Existing Koutoubia Mosque

The existing Koutoubia Mosque was built by Abd el Mumin in 1162. The minaret is 12.5 m wide and 67.5 m to the tip of the cupola on the lantern, and is the mosque's principal feature, rightly ranked alongside later Almohad structures, the Hassan Tower in Rabat (see page 282) and the Giralda in Seville. The minaret, composed of six rooms, one on top of the other, was a great feat of engineering in its day and influenced several subsequent buildings in Morocco. The cupola on top is a symmetrical square structure topped by a ribbed dome and three golden orbs, which are alleged to have been made from the melted-down jewellery of successive Almohad leader, Yaqoub al Mansour's wife, in penance for her having eaten three grapes during the Ramadan fast. The cupola has two windows on each side, above which is a stone panel in the *darj w ktaf*, 'step-and-shoulder', motif. (For a close-up view of the top of the mosque and this design feature, consult a 100dh banknote.) The main tower has a band of coloured tiles at the top.

The Koutoubia, a vast structure for 12th-century North Africa, had to be a mosque equal to the ambitions of the Western Caliphate. It is held to be the high point of Almohad building, a cathedral-mosque of classic simplicity. It is here that the innovations of Hispano-Moorish art – stalactite cupolas, painted wooden ceilings – reach perfection. There are perspectives of horseshoe arches, no doubt an aid to contemplation. Although the prayer hall is off-limits to non-Muslim visitors, an idea of what it is like can be gained at the Tin Mal mosque in the High Atlas (see page 106). The unique *minbar* (preacher's chair), set against this apparent simplicity, is all decoration and variety, and very much in keeping with the elaborate taste of Ummayad Spain. (The original *minbar*, also recently restored, can be viewed at the Badi Palace.) Both prayer hall and chair were to be a source of inspiration for later generations of builders and decorators.

Ultimately, the Koutoubia is striking because it is the work of one ruler, Abd el Mumin. Comparable buildings in western Islam – the Great Mosque of Córdoba and the Alhambra – were built over a couple of centuries.

North of Jemaâ el Fna: souks and monuments

Many of the **souks** of Marrakech retain their original function and a morning's souking is one of the great pleasures of the city. Before leaping into impulse purchases, get an idea of prices in shops in Guéliz, or in the **Ensemble Artisanal** on Mohammed V. Once you have threaded your way up Souk Semmarine, onto Souk el Kebir and past Souk Cherratine, you are in the neighbourhood of some of the city's most important Islamic monuments, the **Almoravid**

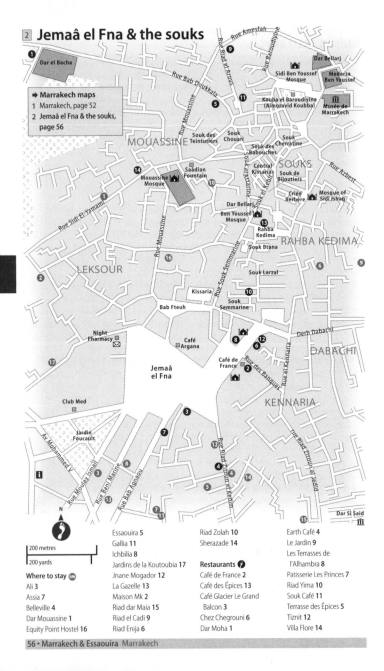

2 Jemaâ el Fna & the souks

Dar el Bacha

➡ **Marrakech maps**
1 Marrakech, page 52
2 Jemaâ el Fna & the souks, page 56

Dar Bellarj

Sidi Ben Youssef Mosque

Medersa Ben Youssef

Rue Amesfah

Rue Riad El Arous

Rue Bab Doukkala

Rue Bab Taghzout

Kouba el Baroudiyïne (Almoravid Koubba)

Musée de Marrakech

MOUASSINE

Rue Mouassine

Souk des Teintutiers

Souk Chouari

Souk des Babouches

Souk Cherratine

SOUKS

Rue Azbezt

Saadian Fountain

Central Kissarias

Souk de Bijoutiers

Mouassine Mosque

Criée Berbère

Mosque of Sidi Ishaq

Dar Bellarj

Ben Youssef Mosque

Rahba Kedima

Rue Sidi El Yamama

Rue Mouassine

RAHBA KEDIMA

Souk Btana

Souk el Kebir

Souk es-Smarrine

LEKSOUR

Souk Larzal

Kissaria

Souk Semmarine

Bab Fteuh

Night Pharmacy

Café Argana

Derb Dabachi

DABACHI

Jemaâ el Fna

Café de France

Rue des Banquets

Rue el Kennaria

Club Med

KENNARIA

Jardin Foucault

Av Mohammed V

Rue Moulay Ismaïl

Rue Bani Marine

Rue Bab Agnaou

Rue Riad Zitoun el Kedim

Rue Riad Zitoun el Jedid

Derb Dabachi

Dar Si Said

N

200 metres
200 yards

Where to stay 🛏
Ali **3**
Assia **7**
Belleville **4**
Dar Mouassine **1**
Equity Point Hostel **16**

Essaouira **5**
Gallia **11**
Ichbilia **8**
Jardins de la Koutoubia **17**
Jnane Mogador **12**
La Gazelle **13**
Maison Mk **2**
Riad dar Maia **15**
Riad el Cadi **9**
Riad Enija **6**

Riad Zolah **10**
Sherazade **14**

Restaurants 🍴
Café de France **2**
Café des Épices **13**
Café Glacier Le Grand Balcon **3**
Chez Chegrouni **6**
Dar Moha **1**

Earth Café **4**
Le Jardin **9**
Les Terrasses de l'Alhambra **8**
Patisserie Les Princes **7**
Riad Yima **10**
Souk Café **11**
Terrasse des Épices **5**
Tiznit **12**
Villa Flore **14**

Koubba and **Medersa Ben Youssef.** (Note that there is a rather bureaucratic enforcement of the order in which you see the three Islamic monuments – Museum, Medersa and Koubba – and the Koubba must be the last of the three.) The **Museum of Marrakech** and the **Fondation Dar Belarj Museum** are also evidence of private money creating new heritage sites.

Souks

The main souks lie to the north of Jemaâ el Fna. The entrance to them is to the left of the mosque. Follow this round to the left and then turn right into the main thoroughfare, **Souk Semmarine**. Alternatively, enter through the small tourist market, further round to the left on Jemaâ el Fna. Souk Semmarine is a busy place, originally the textiles market, and, although there are a number of large, expensive tourist shops, there are still some cloth sellers. To the left is a *kissaria* (small covered alley) selling clothes. The first turning on the right leads past **Souk Larzal**, a wool market, and **Souk Btana**, a sheepskin market, to **Rahba Kedima**, the old corn market, now selling a range of goods, including traditional cures and cosmetics, spices, vegetables and cheap jewellery, and with some good carpet shops. Walk back onto the main souk via a short alley with wood-carved goods. Here the souk forks into **Souk el Attarine** (perfumers' souk) on the left and **Souk el Kebir** on the right.

To the right of Souk el Kebir is the **Criée Berbère**, where carpets and jallabahs are sold. This was where slaves, mainly from across the Sahara, were auctioned until 1912. Further on is the **Souk des Bijoutiers**, with jewellery. To the left (west) of Souk el Kebir is a network of *kissarias*, selling western goods. Beyond this is the **Souk Cherratine**, with leather goods, somewhere to bargain for camel or cowhide bags, purses and belts.

Continuing back on the other side of the *kissarias* is the **Souk des Babouches**, a far better place to buy slippers than in the tourist shops. This feeds into Souk el Attarine, the spice and perfume souk, which itself leads back into Souk Semmarine. West of the Souk el Attarine is the carpenters' **Souk Chouari**. From here, walk on to see a Saâdian fountain and the 16th-century **Mouassine Mosque**. South of Souk Chouari is the **Souk des Teinturiers**, or dyers' market, where wool recently dyed is festooned over the walkways. Nearby are the blacksmiths' and coppersmiths' souks.

Musée de Marrakech

① *Pl Ben Youssef, T0524-441893, www.museedemarrakech.ma, daily 0900-1800, 40dh, 60dh with the Medersa Ben Youssef and Koubba. After the entrance courtyard (good café on left, bookshop on right).*

The entrance to the museum is just off the open area in front of the Almoravid Koubba and it is housed in Dar M'nebhi, the early 20th-century palace of a former Moroccan minister of war. The simple whitewashed walls of the domestic wing shelter temporary exhibitions of generally unimpressive contemporary art. Off the main courtyard, protected by a plexi-glass roof and a brass chandelier the size of a small UFO, are displays of Koran manuscripts, coins, ceramics and textiles. Note the Portuguese influence in the elaborate wooden façades to the rooms on the left. A small passageway to the left of the main reception room takes you through to the restored hammam, now home to a small collection of early engravings on Morocco. The museum as a whole is worth a visit more for the building than the exhibits.

Medersa Ben Youssef

① *Daily 0900-1800, 40dh or 60dh with the Museum and Koubba.*

Standing with the Almoravid Koubba behind you, the minaret of the large 12th-century Ben Youssef Mosque, rebuilt in the 19th century, is clearly visible. Turning right out of the

Museé de Marrakech, follow the street round to the entrance to the city's most important Islamic monument, the 16th-century Medersa Ben Youssef. One of the few Islamic buildings open to the general public, it has been restored by the Fondation Ben Jelloun and is now Marrakech's architectural highlight. Cool, calm corridors, beautiful arches, *zellige* tiles and the light reflecting in the central pool make it a breathtaking place to visit. Founded in 1564-1565 by the Saâdian Sultan Moulay Abdellah, on the site of a previous Merinid *medersa*, it functioned as a boarding school for students of the religious sciences and law. The Medersa is centred around a square courtyard containing a rectangular pool, and with arcades on two sides. Each student had a separate cell with a sleeping loft and a window looking onto the courtyard. Note the much worn but still fine cedar wood of the upper façades around the courtyard. You will see fine *zellige* tiling on the arcade floor, walls and pillars. Inscriptions are in Kufic and cursive lettering, interwoven with floral patterns.

At the far end is the prayer hall covered with an eight-sided wooden dome. Beneath the dome-plaster open-work windows illuminate the tilework. In the *qibla* wall is a five-sided mihrab. Note the stalactite ceiling of the mihrab, and the carved stucco walls with pine cone motif. The inscription here, dedicated to the Sultan, translates as: "I was constructed as a place of learning and prayer by the Prince of the Faithful, the descendant of the seal of the prophets, Abdellah, the most glorious of all Caliphs. Pray for him, all who enter here, so that his greatest hopes may be realized." Note also the massive Carrara marble columns.

On the way out of the Medersa, the toilets on the right of the vestibule have an elaborate stalactite design on the ceiling.

Koubba el Baroudiyine
ⓘ *Pl Ben Youssef, daily 0900-1800, 60dh combined with the Medersa and Museum.*
Now protected by neo-Versailles wrought-iron railings, the 11th-century Almoravid Koubba (Koubba el Baroudiyine) is the only complete Almoravid building surviving in the city. It dates from the reign of Ali bin Youssef (1107-1143) and, perhaps, formed part of the toilet and ablutions facilities of the mosque that at the time existed nearby. At first glance it is a simple building, with a dome surmounting a square stone and brick structure. However, the dome has a design of interlocking arches, plus a star and chevron motif on top. The arches leading into the *koubba* are different on each side. Climb down the stairs to view the ceiling of the dome, noting the range of Almoravid motifs, including the palmette, pine cone and acanthus. Around the corniche is a dedicatory inscription in cursive script. Set into the floor is a small, almost square basin.

Dar Bellarj and around
ⓘ *9 Toulalat Zaouïat Lahdar, T0524-444555, daily 0900-1800, free.*
Turning right out of the Medersa, then left under a covered street, you will come to the entrance of Dar Bellarj, 'the House of Storks', on your left. The building, restored recently by a couple of Swiss artists, dates from the 1930s. Prior to this there was a fondouk on the site which housed the only hospital for birds in North Africa. Here there dwelt a wise man with the gift of curing wounded storks. Today, the building, austerely but simply refurbished, is used primarily as gallery space for contemporary arts.

Just yards from the Medersa Ben Youssef is **Maison de la Photographie** ⓘ *46 Rue Ahal Fès, T0524-385721, www.maisondelaphotographie.com, daily 0930-1900, 40dh, children free*, a recently opened gallery of vintage Moroccan photographs. Thousands of sepia-tinted photos and glass negatives dating to the mid-1800s are displayed over the three floors in a restored riad, with a café on the roof terrace; this is well worth a visit.

North of Medersa Ben Youssef

North of the Medersa Ben Youssef, you can wander through more recent residential neighbourhoods, built on the site of former orchards and market gardens. Whereas Fès has steep and narrow streets, accessible only by pedestrians and mules, flat Marrakech is teeming with bicycles and mopeds, mini-taxis and handcarts. Eventually, your wandering might take you to the open square of Bab Taghzaoute and on to **Zaouïa of Sidi Bel Abbes**. Usually considered the most important of the seven saints of Marrakech, Bel Abbes was born in Ceuta in 1130. He championed the cause of the blind in Marrakech and was patronized by Sultan Yaqoub al Mansour. You are free to wander through the religious complex, though non-Muslims are barred from the mausoleum. It's a striking place, with bright squares and shady alleyways. A series of arches is filled with potted plants and blind people chatting and waiting to receive alms. Nearby is the **Zaouïa of Sidi Ben Slimane el Jazouli**, a 14th-century sufi.

Kasbah quarter

Bab Agnaou, meaning the 'gate of the black people', marks the entrance to the kasbah quarter. To get to it, follow Avenue Prince Moulay Rachid (also known as Rue Bab Agnaou) south from Jemaâ el Fna, or enter the medina at Bab Rob. The kasbah quarter dates from the late 12th century and the reign of the Almohad Sultan Ya'qub al Mansour. Bab Agnaou is also Almohad. The gateway itself is surrounded by a series of arches within a rectangle of floral designs, with a shell or palmette in each corner and an outer band of Kufic inscription.

The road from the gate leads to Rue de la Kasbah, turn right along here and then take the first left. On this road is the much restored **Kasbah Mosque**, dating from 1190. The minaret has Almohad *darj w ktaf* and *shabka* (net) motifs on alternate sides, with a background of green tiles, above which is a band of coloured tiles. Though not as impressive as the tower of the Koutoubia Mosque, the minaret is a notable landmark en route to the Saâdian Tombs. The entrance to these lies directly to the right of the mosque.

Saâdian Tombs

ⓘ *Rue de la Kasbah, daily 0900-1645, 10dh. Try to visit early in the day as the place gets very crowded with tour groups.*

The late 16th-century Saâdian Tombs were discovered thanks to aerial photography in 1917, having been sealed off by Moulay Ismaïl in the 17th century in a vain attempt to condemn the Saâdian rulers to oblivion. A series of chambers around a small garden, decorated with carved cedar and plaster, is the final and, ultimately rather moving, resting place of the Saâdian family. The mihrab of the first main burial chamber is particularly impressive. Here lies the prince Moulay Yazid. The second room contains the tomb of Ahmed al Mansour. The second and older mausoleum was built for the tombs of Ahmed al Mansour's mother, Lalla Messaouda, and Mohammed esh Sheikh, founder of the Saâdians. In the rather dilapidated garden and courtyard are the tombs of numerous other princelings and followers.

El Badi Palace

ⓘ *0900-1645, 10dh plus another 10dh to see the Koutoubia minbar.*

The huge barren spaces of the ruined 16th-century El Badi Palace come as a bit of a shock after the cramped streets of the Marrakech medina. Orange trees grow in what were once enormous pools in the central courtyard, and storks nest noisily on the ruined walls. For five days in July, El Badi comes alive for the annual **Popular Arts Festival** (see page 82), most of the year, however, it is a quiet sort of place, the high thick walls protecting the vast courtyard from the noise of the surrounding streets.

To get there from the Bab Agnaou, head right inside ramparts, and then take the second right. The road leads more or less directly to Place des Ferblantiers, a square with a number of workshops where they make lanterns and items in tin. Pass through Bab Berima, the gate on the southern side. The entrance to the palace is on the right, between high *pisé* walls.

The palace was built by the Saâdian Sultan Ahmed al Mansour ed-Dahbi (the Golden) between 1578 and 1593, following his accession after his victory over the Portuguese at the Battle of the Three Kings, at Ksar el Kebir in northern Morocco. It marks the height of Saâdian power, the centrepiece of an imperial capital. It was a lavish display of the best craftsmanship of the period, using the most expensive materials, including gold, marble and onyx. The colonnades were of marble, apparently exchanged with Italian merchants for their equivalent weight in sugar.

The palace was largely destroyed in the 17th century by Moulay Ismaïl, who stripped it of its decorations and fittings and carried them off to Meknès. No austere royal fortress, the Badi was probably a palace for audiences – and it was at one of these great court ceremonies that the building's fate was predicted: 'What do you think of this palace?' asked the Sultan El Mansour. 'When it is demolished, it will make a big pile of earth,' replied a visionary. El Mansour is said to have felt a sinister omen.

The ruins on either side of the courtyard were probably summer houses, the one at the far end being called the **Koubba el Khamsiniya** (The Fifty Pavillion) after either the 50 cubits of its area, or the fact that it once had 50 columns.

The complex contains a small **museum** whose exhibits include the restored *minbar* (the sacred staired Islamic equivalent of a pulpit, from which the Imam delivers sermons) from the Koutoubia Mosque. Mark Minor, one of the conservators from the Metropolitan Museum of Art in New York who carried out the restoration, called it "one of the finest works of art in wood created by mankind." Constructed in Córdoba in Spain in 1139, it is covered in around 100 carvings. The *minbar* remained in use until 1962. The scattered ruins of the palace, with odd fragments of decoration amidst the debris, include also stables and dungeons.

Royal Palace
ⓘ *Not open to the public.*
To the south of the El Badi Palace is the Dar el Makhzen, the modern-day Royal Palace, one of the late King Hassan II's favourite residences. The present king has had a new palace constructed, close to the Mamounia.

Down Riad Zitoun el Jedid: craft museums and palaces

Two museums devoted to Moroccan artistry, both in spectacular settings, sit close together at the south end of Riad Zitoun el Jedid. From Jemaâ el Fna, follow Rue des Banques from just past **Café de France**. At the first junction, follow through to the right onto Riad Zitoun el Jedid. Eventually, on Riad Zitoun el Jedid, you'll see signs indicating the Dar Si Said off to the left and the smaller Maison Tiskiwine.

Dar Si Said
ⓘ *Derb el Bahia, Riad Zitoun el Jedid, T0524-389564, daily 0900-1630, closed Tue, 10dh*
Built by Si Said, Visir under Moulay el Hassan and half-brother of Ba Ahmed Ben Moussa, Dar Si Said is a late 19th-century palace housing the Museum of Moroccan Arts and Crafts.

The collection includes pottery, jewellery, leatherwork and Chichaoua carpets and is particularly strong on Amazigh artefacts. On the first floor is a salon with Hispano-Moorish decoration and cedarwood furniture, while around the garden courtyard you'll find old window and door frames. Look out for a primitive four-seater wooden ferris wheel of the type still found in *moussems* (country fairs) in Morocco. Those interested in traditional Moroccan artefacts will want to continue to the neighbouring Maison Tiskiwin.

Maison Tiskiwin
ⓘ *8 Rue de la Bahia, T0524-389192, www.tiskiwin.com, daily 0930-1230 and 1430-1800, 20dh, children 10dh.*
Between the Dar Si Said and the Bahia Palace a few streets further south is the fantastic Maison Tiskiwin ('the House of the Horns'), home to a fine collection of items related to Northern African and Saharan culture and society. This small museum was lovingly put together by the Dutch art historian Bert Flint, who still lives here, though he has given the museum to Marrakech University. Flint still spends some of the year travelling and collecting to add to the collection, and there is a strong sense of enthusiasm for the artefacts here (in contrast to some of the state-run museums). There are crafts from the Rif and the High Atlas, though the collection focuses primarily on the Sahara, and includes jewellery and costumes, musical instruments, carpets and furniture. The building itself, around a courtyard, is an authentic and well-maintained example of a traditional riad. There are excellent and copious notes in English. Groups tend to visit in the morning – if you go along in the afternoon you may get the museum all to yourself.

Bahia Palace
ⓘ *0900-1700, 10dh.*
Further to the south is the Bahia Palace (Bahia means 'brilliant', and it is). It was built in the last years of the 19th century by the Vizir Ba Ahmed Ben Moussa, or Bou Ahmed, a former slave who exercised power under sultans Moulay Hassan and Abd el Aziz. Sunlight shines through wrought-iron bars creating beautiful patterns on the *zellige* tiles and, in the courtyard, water ripples over green tiles around a beautiful fountain, surrounded by trees. There are tour groups, but there are also plenty of quiet corners in which lingering until they've passed is a pleasure. The palace is a maze of patios planted with fruit trees, passageways and empty chambers with painted ceilings. Guides will tell you that each wife and concubine had a room looking onto the patio. The story goes that Bou Ahmed was so hated that, on his death in 1900, his palace was looted and his possessions stolen by slaves, servants and members of his harem. Subsequently, the building was occupied by the French authorities. Bareness is still a feature of the palace, but it is one that accentuates the beauty of the architecture.

The Jewish quarter
South of the Bahia and east of the El Badi Palace, the *mellah* or Jewish neighbourhood was created in 1558. The Jewish community has all but vanished, and there is little to tell you of its former role in the life of Marrakech. There were several synagogues and, under the control of the rabbis, the area had considerable autonomy. It is worth asking around to be let into one of the synagogues. See Fès el Jedid, page 141, for the etymology of the term 'mellah'.

Tanneries near Bab Debbagh

The tanneries near Bab Debbagh ('Tanners' Gate') are one of the most interesting (if smelly) sites in Marrakech. Wandering towards the tanners' area, you will in all likelihood be approached by some lad who will offer to show you the tanneries (20dh is a reasonable tip). You will be given a sprig of mint to hold to your nostrils and, through a small metal door, you will be shown an area of foul-smelling pits, where men tread and rinse skins in nauseous liquids and dyes. In small lean-to buildings, you will find other artisans scraping and stretching the skins. Located close to the seasonal Oued Issil, the tanners were on the edge of the city with plenty of water and space to expand away from residential areas.

You will probably be told that there are two tanneries: one Arab, the other Berber. In fact there are several, and workforces are ethnically mixed. There do remain specialities, however, with one set of tanners working mainly on the more difficult cow and camel skins, and the others on goat and sheep skins. Tanning in Marrakech is still a pre-industrial process, alive and functioning not far from the heart of the medina – even though the traditional dyes have largely been replaced with chemical products. See also box opposite.

Ramparts and gates

The extensive ramparts of Marrakech (20 gates and 200 towers stretching for 16 km) are predominantly Almoravid, excepting those around the Agdal Gardens, although they have been extensively restored since. Reconstruction is a continual process as the *pisé*-cement walls, made of the distinctive earth of the Haouz plains, gradually crumble. The ramparts and gates are one of the distinctive sights of Morocco. A ride in a horse-drawn calèche will allow you to see part of the ramparts. In places, there has been much beautification, with fancy wrought-iron railings and rose gardens taking the place of the dust on the Hivernage side of town.

Bab Rob, near the buses and *grands taxis* on the southwest side of the medina, is Almohad, and is named after the grape juice which could only be brought through this gate. **Bab Debbagh**, on the east side, is an intricate defensive gate with a twisted entrance route and wooden gates, which could shut off the various parts of the building for security. **Bab el Khemis**, on the northeast side, opens into the Souk el Khemis (Thursday market) and an important area of mechanics and craftsmen. Check out the junk-market here on a Sunday morning. There is a small saint's tomb inside the gate building. Bab Doukkala, on the northwest side by the bus station, is a large gate with a horseshoe arch and two towers. The medina side has a horseshoe arch and a cusped, blind arch, with a variation on the *darj w ktaf* (step and shoulder) motif along the top. There are occasional exhibitions in the guardroom inside the gate. The esplanade here has been badly neglected and many of the orange trees have died off. A new road across the palm grove north of **Bab Doukkala** completes the circuit of the ramparts.

Gardens

Agdal Gardens
The Agdal Gardens, stretching south of the medina, were established in the 12th century under Abd el Moumen, and were expanded and reorganized by the Saâdians. The vast expanse, over 400 ha, includes several pools, and extensive areas of olive, orange and pomegranate trees. They are in the main closed when the king is in residence, but

Tanning secrets

The tanners are said to have been the first to settle in Marrakech at its foundation, and a gate is named after them, the only one to be named for a craft corporation. 'Bab Debbagh, bab deheb' – 'Tanners' Gate, gold gate' – the old adage goes, in reference to the tanners' prosperity. One legend runs that seven virgins are buried in the foundations of the gate (sisters of the seven protector saints of Marrakech) and that women who desire a child should offer them candles and henna. Another legend says that Bab Debbagh is inhabited by Malik Gharub, a genie who dared to lead a revolt against Sidna Suleyman, the Black King, only to be condemned to tan a cowhide and cut out *belgha* soles for eternity as punishment.

The tannery was considered both a dangerous place – as it was the entrance to the domain of the Other Ones – and a beneficial one, since skins were a symbol of preservation and fertility. Because the tanners spent their days in pits working the skins, they were said to be in contact with the unseen world of the dead and to be masters of fertility, being strong men, capable of giving a second life to dry, dead skin.

The process of tanning skins is strongly symbolic – the tanners say that the skin eats, drinks, sleeps and 'is born of the water'. When the skin is treated with lime, it is said to be thirsty; when it is treated with pigeon dung, it is said to receive *nafs*, a spirit. The *merkel* (treading) stage prepares the skin to live again, while the *takkut* of the tanning mixture is also used by women to dye their hair. At this point, the skin receives *ruh* (breath). Leather is thus born from the world of the dead and the *ighariyin*, the people of the grotto, and is fertilized in the swampy pool, the domain of the dead – who are also said to have the power to bring rain.

In the old days, the complex process of tanning would start with soaking the skins in a sort of swamp – or *iferd* – in the middle of the tannery, filled with a fermenting mixture of pigeon guano and tannery waste. Fermenting would last three days in summer, six in winter. Then the skins would be squeezed out and put to dry. Hair would be scraped off, then the skins would go into a pit of lime and argan-kernel ash. This would remove any remaining flesh or hair, and prepare the skin to receive the tanning products. The lime bath lasts 15-20 days in summer, up to 30 in winter. Then the skins are washed energetically, trodden to remove any lime, and any extra bits are cut off. Next the skins spend 24 hours in a *qasriya*, a round pit of more pigeon dung and fresh water. At this stage the skin becomes thinner and stretches. There follows soaking in wheat fibre and salt for 24 hours to remove any traces of lime and guano.

Then begins the actual tanning process. (The word *debbagh* actually means tannin.) Traditional tanneries used only plants – roots, barks and certain seeds and fruits. In Marrakech, acacia and oak bark are used, along with takkut, the ground-up fruit of the tamarisk. A water and tannin mix is prepared in a pit, and the skins get three soakings.

After this, the skins are prepared to receive the dye. They are scraped with pottery shards, beaten and coated with oil, alum and water. Then they are dyed by hand and left to dry in the sun (traditionally on the banks of the nearby Oued Issil). Finally, the skins are worked to make them smoother and more supple, stretched between two ropes and worked on smooth pottery surfaces.

otherwise can be visited on Fridays and Sundays between 0900 and 1800. Of the pavilions, the Dar al Baida was used by Sultan Moulay Hassan to house his harem. The largest pool, Sahraj el Hana, receives its coachloads of tourists, but at other times is a pleasant place to relax, although not to swim.

Menara Gardens

From the medina and the Agdal Gardens, Avenue de la Menara leads to the Menara Gardens, essentially an olive grove centring on a rectangular pool. A short moped hop from central Marrakech, the area is much appreciated by locals for picnics. The presence of such a large expanse of water generates a pleasant microclimate. The green-tiled pavilion alongside the pool was built in 1866. With the Atlas Mountains as backdrop, it features heavily on postcards.

Jardin Majorelle

① Av Yacoub el Mansour, T0524-313047, www.jardinmajorelle.com, daily 0800-1800 in the summer, 40dh, plus 25dh for the museum.

The Jardin Majorelle, also called the Bou Saf-Saf Garden, is off Avenue Yacoub el Mansour in Guéliz. This is a small tropical garden laid out in the inter-war period by a French artist, Jacques Majorelle, son of a family of cabinet-makers from Nancy who made their money with innovative art nouveau furniture. Majorelle portrayed the landscapes and people of the Atlas in large, strongly coloured paintings, some of which were used for early tourism posters. The carefully restored garden belonged to Yves St Laurent until his death in 2008 and his ashes were scattered here. Strong colours and forms are much in evidence: the buildings are vivid cobalt blue, the cactuses sculptural. Bulbuls sing in the bamboo thickets and flit between the Washingtonia palms. A green-roofed pavilion houses a small **Musée d'Art Islamique**, with a fine and easily digestible collection of objects.

The Palmeraie

Marrakech is surrounded by extensive palm groves. In the original Prost development plan of the 1920s, no building was to be higher than a palm tree. It is also illegal to cut down a palm tree – hence palms have been left growing in the middle of pavements. In recent years the Palmeraie has suffered as the urbanized area round Marrakech has expanded, and certain areas have been divided up for upmarket holiday development. Nevertheless, it is a good place for a drive or a calèche tour. Take the Route de la Palmeraie, off the N8 to Fès, to explore it.

Marrakech listings

For sleeping and eating price codes and other relevant information, see pages 22-28.

Where to stay

Marrakech *p46, maps p52 and p56*

It is a good idea to reserve rooms, as demand for accommodation can outstrip supply in Marrakech, especially around Christmas and Easter holidays. Riads aside, the larger upmarket hotels are located in 3 areas: in the Hivernage garden city area and along the neighbouring Av Mohammed VI; in a development on the Casablanca road in the Semlalia neighbourhood; and in the Palmeraie east of the city. Hivernage is close to Guéliz, and a short taxi ride into Jemaâ el Fna in the old town.

There is a lack of stylish mid-range hotels in the medina; those that do exist are mostly grouped around Riad Zitoun el Kedim, to the southeast of Jemaâ el Fna, but they tend to fill up far in advance. There are, however, some good medium-priced hotels in Guéliz, the centre of the *ville nouvelle*.

The vast majority of cheaper hotels are 5 to 10 mins' walk from Jemaâ el Fna, in the alleys off Rue Bab Agnaou (Av Prince Moulay Rachid), Riad Zitoun el Kedim and the Kennaria neighbourhood behind the Café-Hotel de France.

Riads in the medina

Always double-check your riad reservation at peak times of year (end of year holidays, Easter, May/Jun).

€€€€ Dar Les Cigognes, 108 Rue de Berima, T0524-382740, www.lescigognes. com. Open since 2001, **Dar Les Cigognes** is a luxurious take on the riad-cum-boutique hotel. With just 11 rooms and suites, an award-winning restaurant and cooking school, full-service spa and a superb location next to the palaces, it is one of the very few riads in the old town with street access,

making it very easy to find. Emphasis on service. Part of the Sanssouci Collection.

€€€€ Le Nid, 40 Derb Saka, Mellah, T0524-382740, www.lenid.co. This luxurious modern 4-bedroom riad adjacent to the spice souks offers a 24-hr butler, personal chef, cinema room and sun terrace. Ideal for families or small groups. Part of the Sanssouci Collection.

€€€€ Maison MK, 14 Derb Sebaai, Quartier Ksar, T0524-376173, www.maison mk.com. Vibrant, bright and exceedingly hip, the 6 suites of the luxurious **Maison MK** combine traditional riad decoration standards – *tadelakt* and wrought iron – with contemporary Moroccan design elements and all mod cons. So funky is the place that even the mint teapots are brightly coloured and two-toned. The cinema room has a 2.5-m screen as well as an Xbox and you can put in advance requests for what you'd like in your minibar. Each room has iPod and mobile phone. For 22,000dh you can have the whole riad. Minimum stay of 3 nights, price includes airport transfers.

€€€€ Riad Charaï, 54 Diour Jdad, Zaouïa, T0524-437211, www.riadcharai.com. The former residence of the Pacha of Marrakech's secretary, this elegant boutique riad sleeps up to 16 people in enormous suites, of which some have twin bed arrangements. Decor is full of velvet tones and sultry low-level lighting, and lounge areas and terrace are beautiful. Service is top-notch. There's a hammam, a massage room, a spectacular, turquoise pool (4 m by 9 m – unusually large for a riad) and a huge garden patio. Situated north of the souks, it's a good 15 mins' walk to the main Jemaâ el Fna square.

€€€€ Riad El Fenn, Derb Moullay Abdullah Ben Hezzian, Bab el Ksar, T0524-441210, www.riadelfenn.com. Possibly Marrakech's most spectacularly luxurious riad, **El Fenn** also does the simple things well. The design is striking – deep red walls coexist with more classic riad style, and a fine collection of contemporary art adorns the walls. There are 21 rooms, most of which have private fires, and one of which has a private, glass-bottomed rooftop pool, through which sunlight streams into the room below. Owned by Vanessa Branson, but run with laconic French style, **El Fenn** has some great ecological policies: it uses solar panels and has its own organic garden outside the city which provides the riad with fresh produce. There is a fine restaurant and bar, loads of cosy cushioned seating nooks and 3 pools with shaded terraces. The only danger is that once inside, you'll hardly want to venture out!

€€€€ **Riad el Ouarda**, 5 Derb Taht Sour Lakbir Taht es Sour, Zaouïa el Abbasia, T0524-385714, www.riadelouarda.com. Around 2 courtyards, the larger of which has a small pool, Ouarda has 4 double rooms and 5 suites, all with their own theme. There's a modern feel to the place; plain white walls and low furniture laid out with pebbles combine with restrained use of traditional Moroccan tiles and fabrics. Some suites have their own patio and open fireplace. Twin bed arrangements possible. Located on the northern side of the medina, it's a fair way from the majority of tourists.

€€€€ **Riad Enija**, 9 Derb Mesfioui, Rahba Lakdima, T0524-440926, www.riadenija. com. 15 rooms and suites with fabulously extravagant metal-framed and 4-poster beds around a truly jungliferous courtyard. Swiss- and Swedish-managed, every room is done in a different style, though all share a sense of exotic romance: modern European touches mix with an extravagance of tiles, arches, carved plaster and draped fabrics. Not all rooms have en suite bathrooms, though some have their own private veranda. Central location in medina and excellent service, with breakfast included. Annoyingly, prices are not shown on the website.

€€€€ **Riad Kaiss**, 65 Derb Jdid, Riad Zitoun Kedim, T0524-440141, www.riadkaiss. com. Open since 2000, **Riad Kaiss** was once a wing of the Vizier's harem. Opulent and decadent in equal measure, with 9 rooms and suites, hammam, full service spa, and pool, it's on a quiet side street just steps from Jemaâ el Fna. It also has an award-winning restaurant and cooking school. Part of the Sanssouci Collection.

€€€€ **Riad Zolah**, 114-116 Derb el Hammam, T0524-387535, www.riadzolah. com. Exemplary service sets **Zolah** apart. There are complimentary *babouches*, a mobile phone is lent to guests in case you get lost, and the welcome is warm and friendly. It's also exceptionally beautiful: one courtyard has 4 orange trees, the other a plunge pool, and the 17th-century building retains some original plasterwork. Alan Keohane's black-and-white photos of Morocco decorate the place, there's a selection of Moroccan wines, 3 rooms have working fireplaces, and spectacular silk drapes and romantic lighting add to the special atmosphere. Free Wi-Fi. Free airport transfers.

€€€€-€€€ **Riad Africa**, 94-95 Derb Sakka, Riad Zitoun Lakdim, Tel: +44(0)20-7193 2461, www. riadafrica.co.uk. Individually decorated a/c rooms, with iPod docking stations, have en suite bathrooms with *tadelakt* walls. A plunge pool is set in an attractive palm-filled courtyard. There's a fresh juice bar and rooftop garden, and a massage room with hammam. Moroccan breakfast, Wi-Fi and mobile phones provided for contacting staff when out are included in the price. Dinner is also available.

€€€€-€ **Equity Point Hostel**, 80 Derb el Hammam, Mouassine, T0524-440793, www.equity-point.com. 300 m from Jemaâ el Fna, this is a hostel by name but a riad in style, with lamps and arches, sofas and cushions, big mirrors and shiny red-walled bathrooms. You can stay in an en suite double for about the same price you'd pay in a riad proper (€€€€), or go budget in an 8-bed dorm (€). It's open 24/7, and breakfast and internet is included. Comprehensive online booking system.

€€€ **Dar Hanane**, 9 Derb Lalla Azzouna, T0524-377737, www.dar-hanane.com. iPod docking stations, free Wi-Fi and an honesty bar all contribute to the open, friendly attitude at this place near the Medersa Ben Youssef. There's 1 suite and 4 rooms (all with a/c), all elegantly stylish but also homely and unfussy. A superb terrace view tops the place off. English-speaking staff. If it's full, the owners have 2 more riads in the city: **Riad Tzarra** and **Dar Bel Haj**.

€€€ **Dar Mouassine**, 148 Derb Snane, Mouassine, T0524-445287, www.dar mouassine.com. Spectacular painted ceilings, lots of antiques, old pictures, books and muted natural tones give **Mouassine** a touch of sober class. It's tricky to find initially, but is located close to the main square in Moussaine. Service can be hit and miss and, though there is a/c in some rooms, it is not always working well. Meals available on request.

€€€ **Riad 72**, 72 Arset Awsel, Bab Doukkala, T0524-387629, www.riad72.com. Italian-run **Riad 72** is an exceptionally stylish riad –

traditional *tadelakt* and tiles are used but the colour palette is more muted than most, with lots of greys along with splashes of red. There are only 4 rooms (all a/c), but plenty of space, with huge banana palms in the courtyard, a small splash pool, a hammam and a roof terrace with great views across the medina. There is vehicle access to this smart area in the medina and parking close by. The same people run the equally chic **Riad Due** and **Riad 12**.

€€€ **Riad el Cadi**, 86/87 Derb Moulay Abdelkader, Dabachi, T0524-378655, www.riyadelcadi.com. 14 rooms and suites around 5 courtyards in 7 conjoined houses make the cultured **Dar el Cadi** one of the medina's biggest riads. It was also one of the first riads in the city to open its doors to guests and the years of practice have paid off. Service is efficient and friendly, and cool, simple and scholarly decoration is the order of the day. Library, Wi-Fi, tented roof terrace. Minimum stay of 3 nights. 10 mins' walk from

The riad experience

The riad (*maison d'hôte* or guesthouse) gives you the experience of staying in a small but fine private medina house. Prices are high for Morocco, but you get service, style and luxury in bucketloads. The often painstakingly restored houses are managed either directly by their owners or via an agency which deals with everything from reservations to maintenance. There are hundreds of riads in the city, probably around 1000, though estimates vary wildly.

Guests are met either at the airport, or the edge of the medina. Prices vary enormously, and some are extremely luxurious. Reactions to this type of accommodation are generally very positive. The riads have created a lot of work for locals (and pushed property prices up), so many feel they have a stake in the guesthouse system. (With regard to tipping, err on the generous side.)

Most riads are available to rent in their entirety, making a great base for a group or family holiday. Staff are usually included and food and entertainment (acrobats, musicians, dancers) can often be arranged.

When booking a stay in a riad in winter, check for details of heating. All riads should provide breakfast, included as part of the price, and most will also cook an evening meal on request, though advance warning is usually required. Cooler, darker ground floor rooms are preferable in summer; lighter, warmer first floor rooms in winter. Note too that, in winter, it can rain heavily in Marrakech, turning streets in the old town to muddy tracks.

What riads consider to be high season varies but always includes Christmas and Easter holidays. Rates often fall substantially outside these times. Riads usually quote their fees in euros.

Riad rental agencies

It may pay to shop around and see what is offered by riad rental agencies – they usually add a commission to the price, but they can also have special offers available. **Hôtels & Ryads**, 31 Bis, Rue Victor Massé, 75009 Paris, T+33-(0)1-42 08 18 33, www.riads.co.uk. With 64 riads in Marrakech on their books and one of the easiest to use websites, a good place to get an idea of what's available.

Riads au Maroc, 1 Rue Mahjoub Rmiza, Guéliz, T0524-431900, www.riadomaroc.com. A personalized service for both rooms in riads and whole riads from a range of 55 properties. Prices for a double room are from €45 up to €300, most are around the €70 mark.

Marrakech Riads, 8 Derb Charfa Lekbir, Mouassine, T0524-391609, www.marrakech-riads.net. Friendly and highly recommended agency with 8 excellent riads, including the simple Dar Sara and the beautiful Al Jazira. The headquarters, the beautiful Dar Cherifa, a 17th-century house converted with gallery space on the ground floor, are worth a visit in their own right (see page 78).

Villas of Morocco Immeuble Berdai, 1st floor, Guéliz, T0522-942525, www.villasofmorocco.com. For the ultimate in luxury beyond the confines of the medina, this UK agency has a portfolio of magnificent private villas in the Palmeraie and elsewhere. All are fully staffed to cater for weddings, events and family deluxe holidays. On average from around €3600 per night for exclusivity.

Place Jemaâ el Fna, but there is a porter to carry your luggage on arrival/departure. The **Blue House** is ideal for families/groups (up to 4) at 3300dh per night. Closed in Ramadan.

€€€ Riad Malika, 29 Derb Arset Aouzal, Bab Doukkala, T0524-385451, www.riad malika.com. Featuring lots of eccentric old chairs and art deco touches, **Malika** is the product of years of careful tending and collecting by its French owner. The patio is thick with vegetation, shading the pool and, although reports of the quality of service are mixed, you get character in abundance. Spacious rooms, with a/c and Wi-Fi throughout. Central location in Dar el Bacha area, but quite a walk from Jemaâ el Fna.

€€€ Riad Porte Royale, Derb el Matta 84, Diour Jdad, Zaouïa Sidi bel Abbes, T0524-376109, www.riadporteroyale.com. Owned by an English writer, **Porte Royale** brings a touch of British elegance to the northern edge of the medina. There's no over-the-top decoration or wild kaleidoscope of colours here, just pristine white walls, a few carefully chosen pieces of furniture and occasional rare fabrics. The stylish reserve of the decoration serves to emphasize the beauty of the building and contributes to an atmosphere of serenity. The location is a beautiful part of the medina that few tourists reach and service is superbly friendly and attentive. Excellent value.

€€€ Riad Tizwa, Derb Gueraba 26, Dar el Bacha, T0668-190872 (Morocco) or T+44-7973-115471 (UK), www.riadtizwa.com. Stylish and good value, the Bee brothers' Marrakech riad is an elegant place near Dar el Bacha and claims to be "Marrakech's first environmentally recognized riad", sourcing produce from organic local suppliers. Well-designed without being fussy, the 6 bedrooms, primarily white with splashes of colour, open into a central courtyard with a small fountain. Huge beds are exceptionally comfortable and the dressing areas are a great design feature – bring plenty of clothes in order to make full use of the inventive hanging space behind enormous *tadelakt*

headboards. Bathrooms are luxurious, with innumerable thick towels and soft hooded dressing gowns you may never want to get out of. Wi-Fi, iPod docks and good food.

€€ Les Jardins Mandaline, 55 derb Ferrane Riad Laarouss, T0524-382295, www.lesjardins-mandaline.com. This French-run, good value riad has 8 differently decorated rooms, all with private bathrooms. There's a plunge pool and a pretty *tadelakt* hammam too. Fresh flowers punctuate the mainly white decoration, and the salon has chess and a collection of DVDs. The roof terrace doesn't have any views, but it's quiet and there are sun loungers. Excellent value, though the rooms are a bit cramped.

€€ Riad Dar Maia, 31 Derb Zouina, Riad Zitoune Jedid, T0524-376231, www.riad-dar-maia.com. Tucked into a side alley at the Bahia Palace end of Riad Zitoune Jedid, this pretty little guesthouse has 5 simple colour-themed rooms, each with an en suite shower room. There is a cosy tea salon for guests and 2 roof terraces for breakfast. The English-speaking owner and house manager are exceptional hosts. It's also a bargain.

€€ Riad Marianis, 26 derb el Firane, Riad Laarouss, T0524-383696, www.riad-marianis. com. *Tadelakt*, long narrow rooms and heritage Moroccan rugs and drapes tick all the riad boxes. There's also a good roof terrace, and excellent food is cooked to order. What sets the relaxed **Marianis** apart is the warmth of the welcome. It's also very good value. Check the website for occasional special offers.

€€ Riad tlaatawa-sitteen, 63 Derb el Ferrane, Riad Laarouss, T0524-383026, www.tlaatawa-sitteen.com. This is remarkably good value for a riad. You don't get all the polished edges that come with most riads, but you still get a stylish place to stay in the heart of the medina. Homeliness is emphasized, and the option to go to the market or to a hammam with the staff makes a stay here feel almost like being part of a Moroccan family. There's a salon with books and music, and a kitchen for guests to use. The grey-green colour scheme and Moroccan tiles give the place a young, hip feel. Nearby, the chilled **Dar Najma**, under the same management, has 3 simply styled suites (**€€€**).

Hotels in the medina

€€€€ Jardins de la Koutoubia, 26 Rue de la Koutoubia, T0524-388800, www.les jardinsdelakoutoubia.com. Close to the Koutoubia on the site of one of Marrakech's finest palaces, Dar Louarzazi, **Les Jardins** has a spectacular and elegant central courtyard with a large square pool, off which the lights sparkle at night. As well as the pool, there is a spa, 3 restaurants, an underground car park and a rooftop restaurant with great views. Its size – there are 72 rooms and suites – means that service can be a little impersonal but you're right at the heart of the action. With elevators to all floors and street-level access, this hotel is ideal for wheelchair users. Buffet breakfast is 190dh.

€€€€ La Maison Arabe, 1 Derb Assehbe, Bab Doukkala, T0524-387010, www.lamaison arabe.com. Once one of Marrakech's best restaurants, **La Maison Arabe** is now converted into very swish accommodation, run by an Italian who grew up in Tangier. Despite its size – 12 rooms and 14 deluxe suites – there is something of a private-house atmosphere. There are 2 courtyards and most suites have private terraces and fireplace. A shuttle bus runs to the hotel's own Country Club, set in gardens just outside the city. Cookery classes are recommended, or you can just eat at the in-house restaurant or 1930s themed piano bar.

€€€€ La Mamounia, Av Bab Jedid, T0524-388600, www.mamounia.com. A Marrakech institution, the **Mamounia** was one of the first hotels in the city, built on 8 ha of gardens within the walls and a couple of mins' walk from the Koutoubia. Originally owned and run by Moroccan railways, it has been patronized by the rich and famous ever since opening in 1923. After extensive multi-million pound renovations, the hotel reopened in 2009 and is truly a magnificent homage to Moroccan architecture, design and elegance. Moroccans still talk about it in hushed, awestruck tones, and it looks set to continue as the country's most luxurious hotel for some time. If it's out of your league, you can call in for tea in the gardens for 350dh per head.

€€€€ La Sultana, 403 Rue de la Kasbah, T0524-388008, www.lasultanamarrakech. com. 5 conjoined riads make up this luxury hotel overlooking the Saâdian tombs, in the Kasbah area of the city. From the outside you'd hardly know it was there but inside 28 beautifully crafted rooms and suites open up off enormous corridors, and there are 1200 m sq of roof terrace with a bar. There's a heated pool, a jacuzzi and a *salon de massage* too. Decoration is ornate, with chandeliers, rich sultry colours and the pervasive tinkling of water.

€€€€ Les Jardins de la Médina, 21 Derb Chtouka, T0524-381851, www.lesjardinsde lamedina.com. This hotel in a refurbished palace that once belonged to a cousin of the king has 36 a/c rooms, a heated pool surrounded by trees and good restaurants. While it lacks something of the individuality of a riad, it makes up for it with an extremely high standard of service, exceptional facilities and an exalted setting, with plenty of space for lounging in grand style. There are English newspapers, a licensed bar, lots of books, beautiful gardens overlooked by fitness machines, a hammam, a beauty centre, a jacuzzi and a cookery school, where you can spend a morning learning how to make your own Moroccan tagine. Located in the Kasbah neighbourhood with easy access.

€€€€ Villa des Orangers, 6 Rue Sidi Mimoun, T0524-384638, www.villades orangers.com. At the edge of the medina, the **Villa des Orangers** is a 5-star chic hotel in a 1930s building. Carved plasterwork and tiles give it a traditional riad flavour, while televisions, pools and minibars remind you that this is much more than a *maison d'hôte*. Musicians play every night in one of the 2 courtyards, surrounded by fountains and trees. Rooms are huge and some have private terrace. Prices include many extras, such as airport transfers and tea and pastries. Check the website for special offers for multi-night stays.

€€ Hotel Ali, Rue Moulay Ismail, T0524-444979, www.hotel-ali.com. An old travellers' favourite, this large, rambling hotel is just off Jemaâ el Fna. It's a decent base for those intending to go climbing/trekking, as it is run by people from the Atlas and there are usually guides to be found hanging out here. Don't expect anything stylish; simple rooms have as many beds squeezed into them as possible, but all now have a/c and some have a balcony. Good-value restaurant and discounts for a week's stay. Fabulous views from roof terrace. No credit cards.

€€ Hotel Assia, 32 Rue de la Recette, T0524-391285, www.hotel-assia-marrakech. com. Halfway between a riad and a budget hotel, this good-value place has *tadelakt*, tiles, plants and a fountain, though service can be on the slow side. There are 26 comfortable a/c rooms, but those downstairs are a bit gloomy. Meals available on request. Currency exchange available from reception.

€€ Hotel Belleville, 194 Riad Zitoun el Kedim, T0524-426481, www.hotelbelleville. ma. 4-poster beds are squeezed tightly into some of the 9 en suite rooms in this small hotel not far from Jemaâ el Fna. There's lots of wrought iron, a pleasant roof terrace with tent and a heated Moroccan salon too. Plenty of traditional features, but a bit cluttered and untidy. Free Wi-Fi in the patio and a/c. A good budget option.

€€ Hotel Gallia, 30 Rue de la Recette, T0524-445913, www.ilove-marrakesh.com/ hotelgallia. At the cheap end of the city's stylish places to stay, the **Gallia** is clean and conveniently located in a 1930s building with a beautifully planted courtyard, a huge tree and caged birds. There's plenty of hot water and the 3 floors have carved plaster, peach-painted walls and Moroccan tiles. Though rooms aren't overly fancy, they have

good beds, and breakfast is included, so it's good value. Heading down Rue Bab Agnaou from Jemaâ el Fna, it's at the end of a narrow street on the left. Popular, so reserve well in advance (by fax). English-speaking staff.

€€ Hotel Jnane Mogador, 116 Riad Zitoun el Kedim, T0524-426324, www.jnane mogador.com. So popular that management advise booking 6 months in advance, this place fills a gap in the market between grotty budget hotels and stylish but expensive riads. Theirs is a blueprint that others in Marrakech are now starting to follow, but still nobody else does it quite this well. The 17 rooms aren't large but they have attractive drapes and rugs, and en suite bathrooms. There's a pretty courtyard with a petal-filled fountain, roof terrace with spectacular views to the Koutoubia, free internet access, a hammam with massage and a salon with both a/c for summer and a fire for winter. Great location close to Jemaâ el Fna. Breakfast is 40dh.

€€ Hotel Sherazade, 3 Derb Djama, T0524-429305, www.hotelsherazade.com. Beds are big, fabrics are bold and striped, there's lots of greenery and the vibe is friendly in this hotel southeast of Jemaâ el Fna. It's spotlessly clean and the 23 rooms are arranged around large courtyards. Breakfast is an extra 50dh for a buffet on the roof terrace. The owners also have 2 bungalows for rent 14 km north of the city. The street is the 3rd narrow one on your left as you head down Riad Zitoun el Kedim from Jemaâ el Fna. Good value and very popular, so book well in advance.

€€ Sindi Sud, 109 Derb Sidi Bouloukate, T0524-443337, sindisud@hotmail.com. Just around the corner from **Hotel Médina**, this place has a room on each floor with private shower, a/c and heating, with breakfast included in the price. Other tiled standard rooms (lower end of the € category) are very clean and have basins with shared showers (5dh) on the corridors. There are some nice touches, such as decorated doors and some carved plasterwork. The roof terrace has plants and a laundry area. Even breakfast (15dh) is good value.

€ **Hotel Essaouira**, 3 Derb Sidi Bouloukate, T0524-443805. Clean, simple rooms with coloured glass, basins and mirrors. Shared bathrooms are good and clean and hot showers are included in the price. Tiles and old painted woodwork give the place some style and there are tents, plants and a kitchen on the roof terrace, assuming you can get up the steep spiral stairs. A suite would be a good option for a family.

€ **Hotel Ichbilia**, 1 Rue Bani Marine, T0524-381530. The best of the 32 rooms here have balconies overlooking the street, though these can be noisy. Beds are comfortable but there's little style. The 7 rooms with bathrooms are good value, but those without a/c or en suite bathrooms are even cheaper. No frills, but as cheap as chips. No breakfast available.

€ **Hotel La Gazelle**, 13 Rue Bani Marine, T0524-441112, hotel_gazelle@hotmail.com. The eponymous Gazelle sits on a shelf in the light and pretty courtyard of this friendly budget option south of Jemaâ el Fna. Pink walls predominate and there's a roof terrace, though the beds are rather old and sagging. Rooms have basins, some have bathrooms, otherwise shared showers on corridors.

Hotels in the ville nouvelle

€€€€ **Dar Ayniwen**, Tafrata, Palmeraie, T0524-329684, www.dar-ayniwen.com. Luxury of the ornate, antique sort is on offer at this palm grove guesthouse. Very different to the minimalist riad chic usually found in such places, the decoration creates a more lived-in, but no less elegant atmosphere. 'House cars' with drivers are available to take you wherever you desire in the city. There's a pool, extensive gardens with fruit trees, cacti and English lawn, and a hammam. Minimum stay 2 nights.

€€€€ **Dar Rhizlane**, Av Jnane el Harti, T0524-421303, www.dar-rhizlane.com. The 19 a/c rooms and suites in this Hivernage boutique hotel are decorated in the riad style but the *ville nouvelle* setting on an olive tree-lined boulevard gives an extra spaciousness you rarely find in the medina. There is also a good-sized pool and a rose garden. Some rooms have private gardens, and there is a gourmet restaurant open to non-residents. There is an air of tranquility that is normally found only in the villas of the Palmeraie, but **Dar Rhizlane** is within walking distance of the city centre. Afternoon tea is complimentary. Free Wi-Fi.

€€€ **Bab Hotel**, Corner Rue Mohammed el-Beqal and Blvd Mansour Eddahbi, T0524-435250, www.babhotelmarrakech.com. A funky new boutique hotel in the heart of Guéliz full of trendy 70s retro design. All aesthetically very pleasing and crisp, with minimalist decor and furnishings in shades of white. Roof terrace with Wi-Fi, bar and sun loungers, a small enclosed pool and stylish chill-out lounges with fluffy coloured lampshades and rag-rugs. Restaurant and bar attracts the Marrakech 'arty' types.

€€€ **Diwane**, 24 Rue Yougoslavie (just off Av Mohammed V), T0524-432216, www.diwane-hotel.com. One of the most human of the city's super-hotels, Diwane has a good pool with grassy surrounds, café and a boutique which actually sells some useful maps and books alongside the usual tourist tat. The 115 rooms are a cut above the usual big hotel standard too – they have generous desks, balconies and fridges and tiles and *tadelakt* in the bathrooms for some local style. A good option if you want a big hotel with all the trimmings and don't mind sharing it with tour groups. The Moroccan buffet dinner is worth trying, but skip the 'international' menu. 2 hammams, sauna, gym, hairdresser.

€€€-€€ **Moroccan House Hotel**, 3 Rue Loubnane, T0524-420305, www.moroccan househousehotels.com. The 50 rooms in this modern hotel are decorated in a rather over-the-top recreation of riad style. There are 4-poster beds and lots of purple and bright colours, creating an overall sense of fun. There's a good pool (not heated) and a big roof terrace for breakfast, plus a more traditional hammam in the basement. Service, in contrast to the frilly decor, is staid and professional. Some tour groups. Breakfast is 59dh.

€€ **Hotel du Pacha**, 33 Rue de la Liberté, T0524-431327, www.hotelpacha.net. On a quiet corner of Marrakech's *ville nouvelle*, this 1930s hotel is a good, if old-fashioned establishment, reminiscent of colonial times with its heavy wooden panelling and ornate carved plasterwork. Ground floor rooms have been renovated with en suite marble bathrooms, and all rooms are freshly painted and decorated with Moroccan fabrics; some have small balconies. Double, twin or triple bed arrangements possible. Staff very helpful, and alcohol in the bar is an added bonuses. There's a restaurant too, with a 150dh menu, or à la carte main dishes from 60dh. All in all, good value.

€€ **Hotel Fashion**, 45 Av Hassan II, T0524-423707, fashionhotel@menara.ma. Don't be put off by the ugly exterior, or the naff name; this friendly place combines something of riad style with a convenient location and contemporary mid-sized hotel advantages such as a rooftop pool (albeit a small and rather shallow one; you may bang your knees), a hammam and a good café downstairs for breakfast. Spacious and fairly plush rooms are decked out in warm yellows and reds, with comfortable sofas, big desks and good beds. Showers have a habit of going suddenly very hot, so it may be a good idea to make use of the baths. Free Wi-Fi in reception and breakfast is included.

€€ **Ryad Mogador Opera**, Av Mohammed VI, T0524-339390, www.ryadmogador.com. Situated just across from the Theatre Royal in Guéliz, this branch 4-star link in the Ryad Mogador chain is a good option for those who want a resort-style hotel, as long as the building works next door have finished (still ongoing in 2011). There are 111 rooms here, around an octagonal central atrium with a giant chandelier. Painted wood gives a small touch of local style. Good big pool and a spa, but as with all the Ryad Mogador hotels, no alcohol is served. **Ryad Mogador Menara** offers more of the same just down the road at a 5-star grade, but avoid the **Ryad Mogador Marrakech** near Bab Doukkala. Price includes breakfast.

€ **Hotel Toulousain**, 44 Rue Tarik Ibn Ziad, Guéliz, T0524-430033, www.hoteltoulousain.com. Downstairs rooms open onto a quiet garden courtyard with climbing plants, decorated in pink and blue. There's car parking on the street (paid) and it's a friendly, laid-back place, and very handy for the excellent **Café du Livre** next door. 1st floor rooms can be hot in summer. Rooms without bathroom are cheaper, with breakfast included.

Outskirts of the city

In the Palmeraie, to the north of the centre, the old palm groves are increasingly being taken over by large, smart hotels and villa-style boutique hotels. These can feel a bit far from the action, though there is usually the advantage of large pools and luscious gardens. Many provide transport into the city centre.

€€€€ Amanjena Resort, Route de Ouazarzate Km 12, T0524-399000, www. amanjena.com. This is a top-end complex centring on a large reflecting pool. Featured as the palatial retreat for the girls in the film *Sex and the City II*, this luxurious accommodation starts at 9500dh per night for a 'pavilion' and goes up to 30,000dh for a 'maison' with a private pool. Everything is spectacularly grand and spacious, but, despite the use of local materials, the newness of the place is hard to hide and it therefore lacks something of the soul of a genuine riad. Nevertheless, wood-burning fires, candle lanterns, a gym, clay tennis courts and hammams make the sky-high prices a little easier to swallow, but the continental breakfast is 250dh extra.

€€€€ CaravanSerai, 264 Ouled Ben Rahmoune, T0524-300302, www.hotel caravanserai.com. Elegant and stylish, CaravanSerai (the word means an old roadside inn) has 13 suites, 4 rooms and 40 staff, which gives some indication of the levels of service you should expect. Pale colours and white drapes dominate, creating an atmosphere of calm, and there are vines and jacaranda trees. There's a fantastic vaulted hammam, heated pools, Wi-Fi, 2 daily city centre shuttle buses, billiards, restaurant, bar and airport transfer. Prices have been recently cut and, with frequent special offers, this is affordable luxury.

€€€€ Jnane Tamsna, Douar Abiad, Palmeraie, T0524-328484, www.jnane tamsna.com. Well away from the bustle of downtown Marrakech, the 24 rooms are spread over 5 villas in a walled herb, vegetable and fruit tree garden. The whole ensemble makes an elegant, sophisticated and peaceful place to stay. The design is traditional Moroccan, with lots of personal touches, such as old photos and furniture designed by the owner, Meryanne Loum-Martin. The roll-call of celebrity visitors bears testimony to the highly personalized service and extras, such as organic food, yoga courses, tennis coaching and 5 pools (not always heated). It's one of the best addresses in Marrakech, but the high standards come at a price, although rates include breakfast and soft drinks. Meryanne and her husband Gary, who set up the Global Diversity Foundation, are currently working on a new project, Jnane Ylane, a boutique hotel and natural spa that should be completed in 2014.

€€€€ Les Deux Tours, Douar Abiad, Palmeraie, T0524-329525, www.les-deux-tours.com. Out in the palm groves, this small development was originally designed by Tunisian architect Charles Boccara as second homes for Moroccans tired of the big city. The 35 traditional rooms all have balconies, are surrounded by palms and beautifully decorated in Moroccan style (tiles, fabrics and antiques). Pool suites have own private plunge pool, though there is a 300dh daily charge for heating it. There's a good communal pool too, set in verdant and extensive gardens, though there are mixed reports about the quality of service. Pick-up at Marrakech airport.

€€€€ Palmeraie Golf Palace, Circuit de la Palmeraie, T0524-368722, www. pgpmarrakech.com. The best of the behemoths in the palm groves outside Marrakech, with a frequent shuttle service into town. 5-star luxury directed towards a corporate clientele, but with spacious suites, acres of gardens, golf-course, 5 pools, tennis courts and children's programmes, it's also ideal for families. 286 rooms and 70 suites, with all expected mod cons and either a terrace or balcony. Check the website as there are deals nearly all year offering almost 50% reductions.

🍴 Restaurants

Marrakech *p46, maps p52 and p56*
Upmarket Moroccan restaurants in restored houses with garden courtyards are part of the Marrakech experience. Generally, they are indicated by a discrete wall plaque – taxi drivers know where they are, or someone from the restaurant will come to accompany you. Reservations are usually a good idea. For contemporary eating, the *ville nouvelle* has plenty of good options and, whatever your budget, you shouldn't miss the experience of dining with the locals in Jemaâ el Fna.

Medina

€€€ Dar Moha, 81 Rue Dar el Bacha, T0524-386400, www.darmoha.com. Closed Mon.
One of the best medina restaurants, **Dar Moha** offers inventive Moroccan nouvelle cuisine. Try the sea bass tagine or lemon quail in filo pastry. It's easier than most to locate, being on the busy Rue Dar el Bacha. In summer, try to get a table outside on the patio by the pool. 5-course dinner menu is 530dh per person, set lunch menus from 220dh.

€€€ Dar Zellij, Kaasour Sidi Benslimane, T0524-382627, www.darzellij.com.
Converted from a 17th-century riad guesthouse to a restaurant, **Dar Zellij** now offers one of the most spectacular settings in the city in which to enjoy an evening meal. It's not easy to find but is well worth the effort. Waiters seem to float around the tree-filled courtyard in long white gowns, and the live music is subtle rather than intrusive. Tables come sprinkled with petals, there's an open fire, dark red walls, candles, enormous high ceilings, curtains and calligraphic art. The traditional Moroccan food is good too, though at times it can't quite match the extravagance of the surroundings or the service. Unimaginative vegetarian options. Set menus 300-600dh.

€€€ Ksar Essaoussan, Rue des Ksar 3, Derb el Messoudyenne, T0524-440632, www.essaoussane.com. Evenings only; closed Sun and Aug. Off Rue Fatima Zohra,

where somebody will meet you with a lamp to guide you in. An intimate 18th-century patrician home where Bach plays in an antique-filled interior, **Ksar-es-saoussan** contrasts with the Las Vegas dazzle of some of the medina places. The choice of mains is limited, but it is tasty and authentic cooking. There are 3 set menus (350-550dh) including an aperitif, half-bottle of wine and soft drinks. There are good photo opportunities from the terraces. Reservations recommended.

€€€ Le Tobsil, 22 Derb Abdallah Ben Houssein, Quartier Ksar, T0524-444052.
Evenings only; closed Tue. Elegant Moroccan cuisine is cooked and served with more subtlety than usual in this ochre-walled little riad. The 5-course banquet menu is fixed price and, though it's expensive at 625dh, it does include wine and aperitif. One of the longest established addresses for fine dining in the medina and it continues to maintain its reputation for quality. Reservations are essential as there are not very many tables, and it can get a little cramped. Live gnawa music.

€€€ Villa Flore, 4 Derb Azzouz, Mouassine, T0524-391700, www.villa-flore.com. Wed-Mon, lunch and dinner.
In contrast to the gaudy decor in many riad restaurants, this place is simply and quietly elegant, drawing upon an art deco palette of black, white and wine-red. The Moroccan-French food is beautifully presented, using the freshest of local ingredients. Try the *briouates* of artichoke and prawn for starters, or melt-in-the-mouth lamb. There are mixed reports about the service. Lunch menu is 220dh, dinner 330dh.

€€ Le Foundouk, 55 Souk Hal Fassi, Kaât Ben Hadid, T0524-378190, www.foundouk. com. Tue-Sun 1200-2400. For those for whom insipid, overcooked tagines have become a chore, the succulent, well-spiced versions here will be something of a welcome surprise. Near the Medersa Ben Youssef, the licensed **Foundouk**, in a converted riad, is one of the most elegant restaurants in Marrakech. There are roses in glasses on the tables, contemporary art and mirrors on the walls, and modern jazz plays while a white, dark brown and burgundy colour scheme gives the place an air of contemporary sophistication. As well as the tagines (for around 130dh), there's European food too, and vegetarians can find plenty of choice in the starters to make up an entire meal. Evening reservations recommended.

€€ **Le Jardin**, 32 Souk El Jedld, Sidi Abdelaziz, T0524-378295, www.lejardin.ma. Daily 0900-2300. This large courtyard restaurant enclosed in a 17th-century mansion is 2 steps away from its sister, **Terrasse des Épices**. Under the same ownership and direction, it offers snacks, salads or light meals all day with some enticing vegetarian options. In summer there are outdoor screenings of arthouse movies in the garden, while in winter you can enjoy a meal in front of the crackling fireplace. Alcohol licence pending.

€€ **Les Terrasses de l'Alhambra**, Jemaâ el Fna, T0524-427570. Daily 0800-2300. Almost opposite the **Café de France** is this popular contemporary place for reasonably priced pasta, pizzas and salads. The latter are a good option, including smoked salmon and avocado. If you're in the mood for something more Moroccan, tagine and *pastilla* feature too. It's a smarter venue than many of the places around the square and has a loungey atmosphere and terraces with fab views over the square. Also good for a drink or ice-cream stop during the day. Its prime ringside location means it gets very crowded regardless of food quality or service, so don't expect too much on that front. No alcohol.

€€ **Le Tanjia**, 14 Derb J'did – Hay Essalam, Mellah, T0524-383836. Daily 0800-0100. Describing itself as an oriental brasserie, **Le Tanjia** brings something of chic Paris to the Marrakech medina; dark wood round tables and leather chairs are combined with Moroccan lanterns and palms. Food is high-quality Moroccan, with unusually good salads and vegetarian options. The terrace or the

ground floor bar are good spots for a drink at any time of day. Easy to find near La Place des Ferblantiers and vehicle access to the door. Unfortunately since changing ownership in recent times, the standards have slipped.

€€ **Terrasse des Épices**, 15 Souk Cherifa, Sidi Abdelaziz, T0524-375904, www. terrassedesepices.com. Daily 1200-2300. From the owners of the successful **Café des Épices**, the titular terrace is a surprisingly expansive and open space on the first floor of a building in the middle of the souks. Comfortable, shaded tables and private booths are spaced around the edge and, in the evening, it becomes especially atmospheric, as the sun sets and lanterns light the place. The food is excellent; as well as a traditional 100dh Moroccan menu (lunch only), there are inventive options, such as caramalized prunes with goat's cheese crème fraiche. No alcohol.

€€-€ **Les Premices**, Jemaâ el Fna, T0524-391970. At the southeast edge of the square, a bit away from the main action, Les Premices is a cut above much of its competition. There are 2 levels of terrace overlooking the square or you can sit inside. Try the tasty European dishes, such as mozzarella salad or fried sole, or go for standard Moroccan tagines or couscous from around 70dh. Patchy service. No alcohol.

€ **Chez Bahia**, 206 Rue Riad Zitoun el Kedim, just off Jemaâ el Fna, T0524-378946. Being just off Jemaâ el Fna, **Chez Bahia** gets fewer tourists and also offers better value than some of its competitors right on the square. Tagines are only 30-50dh, and it's also a good spot for breakfast, with freshly cooked pancakes and *bisara*. It's clean, bright, basic, good value and very Moroccan. Call by and order in advance some house specialities, such as spicy aubergine tagine or pigeon *pastilla*. No alcohol.

€ **Chez Chegrouni**, Jemaâ el Fna. Just to the left of the **Café de France**, Chez Chegrouni is well-known for its good couscous. That, combined with its seats out front and upstairs terrace, means that it's

Café culture

Around Jemaâ el Fna there are lots of cafés which exist primarily because of their terraces overlooking the square. None are licensed, and none would be great cafés in other locations, but they are all rightfully popular, especially late in the afternoon, for the opportunity they offer to survey the frenzy below from the relative calm of a terrace. As a response to the hordes of tourists coming up to these cafés just to take photos, many will only let you onto their terraces after you've bought a drink. **Café de France** has several levels and an excellent panorama over the square and the medina beyond.

Café Glacier Le Grand Balcon, on the southeast edge of the square, has perhaps the best views of sunset through the rising smoke from the food stalls below. **Les Terrasses de l'Alhambra**, just opposite the Café de la France, is a strategic meeting place near the entrance to the souks and just beyond the mayhem of the foodstalls. Good views from the top terrace, page 76.

In Guéliz, head to the modern **Marrakech Plaza** at Place du 16 Novembre for people-watching from French-style brasserie-cafés, or spot celebrities during the annual Marrakech Film Festival from the cafés along **Avenue Mohammed VI**.

---

popular, and you'll have to turn up early for the best seats. It's still good value though: a vegetable couscous only 40dh. Vegetarians will be glad to know they do not use meat stock in the vegetable dishes. No alcohol.

€ Earth Café, 2 Derb Zawak, Riad Zitoune Kedim, T0661-289402, www.earthcafe marrakech.com. Daily 1100-2300. The first of its kind in Marrakech and a welcome boost for vegetarians. Organic, vegan and totally animal-friendly food, with Asian influences, served in a colourful courtyard bedecked with paper lanterns. An array of freshly picked salads, such as beetroot salad with goat's cheese, or *pastilla* stuffed with pumpkin and courgette. No alcohol.

€ Jemaâ el Fna food stalls, one of Marrakech's great experiences, eating in Jemaâ el Fna is not to be missed. Piles of salads and steaming tagines are set up under hissing gas lamps from early evening onwards. Each stall has a different variety of cooked food, from sheep heads to snails to fried fish to bowls of soup. It is best to go for the food cooked to order while waiting, and the most popular places obviously have a faster turnover of food. In general, however, eating here is no less safe than in most Moroccan restaurants, and there are rarely any problems. Walking along between the stalls is an experience in itself – you will be cajoled onto benches from all sides by young Moroccans who have somehow picked up a surreal line in mock cockney patter. Don't miss the stalls selling harira soup, served with dates and *gateaux de miel* for 9dh, or fresh fried fish at stall No 14.

€ Nid'Cigogne, 60 Rue de la Kasbah, T0524-382092, Opposite the Saâdian tombs, you climb 2 flights of stairs to reach this roof-terrace restaurant-café, serving good salads and kefta sandwiches. The *salade Maroc* is especially varied and generous for 20dh, and service is continuous 0900-2100. It makes a very handy lunch spot, and you can peer straight across the road into the nests of the eponymous storks. No alcohol.

€ Tiznit, 28 Souk el Kassabine, just off Jemaâ el Fna, T0524-427204. Daily 0800-2300. Just a few doors from **Chez Chegrouni**, heading away from the square, you'll spot a building that juts out a few feet from the main façade. Up the steep tiled steps you'll enter a tiny restaurant jammed with a few plastic tables and locals tucking into the best and cheapest rabbit tagine in town for just 35dh. Closed during Ramadan. No alcohol.

Cafés and patisseries

Café des Épices, 75 Rahba Kedima, T0524-391770, www.cafedesepices.net. Daily 0800-2000. The open space of Rahba Kedima (the Spice Square), thronged with hat, basket and live reptile sellers, makes a great setting for the medina's best café. In a small and usually overflowing building, it offers good sandwiches and salads over 3 floors. The roof terrace is especially popular. Herbal teas also served. Free Wi-Fi.

Dar Cherifa, 8 Derb Charfa Lakbir, Mouassine, off Rue Mouassine, T0524-426463. Daily 1200-1900. Hard to find and when you do you'll probably need to ring the bell to be let in, but that adds to the rarefied air of this gallery café in a tall, spacious riad. Downstairs is a contemporary art space, while the quiet café is on the roof terrace upstairs and serves mint tea and saffron coffee. There are 2 lunch menus (90dh/120dh). Look out for occasional cultural evenings.

Patisserie Les Princes, 32 Rue de Bab Agnaou (also known as Av Prince Moulay Rachid), T0524-443033. Daily 0600-2230. On the pedestrian street south of Jemaâ el Fna, Les Princes has an excellent selection of pastries and petits fours, though the ice creams aren't great. Mint teas come in different varieties in a *salon du thé* at the back.

Riad Yima, 52 Derb Aarjane, Rahba Lakdima, T0524-391987, www.riadyima.com. Daily 0900-1800. Formerly run as a guesthouse, this place is now a small café, gallery and boutique full of quirky pop-art charm. Created by artist, photographer and designer, Hassan Hajjaj, the space is filled with his humorous recycled objets d'art and is tucked down a side-alley near the **Café des Epices**. Serves herbal teas, a variety of coffees and organic fruit juices.

Souk Café, 11 Derb Souk Jdid, Sidi Abdelaziz (near Rue Riad Larousse), T0662-610229. Daily 1100-2300. Tricky to find in the northern twists of the souks, but well worth stopping by for a fruit smoothie on the terrace of this stylishly converted old house. Cinammon-coloured *tadelakt* walls, colourful textiles and authentic Moroccan food served throughout the day. At night the intimate restaurant comes alive with belly dancers, and customers can discreetly bring their own wine/beer.

Ville nouvelle *map p52*

While Marrakech's medina restaurants serve mostly Moroccan food, the *ville nouvelle* has a much wider range of eating and (especially) drinking options. Guéliz (the main *ville nouvelle* area) also has some good cafés, old-fashioned and modern, straight-laced and alternative, many of which also make good eating spots.

€€€ **La Trattoria**, 179 Rue Mohammed el Bequal, T0524-432641, www.latrattoria marrakech.com. Open evenings only from 1830. The city's smartest Italian restaurant, this place is on a leafy side street in the heart of Guéliz and oozes elegance and romance. There's a lush garden terrace for pre-dinner drinks and an excellent selection of wines. The kitchen serves up scrumptious Italian cuisine, from sun-dried tomato and mozzarella tartlets to curried monkfish with pineapple and asparagus. Reservations advisable.

€€ **Al Fassia Guéliz**, 55 Blvd Zerktouni, T0524-434060, www.alfassia.com. Wed-Mon 1200-2230. This excellent Moroccan restaurant is run by a women's cooperative, and all the staff, once you're past the doorman, are female. You can dine à la carte, and there's an excellent choice of tagines – for example, lamb with aubergine and chicken with caramelized pumpkin – for 130dh. Other good options include vegetable couscous and seafood *pastilla* and there's a long wine list too. The interior is elegant, with silk tablecloths and napkins, snug corners and a central area where sunlight filters down in daytime. Reservations recommended. Due to demand, a second **Al Fassia** has been opened in nearby Aguedal, though locals still say Guéliz is the best of the two.

€€ **Bistro Thai**, 8 Av Oued el Makhazine (opposite **Royal Tennis Club**), T0524-457311.

Oriental fusion of Thai, Japanese and Vietnamese cuisine in stylish surroundings. Diners can go for the elegant sunken lounge area, sit up at the sushi bar surveying the chef at work or take a low table out on the wooden decked terrace that looks onto the street. Deliciously fragrant Thai curries, or dramatic flaming wok creations, loads of tasty nibbles, dim sum and steamed rice. Create your own variations ,choosing which meat you want with which style of sauce. Licensed bar and cocktails. The plateau of tasty starters includes satay, *nems* and tiny spring rolls and is enough for 2 people, 130dh.

€€ **Catanzaro**, 11 Rue Tarak Ibn Ziad, next to **Hotel Toulousain**, T0524-433737. Closed Sun. An Italian that's a bit of a Marrakech institution, with excellent wood-fired pizzas and pastas alongside other more complex dishes and meat grills. Reservations are a good idea, but you can usually also turn up and queue. Rustic charm, lively atmosphere and busy with locals and tourists for both lunch and dinner. Good value, with pizzas at 55dh and good Moroccan wines priced from 160dh per bottle.

€€ **Kechmara**, 3 Rue de la Liberté, T0524-422532, www.kechmara.com. Mon-Sat 0730-midnight. Like a very cool contemporary café with a good wine list and exciting food, **Kechmara** is unlike almost all other eating options in Marrakech. The tea menu includes blue and green varieties from Vietnam, and there are omlettes and panini for daytime stops. It's the evening when the place really buzzes, though, with Marrakech's bright young things sitting on designer plastic chairs ordering contemporary European food of the highest order. Live music at the weekends, art exhibitions and a shaded roof terrace bar to escape from all the cigarette smoke. Moroccan Flag beer on tap.

€€ **Le Bagatelle**, 103 Rue de Yougoslavie, T0524-430274, www.bagatellemarrakech. over-blog.com. Daily 0900-2300. Re-opened in 2010, this French brasserie-style restaurant is a favourite with the large expat community and has been popular since it first opened in 1949. Art-nouveau styling, long rows of tables with bentwood chairs and cushion-backed booths, potted plants and loads of old photos give an authentic bistro effect and almost obliterate any sense of the Marrakech street outside. The appetising menu includes trout meunière and quail with raisins and cinnamon. The lunch menu at 110dh is exceptional value and, with free Wi-Fi too, you could make it a working lunch and not feel guilty.

€€ **Le Carioca**, 120 Rue Mohammed Bequal, T0524-431485, www.lecarioca. marrakech.com. Mon-Sat 1200-1600 and 1900-0100. The newest restaurant in town is run by a Moroccan with a passion for Brazilian cooking and South American music. Hey presto! Churrasco barbecued meats roasted on a spit and carved at your table, served with salads and live latin music. As much as you can eat for 230dh and lighter lunches from around 180dh. The bar is open to non-diners and serves tequila slammers and cocktails from 60dh.

€€ **Pizzeria Niagara**, Route de Targa (take a taxi), T0524-449775. Open evenings only. Generally considered Marrakech's best pizza place, Niagara is not exactly central; it's probably worth taking a taxi to get you out to the Lycée Victor Hugo neighbourhood at the far end of Av Mohammed V. Gets crowded in the evenings with local families dining on the street-front covered terrace and serves alcohol at reasonable prices. The chocolate profiteroles are to die for! It's one of a clutch of pizzerias on the same strip, so if you can't get a spot, there are others nearby. Take a moment to stroll along the street outside to admire the sculpted tree trunks.

€€ **Rotisserie de la Paix**, 68 Rue Yougoslavie, T0524-433118. Daily 1200-1500 and 1900-2300. Bow-tied waiters bustle around this popular spot, offering good, freshly grilled meat with a few fish options. There are also pizzas and tagines on the menu, but the whole point is really the meat or grilled fish. In the summer the garden fills up quickly with a mix of expats and tourists, plus a resident peacock, and in winter there's an open fire inside. Service can be hit and miss.

€ **Restaurant Al Bahriya**, 75 Av Moulay Rachid, T0524-846186. Daily 1000-midnight. Just round the corner behind **Café de la Poste** you'll find this street-restaurant, and it's usually packed with Moroccans. Fresh fish, prawns, calamares all fried in batter and served up with wedges of lime and spicy olives. A large mixed plate of fish and chips costs just 35dh. Cash only.

Cafés and patisseries

Café du Livre, 44 Rue Tarik Ben Ziad, T0524-432149, www.cafedulivre.com. 0930-2100 Mon-Sat. Despite the name, **Café du Livre** is a fully-fledged restaurant as well as a café. Unfortunately the standard of cuisine has declined drastically in recent years, but the chocolate-orange tart with good flavoursome coffee is still divine. There are books on Moroccan arts and culture to browse, second-hand novels in English and French for sale, and the free Wi-Fi makes this a popular place for informal business meetings amongst expats. Low ceilings and cigarette smoke are a problem. It's also a good place to pick up information about what's going on in the city. Off a courtyard next to Hotel Toulousaine. Alcohol served.

Café Les Négociants, on the corner of Av Mohammed V and Blvd Mohammed Zerktouni, T0524-435762. Daily 0700-2300. In Guéliz, this busy intersection has popular cafés on each side, but this is the granddaddy, an old-timer still at the heart of *ville nouvelle* life and the place to come for important conversations, for long, lingering mint teas and to watch the world go by.

Grand Café de la Poste, corner of Blvd El Mansour Eddahbi and Av Imam Malik, T0524-433038, www.grandcafedelaposte.com. Daily 0800-0100. Built in 1925, the extravagant **Grand Café** has immaculately restored 1920s colonial styling and a very pleasant outdoor terrace under umbrellas. It's a place people come to be seen but they pay inflated prices for the privilege. Alcohol served.

Kaowa, 34 Rue Yves Saint Laurent (opposite Jardins Majorelle), T0524-330072. Daily 0900-1900. There are potted bamboo plants and a wooden deck terrace outside, or a bright modern interior where you can tuck into fresh organic salads, tasty wraps and fruit smoothies. Nutritious and delicious for a healthy snack.

Le 16, Pl du 16 Novembre, T0524-339670. Daily 0700-midnight. This is one of a new breed of café-restaurant in Marrakech. Its lime-green umbrellas spilling onto the central Pl du 16 Novembre are almost unmissable in the *ville nouvelle*. Worth a visit for its fantastic (and often very imaginative) ice creams and fruit juices. It also makes an excellent lunch spot, with good salads and light meals. Alcohol served.

Vlème Avenue, Residence Palm d'Or, Av Mohammed VI (corner of Blvd Mohammed Zerktouni), T0524-422388. Daily 0700-midnight. On a busy junction at the edge of Guéliz is this modern café that serves a great value full Moroccan breakfast for 35dhs: harira soup, m'smen pancakes, boiled egg, fruit juice and coffee. Also on offer are salads, paninis, pasta and light meals, and there's shaded seating with external a/c for the heat of summer. Set back from the road is a garden with tables, and something of an attraction are the family of ducks that have taken up residence in the small pond.

◑ Bars and clubs

Marrakech *p46, maps p52 and p56*
Dedicated bars are thin on the ground in the city – your best bet for a drink is often somewhere that also functions as a licensed restaurant and stays open late, or the bars within most of the hotels. There are a few sleazy side-street bars in Guéliz around Rue Mauritanie and very expensive bars inside the city's many nightclubs.

Azar, Rue Yougoslavie (corner with Av Hassan II), Guéliz, T0524-430920, www.azar-marrakech.com. Daily 1930-0100. Stylish oriental lounge-bar with chilled world-music mix and occasional live Arabic singers.

Plenty of woven carpets, candlelight and exotic ambience. Cocktails, wines and beers served with Mediterranean-themed food also available in the Moroccan-Lebanese restaurant downstairs.

Bar L'Escale, Rue Mauritania. Mon-Sat 1100-2230. A gritty, all-male environment, this bar is famed for its charcoal-grilled *coquelet* and chips with your Flag beer. Beers and some spirits served, but not for consumption at the outdoor tables.

Café Arabe, 184 Rue Mouassine, T0524-429728, www.cafearabe.com. Daily 1200-2300. Conveniently located on one of the main routes through the medina, this café offers good, if slightly unimaginative, Moroccan and Italian fare on the ground floor in a lush riad setting. Upstairs is where **Café Arabe** really comes into its own, with a rare medina bar and a relaxing rooftop terrace.

Kosybar, 47 Pl des Ferblantiers, T0524-380324. Daily 1200-0100. On several levels on the square traditionally taken up by Marrakech's metal workers, Kosybar functions as a restaurant and café but its roof terrace is a great place to hang out with a drink at sunset. The food is nothing special, cocktails are expensive at around 100dh, but bottles of Moroccan wine are reasonably priced from 150dh. Live music Thu-Sat.

Le Comptoir Darna, Av Echouhada, T0524-437702, www.comptoirdarna.com. Daily 1600-0200. Muted lighting and elegant waitresses in caftans set the tone for this popular, if pricey, drinking spot. There's a mediocre restaurant too but the licence, the live music, the belly dancers and the weekend DJs make it better suited to late-night cocktails. There's even a little boutique.

Pacha, Blvd Mohammed VI, T0524-388400, www.pachamarrakech.com. Daily 2000-0200. A big dancefloor, laid-back bars, chill-out lounge, restaurant and pool. Claims to be the biggest club in Africa. Hefty drinks prices with bottled beers starting at 100dh (admission price of 200dh includes 1 drink).

Sky Bar, La Renaissance Hotel, Av Mohammed V (corner with Blvd Mohammed Zerktouni), Guéliz, T0524-337777, www.renaissance-hotel-marrakech.com. On the 7th floor of the newly refurbished **Renaissance Hotel**, this trendy outdoor bar has the highest vantage point of anywhere in the city and a 360-degree panorama that makes the sky-high prices justifiable.

SO Night Lounge, Sofitel, Rue Haroun Errachid, Hivernage, T0524-425601, www.sofitel.com. Daily 2000-0200. More sophisticated than Pacha, this place comprises a restaurant and club with live music and DJs every night. Chill-out lounges under a pergola in the garden where you can enjoy fresh-fruit cocktails. It's a smart affair and entry costs 200dh (including 1 drink).

Teatro, Hotel Es Saadi, Av El Kadissa, T0664-860339, www.theatromarrakech.com. Daily 2000-0200. Top DJs spin their stuff at this hip club in an ex-theatre in the Hivernage district. Hard house music is the main dramatic theme.

🎭 Entertainment

Marrakech *p46, maps p52 and p56*
Casinos
Grand Casino de la Mamounia, at the **Mamounia Hotel**, Av Bab Jedid, T0524-448811, www.grandcasinomamounia.com. Open 2100-0400. 20 live games and 200 gambling machines in a grand art deco setting. Smart-casual dress code, no jeans or trainers.

Cinemas
The major cinemas showing films in French are the **Colisée**, Blvd Mohammed Zerktouni, T0524-448893 and the **Megarama**, Av Mohammed VI, T0890-102020, a 9-screen complex behind the **Pacha club**. Try also the **L'Institut Français**, Route de Targa, Guéliz, T0524-446930, www.ifm.ma.

Cultural and language centres
Instituto Cervantes, Av Mohammed V, Guéliz (the furthest end from Koutoubia), T0524-422055, www.marrakech.cervantes.es. Spanish cultural and language school, with

Haggling

Part of the fun of shopping in the medina is the haggling that comes with every purchase. To buy in the souks you will have to engage in the theatre and the mind games of the haggle.

In order to come out of the process happy, there are some things to bear in mind. Don't get too hung up on the idea of 'a good price'. The best price is the one you are happy to pay. Have one in mind before you start and don't go above it. Be prepared to walk away if the price is too high – whatever you're buying, there will almost certainly be another stall around the corner selling the same thing.

Be friendly and polite but firm and don't suggest a price you would be prepared to pay for anything you're not sure you want. Once you start talking numbers, you are in negotiation and you may find it hard to extricate yourself. The price you are first quoted might be twice as much as the seller is prepared to accept, but there is absolutely no firm rule about this. A decent starting point from the buyer's point of view is to take about a half to a third off the amount you'd be prepared to pay and start by offering that.

As a very rough guide, and depending on quality, size, etc, expect to pay these sort of prices: *babouches* 50-150dh; leather bag 200-400dh; teapot 50-200dh (more for silver); spices 30-60dh per kg; pouffe 150-450; blanket 300-600dh.

Carpet-buying can be especially complex and has many potential pitfalls – don't be too swayed by offers of mint tea/declarations of antiquity/the years of hard toil the seller's elderly aunt spent making it.

occasional concerts, films, exhibitions and special events.

Institut Français, Route de la Targa, Guéliz, Tue-Sat 1000-1230 and 1500-1900 (library). With a recommended café, open-air theatre and pleasant garden, the French Institute shows films and holds exhibitions and other cultural events. The library has a small stock of books and films in French on Morocco-related subjects. Café open Tue-Sat 0900-1900.

⊛ Festivals

Marrakech *p46, maps p52 and p56*
Jul The Festival National des Arts Populaires (www.marrakechfestival.com) brings together traditional regional music and dance troops from all over Morocco and some international acts.
Dec The Festival International du Film de Marrakech (www.festivalmarrakech. info) is held annually and attracts the stars of Hollywood and world cinema for a truly glitzy gathering.

◯ Shopping

Marrakech *p46, maps p52 and p56*
Crafts, fabrics and clothes
Marrakech is a shopper's paradise. Craft production has taken off in a big way, with a range of new products, notably in metal and ceramic, being added to classic leather and wood items. The influence of the international decorator set can clearly be felt. Close to the Dar el Bacha, in the Bab Doukkala neighbourhood, are plenty of antique dealers and, in Guéliz, the keen shopper will find chic boutiques with clothing, fine leather and other items. Prices in Guéliz are fixed and more expensive than the medina. A feel for prices can also be gained by visiting the workshops in the large craft training centre (L'Ensemble Artisanale), on the right past the Koutoubia as you head to Guéliz. Here, again, prices are non-negotiable, and slightly more expensive than in the old city. In a very short time you can see people at work at practically all the main crafts, including embroidery,

ceramic mosaic and basketry, felt hats, wood painting and slipper making. However, it's a tame experience compared to the sights and sounds of the souks.

In the medina, prices are of course negotiable. If you can approach the process as buying non-essential, decorative items and are prepared to walk away, it is likely to be less painful and you'll probably get a better deal. Keep a sense of humour (remember how absurd it all is when some salesman whom you met 5 mins ago reasons that "you are not my friend because you don't want to buy from me." Always be polite, and you may come away with some bargains. You might even enjoy it.

Good items to buy in Marrakech include thuya wood boxes (though Essaouira is the real home of this craft), painted wood mirrors and side tables, ceramics, carpets, leather bags and *babouches* (shoes/slippers). Hand-woven baskets and woolly hats from the women in the Rahba Lakdima and Jemaâ el Fna can be got at bargain prices. **Sidi Ghanem**, a few kilometres on Rte de Safi, best reached by taxi or bus No 15, www.sidighanem.net. Open Mon-Fri. If you're in the market for serious home decoration, you may want to take a trip out of town to Sidi Ghanem 'industrial zone', where lots of Moroccan contemporary designers have outlets, focusing on home interiors, candles, designer furniture, crafts and fashion. Their main income is from exports but most are also open to visitors.

Medina The souks can be confusing for shopping. Originally each souk specialized in one type of product but this system has largely broken down on the main tourist drag (Souk Semmarine and its continuation, Souk el Kebir) up to the area around the Medersa Ben Youssef. There are shops specializing in slippers, traditional gear, wood and ceramics, and a number of large antique shops.

If you enter the souks from opposite the **Café de France** in Jemaâ el Fna you will pass olive stalls and mint sellers on your right, bend round to the right and you'll find yourself in the eastern corner of a small square called Bab Fteuh. Straight in front of you is the (relatively) wide, paved **Souk Semmarine**. There are some big antique shops and carpet emporia here, some of them very expensive. **Rahba Kedima**, a rare open space off to the right (about 200 m up Souk Semmarine), also has some interesting small shops, as well as the **Café des Épices**. Further on, Souk Semmarine successively becomes **Souk el Kebir**, **Souk el Najjarine** and, under a wooden lintel, **Souk Chkaïria**. Leather goods can be bought here.

The other reasonably major route through the souks is **Rue Mouassine**, which also runs north-south from the western end of Bab Fteuh, past the Mosque Mouassine. You can also get here by entering the souks next to **Café Argana** on Jemaâ el Fna. **Rue Dar el Bacha**, the street running west out towards Bab Doukkala, has many interesting antiques and jewellery shops.

Akbar Delights, Pl Bab Fteuh, T0671-661307, www.akbardelights.com. Tue-Sun 0900-1900. Stunningly embroidered, beaded and bejewelled fabrics, tunics and decorative accessories. Showroom and outlet also in Guéliz at 42c Rue de la Liberté, together with sister company, **Moor** (see below) selling similar beautiful crafted items for the home, but in pastel shades.

Assouss Argane, 94 Mouassine (entrance on Rue Sidi el Yamami), T0524-380125, www.assoussargane.com. Daily 0900-1800. Authentic and undiluted Moroccan argan oil and beauty products, direct from a women's co-operative near Essaouira.

Beldi, 9-11 Rue Laksour (entrance on Rue Mouassine near Bab Fteuh), T0524-441076. Daily 0930-1300 and 1600-1900. This well-known *maison de haute couture* has a fine selection of traditionally tailored caftans, slippers and bags, mainly for women. Waistcoats and flowing shirts for men. High quality at reasonable prices. Credit cards accepted.

Khartit Mustapha, 3 Fhal Chidmi, Rue Mouassine, T0524-442578. Daily 0800-

2100. Specializing in baubles, bangles and beads, Mustapha is the friendly owner of this Berber jewellery shop. He can make necklaces and bracelets to order using the semi-precious stones and colourful beads (once used as currency) that he also sells by weight. Credit cards accepted.

KifKif, 8 Derb Laksour, T0661-082041 (mob), www.kifkifbystef.com. Colourful textiles, jewellery, toys and funky leather bags, selected by expat designer. Manufactured by local crafts workers.

Le Trésor des Nomades, 142-144 Rue Bab Doukkala, T0524-385240. Daily 0900-1930. Run by Mustapha Blaoui, this is a warehouse chock-full of treasures: lanterns, carved wooden doors, goatskin-covered chests in fantastic colours, touareg woven mats, kilims, antique *babouches* and much more. There's no sign outside, but look for the large double wooden doors. Shipping available.

Ministero del Gusto, 22 Derb Azzouz (off Rue Sidi al Yamami), T0524-426455, www.ministerodelgusto.com. Open Mon-Fri. More of a gallery space than a shop, though everything is for sale. One-off furniture creations, jewellery, paintings and vintage clothing displayed within an extraordinary multi-level building full of earthy textures and organic shapes.

Palais Saadiens Tapis,16 Rue Moulay Taïb Ksour (off Rue el Ksour), T0524-445176. Daily 0900-1900. An enormous stock of carpets from all regions of Morocco. Accepts credit cards.

Guéliz There are quite a few souvenir shops and shops selling clothes and luggage on **Av Mohammed V**. There are number of little boutique-type places on **Rue de la Liberté**, **Rue Mauritanie** and **Rue Sourya**, all of which cut across Av Mohammed V between Pl du 16 Novembre (Marrakech Plaza) and Pl Abdelmoumen Ben Ali (**Café Negoçiants** landmark). Also have a quick trawl along the streets around **Rue Mohammed Bequal** (turn left just after the restaurant La Taverne, which itself is almost opposite the **Cinéma**

Colisée). At the new **Marrakech Plaza** on Pl du 16 Novembre are branches of major European chains where young Marrakchis pay high prices for western labels such as Zara, Etam, Mango, Dior and more.

33 Rue Majorelle, 33 Rue Yves Saint Laurent, T0524-314195. Opposite the Jardin Majorelle, this smart new shop has a selection of quality clothing, jewellery and gifts from the new wave of Moroccan designers. Art gallery also attached.

Alrazal, 55 Rue Sourya, T0524-437884, www.alrazal.com. Mon-Sat 0930-1300 and 1530-1930. Exquisite hand-made clothing for children that's somewhere between fancy dress box and party outfit. Silk-embroidered miniature caftans and Ali Baba pants in a rainbow of colours. Smiles aplenty.

Galerie le Caftan, Immeuble 100, No 2, Rue Mohammed Bequal, T0661-765260. Almost opposite the **Galerie Birkemeyer**. As the name suggests, a good choice of upmarket traditional women's gear made to order on the premises. Beautiful *babouches* with a modern touch.

Lun'art Gallery, 106 Rue Mohammed Bequal, T0524-447266. Mon-Sat 0930-1300 and 1530-1930. African masks and carved wooden figures, bronze sculpted curios, hessian wall-hangings and treasures from sub-Saharan Africa. Credit cards accepted and shipping available.

Moor, 42c Rue de la Liberté, Apt 47, 1st floor, T0671-661307, www.akbardelights.com. French elegance with Moroccan influence. Pale shades dominate for lamps, housewares, textiles and cool linen tunics.

Naturelle d'Argan, 5 Rue Sourya, T0524-448761. Open 0930-1300 and 1500-1800. Beauty products and other argan oil-based products, as well as a carefully chosen smattering of handicrafts, such as the exquisite inlaid teaspoons found in several riads in the city.

L'Orientaliste, 11 and 15 Rue de la Liberté, T0524-434074. Mon-Sat 0900-1230 and 1500-1930. Ceramics and perfumes, paintings and semi-antiques.

Books

Marrakech is not the most bookish of towns. Nevertheless, there are a few shops where you can stock up on large coffee table books, maps and recent Moroccan fiction in French. It's also worth trying the **Café du Livre** in Guéliz (page 80). Foreign newspapers, a day or two old, can be bought from the stands along Av Mohammed V – the one next to tourist information has a good selection – and in the large hotels.
Librairie Chatr, 19/21 Av Mohammed V, T0524-447997. Under the arcades at the top end of Av Mohammed V, near the Shell station and the intersection with Rue Abd el Krim el Khattabi. The best choice of books in the city, from coffee table books to novels in English and Atlas Mountain guidebooks (in French).
Librairie Dar El Bacha, 2 Rue Dar el Bacha, T0524-391973. A small but well-stocked shop in the medina, with maps and guidebooks on its shelves.

Supermarkets

Aswak Assalam, opposite the bus station at Bab Doukkala. No alcohol.
Hypermarché Marjane, on the Casablanca road. Stocks just about everything including electrical goods, clothes, household items, food and alcohol. (Non-Moroccans can buy alcohol here during Ramadan).

Country markets

Markets outside Marrakech serve local needs, although there are inevitably a number of persistent trinket pushers. Men from the mountain villages come down on mule, bicycle and pick-up truck to stock up on tea and sugar, candles and cigarettes, agricultural produce, maybe have a haircut or even get a tooth pulled. This is the place to sell a sheep, discuss emigration, or a land sale. There may be some Islamists peddling cassettes of sermons, perfumes and religious texts. At such markets, the difference in living standards between the town and the countryside really hits home. The markets are dusty, rough-and-ready places where people pay with the tiny brass coins hardly seen in the city. You really feel that people are living from the land, and realize how hard drought can hit them.

Country market days as follows: Mon Tnine; Tue Amizmiz, Tahanaoute, Ait Ourir; Wed Tirdouine; Thu Ouirgane, Setti Fatma, El Khemis; Fri Aghmmat, Tameslohte; Sat Asni; Sun Chichaoua, Sidi Abdel Ghiat.

⏺ What to do

Marrakech *p46, maps p52 and p56*
Ballooning
Ciel d'Afrique, Imm Ali, Apt 4, 2nd floor, Av Youssef Ben Tachfine, Route de Targa, Guéliz, T0524-432843, www.cieldafrique.info. An early morning hot air balloon flight over the palm groves and villages to the north of Marrakech is a great way to start the day. Starts from 2050dh per person. They also organize balloon trips further afield in the south of the country.

Climbing and outdoor activities
Terres d'Amanar, 35 km Rte de Asni (30 mins from Marrakech), T0524-438103, www.terresdamanar.com. In the foothills of Mt Toubkal National Park is a new eco-adventure forest park offering professionally supervised outdoor pursuits. Day courses include climbing, abseiling, zip wire, trekking and archery. There's also accommodation in eco-lodge or tents for longer stays.

Golf
Palmeraie Golf Palace Circuit de la Palmeraie, T0524-368766, www. pgp marrakech.com/golf/golf.html. 18-hole, and additional 9-hole course, designed by Robert Trent opened in 2009. Fee 500dh, 7 km north of town in Palmeraie at Hotel Palmeraie Golf Palace.
Royal Golf Club, 7 km south, off the Ouarzazate road (N9), T0524-409828, www.royalgolfmarrakech.com. Three 9-hole interconnected courses set in orchards, fee

A day by the pool

While many of Marrakech's riads have plunge pools, these are often not much bigger than a large bath. And with the coast a long way away for a day trip, out-of-town pools, usually with attached bars and restaurants, or hotels that open their pools to non-residents, can make an attractive day out, especially as the temperature rises in summer.

Beldi Country Club, Km 6, Rte du Barrage, T0524-383950, www.beldicountryclub. com. For a tranquil afternoon lounging by the pool after a delicious three-course lunch on the terrace, this is the perfect spot. 350dh including lunch, 250dh

children. Ring to reserve.

La Plage Rouge, T0524-378086, www. laplagerougemarrakech.com. 3000 sq m of swimming pool makes La Plage Rouge stand out from its competitors. There's sand too and a DJ at night. Waterside beds encourage lounging. Pricey restaurant and bar on site. 250dh entry, 125dh for kids, free shuttle.

Oasiria, T0524-380438, www.oasiria.com. Not just a pool, Oasiria is a large water park, with two pools, a river, huge water slides and a pirate ship. Café-restaurants in acres of gardens. Free shuttle from the city centre, 190dh, 110dh children.

per 18-hole round 550dh including clubs, obligatory caddie 100dh, open daily.

Hammams

The Islamic requirement for ablutions and the lack of bathrooms in many Moroccan homes mean that the city's hammams are well used. They cost around 10dh per person and are either single sex or have set hours or days for men and women. Massage and black soap scrubs cost extra but are not expensive. Remember to keep your knickers or shorts on in the hammam and take a spare dry pair with you.

Try one of those on Riad Zitoun el Kedim or **Hammam Dar el Bacha**, Rue Fatima Zohra. This is a large hammam dating from the early 1930s. The vestibule has a huge dome, and inside are 3 parallel marble-floored rooms, the last with underfloor heating.

Many riads have private hammams, though these offer a different sort of experience compared to the real thing. Riad staff may be happy to accompany you to apply soap and scrub you with a coarse exfoliating mitten. Other deluxe hammams in the medina offer beauty treatments and massages; expect to pay anything from 300dh for a hammam, scrub and massage with argan oil.

Horse riding

Cavaliers de l'Atlas, Rte de Casablanca (opposite Afriquia Station), Palmeraie, T0672-845579, www.lescavaliersdelatlas. com. Riding in the palm groves outside Marrakech or longer treks for several days. Novices and experienced riders catered for.

Trekking and tour operators

Atlas Sahara Trek, 6 bis Rue Houdhoud, Quartier Majorelle, T0524-313901, www.atlas-sahara-trek.com. One of the best trekking agencies in Marrakech, with 20 years' experience. Moroccan-born founder Bernard Fabry knows his deserts well.

Mountain Safari Tours, 64 Lot Laksour, Route de Casa, Guéliz, T0524-308777, www.mountainsafaritours.com. Specialist travel agency with 20 years of experience.

Mountain Voyage, Immeuble El Batoul, 2nd Floor, 5 Av Mohammed V, Guéliz, T0524-421996, www.mountain-voyage.com. Organized and recommended tour operator with English-speaking staff running upmarket treks in the Toubkal area and beyond (5-14 days). Owners of the luxurious **Kasbah du Toubkal** mountain hotel (see page 113).

Omni Tours, 220 Av Mohammed V, T0524-421660, www.omni-tours.com. Organizes 4WD vehicles, minibuses and coach hire. Also runs a range of day excursions and trips countrywide including desert and trekking tours.

SheherazadVentures, 55 Residence Ali, Av Mohammed VI, Guéliz, T0615-647918, www.sheherazadventures.com. English-Moroccan company specializing in tailor-made desert tours. Special interest trips include pottery making, photography, volunteering and date picking.

⊖ Transport

Marrakech *p46, maps p52 and p56*
Air
Airport Marrakech Menara is clearly signposted from the centre. There are direct flights from London and other European cities. **EasyJet** (www.easyjet.com), **Ryanair** (www.ryanair.com) and **Royal Air Maroc** (www.royalairmaroc.com) all fly daily to **London**. There are also flights to **Manchester**, **Bristol**, **Nottingham** and **Edinburgh**. **British Airways** (www.britishairways.com) have 3 flights per week to London. Other destinations include **Casablanca** (2 a day), as well as **Milan**, **Lyon**, **Brussels** (Fri), **Geneva**, **Oslo** and **Copenhagen**. There are daily flights to **Paris** and **Madrid**.

Airline offices Royal Air Maroc, 197 Av Mohammed V, T0890-00080 (call centre). Open 0830-1215 and 1430-1900.

Bus
Local city buses, run by **AlsaCity**, can be caught at the Pl de Foucault, just off Jemaâ el Fna next to the calèches. Stops are elsewhere along Av Mohammed V and Av Hassan II. No 1 and No 7 are the most useful, running from Jemaâ el Fna along Av Mohammed V, through Guéliz. No 3 and No 8 run from the railway station to the bus station, via Jemaâ el Fna; No 10 from Jemaâ el Fna to the bus station; No 11 from Jemaâ el Fna to the Menara Gardens and airport. No 4 goes to the Jardin Majorelle.

For long-distance journeys, the *gare routière* is just outside Bab Doukkala,

T0524-433933, which is easily reached by taxis and local buses. There is often a choice between different companies with varying prices and times. When leaving Marrakech, make sure the number of the booth where the tickets are bought matches the bus stop number where you intend to catch the bus. Always be there in advance. It is wise to call at the station the previous day as some services, notably across the High Atlas to Taroudant and Ouarzazate, leave early in the morning. **CTM** (T0524-448328, www.ctm.ma) departures can also be caught from their terminal on Rue Abou Bakr Seddiq, near the Theatre Royal in Guéliz. **Supratours** (T0524-435525, www.supratours.ma) buses leave from alongside the train station on Av Hassan II, but can be full with pre-booked train travellers. Destinations include **Agadir**, **Casablanca**, **El Jadida**, **Er Rachidia**, **Essaouira** (best with Supratours), **Laâyoune**, **M'hamid** (CTM only), **Oualidia**, **Ouarzazate**, **Rabat**, **Safi**, **Skoura** and **Taroudant**.

Buses to the **Ourika Valley**, **Asni** and **Moulay Brahim** run from Bab Rob.

Calèche
Green-painted horse-drawn carriages can be hailed along Av Mohammed V or from the stands at Jemaâ el Fna and Pl de la Liberté. There are fixed prices for tours around the ramparts, other routes are up for negotiation, but they are not normally prohibitively expensive, and this is a pleasant way to see the city. Expect to pay around 150-200dh per hour. Some carriages have set prices displayed inside.

Car hire
You should be able to get something like a small Dacia or Renault Clio for 350dh per day, unlimited kilometres, but avoid the lesser-known firms, if possible, and make sure there's cover, or at the very least a plan B, in case you break down in the middle of nowhere. A driver will cost you around 250dh a day extra. 4WD hire with driver is around 1200dh per day. If driving, once out

of Marrakech, the roads are rarely crowded. However, the Marrakech–Casablanca road has a notoriously high number of accidents. **Avis**, 137 Av Mohammed V, T0524-433727. **Europcar**, 63 Blvd Mohammed Zerktouni, T0524-431228, and at the airport. **Hertz**, 154 Av Mohammed V, T0524-431394, airport T0524-447230.

Taxi

Petits taxis The city's khaki-coloured *petits taxis* are much in evidence and can take up to 3 passengers. As you get in, check the driver switches the meter on. Be firm but polite about not paying over the odds. From the medina to Guéliz should cost around 10dh during the day, 10-20dh after 2000. Taxis will try and overcharge to the airport; it's worth insisting on them using the meter or agreeing a price first. Major ranks are to be found in Jemaâ el Fna and at the *gare routière* by Bab Doukkala.

Grands taxis These can be found at the railway station and the major hotels. They also run over fixed routes, mainly to the suburbs, from Jemaâ el Fna and Bab Doukkala. They are cheap and convenient for visiting outlying areas and connecting to other cities, such as **Fès** (8 hrs). Prices vary depending on route. 6 passengers are normally squeezed in, but you can make a private trip if you pay for the empty spaces.

For the **Ourika Valley** and **Ouirgane**, they leave from Bab Rob. For **Asni** and **Imlil**, they leave from Av Mohammed VI, near **Pacha** (get a *petit taxi* to take you there). For most other destinations, including **Essaouira** and **Agadir**, go to Bab Doukkala. For destinations east, check out Bab Doukkala or Bab el Khemis.

Train

The railway station is in Guéliz, on Av Hassan II at the corner with Av Mohammed V, T0890-203040 (call centre), www.oncf.ma. Although there are plans for an eventual extension of the line south to Agadir and Laâyoune, at present ONCF operates only bus services to the south, connecting with

the arrival of the express trains. There are express trains for **Casablanca** (3½ hrs), **Rabat** (4 hrs) and **Fès** (7 hrs).

❶ Directory

Marrakech *p46, maps p52 and p56*
Banks The main concentrations of ATMs are on Rue Bab Agnaou (now called Av Prince Moulay Rachid) near the Pl Jemaâ el Fna, and in Guéliz on Av Mohammed V between Pl du 16 Novembre and the roundabout Abd el Moumen. If stuck at weekends and public holidays, then the BMCI, almost opposite the Cinéma Colisée on Blvd Zerktouni, is open 0930-1130 and 1600-1900. Otherwise, Mon-Fri 0900-1300 and 1500-1900.

Medical services **Chemists**: Pharmacie Centrale, 166 Av Mohammed V, T0524-430151. **Pharmacie de Paris**, 120 Av Mohammed V, T0524-447663. The préfecture operates an all-night pharmacy, the **Dépôt de nuit**, which looks like a ticket window on Pl Jemaâ el Fna (with the Koutoubia behind you, turn left after the stone wall of the Club Med compound). You may have to queue for some time. There is also an all-night chemist, **Pharmacie de Nuit**, at Rue Khalid Ben Oualid, Guéliz, T0524-430415 (doctor sometimes available). **Dentists**: Dr Hamid Laraqui, 203 Av Mohammed V, Guéliz, T0524-433216; Dr Gailleres, 112 Av Mohammed V, Guéliz, T0524-449136; Dr Karim Zihri, 117 Rue Mohammed Bequal, Apt 2, Guéliz, T0524-439030. All speak English. **Doctor on call**: T0524-404040 (ambulance service too), SAMU T0524-433030. **Doctors**: Dr Ahmed Mansouri, Clinique Ibn Rochd, Rue de Sebou, T0524-433079, and Dr G Michaelis Agoumi, 7 Rue Ibn Sina, Quatrier de l'Hopital Civile, Guéliz, T0524-448343. Both speak English. **Private hospital**: Polyclinique du Sud, 2 Rue de Yougoslavie, T0524-447999. Polyclinique Les Narcisses, Camp el Ghoul, 112 Route de Targa, T0524-447575.
Useful addresses Emergency services Private ambulance service: 10 Rue Fatima Zohra, T0524-443724. Fire: Rue Khalid Ben Oualid, T150. Police: Rue Ibn Hanbal, T190.

Essaouira

Essaouira, 'little picture', is one of those stage set places: you half expect to see plumed cavalry coming round the corner, or a camera crew filming some diva up on the ramparts. It is a beautifully designed 18th-century military port and, somehow, hasn't changed too much since. The walls are white, the windows and shutters are often cracked and faded blue, while arches and columns are sandy camel-brown. Three crescent moons on a city gate provide a touch of the heraldic, while surfers and fanciful Jimi Hendrix myths hint at Essaouira's hippy days, a few decades ago. (Though stories linking the ruins of Borj el Baroud with Hendrix's 'Castles Made of Sand' are spurious – the song was released 18 months before the singer visited Essaouira.) Tall feathery araucaria trees and palms along the ramparts add a Mediterranean touch. New flights to the airport may further reduce Essaouira's isolation, though currently most visitors still arrive by bus or taxi from Marrakech. Large numbers of foreigners have bought picturesque property and there are two successful music festivals. ▸▸ *For listings, see pages 93-100.*

Arriving in Essaouira → *Colour map 2, B2.*

Getting there

Both **CTM** (www.ctm.ma) and private lines arrive at the bus station about 300 m northeast of the medina at Bab Doukkala – a five-minute walk with luggage or a 10dh *petit taxi* ride (15dh at night). *Grands taxis* also run to the bus station, although arrivals will be dropped off right next to the main entrance to the medina, Bab Doukkala. Drivers may want to use the car park (24-hour warden) close to the harbour next to Place Prince Moulay el Hassan. ▸▸ *See Transport, page 100, for further details.*

Getting around

One of the most appealing aspects of Essaouira is that all the principal tourist sites can be comfortably reached on foot; cars can be left in the car park. There are some good walks along the windswept beach to Borj el Beroud. The walk to Cap Sim is an all-day excursion.

Tourist information   Délégation Provincial de Tourisme ⓘ *10 Av du Caire, T0524-783532, Mon-Fri 0900-1630.* Rather basic office with helpful staff, maps, leaflets and bus timetables.

Background

Essaouira is a quiet sort of place with a long history. There was a small Phoenician settlement here, previously called Magdoura or Mogador, a corruption of the Berber word Amegdul, meaning 'well-protected'. The Romans were interested in the purple dye produced from the abundant shellfish on the rocky coast, which they used to colour the robes of the rich. Mogador was occupied in the 15th century by the Portuguese, who built the fortifications around the harbour. The town was one of their three most important bases, but was abandoned in 1541, from which time it went into decline. Mogador was also visited by Sir Francis Drake in Christmas 1577. In 1765, the Alaouite Sultan Sidi Mohammed Ibn Abdallah transformed Mogador into an open city, enticing overseas businessmen in with trade concessions, and it soon became a major commercial port, with a large foreign and Jewish population establishing the town as a major trading centre.

The sultan employed the French architect Théodore Cornut to design the city and its fortifications. In his design, Cornut chose a rectangular layout for the main streets, resulting in a uniform style, and constructed ramparts in the Vauban style. The fortifications were not always that effective, however. From time to time, the tribesmen of the region would

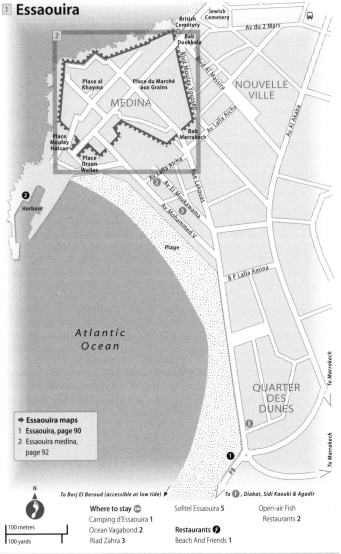

1 Essaouira

Jewish Cemetery

British Cemetery

Bab Doukkala

Av du 2 Mars

Blvd Moulay Youssen

Blvd Al Massira

Place al Khayma

Place du Marché aux Grains

NOUVELLE VILLE

MEDINA

Av Lalla Aïcha

Av Al Akaba

Place Moulay Hassan

Bab Marrakech

Place Orson Welles

Av Lalla Aïcha

Rue La Kouas

2 Harbour

Av El Moukawama

Av Mohammed V

Plage

B P Lalla Amina

Atlantic Ocean

To Marrakech

QUARTER DES DUNES

To Marrakech

➡ **Essaouira maps**
1 Essaouira, page 90
2 Essaouira medina, page 92

N

100 metres
100 yards

To Borj El Beroud (accessible at low tide) ▶

To ❶ *, Diabat, Sidi Kaouki & Agadir*

P8

Where to stay 🛏
Camping d'Essaouira 1
Ocean Vagabond 2
Riad Zahra 3

Sofitel Essaouira 5

Restaurants 🍴
Beach And Friends 1

Open-air Fish Restaurants 2

raid the town, carrying off booty and the merchants' wives – who it is said, were not always that happy to return. Perhaps life in rural Morocco was more pleasant than listening to the wind in the damp counting houses of Mogador.

Orson Welles stayed here for some time, filming part of *Othello* at the Skala du Port. At Independence the town's official name became Essaouira, the local Arabic name meaning 'little picture'. In the 1960s Essaouira had a brief reputation as a happening place, attracting hippies and rockstars, including Jimi Hendrix.

Now the town is emerging from several decades of decline, for on top of fishing, fish processing, a small market and handicraft industries, the town is attracting greater numbers of tourists, notably surfers. The burgeoning number of riads and their accompanying upmarket tourism has also brought some wealth to the inhabitants of this most relaxed town, without spoiling its gentle atmosphere, though an increase in the number of oversized hotels outside the city walls may have a more detrimental effect.

Essaouira has some useful friends in influential places, including André Azoulay, one of HM the King's special advisers, and there is an artistic lobby, too, including gallery owner Frédéric Damgaard and Edmond Amran-Mellah, the writer. Dar Souiri, on Avenue de Caire opposite the Délégation de Tourisme, is the hub of the town's cultural activities.

Places in Essaouira

Medina

Essaouira does not have a lot in the way of formal sights, but has plenty of gently atmospheric streets to compensate. Enclosed by walls with five main gates, the medina is the major attraction. Entering from **Bab Doukkala** the main thoroughfare is Rue Mohammed Zerktouni, which leads into Avenue de l'Istiqlal, where there is the **Grand Mosque**, and just off, on Darb Laalouj, the **Ensemble Artisanal** and the **Museum of Sidi Mohammed Ibn Abdallah**, which houses the **Museum of Traditional Art and Heritage of Essaouira** ① *T0524-475300, Wed-Mon 0830-1200 and 1430-1800, 10dh*. This house, once the home of a pasha, has a collection of weapons and handicrafts, such as woodwork and carpets, and also has an interesting ethnographic collection, including examples of stringed instruments beautifully decorated with marquetry and documents on Berber music.

Avenue de l'Istiqlal leads into Avenue Okba Ibn Nafi, on which is located the small **Galerie d'Art Damgaard**. At the end of the street a gate on the right leads into **Place Moulay Hassan**, the heart of the town's social life. The town's souks are mainly around the junction between Rue Mohammed Zerktouni and Rue Mohammed el Gorry, although there is an area of woodworkers inside the Skala walls to the north of Place Moulay Hassan, where some fine pieces can be picked up with some good-natured bargaining. At the northeast end of Rue Zerktouni, close to Bab Doukkala, is the much-decayed **mellah**, the old Jewish quarter. Although the Jewish community no longer remains, it made a substantial contribution to the commercial and cultural development of the town.

Outside Bab Doukkala is the Consul's **cemetery** for the British officials who died here while converting Mogador into a trading post with strong UK links. Behind the high wall on the road to the bus station is the **Jewish cemetery**. If you find the man with the key, you may discover the resting place of Leslie Hore-Belisha, inventor of the first pedestrian crossing light.

The Harbour and Skala du port

Off Place Moulay Hassan is the small harbour, busy with its fishing fleet. The open-air restaurant stalls serving grilled fish have been smartened up in recent years but are still a great spot for lunch. The sea gate (**Porte de la Marine**), which serves to link the harbour with the medina, was built in 1769, it is said, by an Englishman who converted to Islam during the reign of Sidi Mohammed Ibn Abdallah. The gateway is built of stone in the classical style and the year of its construction (1184 of the Hegira) is inscribed on the pediment. It is connected to the ramparts on the **Skala**, an old Portuguese sea defence and battery, by a bridge which spans small primitive dry docks. Entry to the **Skala du Port** (10dh) is via a kiosk close to the Porte de la Marine, and from the top of the bastion there are extensive panoramic views of the harbour and the offshore islands, the **Îles Purpuraires**.

Skala de la Ville
Further to the north of Place Moulay Hassan, it is possible to get onto the ramparts of the Skala de la Ville from Rue de la Skala close to its junction with Rue Darb Laalouj. Entry here is free, and crenellated walls protect a 200-m-long raised artillery platform and an impressive

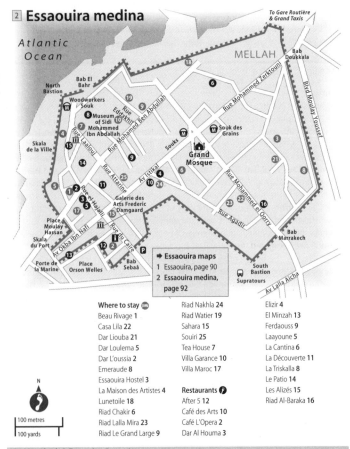

② Essaouira medina

Where to stay
Beau Rivage **1**
Casa Lila **22**
Dar Liouba **21**
Dar Loulema **5**
Dar L'oussia **2**
Emeraude **8**
Essaouira Hostel **3**
La Maison des Artistes **4**
Lunetoile **18**
Riad Chakir **6**
Riad Lalla Mira **23**
Riad Le Grand Large **9**

Riad Nakhla **24**
Riad Watier **19**
Sahara **15**
Souiri **25**
Tea House **7**
Villa Garance **10**
Villa Maroc **17**

Restaurants
After 5 **12**
Café des Arts **10**
Café L'Opera **2**
Dar Al Houma **3**

Elizir **4**
El Minzah **13**
Ferdaouss **9**
Laayoune **5**
La Cantina **6**
La Découverte **11**
La Triskalla **8**
Le Patio **14**
Les Alizés **15**
Riad Al-Baraka **16**

➡ **Essaouira maps**
1 Essaouira, page 90
2 Essaouira medina, page 92

array of decorated Spanish and other European cannon. This is a good spot from which to watch the sunset. From the tower of the **North Bastion** there are fine views of the old mellah, the medina, with its white buildings and blue shutters, and the coastline to the north. The **woodworkers' souks** are situated here in arched chambers underneath the ramparts.

Beaches
Essaouira has fine beaches. The prevailing wind, known as the *alizée*, stirs up a lot of sand and makes it cold for swimming, but ideal for windsurfing, though not necessarily surfing. The northern **Plage de Safi** is fine in the summer, but can be dangerous during windy weather. South of the town, the wide beach is great for football, and there are usually games going on here. Past the Oued Ksob, you will see the waves breaking against the remains of Borj el Baroud, an old fortress. When walking far along the beach it should be noted that the incoming tide makes the Oued Ksob below the village of Diabat into an impassable river.

Diabat
The one-time favourite hippy destination of Diabat, about 5 km from Essaouira, is easily reached by *petit* and *grand taxi*, say 40dh. The ruined palace/pavilion below Diabat is worth a visit. The building is said to have been swallowed by the sand after the people of the Souss put a curse on it because their trade was being ruined. The old fort was built by the Portuguese in the 18th century. A short walk up the road from Diabat will bring you to the **Auberge Tangaro**, one of Essaouira's better known hotels; 500 m further on, and you are at the crossroads with the N1 road from the south, which runs back into town.

Îles Purpuraires
These islands to the southwest are a bird sanctuary, particularly for rare Eleonora's falcons. With a good telescope it's possible to see these falcons from the end of the jetty. Another area frequented by the birds is the mouth of **Oued Ksob**. The river mouth is also noted for a variety of migrating seabirds, including black, little, sandwich, whiskered and white-winged terns. The *oued* can be reached from a track off the N1 south of the town but access to the sea is not easy. Although now a nature reserve, it is possible to visit the main island, **Île de Mogador**, outside the breeding season (it's closed April to October). You can negotiate a private trip with a local fishing vessel to ferry you there and back, but first must obtain a permit (free) from the Port office.

⊙ Essaouira listings

For sleeping and eating price codes and other relevant information, see pages 22-28.

⊙ Where to stay

Essaouira *p89, maps p90 and p92*
The best place to stay is the medina, with its upmarket guesthouses, riads and occasionally damp cheap hotels. It's also possible to stay south of the medina, with a few large hotels and guesthouses stretching along the beachfront as far as the main Marrakech road.

Alternatively, head for a country guesthouse a few miles south in Diabat, Ghazoua or Cap Sim.

When searching for cheap hotels make sure you get a well-ventilated room with windows and, preferably, a view of the ocean.

Riads and guesthouses
Essaouira is second only to Marrakech in the quantity and quality of restored properties in the old town operating as guesthouses. Though many of these are not riads in the strictest sense, they are usually referred to as

such and the style will be familiar to those who have stayed in riads in Marrakech. If you can afford it, these are the best option. The typical Essaouira house has two storeys around a courtyard with rooms opening onto balconies.

Most guesthouses can do evening meals for around 150-200dh, if given advance warning. In many cases, the whole establishment can be rented for a few days for a house party. It is important to book well ahead, especially during the annual **Gnaoua Festival**. Many guesthouses do not accept credit cards; check in advance.

For a selection of apartments and riads, try agency **Jack's Kiosk**, 1 Pl Moulay Hassan, T0524-475538, www.jackapartments.com, or **Karimo**, T0524-474500, www.karimo.net.
€€€€ Casa Lila, 94 Rue Mohammed el Qorry, T0524-475545, www.casalila-riad. com. Exceptionally photogenic, even by riad standards, **Casa Lila** goes big on dusty pastel shades, with lots of purples and lilacs. Rooms come in different colour schemes but all are pretty; the fabrics are luscious, beds are sprinkled with petals, and open fires, floorboards and checkered floors add to the chic quotient. Stunning roof terrace. Minimum 2-night stay.
€€€€ Dar Liouba, 28 Impasse Moulay Ismaïl, T0524-476297, www.darliouba.eu. Homely and French, this is a tall, thin guesthouse with rooms around an octagonal courtyard. The decoration is bright and simple with white walls and splashes of colour, though rooms are rather small. Rustic charm and some rooms with open fireplace. Family suites available. A very warm welcome. Heated in winter.
€€€€ Dar Loulema, 2 Rue Souss, T0524-475346, www.darloulema.com. Centrally situated next to the **Café Taros**, this place has 8 beautifully styled rooms each with a/c and power shower. There's a pleasing mix of antique furnishings, traditional tiled floors and colourful fabrics. Very comfortable. Great views of the fishing port.
€€€€ Riad Watier, 16 Rue Ceuta, T0524-476204, www.ryad-watier-maroc.com. The French owner of this large and spacious riad has filled it with stunning artworks by local painters, aboriginal artists and his own father. The huge rooms are each individually designed and some have mezzanine sleeping platforms. There's a cosy library full of interesting books, a resident tortoise and an air of relaxed charm. White walls add to the sense of light and there are tiles, rugs, terracotta *tadelakt* and big showers in all 10 rooms. Meals upon request. Minimum 2-night stay.
€€€ Villa Garance, 10 Rue Eddakhil, T0524-473995, www.essaouira-garance. com. Well looked after by its French owners, **Villa Garance** has a pretty roof terrace with views over the sea and a plant-draped central courtyard, with an open fireplace for winter. Bright rooms have decorative tiled floors, some have 4-poster beds and all have external windows on a quiet street. A playroom, babysitting service and 4-bedroom suite make it a good option for families.
€€€-€€ La Maison des Artistes, 19 Rue Laâlouj, T0524-475799, www.lamaison desartistes.com. There's an entertaining air of artistic eccentricity at this 7-room guesthouse overlooking the sea, with lots of conversation point pieces of furniture and striking art among the colourful decoration. 'Le Pavilion de Cesar' has stunning wrap-around sea views, as does the roof terrace. An enticing menu of home-made meals prepared upon request. Breakfast and soft drinks included.
€€€-€€ Riad Lalla Mira, 14 Rue d'Algerie, T0524-475046, www.lallamira.net. German-run **Lalla Mira** emphasizes its eco-credentials and also houses a beautiful mosaic-tiled hammam (the oldest in Essaouira), free for guests. The 10 en suite rooms have solar-powered underfloor heating, water-recycling system and hypo-allergenic mattresses, draped with organic cotton. Restaurant serves good vegetarian food. Price includes breakfast.
€€€-€€ The Tea House, 74 Derb Laalouj, La Skala, T0524-783543, www.theteahouse. net. Despite its English name, Alison

MacDonald runs this small guesthouse very much in the traditional Essaouira vein. The 200-year-old house is beautifully decorated, with antiques and pale pastel-painted walls. The 1st and 2nd floors are available for rent, each apartment accommodating up to 4, with kitchen, sitting room, open fire, 2 bedrooms and large bathroom. Shared roof terrace, breakfast and firewood are included. Price is £32 per person, 3rd and 4th guests are half price. Solo travelers can rent apartment for £45. Price calculated in local currency at time of booking.

€€ **Lunetoile**, 191 Rue Sidi Mohammed Ben Abdullah, T0524-474689, www.lunetoile riad.com. Low key and good value, **Lunetoile** is off the beaten track in the mellah, and you'll probably be able to hear the sea and the seagulls from your room. In places the blue and yellow colour scheme is a little jarring but it has a genuine Moroccan feel, it's homely and the large apartments are a great option for families. Up to half price Jan-Mar.

€€ **Riad Chakir**, Rue Malek Ben Morhal (off Av Istiqlal), T0524-473309, www.riadchakir. com. Loads of traditional Moroccan character in these 2 adjoining houses, which offer 20 rooms around stone-columned patios, with colourful painted ceilings, chunky wooden beams and en suite *tadelakt* bathrooms. Some of the rooms are very cramped, but service is friendly and it's very affordable. Central location, close to car park.

€€ **Riad Le Grand Large**, 2 Rue Oum-Rabia, T0524-472866, www.riadlegrandlarge. com. The name is not only tautological, it's not really true, but this is a good, colourful, and good-value option, with 10 cheerful and unfussy en suite rooms, heated in winter, the best of which overlook the street. There's a roof terrace and a restaurant.

€ **Essaouira Hostel**, 17 Rue Laghrissi, T0524-476481, essaouirahostel@gmail.com. Tricky to find, but ring ahead and somebody will come to meet you. A 'boutique' hostel in an 18th-century riad with superb friendly management and youthful vibe. Private rooms and dorms available. Winner of 2nd prize in Hoscar Awards for best hostels in Africa 2008. Dorm from 90dh. Breakfast 20dh or make your own meals in the communal kitchen.

Hotels

€€€ **Hotel Dar l'Oussia**, 4 Rue Mohammed Ben Messaoud, T05234-783756, www.dar loussia.com. A large place for the medina, this offers 20 spacious rooms and 4 suites around a central courtyard. Rooms are stylishly decorated with traditional tiling and fabrics in pale colours. Underfloor heating, free Wi-Fi, free hammam, spa, restaurant and bar.

€€€ **Hotel Villa Maroc**, 10 Rue Abdallah Ben Yassin, T0524-476147, www.villa-maroc. com. Converted from 4 merchants' houses, this was one of the first boutique hotels in Morocco. Beautifully decorated around a central court festooned with plants and greenery, roof terrace with superb views. There are 17 rooms, and an apartment sleeping 4 is available. Restaurant with great food, hammam and spa treatments, free Wi-Fi. Book ahead.

€€ **Hotel Emeraude**, 228 Rue Chebanate, near the little gate of Bab Marrakech, T0524-473494, www.essaouirahotel.com. Small, attractive Franco-Moroccan-run hotel on the dry side of the medina. One of best small hotels in town, with 8 attractive doubles and 2 triples. Stylish and convenient, with guarded car parking just 40 m away.

€ **Hotel Beau Rivage**, Pl Moulay Hassan, T0524-475925, www.beaurivage-essaouira. com. Some of the 21 rooms in this central hotel have balconies overlooking the main square, others have a sea view. The decor is dated and worn out, but it's clean and has friendly, helpful management and a roof terrace. Breakfast 20dh.

€ **Hotel Cap Sim**, 11 Rue Ibn Rochd, T0524-785834. Clean and cheap, just round the corner from Pl Moulay Hassan and a patisserie opposite, which gets noisy at night. Simple rooms with comfy beds, very clean with tiles, coloured glass and a central courtyard. Not all rooms have bathroom. Price includes breakfast.

€ Hotel Riad Nakhla, 12 Rue d'Agadir, T0524-474940, www.essaouiranet.com/riad-nakhla. 18 rooms, all with private bathrooms (though some rather shabby), for a budget price and in a convenient location. The decoration may not be quite up to the level of its riad competitors but there's a courtyard with a fountain and a roof terrace for breakfast. It's attractive, comfortable and has helpful staff. Very good value.

€ Hotel Sahara, Av Okba Ibn Nafi, T0524-475292, www.hotelsahara-essaouira.com. Comfortable and central, Sahara has a range of rooms (70), some of which are fine and functional. Cheaper rooms opening onto the inner courtyard are darker, less well ventilated and can be noisy.

€ Hotel Souiri, 37 Rue Attarine, T0524-475339, www.hotelsouiri.com. A fairly modern hotel, Souiri has 36 bright, clean rooms over 3 floors and a 2-room rooftop apartment ideal for families. It's decorated in a quasi-European style, and all rooms have TV. Category 1 rooms have nicer furniture and en suite bathrooms. There's a roof terrace with sun loungers.

Outside the medina

Outside the medina, most of Essaouira's hotels are big and too characterless to recommend, though there are a few seafront options worth considering if being near the beach is important.

€€€ Ocean Vagabond, 4 Blvd Lalla Aïcha, Angle Rue Moukawama, T0524-479222, www.hoteloceanvagabondessaouira.com. Facing the beach, but only around 200 m from the medina, the **Ocean Vagabond** lacks some of the atmosphere of a medina riad, but is attractively decorated with African-themed bar, library, cosy lounge and gardens with pool. The 14 rooms have marble and *tadelakt* bathrooms, sea-view balconies and plenty of mod cons.

€€€ Sofitel Essaouira Medina & Spa, Av Mohammed V, T0524-479000, www.sofitel.com. Opposite the beach, this is a large and luxurious 5-star hotel, with 117 rooms decorated in a contemporary version of traditional Moroccan style. Big heated pool and sheltered terraces, with palms and a good bar and restaurant. Luxurious spa and access to newly opened **Mogador Golf** course a few kilometres out of town. Multi-night deals often available online.

€€€-€€ Riad Zahra, 90 Quartier des Dunes, T0524-474822, www.riadzahra.com. Spanish-run small family hotel just off the seafront at the very southern end of the beach. 23 spacious rooms around an airy courtyard, with hand-painted furniture and Berber throws. All en suite and some have balconies or sea view. Restaurant and bar, terrace with fab ocean views, good-sized pool (shared with resident turtles), parking. 20 mins' walk to medina. It's more for a sea view.

Outside Essaouira

€€€ Baoussala, El Ghazoua, T0524-792345, www.baoussala.com. A small, pretty eco-guesthouse with a solar-heated pool, surrounded by terrace and gardens. 6 very tastefully designed en suite rooms in a peaceful location 10 km from Essaouira and 10 km from Sidi Kaouki. Purpose-built by owners Dominique and Bruno Maté in extensive grounds. Whole house can be rented. Lunch and evening meals available.

€€€ Jardins des Douars, Douar Sidi Yassine (15 km south of Essaouria, 3 km inland off the road to Agadir), T0524-474003, www.jardinsdesdouars.com. You'll need your own transport to find this delightful hideaway, but well worth the detour. Walls of warm *tadelakt*, hude wooden doors, fireplace and antique furniture. Tranquil surroundings with botanical gardens, spa and 2 pools. Split-level rooms, suites or private *douars* plus a restaurant and bar make this ideal for families.

€€ Auberge de la Plage, Sidi Kaouki, T0524-476600, www.kaouki.com. A colourful, chilled place. 10 bright rooms (2 with shared bathroom). Recently renovated and now full electricity supply, solar-heated hot water and intermittent Wi-Fi. Lovely shaded gardens. Horse riding and camel excursions.

€€ **Dar Kenavo**, 13 km out of Essaouira on Agadir road, after 8 km take the left turn for Casablanca/Marrakech and it's 4 km along on the left, T0661-207069 (mob), www.dar kenavo.com. Out in argan country, a small house with a heated pool and 7 rooms, 2 suites and a private bungalow around a pleasant patio. A quiet corner to see something of Moroccan rural life. There's also a Berber tent. Disabled access.

€€ **Hotel Villa Soleil**, Plage de Sidi Kaouki, about 20 km south of Essaouira (the turn-off for Sidi Kaouki is some 15 km south of Essaouira on the Agadir road), T0524-472092, www.hotelvillasoleil.com. 9 simple rooms and a penthouse apartment arranged around a courtyard. All rooms en suite and with private terrace, shaded by palm trees and conifers. Right on the beach, no pool.

€€ **Résidence Le Kaouki**, 15 km south of Essaouira on road to Agadir, T0524-783206, www.sidikaouki.com. 10 simple rooms and a candlelit restaurant with an open fire. Ideal for windsurfers, 200 m from the beach. Can also arrange other activities and excursions.

Camping

Camping d'Essaouira, 2 km out of Essaouira near the lighthouse, on the Agadir road. Well protected, clean loos.

❼ Restaurants

Essaouira p89, maps p90 and p92
€€€ **After 5**, 7 Rue Youssef el Fassi, T0524-473349. Open daily for lunch and dinner. Formerly 'Le 5', After 5 is no longer under French management, but it's retained the imaginative European and Moroccan menu. There's a 'super brunch' or modern dishes, such as carpaccio of swordfish with ginger. The whole place is very chic and inviting, with striking design features, such as lightshades big enough to live in. There's also a salon de thé and Wi-Fi. Alcohol served.

€€ **Les Alizés**, 26 Rue de la Skala, T0524-476819. Open daily for lunch and dinner. One of the most popular places in town, and

rightfully so. You can't reserve, but waiting at the small tables just inside the entrance with some olives and a bottle of wine is one of the great pleasures of the place. Once you get a table, you'll be plied with great Moroccan food – there's not an enormous choice but it's all good, and the place is run with a rare combination of efficiency and good humour. Alcohol served.

€€ **Elizir**, 1 Rue d'Agadir, T0524-472103. Open daily for lunch and dinner. Creative food using top-notch ingredients, run by a Moroccan recently returned from Italy. In a short time it has gained the reputation as the best restaurant in town. Try the ravioli with ricotta, basil and pistachio, or organic chicken with figs and gorgonzola. Eclectic decor, quirky touches and well-chosen music. Alcohol served. Booking advisable.

€€ **El Minzah**, 3 Av Oqba Ibn Nafia, T0524-475308. Open daily for lunch and dinner. A restaurant and piano bar just inside the walls near the clocktower. Good seafood options, including blue shark. A mellow, sophisticated spot for a drink with live Gnawa music on Sat. Good-value Moroccan fixed menu, or splash out three times as much on the French one. Alcohol served.

€€ **Le Patio**, 28 Bis Rue Moulay Rachid, T0524-474166. Tue-Sun dinner only; closed Jul. Imaginative Moroccan cuisine with a little French influence in their combination of spices and fruit. It's a stylish and atmospheric place, with warm low lighting, arches and flickering candlelight. Alcohol served, try the rum punch.

€€ **Riad Al-Baraka**, 113 Rue Mohammed al Qorry (near Bab Marrakech), T0524-473561. Open daily for lunch and dinner. Courtyard restaurant in what was once a Jewish school. Shaded patio ideal for lunch on a sunny day, or on cooler evenings the restaurant has an open fire. Mostly Moroccan and French cuisine, with live music at weekends. Alcohol served.

€ **Beach and Friends**, Blvd Mohammed V (at southern end of the beach), T0524-474558. Daily lunch and dinner. Right on the shorefront in a modern wooden cabin, a relaxed café-restaurant with sun-drenched indoor or shaded outdoor seating, as well as sun-loungers on the sand. Serves huge salads, tagines, burgers, paninis, pizzas and light snacks. Great for kids. Alcohol served.

€ **Dar Al Houma**, 9 Rue el Hajjali, T0524-783387. Daily lunch and dinner. There's a rare vegetarian set menu (60dh) as well as more standard Moroccan menus at this cosy little place just inside the walls of the medina. Very good value. English spoken. No alcohol. Cash only.

€ **Ferdaouss**, 27 Rue Abdesslam Lebadi, T0524-473655. Mon-Sat lunch and dinner. A popular place for Moroccan home cooking, this place is family run and found in an upstairs apartment. The food is reliable and good value, with the usual selection of *pastillas*, couscous and tagines. Bring your own wine.

€ **Fish stalls**, by far the best cheap eating option is to sample the freshly caught fish, grilled at the open-air restaurants between Pl Moulay Hassan and the port; accompanied by a tomato salad this makes a meal at a reasonable price. The standard of hygiene is good. Prices are fixed by weight and displayed on boards, but make sure you are clear on what you have and haven't ordered. The sales pitch can be a bit aggressive as you try to work your way past the stallholders. A cheaper option is the little fish barbecue place in **Souk el Hout**, the fish market in the town centre (the one on the left as you come from the port area down Av Istikal). No alcohol. Cash only.

€ **Laayoune**, 4 Rue el Hajjadi, T0524-474643. Daily lunch and dinner. Traditional, small and reliable, **Laayoune**, just on the inside of the walls, has a cosy candlelit vibe and great-value fixed menus 60dh-80dh. No alcohol. Cash only.

€ **Restaurant La Découverte**, 8 Rue Houmman, T0524-473158, www.essaouira-ladecouverte.com. Sun-Fri lunch and dinner. A friendly little French-run place offering such delicacies as lentil salad with argan oil and vegetable gratin, as well as meatier Moroccan choices. Wi-Fi. No alcohol. Cash only.

Cafés and ice cream

The best places for breakfast are on Pl Moulay Hassan, particularly **Café L'Opéra** and **Chez Driss**, where it's better value than a cheap hotel, and no one seems to mind if you bring your own cakes. There are beachside cafés, too.

Café des Arts, 56 Av Istikal, T0612-134742. Upstairs on the main street, this place has a young vibe, with live music, art and Moroccan food. Good for a lunch or a quick snack.

Café Taros, 2 Rue de la Skala, T0524-476407, www.taroscafe.com. Mon-Sat till late. Up the street on your left as you face Pl Moulay Hassan with port behind you, this café has a bar and good food. There are lots of books and magazines in the café area. Fabulous roof terrace with bar for sunset cocktails.

Gelateria Dolce Freddo, Pl Moulay Hassan. Right on the main square, this café does a roaring trade in delicious ice cream.

La Cantina, 66 Rue Boutouil, T0524-474515. English-run Mexican bistro-café serving burgers, chilli con carne, veggie food, home-made breads, cakes and scones. Also has book swap and local info. Located in a small square near the mellah.

La Triskalla, 58 Rue Touahen, T0524-476371. A very laid-back café with free internet and Wi-Fi, low lighting, candles and a cat. Plenty of veggie options, snacks and pancakes dominate the menu, and there's an extensive selection of juices, some of which are a tad over-imaginative.

⊕ Entertainment

Essaouira *p89, maps p90 and p92*
Essaouira is not really the place for wild nightlife, although it livens up nicely during the annual **Gnaoua Music Festival** in Jun. The roof terrace lounge bar of **Café Taros** (see above) is usually the liveliest spot after sundown. **El Minzah** (see Restaurants) or the bar in the **Hotel Sofitel** offer upmarket alternatives.

The main alcohol off-licence is near Bab Doukkala. Turn right out of the gate and the off-licence is on your left after about 100 m, identifiable by small black-and-white tiles and beer posters.

✿ Festivals

Essaouira *p89, maps p90 and p92*
May Les Alizés (www.alizesfestival.com) classical music festival.
End Jun Gnaoua Music Festival.
See box, page 30.

○ Shopping

Essaouira *p89, maps p90 and p92*
The main thoroughfares of the southern and central medina are all packed with little boutiques, from traditional jewellery stores and carpet merchants to funky modern designer shops and scrap-metal sculpture studios. Objects made in fragrant, honey-brown thuya wood are everywhere, from small boxes inlaid with lemon-wood to chunky, rounded sculptures. More expensively, you can pick up paintings by the local school of naïve and pointillist artists. Traditionally, the town's women wore all-enveloping cotton/wool mix wraps, in cream or brown, just the thing to keep out the ocean mists. Islamic fashions change and, happily, the weavers have found a new market providing fabrics for *maisons d'hôte* and their denizens. New colours and stripes have been added, and you can get a nice bedspread for 300dh. In Essaouira, you can also find plenty of flowing shirts and pantaloons in psychedelic designs or African cotton print. Raffia-work sandals and handbags and colourful felt accessories are also 'à la mode'. Essaouira is also the place to pick up the much-prized argan oil used for cosmetic and food products.
Argan d'Or, 5 Rue Ibn Rochd. Sells a range of argan beauty products and soaps.
Co-operative Tiguemine Argan, 15 km Rte de Marrakech, T0524-784970. Get to understand the argan oil production process by visiting this women's co-operative 15 km

out of town on the road to Marrakech. There are several other co-ops along this stretch of highway.
KifKif, Pl aux Grains. Locally made accessories, jewellery and knick-knacks with a contemporary edge.
Raffia Craft, 82 Rue d'Agadir. This is a tiny outlet shop for the raffia products of local designer, Miro. His shoes are in demand in Europe and much copied by other local artisans.
Tamounte Co-Operative, 6 Rue Souss (off Pl Moulay Hassan). Sells hand-crafted gifts and games made from thuya wood.

◐ What to do

Essaouira *p89, maps p90 and p92*
Cycling
Bikes, including mountain bikes, can be hired in the old town and from the **Explora** kitesurf shop in the square off Rue Laalouj from €15 per day.

Hammams
There are several public hammams in the medina, with prices from around 10dh for entry (extra for glove, soap and scrub-down). Try the oldest called **Hammam Pabst** on Rue Annasr in the mellah. Orson Welles once used it as a location in the filming of *Othello*. Alternatively, try the more upmarket and very popular **Mounia Hammam**, 17 Rue Oum Errabia. Prices from 50dh for a basic hammam and up to 250dh for the full works.

Horse riding
Ranch de Diabat, Diabat, Quartier des Dunes, T0670-576841, www.ranchdediabat. com. A ranch just 3 km south of Essaouira towards Agadir where you can do short rides along the beach or multi-day treks. Also organizes camel treks.

Surfing
Winter is the surfing season in Essaouira. Apr-Oct the wind is up and the surfers are out in force. If you don't have your own gear,

you can rent but check it carefully. The best surf places are probably:

Club Mistral, right on the main beach at southern end of Blvd Mohammed V, T0524-783934, www.club-mistral.com. Formerly Ocean Vagabond and a long-established professional watersports outfitter.
Explora, T0611-475188, www.explora morocco.com. Next to **Club Mistral** on the main beach. English-speaking staff and good value. Surf lessons from 300dh for 2 hrs. You can buy your gear here too or in their shop in the medina (see under Cycling, above).

Walking
Ecotourism and Randonnées, T0615-762131, www.essaouira-randonnees.com. Half-day and day walks with a picnic through the thuya forest and countryside around Essaouira. Organized from the **Restaurant la Découverte** (see Restaurants). English guide available.

◎ Transport

Essaouira *p89, maps p90 and p92*
Air
RAM run flights to **Paris** and **Casablanca** from the little Aéroport de Mogador, T0524-476709.

Bus
Buses from Essaouira can get very full in summer and during the **Gnaoua Festival** in Jun; see Festivals, above. Check your departure times the day before you travel and try to reserve.
CTM (T0524-784764, www.ctm.ma) and private line bus services operate from the terminal near Bab Doukkala, with connections to **Casablanca** (6 or 9 hrs, depending on route), **Safi**, **Marrakech** (3 hrs) and **Agadir** (3½ hrs). You can also buy CTM bus tickets from their office on Rue de Caire near Bab Sabaa. Lots of touts compete for custom – go inside the terminus and look at ticket windows where departure times are clearly posted. **CTM** has departures

daily at 0745 and 1130 to **Safi**, **El Jadida** and **Casablanca**. Buses south to **Agadir** depart at 1430 (60dh), and twice daily for **Marrakech** at 1230 and 1700 (75dh). The best onward option is the **Supratours** (Essaouira office, T0524-475317, www. supratours.ma) service to **Marrakech** at 0600, 0930, 1145, 1500 and 1800 (70dh) to connect with onward trains to **Casablanca–Rabat**, from the square near the South Bastion. Buy your ticket at the kiosk on the square at least a day before, as this is a popular bus. **Pullman du Sud** has a midnight departure from the bus station for **Casablanca**, arriving at 0630.

Taxi
Grands taxis operate from a parking lot beside the bus terminal. (You may have to wait a while for the vehicle to fill up if you are going to Marrakech.) There are frequent departures for **Diabat**, **Ghazoua**, **Smimou** and other places in the region, also for **Marrakech** and **Agadir**. *Petits taxis* are numerous; 5dh for a short ride in town. There are numerous calèches to be caught from the cab rank outside Bab Doukkala.

● Directory

Essaouira *p89, maps p90 and p92*
Banks Branches of BMCI, BMCE, Banque Populaire and Crédit du Maroc are in and around Pl Moulay Hassan, most with ATM machines. **Medical services Dentist**: Dr ElAcham, 1 Blvd de Fès, T0524-474727; Dr Sayegh, Pl de l'Horloge, T0524-475569. **Doctor**: Dr Mohammed Tadrart, 1 Av Mouqawama, opposite post office, T0524-475954; Dr Said El-Haddad, 5 Av de l'Istiqlal, close to the Wafa Bank, T0524-476910. **Hospital**: Hôpital Sidi Mohammed ben Abdallah, Blvd de l'Hôpital (Emergencies), T0524-475716. **Pharmacies**: Av de l'Istiqlal and on Pl de l'Horloge in medina. Several pharmacies on Av Al Massira near Bab Doukkala. **Useful numbers** Police: main commissariat on Rue du Caire, T0524-784880.

Contents

Footprint features

At a glance

⊖ **Getting around** There are
bus services into the Atlas
mountains, but your own
transport is definitely better.
⏱ **Time required** There are
plenty of day trips into the
mountains from Marrakech.
Otherwise, allow at least a week to
explore the area fully; more if you
want to do some serious trekking.
☀ **Weather** The peaks of the Atlas
mountains remain snow-capped
until at least early summer. The
temperature at night can often
drop below zero.
✖ **When not to go** The Atlas are
best explored in summer or autumn,
as the winter weather can make
getting around difficult. At altitude,
snow lingers through the spring,
though blossom in the high valleys
can also make this a rewarding time
to visit.

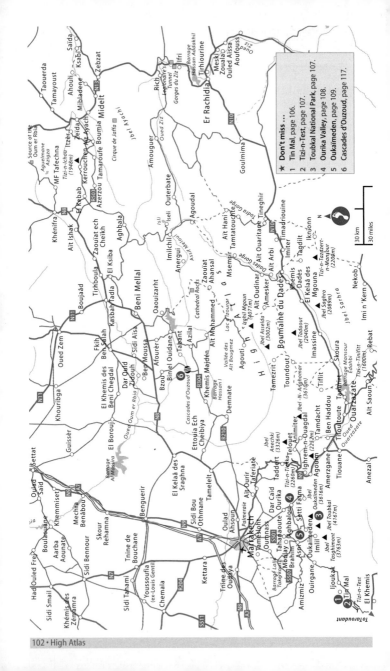

Don't miss ...

★

1 Tin Mal, page 106.
2 Tizi-n-Test, page 107.
3 Toubkal National Park, page 107.
4 Ourika Valley, page 108.
5 Oukaïmeden, page 109.
6 Cascades d'Ouzoud, page 117.

30 km
30 miles

Snow-topped for half the year, the High Atlas rise out of the plains south of Marrakech. West to east they stretch across Morocco from the Atlantic coast just north of Agadir until they fade into the desert on the Algerian border. In many ways they are the dominant feature of Moroccan geography, yet the High Atlas are very different from the Moroccan lowlands, socially as well as topographically.

In winter, there is scope for skiing; in spring, apple and cherry blossom fills the valleys with colour, and, in summer, the cooler air is a draw for escapees from the oppressive cities. All year round there are good walking opportunities, from short strolls to waterfalls, to serious treks to mountain summits.

Within easy day-trip distance of Marrakech, the Toubkal National Park, named for Jbel Toubkal, the highest peak in North Africa, has long been a draw for tourists. The region also has other popular destinations, including the pretty Setti Fatma in the Ourika Valley and the ski resort of Oukaïmeden. The striking, restored mosque of Tin Mal is high on the spectacular road to the Tizi-n-Test pass. Heading south is another dramatic pass, the Tizi-n-Tichka, and the village of Telouet, with its brooding Glaoui fortress.

Further east are the Cascades d'Ouzoud, Morocco's highest waterfalls, and the beautiful high valley of the Aït Bougmez.

Western High Atlas

Three main roads lead south out of Marrakech into the western High Atlas. From west to east, they head over the Tizi-n-Test pass towards Taroudant; up the Ourika Valley to Setti Fatma, Oukaïmeden and the Toubkal National Park, and over the Tizi-n-Tichka pass towards Ouarzazate.

On the R203 to the Tizi-n-Test, Asni is an important market town and Ouirgane is a strung-out holiday destination in the hills. Further south, the road curves and rises through the spectacular mountain valley to the awe-inspiring 12th-century mosque of Tin Mal, one of Morocco's most significant buildings, now partially restored. Back at Asni, a road branches south to Imlil and the Toubkal National Park, centring on North Africa's highest mountain. The landscapes are spectacular, and there are some great walking routes.

The route up the Ourika Valley from Marrakech is, initially at least, a gentler one, splitting to terminate at either the village of Setti Fatma, with its waterfalls and riverside restaurants, or the ski resort of Oukaïmeden.

Most switch-back of all, the N9 climbs to cross through the Tizi-n-Tichka pass at 2260 m. Just east of here is the precipitous Kasbah of Telouet. ►► *For listings, see pages 112-116.*

Southwest of Marrakech → For listings, see pages 112-116. Colour map 2, B3.

Take the main S501 road south out of Marrakech (straight over at the junction near the **Hivernage**). The road forks a few kilometres after the **Club Royal Equestre**. You go left for Asni (S501; see page 105), right for Amizmiz in the foothills of the Atlas. The latter road (S507) passes through a number of small settlements, including Tamesloht, and the Lalla Takerkoust Lake, where accommodation is available. Note that in a wet year, clay from the hillside may crumble onto the upper sections of the Amizmiz to Ouirgane road.

Lalla Takerkoust
Often referred to as 'the lake', Lalla Takerkoust, 40 km to the southwest of Marrakech, is actually a reservoir, formed by a hydroelectric dam (the Barrage Lalla Takerkoust) that provides Marrakech with a good portion of its electricity. It is a popular swimming and picnicking place for Marrakchis wanting to escape the oppressive heat of the city. Lapping at the red-earth foothills of the High Atlas, and with the high peaks as a backdrop, it's a strikingly beautiful place, and there are a couple of places to stay and eat (see page 112) too. If you have a car, the route across the Kik plateau from here to Asni has extraordinary panoramic views across the high pastures to the Atlas peaks beyond.

Amizmiz
Amizmiz, 55 km southwest from Marrakech at the end of the S507, is a growing rural centre interesting as the starting point of some pleasant hikes and for its Tuesday souk.

Turning off right just after the 'administrative zone', you can wind up into the foothills to the *maison forestière*. Parking in the shade, there is some gentle walking along a track above the Assif Anougal, with views down over the villages. From Amizmiz, there is also a road eastwards to **Ouirgane**, via the Tizi-n-Ouzla (1090 m), where you can get a view of the Assif Amassine valley, with the Toubkal Massif as backdrop. There then follows a winding descent to the junction with the S501, where you can go right for Ouirgane or left for Asni and Marrakech.

Un stylo, un bonbon, un dirham

All over the country the sight of children begging is not uncommon. But in the mountains it seems particularly prevalent, spurred on perhaps by generations of well-meaning trekkers who have happily handed out coins, pens or sweets. The mechanical chorus of "Un stylo, un bonbon, un dirham" will follow you, echoing through many remote mountain valleys.

In the past, the advice has been to bring a supply of pens to hand out or, in some worrying cases, medicine. Talk to local community leaders now, though, and they will almost certainly advise against giving the local children anything at all. Even giving out pens encourages systematic begging, damaging the education system and family structures. It also detrimentally affects the way foreign visitors are seen: as resources to be mined, rather than human beings to interact with.

Talk to the local children, teach them something, but save your pen money and donate it instead to organizations like the **Global Diversity Foundation** (www.globaldiversity.org.uk) or the **High Atlas Foundation** (www.highatlasfoundation.org).

Moulay Brahim

With small hotels and eateries, Moulay Brahim is a popular weekend stop for Marrakchis. The village gets particularly busy from June to September, with people coming to visit the shrine of Moulay Brahim, visible with its green-tiled pyramid roof in the middle of the village. Stalls selling various scraggy pelts, chameleons and incense are evidence of the various favours that may be asked of Moulay Brahim. He is said to be particularly good at solving women's fertility problems. There is a festive atmosphere, with whole families coming to rent small semi-furnished apartments.

Asni → *Colour map 2, B4.*

After the rather nerve-racking drive through the gorges of Moulay Brahim, the approach to Asni, with its poplar and willow trees, comes as something of a relief. If you arrive on Saturday, you will be able to see the souk in a big dusty enclosure on your left as you come from Marrakech, with its accompanying chaos of *grands taxis*, mules and minibuses. The village is scattered in clusters in the valley and makes a good place for a quick break en route to Ouirgane, Tin Mal or Taroudant, if you can deal with the attentions of the trinket sellers. There are good walking routes along the Plateau du Kik to the west of Asni, north to Moulay Brahim and southwest to Ouirgane.

A popular driving route goes from Asni up onto the **Plateau du Kik** and then through the villages around Tiferouine, before heading some 8 km northwest cross-country to the settlement of **Lalla Takerkoust** and its reservoir lake (see page 104).

Ouirgane → *Colour map 2, B3.*

Ouirgane is another pleasant place to pause on the R203, about one hour's drive (61 km) from Marrakech. The settlement's houses are scattered on the valley sides, and some have been recently displaced by the building of a new dam on the Oued Nfiss. Ouirgane can be reached by bus from Marrakech (the Taroudant service), or by *grands taxi* from Asni. Hotels in Ouirgane (see page 112) have good food and offer the opportunity to explore the valley on easy rambles.

Tin Mal → *Colour map 2, B3.*

A small settlement high in the Atlas mountains, Tin Mal was once the holy city of the Almohad Dynasty. It offers a rare opportunity for non-Muslims to see the interior of a major Moroccan mosque, with examples of 12th-century Almohad decor intact amidst the ruins. The Koutoubia at Marrakech (the Almohad capital from 1147) was modelled on Tin Mal. At the mosque the guardian will let you in and point out enthusiastically features such as the original doors piled up in a corner. He'll also ask for a donation when you leave.

Background In 1122, Ibn Toumert, after much roaming in search of wisdom, returned to Morocco. He created too much trouble in Marrakech, with his criticisms of the effete Almoravids, and shortly after, when the mountain tribes had sworn to support him and fight the Almoravids in the name of the doctrines he had taught them, he was proclaimed Mahdi, the rightly guided one. In 1125 he established his capital at Tin Mal, a fairly anonymous hamlet strategically situated in the heartland of his tribal supporters. The rough-and-ready village was replaced with a walled town, soon to become the spiritual centre of an empire. The first mosque was a simple affair. The building you see today, a low square structure, was the work of Ibn Toumert's successor, Abd el Mu'min – a student whom the future Mahdi had met in Bejaïa.

Tin Mal was the first *ribat*, as the austere Almohad fortresses were called, and was subject to a puritan discipline. The Mahdi himself was a sober, chaste person, an enemy of luxurious living. All his efforts went into persuading his followers of the truths of Islam, as he conceived them. Tin Mal was subject to a pitiless discipline. Prayers were led by the Mahdi himself and all had to attend. Public whippings and the threat of execution kept those lacking in religious fervour in line. As well as prayer leader, the Mahdi was judge, hearing and trying cases himself according to Muslim law, which had barely begun to penetrate the mountain regions.

After Ibn Toumert's death, his simple tomb became the focal point for a mausoleum for the Almohad sovereigns. Standing in the quiet mosque, today mostly open to the sky, looking down the carefully restored perspectives of the arcades, it is difficult to imagine what a hive of religious enthusiasm this place must have been.

Tin Mal mosque Completed in 1154, under Abd el Mu'min, the Tin Mal Mosque has a simple exterior. The mihrab (prayer niche) is built into the minaret. To the left, as one stands before the mihrab, is the imam's entrance to the right is a space for the minbar, the preacher's chair, which would have been pulled out for sermons. The decoration is simple: there are several cupolas with restored areas of stalactite plasterwork and there are examples of the *darj w ktaf* and palmette motifs, but little inscription. The technique used, plaster applied to brick, is a forerunner of later, larger Almohad decorative schemes.

When the new empire acquired Marrakech, a fine capital well located on the plain, Tin Mal remained its spiritual heart and a sort of reliable rear base. It was to Tin Mal that Abd el Mu'min sent the treasures of Ibn Tachfin the Almoravid. Even after the Merinid destruction of 1275-1276, the tombs of of Ibn Toumert and his successors inspired deep respect.

Eventually, the Almohads were to collapse in internecine struggles. The final act came in the 1270s, when the last Almohads took refuge in Tin Mal. However, the governor of Marrakech, El Mohallim pursued them into their mountain fastness, and besieged and took the seemingly impenetrable town. The Almohad caliph and his followers were taken prisoner and executed, and the great Almohad sovereigns, Abu Yaqoub and Abu Youssef, were pulled from their tombs and decapitated. The Almohads, one time conquerors of the whole of the Maghreb and much of Spain, were destroyed in their very capital, barely 150 years after they had swept away the Almoravids.

In the 1990s, around US$750,000 was put forward for restoration of the ruins. Work now seems to have ground to a halt, though the building is doubly impressive in its semi-ruined, semi-open-to-the-sky way.

Tizi-n-Test → *Colour map 2, B3.*
The R203 from Marrakech to Taroudant is one of the most spectacular routes in Morocco, winding its way up and then down through the High Atlas mountains, above beautiful valleys and past isolated villages, eventually reaching the Tizi-n-Test pass, with its breathtaking views across the Souss valley to the Anti-Atlas mountains. There are buses between the two cities, but check that they are going via Tizi-n-Test. Driving has been possible since the road, a traditional trading route, was formally opened in 1928, following the work of French engineers. Some of its sections are downright scary, but it is a recommended experience, particularly when tied in with visits to Asni, Ouirgane and Tin Mal. Signs on the exit to Marrakech will indicate if the pass is open. The R203 joins the N10 from Taroudant to Ouarzazate (see page 210). For a lunch stop on this route, there is the cheap **Restaurant La Belle Vue**, about 1 km after the pass on the Taroudant side. Cheap rooms are also available, but have a sleeping bag ready – it gets cold at 2100 m altitude.

Imlil and the Toubkal National Park → *See also map, page 108.*

Northern Africa's highest peak is one that many like to tick off their list, but the national park that surrounds it has plenty of other good walks, from afternoon strolls to serious treks. For details of walks in the park see box, page 110.

Arriving in Toubkal National Park
Best time to visit The best time for walking is after the main snows, at blossom time in the spring. Mules cannot negotiate passes until March/April. For some, summers are too hot and visibility in the heat haze is poor. November to February is too cold, and there is too much snow for walking, although frozen ground is often more comfortable than walking on the ever-moving scree. Deep snows and ice present few problems to those with ropes, ice axes, crampons and experience. Without these, stay away in winter.

Information It's wise to purchase specialist hiking books (such as Alan Palmer's *Moroccan Atlas*) and maps. Mules and guides can be hired in Imlil, most easily in the Refuge. Having a local Tachelhit-speaking guide is essential on treks.

Imlil → *Colour map 2, B4.*
Imlil, 17 km south-southeast from Asni, is the most important village of the Aït Mizane Valley. At 1790 m, it is the start of the walks in this area and is also a good place to hang out for a while. In the centre of the village is the car park/taxi area, with the stone-built **Club Alpin Français (CAF)** hut at the corner of the road, a guides hut and the **Café du Soleil**. There are small cafés and shops, a good baker, a highly recommended spice shop and a travel agent. Mules are 'parked' to the south of the village. There is a utilitarian concrete route indicator on the right, should you be unsure of your direction. When you arrive, you may be besieged by lots of underemployed blokes, keen to help you in some way or other. The town's **hammam** has been built with money from the kasbah (see page 113) and is recommended. Information in Imlil is available through the **Hôtel-Café Soleil** and at the **CAF refuge**.

The Ourika Valley is a beautiful area of steep-sided gorges and green, terraced fields along the winding Oued Ourika, about 45 minutes' drive south of Marrakech. The accessibility of the valley makes it a very popular excursion for Marrakchis and tourists, and, in summer, sections of the valley get crowded with campers and day trippers happy to be away from the hot, dusty air of the plain. Just before Aghbalou, the P2017 splits, with a right-hand

Jbel Toubkal region

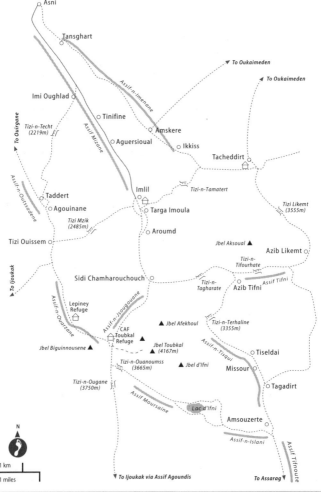

road taking you up to the ski resort of Oukaïmeden. The trail-head village of Setti Fatma is reached by going straight ahead. The valley has occasional problems with flash floods, the worst of which, in 1995, destroyed most of Setti Fatma and killed many people.

Setti Fatma

The road ends at Setti Fatma, famous for its seven waterfalls and 100-year-old walnut trees. There is a small weekly market, a **Bureau des Guides de Montagne** and a good choice of basic accommodation and riverside tagine outlets. Setti Fatma must once have been idyllic. There is breeze-block housing among the older stone homes now, but the stunning setting and the sound of the river make it picturesque nonetheless. The place is set up primarily for Moroccan rather than European visitors, but that gives it an unusual charm, and Setti Fatma would be a good starting point for a trek (see below). It also makes a great day trip from Marrakech.

The main part of Setti Fatma stretches beyond the end of the road. Precarious temporary rope bridges wobble visitors and locals carrying sheep across to a large number of café-restaurants along the bank. The seven cascades are a 30-minute scramble up from Setti Fatma, following the path up behind the first café, and there are plenty of young men and children who will help you find the way. There is another café beside the first waterfall.

Setti Fatma makes a good base for exploring the **Jbel Yagour**, a plateau region famed for its numerous prehistoric rock carvings. See page 115 for trekking details.

Oukaïmeden → *Colour map 2, B4.*

Oukaïmeden, 'the meeting place of the four winds', is Morocco's premier ski resort, and Africa's highest. It's some 2600 m up in the Atlas and a 1½-hour drive from Marrakech, making it a good day trip. The highest lift goes up to 3250 m, and there are various runs down, not always very well marked. There are also four drag lifts and a tobogganing area. The resort is open for skiing from December to March but in summer it's less busy and many places are closed.

The quality of skiing is variable and good skiable snow cannot be counted on, though there's new investment and talk of snow cannons. The hot African sun means that the snow melts easily, only to freeze again at night, leaving slopes icy. Instructors work in the resort, and there are ski shops that rent equipment out and donkeys to carry your gear between lifts

In summer, visitors can walk, climb and even paraglide here. Look out for the prehistoric carvings on the rocky outcrop below the dam wall. There are further carvings on the flat rocks among the new chalets.

Towards Ouarzazate via Tizi-n-Tichka → *Colour map 2, B4.*

Completed in 1936 by the Foreign Legion, the N9 road from Marrakech to Ouarzazate gives stunning views. It runs through the full range of Atlas environments, from the Haouz plains, through the verdant foothills of the Oued Zat, to the barren peaks of the Atlas and the arid regions to the south. Drivers need maximum concentration on this route, especially in the twilight, when you will meet donkeys and flocks of sheep wandering across the road, guided by small children. Clapped out local buses break down, and there are some especially narrow and vertiginous stretches leading up to the pass after Taddert. A further hazard is the group of eager fossil sellers who hang out at viewpoints and café stops. Note that in winter there can be heavy cloud, snow storms and icy rain, reducing visibility and making the road extremely slippery. In such conditions, the road is not much

Walking in Toubkal

It's important to find a guide for longer walks as conditions can be dangerous. The number of people who have to drop out of treks in the area due to stomach problems is high, so try to check on hygiene when deciding who to use. If you're planning a trek in advance, **Mountain Voyage** (www.mountain-voyage.com), based in Marrakech, is recommended; see page 86.

Walking options include the **Aremd circuit**, a refreshing hike through remote villages with breathtaking views, and a hike to the **Lac d'Ifni**. Another is to walk to **Setti Fatma**, in the Ourika Valley.

Much more challenging is to climb **Jbel Toubkal**, the highest mountain in North Africa at 4167 m. It is necessary to break the walk at the **Club Alpin Français Toubkal Refuge** (ex-Refuge Neltner), a simple dormitory place with no meals at 3106 m. In winter this is a difficult trek and full equipment is essential. A specialist hiking book, such as Richard Knight's *Trekking in the Moroccan Atlas* (Hindhead: Trailblazer, 2008), is recommended. Mules and guides can be hired in Imlil, most easily in the Refuge (see Where to stay, page 114).

Imlil to Jbel Toubkal

Day 1 Imlil is the end of the surfaced road but it is possible to reach **Aremd** (also spelt Aroumd) by car up the rough track. It takes about 45 minutes to walk. **Café Lac d'Ifni** makes a good stop here. **Sidi Chamharouchouch** is reached in another 2½ hours, going steadily uphill. It is important to bear right after the *marabout* to find the initially very steep, but later steady, slope up to the **Toubkal Refuge** (3207 m). Allow 4½ hours from Imlil. The Toubkal Refuge, with dormitory space for 30 people, 80dh per night, 150dh in summer, is often crowded. On the plus side, the warden sells bottled water, soft drinks, and can do food (50dh for a tagine). Campers using the level site below the hut can also use the facilities.

Day 2 The usual approach for walkers is via the South Cwm, a long day's walking and scrambling if you want to go up and back. The route is clearer on the map than it is on the ground. First observe the route from the rear of the **Toubkal Refuge**; the large boulders on the skyline are a point to aim for. Leave the refuge

fun at night. If snow cuts the pass, the snow barriers will be down. The total distance from Marrakech to Ouarzazate is nearly 200 km. Good places to stop include upper **Taddert** (busy, 86 km from Marrakech), the **Tizi-n-Tichka** pass (2260 m) itself, which is almost exactly halfway, or **Ighrem-n-Ouagdal**, about 118 km from Marrakech, where there is an old *agadir* (granary) to visit. Driving in good conditions, Marrakech to Taddert will take you two hours, while Taddert to Ouarzazate is about another two.

Telouet

An eagle's nest of a place, high in the mountains, Telouet is something of a legend. It has one of the most spectacular kasbahs in the Atlas. Today, it is on the tourist circuit, as the hordes of 4WD vehicles testify. Within living memory, however, its name was synonymous with the repressive rule of the Glaoui brothers.

The history of Telouet and its kasbah is short but bloodthirsty. It is the story of how two brothers of the Glaoua tribe, sons of an Ethiopian slave woman, by force of arms and character, managed to achieve absolute dominance over much of southern Morocco in the early 20th century. Gavin Maxwell's *Lords of the Atlas* describes the turbulent times in Marrakech and the mountains, as first the Moroccan monarchy and then the French and go down to the river. Cross over and go up the other side to the main path to the foot of the first of the many screes. Take the scree path up to the boulders, which can be reached in just over an hour. From here, there is a choice: the long scree slope to the north of the summit, or the shorter, steeper slope to the south of the summit ridge. Either way, allow 3½ hours.

The summit is not in itself attractive but the stone shelters make fairly comfortable overnight camping for a good view of sunrise. Views are excellent – if there is no haze – to the Jbels Saghro and Siroua but, as the summit here (4167 m) is a plateau, other views are limited. Be prepared for low temperatures at this altitude and for the bitter winds that blow three out of four days in the spring and autumn. The descent is quicker; allow 2-2½ hours.

Toubkal Circuit

In nine days, a good walking circuit can give you a feel for life in the High Atlas and take in Jbel Toubkal too. The map (page 108) shows the main overnights.

Day 1 would take you from Imi Oughlad or Aguersioual to **Amskere**. On **Day 2**, the first full day getting used to the mountains, a five-hour trek takes you to **Tacheddirt**. A long **Day 3** runs via the Tizi Likemt (3555 m) to Azib Likemt. From here, you have another long **Day 4** over to **Amsouzerte**, where there is a difficult-to-find gite or Landrover taxis back down to Marrakech. From Amsouzerte, on **Day 5**, you head for **Lac Ifni** (2290 m). **Day 6** takes you to the **Toubkal Refuge** (3106 m), via the Tizi-n-Ouanoumss (3665 m), and a long **Day 7** is the climb up Jbel Toubkal and back down to the refuge. **Day 8** takes you down to **Aroumd/Aremd** (1920 m), via the shrine of Sidi Chamharouch (2340 m) and its tiny collection of stalls. At the time of the pilgrimage, this shrine is very busy. From Aremd, on **Day 9**, you head back to Imi Oughlad (1300 m). This last long stretching of the legs takes you via the Tizi Oussem (1850 m) and the small settlements of Agouinane and Taddert before the last pass, Tizi-n-Techt (2219 m), taking you down to **Imi Oughlad**.

skirmished with the southern tribal leaders to achieve dominance. The denouement, which came shortly after Moroccan Independence in 1956, was fatal to Glaoui power.

Abandoned before completion, the Kasbah of Telouet as it survives today is mainly the result of 20th-century building schemes by the last great Glaoui lord, T'hami. Generally, as you arrive, someone will emerge to show you around. The great reception rooms, with their cedar ceilings and crumbling stucco, a transposition of 19th-century Moroccan urban taste to the mountains, are worth a visit.

Telouet to Ouarzazate via Aït Ben Haddou → Colour map 2, B4.

For those with 4WD, Telouet is also the starting point for an 80-km route down to Ouarzazate. Ask for the road to Animiter, the first main village. Leaving Telouet, after a few kilometres, a turn-off to the left, near the foot of Jbel Amassine, takes you up to the source of the Glaoui family's wealth, a salt mine. **Animiter**, some 9 km east from Telouet, was famous in the early days of Moroccan tourism as its kasbah, painted by Jacques Majorelle, was featured on an early poster. Here the surfaced road runs out. It should be possible to camp near the Oued Mellah. The next village, **Timsal**, lies a few kilometres to the south. After Timsal, follow the track along the Adrar Taqqat, used when they put in electricity lines. You reach **Tioughassine**, and the track follows the Ounila Valley. At **Assaka**, look out for abandoned granaries under the cliffs. The track then follows up onto a sort of plateau above the canyon. Next, the main track drops steeply down to the valley bottom; **Tizgui-n-Barda** is the next main village, about 29 km from Telouet. Continue along the Assif Ounila to reach **Tamdacht**, meeting point of the *oueds* Marghene and Ounila and the start of the surfaced road. The next stop, **Aït Ben Haddou** (see page 213), is 50 km from Telouet.

This route was used in earlier times by caravans coming up from the south to pick up salt from the Telouet mine. Today, it is increasingly popular as an off-road excursion. In wet weather parts of the track turn to red-clay mud, difficult if you get stuck. As with other off-road adventures, it should be tackled by vehicles in pairs. If you get stuck, you will definitely need someone to help dig you out of trouble.

◉ Western High Atlas listings

For sleeping and eating price codes and other relevant information, see pages 22-28.

◉ Where to stay

Lalla Takerkoust *p104*
€€ Le Flouka, Barrage Lalla Takerkoust, T0664-492660, www.leflouka.com.
14 rooms are scattered around Le Flouka, right at the water's edge of Lalla Takerkoust. Comfortable rooms are simply decorated with lamps and rugs and there are bare beams and open fires. There are also simpler tents and a de luxe *tente de pacha*, with a built-in bathroom. Of the 2 pools, one is reserved for hotel guests, though you can just as easily head straight out into the lake. Swimming straight towards the Atlas mountains is hard to beat. There is a restaurant (**€€**) right beside the lake, serving dishes such as steak or mozzarella and tomato salad, as well as a bar, but it's a peaceful spot, big enough to absorb its visitors with laid-back ease.

Amizmiz *p104*
Before you reach Amizmiz, there are several options for an overnight stop, including **Le Caravan Serai** (**€**), at Ouled Ben Rahmoun, see page 74.

Asni *p105*
€€€€ Kasbah Tamadot, T0208-600 0430 (UK), T877-577 8777 (USA) or T0524-368200 (Morocco), www.kasbahtamadot.com.
One of Morocco's best-known hotels, **Kasbah Tamadot** is run by Virgin and calls itself 'Sir Richard Branson's Moroccan Retreat', though chances are you won't bump into him here. Complete with all the creature comforts you can imagine, the cheapest of the 18 rooms is more than 3000dh a night and for your investment you get indoor and outdoor pools, gardens, spa and a hammam, as well as some spectacular views. The restaurant uses ingredients from the hotel's own gardens and the library comes equipped with a telescope. Despite all its good points, however, it has a little less character than its two rivals, **Kasbah Toubkal** and **Kasbah Bab Ourika**.

Ouirgane *p105*
€€€ Chez Momo II, coming from Marrakech, 800 m past **La Roseraie**, up a road on the left, T0524-485704, aubergemomo.com. After the original **Chez Momo** was engulfed in the water of Ouirgane's new reservoir in 2008, **Chez Momo II** was born, further up the hill, using local craftsmen and materials. Rooms are homely and elegant, with wrought-iron beds, bare wooden beams and lamps in alcoves. There's a beautiful horseshoe arch pool at the front of the house, with trees, roses and sun loungers around, and 'trikking', on foot or on mule, is organized.

€€ Auberge Au Sanglier Qui Fume, T0524-485707, www.ausanglierquifume. com. A small country hotel run by a French couple, 'the boar that smokes' has 22 chalet-style rooms, a restaurant serving excellent French country food, a bar, tennis court and a pool in the summer. There are mountain bikes and quad bikes for rent, and the management will put you in touch with guides should you wish to do some walking or horse riding. The titular boar, complete with pipe, watches over the bar.

€€ La Bergerie, about 2 km before Ouirgane village as you come from Marrakech, turn right at the signpost for Marigha, T0524-485717, www.labergerie-maroc.com. Particularly well set up for families, French-run La Bergerie is spread amongst 5 ha of grounds in a valley away from the village. The restaurant serves a good mix of French and Moroccan food, combining dishes such as kefta and egg tagine with apricots and goat's cheese. There's beer on tap and a good outdoor seating area, and they'll even knock up a fondue on request. The best rooms are the bungalows set in the grounds, with some privacy and more style, nicely worn old furniture and private gardens with peach, apricot and apple trees.

€€ La Roseraie, T0524-439128, www.la roseraiehotel.com. A peaceful hotel set in a 25 ha of exceptionally colourful rose gardens, with 42 rooms and suites, 2 restaurants, a bar next to the pool and 2 tennis courts. The rooms, however, are less spectacular than the gardens, with rather dated peach bathrooms. Horse riding is organized.

Imlil and the Toubkal National Park
p107

The **Bureau des Guides**, in the centre of Imlil, can provide information on accommodation in homes: locals, who are used to walkers, are generally keen to provide a floor or mattresses to sleep on.

€€€€ Kasbah du Toubkal, T0524-485611, Imlil, www.kasbahdutoubkal.com. Imlil's

restored kasbah, perched spectacularly above the village, played the role of a Tibetan fortress in director Martin Scorsese's film *Kundun*. It is run by the UK-based travel agent **Discover Ltd** in conjunction with locals and is often cited as a good example of eco-tourism. There is a range of accommodation, from 3 dorms for groups to 5 deluxe rooms. The best rooms come with CD players, slippers and even Berber clothes to borrow. The building, once HQ of the local *caïd*, is worth a visit; for a 20dh contribution to the local development fund, you can have mint tea and walnuts on the roof terrace. A day trip to the Kasbah can also be arranged form Marrakech for €85, including lunch, a mule ride and a visit to a Berber house.

€€ Riad Imlil, Imlil, T0524-485485, T0661-240599 (mob), www.riaddecharme-imlil. com. Good rooms with TV, room service, Wi-Fi, fridges and a/c. Stone and *tadelakt* are both used, though the rooms are a little dark. There's a restaurant with a fire and a small 'salon Berbere'.

€ Auberge El Aine, Imlil, T0524-485662, T0666-647999 (mobile), iframed@hotmail. com. On the right as you arrive in the village from Asni, this is a bargain. Rooms are small but cute, with windows opening onto a garden with cherry blossom in spring. It's friendly, and the bright colours, topsy turvy stairs and a big tree in the courtyard give the place extra character. Upstairs rooms are best, or there are small apartments with bathroom and kitchen, good for families or small groups.

€ Auberge Imi N'Ouassif, Chez Mohammed Bouinbaden, Imlil, T0524-485126, T0662-105126 (mob), iminouassif@ wanadoo.ma. On the western outskirts of the town, along paths between high stone walls, this is a simple, quiet place that also provides guides.

€ Gite Atlas Aremd, Aremd, T0668-882764, atlastreking@yahoo.ca. Mustapha Ibdlaid runs this basic gîte in Aremd with 12 rooms and good views across the valley to the mountains. There's the option to sleep on sofas in the salon. Hot showers included.

€ Gite Id Mansour, Aremd, T0524-485613, T0662-355214 (mob). A good gite in Aremd, Id Mansour has hot water and towels and is very clean. Beds are comfortable and new and some rooms have mountain views. Stark but fairly comfortable.

€ Refuge du Club Alpin Français, Imlil, T0524-485122, T0677-307415 (mob). Minimal facilities but clean and with a very friendly welcome and good information from Lydia, the French manager. 40 beds in dorms, open all year round.

Setti Fatma and Ourika Valley *p108*
€€€€ Kasbah Bab Ourika, 45 mins from Marrakech off the Setti Fatma road near Dar-Caid-Ouriki, T0524-389797, T0661-252328 (mob), www.babourika.com. Unfussily elegant, this kasbah is in an extraordinary location, perched on its own personal hill overlooking the mouth of the Ourika valley, with craggy red mountain rock to one side and Marrakech in the distance behind. Built, set up and run by the owner of **Riad Edward** in Marrakech, this place is decorated in a similar insouciant style: rooms are huge and have an antique, rustic atmosphere that makes guests feel immediately at home but are also luxurious, with thick rugs, generous bathrooms, open fires and wonderfully comfortable beds. The pool is spectacular, with views to the mountains, and the food is exquisite, with dishes such as chilled carrot soup and lemongrass beef brochette with stir-fried spinach and turmeric expertly mixing flavours. The environmental and social policies of the place are ground-breaking, and guests can take a guided walk through the extraordinarily fertile valley and Berber villages below. The track that needs to be navigated to reach the front door is an eroded adventure, but one that increases the dramatic sense of arrival, and of being in a very special place indeed.
€€ Dar Piano, T0524-484842, T0661-342884 (mob), www.darpiano.com. Closed Jun-Aug. On the right of the road from Marrakech, about 10 km south of Setti Fatma, this cosy, French-run place has simple, homely rooms, good cooking and roof terrace views.
€€ La Perle d'Ourika, T0661 56 72 39, laperledourika@hotmail.com. A couple of minutes downstream from Setti Fatma, the **Perle** has a degree of decoration rare in Setti Fatma, with furry sequined bed covers and painted floors. It's a little over the top, but it is at least an attempt at style. Good shared facilities, 24-hr hot water and a roof terrace with fantastic views up and down the valley. The restaurant is also recommended and has wine.
€ Azilal, Setti Fatma, T0668-883770. Next to Hotel Asgaour, this is a bright and cheerful place, lacking in some creature comforts and with small rooms but with hot water and views over the river. For those on a tight budget, there's a big room you can sleep in for 30dh each.
€ Evasion, Setti Fatma, T0666-640758. Near the bottom of the village, on the opposite side from the river, this is a modern place with good rooms, as long as you're not too disturbed by the strange blue blurry glass. There are balconies with views over the valley and good bathrooms. The attached café has a proper coffee machine and a glassed-in room for rainy days.
€ Hotel Asgaour, Setti Fatma, T0524-485294, T0666-416419 (mob). A friendly place with 20 basic, clean rooms and small but comfy beds. Some rooms have views over the valley, and the hotel has a pretty terrace across the other side of the river, as well as some chairs and tables outside. Rooms with private shower and toilet are more expensive.

Oukaïmeden *p109*
Oukaïmeden has a small but adequate supply of accommodation. In practice, the resort only gets crowded on snowy weekends, and many visitors from Marrakech prefer to return home to sleep. Out of season, rooms in mountain chalets can be found.

€€ **Chez Juju**, T0524 319005, www.hotel chezjuju.com. Open all year (except Ramadan). 8 clean and well looked-after wood-clad rooms, with a decent restaurant serving French as well as Moroccan cuisine, and a bar with cold beer. Half-board is obligatory.
€€ **Hotel Kenzi Louka**, T0524-319080. Open all year round. A large, triangular-shaped hotel, with fairly basic but comfortable rooms. Outside pool (generally heated), information and advice on skiing and trekking.
€ **Refuge of the Club Alpin Francais**, T0524-319036. Open all year. Dorm bunks as well as private double rooms. Skiing equipment, mountain bikes, etc, can be hired and there's a bar and games room.

Telouet *p110*
€ **Auberge Ouahsous**, Anguelz, T0661-199400, www.auberge-ouahsous.com. 10 km from Telouet in the direction of Aït Ben Haddou, this rather imposing hotel has simple, clean, comfortable, rooms, some en suite, a restaurant and a grocery store open 0700-2300.

🍴 Restaurants

Hardly anywhere in the Atlas operates just as a restaurant, though there are cafés, and most hotels also serve food.

Asni *p105*
In the centre of the village are a number of stalls and cafés cooking harira soup and tagines. This is the last major place to stock up on basic supplies for a visit to the Toubkal region.

Ouirgane *p105*
The hotels in Ouirgane all have restaurants attached; **La Bergerie** is a good stopover for lunch.

Tizi-n-Test *p107*
For a nearby lunch stop, the cheap **Restaurant La Belle Vue** (boumzough.

free.fr) is about 1 km after the pass on the Taroudant side.

Imlil and Toubkal National Park *p107*
Most places offer half board, so the standalone eating options are limited, but **Café Soleil** and **Atlas Tichka** offer good lunches. **Les Amis** does good chicken brochettes and genuine coffee; **Café Grand Atlas** is more of a local place, where you can eat tagine on the roof terrace. **Café Imlil** was the first café in town and hasn't changed much since. For something smarter, and for the best views, go to the **Kasbah de Toubkal**.

Setti Fatma and Ourika Valley *p108*
There are a huge number of places in Setti Fatma that set up to catch the lunchtime trade from Marrakech, offering excellent tagines freshly cooked at stalls near the river. There's little to choose between them; wander around and pick one that smells good, or go for a table with a view.

Oukaïmeden *p109*
Chez Juju is probably the best option.

⚙ What to do

Imlil and Toubkal National Park *p107*
Tours and guides
Reckon on about 350dh per day per person and tip generously; about 50dh a day is probably about right.
Brahim Ait Zin, T0667-690903, trekadventurer@yahoo.fr. Brahim knows the mountains very well and speaks good English.
Bureau des Guides, in the centre of Imlil, T0524-485626, bureau.guides@yahoo.fr. Daily 0700-1900 summer, 0800-1700 winter. You can find a guide here.
Hassan Agafay, T0667-842236 (mob). Also recommended is this local outfit.

Setti Fatma and Ourika Valley *p108*
Rafting
Splash Rafting Morocco, Albakech House, Av Mohammed VI, Agdal, Marrakech,

T0618-964252, moroccoadventuretours.com. The best rafting conditions are in the winter and spring. Class III and IV whitewater rafting takes place in the Ourika Valley Dec-May. Splash also run 3-day rafting trips to the Ahansal river Mar-Jun. 650dh per person for a half-day rafting trip.

Trekking

About 10 km from Setti Fatma is Tachedirt, where there is a Refuge du CAF. To set up a trek, contact the **Bureau des Guides de Montagne**, on your right before the hotels. The place is run by the very capable, and English-speaking Abderrahim ('Abdou') Mandili, T0524-291308, T0668-562340 (mob), abdoumandili@yahoo.fr.

Transport

Trips out from Marrakech into the Western High Atlas are fairly easy using buses or shared taxis. In order to do much moving about between villages, your own transport is invaluable, however. Once in the mountains, many of the roads are narrow and winding, with vertiginous drops.

Asni *p105*

There are regular buses, and much quicker *grands taxis*, to Bab Rob in **Marrakech** (2½ hrs).

Tin Mal and Tizi-n-Test *p106 and p107*

The R203 road leaves Marrakech heading south through various small villages on its way to Tin Mal and the Tizi-n-Test pass before dropping down again to Taroudant, gateway to the south, beyond. Tin Mal is about 2 hrs' drive from **Marrakech**, taking things easy, 8 km past the village of Ijoukak. You can also take a Taroudant bus or a grand taxi as far as Ijoujak, where there are several basic cafés with rooms. The pass is another 37 km further southwest.

Setti Fatma and Ourika Valley *p108*

Buses and *grands taxis* go to Bab Rob in **Marrakech**. If driving from Marrakech, head straight for the mountains on the P2017, starting from the fountain roundabout just outside the city walls at Bab Jedid, next to the Hotel Mamounia. Once in Ourika, a possible means of transport is a lift in the open-top vans and lorries which speed along the valley.

Oukaïmeden *p109*

Daily buses to **Marrakech** in winter. From Marrakech, it's reached via the P2017 Ourika Valley road, but forking right 43 km out of Marrakech, instead of left for Setti Fatma. Another option is to walk the piste which leaves the road south of Oukaïmeden, and cross the hills to the R203 to south of Asni.

In a 4WD, you can take winding roads and tracks to **Tahanaoute** and **Asni** on the R203 Tizi-n-Test road. Although the villages and landscapes are beautiful, the villages are very poor, and children are eager for pens, notebooks and dirhams (see box, page 105). When you pull away from a village, watch out that none are clinging onto the back of your vehicle for a thrilling (if dangerous) dare.

Telouet *p110*

A narrow road, in need of resurfacing and with nasty tyre-splitting edges, takes you from the Tizi-n-Tichka road to Telouet; turn left 106 km from Marrakech. For those without their own vehicle, the trip is problematic, though there may be grands taxis up from Ighrem-n-Ouagdal, or you could hire a driver in Marrakech.

Eastern High Atlas

A mountainous hinterland with little of the infrastructure of the Atlas around Toubkal, the Atlas to the east of Marrakech is a wild and little-visited area, with towns along its northern edge, strung out along the N8 from Marrakech to Fès.

Well watered like the High Atlas of Toubkal, the High Atlas south of Azilal has a very different character, due perhaps to the inaccessibility of its valleys, hidden away in the heart of the mountains. The people here are Tamazight-speaking, and more limited contact with mainstream Morocco makes them more conservative. Formal education has had little impact in the high valleys and it was only in the late 1990s that roads began to replace some of the rough tracks. Much of the region's attraction comes from the architecture of the villages, largely unspoiled by concrete. There is also more vegetation here than further west, with conifer forests surviving at high altitude. As well as wide flat valleys, there are deep gorges and small rivers that can easily turn to flood after a rainstorm on the mountains. The highest mountain in the region is the long, rounded ridge of the Ighil Mgoun, which reaches 4071 m.

The town of Azilal gives access to both the beautiful, remote high valley of the Aït Bougmez, an area increasingly popular with walkers, and the Cascades d'Ouzoud, Morocco's highest waterfall. Other attractions include the natural stone bridge of Imi-n-Ifri near Demnate.

Further east is an area of shoulder mountains, snowcapped into early summer, bare plateaux, occasional deep canyons and semi-nomad lifestyles in the high pastures. Gone are the long, deep, winding valleys of the Western mountains, with their terraced fields; highlights include the Jbel Ayyachi and the deep gorges of the Assif Melloul, thick with vegetation.

Imilchil is the most obvious 'capital' of this area and trekking expeditions set off from here. The region is particularly beautiful in late spring, when the greens of young barley and poplars coming into leaf contrast with the creamy-brown nakedness of the cliff-sides above. Near to Imilchil are the calm twin lakes of Isli and Tislit. Tracks lead across the mountains to another major meeting of the ways, Zaouïat Ahansal. ▸▸ For listings, see pages 121-123.

Azilal and the Aït Bougmez Valley

Demnate and Imi-n-Ifri → For listings, see pages 121-123. Colour map 2, B5.

On the R210 about 1½ hours from Marrakech. Demnate was once a picturesque, whitewashed place. These days the crumbling kasbah, once set in the middle of olive groves, is surrounded by unsightly new building. Nearby, **Imi-n-Ifri** ('the door to the cave') is a natural rock bridge formed by the partial collapse of a huge cavern. If you don't have transport, there are transit vans that do the short run up from Demnate. Opposite the closed auberge of the same name, a path winds down to the stream bed and a small reservoir where it's possible to swim and camp. Concrete steps, partly gone, take you up to the **grotto**. Above your head, there are great sheets of calcareous rock and, above that, cawing choughs circling overhead. You may also see the odd Barbary squirrel.

Cascades d'Ouzoud

These waterfalls, about 2½ hours' drive away from Marrakech, make a long day trip. The left turn off the R304, about 20 km before Azilal, is signposted. Tumbling 110 m down cliffs and red with clay after heavy rains, the Cascades d'Ouzoud are an impressive sight and can be seen from above as well as below. The word *ouzoud* comes from the Amazigh *izide*, meaning delicious. After the turn-off from the R304, the road heads north through beautiful

Moussem des fiançailles

Imilchil is famous for its annual summer wedding festival, Moussem des fiançailles, which was traditionally an occasion for people from all over the region to get together. The moussem site is in fact at Allamghou, signed left off the route from Rish, some 20 km before Imilchil and near the meeting place with the mountain piste up from Tinghir.

The local legend goes that two young people fell in love and wanted to marry. Their parents said no, and the couple cried so much that two lakes formed: Tislit for the girl, and Isli for the bridegroom. With such results, the parents could hardly continue to refuse and allowed their offspring to choose

the partner of their choice. The moussem became a great occasion for locals to turn out in all their finery and celebrate marriages with plenty of traditional dances and singing.

In recent years, the occasion has suffered from the incursions of tourists – and drought. In all of Morocco's rural communities, weddings – expensive, once-in-a-lifetime occasions that they are – require a lot of available capital, which always in short supply in drought years. Nevertheless, in villages along the route to Imilchil, there is some new prosperity, lots of new building, for the most part using traditional packed-earth construction methods.

landscapes where the dominant colours are red earth, dark green thuya and the paler grey green of the olive trees. Arriving in the village of Ouzoud, various local men will emerge waving sticks to help you park. For the cascades, head past the riad, and a few metres of market garden land crossed by rivulets of fast-flowing water lead you to the edge of the precipice (watch out for slippery clay). Look out for the traditional water-driven barley mills. There are various paths that will take you down to cafés on the rocks below the falls. It's possible to swim at the base of the falls, but be careful diving in, as the pool is shallow.

Azilal → *Colour map 2, B5.*

Sprawling west from a small core of kasbah and French military buildings, terracotta-red Azilal is less of a one-mule place than it used to be. In fact, it is turning into a major town with stilt-legged buildings, a big *gare routière*, several hotels (see page 122), a Thursday souk and a **tourist office** ① *Av Hassan II, T0523-488334.* From Azilal it is a slow 2¾-hour drive south over the mountains into the Aït Bougmez.

Vallée des Aït Bougmez → *For listings, see pages 121-123.*

The Aït Bougmez is one of the most beautiful valleys of the High Atlas, so far unspoiled by breeze-block building. Electricity arrived in early 2001, and the completion of the black-top road will bring further changes. The stone- and *pisé*-built villages above the fields of the valley bottom are fine examples of housing, perfectly adapted to local environment and needs. One of the most isolated regions of the High Atlas, the Aït Bougmez was until recently annually cut off by snow for part of the winter. Though walking groups are beginning to make a contribution to the local economy, life is still hard.

Tabant, 1850 m up, is the main centre, and the wide, flat-bottomed valley provides pleasant some excellent walking out from here. You could find a local to walk you up to the dinosaur footsteps near Rbat. Tabant to Agouti is an easy 8-km walk along the valley road; look out for the granary of Sidi Moussa up on a mound-like hill. There is another, slightly longer route from Tabant to Ifrane along the old main piste to Aït M'hamed. Longer, more serious treks, head to the **Massif du Mgoun**, Morocco's second-highest mountain massif.

Massif du Mgoun

Although not the most aesthetically pleasing of mountains (it has no soaring peaks), Mgoun has the largest area of land above 3000 m in the whole country. The best time to climb the mountain is probably summer or early autumn, for snow remains late into the year in these highlands. The easiest route to the summit is from the south side of the mountain, which means starting from El Kelaâ des Mgouna in the Dadès Valley (see page 204). The alternative is to head south from the Aït Bougmez to approach the massif from the east. Taking this option, head south from **Tabant** over the Tizi-n-Aït Imi (2905 m) to **Tighremt-n-Aït Ahmed**, and then west to the foot of the mountain along the course of the Assif Oulliliymt on a second day's trek. The ascent to the highest point (4071 m) is not actually difficult. Note that the summit is sacred: in a survival of pre-Islamic tradition, the mountain's help (protection) may be asked, even today.

A popular hiking option is to trek from the Aït Bougmez south to **Bou Thrarar** and **Kelaât Mgouna**. This is a six-day trip, with possible camps at Tarzout, Aguerzka and Bou Thrarar. It will be up to your guide to break up the route as they see fit. Apart from the high pass on the first day, there are no huge climbs, and you will be walking for between six and seven hours a day.

Beni Mellal and around → *For listings, see pages 121-123. Colour map 2, B5.*

One of the major centres of central Morocco, Beni Mellal, on the northern edge of the Atlas, has an important souk on Tuesday. Like a number of other towns in the region, it has grown thanks largely to money sent back by migrant workers in Italy. The main monuments include the **Kasbah Bel Kush**. Built in the 17th century by Moulay Ismaïl, it was heavily restored in the 19th century. It's also worth a walk up to the small, quiet **gardens** below the ruined Kasbah de Ras el Aïn, perched precariously on the cliffside. There is a nice café in the gardens. The **tourist office** ⓘ *1st floor of Immeuble Chichaoui, Av Hassan II, T0523 48 39 81.*

Kasbah Tadla → *Colour map 2, A5.*

Kasbah Tadla, to the northeast of Beni Mellal, was founded in 1687 by the Alaouite Sultan Moulay Ismaïl, no doubt because it is ideally located more or less halfway between Marrakech and Meknès and Fès, the imperial cities of the Saïss Plain. The crumbling terracotta ramparts sit above the shrivelled course of the river and, except for a new social-housing project on the flood plain, the view is little changed since the town's foundation. On the 'plateau' behind the kasbah is a rather derelict public garden, splendid in a quiet sort of way when the purple jacarandas are in flower. Within the kasbah there is a lot of self-built housing, put up by soldiers and their families, and two mosques, one with the distinctive Almohad lozenge design on the minaret. The other has poles protruding from the minaret. Someone might offer to show you into the courtyard building behind the mosque, which was the sultan's residence. Today, it is inhabited by poor residents. The 10-arched bridge over the Oum er Rbia is a fine example of 17th-century engineering. Kasbah Tadla's souk day is Monday.

The best view of the kasbah is from the austere **monument** to four resistance heroes on a low rise on the south side of the town. Four parallel concrete blades rise skywards, but there is no inscription to recall who the heroes were.

Boujaâd → *Colour map 2, A5.*

Just a 25-minute drive from Kasbah Tadla, Boujaâd is something of a surprise. In recent memory, it was an important town – essentially a pilgrimage centre for the semi-nomadic inhabitants of the Tadla plain. The historic medina has an almost Mediterranean character, with its arcaded square, whitewashed walls, shrines, paved streets and white houses. Much of the town was destroyed in 1785. The key buildings are the **Zaouïa of Sidi Othman** and the **Mosque of Sidi Mohammed Bu'abid ech Cherki**, the town's founder.

Trekking from Imilchil to Anergui and Zaouïat Ahansal → *For listings, see pages 121-123.*

One of the best treks in the Atlas takes you from the plateaux of the Imilchil region, via the Assif Melloul and the beautiful village of Anergui, to the former pilgrimage centre of Zaouïat Ahansal. This route, part of the **Grande traversée de l'Atlas marocain**, takes you through remote regions where knowledge of French (and even Arabic) will be rudimentary to say the least. Take a local, preferably Tabant-trained, guide, who will be aware of potentially snowy conditions (if travelling outside summer) and water levels in the Assif Melloul. At Zaouïat Ahansal, you link in with further routes southwest to the Aït Bougmez and north to the Cathedral rocks of Tilouguite and Ouaouizaght. A number of European-based travel companies now do treks in this region. Accommodation is in mountain gîtes, camping out or in locals' homes.

Imilchil → *Colour map 3, A2/3.*

Southeast of Kasbah Tadla, though marginally more easily approached from Rich to the east, Imilchil centres on a beautiful crumbling kasbah topped with storks' nests. The town has a dusty, sloping main street, where you will find a couple of small cafés, the local dispensary and the entrance to the souk. Behind the kasbah, the **Hotel Izlane** can provide a little information on possible treks and may be able to put you in contact with suitable guides. Quiet for most of the year, the town comes alive for the annual marriage fair in September (see box, page 118), when young people descend from the mountains to find themselves a partner.

Lac Tislit, 5 km to the north, is an exquisite if austere oval of blue ringed by reeds, set in an arid hollow of the mountains. The natural splendour is a little marred by a bogus kasbah, complete with plastic ceremonial tents. After Lac Tislit, the larger **Lac Isli** is an easy day's 4WD trip.

Imilchil to Anergui

There are various trek routes from Imilchil to Anergui, a distance of roughly 57 km. The route you take will depend on weather conditions. Some routes require better than average physical condition. If the **Assif Melloul** is not in flood, your guide will take you along the riverside route, which involves some wading and goes via the small settlements of Oudeddi and Oulghazi. After Oulghazi, you may head up out of the river valley to Anergui via the **Tizi-n-Echfart** pass. The other option is a more perilous route high above the river. The river will be in full flood in spring, and ice in shady areas can make high paths perilous for both people and mules.

With the green of its fruit and walnut trees, **Anergui** is one of the most beautiful sites in the eastern High Atlas and a place which now has some accommodation, see page 122.

Anergui to Zaouïat Ahansal

The Assif Melloul continues west from Anergui to meet the **Assif ou Ahansal** near the so-called **Cathedral Rocks** near Tamga. A basic track from Anergui to Zaouïat Ahansal can just about be crossed with 4WD, a distance of around 92 km. For walkers, this route is especially fine, taking you through the beautiful gorges of the Assif Melloul.

Zaouïat Ahansal → *Colour map 3, B1.*

Zaouïat Ahansal (altitude 1600 m) became important due to its location at a meeting of the ways between the eastern and central High Atlas. There are a couple of gîtes. The easiest way to Zaouïat Ahansal is from Azilal, a distance of 83 km. There are fairly frequent 4WD taxis doing this run. About 17 km out of Azilal, a junction is reached where you either go right for the Aït Bougmez or left for Aït M'hamed (Saturday souk), 3 km further on. From here, it's another 63 km to Zaouïat Ahansal. The tarmac runs out a few kilometres out of Aït M'hamed, but the track continues east-southeast towards the **Tizi-n-Tsalli-n-Imenain** (2763 m, 50 km from Azilal), in the shelter of the great Jbel Azourki (3677 m). A further col, the **Tizi-n-Ilissi** (2600 m), comes 16 km further on, below Jbel Arroudane (3359 m). Then comes the drop down to Zaouïat Ahansal.

⚫ Eastern High Atlas listings

For sleeping and eating price codes and other relevant information, see pages 22-28.

⚫ Where to stay

Demnate and Imi-n-Ifri *p117*

€€€ Kasbah Timdaf, T0523-507178, www.kasbah-timdaf.com. A beautiful ecolodge with traditionally designed Berber rooms, flower-filled gardens and a hammam. There's an open fire for when it's cold, free Wi-Fi and good food cooked by the French owners. Cookery lessons are available on request.

€€ Tiziout Maison d'Hôtes, just north of Demnate, T0658-346148, www.tizouit.ma. In a new building made from stone, an elegant but low-key place with 8 spacious, attractive rooms, a pool and great views.

€ Gîte d'étape, at Imi-n-Ifri, T0524-456473. Open only in summer. Take the right-hand fork past the café; it's signposted.

€ Hotel Café d'Ouzoud, on main Av Mohammed V, T0662-239972 (mob) or T0661-241099 (mob). 24 small clean rooms.

Cascades d'Ouzoud *p117*

€€ Hotel Chellal d'Ouzoud, T0523-429180, hotelchellal.weebly.com. A cheerful, colourful place with en suite rooms that are liberally decorated with rugs, fabrics and cushions.

€€ Riad Cascades d'Ouzoud, T0523-459658, www.ouzoud.com. The best accommodation option near the waterfalls, this riad has a combination of whitewashed and rough *pisé*-style walls, 9 tastefully decorated rooms and a spacious roof terrace with panoramic views over the surrounding countryside. There are wooden beamed ceilings and some rooms have open fireplaces. The riad also does decent food, both Moroccan and French, using good local ingredients, either on the terrace or in a traditional Moroccan lounge downstairs.

€ Hotel de France, T0523-459017. Cheap rooms, some of which have en suite bathrooms. Restaurant.

Camping

This is possible at various small sites but you might be better off on the roof terrace of one of the cheap hotels.

Azilal *p118*
€€ Hotel Assounfou, T0523-459220.
Satellite TV and solar-heated water, which
only partly explains why it is generally cold.
Friendly and very pink.

€ Hotel Dadès, T0523-458245. Basic, 3-bed
concrete box rooms, hot showers extra. Just
as you arrive from Marrakech, on your right.

Aït Bougmez *p118*
Options are limited in Tabant itself though
a few attractive options have sprung up in
other villages in the valley. In many villages
there is simple sleeping space in gîtes.

€€€ Dar Itrane, Imelghas, T0523-459312,
www.origins-lodge.com. One of the best
options in the area is this fine, French-
managed ecolodge, a traditional red adobe
building 1800 m up near the village of
Imeghas. There are 17 en suite rooms,
a roof terrace, a hammam and a chef
prepares local Berber dishes. The name
means 'House of the Stars', and it so called
because the remoteness of the place make
it perfect for viewing the night sky.

€€ La Casbah M-Goun, Douar Agerd-
n-ozro, T0662-778148, www.hotel-ait-
bouguemez.com. There's a spectacular
setting for this traditional place. Simple rooms
are generously kitted out with rugs and
blankets, and there are great views of the
surrounding green fields and bare mountains.

€€ Touda, Zawyat Oulmzi. You wouldn't
necessarily know it from the simple,
traditional exterior, but this is a cut above
most of most of the gîtes in Aït Bougmez,
with *tadelakt* bathrooms and carefully
designed bedrooms.

€ Gîte d'étape Imelghas, Imelghas,
T0523-459341. The best of the cheap
gîtes. Accommodation for up to 40,
clean loos and showers.

Beni Mellal *p119*
€€ Hotel Ouzoud, Rte de Marrakech,
T0523-483752, www.sogatour.ma. 28 rooms
and suites with balconies in a modern

but not especially attractive hotel with
restaurant, bar, tennis and pool.

€ Hotel de l'Aïn-Asserdoun, Av des FAR,
T0523-483493. A modern place with en suite
bathrooms, balconies and a restaurant.

€ Hotel Marhaba, on the small square in
the old town (reached by heading up the
souk street which leads uphill to the right
of the big ceremonial gates and square),
T0523-483991. A simple option with 11
rooms around a courtyard. Option to sleep
on roof terrace.

€ Hotel Tasmmet, in the older part of
town, not that easy to find, but if you get
onto the street which runs parallel to the
main street behind the **CTM** offices you
eventually see it down a side street to your
left as you head towards the kasbah, T0523-
421313. Rooms have en suite bathrooms
and the best have balconies. You can also
sleep cheaply on the roof terrace.

Boujaâd *p120*
€ Café-Hotel Essalyn, Pl du Marché, on the
main square.

People on pilgrimages rent rooms in
private houses near the shrines.

Imilchil *p120*
Options are few but adequate. Apart from
the place listed below, there is some simple
dorm accommodation in the village.

€ Hotel Izlane, clearly visible behind the
kasbah, T0523-442806, www.hotelizlane.
com. Run by mountain guide Khalla Boudrik,
the hotel has a large restaurant, 15 rooms,
39 beds, 3 hot showers and 4 loos. Has
regional maps and can advise on treks.

Anergui *p120*
€ Wihalane ('the right place'), pagesperso-
orange.fr/wihalane. For information, contact
Lahcen Fouzal on T0667-265319 via **Studio
La Nature** in Ouaouizaght or via José Garcia,
17 Rue de Sermaize, 90000 Belfort, France,
T+33-384266049.

⊙ Restaurants

Beni Mellal *p119*
Hotel de Paris, a little way out of the town centre on Kasbah Tadla road, T0523-282245. The restaurant serves alcohol.
Salon de Thé Azouhour, 241 Av Mohammed V.

There are also *laiteries* and cafés along the main street.

⊖ Transport

Azilal *p118*
Azilal is the transport hub for the regions of the High Atlas to the south, with a *gare routière* next to the main mosque.

There are buses for **Marrakech**, **Casablanca** and **Beni Mellal**. *Grands taxis* in Landrovers (2 a day) and Mercedes transit vans (2 a day) to **Tabant**; Landrovers for **Zaouïat Ahansal**, too, although for this destination it is probably best to get a Peugeot or Mercedes *grand taxi* to Ouaouizaght and then switch to the less comfortable Landrover.

Beni Mellal *p119*
CTM buses leave from the terminal in the town centre. Connections with **Marrakech** and 3 a day for **Fès**. From the bus station it is a 10-min walk up Av des FAR to the centre. **Casablanca** service irregular.

Grands taxis up to **Ouaouizaght** and to **Azilal**, whence you can pick up tougher transport to the **Aït Bougmez** and **Zaouïat Ahansal**.

Kasbah Tadla *p119*
CTM buses for **Fès**, **Marrakech** and **Beni Mellal** run via Kasbah Tadla. Private line buses from **Agence SLAC** for **Beni Mellal**, **Boujaâd** and **Oued Zem** and **Rabat**. These can all be caught from the bus station on the Boujaâd side of town (ie the far side to the old kasbah).

Boujaâd *p120*
Regular buses and *grands taxis* leave for **Kasbah Tadla** and **Oued Zem** from the main square.

Imilchil *p120*
A long way from anywhere else, Imilchil is hard to reach unless you have your own transport, though you might find a *grand taxi* going that way from the north on the market days of Fri and Sun.

Contents

At a glance

Getting around Fès and Meknès are both spread-out cities – use *petits taxis* to get around. There are buses to towns in the Middle Atlas but you'll need a car to explore further.
Time required Ideally, allow at least a couple of days for each city.
Weather The winters are very cold and the summers very hot. Spring (May or even June) is the best time to visit.

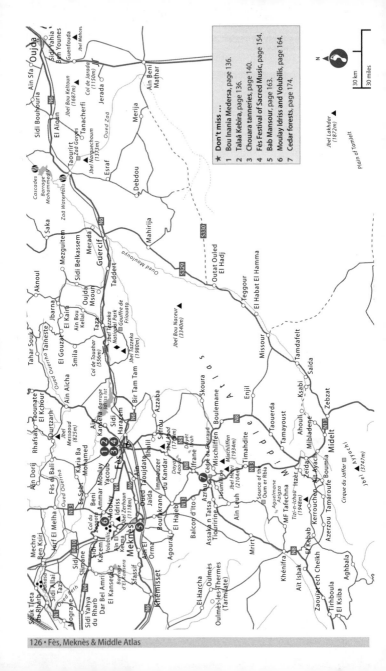

★ Don't miss ...
1 Bou Inania Medersa, page 136.
2 Talaâ Kebira, page 136.
3 Chouara tanneries, page 140.
4 Fès Festival of Sacred Music, page 154.
5 Bab Mansour, page 163.
6 Moulay Idriss and Volubilis, page 164.
7 Cedar forests, page 174.

30 km
30 miles

N

The area of central Morocco around the Jbel Zerhoun and the Saïss Plain was important even in ancient times: a strategic, fertile region on the trade routes leading from eastern North Africa to the Atlantic coast. Power has often been concentrated in this region – witness the ancient Roman city of Volubilis and the imperial cities of Fès and Meknès.

Volubilis is one of the finest Roman sites in North Africa, and its ruins still manage to evoke life in a prosperous frontier town in the second and third centuries AD. Nearby, Moulay Idriss, the father of the Moroccan state, is honoured in the pilgrimage town of the same name, a memorable settlement, with houses cascading down hills on either side of a large mosque.

High on the plateau lands between the Middle and High Atlas, the former mining town of Midelt is another useful base in the region. From here, there are plenty of interesting day trips into the hill country.

Fès

Fès (also spelt Fez in English) is a fascinating city – perhaps as near to the Middle Ages as you can get in a couple of hours by air from Europe. It is not an easy city to get to know, but repays the time and effort spent on it. With three main sections, the city has numerous historic buildings, around the Qaraouiyine Mosque and some memorable souks. Fès is also a base from which to explore nearby regions: Bhalil and Sefrou to the south, the spa towns of Sidi Harazem and Moulay Yacoub, as well as sites further afield, such as the Middle Atlas resorts of Azrou and Ifrane. Also nearby is the other central Moroccan imperial city of Meknès, with Volubilis and Moulay Idriss close by. ▸▸ *For listings, see pages 146-156.*

Arriving in Fès → *Colour map 1, B3.*

Getting there
To get to town from the **Aéroport de Fès-Saïss**, 15 km south of the centre, take a *grand taxi* (150dh) or catch bus No 16. There are two bus stations: the main one is outside the city walls near Bab Mahrouk, while the **CTM** station is on Av Mohammed V in the town centre (*ville nouvelle*). If you come in from Taza and all points east, you will probably arrive at yet another bus terminus, at Bab Ftouh. The railway station is at the end of Boulevard Chenguit in the *ville nouvelle*, T0535-622501. To get to the *ville nouvelle*, head down this road and slightly to the left into Avenue de la Liberté; this joins Avenue Hassan II at Place de Florence. ▸▸ *See Transport, page 155.*

Getting around
Fès is a spread out sort of place, and distances are greater than they may at first seem, so look forward to some considerable hikes from one place to another or *petit taxi* rides. If you are based in a *ville nouvelle* hotel, you can get a taxi from the Place Mohammed V, or the main PTT on the Avenue Hassan II, or simply by flagging one down. Getting around the historic neighbourhoods of Fès, which divide into **Fès el Bali** (the Old) and **Fès el Jedid** (the New), is another matter. You will be dealing with a complex network of lanes and alleys and, in the case of Fès el Bali, much of it is pedestrianized anyway. If time is limited, it may be better to engage an official guide – rather than get lost and have (possibly unpleasant) dealings with an unofficial guide. From the tourist information office on Place de la Résistance in the *ville nouvelle* to Bab Boujeloud, effectively the beginning of Fès el Bali, is a 3-km trot. The train station is a similar distance from Fès el Bali; the **CTM** terminus roughly 4 km.

Tourist information **Office du Tourisme** ⓘ *Pl de la Résistance, T0535-623460.* **Syndicat d'Initiative** ⓘ *Av Mohammed V, T0535-625301.*

Background

Spiritual capital
Fès has a highly strategic location. The city is situated in the Oued Sebou basin, astride the traditional trade route from the Sahara to the Mediterranean, as well as on the path from Algeria and the Islamic heartland beyond Morocco. For centuries, the dominant axis within Morocco was between Fès and Marrakech, two cities linked by their immense power as well as by their rivalry. Even today, while the coastal belt centred on Rabat and

Casablanca dominates the country in demographic, political and economic terms, Fès continues to fascinate, for it has another characteristic, perhaps its dominant feature: Fès is a religious place and is felt to be the spiritual capital of Morocco. The word Fès in Arabic means axe – a possible reference to tools used in its construction.

The influence of a saintly person, the *baraka* or blessing of a protector, was felt to be essential for a Moroccan city in times gone by. Fès, founded by Idriss II, El Azhar, 'the Splendid', had its patron too, and the life of the city once gravitated around the cathedral-mosque where Moulay Idriss and his descendants are buried. In recent memory, the end of each summer saw great celebrations for the *moussem* of Moulay Idriss. The craftsmen's corporations would take part in great processions to the shrine of the city's founder; a sacrificial bull, horns and head decorated with henna the heart of every procession.

The people of Fès were deeply religious. Some early European writers saw the city as a great Mont-St-Michel, a prayer-saturated place with its mosques, *zaouïas* (sanctuaries) and oratories. Dr Edmond Secret, writing in the 1930s, said that "the majority do their five daily prayers. Draped in modesty in the enveloping folds of their cloaks, the bourgeois, prayer carpets under their arms, recall monks in their dignity." This air of religiosity still clings to the city, especially during Ramadan. And, on every night of the year, in the hours which precede the dawn, a time hard for those who are sick and in pain, a company of muezzins maintains a vigil in the minaret of the Andalucían Mosque, praying for those asleep and those awake.

1 Fès: three cities

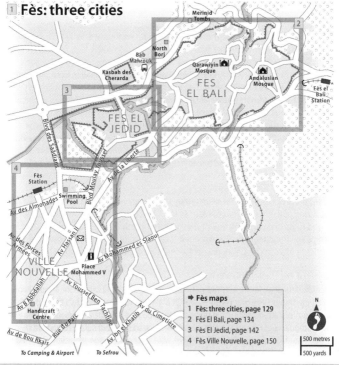

➡ Fès maps
1 Fès: three cities, page 129
2 Fès El Bali, page 134
3 Fès El Jedid, page 142
4 Fès Ville Nouvelle, page 150

Intellectual heritage

The city's religious life was closely tied to education. "If learning was born in Medina, maintained in Mecca and milled in Egypt, then it was sieved in Fès," went the adage. In the early Middle Ages, it was a centre of cultural exchange. One Gerbert d'Aurillac, later to become Pope Sylvester II from 999 to 1003, studied in Fès in his youth and brought Arabic numerals back to Europe. Famous names to have studied or taught in Fès include Maimonides, the Jewish philosopher and doctor, Ibn' Arabi (died 1240) the mystic, Ibn Khaldoun (died 1282), and the mathematician, Ibn el Banna (died 1321).

Thus, Fès supplied the intellectual élite of the country, along with many of its leading merchants and craftsmen, and you will find Fassis (the people of Fès) in most towns and cities. They are rightly proud of their city; their self-confidence, verging at times on self-satisfaction, is a distinctive trait, making them rather different from most other Moroccans. Fès does not have the immediate friendliness of the villages, the mountains or the desert, but it is a city well worth spending time in – like it or not, it will not leave you indifferent. Driss Chraïbi, for one, in his 1954 breakthrough novel *Le Passé Simple*, certainly did not mince his words: "I do not like this city. It is my past and I don't like my past. I have grown up, I have pruned myself back. Fès has quite simply shrivelled up. However, I know that as I go deeper into the city it seizes me and makes me entity, quantum, brick among bricks, lizard, dust – without me needing to be aware of it. Is it not the city of the Lords?"

Settlers from Andalucía and Kairouan

The first settlement here was the village Medinat Fès founded in 789/90 by Moulay Idriss. However the town proper was founded by his son Idriss II as Al Aliya in 808/9. Muslim families, refugees from Córdoba and surrounding areas of Andalucía soon took up residence in the Adwa al Andalusiyin quarter. Later 300 families from Kairouan (in contemporary Tunisia), then one of the largest Muslim towns in North Africa, settled on the opposite bank, forming Adwa'al Qaraouiyine. The Qaraouiyine Mosque, perhaps the foremost religious centre of Morocco, is the centre of a university founded in 859, one of the most prestigious in the Arab World. The influence of the university grew a few centuries later under the Merinids, with the construction of colleges or *medersas*. On the right bank of the Oued Boukhrareb, the Jamaâ Madlous or Andalucían Mosque was also founded in the ninth century and remains the main mosque of Adoua el Andalus.

Almoravids and Almohads

The two parts of Fès el Bali were united by the Almoravids in the 11th century, and Fès became one of the major cities of Islam. In the 12th century the Qaraouiyine mosque was enlarged to its present form; one of the largest in North Africa, it can take up to 22,000 worshippers. The Almohads strengthened the fortifications of the great city. Under both dynasties Fès was in competition with the southern capital of Marrakech.

Growth of Fès under the Merinids

Fès reached its peak in the Merinid period, when the dynasty built the new capital of Fès el Jedid containing the green-roofed Dar al Makhzen still occupied by the monarch, the Grand Mosque with its distinctive polychrome minaret dating from 1279, and the mellah, to which the Jews of Fès el Bali were moved in 1438. The Merinid sultans Abu Said Uthman and Abu Inan left a particularly notable legacy of public buildings, including the Medersa Bou Inania, several mosques and the Merinid Tombs. The Zaouïa of Moulay Idriss, housing

Saving Fès

During the 20th century Fès was largely overshadowed by the growth of Rabat and Casablanca, even though many Fassi notables did well out of the protectorate – witness the palaces and splendid houses of the Ziat, Douh and Batha areas of the medina. The city declined in the post-independence period as the élite moved to the cities of the Atlantic coast, leaving their fine courtyard homes to the poorer members of the family or to rural immigrants. The money for the upkeep of large, ageing buildings has gone elsewhere and, today, much of the medina faces critical problems, not the least of which is the pollution of the Oued Fès and the Oued Sebou, along with the disintegration of the historic, but much decayed, drinking water network.

Today the crumbling houses of Old Fès are home to a poor population. Official figures give 35% of the old city's population as being under the poverty line, the figure rising to more than 40% in some areas. The ADER (Agence pour la dédensification et la réhabilitation de Fès) was set up to improve living conditions – to date with only limited success. With the houses regularly disintegrating after the winter rains, the ADER's main aim is to ensure that people are moved out of the most dangerous housing – so reducing the potential for street protests. In 1981, the city was added to the UNESCO World Heritage List. In the 1990s, the ADER began restoration works on a small number of gates and monuments and a special traditional building crafts training centre was established.

The scale of the problems of Fès is enormous, however. In 1985, UNESCO estimated that US$585 million was needed to save the old city. In 1995, the World Bank came up with US$14 million for infrastructure improvement and works finally got underway. More than 20 years after being listed, the medina continues to decay, with demolitions leading to gaps in the once dense urban fabric. There has been much controversy over the building of two roads into the centre, one leading to Talaâ Kebira and the other over the existing course of Oued Fès. Although some restoration projects seem to go on forever, private and foreign finance has been used to restore a number of buildings at the heart of Fès el Bali, including the Foundouq Najjarine (Fondation Lamrani) and Dar Adil (Italian foreign ministry). To really save Fès, official bodies like the Municipality, the ADER, the Urban Planning Agency and the Ministry of Culture will have to work more closely together. In particular, some sort of housing improvement loan policy will have to be created to persuade the often absent owners to invest in their historic property.

On a much more positive note, however, Fès now has a fast-increasing number of upmarket riads and some European-owned cafés and restaurants. This outside investment and the economic benefits that a flood of new visitors can bring, should help the old city survive.

the tomb of Idriss II, was rebuilt in 1437. In the 15th century Fès consolidated its position as a major centre for craft industries and trade.

From Saâdian Fès to the present
Under the Saâdians (15th to 16th centuries) Fès declined, with a degree of antagonism between the authorities and the people. The Saâdians did, however, refortify the city, adding the Borj Sud and Borj Nord fortresses on the hills to the south and north of the city.

A child's survival guide to Fès

When your parents say to you "son, we're going to Fès," your first reaction might be: "Where's Fès?" The next is: "Will they have pizza?"

In reality Fès is one of the most brilliant cities I've ever been to. Wandering around the medina, you see groups of street children, vibrant coloured washing hanging over into the streets and, best of all, the amazing market. In the markets nothing is fixed-price and there's always some clever deal or haggling going on.

Me and my brother and sister decided to test our haggling skills to the limit by playing a Moroccan version of *The Apprentice* and seeing who could buy the same standard items – a coloured glass, a slipper keyring and a pencil case – for the least money. Sadly, I lost by quite a bit!

At least I was helped in my bargaining by having done the **Café Clock** download course. This is a short session (about 1½ hours, 150dh) that Café Clock runs to teach you some simple Arabic phrases and a bit about the culture and what hand signals mean. My favourite was 'smehily' meaning "sorry", which you pronounce "smelly", and I used a lot bumping into people.

Café Clock is a great place to be, in the heart of the medina, and it does great milkshakes and burgers – and when I say burger I don't mean beef, pork or even lamb – but camelburger! (Which is actually delicious.)

And about the pizza – no, you won't find much in the medina, but they do have Malawi bread, like a thin wide sugary crêpe which is good for breakfast with soft cheese.

Dos

- Have a chocolate and banana milkshake at **Café Clock**.
- Go for a swim in one of the hotels.
- Learn a few phrases of Arabic.

Don'ts

- Go into a carpet shop if you haven't got at least half an hour and don't mind being patted on the head by the owner.
- Run away screaming if your parents even mention it.
- Visit the Roman ruins at Volubilis. Because 1) they are ruins 2) they are Roman 3) you have to drive three hours to get there and back. And no, they're not educational.

by Leo Thomson (age 11)

Under the Alaouites, Fès lost ground to the expanding coastal towns, which were far better located to benefit from trade with Europe. The occupation of Algeria also meant Fès was out of phase with the huge changes taking place to the east. In 1889 the French writer Pierre Loti described it as a dead city. However, the dynasty had added a number of new *medersas* and mosques, and reconstructed other important buildings.

The French entered Fès in 1911, but proved unable to gain full control of the city and its hinterland. Plans to make it the protectorate's capital were thus abandoned. In any case, Rabat on the coast was better located with respect to fertile farmlands and ports. Although the *ville nouvelle*, also often referred to as Dar Dbibagh, was founded in 1916, it dates principally from the late 1920s. French policy was to leave the historic quarters intact, preserved in their traditional form. Since the early 1990s, the city has exploded beyond its former limits, with huge new areas of low-rise housing on the hills behind the Borj Sud at Sahrij Gnaoua and to the north at Dhar Khemis and Bab Siffer.

Places in Fès

Fès is spectacular, but not as immediately attractive as Marrakech. Unlike the capital of the South, a crossroads for caravans and peoples, Fès is more secretive, its old ways hidden behind the cliff-like walls of its alleyways. Its sights are not easily discovered and several days are really necessary to take in the city's atmosphere. Essentially, there are three main areas to visit: **Fès el Bali**, the oldest part of the city, a medina divided by the river into Adwa al Andalusiyin (the Andalucían quarter on the east bank) and Adwa al Qaraouiyine (the Qaraouiyine quarter on the west bank); **Fès el Jedid**, containing the royal palace and the mellah and founded under the Merinids (you need half a day); and the **ville nouvelle**, the city built by the French, which has taken over many of the political, administrative and commercial functions of old Fès. You'd be well advised to save some energy to get up to the Borj Nord/Merinid tombs for views across Fès el Bali at sundown. While Fès el Jedid is fairly flat, Fès el Bali has long sloping streets. In the winter it can rain heavily, turning Talaâ Sghira and Talaâ Kebira into minor torrents. That said, restoration in the old town continues apace (see box, page 131), with areas like the riverfront in r'Cif starting to look quite smart, and its appeal grows with every visit.

Fès el Bali: Adoua el Quaraouiyine

On the left bank of the Oued Boukhrareb, the **Adoua el Quaraouiyine** is a rewarding area to visit, as long as you don't expect too many well-structured heritage sites. If time is very short, then the minimum half-day circuit will allow you to get down the main street, **Talaâ Kebira**, to the central **souks** and main religious monuments, the **Moulay Idriss Zaouïa** and the **Qaraouiyine Mosque** (closed to non-Muslim visitors). At the start or the end of the tour, take a look in at the Dar Batha, a 19th-century Hispano-Moorish palace and now home to a **Museum of Moroccan Arts and Handicrafts**. With more time, you could also take in beautifully restored **Fondouk Nejjarine**, now a museum of wood and carpentry, and head up to the right bank, **Adoua el Andalus**. A couple of days in Fès will give you time to get to know the souks thoroughly and explore the higher, upscale neighbourhoods of **Douh**, **Zerbtana** and **Ziat**, where some of the largest of the city's palaces are located (see box, page 143).

Fès el Bali can only be explored on foot. The layout is complex and it may save time to engage the services of an official guide, as long as the balance between sites of interest and expensive shops is agreed in advance. Avoid unofficial guides and 'students' offering their services. So saying, sometimes you do get lost and need someone to guide you out (10dh is a reasonable tip). The points from which you can get taxis are Errecif, down at the bottom, between the two halves of Fès el Bali, and Batha (pronounced 'bat-Ha'), up at the top.

Towards **Fès el Bali**

Approaching Fès el Bali from the **Boujeloud Gardens** (Jnène Sbil or Jardins de la Marche Verte) ① *Tue-Sun 0900-1800*, you could follow Rue de l'UNESCO right round past the **Dar el Beida**, a late 19th-century palace, on your left. The road continues past a line of early 20th-century buildings (Pension Campini, police station), then the Préfecture on your right, before you reach the rather undistinguished entrance to the **Musée Dar Batha** ① *T0535-634116, Wed-Mon 0830-1630*, on your left almost opposite the Préfecture. The most important displays are the carpets and the distinctive Fès pottery. A 10th-century technique, enabled by the use of cobalt, produced the famous 'Fès blue'. (On Talaâ Kebira there are a couple of shops stocking this traditional pottery.) In the museum also look out for the *minbar* or preacher's chair from the Medersa Bou Inania.

Bab Boujeloud and around
If you're staying in a cheap hotel, it's likely that you'll be somewhere near Bab Boujeloud. The neighbourhood takes its name from the striking gate, which marks the main western

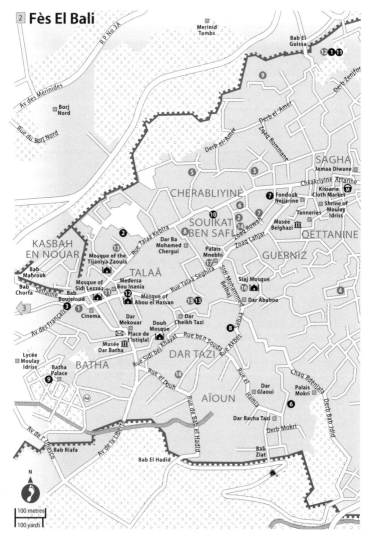

entrance to Fès el Bali. With blue *zellige* tiles on the outside and green on the inside, Bab Boujeloud makes a fittingly stylish access point to the city, and was revamped under the French in 1913. Just to the right of the gate, as you arrive from the Place Boujeloud, there is a small gate in the wall, generally kept closed, which leads into the restored **brick water collector**. Though this may not sound very exciting, it is a good piece of late mediaeval hydraulic engineering, channeling the waters of the Oued Fès into underground pipes,

➡ **Fès maps**
1 Fès: three cities, page 129
2 Fès El Bali, page 134
3 Fès El Jedid, page 142
4 Fès Ville Nouvelle, page 150

Restaurants 🍴
Al Fassia 1
Café Clock 2
Café Médina 3
Café Tabarakallah 4
Cremerie de Place 5
Fez et Guestes 6
Fez Lounge 7
Hotel Batha 9
Le Jardin des Biehn 8
Òuali's Café 10
Palais Jamaï 11
Palais Tijani 14
Riad Fès 13
Thami's 12

Where to stay 🛏
Cascade 1
Dar Bennis 2
Dar Attajalli 3
Dar Bensouda 4
Dar El Hana 5
Dar El Menia 6
Dar Finn 7
Dar Imam 8
Dar Roumana 9
Dar Seffarine 10
Lamrani 11
Palais Jamaï 12
Pension Dar
  Bouanania 13
Riad 9 14
Riad Fès 15
Riad Idrissy 16
Riad Laroussa 17
Riad Tizwa 18

which supplied the distributors of each neighbourhood. The whole system was still in operation in the late 19th century. The two minarets visible from the gate are those of the 14th-century **Medersa Bou Inania** and the simpler ninth-century **Sidi Lazzaz Mosque**.

On your left as you arrive at Bab Boujeloud, the impressive gate flanked by twin octagonal towers is **Bab Chorfa**, leading into Kasbah En Nouar, or Kasbah Filala, so named because it was once occupied by people from the Tafilalet who arrived with the early Alaouite rulers.

There are two main thoroughfares in Fès el Bali. **Talaâ Seghira** leads to the right. **Talaâ Kebira** leads to the left, directly past the Sidi Lazzaz Mosque, and the next major building, the Bou Inania Medersa, one of the most important sites in Fès, and straight on down through the medina to the Qaraouiyine Mosque.

Bou Inania Medersa
ⓘ *0830-1730, 10dh. Open to non-Muslims.*

Fès's most spectacular sight, and one of Morocco's most beautiful buildings, the 14th-century Medersa Bou Inania is located handily close to Bab Boujeloud, the entrance near the top of Talaâ Kebira. Built by the Merinid Sultan Abu Inan between 1350 and 1355, it was used to accommodate students until the 1960s and is now open to the public after a lengthy restoration. You enter through a highly decorated vestibule roofed by a stalactite dome. The building centres on a large, stone-flagged courtyard, at the far end of which is a sort of dry moat, where water taken from the Oued Fès once flowed, which separates the prayer hall from the square courtyard. The mosque area has a highly decorated minaret, indicating that it was far more important than most *medersas*, which normally do not have minarets or even pulpits for the Friday prayer. Indeed, the *medersa* has the status of a Friday mosque and, for a time, rivalled the Qaraouiyine Mosque. For the best view of the minaret, go for a coffee and a cake on the roof terrace of **Café Clock**, opposite (see page 153). The courtyard is decorated with ceramic mosaic, Koranic inscriptions and some fine carved woodwork. On the ground and first floors are the students' cell-like rooms, some with decorated ceilings.

There used to be a complex 14th-century *clepsydra* (**water clock**) built in the wall opposite the *medersa*. Using brass bowls and the dripping of water, and complete with chimes, it is said to have been used to allow the Medersa Bou Inania, visible from both the Qaraouiyine Mosque and the Mosque of Fès el Jedid, to signal the correct time for prayer. The wooden structure has been restored and, at some point, the clock may actually be made to work again.

Down Talaâ Kebira to the Qaraouiyine, the souks and medersas
The narrow Talaâ Kebira, the principal street in Adoua el Qaraouiyine, descends steeply towards the spiritual and commercial heart of the city, a tangle of streets and alleys around the shrine (*zaouïa*) of Moulay Idriss and the Qaraouiyine Mosque. The 20-minute walk from Bab Boujeloud is many people's most memorable experience of Fès, an extraordinary wander through noises, smells, sights and a mass of humanity, from camels' heads on display at the butchers to aged mint sellers to heavily laden mules carrying goods across the city, guided by muleteers crying out 'Balak!' to warn pedestrians. Once you get to the bottom of Talaâ Kebira, the main religious monuments are off limits to non-Muslims, though the doors to the Qaraouiyine Mosque are often open, allowing a quick glimpse of the interior. It may be possible, depending on restoration works, to get into one of the *medersas* that ring the Qaraouiyine Mosque. Try to see the Medersa el Attarine, and don't miss the restored Foundouk Nejjarine, the Carpenters' Fondouk, which is the main accessible historic building in the central part of Fès el Bali. The other don't-miss sight is the main tannery, Dar Debbagh, located quite close to the well-signed Musée Belghazi.

Saintly Sultan Abou Inane

A number of ancient colleges in the medinas of Morocco – among them *medersas* in Meknès, Salé and Fès – bear the name Bou Inania, after their royal founder. Sultan Abou Inane's most important building works were in Fès: he constructed the Jamaâ Zhar, a fine mosque close to his palace, and the Koubba of the Karaouiyine Library. Today's non-Muslim visitor can see the Medersa Bou Inania, considered to be one of the finest in existence. Tradition has it that when the sultan was presented with the final accounts, he tore up the paperwork, declaring that "Beauty is not expensive, whatever the sum may be. A thing which pleases man cannot be paid too dear."

Born in Fès in 1329, Abou Inane Faris de-throned his father at the tender age of 20, and had himself proclaimed sultan at Tlemcen in June 1348. By all accounts he was an imposing figure. Wrote Ibn el Ahmar, chronicler of the Merinids: "He was taller than everybody else. His body was slim, his nose long and well-made. He had hairy arms. His voice was deep, but he spoke quickly in a staccato manner, so that it was sometimes difficult to understand him. He had beautiful, finely shaped eyes, full eyebrows, and an agreeable face of great beauty … My eyes have never seen in his army a soldier with a fuller beard, a finer and more pleasing figure." Abou Inane was also, by all accounts, a skilled horseman, and had a good knowledge of law, arithmetic and Arabic. Ibn el Ahmar also mentions that he left behind 325 children.

On being proclaimed sultan, Abou Inane took the throne name of El Moutawakkil, 'he who places trust in God'. Although a strong ruler, he was also a pious man (he knew the Koran by heart), and this was reflected in a number of ways. He instituted a tradition of having a blue flag hoisted to the top of the minarets on Friday to indicate prayer time, and had oil-lamps placed on the minarets to show prayer times at night.

Like many a medieval ruler, however, Abou Inane had an unfortunate end. In 1358, returning to Fès from Tunis, he fell sick. Arriving in his capital on the eve of Aïd el Kebir, he had sufficient strength to lead the great prayers on the *musalla* outside the city. He was too ill, however, to receive homage from the notables of the realm. The vizier, Hassan el Foudoudi, who had been plotting in the wings had the sick sultan smothered in his bedclothes.

The burial place of Abou Inane, however, remains something of a mystery. Perhaps it was too risky to allow such a good ruler to have a mausoleum, which might then become a focus for public gatherings and discontent.

As Talaâ Kebira descends, it goes through frequent identity changes, taking on the name of the different crafts which are (or were) practised along different sections of the street. First it becomes **Rue Cherabliyine** (slippermakers), where each afternoon except Friday people hawk second-hand shoes and slippers. The **Cherabliyine Mosque** dates from 1342, the reign of Sultan Abul Hassan, and has a small and attractive minaret tiled in green and white including the *darj w ktaf* motif. Further on, Rue Cherabliyin is called **Aïn Allou**, where leather articles are auctioned every day except Friday. After Aïn Allou, the street is named for the basket weavers (Msamriyine) and bag makers (Chakakyrine), before becoming the **Souk el Attarine**, the former perfumers' souk, the most prestigious in the medina. Between Attarine and the Zaouïa of Moulay Idriss is the lively main **kissaria**, the place to buy traditional clothing.

Before getting tangled up in Souk el Attarine, take a right and then a left down some steps off Cherabliyine to get to the square in front of the 18th-century **Fondouk Nejjarine**, an impressive building now home to the **Musée du Bois** ⓘ *38 Rue Abdelazuz Boutaleb, T0535-621706, open 1000-1700, 20dh*, an interesting museum of wooden crafts and tools. The beautiful space is filled with some impressive pieces that showcase Fassi carpentry to great effect, such as carved doors and windows, handsome coffers and musical instruments. There's also an impressive doorknocker carved from one piece of wood. The fondouk is also worth a visit for its roof terrace, where there's a good, if rather pricey, café – a good spot to take a break from the frenetic activity of the souks. Back on the square, the **Nejjarine Fountain**, also carefully restored, is reputed for the fever-curing properties of its waters. On the far side of the square from the fondouk is **Hammam Laraïs**, the wedding baths, once much used by grooms and brides before a pre-marriage trip to the Zaoüïa of Moulay Idriss. The tanneries of **Dar Debbagh** are close by. To get there, go right at the far end of the Nejjarine square and follow the street round.

Surrounded by narrow streets, the 18th-century **Zaoüïa of Moulay Idriss**, last resting place of the ninth-century ruler Idriss II, is off-limits to non-Muslim visitors, although parts of the interior can be seen by tactful glances through the large, unscreened doorways. Shops around the *zaoüïa* sell candles and other artefacts for pilgrims, the distinctive nougat sweets which are taken home as souvenirs of a pilgrimage, and silverware. Each entrance to the precinct is crossed by a wooden bar, ensuring no pack animals go wandering into the sacred area. On your way round, note a circular porthole through which offerings can be discreetly passed.

The Qaraouiyine Mosque (see below) is also surrounded by narrow streets on all sides. In the immediate vicinity of the mosque are four *medersas*: going clockwise, **Medersa Attarine** (the most important and visitable, see below), **Medersa Mesbahiya** (partly ruined), **Medersa Seffarine** (the Coppersmiths' Medersa, recently restored), and **Medersa Cherratène** (more modern, three storeys). All were in use well within living memory.

Dating from 1323, the **Medersa Attarine** (currently undergoing restoration) was built by Merinid Sultan Abu Said. It used to accommodate students studying at the nearby Qaraouiyine University. The courtyard is one of the most elaborately decorated in Morocco, with the usual carved stucco and cedar wood, and *zellige* tiling. The courtyard has a solid, white marble fountain bowl. In the dark prayer hall, a chandelier bears the name of the *medersa's* founder and the date. As with most *medersas*, the second floor has a succession of students' cells. From the roof (if accessible) there is a good view of the minaret and courtyard of the Qaraouiyine Mosque.

Qaraouiyine Mosque
ⓘ *Inaccessible to non-Muslims. From the narrow streets, you may be able to take diplomatic glances through unscreened entrances.*

At the end of Souk el Attarine, the Quaraouiyine Mosque, the focal point of Fès el Bali, is probably the most important religious building in Morocco and was once a major centre of medieval learning, with professors in law, theology, algebra, mathematics, philosophy, and astronomy. With space for some 20,000 worshippers, it is one of the biggest mosques in North Africa. Original funding to build this mosque was provided in 857 by a wealthy immigrant family from Kairouan (in present day Tunisia), hence the name. The building was enlarged in 956 and again – most importantly – under the Almoravids between 1135 and 1144. The Almohads added a large ablution hall, the Merinids rebuilt the courtyard and minaret. The twin pavilions in the courtyard are 17th-century Saâdian additions. While the

Bathtime blues

Early in the 19th century, Fès was visited by the Spaniard Domingo Badia y Leblich, travelling under the pseudonym Ali Bey el Abbassi. He noted the importance of the public baths or hammams of Fès: "The baths are open to the public all day. The men go in the morning, the women in the afternoon. I generally used to go in the evening, taking the whole bathhouse for myself so that there would be no outsiders … The first time I went there, I noted that there were buckets of water placed symmetrically in the corner of each room and each cubicle. I asked what they were for. 'Do not touch them, sir,' the personnel of the hammam replied in haste. 'Why?' 'These are buckets for the people down below.' 'Who are they?' 'The demons who come to wash during the night'."

A few centuries earlier, Leo Africanus described the traditions of the hammams of Fès: "The companions and the owners of the steam-baths hold festivities once a year, celebrating in the following way. First of all they invite all their friends, and go through the city to fife, tambourine and trumpets, then they take a hyacinth bulb, placing it in a fine copper container which they cover with a white cloth. Then they go back through the city, accompanied by music, to the door of the hammam. There they put the bulb in a basket which they hang over the door, saying, 'This will bring seed to the hammam, because of it there will be many visitors'."

Traditions related to the hammam seem to have died away today. But, even in the 1920s and 1930s, superstitions were very much alive. Dr Edmond Secret, a French doctor working in Fès, noted how those who went to the hammam very early, washing alone, were considered courageous, and genies were held to live in damp corners and the water pipes.

---

minaret goes back to 956, the 'Trumpeters' Tower' or Borj an-Naffara is later and is used during Ramadan to signal the time to begin fasting again. Built under Sultan Abou Inan in the second half of the 14th century, the tower originally functioned as an observatory. There are said to be plans to convert the tower into a museum dedicated to astrolabes and astrology – an important science in the Muslim world given the religion's use of a lunar calendar and the need to calculate the precise direction of Mecca for prayer. The Qaraouiyine has 14 doors, 275 pillars and three areas for ablutions. Features include elaborate Almohad carving and a venerable wooden pulpit. Some of the chandeliers were made from church bells. Women have a separate worship area, on a mezzanine floor, behind the men.

A minor sight on the Derb Bou Touil, the street running along the eastern side of the mosque, is the 14th-century three-storey **Fondouk Titouani**, originally built to accommodate merchants from Tetouan and, today, used by artisans and a carpet shop. Both this and the nearby **Palais de Fès** restaurant have good views of the Qaraouiyine's courtyard.

Place Seffarine

On the southeast side of the Qaraouiyine, the triangular Place Seffarine (Brassworkers' Square) is marked by a tree visible from the north or south Borj. On the right is the **Qaraouiyine Library**, founded in 1349 and still operational. You can usually enter the courtyard and entrance hall; non-Muslims are not allowed in the library itself. Of passing interest, behind the tree on Hyadriyine are two of the oldest **hammams** in Fès, which are currently being renovated, though an opening date remains elusive.

The **Medersa Seffarine**, built in 1271, was the first in the city and is much simpler in style than the later *medersas*. It continues to be used by students and, for a 10dh tip to the man on the door, you can have a quick guided tour – it's interesting to see a working *medersa* but it's a little like looking around a youth hostel, albeit a very ancient one.

If you head left of the tree on Seffarine, you can follow through to one of the bridges over the Oued Boukhrareb, either Qantrat Kharchifiyine or, after Sebbaghine, Qantrat Tarrafine. Here you come out onto **Rcif**, home to the best fresh produce market in the medina and a useful point for getting a *petit taxi*.

Chouara tanneries

The most colourful sight in Fès, the Chouara tanneries have not really changed since medieval times. At the bottom of the valley, they use the water of the Oued Boukhrareb, as well as a smelly mix of urine and guano to turn animal hides into dyed, usable leather. To get there from the Medersa Seffarine, follow Derb Mechattine (the narrow right-hand street of the two at the top of the square) around to the left onto Zanka Chouara. The best views of the tanneries are from leather shops that have terraces from where you can view the work going on below. Afterwards, you'll be expected to have a look at the handiwork for sale; there's no obligation to buy anything, although the quality is high, and you could do much worse for a souvenir of the city. See box, page 63 for a full account of the traditional tanning process.

Adoua el Andalus

Probably the poorest area of the medina, the Andalus quarter, the right bank of Fès el Bali, has fewer obvious sights than the left bank. However, the Medersa Sahrij, next to the Mosque al Andalus, is worth a visit. You can approach the neighbourhood from the southeast, taking a *petit taxi* to Bab Fettouh, or by climbing up out of Bab Rcif, losing yourself in the maze of streets of the Qouas neighbourhood.

With its green and white minaret, the **Mosque al Andalus** is a distinctive building dating from the same period as the great Qaraouiyine Mosque. The minaret dates from the 10th century, and the mosque was enlarged in the 13th century, with an architect from Toledo designing the grand main doorway, particularly impressive if you approach the mosque coming up the steps from below. If interested in a relic of the city's commercial life, take a look in at the **Fondouk el Madlous**, a few steps down from the mosque entrance on the left. Restored under Moulay Hassan I in the 19th century, this fondouk is still used for accommodation and storage.

As you face the main door of the mosque, go right along Derb Yasmina to reach the entrance of the nearby **Medersa Sahrij** ('School of the Reflecting Pool'), built 1321-1323 to house students studying at the mosque. There has been no major restoration campaign here yet and cats snooze on the weathered wood screens topped with scallop designs. The white marble basin, after which the *medersa* was named, has been removed from the courtyard. The large prayer hall contained the library against the *qibla* wall at either side of the mihrab. Try to get up onto the roof for the view. In between the mosque and the *medersa* is the **Medersa Sebbayine**, now closed. After visiting the Medersa Sahrij, you could carry along the same street, past the unmarked Medersa el Oued on your right. A few metres further on, a sharp right will take you onto Derb Gzira. Just after the turn is a house which bears the strange name of **Dar Gdam Nbi**, the 'house of the Prophet's foot', so called because a sandal which supposedly once belonged to the Prophet Mohammed was conserved there. Once a year, just before the Prophet's birthday or Mouloud, the Tahiri family would open their home to allow the faithful to approach the semi-sacred item of footwear. Unfortunately, the owners have sold up and the property has been divided. Continue therefore on Derb Gzira, which winds back down to Rcif, where you could find a bus (No 18) to take you back up to Place de la Résistance in the *ville nouvelle*. There are plenty of red *petits taxis* here as well.

Fès vantage points

The **Borj nord**, built by the Saâdian Sultan Ahmad al Mansour in 1582, is a small but interesting example of 16th-century fortress architecture. There are good views of parts of Fès el Bali from the roof. Inside, the **Arms Museum** ⓘ *T0535-645241, closed Tue*, has displays of weapons and military paraphernalia from all periods, including European cannon. The collections have been built up mainly as a result of royal donations and include a number of rare pieces. Many of these killing tools have a certain splendour as crafted items. Look out for the largest weapon of all, a 5-m-long cannon weighing 12 tonnes used during the Battle of the Three Kings. From the Borj nord, you can head along the hillside to the 14th-century **Merinid Tombs**. The tombs are ruins, and much of the ornamentation described by earlier visitors has not survived. (Note that this is not a safe place to go alone at night.) In the late afternoon, the garden promenade behind the Borj nord and tombs is busy with locals out for a stroll. The views over Fès el Bali are splendid. Nearby is the **Hotel des Merinides**, also with an excellent view and a pool, which non-guests can use for a small fee in the summer.

From the 13th-century **Borj sud**, south of the centre, occupied by the military, you can look north over Fès. The nearby *son et lumière* auditorium bathes Fès el Bali in white light. Unfortunately there are no lasers to pick out the parts of the city being described in the commentary. Until the late 1990s, this southern military outpost of the city stood in isolation but nowadays the low-rise flats of the sprawling Sahrij Gnaoua neighbourhood have marched up the hills, threatening to engulf it.

Fès el Jedid

The one-time Merinid capital, containing the Royal Palace and the old Jewish quarter (the *mellah*) is now a pleasant haven between the hustle and bustle of Fès el Bali and the *ville nouvelle*. Allow half a day here, perhaps in the late afternoon, before heading for the Borj Nord at sunset.

Mellah

The best place to start is probably at the **Place des Alaouites**, close to the Royal Palace, and instantly recognisable by its spectacular doors giving onto a vast esplanade, used essentially on ceremonial occasions – or, in the early 1990s, during urban riots. Over on the right, at the edge of a small garden terrace, is the elegant **Bab Lamar**. Between this and the Rue Bou Ksissat, opt for the small gate which takes you into Rue des Mérinides in the **mellah**. The term, used throughout Morocco, probably derives from the Oued Melah, literally 'salty river', which once ran close to this part of Fès, but which, like so many of the watercourses in the region, has disappeared. Off Rue des Mérinides, the streets once had names that reflected the area's Jewish past. Take the fourth street on the right, Rue de Temara, which will take you to the **Synagogue Aben-Danan**. (There used to be two other synagogues, the Em Habbanim and the Mansour.) In fact, until the 13th century, the Jews lived in Fès el Bali in the Bab Guissa area, still referred to as Fondouq el Yahoudi. In the main hall of the synagogue, there is a collection of objects giving some idea of the material context of

Fassi Jewish life. After the synagogue, past a small square, head across to the **Nouaïl** area. Next to the Jewish cemetery, the **Jewish Museum** is an intriguing collection of photos, newspaper clippings and artefacts of the community that lived here. (If you go right here, the street leads down to a door which will take you down to the American animal hospital or **Fondouk el Amerikan**.) From the Nouaïl area try to cut through to the continuation of Rue des Mérinides, Rue Sekkakine and the imposing **Bab Semmarine**, which leads you to Fès el Jedid proper. (If you double back on Rue des Mérinides, you'll find **Bab Magana**, the 'clock gate', whose scruffy timepiece stopped a while ago.) All along the street are the elegant façades of the houses built by prosperous Jewish families in the early 20th century.

Bab Semmarine to Bab Sba'

Bab Semmarine, a chunky structure characterized by a double horseshoe arch and lozenge motifs, takes you through into the wide main street of **Fès el Jedid**, often referred to as Avenue Moulay Slimane. This divides the *madina al bayda*, the white city founded by the Merinids in 1276, in two and takes you through to **Bab Dekakene**. On the right, **Jamaâ el Hamra** 'the red mosque' is the first of the two mosques, so called because it was founded by a red woman from the Tafilalelt. The second mosque on your right is the **Jamaâ el Bayda**. Continue straight ahead and, at the end of the avenue, you can cut through an arched gate in the walls to your right taking you past the dry course of the Oued Chrachar to a decrepit waterwheel and a small café-restaurant. Double back, cut through left, and you are at **Bab Dekakene**. Here you want to go through to the right to the walled square referred to as

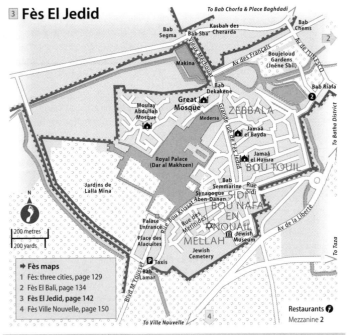

3 Fès El Jedid

To Bab Chorfa & Place Baghdadi

Bab Segma
Kasbah des Cherarda
Bab Sba'
Bab Chems
Vieux Méchouar
Av de l'UNESCO
Makina
Av des Français
Boujeloud Gardens (Jnène Sbil)
Bab Riafa
Bab Dekakene
Great Mosque
ZEBBALA
Moulay Abdullah Mosque
Medersa
Grande rue de Fès Jedid
Jamaâ el Bayda
Royal Palace (Dar al Makhzen)
Jamaâ el Hamra
BOU TOUIL
To Batha District
Jardins de Lalla Mina
Bab Semmarine
Rue Sidi
N
Synagogue Aben-Danan
SIDI BOU NAFAI
Rue des Mérinides
EN NOUAÏL
Av de la Liberté
200 metres
200 yards
Palace Entrance
Rue Bou Ksissat
MELLAH
Jewish Museum
To Taza
Place des Alaouites
Jewish Cemetery
P Taxis
Bab Lamar
Blvd M Youssef

Fès maps
1 Fès: three cities, page 129
2 Fès El Bali, page 134
3 Fès El Jedid, page 142
4 Fès Ville Nouvelle, page 150

To Ville Nouvelle
4

Restaurants
Mezzanine 2

The palaces of Fès

Hidden in the narrow streets of the Douh, Zerbatana and Ziat neighbourhoods, just east of the Batha, are some truly huge 19th- and early 20th-century palaces. The heirs have long since migrated to more promising elsewheres, and the high-ceilinged rooms are semi-squatted by poor relatives or rural migrants. If your time is limited, try to see Dar el Glaoui and Dar el Mokri. You will need to find a local to guide you in and a tip to the owner of around 20dh per visitor is probably reasonable for the disturbance. **Riad Fès** guesthouse, T0535-741012, may be able to put you in touch with a suitable guide. Try also the multilingual Abdellatif Riffi Mbarki, T0668-220112 (mob).

Most often visited, as it is right on Talaâ Seghira, is the **Palais Mnebhi**, which now functions rather efficiently as a restaurant. Its former owner was a minister of war under Sultan Moulay Abd el Aziz, and Maréchal Lyautey, first résident-général, resided here. Try to get a peek at the garden patio of **Dar Ba Mohamed Chergui**, on Derb Horra, linking Talaâ Kebira to Talaâ Seghira. The overgrown raised flowerbeds are laid out according to the *mtemmen*, figure-of-eight motif traditional in *zellige* (ceramic-mosaic). On Rue Sidi Mohammed el Haj, a right off Talaâ Seghira as you descend, is **Dar Ababou** which has a garden courtyard overlooked by balconies.

Dar el Glaoui is the most easily visited of the big palaces. Three tennis courts, if not four, would have easily fitted into the main courtyard. From the roof terraces there are views across the city. When the Glaoui family fell from favour after independence, the palace was abandoned. No less splendid is **Dar el Mokri**, named for the grand vizir El Mokri who held office for the whole of the French period. There are some 1930s additions and a sadly run-down garden. Off the big courtyard, the rooms are partly converted to workshops, partly squatted. There is an off-chance that if you are passing down Derb Chaq Bedenjala on your way to Bab Jedid a lad will spot you and ask if you want to take a look at the palace.

Close to the Batha (*batha* is Arabic for open area) are a number of easily located patrician residences. Right on the square, **Dar Mekouar**, once a cradle of the nationalist movement, is a few metres to the left of the **Maison Bleue** guesthouse (see plaque on wall). Next to the café to the right of the Maison Bleue, a narrow street, Derb Salaj, runs directly into Fès el Bali. Follow along and you will find, down a blind alley, the house used by the local **Institut Français** for occasional concerts. Further along, the very chic **Riad Fès** guesthouse is signposted, and you will find **Dar Cheikh Tazi**, now headquarters of the Association Fès-Saïss, an organization working to promote the region.

the **Vieux Mechouar**. On the left are the Italianate entrance gates to the **Makina**, originally built in the 19th century to house an arms factory; it now has various functions, including a rug factory and youth club. Going straight ahead, you come to **Bab Sba'**, which takes you through onto the main road running along the north side of the city, linking the *ville nouvelle* to Fès el Bali. You might take a look at the unusual twin octagonal towers of **Bab Segma**, flanking the ring road. The fortified structure to the north is the **Kasbah des Cherarda**, built 1670 by Sultan Moulay Rachid and today housing a branch of the university and a hospital.

For those with plenty of time, the trail through Fès el Jedid should include a dawdle through the **Moulay Abdullah** neighbourhood, north of the palace. There are a couple of mosques for non-Muslims to look at from the exterior here. Those with plenty of energy should head through the Boujeloud gardens and along Avenue des Français to **Bab Boujeloud** at the western end of Fès el Bali (see page 134).

Around Fès → *For listings, see pages 146-156.*

Moulay Yacoub → *Colour map 1, B3.*
Every bit a country spa town, Moulay Yacoub, 20 km northwest of Fès, is a short 45-minute journey through rolling countryside and some interesting capital-intensive irrigated farming. Taxis from Bab Boujeloud stop near the car park above the village. Steep flights of steps lead down into the village. There are plenty of hammams, small shops, cafés and a number of cheap lodging houses, some with rudimentary self-catering facilities.

Moulay Yacoub is a destination for local tourists, and a visit to one of the **hammams** can be quite an experience. There are baths for both men and women. The buildings date from the 1930s and could do with some maintenance but, at the price, you can't complain. The men's hammam has a pool of extremely hot sulphurous water – a bucket of Moulay Yacoub water poured on your head is guaranteed to boil your brains. There are few foreigners; beware the masseur, who may well delight in making an exhibition of you with a poolside pummel and stretching designed for Olympic athletes. Merely bathing in the hot spring water will leave you exhausted – and hopefully rejuvenated. There is also a luxury spa down in the valley.

Sidi Harazem → *Colour map 1, B3.*
In restaurants all over Morocco, Sidi Ali and Sidi Harazem are the most widely available mineral waters, along with sparkling Oulmès. The saintly Sidi Harazem is said to have died in Fès in 1164. He taught at the Qaraouiyin Mosque and, it is said, his classes and lectures were so interesting that even the *djinn*, the mischievous spirits of Moroccan folklore, attended. The village of Sidi Harazem, with its spring and spa centre, is only 4 km along the N6 from Fès, with buses leaving from the **CTM** bus station and Bab Boujeloud, and other buses and *grands taxis* from Bab Ftouh. The area around the thermal baths is still very popular for swimming and picnics. There is a 17th-century *koubba*, dating from the time of the village's establishment as a resort under Sultan Moulay Rachid.

If you want to stay, there is the pricey (for what it is) **Hotel Sidi Harazem** (T0535-690135, www.sogatour.ma), with 62 air-conditioned rooms, health facilities, restaurant and bar (**€€**).

Bhalil → *Colour map 1, B3.*
En route to Sefrou, 5 km before the town off the N8, is Bhalil. This small hill village may have had a Christian population before the coming of Islam. Behind the picturesque village are several **troglodyte dwellings**, with people still inhabiting the caves. The road takes you round the town, giving excellent views on all sides, and there are two good, clean cafés on the outskirts when approaching from the east.

Sefrou → *Colour map 1, B3.*
Sefrou is 32 km south of Fès along the N8. It is not the sort of place you would visit if travelling south, as the N8/N13, via Ifrane and Azrou, is a better route from Fès to Er Rachidia and the South. However, Sefrou is certainly worth visiting as a side trip from Fès or even for an overnight stay, as it is one of the most appealing towns in Morocco, a poor but relatively unspoilt historic walled town lying in a beautiful wooded valley, with a calm and genuinely friendly atmosphere.

Arriving in Sefrou Both buses and taxis arrive and leave from Place Moulay Hassan, by Bab Taksebt and Bab M'kam, where the road from Fès meets the old town. Buses from Fès leave from Bab Boujeloud and many go on to Er Rachidia. *Grands taxis* from Fès leave from Bab Ftouh. **Syndicat d'Initiative** ① *past the Jardin publique, T0535-660380.*

Background Although now bypassed by new roads, Sefrou once lay astride the major caravan routes from Fès and the north, to the south and the Sahara beyond. It does, however, remain an important market place for the surrounding agricultural region. Like Debdou and Demnate, Sefrou was one of those small inland Moroccan towns that had a distinctive character because of its large Jewish population, which predated the Islamic conquest. Although many Berbers and Jews were converted to Islam by Moulay Idriss, Sefrou's Jewish element was reinforced with the migration of Jews from Tafilalet and Algeria in the 13th century. After the Second World War, large numbers of Jews emigrated to Morocco's large cities, Europe and Israel. The 1967 Arab-Israeli War was the final blow. Sefrou has fascinated American academics, with the likes of anthropologists Geertz, Rosen and Rabinow carrying out research here. Recently Sefrou was created capital of a new province, receiving new and badly needed investment. A town declining into shabby anonymity, it may yet rescue something of its heritage and find a place on the tourist map.

Places in Sefrou The market place below and east of Avenue Mohammed V is a relaxed area to wander, best during the Thursday **market**. The town, which is known for olive and cherry production, has a large **Fête des Cerises** in June, and other smaller *fêtes* during the year. There is a *moussem*, or religious gathering, for Sidi Lahcen Lyoussi.

Entering from the north, the road curves down to the Oued Aggaï, past the **Centre Artisanal** ① *Mon-Sat 0800-1200 and 1400-1900*, into the busy Place Moulay Hassan. From here, **Bab M'kam** is the main entrance to the medina, which lies north of the river, and **Bab Taksebt** is the main entrance, over the bridge, into the *mellah*. Both are small, maze-like quarters, but it is difficult to get seriously lost. The **mellah** can also be entered from the covered marketplace through **Bab M'Rabja**. Beside a mosque built into the wall, turn right and down the main street, beside small restaurants, butchers', shops and craftsmen, and then left to reach one of several small bridges over the Oued Aggaï. Alternatively, take one of the small side turnings to discover the cramped design of the *mellah*, now mainly occupied by poor rural migrants, with houses often built over the narrow streets.

In the medina, the **Grand Mosque**, restored in the 19th century, lies beside the river and the souks just upstream. Past the souks is the **Zaouïa of Sidi Lahcen ben Ahmed**. In the medina there is a clearly discernible difference in the design of the quarter, reflecting the strict regulations and conditions under which Jews in the *mellah* lived. Sefrou is quite remarkable, however, in that the mellah is as large as the medina.

Avenue Moulay Hassan crosses the Oued Aggaï, where there is a **Syndicat d'Initiative** which has a **swimming pool** and continues as Avenue Mohammed V, the main street of the unexciting new town, with the post office and a few shops and simple café-restaurants. Turn into Rue Ziad by the post office, past **Hotel Sidi Lahcen Lyoussi**, and continue uphill on the black-top road. Camping is signed to the left but continue up to the **koubba of Sidi Bou Ali**, with its white walls and distinctive green-tiled roof. There is a café, a few stalls and a magnificent view. Another small excursion beginning south of the river leads west to a small **waterfall** (*les cascades*).

For sleeping and eating price codes and other relevant information, see pages 22-28.

● Where to stay

There are hotels and riads in Fès to suit all budgets, including some very luxurious ones in and around the tangled lanes of the medina – certainly the best place to stay if you want to get a real feel of old Fès. If you want to stay in a riad, a reservation is essential and someone will be sent to meet you.

New riads are opening all the time, and they tend to be owned by a slightly younger crowd than in Marrakech. Fès also has a disproportionate number of British riad owners compared to other Moroccan cities. **Fez Riads**, T0672-513357, www.fez-riads. com, is an excellent agency offering luxury accommodation in the medina.

Fès El Bali *p133, map p134*
Riads
€€€€ **Riad 9**, 9 Derb Lamside, Souiket Ben Safi, Zkak el Ma, T0535-634045, www.riad9.com. Sophisticated and elegant, **Riad 9** has everything necessary to make a stay in Fès unusually stylish, from books, jazz, Chinese lanterns and panoramic views to a hyperactive cat. Run by a French designer, it has the rugs and architectural features but goes a step further, with great touches like tree trunk underwear drawers, dentists' chairs in bathrooms, canary yellow python skin pouffes and turtle doves on the roof. Old antiques mix with inventive contemporary design to create something very special. A second house that will bring the 3 rooms up to 5 is due to open in Apr 2012, along with the restaurant **Bruno**, which will feature modern French-Arabic cuisine. Rooms are rented individually or you can rent the whole place.
€€€€ **Riad Fès**, 5 Derb Ben Sliman Zerbtana, T0535-741206, www.riadfes.com. This vast house, originally built in 1900, was one of the first in Fès to be transformed into upscale accommodation, and it remains one of the city's most luxurious places to stay. Particularly at night, its poolside bar is spectacular and seriously hip. The 26 rooms are split into 3 different design themes depending on your tastes – Baraco Andalous, traditional Moroccan or Oriental – and although they don't quite live up to the wow-factor of the rest of the place, they still feel special. The roof terrace provides a more upmarket spot in the medina for lunch and has fantastic views.
€€€€ **Riad Laaroussa**, 3 Derb Bechara, T0674-187639, www.riad-laaroussa.com. One of the first wave of contemporary riads in Fès, this 17th-century riad opens out around a grass and pebble courtyard with fountains and orange trees. As well as 4-poster beds, fireplaces in some of the rooms (a huge bonus during the rather damp and cold winters) and a striking *tadelakt* roof terrace, there are plenty of quirky touches like kettles for taps, adding an air of the unexpected. The dining room has black-and-white photos and jazz playing, while the 7 bedrooms are all themed around a colour. There's an elegant hammam and spa and copious amounts of intricately carved plaster.
€€€€-€€ **Dar Bensouda**, 14 Zkak El Bghel, Quettanine, T0535-638949, www. riaddarbensouda.com. This chic hotel is in one of the more obscure parts of the medina and is well worth the effort of finding. Owned by Moroccan hotelier Abdellatif Aït Ben Abdellah, who made his mark with several respected riads and restaurants in Marrakech, he's brought his own sense of style to Fès. A large courtyard is minimally furnished with butterfly chairs, linen drapes and saffron-coloured rugs. Rooms are individually decorated with pared-down elegance, and 1 luxury suite has a private courtyard at an accessible price. Another courtyard is home to an inviting

plunge pool, the restaurant (warmed by a log fire in the winter) serves a wide range of Moroccan cuisine, while the roof terrace provides a full 360-degree view of the medina and surrounds.

€€€ Dar Attajali, 2 Derb Qettana, Zqaq Rommane, T0535-637728, T0677-081192 (mob), www.attajalli.com. **Attajali** is one of the most exquisite renovations in the medina, highly traditional with a feminine feel. Think lots of pinks, purples and silky fabrics, soothing Arabic music and an air of quiet serenity. 5 individually decorated rooms have wooden ceilings, pretty *zellige* tiles, antiques, comfortable mattresses, imported German duvets and traditional Moroccan beauty products in the bathrooms. The 'purple suite' has a spectacular draped 4-poster bed, if you're after a romantic weekend away. This is the only vegetarian guesthouse in Fès, and the food is excellent, making good use of locally sourced fruit and vegetables. Breakfast and dinner are served in a rooftop dining room, with wonderful views across the medina.

€€€ Dar Bennis, just off Talaâ Seghira, T0661-564364, www.houseinfez.com. Available only to rent in its entirety, **Dar Bennis** sleeps 2-4 very comfortably and 5 at a push, a great base for a couple or a family. Owned by the Director of the American Language Centre, it is a simple but beautiful house on 4 levels around a small courtyard. You also get Hafid, the manager, to make you breakfast and be around if and when you need him. It's €80 per night for one person, plus an extra €20 for each extra person.

€€€ Dar Roumana, 30 Derb el Amer, Zkak Roumane, T0535-741637, www.darroumana.com. One of the first foreign-owned guesthouses to open in the medina (and still one of the best). The American owner Jennifer Smith has created one of the friendliest places you could hope to stay. Big on traditional Moroccan decor, such as *zellige*, intricate plaster work and painted ceilings, it has a wonderful feeling of space and light, with a large central courtyard,

library, TV room and sprawling roof terrace with excellent views of the Merinid tombs. All 5 suites are large, well proportioned and feature the works of local craftsmen, as well as unique characteristics, such as the claw-footed bath in the Roumana suite, or the private balcony off the Yasmina suite. Jennifer has always been known for her excellent cuisine and, as well as offering cooking lessons, she's upped the ante again recently by bringing in a French chef, Vincent Bonnin, to head the restaurant (now also open to the public), which offers a daily changing menu Tue-Sat. Booking recommended.

€€€ Dar Seffarine, 14 Sbaa Louyate, T0535-635205, www.darseffarine.com. Widely recognized as being the most spectacular renovation in Fès, the 750-year-old Dar Seffarine is an architectural gem built around a spectacular tiled courtyard with high arches. The creation of Kate (a Norwegian graphic designer and photographer) and Alla (an Iraqi architect), their attention to detail from the restoration of the house's intricate features to the choosing of antique carpets, furniture and linens is impeccable. Decor is minimal to allow the house to speak for itself, but a museum it's not. The couple are gregarious hosts and every evening guests are invited for drinks in their small, homely courtyard just off the kitchen, or can dine together in the rooftop dining room (the food is excellent). Located just around the corner from the Qaraouiyine Mosque, it's also well positioned for some of the medina's key sights, and with easy access to the parking and taxis at Rcif.

€€€ Riad Idrissy, T0649-191410 (Robert), T0535-633066 (the riad), www.riadidrissy.com. Another good example of the laid-back new vibe of the Fès medina, this 4-suite riad feels more like a private home than a hotel, with a big personality, thanks to lots of irreverent personalized touches and quirky finds by owner John Twomey and interior designer and gardener Robert Johnstone. Check out the beaded animal tables from Cameroon and the raffia wedding cake covers refashioned as lampshades, or the 4-poster bed that needs box steps to climb onto it. Johnstone has recently added 'The Ruined Garden', which is accessible from the house. He grows fresh produce that creates a cooling oasis, framed by trees and ancient columns for afternoon tea parties and street food stalls for dinner (ruinedgarden.com).

€€€ **Riad Tizwa**, Derb Guebbas 15, Douh Batha, T07973-238444 (UK mob) or T0668-190872 (Morocco mob), www.riadtizwa. com. Sibling to the more established Tizwa in Marrakech, Tizwa Fès has 9 chic double bedrooms and a sprawling, lushly planted roof terrace, where excellent breakfasts are served. All rooms are generously appointed with some useful modern details, such as iPod docking stations, which is indicative of the Bee brothers' laid-back approach to hospitality that makes the place so pleasurable. Bathrooms are all done out in *tadelakt*, with organic rose petal soap and luxuriously thick bathrobes, and tea and coffee is secretly delivered to your door in the mornings, a nice touch. Communal spaces are warm and welcoming, with an open fireplace in the living room and a richly furnished courtyard for chilling out over mint tea in the afternoons. A truly comfortable home-away-from-home.

€€€-€€ **Dar el Hana**, 22 Rue Ferrane Couicha, Cherabliyine, T0535-635854, T0676-286584 (mob), www.darelhana.com. A homely little riad, you'll be fantastically well looked after here, whether you rent the whole place or just a room. Carefully restored, Dar el Hana has wooden beamed ceilings, shuttered windows and a 'secret' window just above the pillows. All rooms have private bathrooms but in the smaller rooms they are not en suite. Guests breakfast together in the courtyard or on the terrace. The whole place can be rented out for €215.

€€€-€€ **Dar El Menia**, T0535-633164, T0655-206961, www.medinafes.com. This small but immaculately renovated little guesthouse, just off the Talaâ Kebira, has just 4 rooms, each with their own character.

Around 250 years old, you'll find plenty of traditional Moroccan decoration here, from painted wood and intricate plasterwork, to pristine *zellige* tiles and carved cedar wood doors. It's a great place to get a taste of traditional Moroccan living while being perfectly placed at the heart of the medina for exploring. There's a roof terrace for chilling out, and the sumptuous traditional dinners of couscous and tagine (by prior arrangement) are a bargain.

€€€-€€ **Dar Finn**, 27 Zqaq Rowah, Cherabliyine, T0655-018975, www.darfinn. com. **Dar Finn** is one of the hippest openings of 2011 and is ideal for style-savvy travellers who want to get off the beaten path. Owners Rebecca Eve and Paul O'Sullivan, who named it after their son, have brought an upbeat boutique concept to the medina. Half the house has retained its traditional architecture – such as in the courtyard and tearoom – but there is a modern façade, garden and plunge pool, and an intimate dining room to create a more groovy hangout for guests. Large balconies off the suites have the clean lines of nouveau art deco, while the upper floors and three roof terraces offer softer, chill-out zones with jaw-dropping views. The vibe is laid-back and relaxed, and there's an honesty bar.

€€ **Dar Imam**, 6 Derb Ben Azahoum, T0535-636528, www.fes-hostel.com. A good choice for style on a budget, this 400-year-old place has 9 en suite rooms with comfortable beds, and many can sleep 3-4 people. There's also a pretty terrace.

Hotels

Budget accommodation in the medina, mostly in the Bab Boujeloud area, fills up very quickly in spring and summer.

€€€€ **Hotel Palais Jamaï**, Bab el Guissa, T0535-634331/3, www.sofitel.com. A former palace with superb views of the medina and a beautiful garden, Jamaï has 123 rooms, 19 suites, 2 restaurants, bar, hammam, sauna, tennis court and a pool that is heated in winter. Rooms don't quite come up to a 5-star standard, service is pleasant but can be slow, and breakfast is disappointing. However, if you want to be in the medina but can't deal with the maze-like streets, this is a good choice; a taxi will take you right to the door.

€€-€ Pension Dar Bouanania, 21 Derb Ben Salem, Talaâ Kebira, T0535-637282. A rarity in the medina, **Dar Bouanania** is a good-value hotel with some style. Packed with painted wood, plaster and traditional tiles, it's a great way to get a taste of the architecture on a budget. Rooms – some en suite – sleep up to four and have big rugs and ornate furniture. Great value if you're travelling as a family or a group.

€ Hotel Cascade, 26 Rue Serrajine, T0535-638442. A backpackers' institution, the busy **Cascade** is in the very heart of the action, just inside the main gate of Bab Boujeloud. Rooms are very basic but OK for the price and, on the upside, it's a great place to watch over the comings and goings down below. If money is really tight, you can also sleep cheaply on the roof terrace.

€ Hotel Lamrani, Talaâ Seghira, T0535-634411. Next to the fountain on the left on your way down Talaâ Seghira, Lamrani is a decent budget option, with 16 light and impeccably clean rooms, some with up to 4 beds. Hot showers are included (not always the case in budget places in Morocco) and it's a good place to meet fellow travellers. Management is friendly if a little erratic service-wise.

Fès ville nouvelle *map p150*
€€€€ Atlas Fès and Spa, www.hotels atlas.com. The new, European-style **Atlas** is a well-established Moroccan chain with properties all over the country. Its latest opening in Fès promises proper 5-star comforts and old school hospitality rather than hipness, though the contemporary decor will appeal to design-conscious travellers. Rooms are pared-down and elegant, with mod cons like flat-screen

TVs and satellite channels. Between the new town and the medina, it's handy for exploring both sides of Fès. The spacious grounds, a large pool area, luxury spa and gourmet dining place it firmly at the top of the 5-star list.

€€€€ Hotel Jnan Palace, Av Ahmed Chaouki, behind the craft centre off Av Allal Ben Abdallah, T0535-652230. One of the better of the 5-star hotels in the *ville nouvelle*, the Jnan has beautiful grounds, a decent-sized pool, 195 modern rooms, 51 suites, 3 restaurants, a cigar and piano bar, library and a disco. It's a popular spot for expat residents on a Fri night. It doesn't have the character of hotels in the medina, but if you're looking for a 'soft' introduction to this most intense of Moroccan cities, it's a reliable choice.

€€€€ Royal Mirage Fès, Av des FAR, T0535-625002. The **Royal Mirage** group has hotels in Fès, Marrakech and Agadir and is a favourite among moneyed Moroccans and tour groups. This one has 271 plush if somewhat kitsch rooms, many with balconies overlooking the large pool area, extensive gardens, 2 restaurants, coffee shop, bar, tennis and even car rental on site. Even if you're not planning to stay, it's a handy place to escape the heat for a day by the pool (100 dh) and lunch.

€€€ Barceló Fès Medina, 53 Av Hassan II, T0535-948800, www.barcelo.com. This brand spanking new 5-star handily located between the *ville nouvelle* and the medina brings a breath of fresh air to the new town hotel scene. It's decorated in contemporary style, with all mod cons, designer furniture, a top-flight spa and impeccable service. It also offers gourmet dining in the **Azahar** restaurant, a jazz bar and café, free Wi-Fi throughout, a business centre and a small but pretty pool.

€€ Hotel Moussafir Ibis, Av des Almohades, T0535-651902/08. Part of the Accor group, this hotel is next door to the train station so is useful for early departures or late arrivals. It lacks authentic Moroccan

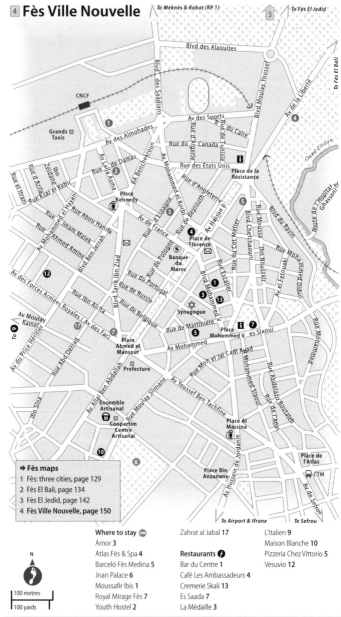

4 Fès Ville Nouvelle

To Meknès & Rabat (RP 1)

To Fès El Jedid

To Fès El Bali

Blvd des Alaouites

CNCF

Grands Taxis

Av des Almohades

Av des Sports

Rue du Caire

Rue de Tunisie

Rue du Nigerie

Rue du Canada

Rue des Etats Unis

Blvd des Saâdiens

Blvd Yemen Moulay Youssef

Av de la Liberté

To Fès El Bali

Oued Zitoun

Route de l'Hôpital el Ghassani

Rue de Damas

Ibn Zeïdane

Rue el Achir

Rue el Irfam

Rue Ksar el Kebir

Rue Lalla Asma

BA Benchekroun

Av Mohammed el Korb

Rue d'Angleterre

Place de la Résistance

Place Kennedy

Rue Abou Hanifa

Rue el Hayani

Av Mohammed el Imam Malek

Av Mohammed Amine Ben Jerran

Blvd Tarik Ibn Ziad

Av des Forces Armées Royales

Rue Ibn Aïcha

Av d'Espagne

Av de France

Rue de Beyrouth

Av Hassan I

Rue du Cot Mettier

Blvd Chefchaouni

Rue Moussa

Ibn Roussair

Av el Fetouaki

Blvd Mohammed Diouri

Place de Florence

Banque du Maroc

Rue de Fouquel

Rue de Portugal

Rue de Russie

Rue de Belgique

Synagogue

Rue de Martihière

Place Ahmed el Mansour

Place Mohammed V es Sfaoui

Av Mohammed

Rue Moh el Jal Cadi Ayad

Prefecture

Av Allal Ben Abdallah

Rue Moulay Slimane

Av Youssef Ben Tachfine

Ibn Sina

Av Moulay Kamel

Av du Price Héritier

Rue Abou Derai

Ensemble Artisanal

Coopartim Centre Artisanal

Place Al Massina

Av Mohammed Sfaoui

Rue Mohammed

Rue Abdelaziz Bouaaleb

Rue de l'Atlas

Place de l'Atlas

CTM

Place Bin Anzanane

Av Hussein de Jordanie

Av de Sefrou

To Airport & Ifrane

To Sefrou

Fès maps
1 Fès: three cities, page 129
2 Fès El Bali, page 134
3 Fès El Jedid, page 142
4 Fès Ville Nouvelle, page 150

To Meknès & Rabat

To 9

100 metres
100 yards

Where to stay
Amor **3**
Atlas Fès & Spa **4**
Barceló Fès Medina **5**
Jnan Palace **6**
Moussafir Ibis **1**
Royal Mirage Fès **7**
Youth Hostel **2**

Zahrat al Jabal **17**

Restaurants
Bar du Centre **1**
Café Les Ambassadeurs **4**
Cremerie Skali **13**
Es Saada **7**
La Médaille **3**

L'Italien **9**
Maison Blanche **10**
Pizzeria Chez Vittorio **5**
Vesuvio **12**

N

character, but the 122 rooms are clean and comfortable, and the gardens surrounding a small pool are quite lovely. Just think of it as somewhere reasonable priced and practical, rather than a Fès 'experience'.

€€ Zahrat al Jabal, Av des FAR, T0535-944646. This funky little hotel offering 62 modern a/c rooms with TV is very friendly and eager to please. Centrally located, there's a rooftop bar and restaurant serving international and Moroccan dishes. A pleasant place to relax.

€ Hotel Amor, 31 Rue d'Arabie séoudite, coming from the train station, take a left as you come onto the Pl de Florence, T0535-622724. A small hotel with just 35 rooms, most with showers though there are a handful of cheaper, shared bathroom options. Rooms are simple but clean and comfortable, with colourful decor, bed linen is provided (not always the case in some of the cheaper Moroccan hostels) and they are super friendly. It also has a café-pâtisserie in the street below. Avoid street-facing rooms if traffic noise bothers you. Good value.

€ Youth hostel, 18 Rue Abdesslam Serghini, in the *ville nouvelle*, T0535-624085, www.fesyouth-hostel.com. Widely considered to be Morocco's best youth hostel, this is a spotless and very professional outfit, worth considering even if you don't usually stay in youth hostels. There's a very pleasant courtyard and garden, with lilies, trees and birds, and they have single-sex dorms and smaller rooms for 2-7. You can do laundry on the roof and they offer good information. Reception open 0800-2200 but rooms closed 1000-1200 and 1500-1800. No HI card necessary.

Camping

Camping du Diamant vert, near Aïn Chkeff, right off the N6, is comparatively expensive by Moroccan standards, but it does have some extra facilities like a shop and snack restaurant. There is plenty of shade, though the washing blocks are poorly maintained. To get there take bus No 19 from Fès from

outside the **PTT**. If you do stay here, you can use the aqua-fun complex next door during the summer, but bear in mind this means the campsite gets packed and noisy during peak periods.

Camping international, on the Sefrou road, some 3 km from Fès. This is possibly a better option. It is a well maintained but expensive site with a pool, shops and even a bar serving alcohol. To get here take bus No 38 from Pl Atlas, T0535-731439.

Moulay Yacoub *p144*

Like many smaller towns and villages in Morocco, it is possible to find a room to rent at a very reasonable price in private homes here, which can be a hugely rewarding experience. There are also a few basic options.

€€ Hotel Moulay Yacoub, T0535-694035, www.sogatour.ma. Part of the Sogatour group, this comfortable 60-room hotel offers TV, bath and terrace in each, as well as 60 bungalows. It also has a restaurant with magnificent views, bar, tennis, pool, and a pretty, new tree-lined road leads down to the medical treatment centre that makes use of the thermal springs, with neat gardens, café and practice golf. Unfortunately service doesn't always come up to scratch.

Sefrou *p144*

€ Dar Attamani, 414 Bastna, T0645-298930, T0660-492442, www.darattamani.com. A friendly little guesthouse with bags of charm in the centre of the medina. The 5 rooms are individually decorated in rich Moroccan blues and greens and complemented by different living spaces. The roof terrace has glorious views over the surrounding hills, food is cheap and tasty and there's Wi-Fi.

Camping

Camping de Sefrou, 2 km from the town, follow Rue Ziad, by the post office on Av Mohammed V, T0535-673340. In site of 4 ha, bar/snack, groceries, showers, laundry, petrol at 2 km.

🍴 Restaurants

Fès El Bali *p133, map p134*

The medina is changing fast and although the majority of places to eat are still traditional Moroccan restaurants or street food, there are also increasing numbers of hip, foreign-owned places. Since opening in 2006 the British-run **Café Clock** (see Cafés below) has become the essential meeting point of anyone travelling to Fès. But for fine dining, visit the new boutique hotels like **Dar Bensouda** (see page 146) and **Dar Roumana** (see page 147).

€€€ Al Fassia, in the **Hotel Palais Jamaï**, Bab el Guissa, T0535-634331. Open lunch and dinner. Cooling views of the pool and verdant gardens make a lovely setting for a high quality buffet lunch. Choose from a wide variety of salads, Moroccan and international dishes and fresh fish and meat grilled on the spot. They also have a good wine list, including some very drinkable Moroccan bottles.

€€€ Le Jardin des Biehn, 13 Akbat Sbaa, Douh, T0664 647 679, www.jardindes biehn.com. Open breakfast, lunch and dinner. The **Jardin des Biehn** combines several riad-style suites around a private organic garden with the colourful **Café Fès** at one end. Once a Pasha's summer palace, it is a wonderfully atmospheric place for a lazy lunch (yes, they do serve wine), or dinner beneath the stars. Michel Biehn, a well-known collector of antique textiles, lends his touch throughout, and you can see the art gallery and or stroll in the gardens. The traditional Moroccan, or lighter French and Italian dishes, feature many home-grown products, and there are also pizzas baked in a wood-fired oven.

€€€ Palais Tijani, 51-53 Derb Ben Chekroune Lablida, T0535-741128. Open lunch and dinner. A classic palace restaurant, with lots of intricate ornamentation, low tables, scattered rose petals and a focus on providing a true taste of Morocco. Service is charming, and dishes include celebratory pigeon *b'stilla* (pie), hearty tagines and couscous. No alcohol licence.

€€ Café Medina. Open 1000-2300. Located just outside Bab Boujeloud, this is a peaceful spot to hang out on a roof terrace. It is a little bit more upmarket than its neighbours and offers good-quality Moroccan options.

€€ Café Tabarakallah, Blvd Ahmed ben Mohammed Alaoui, Rcif. Open 0800-2200. Opposite the **Cinema Amal** in bustling Rcif this is a useful lunch-stop after a morning exploring the Andalous Quarter. Spread over several floors with sprawling terraces and friendly service, the order of the day here is the rotisserie chicken stuffed with fresh coriander and spices with chips and a plate of stewed white beans. They also have a vast range of Moroccan cakes and pastries.

€€ Fez Lounge, 95 Zkak Rouah, www.fez lounge.com. Open 1000-midnight. If ever there was a clear sign of the new Fès that is about to emerge, the medina's first 'bar' concept, **Fez Lounge**, is it. A popular meeting point for expats and groovy locals, you can get a proper cocktail here, too, if you're discreet (ask for the 'special' menu) and sample some decent Moroccan snacks with a modern touch. Decor-wise think Marrakchi style, with dark *tadelakt* walls, funky pouffes, low tables in intimate booths and groovy music.

€€ Mezzanine, 17 Kasbat Chams, in front of the entrance to the Jnan Sbil Gardens, near Bab Boujeloud, T011-078336. Open 1100-0100. A stylish place for a sundowner, this fashionable lounge and bar, with its sleek rooftop terrace, overlooks the Jnan Sbil Gardens. The tapas-style menu features a mix of flavours from Morocco, France and Spain, from grilled sardines and chorizo skewers, to grilled goat's cheese, marinated aubergines and tapenade. Booze is expensive, though.

€ Fez et Gestes, 39 Arsat El Hamoumi, Ziat, T0535-638532, T0668-601791, www.fes-et-gestes.ma. Open lunch and dinner. Housed in an Italian-style villa, with a pretty, walled garden, this is one of the loveliest spots in the medina and is the creation of charming French expat, Cecile. In the shade of a jacaranda tree, refuel on perfectly executed Moroccan salads, tagines and pastries. In winter, 2 plump leather armchairs in the library provide a cosy nook for hot mint tea and a good book.

There is no shortage of cheap eats in Fès el Bali, particularly just inside Bab Boujeloud, where there is a busy row of cafés with outdoor tables, all of which are good for an evening meal. Of these, local celebrity € **Thami's**, tucked into a corner under the tree, is the most often recommended and the tastiest. His kefta and egg tagine is excellent, as are his steaming great cauldrons of *lobia* (white bean stew) and *maakouda* (potato pancakes with hot chilli sauce). It's also arguably the best place in town for a spot of people watching. Open noon-midnight.

Cafés

Café Clock, 7 Derb el Magana, Talaâ Kebira, T0535-637855, www.cafeclock.com. Daily 0900-2300. In a beautiful old building just off Talaâ Kebira, in the heart of the medina, **Café Clock** is so much more than just a café. It has become the epicentre of traveller and expat Fès since opening in 2006, and understandably so. Hip, young, and energetic, there always seems to be something going on, whether it's a photo exhibition by a local artist, Arabic conversation classes or a calligraphy lesson in one of the upstairs lounges. It's also a great place to eat, with a contemporary rif on Moroccan classics. People come from far and wide to get a taste of their eponymous camel burger, or for afternoon tea and home-baked cakes on the roof with its stunning view of the minaret of the Medersa Bou Inania across the other side of Talaâ Kebira. There's even free Wi-Fi and, if you want to find anything out about the city, you'll probably find someone here who will be happy to tell you.

Cremerie de Place, on the northern point of Pl Seffarine. A well-loved little spot for sitting out on the square and watching the copper beaters at work. There's something almost musical about the chink, chink, chink of so many little hammers, and it's a good place to get to know locals who stop for a chat minus the endless haggle. Coffee, *panache* (mixed fruit juice) and cakes are all good here, and it's ideal for catching your breath after a couple of hours losing yourself in the souks. **Óuali's Café**, Pl Bouros, Talaâ Kebira. An unmarked and unprepossessing café with a few rickety outdoor tables on the right as you head down Talaâ Kebira, the much-photographed and rather ancient Óuali will serve you an exquisitely spiced coffee with commendable panache. You even get a home-made leather holder to stop your hands from burning.

Fès ville nouvelle *map p150*

Fès is far from having the same variety and choice of international restaurants as Marrakech, although this is changing. In the last few years a handful of restaurant-cum-lounge clubs have opened up, like **Andalous Fès** and **O' Club**, and dining out in the *ville* gets more chic by the week. It's also the place to come if you feel like a change from more traditional Moroccan fare.

€€€ Maison Blanche, 12 rue Ahmed Chaouki, T0535-622727, www.maison-blanche.ma. Open lunch and dinner. Arguably Fès's best restaurant, it is also its trendiest, combining a large, slate-clad dining room with an elegant 1st floor bar and lounge. It is hugely popular among the city's groovers and shakers and is a satisfying choice if you're looking for somewhere special to splash your cash. Food is Franco-Moroccan with lots of creative touches, such as grilled John Dory with a preserved lemon marmalade or fillet of beef with pistachio butter. The wine list and cocktails are excellent, and there's even a cigar bar for lovers of a nice, fat Cubano, but it can get pricey. The 2-course menu for 200dh is a more affordable option.

€€€ **L'Italien**, Residence Longchamp, Av Omar Ibn Khattab, T0535-943384, www.restaurant-litalien.com. Open noon to midnight. This Scandinavia-meets-Italy newcomer fast became the restaurant du jour among the city's beautiful people when it opened in mid-2011. The blonde wood, natty furniture and large communal table are about as far from Fès as you could hope to be, but a welcome respite from tagines. They serve top-notch homemade ravioli stuffed with spinach and ricotta, bread rubbed with rosemary and salt, and crisp-based wood-oven fired pizzas.

€€ **La Médaille** 24 Rue Med el Hayani, T0535-620183. Open lunch and dinner. Located near the central market, off Blvd Mohammed V to your right as you come from Pl de Florence, this is a lively bar-cum-restaurant with lots of soul. It's popular with Moroccans and tourists, who come to feast on high-quality traditional fare. It's reasonably smart and licensed.

€€ **Restaurant Pizzeria Chez Vittorio**, 21 Rue Brahim Roudani/Rue Nador, T0535-624730. Open lunch and dinner. This bistro-style restaurant with dark wood panelling and gingham tablecloths serves solid Italian food, decent steaks in old-fashioned French sauces, and a perfectly drinkable bottle of local wine. It does pizza less well, but its friendly service and cosy, laid-back atmosphere are popular with expats. No credit cards.

€€ **Vesuvio**, 9 Rue AbiHayane Taouhidi, T0535-930747. Open lunch and dinner. Similar looking to **Vittorio**, this down-to-earth place serves reasonably priced pizza. Service is friendly and, until **L'Italien**, opened, it was the place for a pie and a glass of wine. Takeaway pizzas are also available (it's a 20dh cab ride from the medina).

There are several good cheap options along **Av Chefchaouni** selling piping hot brochettes, lentils, Moroccan salads and other tasty street food.

Cafés

In the *ville nouvelle* the wide boulevards lend themselves well to café society and there are innumerable places to sit back with a *café noir* (black coffee) or a *nous nous* (half and half). The better ones include L'Elysée, 4 Rue de Paris; Café Les Ambassadeurs, Pl de Florence, and Cremerie Skali, Mohammed V, which has a huge juice and shakes menu, all freshly made on the spot.

⒪ Bars and clubs

Fès *p128*

A drink in the **Hotel Palais Jamaï** is a good break in the medina, and the **Hotel des Merinides** has a good view of the city, but for the classiest bar, go to **Riad Fès** and sit by the pool. Many of Fès's expats favour the bar in the **Hotel Batha** for a beer, or there's the newly opened **Mezzanine** (see page 152).

In the *ville nouvelle* try **Es Saada**, on Av Slaoui; and **Bar du Centre**, Av Mohammed V, for ice-cold beers (Casablanca and Special Flag are both good local brews). If you want to glam it up, **O'Club** at Andalous Fez, 2.5 Rte d'Imouzzer, T0661-562978, www.oclubfez.com, combines the bar-club-lounge experience and attracts hip young Fassi's and expats with their European-style DJs and 'club' nights.

⊛ Festivals

Fès *p128*

Jun For 10 days Fès vibrates to the rhythmic drumming and soaring voices of the **Festival de Fès des musiques sacrées du monde** (Fès Festival of Sacred Music). From sufi to gospel, the range is wide, and there is a scattering of dance too. Free open-air concerts take place in the square outside Bab Boujeloud, with other ticketed events at locations such as the Batha Museum and Bab Makina. Prices for individual concerts range from around 150dh to 600dh, or you can buy a pass for all the concerts for 2900dh. Tickets are available online at www.fesfestival.com.

◯ Shopping

Fès *p128*
Books and newspapers
Newspapers from the stalls in
Av Mohammed V.
English Bookshop, 68 Av Hassan II, near Pl
de la Résistance. New books in English.

Moroccan goods

Fès has for long been one of the great trading
centres of Morocco. The souks, *kissaria* and
boutiques offer a splendid selection for
visitors. Many of the boutiques in the hotels,
the *ville nouvelle* and near the important
tourist attractions will try to charge inflated
prices. As elsewhere, the large carpet shops
have very experienced salesmen who work
with guides to whom they pay a commission
for sales completed. Best buy in Fès is
probably the blue-and-white painted, quite
rustic pottery once typical of the city. For
smaller gift items, slippers and traditional
clothing wander in the *kissaria* (clothes
market) area between the Zaouïa of
Moulay Idriss and the Qaraouiyine Mosque.
Coopartim Centre Artisanal, Blvd Allal Ben
Abdallah, T0535-625654. Open 0900-1400
and 1600-1900. A good selection of crafts
in the *ville nouvelle*.

◯ What to do

Fès *p128*
Tour operators
There are several good tour companies
offering a break from the norm with
specialized niche trips aimed at independent
travellers who want to experience a more
authentic side of Morocco.
Fez Food, www.fez-food.com. Designed
for foodie travellers who want to experience
the gourmet delights of the medina or learn
about spices, taste wine in the vineyards
of Meknès, or try rolling couscous in the
Atlas. They also have more traditional
cooking lessons.

Tours Around Fez, www.toursaroundfez.
com. Offers hikes and sunset picnics on
Mt Zalagh to 4WD trips through the Middle
Atlas, with a focus on responsible tourism.
Yomikha Morocco, www.yomikhamorocco.
com. Offers bespoke tours in and around
Fès and further afield, including day trips to
the cedar forests near Fès, educational visits
to the ancient Roman ruins of Volubilis and
more extensive journeys to the Sahara.

◯ Transport

Fès *p128*
Air
The small **Aéroport de Fès-Saiss** is 15 km to
the south of the city, off the N8, T0535-
624712. There are flights to **Casablanca**
with connections to domestic and
international destinations, but for now no
other direct flights to cities elsewhere in
Morocco. There are increasing numbers of
budget airlines, such as **Ryanair** and also
Royal Air Maroc (RAM), connecting with
cities in Europe. **Jet4you** fly to **Brussels**
and **Paris**, and Ryanair fly to **Alicante**,
Barcelona, **Bologna**, **Brussels**, **Düsseldorf**,
Frankfurt, **London (Stansted)**, **Marseille**,
Milan, **Paris**, **Pisa** and **Rome**. Routes change
frequently. To get to the airport take bus
No 16 from the train station. **RAM** office,
54 Av Hassan II, in the *ville nouvelle*, T0535-
625516/7, reservations T0535-620456/7.

Bus
Local buses cost 2dh. No 1 runs from Pl des
Alaouites to Dar Batha, No 3 from Pl des
Alaouites to Pl de la Résistance, No 9 from
Pl de la Résistance to Dar Batha, No 10 from
Bab Guissa to Pl des Alaouites, No 18 from
Pl de la Résistance to Bab Ftouh and No 20
from Pl de Florence to Hotel les Merinides.

CTM buses depart from the station
on Av Mohammed V, T0535-622041, for
Beni Mellal, **Marrakech** (early morning
departure, 8-9 hrs), **Tetouan**, **Tangier** (in the
small hours, 6 hrs), **Taza**, **Oujda**, **Nador**. For
Casablanca, 8 departures a day, 0700-1900,

for **Rabat**, 7 a day, and for **Meknès**, 8 a day, 0700-1900. Most other private line buses leave from the new terminal off the Route du Tour de Fès, below the Borj Nord and not far from Bab Boujeloud. Buses for the **Middle Atlas** leave from the Laghzaoui terminal, Rue Ksar el Kebir.

Car hire
Fès lies at a crossroads in Morocco and is an excellent base from which to plan and carry out the next stage of travels. It is a fairly easy city to navigate and there are several car parks dotted around the medina, usually fairly close to the one of the babs, where you can safely leave your vehicle for a day or two. Note: a tip to the 'guardian' (security person) on leaving is expected.

Avis, 50 Blvd Chefchaouni, T0535-626746. **Budget**, adjacent Palais Jamaï Hotel, T0535-620919. **Europcar-Inter-Rent**, 41 Av Hassan II, T0535-626545. **Hertz**, Kissariat de la Foire No 1, Blvd Lalla Meryem, T0535-622812; airport T0535-651823. **Holiday Car**, 41 Av Mohammed V, T0535-624550. **SAFLOC**, Hotel Sheraton, T0535-931201. **Zeit**, 35 Av Mohammed Slaoui, T0535-625510.

Taxi
Grands taxis leave from Pl Baghdadi, except for those to Sefrou and Azrou, which leave from Rue de Normandie. Red, cheap and a quick way to get around Fès, *petits taxis* generally have meters. Sample fares, Bab Boujeloud to Pl Mohammed V, 10dh; Pl Mohammed V to Hotel Les Merinides, 15dh.

Train
The railway station is at the end of Blvd Chenguit, in the *ville nouvelle*, T0535-622501. If you arrive by train, check your departure time at the station. There are direct train services to **Marrakech** (4 hrs), **Rabat** (5 hrs)

and **Casablanca** (8 hrs), all via **Meknès** (1½ hrs). To **Tangier** (6 hrs), you will change at **Sidi Kacem** or **Sidi Slimane**. There are also services to **Taza** and **Oujda**.

❶ Directory

Fès *p128*
Banks Lots of banks in *ville nouvelle* on Pl Florence and Av Mohammed V. The most reliable ATM is the **Wafa Bank**, Av Mohammed V, T0535-622591. Other banks with ATMs are in the big **Immeuble Mamda**, Pl de Florence. ATMs in Fès el Bali can be found at the entrance to Bab Boujeloud (both inside and outside the gate) and at Rcif (near the main square). There are also a couple of well-signposted ATMs in busier parts of the souks, such as Attarine. **Cultural and language centres** Institut Français, 33 Rue el Bahrein, T0535-623921, library and films. **Alif** (Arabic Language in Fès), in the *ville nouvelle* at 2 Rue Ahmed Hiba (close to the Hotel Zalagh), T0535-624850. Good reputation for organizing courses in Arabic, both literary and spoken Moroccan. They can cater for specific language needs, and at any one time have around 30 or more students, from various backgrounds. See also Café Clock, in Restaurants above. **Medical services Chemists**: there is an all-night chemist at the Municipalité de Fès, Blvd Moulay Youssef, T0535-623380 (2000-0800). During the day try **Bahja**, Av Mohammed V, T0535-622441, or **Bab Ftouh** at Bab Ftouh, T0535-649135. **Hospital**: Hôpital Ghassani, Quartier Dhar Mehraz, T0535-622776. **Useful addresses** Fire: T15. **Police**, Av Mohammed V, T19. **Garages** Try Mécanique Générale, 22 Av Cameroun. Fiat repairs at **Auto Maroc**, Av Mohammed V, T0535-623435.

Meknès

Meknès never set out to be an 'imperial city'. But, as chance would have it, the inhabitants of Fès and Marrakech showed little enthusiasm for 17th-century ruler and builder Moulay Ismaïl, and so he turned his attentions towards Meknès. Strategically situated at the heart of Morocco, Meknès became his capital, and he embarked on a massive building programme. Meknès is known as a city of minarets – gentle green or grey in colour, the tall, angular, linear towers dominate the old town, which, with its cream colour-washed houses and terraces sits above the narrow valley of the Oued Boufekrane. There are pleasant souks, a medersa – but, above all, an easy pace that is almost relaxing after the tension and press of Fès. The most famous monument is the great Bab Mansour el Aleuj and, although today little is left except for vast pisé walls, once upon a time this great gate to a palace complex was worthy of the Thousand and One Nights. Meknès also offers some rewarding side trips – to the Roman site of Volubilis, and to the pilgrimage centre of Moulay Idriss.» For listings, see pages 168-172.

Arriving in Meknès → *Colour map 1, B3.*

Getting there

The new bus station (private long-distance buses) is at Bab el Khemis, on the far side of the medina from the *ville nouvelle*. The old **CTM** bus station is at 47 Avenue Mohammed V in the *ville nouvelle*, and some *grands taxis* leave from nearby on Avenue des FAR. Private local buses arrive at the terminal below Bab Mansour. The main train station is some way from the centre and 1 km from the medina. If you are going to stay in *ville nouvelle*, get off at the **Meknès Amir Abdelkader** station, the first of the two stations in Meknès as you come from Casa/Rabat. This station is just below Avenue Mohammed V and closer to the centre of the *ville nouvelle* than the other main station.» *See Transport, page 171, for further details.*

Getting around

Meknès is a fairly spread-out place. The medina, along with the ruined palace complexes of the 17th century, is situated across the valley of the Oued Boufekrane. When visiting Meknès in summer, it can get hot, and the distances between the different parts of the 17th-century palace city are considerable. You will probably need a full day, with most of a morning dedicated to the palace complex. In half a day, you could do the medina easily.

Tourist information Office du Tourisme (ONMT) ① *27 Pl Batha-l'Istiqlal, T0535-521286.* Helpful, although not overly endowed with information.

Background

Coming up to Meknès by road from Rabat, you get a good idea of why Moulay Ismaïl chose the town as his capital. The N6 passes through the Mamora Forest and a belt of fertile, relatively prosperous countryside. Meknès was originally a kasbah from the eighth century, used by the Kharajite Berbers against the Arabs. The town itself was founded by the Zenata Amazigh tribe called Meknassa in the 10th century and then destroyed by the Almoravids in 1069. A later kasbah was destroyed by the Almohad Sultan Abd el Moumen in order to build a new grid-patterned medina, some features of which still remain. This city was ruined during the conflict between the Almohads and the Merinids, but was partially rebuilt and repopulated in 1276 under Sultan Moulay Youssef. A fine *medersa* was built under the Merinids, as they sought to expand Sunni orthodoxy to reduce the influence of Soufi leaders.

The reign of Moulay Ismaïl

The reign of the Alaouite sultan, Moulay Ismaïl (1672-1727), saw Meknès raised to the status of imperial capital. Even before his succession to the imperial throne, Moulay Ismaïl developed the city. Meknès was chosen as his capital rather than the rebellious and self-important rivals of Fès and Marrakech. Moulay Ismaïl is renowned for his ruthless violence,

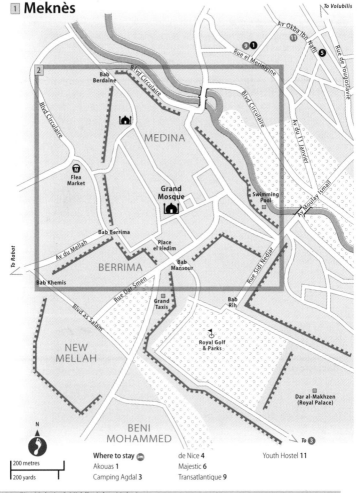

1 Meknès

Where to stay
Akouas **1**
Camping Agdal **3**
de Nice **4**
Majestic **6**
Transatlantique **9**
Youth Hostel **11**

200 metres
200 yards

but many of the stories recounted by the guides may be apocryphal. What is certain is that he made an impression on European visitors to the court. Meknès was described as a Moroccan Versailles. Indeed, some suggest that the sultan was trying to rival Louis XIV, then involved in building his palace complex outside Paris. Having conquered Morocco, Moulay Ismaïl left his mark all over the country. Kasbahs were built by his troops as they pacified the tribes, cities acquired mosques and public buildings.

Moulay Ismaïl's vision of Meknès was vast and, although much of the *pisé* and rubble walls are in ruins, those still standing are testimony to its original scale. The city was built by a massive army of slaves, both Muslim and Christian, and the sultan was notorious

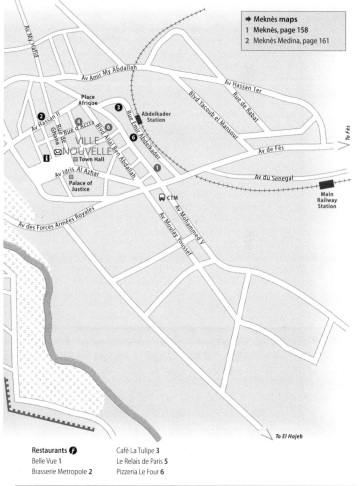

➡ **Meknès maps**
1 Meknès, page 158
2 Meknès Medina, page 161

Restaurants ❶
Belle Vue 1
Brasserie Metropole 2

Café La Tulipe 3
Le Relais de Paris 5
Pizzeria Le Four 6

for his barbaric treatment of these people, supposedly having them buried in the walls among other horrors. He built several palaces to accommodate his wives, concubines, children and court, as well as quarters for his army, the Abid Bukhari, an élite praetorian guard of black slaves, the chief instrument of his power. The city contained within it all that was necessary for such a large military machine, with store houses, stables, armouries, gardens and reservoirs.

After Moulay Ismaïl

After Moulay Ismaïl's death, Meknès gradually declined. His huge court and army could not be held together without his immense ego, and his successors, Moulay Abdallah and Sidi Mohammed, returned the emphasis to Fès and Marrakech. Furthermore, the earthquake of 1755 destroyed many of Moulay Ismaïl's creations. The French revitalized Meknès, appreciating its strategic position in the corridor linking eastern Morocco and Algeria with the coastal belt around Rabat and Casablanca. They built their *ville nouvelle* apart from the medina and the imperial city, on the east bank of the Oued Boufekrane, as part of their policy of separate development of Moroccan and European quarters. During the protectorate, Meknès became the most important garrison town in Morocco and continued as an important military town after independence.

Meknès today

Although Meknès is perhaps overshadowed by its near-neighbour Fès, it is today the fifth largest city in Morocco, with both tourism and industrial activities, and is the centre of a highly productive agricultural region. After a period of relative stagnation, Meknès is re-emerging as an important town. National planners made the city capital of the Meknès-Tafilalelt region, which extends southeast to Er Rachidia, Erfoud and Rissani down one of the country's most strategic lines of communication. The late 1990s saw a spate of new building, not all of it in keeping with the city's character. Along with assorted concrete blocks, a McDonald's has gone up on the corridor of parkland designed as a green lung for the heart of the city. And, horror of horrors, some philistine has put up a low-rise housing block in the heart of the medina, higher than some of the minarets.

Lovers of Moroccan red wines will find place names in the region south of Meknès familiar. The country's best vineyards are located here, near settlements like Aït Souala, Aït Yazm and Agouraï. Quality is improving, with foreign investors putting money into improved vinification methods and makers from Bordeaux and other renowned wine regions bringing their knowledge to the industry.

Places in Meknès

Meknès is a striking town, a fact accentuated by the distant backdrop views of the **Jbel Zerhoun**, which rises to over 1000 m to the north. The wooded foothills and orchards of olives, apples and pears below provide a green setting to the city for much of the year. One of the great imperial cities of Morocco, it is now more memorable for the impressive sense of scale and feeling of space than for any existing historic architecture. Another distinct part of Meknès is the **medina**, which includes the intricately decorated Medersa Bou Inania, vibrant souks, the Dar Jamaï palace museum and numerous mosques. The cream-washed walls and daily life of the residential areas just behind Rue Dar Smen still carry an antiquated 'Morocco that was' feel about them. To the east of the medina, on the opposite bank of the Oued Boufekrane, there stands the early 20th-century *ville nouvelle*. Carefully laid out by planner Henri Prost, the new town commands impressive (and as yet unspoiled) views over both medina and the imperial city. It has a relaxed atmosphere and is a calm place to drink a coffee or tea and watch the evening promenade. Meknès is one of the easiest imperial cities to explore independently, but there is no shortage of faux guides offering their services in Place el Hedim and nearby. If you need assistance, obtain an official guide from the tourist office or one of the larger hotels. About 150dh is a realistic fee.

Medina

Place el Hedim (the Square of Destruction), opposite Bab Mansour, is the centre of Meknès' old city and the best starting point for exploration. The biggest open square in the city, it was once as busy as the Jemaá el Fna in Marrakech (see page 50), filled with acrobats, storytellers and snake charmers plying their trade. Despite its name, the square is now a quiet place with some cheap cafés at the far end, opposite Bab Mansour. Renovation works are underway and, hopefully, the square will remain the central place to stroll on a Meknès evening rather than becoming a car park. To the left of the square is a crowded, covered **food market**, with bright displays of fresh vegetables and pickles; definitely worth a look. On the right-hand corner of the square down a few steps is **Dar Jamaï**, a 19th-century

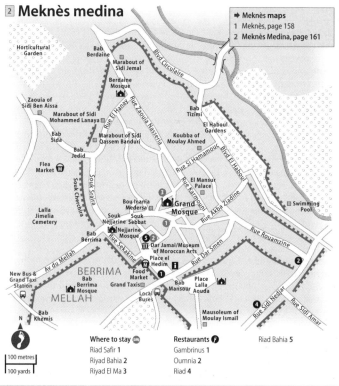

2 Meknès medina

➡ Meknès maps
1 Meknès, page 158
2 Meknès Medina, page 161

Horticultural Garden
Bab Berdaine
Marabout of Sidi Jemal
Blvd Circulaire
Berdaine Mosque
Rue El Hanah
Rue Zaouia Nasseria
Zaouia of Sidi Ben Aissa
Marabout of Sidi Mohammed Lanaya
Bab Tizimi
El Haboul Gardens
Bab Sida
Marabout of Sidi Qassem Banduri
Koubba of Moulay Ahmed
Rue Sti Hamamout
Blvd El Haboul
Bab Jedid
Flea Market
Souk Cherchira
Souk Sraila
Rue Karmouni
El Mansur Palace
Rue Akba Ziadine
Swimming Pool
Lalla Jimelia Cemetery
Bou Inania Medersa
Grand Mosque
Souk Nejjarine Sebbat
Nejjarine Mosque
Rue Rouamzine
Bab Berrima
Rue Setakine
Dar Jamai/Museum of Moroccan Arts
Rue Dar Smen
Ay du Mellah
BERRIMA
Bab Berrima Mosque
Food Market
Place el Hedim
Place Lalla Aouda
New Bus & Grand Taxi Station
MELLAH
Grand Taxis
Bab Mansour
Rue Rouamzine
Local Buses
Rue Sidi Nedjar
Rue Sidi Amar
Bab Khemis
Mausoleum of Moulay Ismaïl

N

100 metres
100 yards

Where to stay
Riad Safir 1
Riyad Bahia 2
Riyad El Ma 3

Restaurants
Gambrinus 1
Oumnia 2
Riad 4

Riad Bahia 5

palace, owned by officials at the court of Sultan Moulay Hassan, and now the **Museum of Moroccan Arts** ⓘ *T0535-530863, Wed-Mon 0900-1700, 10dh*. Built in 1882, it was the residence of the Jamaï family, two members of which were ministers to Moulay Hassan. It was used as a military hospital after 1912 and in 1920 became a museum. Exploring the house gives an insight into the lifestyle of the 19th-century Muslim élite. On display are wrought iron, carved wood, weaving, leather and metal work, and various antique household items. Look out for richly painted wooden chests and panels. Upstairs is a furnished reception room. The garden planted with cypress and fruit trees is a pleasant halt in the heat of the day.

The medina of Meknès has seven traditional **souks**, which, while not quite of the order of those in Marrakech or Fès, are nevertheless well worth exploring. Immediately to the left of the Dar Jamaï a small entrance leads to the souks. The alley bends around to the right behind Dar Jamaï past some undistinguished clothes shops. Just before a carpet shop turn left. The passage, now covered, widens slightly, and continues past a range of shops selling modern goods, a bank, and various minor side turnings. At the junction, on the left, is **Souk Nejjarine**, which includes textile-sellers and carpenters, another entrance to the carpet souk and a fondouk hardly changed since it was built. This route passes the Almoravid **Nejjarine Mosque**. At the end, one can turn left towards the mellah or Place el Hedim or right into the dusty and noisy **Souk Sraira**, just inside the city walls, used by carpenters and metalworkers. At the very end, on the left, is the 12th-century Almohad **Bab Jedid** gate, around which are some interesting stalls selling musical instruments. **Souk Cherchira**, initially occupied by tent-makers, runs parallel to Souk Sraira but outside the city walls. **Souk Sebbat** is the right-hand turning opposite Souk Nejjarine and includes sellers of *babouches*, modern clothes and caftans, several tourist and handicraft shops, a *fondouk* on the right and another on the left, before the Bou Inania Medersa. A turning on the right opposite the *medersa* leads directly onto Rue Dar Smen, a good alternative route to remember.

Best approached from Souk Sebbat is the **Bou Inania Medersa** ⓘ *0900-1200, 1500-1800. Climb up onto the roof for a view of the medina, including the roofs of the Great Mosque, the minaret of the Nejjarine and other mosques.* Founded circa 1345 by Merinid Sultan Abou el Hassan, this former college dispensing religious and legal instruction is a must-visit. The door to the *medersa*, part of a cedar screen, is just under a dome (notable for its ribbed design) at an intersection in the souk. Altogether, the college had 40 cells for its students, on both floors, around an oblong courtyard including a pool, with arcades surrounded by a screened passageway. As with many of the *medersas*, there is eye-catching *zellige* tiling and carved wood lintels. Take a look at the green-and-yellow tiled prayer hall. The doorway is ornamented with *zellige* tiling, as well as the customary and, perhaps, a little over-the-top stalactite-style plasterwork.

Nearby, the **Grand Mosque**, situated in the heart of the medina, is a 12th-century Almoravid foundation with 14th-century alterations. It is one of the oldest in Meknès and also the largest. Although non-Muslims are not permitted to enter the mosque, it is possible to view its lovely green-tiled roof and the minaret from the neighbouring Medersa Bou Inania (see above).

Mellah

To the west of Place el Hedim, through a street popular with hawkers of household goods, turn left into Avenue de Mellah. On the left is the mellah, a quarter built by Moulay Ismaïl in 1682 for his large Jewish community, which was walled off from the Muslim medina. The

Bab Berrima Mosque dates from the 18th century, a time when the mellah was becoming increasingly Muslim. Few members of Meknès's once important Jewish community remain today, however.

Bab el Khemis

Heading southwest towards Rabat, the city wall is broken by Bab el Khemis, built by Moulay Ismaïl, with a range of different arches, decoration and calligraphy. This is the only remaining piece of the garden quarter attributed to Moulay Ismaïl. The rest has gone. It was destroyed by Moulay Abdallah, son of the great Moulay Ismaïl, who was not pleased by the reception he received from the inhabitants when he returned from an unsuccessful campaign. After this, the Boulevard Circulaire leads past a cemetery containing the 18th-century tomb of Sidi Mohammed Ben Aissa, founder of the important religious brotherhood of the Aissoua. It's closed to non-Muslims but worth a look from a respectable distance. The Ben Aissa religious ceremonies are still held on the Mouloud (Prophet Mohammed's birthday). The Boulevard Circulaire continues round to Bab Berdaine, the entrance to the north medina.

Northern medina

Less frequented by tourists, the northern medina is reached by either weaving through the streets from the *medersa* or the souks or, more easily, coming round on the Boulevard Circulaire. **Bab Berdaine** dates from the 17th century, a building decorated by Jamaâ el Rouah and flanked by two immense towers. Inside, on Place el Berdaine, is the **Berdaine Mosque**. Travelling south, the streets continue through an area of the traditional medina, only occasionally spoilt by insensitive new building. Here you are in traditional neighbourhoods where private and public space are clearly differentiated, each quarter having its own mosque, hammam and public oven.

Back on the Boulevard Circulaire, the next major gate around towards Oued Boufekrane is **Bab Tizmi**, near to **Restaurant Zitouna**. Opposite Bab Tizmi is the quiet **Parc el Haboul**, part of an area of gardens and recreational facilities in the valley, dividing the medina and the *ville nouvelle*.

Bab Mansour

Claimed by some to be the finest gateway in North Africa, Meknès is dominated by this monumental gate at the top of the hill in the medina, opposite Place el Hedim. It dates from the reign of Sultan Moulay Ismaïl and was completed by his son Moulay Mohammed Ben Abdallah in 1732, and marks the entrance to the huge grounds of his imperial city. The gate is named after one of the sultan's Christian slaves, Mansour the Infidel. The huge size is more of a testimony to its sultan than a reflection of defensive strength. The gate is clearly more about imperial splendour than anything else. The decorated flanking towers do not even have firing posts. The outrepassé arch is surrounded by a blind arch, including the usual lozenge network motif and *zellige* tiling. Between the arch and framing band is a black-tiled area with floral patterns. The overall effect of the main gate is exuberant and powerful. The gate has come to be a symbol of Meknès, even of Morocco as a whole.

Imperial city

The imperial city of Moulay Ismaïl is a massive area of crumbling walls and ruins, well worth taking a day to explore at leisure. Immediately through Bab Mansour from Place el Hedim is **Place Lalla Aouda**, once the public meeting point during the period of Moulay

Ismaïl and now a relaxing and pleasant area to rest. In the far corner is the **Lalla Aouda Mosque**, the story being that it was built by Princess Aouda as penance for eating a peach during the Ramadan fast.

Directly opposite Bab Mansour, in the right-hand corner of the square, a space in the walls leads through to a second square, the **Mechouar**. To the right note the domed **Koubat al Khayyatine** ⓘ *on the left of the entrance to the building, tickets 10dh,* a plain building with pleasing simple decor situated in a small park behind a fence. In the 18th century this was used to receive ambassadors and, later, to make uniforms. Koubat el Khayyatine translates as 'the tailors' dome'. Inside is a display of photos of old Meknès. Outside, right of the entrance, a flight of stairs leads down to dank and vaulted underground chambers, said by guides to be the prison of the Christian slaves, although why one should want to keep a workforce down here is anyone's guess.

In the wall opposite the small park the right-hand gate leads to a golf course. This was originally to have been a lake, but was converted to its present use by the king. Behind the golf course is a later palace of Moulay Ismaïl, the **Royal Palace** or **Dar al Makhzen** ⓘ *closed to visitors*, still in use and now heavily restored.

South of Place Lalla Aouda, the **Mausoleum of Moulay Ismaïl** ⓘ *access via the monumental entrance in the cream wall opposite an arcade of craft shops (stock-up on film here), entrance fee (sometimes),* contains the tombs of Moulay Ismaïl, his wife and Moulay Ahmed. Unusually for religious buildings in Morocco, the mausoleum is open to non-Muslims. These visitors can enter as far as an annex to the mosque section and admire from there the plaster stucco, *zellige* tiling and distinctive and exuberant colouring. The guardian normally allows visitors to take photos of the interior of the mosque from the annex.

Just past the mausoleum is an entrance to **Dar el Kebira** ('the big house'), Moulay Ismaïl's late 17th-century palace. The palace is in ruins, but the nature of the original structure of the building can be discerned. Since the 18th century, houses have been built into the walls of the palace. Back out on the road, pass under the passage of the **Bab ar Rih** ('Gate of the Winds'), a long, arched structure. Follow the walled road, running between the Dar el Kebira and the Dar al Makhzen and turn right at the end. Carry straight ahead through another arch and, after around 200 m, you reach another chunky *pisé* wall, the Heri es Souani building.

Heri es-Souani
ⓘ *0830-1200, 1430-1830.*
Close to the city campsite and a hefty 35-minute walk from the medina, Heri es Souani, also called Dar el Ma ('the Water Palace'), is a large, impressive structure, also dating from the reign of Moulay Ismaïl and used variously as granary, warehouse and water point to provide for the court, army and followers in either the normal run of events or in case of emergencies, such as conflict or drought. It is a good indication of the scale of Moulay Ismaïl's imperial ambitions. From the roof there would be a good view, if one were allowed up. The nearby Agdal basin is now used for storing water for irrigation purposes. Once it was presumably a vital reserve in case of siege. Popular with strollers at weekends and on summer evenings, the location is a little stark on a hot summer afternoon, so have a post-visit drink at the café in the nearby campsite.

Moulay Idriss and Volubilis → *For listings, see pages 168-172. Colour map 1, B3.*

The shrine town of Moulay Idriss and the Roman ruins at Volubilis are an easy day trip from Meknès, although there is a hotel at Volubilis and more at Moulay Idriss for those who want to stay over and get a really early start, a good idea in summer when the heat can be oppressive. Volubilis, set in open fields, is a delight in spring, with wild flowers abounding. The ruins, covering over 40 ha, have poetic names – the House of Orpheus and the House of the Nymphs, the House of the Athlete and the House of the Ephèbe, and there is a noble forum, a triumphal arch to Caracalla as well as ancient oil presses. The vanished splendour of Volubilis is echoed by legendary evocations of early Islam at Moulay Idriss nearby. This most venerable pilgrimage centre, set between steep hillsides, was founded in the eighth century by one Idriss Ibn Abdallah, great-grandson of Ali and Fatima, the Prophet Mohammed's daughter. Today he is referred to as Idriss el Akbar, 'the Great'. His son, Idriss II, is buried and venerated in Fès.

Arriving in Moulay Idriss and Volubilis

Getting there Moulay Idriss is 30 km north of Meknès; Volubilis a little further north. For Moulay Idriss, take a *grand taxi* from Rue de Yougoslavie, or from the square below Place el Hedim (a 10dh ride). There are also regular buses from below Bab Mansour. The last bus back is at 1900. Volubilis is a clearly signposted 5-km drive from Moulay Idriss, a pleasant walk on a nice day, or a short taxi ride. Alternatively, for Volubilis bargain in Meknès for a *grand taxi* (split cost with others, say 50dh the trip), or take a bus for Ouezzane and get dropped off near the site. If travelling by car, leave Meknès by Rue de Yougoslavie in the *ville nouvelle*, and follow the R410 as far as Aïn el Kerma, and from there the N13 to Moulay Idriss.

Moulay Idriss

Coming round the last bend from Meknès, Moulay Idriss is a dramatic sight; houses and mosques piled up around two rocky outcrops, with the *zaouïa*, or sanctuary, in between. The centre of the Jbel Zerhoun region, Moulay Idriss is a pilgrimage centre, including as it does the tomb of its namesake, Idriss Ben Abdallah Ben Hassan Ben Ali, the great-great-grandson of the prophet Mohammed. The town is an alternative to Mecca in Morocco for those unable to do the ultimate pilgrimage. Moulay Idriss came to Morocco from Arabia, after defeat at the Battle of Fakh in 786. In 788 he was accepted as imam by the Amazigh Aurora tribe at Volubilis and continued the rest of his life in Morocco, before he was poisoned in 791, to win over the loyalty of the tribes to the Idrissid Dynasty he established, and to spread the faith of Islam. This town and Fès were two of his major legacies.

However, the town of Moulay Idriss was mainly developed in the 18th century by Sultan Moulay Ismaïl, in part using materials lifted from nearby Volubilis, which the sultan plundered without restraint. Moulay Idriss was closed to non-Muslims until 1912 and, even today, is primarily a Muslim sanctuary, best visited during the day as an excursion and, although not unfriendly, certainly a place to be treated with cautious respect. A religious festival, or *moussem*, is held here in August, when the town is transformed by an influx of pilgrims and a sea of tents.

Buses and taxis stop in the main square, where there are some basic restaurants and cafés. Above it is the **Zaouïa of Moulay Idriss**, as well as shops for various souvenir items associated with pilgrimage: rosaries, scarves, candles and a delicious array of nougats, candies and nuts. The sanctuary itself, with its green-tiled roofs, a succession of prayer halls, ablution areas and tombs, is closed to non-Muslims.

Looking up from the square, the medina clings to the two hills, on the left is Khiba, while Tasga is on the right. Steep paths climb through the residential areas. After the climb, there is a rewarding view over the sanctuary, showing the courtyards and roofs, and the adjacent royal guesthouse. The road through the town, keeping right, leads to a Roman bath just above the stream. Further on, beyond the road, there is a ruined 18th-century palace with a good view of the town.

Volubilis

ⓘ *Below the Jbel Zerhoun and 5 km from Moulay Idriss along the N13, the site is signed from the road, has parking (10dh usually), a café and ticket office but little else. It can be viewed in a day trip. In summer, start early to avoid the heat. On the way in, note the collection of mosaics and sculptures, an 'open-air museum'. Open 0800 to sunset. 20dh.*

Volubilis is by far the most impressive Roman site in Morocco and sits in a spectacular spot, with the hills and Moulay Idriss behind, vast views over the plain below. While much has been removed to adorn other cities over the centuries, or taken to museums such as the one in Rabat, the structure of the town is largely intact, the design of the buildings clearly discernible from the ruins. Many floor mosaics remain, remarkably unaffected by the passing centuries.

Background Archaeological evidence points to the possibility of a Neolithic settlement at Volubilis, while tablets found show there was a third-century BC Phoenician settlement. In AD 24 it was the western capital of the Roman kingdom of Mauretania, and from AD 45 to 285 the capital of the Roman province of Mauretania Tingitana. Under the Romans the immediate region prospered from producing olive oil. However, as Volubilis was at the southeastern extremity of the province, connected to Rome through the Atlantic ports, its weak position necessitated extensive city walls.

Under the Emperor Diocletian, Rome withdrew to the coastal areas, leaving Volubilis at the mercy of neighbouring tribes. The city survived but its Christian and Jewish population diminished in importance, becoming the Christian enclave of Oualila during the eighth century. Though proclaimed sultan in Volubilis, Moulay Idriss preferred Fès. By the 11th century, Volubilis was totally deserted. It suffered again when Moulay Ismaïl ransacked the ruins to build Meknès and, further, in the earthquake of 1755. French excavations and reconstruction began in 1915. The metal tracks on the site date from this period.

The site From the ticket office the entrance to the city is by the southeastern gate. A path, with sculptures and tombstones alongside it, leads down to a bridge across the Oued Fetassa. Up on the other side the first important remains in an area of small houses and industrial units are of an **olive press complex**. The mill stones, for crushing the olives, and the tanks for collecting and separating the oil, can be seen. Olive presses can be found through much of the city, as olive oil production was as essential an element in its economy as it is in the area today. Many of the same techniques are still used.

Right of the olive press is the **House of Orpheus**, a large mansion. In this building, as in most, some areas will be clearly roped off, and it is advisable to respect this, to avoid the whistle and wrath of the otherwise very friendly guardian. The first entrance gives access to a room with an intricate dolphin mosaic, to a kitchen with a niche for religious figures, and to a paved bathroom and boiler room. Note the complex heating system. The second entrance leads to an open court with a mosaic of the goddess Amphitrite, with living rooms around it, including a dining room with an Orpheus mosaic, showing the hero playing his harp.

Roman imperial settlements, even the most provincial, had impressive arrays of public buildings to cement a general feeling of Romanity. This was architecture as identity, and Volubilis was no exception. Heading further down into the site, and then to the right, lie the **Baths of Gallienus**, public baths which are the distant ancestor of the Moroccan hammam. Beyond this, the large public square in front of the Basilica is the **Forum**. In this area are a number of monuments to leading Roman figures. The **Basilica** is one of the most impressive ruins, with a number of columns still intact. This third-century building was the court house for the city.

Beside the Basilica is the **Capitol**, also with columns. In the court in front there is an altar and steps leading up to the **temple** dedicated to Juno, Minerva and Jupiter Optimus Maximus. This building had great state importance, being the place where the council would assemble on great occasions.

Volubilis

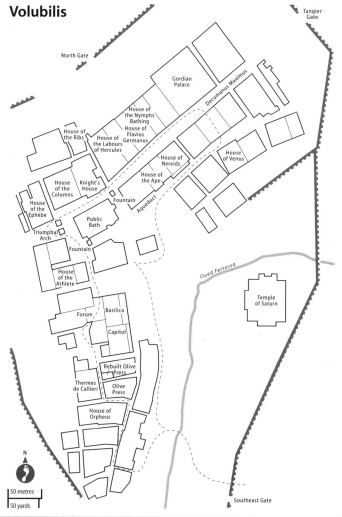

Adjacent to the Forum is the **House of the Athlete**, named after the mosaic of an athlete winning a cup. The Triumphal Arch dominates the skyline, as well as the Decumanus Maximus, the roadway leading to the Tangier Gate. This was built in AD 217 to honour Emperor Caracalla and his mother Julia Domna. Originally finished with fountains and medallions, the arch was heavily reconstructed by French archaeologists. Although not of the same finesse as the honorary arches surviving in the Roman cities of Tunisia and Libya, it is nevertheless impressive. The Decumanus Maximus, the main street, had a colonnade with small shops, in front of a series of large houses, some containing interesting mosaics.

Starting on the left, from just beside the Triumphal Arch, the **House of the Ephèbe** was built around a courtyard with a pool. The house is named after the bronze statue of a beautiful boy or *ephebos* found in the ruins. Adjacent is the **House of Columns** and then the **Knight's House**, which has an interesting mosaic of Bacchus, good-time god of wine. In a more serious taste, the **House of the Labours of Hercules** has a mosaic with individual pictures of Hercules's life, and another of Jupiter. Further up, the **House of the Nymphs Bathing** has a mosaic showing nymphs undressing. The largest house on this side, the **Gordian Palace**, is fronted by columns, but the remains are quite plain. This may have been the governor's residence from the time of Gordian III, with both domestic quarters and offices.

On the right-hand side of Decumanus Maximus from the Triumphal Arch there is a large **public bath and fountains**, fed by an aqueduct. Three houses up is the **House of Nereids** with a pool mosaic. Behind this and one up is the House of Venus, which has one of the best arrays of mosaics. The central courtyard pool has a mosaic of chariots. There are also mosaics of Bacchus, on the left, and Hylos and two nymphs, on the right. Nearby is a mosaic of Diana and the horned Actaeon. From the House of Venus cross back over the Oued Fetassa to the remains of the **Temple of Saturn**, a Phoenician temple before the Romans took it over. From here, follow the path back to the entrance, perhaps for refreshments in the café.

☻ Meknès listings

For sleeping and eating price codes and other relevant information, see pages 22-28.

☻ Where to stay

Meknès medina *p161, map p161*
At peak times, especially spring holidays, book in advance or arrive early.

€€€ Riad Safir, 1 Derb Lalla Alamia, Bab Aissi, T0535-534785, www.riadsafir.com. This riad expanded recently to incorporate the house next door and now combines 2 quite different, though equally stylish, spaces. The first house is cosy and bohemian, filled with warm red and orange textiles and lots of carved wood detailing. The second offers a more contemporary interpretation of Moroccan architecture, with cooling greys and greens. All 7 rooms have bags of character and plenty of space.

The food is good too, but needs to be booked 3 hrs in advance (better still in the morning) and there are lounges for relaxing, a massage room and spacious roof terrace.

€€ Riyad Bahia, 13 Tiberbarine, T0535-554541, www.ryad-bahia.com. This is a pretty little guesthouse with a comfortable, laid-back vibe. Owners Abdellatif and Bouchra are well travelled themselves and so understand the needs of other like-minded souls. Rooms are decorated with antique wooden doors, low tables and cushions, and all have big beds with soft linens; suites have fireplaces. Some have windows onto the street as well as the lushly planted courtyard. There's also Wi-Fi and a multi-levelled terrace with good views over the city, but the best thing is Bouchra's cooking, among the best in Morocco.

€€-€ **Riad El Ma**, 4 derb Sidi Besri, T0661-514824, www.riad-el-ma.com. An atmospheric riad, big on original details, such as ornate plasterwork, painted doors and *zellige* tiles, complemented by home-away-from-home service. The 6 rooms have colour themes, private bathrooms and big, comfortable beds. The large central courtyard creates a great sense of space. There's also a library, a dining room for breakfasts and evening meals (book in advance) and a small, corner rooftop pool.

Meknès ville nouvelle *map p158*
There are some very reasonably priced central hotels here. Some of the older ones near the top end of Av Mohammed V and the Av des FAR, however, tend to be noisy, due to the number of bars in the vicinity.
€€€ **Hotel Transatlantique**, Rue el Meriniyine, T0535-525051, transat@iam.net. ma. This centrally located hotel is one of the better choices in Meknès if you're looking for European-style comforts, though it falls short of its 4-star status. It has 120 a/c rooms, 2 restaurants, a bar, tennis courts, and 2 fair-sized pools, and they accept credit cards. It dates back to the 1930s, when it was probably quite smart, and retains a certain faded glory, particularly in the old wing (*l'aile ancienne*), where rooms have balconies and views over the gardens or the medina. They are a little tatty, however, and the 60 rooms of the new wing, built in the 1960s, have been modernized with a few more creature comforts.
€€ **Akouas Hotel**, 27 Rue Emir Abdelkader, T0535-515967, www.hotelakouas.com. This mid-sized, modern hotel is a good deal, especially for those looking for nightlife. Spread over 7 floors with uninspired but perfectly decent decor, it has a small pool and bar, although the on-site nightclub can be noisy.
€€ **Hotel de Nice**, 10 Rue d'Accra, T0535-520318. This is a reasonable mid-range option, centrally located, squeaky clean and comfortable, with some welcome modern

touches. Although it's not exactly brimming with personality, all rooms are en suite with pretty, planted balconies. It also has a restaurant (breakfasts are generous and varied), a licensed bar and safe parking.
€ **Hotel Majestic**, 19 Av Mohammed V, T0535-522033. A quirky, but in some ways quite fabulous old 1930s-style place, this is a great pad for lovers of kitsch. There are 47 clean rooms, each panelled in dark wood beneath layers of varnish and purple bedspreads. Rooms on street are on the noisy side, so it's worth opting for a quieter inner room. Although most only stay here 1 night for its location to the station, it does provide a taste of old Morocco, is good value and reasonably friendly.
€ **Youth hostel**, Av Okba Ibn Nafii, near the municipal stadium and **Hotel Transatlantique**, T0535-524698, www. hihostels.com. Open 1000-1200 and 1600-1700. This is the HI's headquarters in Morocco and is one of the best and most friendly hostels in Morocco, with dorms arranged around a garden. Clean, comfortable and well maintained, it has a total of 60 beds costing 25-35dh per night, a communal kitchen and meals available on request. It's 25 m from the bus stop, and just over 1 km from the train station.

Camping
Camping Agdal, 2 km out of Meknès centre, opposite the Heri es Souani, T0535-551828. To get here take buses Nos 2 or 3, or better, a *petit taxi* from Meknès town centre. The 4-ha site has a shop, café, laundry, electricity for caravans, hot showers, plenty of shaded areas for pitching a tent and is clean and well organized. It now offers some rooms, which are a cheap alternative to a hotel. The site serves alcohol and it can get a bit noisy near the café area, especially once the piped music gets going, but it's a great little site for one so close to the city.
Camping Belle-Vue, on the road to Moulay Idriss some 15 km north, T0668-490899. This is a smaller site of around 3 ha set

in beautiful countryside. It costs 60dh for 2 people with car and tent, and has a small shop, showers, laundry, electricity for caravans, and petrol just 100 m away. But the toilet blocks could do with some maintenance.

Moulay Idriss p164

Since the king suggested that the notion that non-Muslims couldn't stay overnight in Moulay was outdated, riad owners have started moving in on Moulay and accommodation is slowly improving, though much of it is still fairly basic.

€€ **Dar Zerhoune**, T0642-247793, http://buttonsinn.com. Far and away the best place in town. A boutique-style guesthouse with just 4 rooms, all simply but very comfortably decorated, with large bathrooms, quality bed linens and some great details, such as the sea serpent table legs and flea market finds. The New Zealand owner Rose Button makes the experience a special one, and you'll find lots of great homely touches here from highly sociable breakfasts and dinners on the roof, to arranging henna sessions, carpet-buying trips and cooking classes with local women.

€€ **Hannaoui**, 5 Rue Ben Yazgha, T0535-544106, zakia_hanaoui_5@hotmail.com. Contemporary Moroccan style, this is a friendly and enthusiastic place with views over the stream and mountain. The 'hammam' is little more than a bathroom with a big heater, but it has lots of well-labelled herbs and local plants.

€ **Scorpion House**, 54 Drouj El Hafa, T0655-210172, www.scorpionhouse.com. Mike Richardson of Fès's famed **Café Clock** expanded his business to Moulay Idriss in 2011 opening this place as Café Clock II. It's well worth the steep climb to get up to the café decorated in trademark Richardson style with specially commissioned tiles from the village, art deco finds from the mellah in Fès and natty furniture giving it a contemporary feel. It has a couple of gardens and terraces cascading off the main

dining room and serves excellent fresh soups, salads and sandwiches from produce grown in the garden as well as traditional *mechouia* (Moroccan-style barbecue).

Camping

Zerhoune Belle Vue, en route to Meknès. Also, the proprietor of the café allows people to camp opposite the turning to Volubilis.

🍴 Restaurants

Meknès medina *p161, map p161*
Meknès has a small but growing range of Moroccan restaurants catering mainly to tour groups.

€€ **Café Restaurant Gambrinus**, Av Omar Ibn el Ass, opposite the market, off Av Hassan II, T0535-520258. This friendly little place serves French, Spanish and Moroccan cuisine, and it's a reliable lunch stop for refuelling. Interesting wall murals give it the edge over similar places.

€€ **Restaurant Riad**, 79 Ksar Chaacha, T0535-530542. This rather good medina restaurant offers a range of traditional Moroccan menus concentrate on the classics, such as beef and prune tagine, pigeon *pastilla* and couscous on Fri. It has no alcohol licence and can fill up with tour groups, but one of its great advantages is being able to eat outside in a garden filled with flowers and cacti and a small, slightly unkempt pool.

€€ **Riad Bahia**, 13 Tiberbarine, T0535-554541, www.ryad-bahia.com (see also Where to stay, above). One of the best places in the medina, offering an excellent and varied range of tagines including lamb and aubergine or apricots, chicken and preserved lemon, and beef with prunes. It's all very calm and orderly, yet authentically Moroccan, with leather pouffes, abundant carved wood and a well-planted courtyard. Advance booking essential.

€ **Oumnia**, 8 Ain Fouki Rouamzine, T0535-533938. A cosy little family-run place with a good-value fixed menu of Moroccan staples. Follow the signs off Rue Rouamzine.

Two sides of Pl el Hédim fill up with street foodstalls hawking a preponderance of brochettes. There's not much to choose between them, so take a wander and see what takes your fancy.

Meknès ville nouvelle map p158

€€€ **Le Relais de Paris**, 46 Rue Oqba – Ibn Nafia, T0619-210210. This smart French restaurant is considered one of the best in Morocco, even among the French. Impeccable decor, a romantic atmosphere and the attentive service of manager Philippe add to the sense of occasion, with classy bistro-style dishes served. All products are sourced locally and freshly made each day. Try the goat's cheese salad, grilled duck breast and gooey tarte tatin.

€€€ **Restaurant Belle Vue**, in Hotel Transatlantique, Rue el Marinyen, T0535-525051. The restaurant has an extensive international menu of varying quality – it's better to stick to Moroccan dishes – but the wines are good and it has wonderful views over Meknès medina from its hilltop location, which is the main reason to come here.

€€ **Pizzeria Le Four**, 1 Rue Atlas, T0535-520857. A licensed place around the corner from the station, it's popular with expats, local businessmen and students, and independent travellers, largely for a cool beer and a pizza. The atmosphere is fairly lively and it's a good place to meet people (and take a break from Moroccan tagines and couscous if you've been on the road a while).

€€ **Restaurant Bar Brasserie Metropole**, 12 Av Hassan II, on the corner near the Central (food) Market, T0535-522576. Serves good brochettes, roast chicken, and it's licensed.

Otherwise, try the cheap and cheerful roast chicken shacks (€) on Av Mohammed V, uphill from the Hotel Majestic, opposite the BCM: **Coq Magique** and **Restaurant Sana**.

Cafés
Meknès produces the best mint in Morocco, so don't pass up a chance to get your fix of mint tea here. Try one of the noisy cafés on Rue Dar Smen.

Café la Tulipe, Pl Maarakat Lahri, T0535-511094. This big bustling place with plush wicker chairs under the trees is a charming place for a pot of mint tea watching the world go by. It also serves excellent cakes and pastries and good ice cream in the summer.

🎶 Bars and clubs

Meknès p157, map p158 and p161
As a traditional Moroccan town, Meknès is surprisingly lively, with a fairly upbeat scene. It has several bars and nightclubs and a comparatively happy-go-lucky attitude to drinking and dancing.
Bar Continental, Av Hassan II.
Hotel Transatlantique, Rue el Marinyen. An excellent place for a relaxing drink, not least because of the view over the medina.
Hotel de Nice, 10 Rue d'Accra.
La Caravelle, 6 Rue de Marseille.
La Coupole, Av Hassan II.

⚙ What to do

Meknès p157, map p158 and p161
Hammam
Hammam des Jardins, aka Hammam Maha, very handy for the *ville nouvelle*. Heading towards the medina on Av Hassan II, take a right between **BCM** and **Agora** salon de thé. After 25 m, drop left down some steps, then go right. The hammam, with separate entrances for men and women, overlooks a semi-abandoned small park.
Hammam Sidi Omar Bou Aouada, turn right as you face Dar Jamaï museum on Pl Hedim, baths on your right about 25 m further on, unmarked.

⊖ Transport

Meknès p157, map p158 and p161
Bus
Local buses No 5, 7 and 9 run between the *ville nouvelle* and the medina. **CTM** buses to **Rabat** (5 hrs), **Casablanca** and **Fès** (7 a day), **Tangier** (7 hrs), **Ifrane**, **Azrou**, **Ouezzane**

and **Er Rachidia** (daily) leave from 47 Av Mohammed V, T0535-522583/4. Private lines go from the terminal below Bab Mansour.

Car hire

Stop Car, 3 Rue Essaouira, T0535-525061, and **Zeit**, 4 Rue Antsirebe, T0535-525918. If driving up from Marrakech, there are some beautiful views on the Azrou to Meknès route (the N13), with the Belvédère d'Ito, or you can turn onto the R212, which will take you from Mrirt through fine landscapes to join the N13 north of El Hajeb.

Taxi

Grands taxis, which are a particularly good option to both **Fès** and **Azrou**, leave from the car park below Pl el Hedim, opposite the private line buses. Ask the drivers hanging around for the destination. For **Moulay Idriss** (and then a short walk to **Volubilis**) they leave from near the Shell station on your right as Av Hassan II descends. Negotiations over prices can be long and painful, with various people hanging around to act as intermediaries and take their cut. See also the taxi rank near the Palais de la Foire. Light blue *petits taxis* hop between *ville nouvelle* and medina.

Train

The main station is some way from the centre, T0535-520017/520689. Regular departures for **Rabat** and **Casablanca**, **Tangier** (with a change at Sidi Kacem), and eastwards for **Fès**, **Taza** and **Oujda**.

❶ Directory

Meknès *p157*, *map p158 and p161*
Airline offices Royal Air Maroc, 7 Av Mohammed V, T0535-520963/523606. Closest airport is at Fès. **Banks** Banque du Maroc, 33 Av Mohammed V. BMAO, 15 Pl 2 Septembre. BMCE, 98 Av des Forces Armées Royales, T0535-520352. Bureau de change open daily 1000-1400, 1600-2000. Credit du Maroc, 33 Av Mohammed V. SGMB, Pl Al Wahda Al Ifriqiya, T0535-527896. Wafa Bank, 11 Av Mohammed V, T0535-521151, as usual, the most useful. **Cultural centres** Institut Français, zankat Farhat Hachad, Av Hassan II, T0535-524071. Organizes lectures and films, hosts occasional concerts and plays. Closed mid-Jul to early Sep. A bright note in Meknès' rather sleepy cultural life. **Medical services Chemists**: Pharmacie d'Urgence, Pl Administrative, T0535-523375, 0830-2030. Depot de Nuit: Medicaments d'Urgence, Hotel de Ville, Pl Administrative, 2030-0830. **Hospitals**: Hôpital Mohammed V, T0535-521134. Hôpital Moulay Ismaïl, Av des FAR, T0535-522805. Probably the best of the bunch is Polyclinique Cornette-de-St-Cyr, 22 Esplanade du Docteur Giguet, T0535-520262. **Useful numbers** Ambulance: T15. Fire: T15. Police: T19.

Middle Atlas

From Fès or Meknès there are a number of interesting towns to visit in the Middle Atlas, possibly as stopovers to break a journey south to Marrakech, or as places to escape the summer heat and do some walking in the hills and cedar forests. In a week you could comfortably combine Fès and Meknès (plus Volubilis and Moulay Idriss) with a circuit southwards, which might include overnights in Azrou, Ifrane, Sefrou or Immouzer du Kandar. A loop southwest of Azrou would take you down to Khénifra and back up via the Aguelmane Azigza and Oum er Rbia, Morocco's largest river, which flows into the Atlantic at Azzemour. Strategically located on the road between the imperial cities and Tafilalet, and next to magnificent mountains, Midelt at an altitude of 1525 m, looks as though it will have a good future as a base for hikers.
▶▶ *For listings, see pages 177-180.*

Azrou and around → *For listings, see pages 177-180. Colour map 1, B3.*

Azrou, 70 km south of Meknès, is a small Amazigh market town and hill resort at the heart of the Middle Atlas. The name means rock in Tamazight and refers to the rock in the middle of the town next to the large new mosque. The town has a relaxed air and good hiking in the wooded vicinity. The ruined kasbah was built by Moulay Ismaïl. If you have a car, there are some very scenic routes south of Azrou where the landscapes are truly spectacular. One loop would take you up to **Aïn Leuh**, past Lac Ouiouane and across the **Plateau des cèdres** to the source of the **Oum er Rbia** (Morocco's major river) and onto the **Aguelmane Azigza** and **Khénifra** (a possible overnight stop), or back up from Khénifra on the main N8 to Azrou via Mrirt (large Thursday souk).

Arriving in Azrou

All buses, except those of **CTM**, arrive at the bus station opposite the Grand Mosque, near Place Mohammed V. The *grand taxi* station is close by, near the roundabout. Azrou is a one-horse sort of place, so there are no difficulties getting around.

Background

One of Azrou's claims to fame is that under the French protectorate, it was chosen to be home to the Collège berbère, a training school for Moroccan Berbers, which was founded on the premise that Arabs and Imazighen were fundamentally different – and should be educated and ruled as such. The divide-and-rule policy backfired – it was in the interests of neither Arabs nor Imazighen for a colonial regime to continue to control Morocco; in any case, loyalty to Islam and the Alaouite throne proved to be stronger than ethnic ties, a fact which somehow escaped French colonial ethnographers. After Independence, the Collège berbère became the Lycée Tarik Ibn Zayid, symbolically named for the Arab conqueror of Andalucía. In the late 1990s, Amazigh cultural movements began demanding more official recognition of their cultural identity; it will be interesting to see how Morocco handles its large Amazigh minorities in coming years.

Places in Azrou

Azrou's traditional character, once created by the green-tiled roofs of the arcades round the market square, has taken a beating. Although there are a few good hotels and it is ideally located as a base for exploring the cedar forests, it has yet to find its place in the tourist market. It seems to function as a sort of suburb to its more upmarket neighbour, Ifrane. The heart of Azrou, **Place Mohammed V**, is to the right on leaving the bus stop. There is a covered **market** near Place Mohammed V, while the **Ensemble Artisanal** ① *0830-1200, 1430-1800*, is situated off Avenue Mohammed V, with a fixed-price shop and a number of craftsmen working on the premises – look out for the Middle Atlas carpets. A large **Amazigh souk** is held just above the town on Tuesday, with vegetables, textiles and some interesting Middle Atlas carpets, as well as traditional entertainment from musicians and others. The town also has a small pool for summer use.

Around Azrou

If you have time, seek out the region's largest and most famous cedar, the **Cèdre de Gouraud**, named after some half-forgotten French military commander. This is signposted to the right off the Azrou to Ifrane road, down a narrow, winding road. Barbary apes will be eagerly waiting among the trees to share the contents of your picnic.

Of more specialized interest is the abandoned **Benedictine monastery** at **Tioumliline** ① *turn right a few hundred metres up the hill after the Ifriquia petrol station above Azrou on the Midelt road.* The monastery, founded in 1920, was finally relinquished in 1963, becoming a vocational training centre, abandoned along with the dispensary in the 1980s. Low stone buildings, a cloister planted with cypress, lilac, and a Judas tree survive on this beautiful site, as does the church building and the graves of five fathers. The monastery was important as a meeting place for Moroccan intellectuals in the heady days after independence, providing a refuge to abstract painter Gharbaoui, amongst others. The location is lovely, and birdwatchers may find things of interest in the mixed deciduous/cedar woodlands here.

At 19 km south of Azrou, a turning off the N8 leads to **Aïn Leuh**, an Amazigh village with a Wednesday souk important to the semi-nomadic Beni M'Guild tribe, a ruined kasbah from the reign of Moulay Ismaïl, and nearby waterfalls. You then follow a narrow road through cedar forest and across a plateau, past **Lac Ouiouane** and its 1930s chalets to the source of the River Oum er Rbia, 20 km away. In places, the cedar forest has been cut back to form a thick green crown on the tops of the hills. The villages here are desperately poor, there is little traffic and children will come racing out at the first sign of a passing vehicle. Many of the houses are little more than stone shelters with crude plank roofs, now partly rendered more watertight with plastic. Drive slowly as the road is narrow. Eventually, you drop down to the source of **Oum er Rbia**, clearly visible with its water works from above. There is a car park (lots of men wanting to warden your car) and steps leading to a series of concrete platforms built on the rocks where the river waters come boiling out from between the boulders. (Some of the springs are said to be sweet, others salty.) After the platforms, you can clamber up to see where the water comes crashing into a small, but not actually very deep pool (no diving). After the source, you can head west on a narrow and in places much deteriorated metalled road through beautiful landscape to join the main N8 south of Mrirt. The other option is to continue on south to **Aguelmane Azigza**, a crater lake surrounded by forest and ideal for swimming. The tree-lined spot has its devoted followers among Moroccan campers and is a fine location for some birdwatching. There also may be accommodation on offer in a local café. The road continues to rejoin the N8 at Khénifra.

Khénifra → *Colour map 1, C2.*

Khénifra, capital of the Zaïane region and 96 km southwest of Ifrane, is a relaxed (if rather dull) Middle Atlas town with a population of around 100,000. The town's men are famed for their horsemanship. It has large Wednesday and Sunday **souks** – the place perhaps to pick up an Amazigh rug. The town, with its strategic location at the heart of the Middle Atlas, was developed by Moulay Ismaïl in the late 17th century. In the late 19th century, Sultan Hassan I named local strongman Moha ou Hammou ez Zaïani as caïd. The French had considerable difficulty in bringing Khénifra under their control and suffered a major setback there in 1914, at the hands of Moha ou Hammou. The town only came under the protectorate's control in 1921, when he was killed in a battle with French forces. A few kilometres south of the town on the N8 is a **monument** to this resistance hero.

Khénifra still has a somewhat military feel to it. There is a main avenue with the usual buildings on stilt-legged arcades (cybercafés here). At the north end of town near the horse-monument roundabout are a large number of steep-roofed French buildings, often topped with storks' nests, while, over the river, is the **kasbah** area with an old bridge and one or two historic buildings drowned in a mass of new construction. A possible place for a coffee stop might be the **Café des Cascades**, on a low rise between town centre and horse roundabout. There is a **tourist office** at Immeuble Lefraoui, Hay Hamou-Hassan.

Ifrane and the lakes → *For listings, see pages 177-180. Colour map 1, B3.*

Ifrane, 17 km north of Azrou and 63 km south of Fès, is a mountain resort founded by the French in 1929 which today has numerous large villas and chalets, as well as a royal palace and hunting lodge. It still manages to have something of a colonial hill-station feel to it, despite the arrival of a large new campus university housed in chalet-type buildings and vast new social housing developments on the Azrou side of town. When the palace is occupied by the king, the town becomes busy with staff and politicians. From the town there are good walks in the cedar forests, and a drivable excursion round the *dayats* (crater lakes). There is some skiing to be had at the nearby resort of **Mischliffen** and there is a small airport maintained for private and royal flights.

The dayat lakes

North of Ifrane, leave the N8 to the east for a tour of the dayats, seasonal limestone lakes which are a haven for wildlife, especially birds. There are four lying between the N8 and the R503: Aaoua and Ifrah are the largest but you can also visit Afourgah and Iffer. **Dayat Aaoua**, 12 km from Ifrane, is a scenic place to picnic if the lake is full, which is not the case in drought years and can make the area disappointing for birdwatchers. In good circumstances, however, the dayats are home to coots, herons and egrets; look out for the black-winged stilt and numerous reed warblers. The surrounding woodland, made up mainly of holm-oak and cedar, is alive with birds: tits, chaffinches, short-toed treecreeper, jays, greater spotted woodpeckers and raptors including black and red kite, Egyptian vulture and booted eagle. In the woodland Barbary apes can be seen and, where the woodland gives way to more open plateau, look out for the jackals.

Immouzer du Kandar

A small hill resort, 80 km south of Fès and beautiful in spring with the apple blossom, Immouzer is a popular excursion from Fès, easily accessed with regular buses and *grands taxis*. It is also a lively place during the **Fête des Pommes** in July. Market day takes place on Mondays in the ruined kasbah. Just north of Immouzer du Kandar are the popular picnic/camping springs, **Aïn Seban** and **Aïn Chifa**, clearly signposted to the west of the road. In drought conditions they are less attractive.

Midelt → *For listings, see pages 177-180. Colour map 3, A3.*

For many, the rough-and-ready mining town of Midelt is a handy overnight stop about halfway between the imperial cities and the Tafilalet. Despite high unemployment, the town has a calm, friendly atmosphere and a souk on Sunday. Those in need of a little retail therapy should think carpets in Midelt. These can be bought from the weaving school (*atelier de tissage*) of the **Kasbah Meriem**, the local name for the monastery/convent of **Notre Dame de l'Atlas** ① *T0535-580858,* which is run by Franciscan sisters in premises off the road to Tattiouine. There is also a tiny community of Trappist monks here who relocated from Algeria. The sisters may also be a good source of information about the region. To get there, head north out of Midelt town centre, take a left turn onto the track after the bridge, follow the track towards the kasbah village, where you then take a sharp right and go almost immediately left up the hill. After about 1 km, the Kasbah Meriem is signed on the left, down a dip and up again, its presence indicated by trees. The atelier is left of the large metal gate. Inside, there is a simple church with a small icon of the seven sleepers of Ephesus, symbol of a myth present both in Christianity and Islam. The Franciscan sisters do lots of good work in the region, travelling off into the countryside with mules and a dispensary tent. While the covert funding by USA churches of Protestant missionary activity has attracted criticism in the Moroccan press, the Franciscans' efforts are much appreciated by locals.

For more on **hiking** opportunities and other possible excursions in the area, head for **Aït Ayach**, halfway between Midelt and Zeïda on the N13, where the **Auberge Timnay** can help with vehicle hire and guides (see page 179).

Around Midelt → *Colour map 3, A3.*

Midelt works well as base for excursions, to the abandoned mines of Ahouli in a defile of the Oued Moulouya, or an off-road trip to the Cirque de Jaffar, a natural amphitheatre in the side of Jbel Ayyachi, paramount peak of the region. In the heart of the eastern High Atlas, Imilchil is now feasible as a long day trip on the metalled road via Rich (see page 120). Note that, as elsewhere in this plateau region, the winters are very cold and the summers very hot, so the best time to visit is the spring. Here the spring is later, and May or even early June are recommended for walking.

Mines of Ahouli

For those with a hire car, this excursion north from Midelt goes along the S317 to **Mibladene** (10 km) and over the head of the Oued Moulouya to the abandoned mining settlement of Ahouli. The road is signed right a few metres north from the central bus station junction in Midelt. The first long straight section to Mibladene is badly potholed but it then improves slightly after Mibladene, a former mining community, to the right of the road. You then wind into spectacular gorges. The road deteriorates again after an Indiana Jones-style bridge, parts of it washed away by floods.

Ahouli must once have been a hive of activity. Copper and lead were the main products. The gorge is beautiful, with poplar, oleander and even the odd weeping willow. Mine infrastructure and housing clings to the cliffs. The community even had its own rather splendid cinema (now sanded up) and swimming pool. The lower floors of the houses had heavy metal doors, to keep out eventual floodwater. There is a caretaker here, and he or his son may show you round.

After Ahouli, you can drive up out of the gorges on a well-made track, turning left to more abandoned dwellings on the plateau. Turning left, a couple of kilometres brings you to the small village and semi-abandoned *ksar of* **Ouled Taïr** next to the *oued*, reached by a wobbly footbridge.

Note When driving out to Mibladene, men will try to flag the car down. Most will be selling fossils or stones of some kind. With all three mines in the region (Mibladene, Ahouli and Zaïda) now closed, there is a lot of poverty; selling stones is about the only thing left to do for many.

Jbel Ayyachi

Midelt is also the jumping-off place for treks up to Jbel Ayyachi, which at 3747 m is eastern Morocco at its highest, an impressive 45 km stretch of solid mountain, unbroken by any peaks. First conquered in July 1901 by the Marquis de Segonzac, the heights can remain snow-covered well into late June. In the right conditions, on a long summer's day, the climb can be done in a day, but it's probably better to take two days and bivouac out on the mountain. To tackle the Jbel Ayyachi, head first for **Tattiouine**, 12 km from Midelt (*grand taxi* transport available). Here it should be possible to find mules and a guide. For a fit party, the climb and back should take around 12 hours. Make sure you have plenty of water. Even in summer, it can be very cold at the summit.

Impressive and seemingly impenetrable with its snow-capped heights, the Jbel Ayyachi functions as a water tower for southeastern Morocco, its meltwater feeding both the Moulouya to the north and the Oued Ziz to the south. Jbel Ayyachi derives its name from the local Aït Ayyach tribe. Within living memory, caves in the cliffs were occupied by freedom fighters resisting the Makhzen and the incoming French. The last of such mountain strongholds were only finally taken by the central authorities in 1932.

Cirque du Jaffar

One of Morocco's best known 4WD excursions takes intrepid off-roaders up to the Cirque de Jaffar (map NI-30-II-3), one of the natural arenas hollowed out on the north side of the Jbel Ayyachi. In fact, in a good off-road vehicle, it is just about possible to travel over from Midelt, via the Oued Jaffar, to **Imilchil**, a distance of 160 km (see page 120). The initial part through the Oued Jaffar gorges is the most scenic. The route is not to be attempted in winter, however, and certainly not risked in spring if there are April snows. Consult the **Gendarmerie royale** in Midelt or the people at **Auberge-Restaurant Timnay** on the Zeïda road (see page 179).

◉ Middle Atlas listings

For sleeping and eating price codes and other relevant information, see pages 22-28.

◉ Where to stay

Azrou and around *p173*
€€ Hotel Panorama, T0535-562010, panorama@extra.net.ma. This is the best hotel in Azrou and, as the name suggests, the one with the best views. All of the

38 rooms have a balcony or terrace from which to admire them and, slightly less attractively, they also have large TVs should your penchant be for late-night Arabic TV. Elsewhere the hotel is pleasant enough, with some good quality contemporary photographs decorating the walls and a good restaurant and bar for a sundowner. It's good value for money too.

€ **Hotel Azrou**, Rte de Khénifra opposite the **Crédit agricole**, about 600 m down from central mosque, T0535-562116. This is simple, no-frills accommodation at its best, with freshly painted walls and clean en suite rooms with single beds (but not 24-hr hot water). There's a bar and restaurant that seems to open depending on business. Private parking.

€ **Hotel Salam (Chez Jamal)**, Pl Saouika off Pl Mohammed V, T0535-562562. This is quite a sweet little place overlooking the main square (the entrance is at the rear), if you don't mind getting back to basics. The decor is of the colourful birthday cake variety so beloved by Moroccans, but the management is friendly and willing and they'll do their best to ensure a happy stay. Some rooms are en suite (hot water costs 8dh) and it has a pleasant roof terrace.

€ **Youth hostel**, Rte de Midelt, Azrou, BP147, to get to it follow the signs from Pl Mohammed V, and turn left off the road to Midelt, T0535-563733, www.hihostels.com. Clean and friendly, 40 beds, kitchen, overnight fee 20dh, about 1 km from town centre.

Khénifra *p174*

There is little to choose from in Khénifra (for now), and what there is is of similar quality.

€€ **Hotel Najah**, on the N8, T0535-588331. Probably the most upmarket. A modern place with plenty of hot water and clean, comfortable rooms. A café and restaurant are attached.

€ **Hotel-Restaurant de France**, Quartier Forces Armées Royales, T0535-586114. This is more basic but has good-sized double rooms (twins are a little more cramped), loads of pink paint and some fairly garish carpets and tiles. It's comfortable nonetheless and a bargain. Added bonuses are a large pool and a decent restaurant.

Ifrane *p175*

€€€€ **Michlifen Ifrane Suites and Spa**, Av Hassan II 18, T0535-864000, www.michlifenifrane.com. Under the same ownership as **La Moumounia** in Marrakech, this is one of the swankiest new openings in Morocco and brings a touch of glamour to the alpine-esque town of Ifrane. Expect 5-star service with bells on. There's a luxury spa and hamman, beautiful bedrooms, several excellent restaurants and stunning views of snow-capped mountains. Design-wise, think American lodge luxury and sleek, Nordic minimalism, with plenty of wow-factor. There's even a log-fire by the indoor pool.

€€ **Hotel Le Chamonix**, T0535 566028. A good, mid-range option, with 64 bright clean rooms, with fairly chintzy communal areas and simple, comfortable decor in the rooms. It could do with a bit of TLC these days, but friendly service and a willing attitude make up for it. The restaurant serves alcohol, and you can hire skis from the bar.

€€ **Hotel Perce Neige**, Rue des Asphodelles, T0535-566210, www.hotel-leperceneige.com. This is a friendly little place of just 22 rooms and 5 suites, which is good value if a little jaded. In the centre of town, it's a good base for exploring and has a good-value restaurant and bar.

€ **Gite Dayet Aoua**, Rte d'Immouzer a Ifrane, Km7, T0535-604880, T0661-351257, www.gite-dayetaoua.com. Located about 7 km outside Ifrane, this basic gîte is set in stunning countryside. Peacocks and chickens roam the gardens, decor is a cut above most gîtes of this level, each room individually and carefully decorated with local textiles and crafts. Don't expect modern luxuries but if you want to get away from the mob, sample home-cooked Moroccan food served in a Berber tent, or go on long walks from your back door, it's a winner. They can also arrange bivouacs for camping in the hills, canoe trips and guides.

Camping

Camping International, signposted from the town centre, T0535-566156. Very busy in the summer but open year round for those brave enough to face the winter chill. The 6-ha site is fairly basic with no shop or restaurant, though it does have laundry facilities and showers. Petrol is only 2 km away.

Midelt *p176*

There is only the most basic of accommodation in Midelt itself, and it's worth getting off the beaten path a little for the best of it. Reservations are recommended in the spring.

€ **Auberge-Restaurant Timnay**, Aït Ayach, halfway between Midelt and Zeïda on the N13, 20 km from Midelt, T0535-583434, timnay@iam.net.ma. This is an efficient set-up, with a range of accommodation, including simple rooms, camping, nomad tents and sites for campervans. There is a restaurant, shop and pool, also 4WD rental, with guide for exploring the region. For a 4WD, you may feel that 4 people are necessary to cover costs. Possible circuits on offer include Zaouïa Sidi Hamza and the upper Taâraârt Valley (2 days, 415dh per person). There are also good day trips to Canyon de Tatrout.

€ **Hotel Atlas**, Rue Mohammed Amraoui, T0535-582938. This small family-run hotel is very clean, with pale blue rooms, colourful bedspreads and a roof terrace with mountain views. Shower 10dh, besara soup 5dh. Great value for money.

€ **Hotel Bougafer**, 7 Av Mohammed V, T0535-583099. Up the hill round behind the bus station, this place has good, clean en suite rooms and simple 3- and 4-bed rooms on the top floor. There's internet access from 2 computers and the restaurant has a cinema-sized TV screen, which pulls in locals as well as tourists.

Camping

You may be able to camp in the grounds of the **Hotel Ayachi**, but the Timnay (see above) is really the best option.

🍴 Restaurants

Azrou and around *p173*

€€ **Hotel Panorama**, T0535-562010 (see also Where to stay, above). With its crackling wood fire and 100dh menu, including mountain delicacies such as Middle Atlas trout and *lapin à la moutarde*, this is a great choice, especially after a hard day hiking.

€€ **Hotel Restaurant des Cèdres**, Pl Mohammed V, T0535-562326. Behind the net curtains, there are 2 fixed menus, one 'gastronomique', one 'touristique', though you may find that you can order the same things à la carte for cheaper. Service is attentive and the fish is good.

€ **Boulangerie Pâtisserie L'Escalade**, 5 Pl Hassan II, T0535-563419. Excellent little baker with very good cakes and biscuits.

Ifrane *p175*

Ifrane is not exactly a gastronomic destination but there are some reasonable options, lots of mid-range places and a handful of cafés.

€ **Café-Restaurant de la Rose**, 7 Rue des Erables, next to the Mobil station, T0535-566215. This is a fairly basic place that nevertheless offers a hearty menu (70dh) that hits the spot. The special is the *truite en papillottes*. No alcohol. You can also ask for obliging local mountain guide Izem here, who knows some good routes in the local outback.

Le Croustillant Boulangerie Pâtisserie, does reasonable coffee and has a good selection of pastries in a setting reminiscent of a European cafeteria.

Midelt *p176*

€ **Hotel Roi de la Bière**, Av des FAR, T0535-582625. This Moroccan salon offers free internet and lots of Barbie-pink decor, along with a good-value 80dh fixed menu.

€ **Restaurant de Fès**, 2 Av Mohammed, T0662-057754. Couscous is the order of the day here, along with some excellent options for vegetarians. Choose from 7 different *salades Marocaine* and an excellent 10-vegetable tagine. Small, welcoming and enthusiastic, it gets filled up with groups, so it's worth trying to bag your table early. 3-course menu for 80dh.

There are some cheap roadside places just up from the station offering mainly tagines – try Restaurant Lespoir or du Centre.

⚙ What to do

Ifrane *p175*
Skiing at Mischliffen Near Ifrane, the season is Jan-Mar, and the resort has good, but short, slopes, sometimes with patchy snow cover. Hire equipment from the Chamonix restaurant in Ifrane and take a taxi to the resort. This is a small area with cafés and ski lifts but little else. During summer the area is popular with walkers.

Midelt *p176*
For guides and hiking options, see Auberge-Restaurant Timnay, page 179.

⊖ Transport

Azrou and around *p173*
There are plenty of buses from **Meknès** and **Fès** to Azrou, which is situated at a crossroads of routes leading up from Marrakech (via Beni Mellal and Khénifra) and **Er Rachidia** (via Midelt). Coming from Marrakech, you will have to change at Beni Mellal if you don't get a direct bus. CTM buses depart from near Pl Mohammed V, with early departures for **Casablanca**, **Midelt**, and **Meknès**. There are further CTM and private line services from Azrou to **Rissani**, **Er Rachidia**, **Marrakech**, **Khénifra** and **Fès**, and numerous *grands taxis* to **Khénifra**, leaving from close to the rock, **Ifrane**, **Immouzer du Kandar**, **Meknès** and **Fès**.

Ifrane *p175*
There are regular buses from Ifrane to both **Azrou** and **Fès**.

⊕ Directory

Azrou and around *p173*
Banks The Banque Populaire and the BMCE (cashpoint) are on Pl Mohammed V.

Ifrane *p175*
Internet Le Croustilant café opposite the Mobil station has internet access. For wines and beer, there is a *débit d'alcohol* next to Le Croustillant. For films and photography equipment, there is a shop next to the Hotel Le Chamonix.

Taza and around

*There was a time when Taza was quite a happening place, given its strategic location
controlling the easiest route from the Moroccan heartland of Fès and Meknès to the eastern
plains. The town, rather quiet today, is divided into three quite separate parts: the area
around the railway and bus station; the* ville nouvelle *around Place de l'Indépendence, and
the quiet medina on the hill with its narrow streets. After the hurly-burly of Fès, low-key Taza
makes a good base from which to explore up into the hills of the Jbel Tazzeka National Park.*
▶▶ *For listings, see pages 186-188.*

Arriving in Taza ➜ *Colour map 1, B4.*

Arriving by train, bus or *grand taxi*, you will come into the north of the *ville nouvelle*. The
medina is a fair 3-km trek away and, as there is only one hotel there, you will probably stay
in the *ville nouvelle*. (Go straight down Avenue de la Gare; there are three hotels on Place
de l'Indépendence at the end.) There is a regular bus service from Place de l'Indépendence
to Place Moulay Hassan in the medina. A light blue *petit taxi* will cost you around 3dh from
station to Place de l'Indépendence, and 6dh from the station to the medina.

Background

The site was first settled in Neolithic times. Later it was developed by Meknassa Amazigh
groups, eventually becoming an important, but ultimately unsuccessful fortification
against the advance of the Fatimids from the east. The Almohads under Sultan Abd el
Moumen captured the city in 1141-1142, making it their second capital, and using it to
attack the Almoravids. The Almohads built a mosque and expanded the fortifications.

Taza was the first city taken by the Merinids, who extended the Almohad city
considerably. Its important defensive role continued under the Merinids and the Saâdians,
and was again pivotal in the rise to power of the Alaouites, who further extended and
fortified the city, later using it as a strong point in their defence against the threat from
French-occupied Algeria to the east.

The eccentric pretender, Bou Hamra, 'the man on the she-donkey', proclaimed himself
sultan here in 1902 and controlled much of eastern Morocco until 1912, when he was
caught and killed. He was known as a wandering miracle-maker, travelling Morocco on
his faithful beast. Taza was occupied by the French in 1914, and became an important
military centre, located on the route linking Algeria with the Atlantic plains of *le Maroc
utile*, between the remote mountains and plateaux of eastern Morocco and the great cities
to the west. Today, with the decline in cross-border trade with Algeria, Taza, like its distant
neighbour Oujda, sees far less passing traffic than it did and has a distinctly sleepy feel to
it. A couple of the hotels have been upgraded, however, and you could well stay here for a
couple of nights if exploring or birdwatching up in the Jbel Tazzeka National Park.

Places in Taza

The **ville nouvelle** – for hotels, restaurants, banks and other services – is a quiet place
centred around early and mid-20th-century buildings on Place de l'Indépendence. The
older buildings are in the small, attractive **medina** perched on the hill 3 km away from
the railway station and 2 km from the centre of the new town. From the bottom of the
hill there is an interesting short cut to the **kasbah** via a flight of steps which provide

remarkable views. Beyond this point, further along the main road on the right, are the **Kifane el Ghomari caves**, inhabited in Neolithic times. Note that the main historic buildings in the medina are closed to non-Muslims.

Medina

The transport hub of the old town is **Place Moulay Hassan**, just outside the main entrance to the **souk**. The focus of the old quarter is the main street, commonly called the Mechouar from end to end, which runs behind Place Moulay Hassan along the entire length of the medina, from the Andalucían Mosque to the Grand Mosque at the opposite end of town by the Bab er Rih gate. Between the two mosques are the various souks. Hassle is practically non-existent, as there are few articles thought to interest the tourist. The fact that there is no motor traffic in the medina makes it all the more pleasant. The best thing to do is just wander – the old neighbourhoods are quite small and sooner or later you will come out on the outside road ringing the town.

Turning left just past the main gate to the souk, by the **Cinema Friouato**, is the jewellery section of the souk. From here you can turn left along a very straight and narrow section of road towards the Andalucían Mosque, or right towards the Grand Mosque. Following the latter route, the food and spice souk is off to the left, behind the broader section of the Mechouar. Further along, you may get a glimpse of the **Zaouïa of Sidi Azouz** (note its beautiful wall-basin by the door). It is difficult to gain a good view of the **Grand Mosque**, built by the Almohads in the second half of the 12th century, with further elaboration by the Merinids in the late 13th century, and the Alaouites in the 17th. In its classic proportions of 1:5, the minaret resembles that of the Koutoubia Mosque in Marrakech. Only Muslims can view the beautiful chandelier bearing 514 oil lamps, which lights the mosque.

Taza medina

200 metres
200 yards

Restaurants ❶
Café Andalous 1
Café en Ghissani 2

To the right of the Grand Mosque, down a steep flight of steps, you reach a section of the **ramparts**, with good views over the surrounding countryside, lower Taza, and the mountains beyond. Going left after the steps to start a rampart tour, the first section, with some steep drops, is referred to as **Bab er Rih**, 'the Gate of the Wind'. From here you have perhaps the best view of the Almohad minaret. Eventually, keeping to the outside of the town, you could look out for the circular **Sarasine Tower**, also dating back to the Almohad times – and showing clear European influence.

At the far end of the mechouar from Bab er Rih is the **Andalucían Mosque**, with its 12th-century minaret. Just before, on the right, stands the 14th-century **Medersa of Abu el Hassan**, named after a Merinid sultan. This is closed, but the exterior shows a carved lintel in cedar wood and a porch roof overhanging the road. In a lane to the right of the mosque, Zankat Dar el Makhzen, there is the former house of Bou Hamra the pretender. The weekly **market** takes place outside the walls at this end of town, outside **Bab Titi**.

Jbel Tazzeka National Park → *Colour map 1, B4.*

An area of fine mountain scenery, the Jbel Tazzeka National Park, south of Taza and the N6, can also be visited with your own transport on a long but rewarding day trip from Fès. The region's cork-oak forest and its undergrowth has plenty to keep ornithologists happy – look out for the rare black-shouldered kite. Scenery and kites apart, however, the main reason for doing this trip is to go intrepidly down into the **Gouffre de Friouato**, an immense series of hobbity caverns with scrambles, stalactites and mud aplenty.

From the plateau of old Taza, the S311 winds its way south and west, eventually linking up with the the N6 some 31 km further west. If you have parked close to the walls of Taza, head back as though you were returning to new Taza, leaving the Préfecture on your left, and go straight ahead at the next roundabout. (Without a car you might bargain for a *grand taxi* to take you part of the way, from the rank by the railway station.) With no stops, a careful driver will take 1¾ hours to reach the N6. (Take water in case the engine overheats.)

After a rainy winter, the **Cascades de Ras el Oued**, a few kilometres out of Taza and a popular picnic spot, might be worth a look. Next stop, some 14 km along the route, is the **Vallée des oiseaux**, which starts with a thick stand of cork oak. Nearby lies the **Dayat Chiker**, a seasonal lake. Next you will reach a fork in the road signed Maghraoua (left) and Bab Boudir (right). Go right, and 3 km further on, about 35 minutes from Taza, you will reach the turn-off right heading uphill to the Gouffre de Friouato.

Gouffre de Friouato

A descent into this magnificent cave system is not for the weak-kneed. Near the car park is a stone-built *guichet* building, where smiling, bright-eyed Mustapha Lachhab presides over piles of biscuits, sweets, torches and batteries – everything an amateur caver could need. The officially authorized organizer of guides, he also has photocopied sheets with a cross section of the caverns. Access to the first flights of steps costs 3dh; 100dh gets you a guide to take a small group (up to four people), down the 230 m and 520 steps of the first section, through a narrow squeeze and scramble bit and into the **Salle de Lixus**, as the first main cave is rather grandly known, after the Roman site near modern Larache. Here there are stalactites, including a sort of crystal platform looking for all the world like a Renaissance pulpit, a be-turbaned individual (use your imagination) and a *hallouf* (pig). From here the caves run on at least a further 2 km, an exploration best left to the enthusiastic and well equipped. Getting down and back from the Salle de Lixus will take you about an hour. The squeeze to this section is easier coming up, by the way. If you're a real speleologist, it would definitely be worth spending time in the region as there are further caverns elsewhere. Note that, having done the descent so many times, the local guides really do know how to pace a group. They now also have quite a lot of ropes and other material left behind by cavers.

After the caves, the next major stopping point, 30 km from Taza, is an unlikely *station estivale* with red-roofed houses and various seasonal eateries, including the **Café Bouhadli**. Continue on to the Bab Taza pass, from which a rough and challenging track goes north up to the **Jbel Tazzeka**, where there are incredible views of the surrounding mountains. After, or avoiding, the Jbel Tazzeka, the road continues through cork forest, past another signed picnic area, the **Vallée des cerfs**, and then down and through the narrow gorge by the Oued Zireg and back to the N6. The map shows distances between major points and the quality of the roads. For excursions south to Immouzer du Kandar and the Dayats of Aaoua, Afourgah and Ifrah, see page 175.

East of Taza → *For listings, see pages 186-188. Colour map 1, B5.*

Oujda Msoun
Some 20 km to the east of Taza along the N6 is the fortified farming village of Msoun. Built around 1700 in Moulay Ismaïl's reign to guard the approaches to the strategic Taza Gap, it is still inhabited by members of the semi-nomadic Houara tribe. The village has a shop, post office and even a teahouse. The compact, walled settlement stands isolated on a hillside, clearly visible from the main road where there is the convenient **Motel-Restaurant Casbah** and a petrol station. It is possible to walk to the village from here, just 2 km.

Jbel Tazzeka National Park

Guercif

Guercif is an unremarkable modern agricultural town noted for its olives and shoe industry. In the 14th century, it became a stronghold of the Beni Ouattas Tribe, who later overran Taza and replaced Merinids to form the Ouattasid Dynasty. The main part of town, which lies to the south of the main road, is centred around Boulevard Mohammed V, its solid 19th-century mosque and two adjacent squares. The railway station is reached via a driveway from the opposite side of the main road. Market day is Sunday.

Taourirt

Halfway between Taza and Oujda, Taourirt is an important commercial centre with a large **market** on Sunday. In the past the town functioned as the junction between two major trade routes: the east–west trans-Maghreb route and the route from Melilla to the Tafilalet. The centre of town is located around the junction of the N6 and the Debdou road (the ancient caravan route to the south which is packed with shops, garages, cafés and small workshops). The only tangible historic attraction is the remains of the **kasbah** on the hill 1 km to the northwest, unfortunately spoiled by electricity pylons but with excellent views.

There are several excursions around Taourirt that make it worthwhile stopping for a day or two, if you have time. The mountain village of **Debdou** (see below) and the **Zaâ waterfalls** and gorges. Providing there is enough water in the *oued* (unlikely between August and December), the falls make an enjoyable picnic and bathing excursion and camping is possible. To get there, turn right at the signpost 6 km along the Taza road. It is a further 9 km to the waterfalls. The track continues to Melga el Ouidane and the large lake known as **Barrage Mohammed V**. There are a number of picnic spots along the route. The **Zaâ Gorges** are deep, very impressive and well worth the journey. As you leave Taourirt on the Oujda road, there is a turning off to the right. You cannot drive through the narrow defile. Leave the car where the road ends and walk from there.

Debdou

Nestling in a verdant bowl formed by the surrounding massif, Debdou, 50 km southwest of Taourirt, is an island of rural tranquillity. The fact that it's on a road to nowhere has helped to preserve its identity. The surrounding area is very scenic and provides good opportunities for walking and exploration. There is an interesting kasbah halfway up the mountainside above the main village. There are no tourist facilities, and transport links are poor.

Until the 1960s over half the population of Debdou were Jewish, and most were the descendants of Jews from Taza who fled the persecution and chaos of Bou Hamra's rule (1902-1908). The 'main street' branches off the main road at the entrance to the village and zig-zags for about 1 km, past store houses, to a square at the top end of the village known as **Aïn Sbilia**. Overlooking the square is a balcony shaded by plane trees. A small sluice gate allows water to flow into a channel bisecting the square below, which has a café. It is all very restful, the locals playing cards or backgammon and drinking mint tea.

High above the village is the still-inhabited **kasbah of Caïd Ghomriche**, built by the Merinids in the 13th century and subsequently handed over to the Beni Ouattas, a related tribe, around 1350 when the Merinids ruled Morocco. Follow the signposted track (2 km) starting from the bottom end of the village. Note the colourful hammam, which is still heated by a wood stove. Along the way there are pretty views of the town on the right and the waterfalls high above on the left. Just before the kasbah there is a grassy ledge with good views over the valley, and the entrance to a **cave**. The settlement is a mixture of ancient ruins, small vegetable gardens and mud houses.

At the back of the village, past the walls and a dry moat, is a field where jagged stones stick out of the ground – the sunken headstones of tombs. By crossing the field and turning left for 30-40 m and then sharp right, there is a path (1 km) linking up with the main road and the source of the Oued Debdou. The same location can be reached by the main road, which swings to the left just before Debdou and runs along the mountain crest, or **Gaada de Debdou**, for 5 or 6 km. There are fantastic views from here and good walking opportunities. Beyond this, the road descends from the plateau down into the arid Rekkam plain where it becomes a rough track, eventually leading to Outad Ouled el Hadj. **Market** day is Wednesday.

El Aïoun

Halfway between Taourirt and Oujda, and within easy reach of the **Beni Snassen Mountains** (see page 411), El Aioun was founded by Moulay Ismaïl in 1679. It has a small kasbah, restored in 1876 by Sultan Moulay Hassan in response to the threat of French expansion from Algeria. To the south of the town is a **cemetery**, where those who died fighting colonialism are buried. During the first half of the 20th century, El Aïoun became a centre of the Sufi Brotherhood of Sheikh Bou Amama, whose *zaouïa*, or sanctuary, is located here. The weekly **souk** is held on Tuesday and frequented by members of the local Ouled Sidi Sheikh tribe.

Missour

A tranquil town with many donkeys and unpaved roads, Missour comes alive for the weekly market. There is a fair medium-priced hotel here and, although unaccustomed to foreigners, locals are helpful. If you are lucky enough to be here on a Wednesday, there is a large local **souk** situated on the hill by the water tower, past the new mosque. The lower part of the market is disappointing, but the top end of the main enclosure has the fruit and vegetable market, and a separate area beyond encloses the livestock market. Both enclosures have tea tents. There is a view of the town and the mountains from the adjacent hill.

Oued Moulouya

Past Missour, the road continues for about 30 km through a still bare but slightly more dramatic landscape that would make a good Western film set. After Tamdafelt, the road runs along an attractive stretch of the Oued Moulouya, with *pisé* villages and richly cultivated riverbanks. Two fortified kasbahs built by Moulay Ismaïl around 1690 to guard the imperial route from Fès to Sijilmassa are still inhabited: **Saida** and **Ksabi**. The inhabitants, originally forming an agglomeration of 10 *ksars*, are mostly descendants of Alaouite guardsmen from the Tafilalet. At over 1000 m, the freshness of the air and quality of light in this remote region are exhilarating. After Ksabi, the road swings away from the river and crosses the high plain of Aftis until it joins the N13, 15 km east of Midelt.

◉ Taza listings

For sleeping and eating price codes and other relevant information, see pages 22-28.

◉ Where to stay

Taza *p181, map p182*
€ Grand Hotel du Dauphiné, Av de la Gare and Pl de l'Indépendance, T0535-

673567. Handily located in the centre this 26-room place was renovated a few years ago and, although all its period details have gone, there are some modern touches that make it more comfortable. Best used as an overnighter, there's a large café next door for stocking up on breads and pastries for travelling.

€ **Hotel de la Gare**, at the main crossroads near the station, T0535-672448. This cheap and cheerful hotel is adequately clean (if you're not too fussy) and has very friendly owners. There's a decent café and *téléboutique* next door. The best rooms are on the 1st floor, but have cold showers only. The main reason to stay here is for early starts with *grand taxi*, bus and train stations close by.

Jbel Tazzeka National Park *p183*
€€€-€€ **Auberge Aïn-Sahla**, 59 Oued Amlil, T0661-893587, T0670-196094. Located in the heart of the Tazzeka National Park, this place is a gem for those who like to get out into the wilds in style. It has 17 rooms and 3 suites, some with private gardens or terraces, all beautifully decorated with lots of outdoor spaces for chilling out. The pool is fed by the Aïn-Sahla spring, and the home-cooked food is excellent. It's a great base for keen walkers, and the friendly owners are an excellent source of information on the hidden corners of the park.

Taourirt *p185*
€ **Hotel Mansour**, on the Debdou road just off main crossroads, T0536-694003. Large rooms, adequately clean, good café below. Hot water available.

🍴 Restaurants

Taza *p181, map p182*
€€ **Grand Hotel du Dauphiné**, junction of Pl de l'Indépendence and Av de la Gare, T0535-673567. Huge 1950s dining hall, good value if you don't mind a limited menu (sometimes only steak and chips), but on the plus side they do serve a nice cold bottle of beer.

For more basic eats try **Café Restaurant Majestic** (€), Av Mohammed V, which does solid Moroccan food, while the **Snack Bar Youm Youm** (€), behind Hotel de la Poste on Blvd Moulay Youssef, serves tasty brochettes.

Cafés
Taza is a great place for people-watching and has a thriving Moroccan style café scene.
Café Andalous, in the old town. With a terrace overlooking the animated Pl Moulay Hassan, this is probably the top spot to sit and observe the local scene.
Café des Jardins, Av Ibn Khatib. Located in the municipal gardens en route to the old town. Chill out on the shady terrace with views, after a morning in the medina.
Café el Ghissani, opposite **Café Andalous** by the main entrance to the souk. This is a good place to catch your breath and is hugely popular with locals.
Pâtisserie des Festivités, 1 Blvd Mohammed V, just off Pl de l'Indépendence. Provides a cosy nook and is good for breakfast and cakes.

Guercif *p185*
The best eateries are the group of transport cafés known as 'le complexe' on the main road, the meat used for the brochettes is very fresh, direct from the in-house butcher.
Place Centrale has several snack places and grocery stores catering for travellers.
Café Nahda is a small, friendly, efficient place on the corner of Rue Mohammed V and Rue Ibn Battuta near the mosque. The café opposite is also good.

🛍 Shopping

Taza *p181, map p182*
Pistacherie Rayane, 5 Av Moulay Hassan, by the entrance to the old town. Sells factory-fresh nuts, much cheaper than elsewhere.

🚍 Transport

Taza *p181, map p182*
Taza is easily accessible by public transport from Fès, 120 km to the west. Coming from eastern Morocco, you will necessarily pass through Taourirt and Guercif, a major meeting of the roads some 40 km from Taza.

Bus

CTM buses leave from their office on Pl de l'Indépendence for **Oujda** and **Fès/Meknès/Casablanca**. Other companies operate from near the railway station, turn right at the end of Av de la Gare. Regular services to **Oujda/Guercif/Taourirt** (4 hrs), **Fès** every hour (2 hrs), **Nador** (4 hrs), **Al Hoceïma** (4 hrs) and **Aknoul** (1 hr). Make sure you take a new-looking bus by a reliable company for Al Hoceïma and Nador.

Taxi

Grands taxis leave from the transport cafés by the bus station to **Oujda**, **Fès**, **Al Hoceïma** and **Nador**, amongst other places.

Train

At Taza the ONCF locomotives switch from electric to diesel, hence speed heading eastwards is slow. There are at least 3 daily departures for **Oujda** (4 hrs), stopping at **Guercif** and **Taourirt**. **Casablanca** is 7 hrs away; **Tangier**, a good 8 hrs away, if you are lucky with the connection at **Sidi Kacem**. **Fès** is 2 hrs by train, **Meknès** 3 hrs.

Guercif *p185*

CTM bus connections to **Oujda**, **Fès**, **Midelt** and **Er Rachidia**. CTM offices are between the central square and Pl Zerkatouni. Private lines: **Taourirt/Oujda** and **Taza/Fès**, **Nador**. **Er Rachidia** departs from 'le complexe' on the main road. ONCF train services to **Taourirt/Oujda** and **Taza/Fès/Casablanca**.

Taourirt *p185*

Buses for **Oujda** (every ½ hr) and **Nador** (around 5 a day) depart from the Agip petrol station past the main crossroads. **Guercif/Taza/Fès** (virtually every 30 mins during the day and hourly at night) depart from

near the Shell petrol station on the same road, as do the *grands taxis* that ply the N6. *Grands taxis* for **Debdou** leave from the rank on the Debdou road. There are trains to **Oujda** 0530, 0800, 1800, 1930 (approximate times); **Taza/Fès/Casablanca** 0830, 1045, 2030, 2230 (approximate times). Once the new Nador line opens, Taourirt's transport options will increase.

Debdou *p185*

There's an early morning and an early afternoon bus departure to **Taourirt** as well as taxis (most frequent in the morning and early evening – if you don't want to get stuck here, try to leave before 1800).

❸ Directory

Taza *p181, map p182*
Banks Banks with ATMs include the BMCE, near the Hotel du Dauphiné, in the new town.

Guercif *p185*
Banks Banque Populaire, on market square. BM and BMCE, near Shell petrol station on Oujda road. **Medical services** Chemists: Pharmacie centrale on the market square.

Taourirt *p185*
Banks Banque Populaire, on the main road. **Medical services** Chemist: Pharmacie Echifa, opposite the new mosque. **Petrol** At the south end of the main boulevard before the bridge.

Missour *p186*
Banks BMCE, CMD and Wafabank next to Hotel Mansour. **Medical services** Chemist: on the road out to Debdou: Al Jabri and Al Qods.

Contents

Footprint features

Desert & gorges

At a glance

⊖ **Getting around** You will need a 4WD vehicle to fully explore this area.
⏱ **Time required** Allow a week.
☀ **Weather** Very hot in summer, although cold at night. Beautiful in spring and early summer, although melt water from the mountains can be a problem if going off-road.
✖ **When not to go** In the middle of summer much of the tourist infrastructure around Merzouga shuts down as it becomes too hot to venture out onto the dunes.

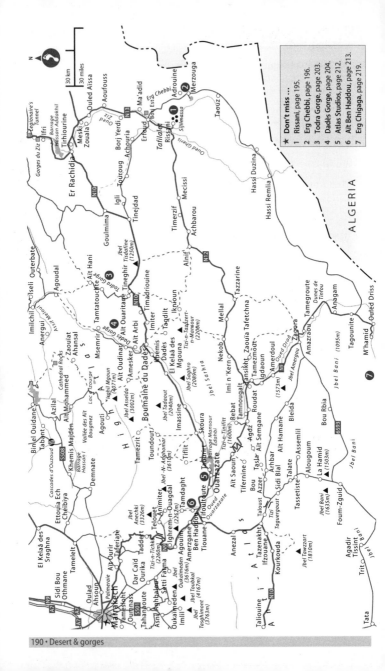

With their arid mountains and gentle oases, a volcanic massif and some splendid canyons, the great valleys south of the High Atlas have some of the finest scenery in Morocco. Whether heading south from Fès, via the crumbling *ksar* at Rissani, or east from Marrakech, many people's aim is Erg Chebbi, the cinematic sand dunes near Merzouga. Here you can sleep in nomad tents and ride out on camels into the sunset. To the west, the spectacular, winding valleys of Dadès and Todra become narrow gorges before they rise into the High Atlas, their red rocks glowing in the southern sun. To the south there are alternative tastes of desert life to be had as you follow the Drâa Valley through miles of lush oases and sleepy villages until the ribbon of tarmac finally stutters to a halt at M'Hamid el Ghizlane and the Sahara beckons. Here, the dunes of Erg Chigaga are the star attraction, some 50 km away across turbulent desert pistes and stony hammada.

Almost all travellers will pass through Ouarzazate, where the Tizi-n-Tichka route over the mountains from Marrakech meets the main east–west Er Rachidia to Agadir axis running parallel to the south side of the High Atlas. Ouarzazate is the centre of Morocco's film industry, the desert surroundings standing in as various parts of this and other planets. Nearby, Aït Ben Haddou is the biggest film star of all, a stunning sand castle of a kasbah.

Er Rachidia to the dunes of Erg Chebbi

The variety and scale of the landscapes is the attraction of east-central Morocco. South of the Gorges of the Ziz and relaxed Er Rachidia are the palm-filled canyons of the Tafilalet on the Ziz river, one of the biggest oases in the world and famous (as well as historically important) for its dates. Further south, there is a crumbling ksar (fortified kasbah) at Rissani and the high dunes of Merzouga, site of many a Saharan fantasy – both cinematic and personal – as travellers flock to ride camels out into a photogenic ideal of the desert. ➤➤ For listings, see pages 197-201.

Er Rachidia and around → For listings, see pages 197-201. Colour map 3, B3.

Er Rachidia was previously known as Ksar es Souk or 'the village of markets', due to its importance as a trading crossroads for the trans-Saharan caravans. It was renamed after independence for the first Alaouite leader, 17th-century sultan Moulay Rachid. The present town was established by the French, initially by the Foreign Legion, as a military and administrative centre, a role it retains today. The town, with its mix of new concrete and older mud-walled buildings, has little in the way of sights beyond a 19th-century *ksar* near the Erfoud exit, but it is a convenient stopping point at the meeting of routes to Ouarzazate, Erfoud (south), Midelt and Meknès (north), and distant Figuig (east), and so has reasonable facilities and a relaxed atmosphere. It is generally used by visitors as an overnight stop on a 'round the High Atlas' circuit and makes a good place to pause before heading down to Rissani (more crumbling kasbahs) and the dunes of Merzouga. If you can't get accommodation at Merzouga or Erfoud, the dunes are visitable from Er Rachidia on a long day out. Evenings in the town are pleasant, with lots of people out strolling in the streets after the heat of the day, and the main market days are Sunday, Tuesday and Thursday.

Arriving in Er Rachidia
Getting there There are several buses a day for Erfoud and Rissani (two hours), Midelt (three hours), Tineghir (3½ hours), Fès (nine hours) and Meknès (eight hours), and one each morning to Figuig (eight hours). There are frequent *grands taxis* to Erfoud and Meski, Goulmima and Tinejdad, from the taxi rank opposite the bus station.

Getting around The grid-iron street pattern, so typical of French garrison towns in the Sahara, makes orientation simple. The main road, Avenue Moulay Ali Cherif, leads down to the new bridge over the Oued Ziz, after which it becomes Avenue el Massira. The *gare routière* is on the right in the town centre on Rue M'Daghra as you head east. The **CTM** bus company is located here too (T0535-572024). *Grands taxis* are 200 m further north along the main road.

Tourist information **Tourist office** ① *44 Rue My Abdellah (near bus station), T0535-570944, Mon-Fri 0830-1630.*

Places in Er Rachidia
Er Rachidia is not blessed with myriad sights. You may want to take a look at the historic **Ksar Targa**, about 5 km from the centre. Also of passing interest are the social housing developments on either side of the Midelt road. Here the architects put new homes within

neo-*ksar* type walls, which are painted a strong, Marrakech terracotta colour. As the largest town in the southeast, close to the Algerian frontier, the modern Moroccan state clearly needed to mark its presence by such projects. You will also notice quite a number of soldiers – there is a large garrison – and lots of shoeshiners, who will readily apply black polish to dusty walking boots.

Gorges du Ziz

The N13 north to the Gorges of the Ziz is a superb route. For the first 20 km the road follows the Oued Ziz. Caves can be seen cut into the cliff, no doubt used to store crops. On your right is the western shore of the **Barrage de Hassan Addakhil**, completed in 1971. The dam supplies water to Er Rachidia and the region's oases. It also limits the potentially destructive flash flooding of the Oued Ziz. Migrating birds stop over on the lake, too. If you travel along this route in the evening, the sun accentuates the landforms, highlighting bands of hard rock with screes between. Then you come to the **Gorges of the Ziz**, a spectacular ride in a narrow defile 2 km in length. At around 29 km from Er Rachidia, where a bridge crosses the river, there is the small settlement of **Ifri** where picnicking and camping are possible.

If you have lots of time, then continue on the N13, through the Legionaire's Tunnel, to the hot springs of **Moulay Ali Cherif**, 42 km north of Er Rachidia. Follow through to the gardens of **Tirhiourine**. The surfaced road links with the N10 a few kilometres east of Er Rachidia, near the airport.

If you are travelling north on the N13 from Er Rachidia to complete a High Atlas circular tour, Midelt (see page 176) is the next major town with decent accommodation, 156 km from Er Rachidia.

Tafilalet

The southern stretches of the Ziz valley, known as the Tafilalet, are particularly fertile. Historically, the region was of considerable importance, due in part to its location on the trans-Saharan trade routes. In the eighth and ninth centuries the region was a separate kingdom and became known as a centre of religious unorthodoxy – of the Kharijite Berber heresy and later of Shi'ism. The ruling Alaouite Dynasty originated in Rissani. From 1916 to 1931 French control of the region was challenged and effectively thwarted by local forces. Many of the settlements of the valley were destroyed in a flood in 1965. Today the region produces figs, olives and dates, but is noted especially for its tamarisk trees. (Dried tamarisk fruit is used in the leather industry for its tannin, essential to the curing process.)

Meski → *Colour map 3, B3.*

Heading for the Tafilalet from Er Rachidia, it's a 94 km journey to Rissani. Meski, lying to the west of the Erfoud road about 18 km east of Er Rachidia, is the first halt, famed for its **Source Bleu**. Developed by the Foreign Legion, Meski has a springwater pool surrounded by palms, and a popular camp site, the **Camping de la Source Bleu**. The **Ksar of Meski** is around 500 years old and the ruins make an attractive silhouette. To get to Meski from Er Rachidia, take a *grand taxi*, paying the same price as for Erfoud – the Source and campsite are a few hundred metres from the road. Moving on from Meski, you might be able to get a bus, or (easier) hitch a lift with other tourists.

Continuing south on the N13 towards Erfoud, you could easily miss one of the most spectacular views in Morocco. Keeping an eye out, you will eventually glimpse the huge oasis-canyon of the Oued Ziz to the right (west). There is a track, marked by a small cairn, which runs to the edge of the gorge. The view is magnificent – and there will be others there admiring the scenery too.

Along the Ziz Canyon → *Colour map 3, B3.*
After the viewpoints, the road soon drops down into the valley, some 20 km long, where a succession of *ksar* house the farming people who make their living from the area.

If you have time, take a 4WD and a guide along the small roads by the river through the small settlements rather than speeding along the N13. Here you will see a great contrast between the green fertile ribbon of palms and oasis gardens and the surrounding scorched landscape. In each loop of the river stands a *ksar* (fortressed village) made of mud brick guarding the valley and providing protection for the village as well as supervision for the trade in slaves and precious metals that once used this route.

At 28 km from Er Rachidia, the route drops to the valley floor along a road descending down the cliff face. **Zouala** is the first settlement. You could take time to explore the oasis here. Above are soaring crags, below are palms and water: a fine dual environment for birds, the green contrasting with the rock faces. Further on, the large settlement strung out along the road is **Aoufouss**, about 45 km from Rachidia. There is an **Afriquia** petrol station and a **CTM** stop. Red-washed concrete houses line the road; the old *pisé* dwellings are clearly visible further back. For a break, try the café attached to the petrol station where food is usually good and the bathrooms are clean. The road then rises out of the canyon floor onto an arid plain for the final approach to Erfoud.

At **Borj Yerdi**, 14 km north of Erfoud, the first small dunes come into view and, if driving, watch out for sand on the road, despite the tiny fences of palm fronds put up to control the shifting dunes.

North of Erfoud, on the eastern side of the road, is the *ksar* of **Ma'adid**. Here it is said the streets are so narrow and the arrangement so complicated that only locals can find their way in and, more importantly, out. Take a guide if you visit. There will be crowds of excitable children, eager, as usual, for *bonbons* and *stylos*.

Erfoud → *For listings, see pages 197-201. Colour map 3, B3.*

Erfoud is a southern Moroccan garrison town, founded by the French in the 1930s to administer their desert territories. The modern centre of the Tafilalet region, it makes an excellent base for exploring the valley and nearby desert areas. The small town of Rissani and its *ksar* and the dunes of Erg Chebbi are close by, though to see the latter at their best, you're probably best continuing to Merzouga. Lovers of dates may try to time their visit to coincide with the annual date festival held in October, though it is a movable feast and hard to pin down.

Arriving in Erfoud
Getting there Erfoud is easily accessible from Ouarzazate and the Dadès Valley further west. You can travel by bus from Tinghir to Tinejad, changing there for Erfoud (two hours). Er Rachidia to Erfoud is 1½ hours. There is also a daily bus from Fès (11 hours).

Getting around Erfoud is a small place, easily explored on foot. You will probably want to visit the *ksar* at Rissani, however, which is easily accessible by *grand taxi*. A number of other *ksar* are a few kilometres outside the main settlement. The Erg Chebbi dunes can be reached by 4WD excursion, with most hotels in Erfoud offering the trip, as well as local desert tour agencies. Otherwise, try to join up with some people with a car. There are *grands taxis* and minivans in the early morning between Merzouga and Rissani, leaving from next to the bus station.

Places in Erfoud
On the other side of the river from the town of Erfoud is the **Borj Est**, a military fort (no admittance, but get a taxi up to the top for the view) overlooking the village and palms, the Tafilalet oasis and the desert. There is a **market** on Sunday in the centre.

At the **Marmar Marble Factory** they polish a black rock estimated to be about 650 million years old, embedded with fossilized shells known as goniatites (ammonites). The slabs, rather reminiscent of tombstones, appear in all the hotels and bars in town. The main quarries are out of town on the road to Merzouga.

Rissani → *For listings, see pages 197-201. Colour map 3, B3.*

Rissani, 22 km south of Erfoud and birthplace of the Alaouite Dynasty, is a sprawling modern village close to the site of the ruined town of Sijilmassa. It has a 17th-century *ksar* which houses most of the population, and the main street has a bank and a few cafés. If you are feeling energetic and have your own transport, you may want to explore other local *ksar* on a heritage trail, the *circuit touristique*.

Places in Rissani
Sijilmassa was once the Berber capital of the Tafilalet region, and a major trading centre. It was founded in 757 by the Arab leader Moussa ben Nasser and its location on the major Sahel to Europe trade route, from Niger to Tangier, gave it considerable importance and prosperity, trading in gold. Its fame grew, as did its size. The ruins, little of which remain, are between the town and the river. A major new kasbah was put up by Moulay Ismaïl, but the Aït Atta tribe destroyed the town in 1818. The current Alaouite Dynasty settled in the surrounding region in the 13th century before gaining the Moroccan Sultanate in the 17th century. The ruins are really of historical interest only and the guides are often not very well informed – although they can be entertaining. Tales of earthquake destruction are on the fanciful side.

To find out more about Rissani's past, you might call in at the **Centre d'Études et Recherches Alaouites (CERA)** ① *T0535-770305, Mon-Fri 0830-1630*, located in the large austere *ksar* on the main square, just along from the **Hotel Sijilmassa**. There is a library and a small museum, which is just a few small cases of pots from recent excavations and large panels with information in French about the region's history. There is a detailed 1:100,000 scale map of the region, and some of the staff may helpfully speak English.

The Ksar circuit around Rissani
The whole feel of the Rissani oasis is rather Mesopotamian, with mud monuments crumbling away to fine dust. The region was once obviously very prosperous, as the palace buildings dotted around here were designed by architects, unlike the *ksar* villages. And in the light of the isolation of Rissani, separated from Erfoud by salt flats, these remains become even more fascinating. Much eroded by the action of the wind, sun and occasional floods, the lost Alhambras of the Tafilalet must have been truly impressive for wandering nomads and caravans coming up from far distant Mali. It was clearly the Arabian Nights city of the medieval imagination.

To the southeast of Rissani is the **Zaouïa of Moulay Ali Cherif**, the founder of the Alaouite Dynasty. This is a new building as the previous one was destroyed by flash flood. Non-Muslims may not enter and are prevented therefore from viewing the beautiful glazed tilework, the central courtyard with fountain and surrounded by palms. Moulay Ali Cherif was buried here in 1640. Near here is the **Ksar Akbar**, a ruined Alaouite palace from the 19th century, which once held vast treasures and the rejects of important families. It is also said to be the palace of Moulay Abd el Rahmane, brother of reforming 19th-century sultan Hassan I.

About 2 km to the south is the **Ksar Ouled Abd el Helim**, nicknamed the 'Alhambra of the Tafilalet'. It was built in 1900 by Moulay Rachid, elder brother of Moulay Hassan, as a governor's residence. Its decorated towers, monumental gateway and cloistered courtyards provide a little grandeur in the oasis.

Tinrheras is the most southerly *ksar* at 770 m above sea level. There is a splendid view from the walls of the hammada to the south and the panorama of the oasis to the north. Off the road to Erfoud, in the vicinity of the **Hotel Kasbah Asmaa**, are some more minor sights, including **Ksar Jebril**, a large, still-populated village to the west, and **Al Mansouria**, another village to the east, about 300 m into the palm groves. Here there are yet more crumbling remains of vanished palaces, including a rather spectacular gate.

Merzouga and the dunes of Erg Chebbi → *For listings, see pages 197-201.*
Colour map 3, B3.

Some 61 km southwest of Erfoud, Merzouga has one attraction: the 150-m-high dunes of Erg Chebbi, a vast pile of sand stretching into the Sahara. The dunes are an offshoot of a much bigger area of dunes across the border in Algeria but, because of the relative accessibility of Erg Chebbi, they have often been used as a film set by Hollywood directors. And it's not hard to see why. As the sun shifts across the sky during the day, the dunes change colour, from the palest cream to deep oranges and reds, and their beautiful shapes and patterns are constantly sculpted by the wind. Despite the popularity of the dunes, it's easy to escape any sign of human habitation, especially if you get up early for a walk. Bear in mind, however, that what might at first appear no more than a lifeless expanse of sand is, in fact, a fragile ecosystem and one that quad bike tours are in danger of destroying.

All of the hotels along the edge of Erg Chebbi organize **camel treks** into the dunes – usually out to semi-permanent tent encampments where you stay a night before coming back to the hotel. The cheaper trips tend to go a short distance to a communal camp where you may find that the romance of a night under the bright Saharan stars is spoiled by the crowds. Pay a bit more and you should get a small camp, with varying degrees of comfort. Camps to the northern or southern slopes of the dunes tend to be quieter. There is little else, beside the other tourists and a small village with a Saturday souk, but the calm and the wilderness are a big part of the appeal. There is occasionally good birdwatching in the adjacent **Dayat Merzouga**, when it has water. Another (summer) option is to have a sand bath, said to be good for rheumatism.

The *piste* continues south to **Taouz**, and the 4WD brigade now travel along the once 'forbidden track' (shown as the *piste interdite* on the maps) west to Remlia and the confluence of the dry river valleys of the Gheris and Ziz. More simply, a *grand taxi* from Rissani to Merzouga will cost around 50dh.

For sleeping and eating price codes and other relevant information, see pages 22-28.

● Where to stay

Er Rachidia and around *p192*

There is not a huge choice of hotels in Er Rachidia, especially at the top of the range.

€€€ Hotel Kenzi-Rissani, Av Moulay Ali Cherif, in the direction of Erfoud, T0535-572584, www.kenzi-hotels.com. Pleasant location on the town's outskirts, 62 rooms, restaurant, bar, tennis and pool, open to non-residents for 50dh daily. Can get very booked up by tour groups at peak times. Better deals available online.

€€€ Hotel Le Riad, Zone touristique d'Errachidia, Rte de Goulmima, T0535-791006, www.hotelleriad.com. A smart place outside the city, with 24 a/c rooms around a good-sized pool.

€€ Auberge Palma Ziz, 30 km north of Er Rachidia on N13, near village of Aït Menzou, T0535-576160, www.palmaziz. com. Simple Berber guesthouse, with 12 satisfactory rooms, tiled floors and pine furniture. Some triple rooms. Most have en suite bathroom. No a/c. Terrace overlooks village and surrounding countryside. Price includes breakfast; half-board and full-board options are available.

€ Hotel Ansar, 34 Rue Ibn Batouta, T0535-573919. Clean hotel with 14 cheap rooms on street leading away from the main street behind bus station. Shared bathrooms.

€ Hotel Errachidia, 31 Rue Ibnou Batouta, T0535-570453. This is a reliable, clean, modern place just behind the bus station. Rooms have TVs, desk and comfy beds. It's far from beautiful, but it does the job.

€ Hotel M'Daghra, Rue Allal Ben Abdallah (if coming from west, turn left at Café Lipton on main drag, hotel is 100 m down on right), T0535-574047. Another modern option in the centre, with 26 rooms with decent showers, good beds and some with balconies.

Tafilalet *p193*
Camping

Camping Tissirt, 30 km south of Er Rachidia, heading to Erfoud, T0662-141378, www.campingtissirtziz.free.fr. On the edge of the Ziz Canyon, the site has great views, shaded garden, a big Berber tent and a couple of *pisé* bungalows. It's 65dh for a caravan, 2 people and electricity.

Erfoud *p194*

Erfoud has a clutch of pricey hotels at the Rissani (southern) side of town, facing towards the distant Merzouga dunes. Many are slightly garish modern takes on the traditional kasbah. Coming from Er Rachidia, cheaper hotels and eateries in the town centre are reached by going left onto Av Mohammed V, at the crossroads with the post office.

€€€ Kasbah Hotel Chergui, 5.5 km from Erfoud heading north to Er Rachidia, T0535-578504, www.hotelchergui.com. Brand new kasbah-style hotel with 100 rooms including 4 'royal' suites. Amenities include huge pool (shaped like the African continent), spa, bar, restaurant and well-kitted out rooms. Shame about the clichéd paintings and some of the decor. Half-board only.

€€€ Kasbah Xaluca Maadid, 205 Rte Errachidia, T0535-578450, www.xaluca.com. Part of a Spanish chain, this super neo-kasbah is 7 km north of town in village of Maadid. It has spacious rooms and large suites with all mod-cons, decorated in local traditional style with palm beams and marble bathrooms. Huge oudoor pool and indoor pool with spa. Service is impersonal. Restaurant and bar.

€€ Hotel Kasbah Tizimi, 2 km out of town on the Tinghir road, T0535-576179, www.kasbahtizimi.com. 65 rooms, 8 suites around patio, pleasant pool, good restaurant. Wrought-iron furniture and *beldi* tiled floors. Some of the bathrooms very scruffy. Popular with package tour groups.

€€ Hotel Tafilalet, Av Moulay Ismail, in town, on left as you arrive from Rachidia, T0535-576535, www.hotel-tafilalet.com. 60 a/c rooms, bar, restaurant, pool and garden. Has had mixed reports – a bit run down and also used by tour groups.

€ Hotel Farah Zouar, Av Moulay Ismail, on right as you leave Erfoud for Rissani, T0535-576230. This has 30 a/c rooms, restaurant serving European and Moroccan food, good views from roof terrace. 17 small rooms, caters more to independent budget travellers and locals than groups.

€ Hotel Merzouga, 114 Av Mohammed V, T0535-576532. Basic but friendly, you can sleep on roof terrace for 25dh. Rooms with shower.

Camping

Tifina Camping, 8 km from Erfoud towards Rissani, T0610-231415, www.tifina-morocco.com. Newly constructed from local materials in vernacular style, an excellent camping complex with premium, comfort and luxury options. Pool, restaurant and clean bathroom facilities. Disabled access.

Rissani *p195*

There are few hotels in Rissani and at peak times of year, they tend to get booked up. It is probably better to stay in Erfoud, where there is much more choice, and make Rissani a day out. Another option would be to stay at one of the various dune hotels at Merzouga.

€€€ Kasbah Ennasra, Rte de Rissani, 2 km north of Rissani, T0535-774403, www.kasbahennasra.it. A very pleasant hotel for a couple of nights, or even just for lunch at its restaurant by the pool. Rooms are spacious with *pisé* walls and some have 4-poster beds. En suite bathrooms and a/c. Family room available. Pool, terrace and bar.

€€ Hotel Kasbah Asmaâ, north of the town at road junction, 15 km from Erfoud, T0661-206336 (mob). 25 a/c en suite rooms. Pool and restaurant. Disorganized management. Can arrange sorties to the dunes at Merzouga for small groups.

€ Hotel-Café-Restaurant Sijilmassa, Pl Massira el Khadra, T0535-575042. Pass through the triumphal arch, the hotel is over on the left, near the mechanics. 10 high-ceilinged rooms with en suite bathrooms, some with 2 double beds. Roof terrace and adequate food, though service and cleanliness is poor. A last option only.

Merzouga and Erg Chebbi *p196*

Spread out along the edge of the dunes, most of Merzouga's hotels are north of the village itself. In fact those further away tend to be preferable – they generally have more space and easy access to the less visited areas of the dunes. Most have obligatory half-board and do their own excursions out onto the dunes. Many close in the summer, when it becomes too hot to go out on the dunes. Flash floods in 2006 destroyed several hotels, some of which have since been rebuilt.

Signs off to the east of the new sealed road from Rissani lead across the sand on bumpy pistes, to ubiquitous *pisé*, kasbah-style accommodation, with high walls around a large central courtyard. Most hotels will offer to meet you out on the main road, which is highly advisable. Note that there are numerous faux guides in the area who will do their best to convince you that certain auberges are closed and lead you elsewhere. If you have GPS, contact the auberge for their precise location.

€€€ Auberge Atlas du Sable, T0535-577037, www.alielcojo.com. 40 colourful rooms, some with a/c (100dh more) around a courtyard pool. Large restaurant that can be noisy with tour groups and motor rally events. Spanish owned, with little English spoken. Overpriced rate for half-board with a/c. Trips go to 2 bivouacs out in the dunes, reachable by camel or 4WD.

€€€ Auberge Kasbah Derkaoua, T0535-577140, www.aubergederkaoua.com. At the northern end of the dunes, Derkaoua is best reached heading southeast out of Erfoud, rather than from the Rissani–Merzouga road. Popular, and a cut above most of the other options, there's a licensed restaurant, a pool, hammam and a tennis court. Rooms are decorated with Moroccan fabrics and the food is magnificent. Book in advance. Bivouac from 550dh per person.

€€€ **Hotel Kasbah Tombuctou**, Hassi Labied, Merzouga, T0535-577091, www. xaluca.com. Rising from the foot of the dunes like a Sahara theme park, this Xaluca-owned hotel is a bit garish, but full of luxury. Rooms are cool, finished in coloured *tadelakt*, some with enormous bathrooms. Huge pool, restaurant and its own bivouac for getting deeper into the sand. All mod cons. Live the dream in the Royal Suite (€€€€).

€€ **Auberge du Sud**, T0661-216166 (mob), www.aubergedusud.com. 20 differently themed rooms and a big dining area. Camel trips (600dh per person) involve 2 or 3 hrs' trekking to a camp with showers and toilets. Each room has its own terrace overlooking the dunes. Solar panels provide electricity and hot water. Free collection from Rissani.

€€ **Auberge Ksar Sania**, by the Grand Dune and the seasonal lake, T0535-577414, www.ksarsaniahotelmerzouga.com. Run by Gérard and Françoise Tommaso, Ksar Saniya was among the places destroyed by flooding in 2006, but has been rebuilt as an unusual hexagonal eco-lodge, with attractive rooms shaped from traditional materials, palms and *tadelakt*. Also offers cheaper self-cooling mud-built 'huts' in the garden. Pool.

€€ **Auberge Le Dunes D'Or**, T0661-350665 (mob), www.aubergedunesdor.com. Comfy *pisé* rooms around a good courtyard with trees around a pool. Cosy eating area. Sand-skiing organized. Half board available.

€€ **Chez Julia**, right in the village of Merzouga itself, T0535-573182. This place offers a very different experience to all the kasbah-style hotels. Small and personal, it's run by the eponymous Austrian owner. The 9 rooms, decorated in pastel tones, have good big beds; the room at the top has good views over Merzouga to the dunes. Facilities are shared but everything is spotlessly clean.

Breakfast (40dh) is taken on the roof terrace and there are lots of Moroccan choices for dinner – especially good for vegetarians – and Austrian desserts too.

€€ **Haven la Chance Desert Hotel**, Hassi Labied, 4 km from Merzouga, T0535-577269, www.desert-hotel.com. Lots of local info and good connections with guides. Rooms are unattractive, but most are en suite with a/c. Nomad-style *khaima* tents on site from 190dh per person half-board, or DIY camping. Also run **Blue Men of Morocco**, see page 200.

€€ **Kasbah Mohayut**, T0666-039185 (mob), www.mohayut.com Colourful rooms with bathrooms and roof terrace. Rooms have a/c and some have private terraces overlooking the dunes. 4 suites added in 2008. There's a pretty pool with a camel fountain, plus restaurant and bar. A popular mid-range option. Half board available.

€ **Auberge Camping Sahara**, Hassi Labied, T0535-577039, www.aubergesahara.com. Simple family-run auberge with shaded camping sites (25dh per person), showers and respectable washing facilities. Also has 20 homely guest rooms, a pool and a restaurant.

Restaurants

Er Rachidia *p192*

€ **Hotel-Café La Renaissance**, 19 Rue Moulay Youssef, T0535-572633. Reliable, with excellent couscous.

€ **Hotel Oasis**, 4 Rue Sidi Abou Abdallah, T0535-572519. Serves Moroccan food and alcohol.

€ **Restaurant Imilchil**, Av Moulay Ali Cherif, T0535-572123. Moroccan standards served on a terrace overlooking the main drag.

€ **Restaurant Lipton**, Av Moulay Ali Cherif. Good food throughout the day and night – and handy for the bus station.

€ **Restaurant Sijilmassa**, Av Moulay Ali Cherif. The most economical place, with a simple but good menu.

There are other cheap places along Av Mohammed V.

Erfoud *p194*

You can eat in (relative) luxury at any of the hotels in Erfoud. The **Kasbah Xaluca** lunch-buffet is delicious for 210dh (see Where to stay, above). For those on a budget, there are places on Av Moulay Ismail and Av Mohammed V.

€€ Dadani, 103 Av Mohammed V, T0535-577958. An excellent little café-restaurant with traditional (and comfortable) Moroccan seating upstairs and a Western-style café downstairs. Very good *kalia*, though don't expect it to come in a hurry. There's even an apartment for rent, should you like it so much you want to stay.

€ Café-Restaurant des Dunes, Av Moulay Ismail, near the Ziz petrol station. Well known.

€ Restaurant-Café du Sud. Very handy for the bus station on Av Mohammed V.

Rissani *p195*

There are not that many eating options in Rissani but the restaurant at **Kasbah Ennasra** is open to the public and serves good Moroccan set menus. Also the **Restaurant Café Merzouga** on Av Moulay Ali Cherif, near the main market, is recommended.

Merzouga *p196*

Most people eat where they're staying, so there's not much in the way of standalone eating options. However, the **Café Nora**, T0667-612191, in Khamlia, just 7 km south of Merzouga on the Taouz road is well worth a visit for a tasty organic lunch or mint tea prepared by Hassan and Souad. Combine it with a visit to the Dar Gnawa next door.

⚐ Shopping

Rissani *p195*

Rissani has a lively market on Sun, Tue and Thu, and there are several handicraft shops. People with large vehicles may like to pick up a hefty chalky-white *khabiya* (water jar) or two, as still used in the region. You could also kit yourself up with full touristic 'blue man' gear, including *gandoura* 'air-conditioned' robe, slit down the sides, baggy *seroual* and a *chèche* (3 m of cotton, sand-proof scarf).

⚙ What to do

Erfoud *p194*

There is a men's **hammam** next to the Hotel Sable d'Or.

Merzouga and Erg Chebbi *p196*

Blue Men of Morocco, www.bluemen ofmorocco.com. Customized tours throughout Morocco. Also run **Haven la Chance Desert Hotel**, see page 199.

Dar Gnawa Khamlia, T0668-247150, www.khamlia.com. 7 km south of Merzouga on road to Taouz, next to **Café Nora** is this open house of local Gnawa musicians, the music that was brought to this region by slaves from sub-Saharan Africa. Hamad Mahjoubi will even teach you to play, or organize a ceremony for you. Ideal for sandstorm days.

⊖ Transport

Er Rachidia *p192*
Leave from the bus station off Av Mohammed V, T0535-572760. Early morning departure for the long ride to **Figuig**. There are also buses to **Casablanca**, **Marrakech** and **Meknès**.

Erfoud *p194*
There are buses each day to **Er Rachidia** and on to **Meknès**. Transport onwards to **Rissani** is by bus, *grand taxi*, or by a hired 4WD.

Rissani *p195*
Although there is a new *gare routière*, before the ceremonial arch as you come into town

from the north, lots of buses still come into the main square. There is a **CTM** bus (T0535-770238), leaving from the Marché Verte, for **Er Rachidia** and **Meknès** every evening, plus occasional *grands taxis* across to places on the Zagora to Ouazarzate road.

❶ Directory

Er Rachidia *p192*
Car parts Renault and other vehicle parts, also tyre repair, at place opposite the Hotel Meski. **Medical services** Chemist: Blvd Moulay Ali Cherif, open all night, and one near Café Lipton and next to bridge in same building as Café Bousten. **Useful numbers** Fire: T15. Police: T19.

Erfoud *p194*
In the town centre near the Av Moulay Ismail/Av Mohammed V junction are a pharmacy and doctor. There is a BMCE ATM next to the Total garage on the east side of the main drag, just before the Hotel Tafilalet, as you go north.

Todra and Dadès gorges

The 'Road of the Thousand Kasbahs', as it is marketed, runs between Er Rachidia and Ouarzazate, through arid plains and oases with a backdrop of harsh mountain landscapes, where semi-nomadic Berbers pasture their flocks. The modern world has arrived, however: tourist buses and 4WDs bring their flocks to the growing villages at the start of the spectacular gorges, and the new buildings replacing the crumbling kasbahs these days use concrete breeze blocks rather than pisé. Nevertheless, there is plenty to see, as well as walking opportunities along this route. Skoura is an oasis town with old kasbahs and El Kalaâ is the centre of Morocco's rose-growing industry. Those with 4WDs can try the bumpy mountain tracks leading into the Massif du Mgoun, or the rugged gorge-to-gorge route from Tineghir to Boumalne. ▶▶ *For listings, see pages 205-209.*

West from Er Rachidia → *For listings, see pages 205-209.*

Goulmima → *Colour map 3, B3.*
Goulmima (not to be confused with Goulimine, south of Agadir, see page 258) is one of a series of expanding small towns, mainly Amazigh in population, around the eastern side of the High Atlas. There is a lot of new property on the outskirts and the town is well served with water, electricity and telephones. For visitors, the main attraction is the large number of *ksar* out in the palm groves (ask at **Les Palmiers**, page 205, about a guide). Much of the town is to the north of the road in the main oasis. Market day is Monday.

There is a road north from Goulmima leading to the villages of the High Atlas (only suitable for 4WD). It is surfaced for the 55 km to Amellago, from where it is possible to circle back to the Todra Gorge and/or the Dadès Gorge.

Tinejdad → *Colour map 3, B2.*
At the junction of the Er Rachidia, Tineghir and Erfoud roads, Tinejdad is an Amazigh and Haratine town in a large oasis, with some significant kasbahs, notably the Ksar Asrir. There are a lot of bicycles in Tinejdad, so be particularly careful if driving through. The central square has a post office, the town gardens, town hall, telephones, taxis and petrol station.

Tineghir → *Colour map 3, B2.*
Once a tiny oasis settlement, Tineghir is now a modern administrative centre, its population swelled by technicians and staff working for the local mining company. Tourism is taking on importance, and the town is an ideal stay on the road east to the Tafilalet. It also makes a good first night stop on a walking holiday.

Tineghir is an unexpectedly large place. There is the modern hub, now ribboning east and west along the N10, as well as the older kasbah settlements a few kilometres north from the town, overlooking the irrigated plain as one climbs out of the town towards the Gorge du Todra. The contrast of magnificent barren mountains and verdant oases is stark. For the rushed, there are views from the gorge road, otherwise you might explore on foot; hire a guide for 40dh. You will find olive and fruit trees inter-cropped with cereals and vegetables, herds of sheep and goats out to pasture in the foothills. As elsewhere in the region, there is much new building along the roads, the old *ksar* partly abandoned to the side. The main population belong to the Aït Atta tribe. Try to visit the **Kasbah el Glaoui** on the hill above the town. Although officially closed, it is normally possible to get in.

South from Tineghir

The village of **Aït Mohammed** is southeast of Tineghir and clearly visible from the main road. It stands on the minor road that goes along the *oued* to El Hart-n'Igouramène. A track due south leads into the **Jbel Saghro**, aiming for the village of **Iknioun**, which nestles under the central heights. It eventually connects with the desert road from Erfoud to Zagora.

Todra Gorge → *For listings, see pages 205-209. Colour map 3, B2.*

The Todra Gorge, particularly spectacular in the evening, when the rocks are coloured in bands of bright sunlight and dark shadow, is narrower and more winding than the Dadès Gorge. There are campsites and places to stay near the narrowest part of the gorge, a highly recommended break from the activity of the major towns.

The 14-km route up the gorge is very narrow, and you will have to slow down for kids playing near the road. Also watch out for the tyre-splitting road edge when you move over for a bus thundering towards you. (Tourist buses and 4WDs head up to the gorge for lunch.)

Just north of Tineghir, as the road climbs up, is the village of **Aït Ouaritane**. There are many good views and some stopping places on the road. The safest place to stop is generally picketed with camels; the most spectacular has fossil and scarf sellers. Neat strips of crops in the oasis gardens and crumbling kasbah villages spread out below.

Some 9 km from Tineghir are campsites in an idyllic location in a palm grove. About 6 km further on is the most visited section of the gorge, where the high cliffs leave just enough space for the road and river. As you might imagine, rocks, palm groves and river make this a good environment for birds. There are some hotels (eg **La Vallée**) before the ford (which should present no problems for ordinary cars) and you can then carry on up to the next two hotels, **Les Roches** and **Yasmina**, which squat in bogus kasbah style under a spectacular overhanging bit of gorge.

Tamtatouchte and beyond

The more adventurous will want to continue beyond the narrow confines of the Gorge du Todra. The village of Tamtatouchte is a steady climb of about four hours. The **Auberge Baddou**, the **Auberge Bougafer** and various other rudimentary establishments provide food and accommodation. A few lorries returning from the souk use this route and may provide you with a lift, if necessary. With 4WD, many of the smaller villages to the north can be reached. With a good driver, connections can be made westwards to the Dadès Gorge or northwards to Imilchil (see page 120).

Gorge to gorge

Though rough, the 42 km west to **Msemrir** and the Dadès Gorge from Tamtatouchte, rising to 2800 m, is popular with the 4WD brigade. It can be done in five hours. This journey is best undertaken in a good 4WD vehicle with reliable local driver. Ensure that tyre pressure is higher than normal, as tracks are very stony, and that you have a full petrol tank. Find out about the condition of the piste before departure. This route is best undertaken between May and September. At other times of year, potential flash floods make it dangerous. It is probably best to do this route starting at the Todra Gorge so you do the most difficult pass, the one after Tamtatouche, 2800 m, first. At Msemrir, a popular base village for treks, there are a couple of simple places to stay, including the **Auberge el Ouarda** and the **Auberge Agdal**.

Boumalne du Dadès

Boumalne is a small town, with a reasonable selection of hotels, though most people prefer to head on up the Dadès valley and stay there. The town grew from a very basic settlement to its current size mainly in the second half of the 20th century. In the Muslim cemetery there is the domed shrine of one Sidi Daoud. He is commemorated in an annual festival, when bread is baked from flour left at the grave and fed to husbands to ensure their fertility. Wednesday is market day. Approaching from the west, there is usually a Gendarmerie royale checkpoint at the intersection before the bridge, so slow down.

From a high point above the town, a barracks and some hotels look out over the harsh and rocky landscape. If you are a birdwatcher, you may well want to head off south to the **Vallée des Oiseaux** (on the road from Boumalne to Iknioun). The track southeast which leaves the N10 road just east of Boumalne gives easy access into the desert. It rises steadily to Tagdilt and provides possibilities for spotting desert birds and, less likely, desert fauna.

Through the gorge → *Colour map 3, B2.*

The R704 leaves the N10 at Boumalne and follows the Oued Dadès through limestone cliffs, which form the striking Dadès Gorge. The principal destination is the section of the gorge following Aït Oudinar, but the track continues up into the High Atlas, with public transport as far as Msemrir. There are very basic pistes into the mountains and around into the Todra Gorge (see page 203).

Just beyond Boumalne is **Aït Arbi**, where there are a series of striking *ksar* above the road. The road continues past areas of unusual rock formations, through Tamnalt and **Aït Oudinar**, where there is basic accommodation. The valley narrows after Aït Oudinar, creating the most striking area of the gorge, where the cliffs are vivid shades of red. The road continues alongside the *oued* as far as **Msemrir**, just beyond which it branches. The right-hand branch turns into a difficult track, running east across the pass (2800 m) and continuing to link with the R703 through the Todra Gorge, or up into the High Atlas. The gorges and crags offer a good environment for golden and Bonelli's eagles and lammergeiers, and the scree slopes for blue rock thrushes.

El Kalaâ des Mgouna and the Vallée des Roses → *For listings, see pages 205-209. Colour map 3, B1.*

A ribbon-development place, El Kalaâ des Mgouna, 1¼ hours' drive from Ouarzazate, is the capital of the Moroccan rose-essence industry and centre of the Mgouna tribe. (The name means 'Citadel of the Mgouna' and is also spelt Qalat Mgouna.) The former French administrative centre has become a sprawling town, with banks, police, small shops for provisions, petrol and a Wednesday market. The blooms in the Vallée des Roses flower in late spring. The rose festival is held in early May, with dances and processions under a shower of rose petals to celebrate the harvest. The children at the roadside will try to sell bunches of roses and garlands of rose petals, and there are plenty of shops selling rose water, *crème à la rose*, rose-scented soap and dried roses.

Background

A picturesque local legend runs that pilgrims travelling back from Mecca brought with them 'the Mother of All Flowers', the Damascus rose, initiating the rose industry. It may be, however, that sometime in the 20th century, French perfumers realized that conditions in this out-of-the-way part of southern Morocco would be ideal for the large-scale cultivation of the bushy *Rosa centifolia*. Today, there are hundreds of kilometres of rose bush hedges, co-existing with other crops, and two factories, distilling rose essence. The one in a kasbah-like building can be visited. To produce a litre of good quality rose oil requires around five tonnes of petals, you will be told. The locals feel, however, that the price paid by the factories is too low and prefer to sell dried rose petals on local markets. Pounded up, the petals can be used mixed with henna or other preparations.

Places in El Kalaâ

While based in El Kalaâ, if you are feeling energetic you may want to head northwards 15 km up the Mgoun Valley to the **Ksar de Bou Thrarar**, at the entrance of the **Mgoun Gorges**. Less adventurously, there is a dagger-making workshop and showroom, **Co-operative Artisan du Poignards Azlag**, on the eastern outskirts of the town. For trekking options in the Massif Mgoun, see Azilal High Atlas section, Vallée des Aït Bougmez, on page 118.

Skoura oasis → *Colour map 2, B5.*

The large oasis fed by the Oued Idelssan has irrigated land growing palms, olives and cereals. The Oued Hajag crosses the road on the western side of Skoura. The small settlement here has a white square mosque with white cupola. You can now bypass the town on the main road. Nevertheless, the palm groves are worth stopping to explore on foot, bicycle or even on horseback (See What to do, page 209).

Before the actual village, to the left of the road (if coming from Ouarzazate), is **Kasbah Amerhidl**, the largest of Skoura's kasbahs. The village also includes two kasbahs formerly occupied by the El Glaoui family, **Dar Toundout** and **Dar Lahsoune**.

◉ Todra and Dadès gorges listings

For sleeping and eating price codes and other relevant information, see pages 22-28.

◒ Where to stay

Goulmima *p202*

€€€ Chez Pauline, Tadighoust, 15 km from Goulmima, T0535-885425, www.gite chezpauline.com. French-run guesthouse surrounded by peach, fig and olive trees, with the odd chicken scuttling across the farm. 4 rustic whitewashed en suite rooms in the main house sleep 2-5 people and are tastefully decorated with African artefacts. Each has a/c. 2 annexes offer dorm-style accommodation at 120dh per person. Camping also available. Excellent food.
€€ Les Palmiers, T0535-784004, www. palmiersgoulmima.com. 5 bright, clean en suite rooms. Space for small tents in

the verdant garden. Franco-Moroccan management. Recommended.

Tinejdad *p202*

€€€ Ksar el Khorbat, T0535-880355, www.elkhorbat.com. Built within an 18th-century *ksar*, there are 10 huge, characterful rooms with bathrooms and plenty of Moroccan rugs. Pool, restaurant and library. Winner of the 2010 Responsible Tourism Award. Obligatory half-board.

Tineghir *p202*

€€ Hotel Kenzi Bougafer, Blvd Mohammed V, T0524-833200, www. bougafer-saghro.com. An early 1990s hotel, lacking personality, located 2 km west of town. Comfortable, clean, good pool, alcohol, noisy with tour groups. Mixed reports. Doubles 680hd half-board.

€€ **Hotel Tomboctou**, 126 Av Bir Anzane (take 1st major left coming into Tineghir from west), T0524-835291, www.hoteltomboctou. com. Good cool rooms in a restored kasbah, small pool, secure car parking available. Eco-savvy. Mountain bikes for rent, plus sketch maps of region. The best option in town.

€€ **Kasbah Lamrani**, Zone Touristique, Blvd Mohammed V, T0524-835017, www. kasbahlamrani.com. A modern hotel with nods to the local traditional style, such as a fountain in the reception and beamed ceilings. Large rooms, all with a/c or heating and some with balcony overlooking the pool. Bar and restaurant.

€ **Hotel l'Avenir**, on the 2nd square, T0524-834599. On 1st floor above a pharmacy, 12 small rooms, very clean, good beds, roof terrace. Some rooms only open onto corridor, square below is noisy. Bike hire.

€ **Hotel Oasis**, Pl Principale, T0524-833670. Cheap, clean, central, welcoming, upstairs restaurant with good food and views over town. Price includes breakfast.

Camping

Camping Almo, centre of town on south of road. Very secure, pool, shop. Summer only.

Camping Ourti, south of road at western end of town opposite **Hotel Kenzi Bougafer**, T0524-833205. Very secure, restaurant, bungalows, pool but quite a walk from town. All sites have electricity for caravans. Perhaps the best of the bunch.

Todra Gorge *p203*

In winter it gets pretty chilly at night and, in late summer, the river can swell suddenly after thunderstorms in the mountains, so choose your camping place with care.

€€ **Dar Ayour**, 13 km up the gorge, just before the narrowest point, T0524-895271, www.darayour.com. Stylish guesthouse with plum-coloured *tadelakt* walls, Berber rugs and a warm welcome. Built right on the edge of the river, overlooking the gardens. Rooms are colourful, with tiny en suite bathrooms. Recommended.

€€ **Hotel Kasbah Amazir**, just after Camping Les Poissons Sacrés, stone building, T0524-895109. 15 a/c rooms (6 triple, 9 double), garden terraces shaded by towering date palms, and a pool. Anxious to please. Recommended.

€€ **Hotel Yasmina**, T0524-895118. Near the top of the valley, **Yasmina** has 50 functional rooms, all renovated with heaters and a/c. Fake *pisé* walls, lots of blankets, very blue bathrooms and candles. Not the most beautiful hotel but a fair mid-range choice. Camping by arrangement. Sleeping on roof is also a possibility. Hot water is only provided when the generator is working to produce light, so have your shower in the evening and take a torch. Rooms are heated in winter.

€ **Hotel-Camping Atlas**, just opposite *téléboutique*, T0524-895046. Has 6 rooms, also camping. Rooms are in small building overlooking site, meals cooked to order. Same management as **Hotel Kasbah Amazir**.

€ **Hotel-Camping du Soleil**, aka Chez Bernard, T0524-895111, www.hotelcamping lesoleil.com. A bit lacking in shade, otherwise an excellent site. Has a small pool, washing machines and they can put you in contact with a local for mule rides in the region.

Boumalne du Dadès *p204*

€€€ **La Perle du Dades**, 5 km from town centre on very rough track on the Er-Rachidia side of the river, T0524-850548, www.perledudades.com. Beautifully restored Kasbah opened in 2007, with 14 spacious rooms, split-level suites and novel 'troglodyte' cave-rooms. Full of homely furnishings, basketware, books, an old piano and cosy nooks. Pool. Great views from terrace and loads of activities. Food can be disappointing. Not much English spoken. Breakfast included.

€€€ **Xaluca Dades**, heading out of town on the Er Rachidia road, signposted off to the left, T0524-830060, www.xaluca.com. Former 1970s state-owned hotel given a heavy-handed Afro revamp. 110 rooms with stone walls, *tadelakt* shower and vibrant printed fabrics. Plenty of facilities, pool, restaurant, bar and ideal for families needing space.

€€ **Auberge de Soleil Bleu**, up a slightly rough track past **Hotel Xaluca**, T0524-830163, www.hotelsoleilbleu.com. 12 rooms with bath, good restaurant, fine views, camping permitted, treks organized into High Atlas and Jbel Saghro. Popular with walkers and birdwatchers.

€€ **Kasbah Tizzarouine**, T0524-830690. A large hotel complex on the plateau overlooking Boumalne from the south (at top of slope, turn right just before large mural). Fine views over the Oued Dadès and the mountains to the north. Accommodation includes fairly traditional buildings with all modern comforts, tiny underground rooms (troglodyte), cool in summer and cosy in winter, or even nomad tents kept cool by the breeze.

€€-€ **Auberge Al Manader**, Av Mohammed V, on the Er Rachidia road, a pink building overlooking the valley near the **Hotel Chems**, T0524-830172. Has 12 good clean rooms, 4 with bathroom and a/c, panoramic views.

€ **Hotel-Restaurant Chems**, Av Mohammed V, at the top of the slope heading for Er Rachidia, on the right on the bend, T0524-830041. Has 10 double rooms, 5 single rooms with bathrooms. Well maintained, nice reception, restaurant.

Dadès Gorge *p204*
Make sure you have enough blankets, as it gets cold at night. Most places here offer half-board. The better places are mostly further up the valley, though there are plenty of choices.

€€ **Auberge des Gorges Dadès**, T0524-831719, www.aubergeaitoudinar.com. Good camping under trees on grass by the stream. Alternatively, go for one of the 32 rooms with slightly sagging beds and little balconies.

€€ **Kasbah de Victor**, 31 km north from Boumalne, T0622-290268, www.lakasbah devictor.com. 4 bright rooms in a French-run guesthouse perched out on the rocks. Heated in winter, pool, Berber tent and restaurant with interesting variations on Berber standards, such as lamb tagine with apple, or camel tagine with harissa.

€€ **Le Vieux Chateau du Dadès**, T0524-831261, www.hotellevieuxchateau.com. 30 rooms, all with bathrooms and views over the canyon. There's also a big, wood-clad dining room and a covered terrace over the stream.

€€ **Les 5 Lunes**, Ait Oudinar, T0524-830723, www.les5lunes.com. Belgian-Moroccan run, this traditionally built little place has a different vibe to most of the accommodation in the valley. Flamenco music plays, there are old Berber wooden locks on the doors and the freshly made pancakes for breakfast are excellent. There are only 5 rooms, a salon with a fire, and a roof terrace with good views over the greenest part of the valley. Thoroughly laid-back.

€€ **Timzillite**, T0677-264347. Up above the much-photographed hairpins at the top of the canyon, **Timzillite** has views that are hard to beat, as long as you don't suffer from vertigo. 6 rooms are small but cosy, and there's solar power for electricity and water. The roadside café is a popular stopping place.

€ **Atlas Berbere**. T0524-831742. All rooms here have heating and a view, and some have two: over the stream and down the valley. The food is good and there are veggie options, such as ratatouille. The friendly owner will proudly tell you that he is the creator of the fake *pisé* wall effect ubiquitous in the Dadés valley. There's music every evening and a wood fire. It's worth trying to bargain on the price. You can sleep on the roof terrace for 25dh.

€ **Auberge des Peupliers**, T0524-831748, www.hoteldespeupliers.com. 12 traditionally styled rooms with heating in winter. Good tiled bathroom and mock *pisé* walls carved with Berber motifs. Open fire in the salon/restaurant. Camping by the river is also an option.

€ **Auberge Tissadrine**, T0524-831745, www.auberge-tissadrine.com. The hotel faces a side canyon that you can walk up across the other side of the stream. All 14 rooms have en suite bathrooms; the best rooms have a little balcony over the stream, while some look onto the road.

€ **Kasbah de la Vallée**, T0524-831717, www.kasbah-vallee-dades.com. Of the 40 rooms, 15 have generous balconies overlooking the silver poplars and fruit trees in the valley and there's a/c and heating. When it's warm enough, breakfast can be taken on the terrace. The restaurant has an open fire and live music but big groups mean the atmosphere is less than intimate. Trips are organized up into the mountains or down to the Vallée des Roses. Mountain bikes for hire.

El Kalaâ *p204*

€€ **Kasbah Assafar**, 5 km from El Kelaâ des Mgouna on the road to Bou Tharar, T0524-836577, www.kasbahassafar.com. Fantastic views of the Rose Valley from this authentic converted kasbah. 8 rather cramped rooms sleeping up to 3 people in each. Shared bathrooms, loads of character and excellent local knowledge. Official mountain guides on hand.

€€ **Kasbah Itran**, 3 km from El Kelaâ des Mgouna heading to Bou Tharar, T0524-837103, www.kasbahitran.com. A tiny auberge run by a Spanish-Moroccan partnership, perched up on a cliff on the road up to Bou Tharar and into the Massif du Mgoun. 6 attractive, homely rooms, 3 with en suite bathrooms. Great views of Kasbah Mirna to the south and Kasbah du Glaoui to north. Can organize local treks. Recommended.

Skoura oasis *p205*

€€€€ **Dar Ahlam**, T0524-852239, www.maisondesreves.com. One of the most exclusive addresses in Morocco. Prices start at around 12,600dh per night all inclusive. Special 'discovery' offers off-season.

€€€ **Dar Lorkam**, T0524-85 2240, www.dar-lorkam.com. Over the river in the *palmeraie*, an attractive place with 6 rooms and 1 family suite with attached bathrooms. Pool.

€€€ **Jardins de Skoura**, www.lesjardins deskoura.com. Hammocks by the pool, breakfast in the gardens and open fires for cold winter evenings. Beautiful *pisé* rooms and *tadelakt* bathrooms. A popular stopping-off point deep in the *palmeraie* and from where you might not want to move on.

€€€ **Kasbah Aït Ben Moro**, 3 km west of Skoura proper, T0524-852116, www.aitben moro.com. A beautifully refurbished building a few metres off the main bypass. Rooms are dark, as kasbah rooms tend to be, decor is austere and elegant. From the roof terrace and garden there are views over the palm groves to the Kasbah d'Amerdihil. 13 rooms, 4 suites and 3 tower rooms (660dh) with shared bath. Can organize horse riding.

€ **Chez Slimani**, T0661-746882 (mob), www.chezslimani.com. A simple gîte-type place with 7 basic rooms in an old kasbah somewhat hidden in the *palmeraie*, some 200 m from the Kasbah d'Amerdihil.

🍴 Restaurants

Tinejdad *p202*

Café el Fath, **Café Assagm** and **Café Ferkla** are possibilities for refreshment. **Café Oued Ed-Dahab**, stands north of Tinejdad at the junction with the road to Erfoud.

Tineghir *p202*

There are no exciting gastronomic choices here. **Hotel Oasis**, Pl Principale, is a little cheaper than the other hotel restaurants. **Hotel Saghro** has a fair though expensive restaurant. **Hotel Todra**, 32 Av Hassan II, is cheaper. **La Gazelle d'Or**, in the town centre, is also good. **La Kasbah**, Av Mohammed V, is a friendly place with good food.

Boumalne du Dadès *p204*

A few decent options frequented by tourists are along the main road, just across the river and at the bottom of the Av Mohammed V. **Café Atlas**, in the centre, is good for food or just a tea or coffee. **Hotel-Restaurant Salam**, in the centre, serves food, tea or coffee. **Restaurant Chems**, just outside Boumalne, on the Er Rachidia road, is perhaps the best option with its pleasant terrace.

El Kalaâ *p204*

Café-Restaurant Rendez-Vous des Amis, Av Mohammed V, T0661-871443. Popular and reliable for tasty tagines and snacks.

O Shopping

Tineghir *p202*

There is a souk on Tue, behind the Hotel Todra and there are small shops on the main square (Pl Principale).
Chez Michelle Supermarket, T0524-834668. For alcohol, snacks and trekking supplies.

El Kalaâ *p204*

Apart from the ubiquitous rose products (best buy: large pink heart-shaped rose-flavoured soap), you could try:
Coopérative du poignard, the Dagger Makers' Cooperative, on the right shortly after the centre. Making daggers is a craft tradition carried on from the now-departed Jewish communities in the region, and most of the artisans are concentrated in Azlague, south of the Coopérative.

O What to do

Boumalne du Dadès *p204*
Trekking
Bureau des Guides, bottom of Av Mohammed V, main street, T0667-593292.

El Kalaâ *p204*
Trekking
El Kelaâ is a good base town for trekking; call the **Bureau des Guides de Montagne**,

1 km before the town centre, on south side of road, T0524-836577, T0661-796101 (mob). The Kasbah Assafar also has plenty of contacts with guides. Ambitious walkers in late spring and summer may want to try to climb **Irhil Mgoun**, at 4068 m one of the highest peaks in the central High Atlas. A good 7-day circuit would take you up to Amesker and back via Aït Youl.

Skoura oasis *p205*
Horse riding
Skoura Equestrian Centree, 2 km from Skoura on Toundout road, T0661-432163 (mob). Lessons and treks through the Skoura oasis. For beginners and experienced riders.

O Transport

Tineghir *p202*
There are buses to many locations, including **Ouarzazate** (5 hrs), **Erfoud** (3 hrs) and **Er Rachidia** (3 hrs). Grands taxis go to **Boumalne du Dadès** (1 hr). Buses leave from Pl Principale. *Grands taxis* and mini-vans run from the eastern end of the town gardens in Tineghir up through the Todra Gorge. Some of the hotels will happily organize trips to the Gorge for you, but check out the prices locally to avoid being overcharged.

If driving, pass through ribbon settlements in this region with care, especially in the evenings; watch out for small children, bicycles, mopeds and donkeys.

O Directory

Tineghir *p202*
Banks Banque du Maroc, along with other banks, on the Av Mohammed V. **Post** Poste Maroc, on main square.

El Kalaâ *p204*
Banks Wafa Bank and Banque populaire right on main intersection. **Medical services Pharmacy**: Blvd Mohammed V, T0524-836392. **Doctor**: Dr Brahim Charaf, T0524-836118, home T0524-850061.

Ouarzazate

The name 'Ouarzazate' (pronounced wah-za-zatt) may be highly evocative of a dusty desert fort but the reality is unfortunately a little more prosaic. As a result of the lucrative film industry that blossomed here in the 1990s and early 2000s, infrastructure was radically improved to cater for visiting stars, crews and local workers. The once-isolated French military outpost now has an international airport, a core of luxury hotels alongside its kasbah and a Cinematography School. Though the garrison remains, the needs of the regional administration and migrant worker remittances have since created a large town. Ouarzazate should thus be seen as a pragmatic base for exploring valleys and oases south of the High Atlas, a transit point for mountain and desert. The region is at its best in early spring, when blossom is on the almond trees and snow still covers the summits of the Atlas. ➤➤ For listings, see pages 214-217.

Arriving in Ouarzazate ➔ Colour map 2, C5.

Possible routes Local tour companies often sell Ouarzazate as a long day trip from Marrakech. This is only really worthwhile if the journey includes **Telouet** (see page 110). It would be better to make an overnight stop in Ouarzazate, after a leisurely drive over the Tizi-n-Tichka pass, taking in the kasbahs at Telouet and Aït Benhaddou. The following day, you could explore sights east from Ouazarzate (Skoura, El Kelaâ des Mgouna and the Rose Valley), making a loop via Bou Thrarar and the Dadès Gorge if you have a 4WD vehicle, before the long drive back. Alternatively, Ouarzazate or any of the Dadès towns and

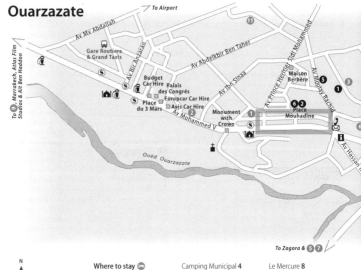

Ouarzazate

N

Not to scale

Where to stay		
Amlal 1	Camping Municipal 4	Le Mercure 8
Azoul 2	Dar Daif 5	Oscar 9
Berbere Palace 3	Kenzi Azghor 6	Royal 10
	La Vallée 7	Villa Kerdabo 11

Tineghir can be used as overnight stops on the Atlas tour from Fès to Marrakech or vice versa, other possible overnights being Er Rachidia, Midelt, Beni Mellal or Azilal. Another option, if you are more of a day walker, is to spend a couple of nights in Skoura, Boumalne or Tineghir in order to explore palm groves and gorges. The narrow roads that lead up both the gorges of Dadès and Todra have a scattering of auberges and small hotels that place you near to the best trekking. There's some good mountain biking from Skoura and Boumalne. Those driving should take great care; the main roads are narrow, wind up and over high passes and get busy with vehicles driven too fast by experienced local drivers.

Getting there Although Ouarzazate is served by charter flights from France, most visitors come in by road. **Taourirt airport** is 2 km northeast of Ouarzazate. From the airport, get a *petit taxi* to your hotel for around 10-20dh. The **CTM** bus terminal is on Avenue Mohammed V, on the corner of Avenue Moulay Rachid, next to the Post Office. Private line buses and *grands taxis* arrive at the bus station at the western end of town, on Avenue Moulay Abdellah. It is a hefty walk from this bus station to the main hotels; best take a *petit taxi*.
▸▸ *See Transport, page 217, for further details.*

Getting around Hotels in the town centre are mainly along Avenue Mohammed V and Avenue Moulay Rachid or over the causeway in Hayy Tabount. As you come down Avenue Mohammed V, heading east from the bus station, is the large **Place du 3 Mars**, a large square on your left. Here there are a few tour agencies, cafés and the Palais des Congrès. Further along the main street are banks, hotels, restaurants, cafés, shops, car rental agencies, tour companies and petrol stations. The **old market** area is now closed to traffic

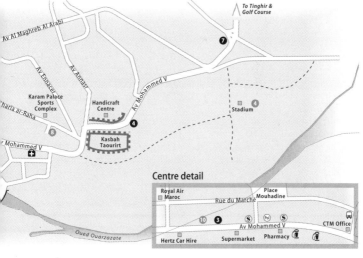

Restaurants 🍴
Accord Majeur **1**
Café Restaurant Aux
  Bons Amis **2**

Chez Dmitri **3**
Douyria **4**
La Datte D'Or **5**
Patisserie Habouss **6**

Relais de Saint-Exupèry **7**

and offers some interesting clothing, jewellery, spice and ceramics stalls before opening out onto to the **Place Al Mouahadine**, which in turn offers pavement snack-restaurants, an excellent patisserie and several desert tour agencies. The famous **Kasbah Taourirt** is located at the eastern edge of town and is an easy walk from the town centre.

Getting to the spectacular kasbah at **Aït Ben Haddou** is awkward without your own car. You could club together with other tourists and hire a *grand taxi*, or you could get a bus going up the N9 Marrakech road, get off at the turn-off for the kasbah – and walk the rest. A few kilometres out of Ouarzazate, just off the Marrakech road, **Tifoultoute Kasbah** and the **Atlas Film Studios** are easily reached by *grand taxi*. Skoura, east along the Boumalne du Dadès N10 road, is easily accessible by local bus or *grand taxi*. Both Aït Ben Haddou and Skoura have good accommodation options.

Tourist information Délégation du Tourisme ① *Av Mohammed V, opposite CTM bus terminal, T0524-882485, Mon-Fri 0900-1200, 1430-1830.*

Places in Ouarzazate

Strategically placed at the confluence of three rivers, Ouarzazate has had a military presence since the Almohad period. In the late 19th century, the kasbah came under control of the Glaoui family, who used it as a power base to develop their control of the South. In 1926, the first airfield was built and, in 1928, a regular French military garrison was installed. Ouarzazate was henceforth the main administrative town for the region, the nerve centre for the Lyautey method of expanding French influence into tribal areas. A few buildings from this period straggle along the main street. Around and above them are the large hotels, built mainly in the 1980s. Today, Ouarzazate is a solid, if sleepy, little town with a **market** on Sunday and Tuesday.

The immediate vicinity of Ouarzazate is often used as a film location. Since *Lawrence of Arabia* was filmed at Aït Ben Haddou, the region, close to mountains and desert, has been a popular director's choice. **Atlas Studios** ① *5 km along the road to Marrakech (look out for the mock Egyptian statues signalling the studios), T0524-882212, www.hotel-oscar-ouarzazate.com, 0830-1900, 50dh*, never seem to be out of work, and the town is keen to market itself as a kind of Moroccan Hollywood. *Hideous Kinky, Gladiator, Kundun, The Last Temptation of Christ, Babel* and *Alexander the Great* were all made here; you can see various bits of set and props on a 30-minute guided tour, as long as there's no filming in progress.

The historic highlight of Ouarzazate is the **Kasbah Taourirt** ① *east of the town centre along Av Mohammed V, daily 0800-1830, 20dh*. Constructed largely in the 19th century, the building had its heyday in the 1930s and would have housed the Glaoui chief's extended family, servants and followers, as well as a community of tradesmen, artisans and cultivators. Today it's one of Ouarzazate's poorest areas. The part adjacent to the road, probably quarters for the Glaoui family, has been maintained and can be visited.

Around Ouarzazate

Mansour Eddahbi Dam → *Colour map 2, C5.*
To the east of Ouarzazate, the Mansour Eddhabi Dam on the Oued Drâa has created a lake over 20 km long. Birdwatchers come here to see the wintering and migrating wildfowl. Visitors include spoonbills and flamingos, when there is sufficient water in the dam. In recent years, water levels have fallen spectacularly (the lakeside golf course is a ghost of

its former self) and the villas built as pricey lakeside retreats are now a fair way from the water. About 13 km from Ouarzazate, tracks from the N10 lead down towards the northern shore; one is signed into a gated reserve. (You should be able to enter if you show your binoculars and say you are a birder.) Another access point is via the Royal Golf club. The southern shore is more difficult to reach and access to the dam itself is prohibited. The best time to visit the lake is in spring or autumn.

Kasbah of Tifoultoute

Take the N9 from Ouarzazate north towards Marrakech. After 6 km, turn left on the road marked for Zagora and Agdz. After 1 km turn left again and after about 7 km you will come to the village of Tifoultoute with its splendid **kasbah** ① *T0524-882813, www.kasbah-tifoultout.com*, built for the Glaoui family in the early 20th century. It stands alongside the Oued Igissi. Still owned by the family, it has adequate food, guesthouse accommodation and magnificent views. You can visit for 10dh and climb up to the roof terrace for views of the countryside and a stork's nest on one of the turrets. A visit to the kasbah of Aït Ben Haddou (see below) could be combined with a visit here.

Oasis of Fint

For those with 4WDs or hardy cars, the oasis of Fint is a possible destination, a few kilometres out in the desert west of Ouarzazate, across the Tabount causeway.

Aït Ben Haddou → *Colour map 2, B4.*

Up on a dramatic hillside, the kasbah of Aït Ben Haddou, 30 km from Ouarzazate, is one of the largest complexes of traditional packed-earth buildings in Morocco, hence its place on the UNESCO-sponsored World Heritage List. The place's fame has spread far and wide and, in high season, coach load after coach load of visitors drive up, pause for a few photographs to be taken and then leave.

The turn-off for Aït Ben Haddou is clearly signed from the N9, 22 km from Ouarzazate. A large *marabout* with ridged cupola and crenellated edges on the tower is a prominent landmark to make sure you don't miss your way. The route follows the valley, with the *oued* on the right. The first village is **Tissergate**. After a further 10 km the much-filmed kasbah comes into view on the right, set up above the bright green of the irrigated fields. The kasbah towers offer views across the area, and the old village also includes a large *agadir*, or store house.

Aït Ben Haddou grew because of its strategic location on the south side of the Atlas, near the convergence of the Drâa and Dadès Valley routes. The village is a must for tourists, both because of its unique architecture and its role in the film industry, with *Lawrence of Arabia*, *Jewel of the Nile* and *Gladiator* all having been filmed here, as well as *Jesus of Nazareth*, for which part of the settlement was actually rebuilt. Despite all the visitors, the place is an awesome sight, and largely unspoilt.

Tamdaght → *Colour map 2, B4.*

The road continues north from Aït Ben Haddou into the mountains and to the ford at Tamdaght. A bridge has been constructed and the road re-surfaced recently, allowing most vehicles to carry on for the remaining 40 km or so up to Tourhat, along the Asif Ounila and then west to Telouet (see page 110).

⊙ Ouarzazate listings

For sleeping and eating price codes and other relevant information, see pages 22-28.

● Where to stay

Ouarzazate *p210, map p210*
A lot of streets in Ouarzazate have yet to get name plaques, which can make navigation tricky. If you are travelling by public transport, you come into the *gare routière* on the Marrakech side of Ouarzazate. After a hot bus journey, you may want to take a *petit taxi* to run you into town, a couple of kilometres away. (**CTM** buses come into Av Mohammed V.) Hotels are basically in 3 areas: around Av Mohammed V; further east in the Av Moulay Rachid (big neo-kasbah hotels); and over the causeway in Hayy Tabount.

€€€€ Hotel Berbère Palace, T0524-883105, www.hotel-berberepalace.com. 'Luxury' hotel with 249 bungalow rooms and suites off garden patios. Pool, bar, tennis, restaurants (Moroccan, Italian, international), piano bar, even a hammam, prices start at 2300dh. Clientele includes tourists, business people, film producers and even the odd star. Smooth but impersonal.

€€€ Dar Daïf, Talmasla, next to the Kasbah des Cigognes on the Tabount side of town, T0524-854232, www.dardaif.ma. About 5 km out of town, a traditional restored kasbah with 15 rooms and a pool, well looked after by its French-Moroccan owners. Some rooms with private terrace. Half-board only.

€€€ Hotel Kenzi Azghor, Av Moulay Rachid, T0524-886501, www.kenzi-hotels.com. 110 modern rooms, restaurant, bar, pleasant pool, used mainly by tour operators so often full. Comfortable, but lacks character. Better rates online.

€€€ Villa Kerdabo, 22 Blvd Sidi Bennaceur, near the airport, T0524-887727, www.villakerdabo.com. Far from town centre, this place has 7 simple en suite rooms around a pleasant patio and pool. Restaurant. Airport transfers arranged.

€€€-€€ Le Mercure, Av Moulay Rachid, T0524-899100, www.mercure.com. An upmarket, yet good-value option from the French hotel chain. The modernist design hotel has more character than most, a good range of facilities and a chic lounge-bar that has fabulous views of the adjacent kasbah. Bar open to non-residents, pool, spa, parking and decent buffet restaurant. Book ahead.

€€€-€€ Hotel Oscar, T0524-882212, www.hotel-oscar-ouarzazate.com. On the northern outskirts of town, right in the Atlas Corporation Studios, this is a film set hotel, used by film crews and with various slightly surreal bits of film paraphernalia around the place. A recent change of ownership and a welcome facelift throughout makes this a good option for families. 57 rooms, 8 suites, a/c, lush pool with Egyptian gods to watch over you. Breakfast 90dh.

€€ Hotel Azoul, Av Mohammed V (near Place 3 Mars), T0524-883015, www.hotel azoul.com. A new city centre hotel with 14 rooms around a central courtyard. The contemporary take on kasbah architecture and decor is a bit questionable, but rooms are pleasant and clean and staff are keen to help. Sun terrace and mini-cinema. Price includes breakfast.

€€ Hotel La Vallée, 1 km, Rte de Zagora, Tabount, T0524-854034, www.hotellavallee maroc.com. Very good option with 51 large, simply furnished rooms and some family rooms. Much used by passing tour groups. Lunch and dinner served. Friendly service. Pleasant small pool.

€ Hotel Amlal, 24-25 Rue du Marché, T0524-884030, www.hotelamlal.com. 28 rooms, central location and easily located on side street behind RAM office. Good clean, basic rooms with a/c, showers, some family rooms.

€ Hotel Royal, 24 Av Mohammed V, T0524-882258, near the BMCE bank. Friendly place with clean rooms with shower, also some more basic rooms. Well located, budget prices, 1st floor rooms slightly better but hot in summer. Some rooms have a/c. Breakfast extra in café downstairs.

Camping
Camping Municipal, next to the Stade Municipale, off the N10 heading out of town on the Skoura road, T0524-888322, www.circuitsudmaroc.com. Running water, café, restaurant, pool at complex next door, hot showers, electricity for caravans, grocery shop and petrol 800 m away. Caravan parking 49dh per night with electricity, camping 13dh per person.

Aït Ben Haddou *p213*
Aït Ben Haddou has a number of decent hotels, most offering half-board. None are in the actual kasbah itself, which is inaccessible by vehicle, but many offer good views of it across the river, and staying here gives you the opportunity to see it late evening and early morning when the tour buses have gone. At peak times of year, try to reserve accommodation in advance.

€€€ **Dar Mouna**, T0524-843054, www.dar mouna.com. With a pool in an internal garden and views of the kasbah (for which you pay extra), this is a classy place with big beds and a restrained riad style, though the warmth of the welcome may not match the quality of the accommodation.

€€€€ **Kasbah Ellouze**, Tamdaght, T0524-890459, www.kasbahellouze.com. 4 km north of Aït Ben Haddou, out of sight of the kasbah, Ellouze is a new building but is built in traditional fashion and overlooks almond orchards. Cosy and warmly lit, with plentiful arches and tiles, it is quiet and well away from the tourist buses. Small pool with shaded terrace. Half-board only.

€€€€ **Riad Maktoub**, T0524-888694, www.riadmaktoub.com. Though on the 'wrong' side of the road, and therefore a distance from the kasbah, Maktoub is a well-designed place, with *pisé* walls around a courtyard with a pool. Delicious food served. Suites have lounge with open fireplace. Large family rooms also available.

€€ **Auberge Etoile Filante d'Or**, T0524-890322, www.etoilefilantedor.com. Recently renovated, a great base for a few days exploring the region on foot or by bike (which can be rented here).19 spacious en suite rooms with a/c, solid pine furniture and traditional bamboo ceilings. There's a remarkably elegant TV lounge and restaurant, Wi-Fi and roof terrace for star-gazing. Half-board and full-board options too.

€€ **Hotel La Kasbah**, T0524-890308, www.hotel-lakasbah.com. A big place with a restaurant, pool and hammam near to the kasbah. Too large to be very personal, but in a great position and with plenty of facilities. Used mostly by tour groups. Rooms in the new wing are far better and more attractive.

€ **Auberge Kasbah du Jardin**, T0524-888019, www.kasbahdujardins.com. Well located at the far end of town and near the footbridge across to the Kasbah. A friendly auberge with 15 simple en suite rooms, pool and terrace with great view. Nothing fancy, but well priced and clean. Rooms by the pool are the best. Breakfast included; set meals available for 80dh.

🍴 Restaurants

Ouarzazate *p210, map p210*
There are a growing number of eateries doing more than just multiple tagines and couscous. The cheapest places are around the Rue du Marché and on the Pl al Mouahidine. Near the kasbah there are a few newer restaurants worth checking out.

€€ **Chez Dmitri**, 22 Av Mohammed V, T0524-887346. Daily lunch and dinner. Once the focus of Ouarzazate, as the bar of the Foreign Legion, the restaurant serves excellent Italian and Greek food, as well as some Moroccan choices. Alcohol served.

€€ **La Datte d'Or**, Av Moulay Rachid, T0524-887117. Daily lunch and dinner. Alpine-Berber chalet decor, fixed price menu and attentive and efficient service.

€€ **Le Relais de Saint-Exupéry**, aka Le Petit Prince, 13 Av de Moulay-Abdallah, Quartier el

Qods, T0524-887779, www.relais-ouarzazate. com. Daily lunch and dinner. For varied French and Moroccan cuisine in a setting dominated by old photos of flight and flying. Good-value set menus around 150-300dh. In the Skoura direction, leaving Ouarzazate on your left just on the main junction that links to the road to the airport. Alcohol served.

€€-€ Accord Majeur, Av Mansour Eddahbi (opposite **Hotel Berbère Palace**), T0524-882473. Mon-Sat lunch and dinner. International menu includes Italian, French and Chinese dishes, with some Moroccan options. The tatin de tomate comes recommended. High-quality food, fresh produce and friendly service from the French owners. Alcohol served.

€ Café Restaurant Aux Bons Amis, Pl Al Mouahidine. One of a string of cheap eateries on the plaza offering similar Moroccan fare of brochettes, tagines, crispy pizzas and salads. Warming harira soup recommended in winter.

€ Douyria, next to Kasbah Taourirt, T0524-885288, www.restaurant-ouarzazate. net. Daily lunch and dinner. Contemporary Moroccan cuisine in a converted old house, with roof terrace and stylish salons. Imaginative menu includes camel and goat dishes. Alcohol served.

€ Patisserie Habouss, Pl Al Mouahidine, T0524-882699. Famed for its scrumptious cakes and Moroccan patisseries, but great spot just to sip mint tea or freshly squeezed fruit juice while people-watching. Pizzas and light meals also served. No alcohol. Cash only.

🍸 Bars

Ouarzazate p210, map p210
Hotel La Perle du Sud, Av Mohammed V (near Pl 3 Mars). The only hotel in town with nightclub and bar open to locals and tourists alike.
Hotel Le Mercure, see Where to stay, above. Stylish and contemporary lounge bar in hotel, with open fireplace. Good range of wine, beer and cocktails. Open to non-residents.

✪ Festivals

Ouarzazate p210, map p210
Events tend to be a bit ad hoc, so always check in advance with the tourist office (see page 212) to confirm dates.
May Small handicrafts fair.
Sep Moussem of Sidi Daoud.
Oct African music festival, www.festivalazalay.com.

✪ Shopping

Ouarzazate p210, map p210
Sun cream, batteries, writing paper and stamps etc can all be obtained on Av Mohammed V at the supermarket (opposite **Chez Dimitri**). It even sells alcohol – the last place to do so before the deserts south beyond M'Hamid, or Tineghrir to the east. Along this strip there are also a number of shops selling the ubiquitous 'cadeaux berbères': carpets, babouches, knick-knacks, jewellery and traditional desert robes or gandoura. The covered market and the shops around the edge of Pl al Mouahidine have some cheap Western clothing, household goods as well as a few spice sellers. There is a reliable pharmacy next to the Shell petrol station, opposite Pl al Mouahidine. Local **markets** take place on Sat and Sun.
Ensemble Artisanal, opposite the kasbah. Daily. Sells a good range of local handicrafts and African artefacts.
Coopérative des Tissages de Tapis, at the rear of the **Ensemble Artisanal**. Closed weekends. Another fixed-price shop selling carpets hand-made by local women of the Ouzgita tribe.

✪ What to do

Ouarzazate p210, map p210
Quad biking
Kart Aventure, Av Moulay Rachid, between hotels Berbère Palace and Ibis, T0524-886374, www.kart-aventure.com. Full-day and multi-day excursions in sand-buggies.

Quads Aventures, in Hayy Tamassint, near Atlas Studios, T0524-884024, www.quads aventures.com. Around 450dh for 2 hrs. Also rents mountain bikes and organizes kayaking on the lake.

Tour operators
Amzrou Transport Touristique, 41 Av Mohammed V, T0524-882323. Rental of 4WD vehicles with driver; treks and circuits for small groups.
Daya Travels, T0524-887707, www.daya travels.com. Day excursions, longer tours and trekking/cycling trips. Also rent bikes.
Ksour Voyages, 11 Pl du 3 Mars, T0524-882840, www.ksour-voyages.com. Turn left before the Palais des Congrès as you come from Marrakech. 4WD tours, desert trips and mountain trekking.

Trekking agencies and guides
Désert et Montagne Maroc, contact via Dar Daïf guesthouse, see Where to stay above, or on T0524-854947. Sets up mule and camel treks.
Iriqui Excursions, Pl du 3 Mars, T0524-885799, www.iriqui.com. In-depth knowledge of region and specialist in desert trekking.
Ouarzatrek, based in Hotel La Vallée, T0666-177610, www.ouarzatrek.com. Can arrange trekking excursions on foot or by mule in the region.

⊖ Transport

Ouarzazate *p210, map p210*
Air
Flights from **Taourirt airport**, northeast of the city, T0524-882348, to **Casablanca** (600dh) and shuttles connecting Casablanca to Zagora, via Agadir and Ouarzazate (Mon, Wed and Sun) with **RAM**. International flights to **Europe** (mainly France), both charters and regular. For internal flights, airport formalities are confusing. **Airline offices**: RAM, Av Mohammed V, T0890-000800.

Bus
To **Marrakech** (5 hrs) across the High Atlas via Tizi-n-Tichka (occasionally closed in winter). Several services a day to **Zagora**, east to **Boumalne**, **Tineghir**, **Er Rachidia**, and west to **Taroudant** (5 hrs) and **Agadir** (7½ hrs). **CTM** buses, T0524-882427, leave from the offices on Av Mohammed V, next to the Post Office. **Supratours** from their office near RAM offices, and private line buses from the *gare routière* outside town. For distant destinations, get your ticket the day before.

Car hire
Budget, 4 Av Mohammed V, near RAM offices, T0524-884202. Hertz, 33 Av Mohammed V, T0524-882084. Europcar, Pl du 3 Mars, T0524 882035. Other agencies around Pl du 3 Mars. For petrol, there is Shell in the centre and service stations at the main exits to the town.

Taxi
Grands taxis have 2 departure points: from behind Pl Al Mouahidine, where destinations include **Skoura**, **El Kelaâ des Mgouna** and **Boumalne**. Alternatively, the taxi rank across the *oued* in Tabount serves **Agdz**, **Zagora** (3 hrs) and **M'Hamid**; for destinations west and north, head for the *gare routière*.

❶ Directory

Ouarzazate *p210, map p210*
Banks ATMs near the RAM on Av Mohammed V. BMCE, Av Mohammed V, has a bureau de change open Sun. Otherwise try the large hotels to change money. **Medical services** Chemist: Pharmacie du nuit, Av Mohammed V (opposite Post Office), T0524-882490, also on Av al Mouahidine. **Police** Av Mohammed V, T190. **Useful numbers** Fire: T150.

Drâa Valley

The road southeast from Ouarzazate to Zagora is spectacular, first winding its way across the Jbel Anaouar mountains, and then down along the Drâa Valley, a strip of intense cultivation and a band of vivid colour weaving through the desert. Here and there are red earth-coloured kasbahs and villages of flat-roofed houses, their rooftops edged with crenellations. Once, the Drâa was one of the longest rivers in Northwest Africa. Today, the cultivated areas give way to the desert near M'hamid, south of Zagora. In this region, the classic sights are the village of Tamegroute, once famed as a centre of Islamic learning, and the dunes of Erg Lehoudi and Chigaga. ▶ *For listings, see pages 221-224.*

Arriving in the Drâa Valley

Getting there
The N9 is a good road, much improved by recent works. Regular buses and *grands taxis* connect Ouarzazate, Agdz, Zagora and M'Hamid. A car allows you to make photo stops at will and to visit the smaller, less spoilt oases and villages. The most difficult section of this route is between Ouarzazate and Agdz, with a winding climb up to the Tizi-n-Tinifitt.

Getting around
Zagora can be explored on foot. Tamegroute is 20 km away and you might be able to get a *grand taxi* or a lift, if you don't have your own transport. There are also daily buses via Tamegroute and a slow local stopping bus between M'hamid and Zagora. **CTM** buses run between Ouarzazate, Zagora and M'Hamid. The **Supratours** service only runs as far as Zagora. The dunes of Chigaga require a 4WD.

Background
The Drâa Valley was not always so arid – as is attested by the rock carvings of animals which have been discovered in the lower Drâa. The river was known to the ancient writers: for Pliny, it was the *flumen Darat*; for Ptolomey, the *Darados*, and Polybius mentions it as a river full of crocodiles. After Zagora, near M'Hamid, the Drâa disappears into the sandy Debaïa plain. The river only very rarely runs its full course to the Atlantic coast near Tan Tan, some 750 km away (the last time was in 1989). In years of sufficient rainfall, however, there is good grazing for the nomads in the Debaïa, and even some cultivation.

Heading south of **Agdz** (see Where to stay, page 221), you are entering real kasbah land, one of the most beautiful oasis valleys in Morocco. With a 4WD, there are opportunities for some off-road driving here. Try to take in the kasbah at **Tamnougalt** (10dh), some 6 km south of Agdz, on the north bank of the Drâa, and the museum at **Ksar Tissergate**, around 8 km north of Zagora.

Zagora → *For listings, see pages 221-224. Colour map 2, C6.*

Zagora is the main town at the southern end of the Drâa Valley and the best place to overnight before heading off into the desert. In the 1990s, the town woke up to tourism. The arrival of 4WD vehicles and the improvement of the N9 road have allowed an influx of visitors. In the space of a decade, the desert settlement founded by an Arab tribe in the 13th century has been transformed out of all recognition. A new tourist information office is due to open soon at the southern end of Avenue Mohammed V, near the very grand provincial administration building and the famous '52 Days to Timbuktu' road sign.

Arriving in Zagora
Hassle Given the poverty levels here, many locals compete fiercely for the tourist trade. To avoid potential hassle, try to make travel arrangements into the desert in advance, either through your hotel or through recommended agencies.

Places in Zagora
Although there are few architectural traces of the town's life before tourism, the paths through the date palm groves to the various *ksar* can help you imagine a time when the world was slower. Of these promenades, one of the more pleasant, despite the potential pestering, is around the **Amazrou** date palm oasis across the river. There is also some accommodation here and a kasbah once famed for its silverwork. Above Zagora and within walking distance are two hills, from which there are excellent views over the valley and towards the desert. Nearby are the ruins of an 11th-century **Almoravid fortress**.

During the *moulid* there is a major religious festival held in Zagora, the **Moussem of Moulay Abdelkader Jilala**. The town's **market** days are on Wednesday and Sunday. The souk is an important place for the exchange of produce and livestock for the surrounding region. **Musée des Arts et Traditions de la Vallée du Drâa** ① *8 km north of Zagora in the Ksar Tissergate, T0661-348388 (mob), 20dh*, is a very worthwhile museum of local antiquities housed in the ancient Kasbah. Displays tagged in English.

South of Zagora → *For listings, see pages 221-224.*

Tamegroute and Tinfou dunes → *Colour map 2, C6.*
Tamegroute lies on the left bank of the Oued Drâa, 20 km southeast from Zagora, and is visited mainly because of the *zaouïa*, founded in the 17th century. It is the headquarters of the influential Naciri Islamic brotherhood, which had great importance in the Drâa region until recently, and is visited by scholars from the Islamic world. The outer sanctuary and library are open to public view (closed 1200-1500), the latter containing a number of impressively old Korans and 12th-century antelope hide manuscripts. The village is also interesting to explore, with its inhabited underground kasbah, and there's a community pottery that for centuries has been producing the green-glazed and brown ceramics typical of the region.

Some 8 km south of Tamegroute, the **Tinfou dunes** are a small and popular but nevertheless memorable area of Saharan sand.

Tagounite → *Colour map 2, C6.*
Driving south from Tinfou, the road takes you up over the Jbel Bani and down into oasis country again and the village of Tagounite. There are basic shops here and the last petrol station before the desert. Tracks to the east connect to **Merzouga** (see page 196), or **Foum Zguid** to the west (only advisable with a guide and 4WD; see box, above).

M'Hamid → *Colour map 2, C6.*
An alternative to Merzouga in the east, M'Hamid is popular as a base for camel trips into the dunes. The village of M'Hamid itself marks the end of the tarmac road and has a few basic shops, souvenir shops and desert tour agents. Across the river in 'old' M'Hamid is an

4WD tracks around Zagora

Always check that you have a good spare tyre before setting out on piste into rough country.

From the N12 to the N10

With a solid 4WD, there are a couple of routes from the N12 across wild country to the N10 Er Rachidia to Ouarzazate road. Heading east out of Nekob, you will find a sign showing right for Tazzarine and left for Iknioun, a settlement lying some 65 km to the north in the Jbel Saghro. It is best to travel this route with a local as the tracks are confusing. Some of the better ones lead up to mines, in fact. After crossing the Tizi-n-Tazazert-n-Mansour (2200 m), you will have the option of going north on a rather better piste to Boumalne (about 42 km), or right to Iknioun and then Tineghir, via the Tizi-n-Tikkit, a rougher but more beautiful route.

The easiest route up from the N12 to the N10 heads north from Alnif, however.

Although it is best tackled in a 4WD, it can just about be done in a hire care with high clearance. After the Tizi-n-Boujou, the track takes you onto the N10 some 20 km east of Tineghir, 35 km west of Tinejdad.

West from Zagora to Foum Zguid

This route was off-limits for years due to the risk of Polisario rebel incursions from neighbouring Algeria. It is another difficult journey best attempted in a 4WD with accompanying vehicles. Much of the road (the 6953) is a very poor surface and 124 km in these conditions are not to be undertaken lightly. The thrill of the open spaces, the wide horizons and the faint prospect of sandstorms make this a memorable journey. Basically, the road runs east–west, following the line of the Jbel Bani to the south. From Foum Zguid, further rough tracks take you southwest and west towards Tata in the Anti-Atlas.

interesting kasbah to explore and outlying villages. The most common destinations are the sands of the **Erg Lehoudi**, some 8 km north of M'hamid, and the magnificent unspoiled dunes of **Chigaga**, 55 km out towards the Algerian frontier, a two-hour drive by 4WD, or a three-day camel trek. There are plenty of outfits (and hustlers) here who will set you up with a trip of any length, from a short camel ride and a single night in a camp under the stars to a week-long camel trek west to Foum-Zguid. Shop around and make sure you know what you're getting, see What to do, page 224. M'hamid itself has basic facilities and a Monday souk. If visiting on this day, there may be some 'blue men of the desert' around, more for the benefit of tourists than tradition. The days of the great camel caravans led by indigo-swathed warriors are a mirage from the past, but you can get an idea of this cultural heritage at the annual **International Nomads Festival** in March (www.nomadsfestival.org).

North of Zagora → For listings, see pages 221-224.

Nekob and Tazzarine → Colour map 2, C6.

Leaving Zagora, there are two main options if you want to avoid retracing your track back along the Drâa Valley. The first route, the rough track running northeast from Zagora to Tazzarine, a settlement on the main metalled west to east route to Rissani in the Tafilalet, is for 4WD only and needs careful planning. Ask at Zagora hotels for details of the vans and lorries covering this route.

In a hire car, there is a better route to Rissani which, although it means retracing steps 60 km up the Ouarzazate road as far as **Tansikht**, takes you across some wonderful arid scenery on metalled road all the way east to Rissani. Although the route can easily be driven in a half-day, there are a number of auberges and converted kasbahs offering an overnight halt at **Nekob** (42 km from junction). There is a helpful **Bureau des Guides** in Nekob who can organize trekking excursions in the Jbel Sarhro area. For 4WD routes from here, see box, opposite. After Nekob, Mellal is the next settlement before **Tazzarine** (conveniently located 75 km from the junction), a small settlement with petrol station and basic shops, where the direct north–south track from Zagora joins the road. Tazzarine is a good base for searching out the *gravures rupestres* (prehistoric rock carvings) at **Tiouririne** or **Aït Ouazik** (see Where to stay, below, for details about guides).

◉ Drâa Valley listings

For sleeping and eating price codes and other relevant information, see pages 22-28.

◎ Where to stay

Agdz *p218*
€€€ **Kasbah Azul**, T0524-843931, www.kasbahazul.com. Beautiful kasbah-style guesthouse in the palm groves, run by a French artist and a Moroccan musician. Style in abundance and traditional features. Gardens and pool. The best place around by miles.

€€ **Chez Yacob**, Tamnougalte (4 km south of Agdz on road to Zagora), T0524-843394, www.lavalleedudraa.com. In a restored house right next to the 18th-century Tamnougalte kasbah, **Chez Yacob** has a busy restaurant popular with passing tour groups. From the terrace and the restaurant there are lovely views over the surrounding Drâa oases. Built in the traditional *pisé* style, rooms are cool in summer and warm in winter. Simply furnished en suite rooms with a central courtyard.

€ **Hotel Kissane**, Av Mohammed V, T0524-843044, www.hotel-kissane.m1.ma. Named after the neighbouring Jbel Kissane, budget option with 29 simple en suite rooms. Lacks charm, but has a pool and a restaurant. Breakfast 35dh.

Camping
Camping Kasbah de la Palmeraie, 2 km from Agdz, T0524-843640, www.casbah-caidali.net. Camping facilities in the palm groves run by local family in conjunction with their restored kasbah guesthouse, Casbah Caïd Ali. Meals upon request, electricity, showers and toilets. Can organize local excursions and trekking.

Zagora and Amazrou *p218*
€€€ **Riad Lamane**, Amazrou (off the road to M'Hamid just after the bridge, turn right at the mini-roundabout), T0524-848388, www.riadlamane.com. Individually designed bungalows with coloured *tadelakt* walls and huge beds, all with African or Berber decorative touches. Also luxurious 'tent' rooms with bathrooms. Gorgeous gardens with pool and 2 restaurants. Very special. Desert excursions and camel trips offered.

€€€ **Villa Zagora**, www.mavillaausahara. com. An oasis within an oasis, this tiny guesthouse has 6 elegant rooms and a Berber tent for budget travellers (250dh per person). Eat locally grown food, freshly cooked, in the garden, on the terrace or in the dining room. Rooms have contemporary touches and there is art, an open fire, good views and a pool.

€€ **Hotel Zagour**, Amazrou, T0524-846178, www.zagour.ma. Overlooking the palm groves in Amazrou just outside Zagora. Friendly service, clean rooms in local mud-built style, all with bathrooms and a/c. Moroccan cuisine, terrace café and pool. Good budget option.

€€ Kasbah Asmaa, 2 km from centre, just over the bridge to Amazrou on eastern side of and adjacent to Oued Drâa, T0524-847599, www.asmaa-zagora.com. The 3-star kasbah-style sister to the more upmarket **Palais Asmaa** nearby. This hotel has plenty of spacious rooms, though they are looking a bit worn out. Tented Moroccan restaurant, bar, pool and gardens.

€€ Kasbah Sirocco, Amazrou, T0524-846125, www.kasbahsirocco.com. Good views and freshly painted rooms with brightly coloured Berber throws over pine beds. Nice pool, licensed restaurant and desert trips organized. From Zagora heading in the direction of M'Hamid. Turn left at mini-roundabout at Amazrou, hotel is 150 m on left.

€€ La Perle du Drâa, 4 km south of Zagora on Rte de M'Hamid, T0524-846210, www.perledudraa.ma. Just out of town, an impressive kasbah-style hotel that's hard to miss. Single, twin, double and family spacious en suite rooms with a/c and Wi-Fi. Clean and functional. Large outdoor pool, restaurant and bar.

€ Auberge Chez Ali, Av Atlas-Zaouite, T0524-846258, www.chez-ali.com. Simple, colourful, comfortable rooms in Saharoui style. Range of prices; pay more for showers, or less to sleep in a Berber tent. Large gardens, great food and a good place to book camel treks. Popular, so book ahead.

€ Hotel La Palmeraie, Av Mohammed V, near road junction to south of town and bus station, T0524-847008, www.lapalmerie-zagora.com. It's fallen out of favour lately and certainly needs some updating, but the oldest hotel in town is still reliable for its friendly service, good value and comfortable rooms, some with a/c. Pool and bar/restaurant.

Camping

Camping Les Jardins de Zagora, Av Hassan II, next to **Hotel Ksar Tinzouline**, T0524-846971. Camping in Berber tents available

from 40dh per person, or pitch your own, or park your caravan. Meals on request for 80dh. Close to town centre.

Camping Prends Ton Temps, Hay El Mansour Dahbi, T0524-846543, www.prendstontemps.com. Pitch up or park up here in well-run site open all year. Toilets and washing facilities. Restaurant and garden; shared nomad tents and simple guest rooms in the auberge also available.

Tamegroute and Tinfou dunes *p219*

€€ Kasbah Sahara Sky, Tinfou, T0667-351943 (mob), www.hotel-sahara.com. Closed Jul. A well-appointed observatory on the roof, as well as very dark skies (and cold beer) attract astronomers to this comfortable and friendly hotel next to the dunes. Spacious en suite rooms and ground-floor rooms with disabled access.

M'Hamid *p219*

There are now a sprinkling of boutique guesthouses and hotels in the palm groves of Ouled Driss just before the village, and a few simple hotels in the village itself.

€€€ Dar Azawad, T0524-848730, www.darazawad.com. Closed Jul. A luxury boutique hotel in the oasis 5 km before M'Hamid, with 9 charming kasbah-style rooms and 6 super-chic suites, French restaurant, pool, hammam and bar. They also have a deluxe tented bivouac at Chigaga dunes for exclusive hire.

€€€ Kasbah Azalay, T5024-848096, www.azalay.com. A fairly new, Spanish-owned, kasbah-style hotel, **Azalay** has 22 good-sized a/c rooms, bar and restaurant. Magnificent indoor pool and huge marble hammam. Transfers from Ouarzazate or Marrakech airport and they offer their own excursions into the desert.

€€€-€€ Riad Ma Bonne Étoile, Ouled Driss, T0524-848498, www.riadmabonne toile.com. In the oasis before M'Hamid, a well-run guesthouse with 7 comfortable rooms, 4 bungalows and a pool. Organizes painting courses and cultural activities. You can also sleep in bivouac tents nearby, run by a local family.

€ **Hotel el Ghizlane**,T0668-517280. Has 7 very basic rooms, some en suite. Family run and ideal for a night before or after a trek into the dunes. Popular with backpackers. Tasty meals available. Also have a bivouac outside the village and a high-quality camp in Chigaga. Price includes breakfast.

Camping

Auberge al Khaima, T0667-414502 (mob), www.aubergeelkhaima.com. Camping, caravan park and much more besides. At the edge of the palm groves, just across the bridge, the auberge has recently added comfortable self-catering bungalows built in traditional style. There is a pool on site and they also run a small guesthouse and café in the main village.

Auberge Hamada du Draâ, T0524-848086, www.hamada-sahara.com. Yet another campsite upgrading its sevices. The caravan park has shaded sites, with shared toilet block and showers. There are also very solid and comfortable nomad 'tents' with woven roofs and mud-built walls, which are good for families at 220dh per person. Additional new auberge with 10 suites with a/c and bathrooms from 330dh per person. Pool, restaurant and desert excursions.

Nekob and Tazzarine *p220*

€€€ **Ksar Jenna**, 2 km west of Nekob, T0524-839790, www.ksarjenna.com. A relaxed and elegant retreat, with 6 gorgeous rooms, mosaic tiled bathrooms and cool gardens. Restaurant with magnificent painted ceiling, fountain and bar.

€€-€ **Kasbah Ennakhile**, T0524-839719, www.kasbah-nkob.com. Friendly service and a choice of 10 bright 'auberge' rooms with shared bathrooms, or 5 newly added 'kasbah' suites with traditional *tataoui* ceilings, stone floors and attached bathrooms with inventive use of Berber water pitchers. Views over the oasis from the terrace salon and some rooms. Local trekking organized.

Camping

Camping Amasttou, Tazarine, T0524-838078, www.amasttou.com. Signposted as you arrive from Nekob. 150dh per person half-board in a large Berber tent. Simple rooms available, caravan parking or pitch your own tent. Shower and toilet block. Small pool and restaurant.

4WD tracks around Zagora *p220*

€€ **Kasbah Meteorites**, 13 km west of Alnif, T0535-783809, www.kasbahmeteorites.com. A good place for lunch, the pool or an overnight stop in their new wing of 16 large, clean en suite rooms with fossil basins. Plenty of local information for trekkers and geologists.

🍴 Restaurants

Zagora *p218*

As in many southern towns, cheap eateries need to be treated with caution. If worried, stick to food cooked before you like brochettes, grilled meats and tagines that have been simmering for hours. Almost all of the good places to eat or drink in Zagora are attached to hotels.

Hotel La Palmeraie, Av Mohammed V. Welcomes non-residents for a drink and a dip in the pool.

Hotel La Fibule du Draâ, in Amazrou. Good place for a drink.

Le Dromadaire Gourmand, Av Mohammed V. At the entry to town coming from Ouarzazate, a popular new restaurant for locals and tourists. Good food and local specialities. Around 70dh for a main course. Bring your own alcohol.

Restaurant Timbuctou, in the town near the minibus terminal. Reliable cheap food and popular with tourists.

Riad Lamane, Amazrou (see page 221). Set 3-course lunches and dinners in fabulous gardens for 150dh. Alcohol served. Non-residents welcome.

○ What to do

Agdz *p218*
Agdez Aventures, on the main square,
T0671-732622 (mob), www.agdez.com.
Rents out mountain bikes and arranges
hiking and biking tours.

Zagora *p218*
Caravane du Sud, Amazrou, T0524-847569,
www.caravanesud.com. Camel-trekking,
mountain-biking, 4WD and quad-biking
in the desert around Zagora.

Nekob *p220*
Bureau des Guides, T0667-487509 (mob),
www.moroccotrek.net. Official local guides
for trekking in Jbel Sarhro Oct-May.

M'Hamid *p219*
Sahara Services, T0661-776766,
www.saharaservices.info. Has a good
reputation – their 'sunset tour' is €38
per person, including food and a night's
accommodation, or you can do a whole
day's trek, getting you deeper into the
desert, for €55.
Zbar Travel, T0668-517280, www.zbar
travel.com. Reliable local operators with day
treks by camel, multi-day safaris in 4WD,
sandboarding and a super bivouac at Erg
Chigaga with sand-proof tents. Office in
Ouarzazate also.

○ Transport

Zagora *p218*
Daily **CTM** bus departs at 0600 from
M'Hamid to **Casablanca** (14 hrs) via Zagora
(2 hrs), **Ouarzazate** (5 hrs) and **Marrakech**
(10 hrs). There is also a slower private bus
departing M'Hamid at 0700 along the same
route as far as Marrakech. There are *grands
taxis* between Zagora and **Ouarzazate** and
minibuses shuttling between **M'Hamid**,
Tagounite and Zagora.

○ Directory

Zagora *p218*
Banks Anything of any importance is on
Av Mohammed V, including the Banque
Populaire. **Medical services** Dr Brahim
Bouassou, 6 Av Mohammed V, T0524-
847395. **Useful addresses** Total station
on the Ouarzazate road can do minor
vehicle repairs, while there is a larger garage
opposite the police station, on your left as
you come from the Ouarzazate direction.

Contents

At a glance

⊖ **Getting around** The whole
area is accessible by bus or *grand
taxi*. It may be worth considering
a flight to Laâyoune in the deep
south, however.

⟡ **Time required** Allow a week or
two to do the area justice and bear
in mind the distances involved.

☼ **Weather** The Atlantic usually
keeps the coast from getting too
hot, and Agadir is sunny just about
year-round. Further south, mists can
shroud the beaches in winter. The
best surfing waves are usually found
from late autumn to early spring.

✖ **When not to go** Agadir can get
busy with package holidaymakers
during winter holidays.

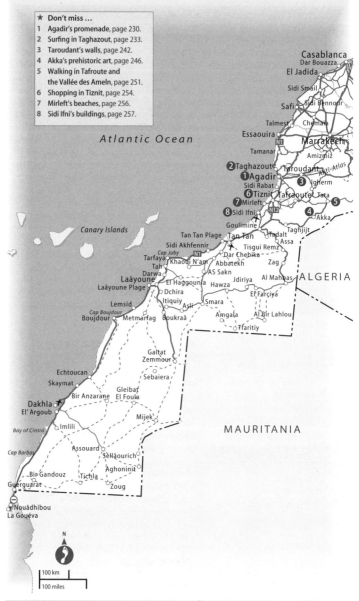

★ **Don't miss ...**
1 Agadir's promenade, page 230.
2 Surfing in Taghazout, page 233.
3 Taroudant's walls, page 242.
4 Akka's prehistoric art, page 246.
5 Walking in Tafroute and
  the Vallée des Ameln, page 251.
6 Shopping in Tiznit, page 254.
7 Mirleft's beaches, page 256.
8 Sidi Ifni's buildings, page 257.

Atlantic Ocean

Casablanca
Dar Bouazza
El Jadida
Sidi Smail
Safi   Sidi Bennour
Talmest   Chemaïa
Essaouira
N1   **Marrakech**
Tamanar
Amizmiz
❷ Taghazout   Taroudant   Anti-Atlas
❶ Agadir   Igherm
Sidi Rabat   ❸
❼❻ Tiznit   Tafraoute   Tata
❽ Sidi Ifni   Mirleft   ❹
Goulimine   Akka
Taghjijt
Tadalt   Assa

Canary Islands

Tan Tan Plage   Tan Tan
Sidi Akhfennir   Tisgui Remz
Cap Juby   Dar Chebika
Tarfaya   Khaoui N'am   Abbatekh   Zag
Tah   AS Sakn
Darwa   Jdiriya   Al Mahbas
Laâyoune   El Haggounia   Hawza
Laâyoune Plage   Dchira   El Farçiya
Lemsid   Itiquiy   Asli
Cap Boujdour   Boukraâ   Smara
Boujdour   Metmarfag   Amgala   Al Bir Lahlou
Tfaritiy

Galtat
Zemmour

Echtoucan   Sebaiera
Skaymat
Bir Anzarane   Gleibat
Dakhla ✈   El Foula
El' Argoub   Mijek
Bay of Cintra   Imlili

MAURITANIA

Cap Barbas   Assouard
Sellaourich
Bir Gandouz   Aghoninit
Guerguarat   Tichla   Zoug

ⓝ Nouâdhibou
La Gouéva

ALGERIA

N
100 km
100 miles

South of the High Atlas, the landscapes are worthy of some yet-to-be-made Moroccan road movie. The scenery of the Anti-Atlas is like a geology dissection, with the mountains' inner workings turned out and laid bare, the land risen and folded over on itself. The Saharan coast is flatter and bleaker, but it has an austere magnificence, too.

Oceanside Agadir – Morocco's package holiday resort – has beach life and bar life, a long bustling promenade and a smart new marina and pizza restaurants. Just to the north are the surf beaches and surf schools around Taghazout and winding mountain routes into the more remote interior. Inland from Agadir, in the densely fertile agricultural Souss Valley, lies walled Taroudant, often compared to Marrakech. From here you can travel up into the Jbel Siroua, or down across wild hills via Igherm to Tata, a good base from which to reach south, to the prehistoric rock art sites at Akka and Oum el Aleg, or east to Tissint. Moving west, there are fortified granaries at Amtoudi and in the great natural rock amphitheatre of Tafraoute, an excellent centre for climbing, walking and trips to nearby canyons. On the coast, there are more good surfing waves around the whitewashed, one-time Spanish enclave of Sidi Ifni and, nearby, the hipsters of Mirleft are hard at work turning a one-camel town into a celebration of Moroccan cool. Further south still, sports fishing and huge empty landscapes are on offer at remote Dakhla, the last stop before the border with Mauritania.

Though bumpy tracks are slowly giving way to tarmac, Morocco's southern provinces are little visited. This may change as new palm-dotted golf courses and tourist zones near Agadir rise out of the dust. For the moment, however, the great horizons and mountainscapes are the preserve of a handful of more determined visitors.

Agadir and around

Atlantic Agadir, at the mouth of the Souss Valley, is named after a Berber fortified granary. But simple rural life is long forgotten in today's city of around 200,000 people, which has grown up along the sweeping 9-km beach. A further half a million live in the surrounding area. A microclimate of year-round sun and swimming ensures that Agadir receives the largest number of tourists in all Morocco. And, while most of its visitors don't stray far from its large package holiday hotels, the city has the advantage of being near interesting villages and natural sights – as well as having good onward connections.➤➤ *For listings, see pages 236-241.*

Arriving in Agadir ➔ *Colour map 2, C2.*

Getting there
The vast majority of tourists arrive in Agadir by air. **Aéroport d'Agadir-Massira** ⓘ *on the Taroudant road, T0528-839122, www.agadir-airport.com,* is 26 km inland from the city. Package holiday companies have buses to shuttle clients to their hotels, and car hire companies have offices at the airport. Otherwise, there are six-passenger *grands taxis* outside the airport (170dh to the town centre, 220dh at night; you could arrange to share). If Agadir is not your main holiday base, then you could take a *grand taxi* to Inezgane, a transport hub south of the city with good connections to various destinations. There is also a bus, No 22, for Inezgane, but no bus that goes direct to Agadir.

Intercity buses arrive at the *gare routière*, outside the town. Some buses from southern destinations only go as far as Inezgane, so you will need to take a *grand taxi* (around 5dh a place) or a local bus (Nos 5 and 6) to get into the city. Local buses and *grands taxis* arrive at the southern edge of the city centre on the Rue de Fès, close to the Avenue el Mouqawama.

Arriving by road, from the north you will come in on the N8, leading into Avenue Mohammed V; from Marrakech and the N8, turn left along Boulevard Mohammed Cheikh Saadi into the town centre. From the airport and Inezgane, and beyond along the N10 to Taroudant or the N12 to Tiznit and the South, the route goes along either Avenue Hassan II or Avenue Mohammed V.➤➤ *See Transport, page 241, for further details.*

Getting around
Agadir is not a huge place, and most things can be done on foot. There are plenty of *petits taxis*, useful for getting to some of the more distant hotels.

Tourist information **Office du Tourisme** ⓘ *Av Mohammed V, T0528-846377, Mon-Fri 0830-1630.* Near the north end of town, the tourist office is almost entirely useless.

Background

Agadir has little that is distinctively Moroccan. The old town was almost totally destroyed in the earthquake of 1960, and has been rebuilt as an international beach resort.

Agadir's rise and fall
Agadir first features in written history in the early 16th century, when a Portuguese noble built a fortress named Santa Cruz de Cap de Gué, somewhere close to the present city. The fort was sold on to the King of Portugal in 1513 and, for a while, it became a link in a chain of

trading posts the Portuguese established along the Atlantic coast of Africa. The Imazighen of the Souss valley launched a jihad against this isolated fort, and the Saâdian Emir of the Souss, Mohammed Echeikh el Mehdi, captured it in 1541, heralding the Portuguese departure from most of their other Atlantic strongholds. His son, Moulay Abdallah el Ahalib, built the kasbah on the hill overlooking the city, the ruins of which still stand.

As the Saâdians developed farming in the Souss valley, Agadir grew in importance, eventually becoming a big trading centre in the 17th and 18th centuries. Exports were sugar cane, olive oil, gold and spices, both from the Souss valley and the Sahara. However, Agadir declined during the reign of Sidi Mohammed Ben Abdallah, who preferred to develop Essaouira, to the north, and closed down Agadir's port. By the beginning of the 19th century, Agadir had all but disappeared.

In the early 20th century, Agadir briefly hit the international headlines. The European powers were running out of places to colonize, and Germany, under Kaiser Wilhelm II, was annoyed at the growing influence of France and Spain in Morocco. In 1911 an incident

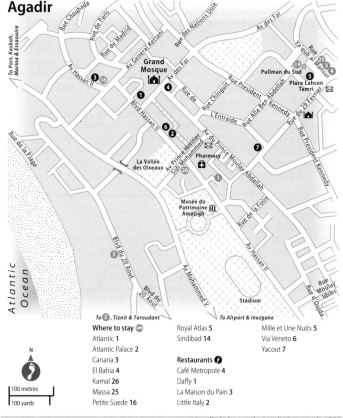

Agadir

Atlantic Ocean

To Port, Kasbah, Marina & Essaouira

Grand Mosque

Pullman du Sud

Place Lahcen Tamri

L'Entraide

La Vallée des Oiseaux

Pharmacy

Musée du Patrimoine Amazigh

Stadium

To Tiznit & Taroudant

To Airport & Inezgane

N

100 metres
100 yards

Where to stay
Atlantic 1
Atlantic Palace 2
Canaria 3
El Bahia 4
Kamal 26
Massa 25
Petite Suede 16

Royal Atlas 5
Sindibad 14

Restaurants
Café Metropole 4
Daffy 1
La Maison du Pain 3
Little Italy 2

Mille et Une Nuits 5
Via Veneto 6
Yacout 7

occurred in the Bay of Agadir when a German gunboat appeared 'to protect German interests'. The crisis was settled by negotiations between the French and Germans which recognized France's rights in Morocco in exchange for territorial concessions in the Congo. The French occupied Agadir in 1913. They constructed the port in 1914 and enlarged it in 1930 and 1953.

On 29 February 1960, disaster struck: old Agadir was completely destroyed by a terrible earthquake, killing an estimated 15,000 people. Newly independent Morocco faced the challenge of rebuilding the town. An entire new settlement was laid out south of the old centre and planned for development as a major tourist resort, with distinct functional zones separated by green swathes, the large hotels carefully distanced from the local residential areas. The ruined kasbah was encased in concrete. Set in the wall are Mohammed V's words, commemorating the dead: "If destiny desired the destruction of Agadir, its reconstruction depends on our faith and our determination." More clearly visible on an arid hillside, in giant Arabic letters, is the national motto: "Allah, Al Watan, Al Malik" ("God, the Nation, the King"). With reconstruction, the city gained some functional buildings, all brutalist concrete, by the likes of star 1960s Moroccan architect Jean-François Zevaco. The port, which escaped total destruction, was developed as the base for a large fishing fleet and as the centre of an industrial zone.

Agadir today

In the 1990s, tourism in Agadir suffered from the impact of the Gulf War and the huge growth in the popularity of Marrakech. Agadir had no nightlife to compete with the Balearics or the Canaries and, instead, the town became a destination for a wealthy Gulf Arab clientele. From the town's nightclubs, prostitution developed. Poor housing areas on the margins expanded, with rural people fleeing the drought-stricken countryside in the late 1990s. Thanks to this exodus, Agadir is now the largest Tachelhit-speaking city in Morocco, and its people, the Gadiris, are proud of their Amazigh origins. There is a dynamic local bourgeoisie with business interests across Morocco. Since the turn of the millennium, tourism in the city has attempted a move upmarket, with the Agadir Marina development at the northern end of the bay.

Places in Agadir

The beach and promenade

The beach is Agadir's main asset, groomed daily and well provided with cafés, camel rides and watersports. A long swathe of sand, it stretches around the bay as far as Agadir itself. It's usually fairly well sheltered from wind and waves, and hassle is kept to a minimum. Due to the preponderance of superhotels at the edge of the sand, the beach can feel removed from the centre of the town, especially at its southern end. The beach in front of the hotels is patrolled by wardens who keep trinket-sellers at bay. On the more public stretches of sand you may get more attention from salesmen. There can be a strong undertow in the sea and small children should not be left to paddle unattended.

At the edge of the sand, Agadir's promenade has been much improved over the years and makes for a fascinating wander, especially in the early evening, when you might see jugglers, visiting Casablancans in high heels and gold clothes, toy sellers and European families with ice creams. Brick-tiled and palm-fringed, there are plenty of cafes and restaurants alongside.

Sunbed hire, around 30dh per day, often includes toilet and shower facilities, usually attached to snack bars and restaurants.

The Marina
Beyond the beach's northern end, the new yacht-filled marina has Western shops and some smart cafés and restaurants. A couple of boats here, including the **Jolly Roger** ① *T0654 310 159*, offer tours and fishing trips.

Kasbah
The kasbah was a densely populated area of the old town and many died here in the 1960 earthquake. It's reached by a winding road to the north of the centre, off Avenue Mohammed V, a *petit taxi* ride for all but the most energetic. The kasbah was built in 1540 to launch an attack on the Portuguese city and was retained after the victory as a fortification against local insurrection. The ramparts and entrance have been maintained in a reasonable condition, as Agadir's one historic site and a memorial to those who died. Despite its view over Agadir, it was not resettled after 1960.

City centre
Architecturally the city is memorable for the buildings from the 1960s reconstruction period. The main post office, by Zevaco, is typical of the minimalist reinforced concrete austerity. The modern **Grand Mosque** is on Avenue des Forces Armées Royales.

The **Vallée des Oiseaux** (Valley of the birds), between Avenue Mohammed V and Boulevard du 20 Août, is a pleasant place to wander and listen to bird song, although the llamas and mountain goats look rather as if they're missing life in the countryside.

Musée Amazighe ① *Passage Aït Souss, between Blvd Hassan II and Blvd Mohammed V, T0552-821632, open 0930-1730, 20dh*, has a small but interesting display of jewellery, carpets, pottery and wooden craftwork from southern Morocco, as well as occasional temporary displays. The collection was assembled over the years by Dutch local art specialist Bert Flint, one of the founders of the Casablanca École des Beaux Arts, who now runs the Maison Tiskiwine in Marrakech (see page 61).

Jardim de Olhāu ① *corner of Rue Kennedy and Av des FAR, Tue-Sun 1430-1830*, is a small park that was created to mark the twinning of Agadir and the Portuguese town of Olhāu. It's a cool and peaceful oasis of green with a playground. A small exhibition shows photos of Agadir before the 1960 earthquake.

Beyond the centre
Souk al Had ① *Av Abderrahim Bouabid, Tue-Sat, a 20-min walk or a short taxi ride from the centre*, is Agadir's Moroccan market. It doesn't give quite the same shopping experience as Marrakech or Fès, but it does offer a taste of local life, with stalls selling carefully piled spices, boxes, shoes, crafts and tagines.

Médina d'Agadir ① *T0528-280253, www.medinapolizzi.com, open 0900-1800, 40dh*, is a small, village-sized and spotlessly clean version of the old medina of the city between Agadir and Inezgane, designed and built by an Italian architect. Traditional methods and materials have been used, and the project includes workspaces for artisans and a restaurant.

The coast to the north of Agadir has great surfing beaches, especially around Taghazout. Although developers are moving in, the area remains largely tranquil, with Paradise Beach and others stretching 30 km northwards from Agadir. Inland, Paradise Valley is a beautiful gorge and river basin, dotted with palm trees and waterfalls, leading up into the mountains and the village of Immouzer des Ida Outanane.

Taghazout → *Colour map 2, C2.*

Morocco's surfing centre, Taghazout (19 km north of Agadir) was once a sleepy, hippy village. Today, it is waking up to making money out of its fame, but for now it remains a laid-back, pretty little town, centred on a small bay where fishermen hang out, smoking around their upturned boats. Surfers from all over the world gather and discuss the waves, and a handful of cafés and restaurants sell banoffee pie and smoothies alongside the tagines. The nearby beaches are superb, and you don't have to go far to get more great surfing away from the crowds. The accommodation is excellent, and there are good surf schools too, offering equipment hire, beginner's lessons and tips and transport for experts. The best surfing, and therefore Taghazout's high season, is from autumn to spring when the Atlantic winds work their magic. Summer is quieter and hotter, but there are usually still some waves to be had. All year round there are possibilities for horse riding and quad biking, too. To get there, catch bus No 12 or 14 from Place Salam in Agadir. Bear in mind that the nearest ATM is in Aourir, a couple of kilometres down the coast.

Rocky reefs, sandy beaches and the Atlantic swell combine here for some fantastic surfing conditions. There's plenty of space for hanging out on the wide sands too. The beach in Taghazout itself is picturesque but has sewage problems. **Panorama's** is immediately south of the town, a short stroll to a big expanse of beach with decent waves for all abilities, especially when there's a big swell. Further south, just before Aourir, **Crocs** is good for beginners. Famous surfing spots, **Anchor Point**, **Killers** and **Mysteries**, are all within walking distance to the north, though they can be crowded. It's worth taking a bus from the square to **Aourir** to the south or to **Boilers** and **Tamri Plage** to the north. Tickets are cheap and the buses run every 30 minutes. Having a car opens up other seldom-surfed possibilities along the N1; there are plenty of hire options. See box opposite for more details on the best breaks. For beginners, Taghazout is a good place to learn; see What to do, page 241 for details.

Immouzer des Ida Outanane → *Colour map 2, C2.*

Named after the local confederation of Berber tribes, Immouzer des Ida Outanane is small mountain town at the end of a spectacular winding drive up from the coast through the palm-filled **Paradise Valley** (where there are some good walking opportunities and possibilities for wild swimming) into the hills. Around 50 km northwest of Aourir, at an altitude of 1160 m, Immouzer is a cool, relaxing place for a day trip or a short stay, with pine, olive and eucalyptus trees, terraced fields and little or no hassling of visitors. It is a markedly Moroccan and rural experience in contrast to the international cafés and surf schools on the coast. The local claim to fame is honey: there's a festival in May and plenty of roadside honey stalls on the road from the coast. If you stop and ask, someone will probably be happy to show you their hives. Thursday's market is a bustling local affair, with the village filled with sellers of meat, homemade metal buckets and plastic furniture. Immouzer's most famous sight, however, is its seasonal waterfall, impressive in spring

Surf breaks

Anchor Point

Anchor Point at Taghazout is a wave of world renown. The relaxed Vee-Dub camper vibe of the 1970s may have gone – and expect the line-up to be packed every time the wave breaks – but the wave is the same. It still offers that big, green wall, those long, leg-aching rides and, at eight foot plus when the wave really comes into its own, a world-class challenge. Stretching north from the edge of Taghazout, this rocky ledge of a point leads out to the old anchor factory that gives the place its name. Don't expect many barrels, as this wave is all about big walls.

Boilers

This right-hander north of Taghazout, off the N1, is probably the most consistent point in the region and, while not exactly the longest, it certainly is a rewarding wave. Named after the huge ship's boiler that sits next to the peak, this spot is a great indicator reef and is clearly visible from the coast road. The main downside is the crowds and, at times, the line-up is packed and can get hassley. If Boilers is too crowded, head for Taghazout; if it's too small, head for Tamri.

Immessouane

The days of catching Immessouane to yourself are long gone, the line-ups are now crowded whenever the swell kicks in (and even when it doesn't) but this headland, about 30 km north of Taghazout, boasts at least three waves that will tempt you to pitch up on the dusty, godforsaken campsite. The first fills your view from the basic campground: walls wrapping off the end of the rocky headland through to the inside of the bay. A few hundred metres to the south, a stark defensive wall guards the harbour.

Firing across in front, this second right is a hollow and powerful wave with a steep take-off that offers adrenalin-fuelled barrels. Inside the bay lies the most popular and longest of the three right-handers. It starts to break at the southern end of the harbour mouth and peels through to the beach at low tide. Suitable for all surfers, this is an excellent, long-walling wave breaking over sand and rocks.

Killer Point

The points around the Taghazout region all have a similar geological make-up. The flat rock reefs have a deposit of sand that builds up over them during the quiet of the summer and is then groomed by the season's early swells into long sandbars. Some years these can be epic, while in others a wave may not break at all. Killer Point is one such place: catch it good and you'll be rewarded with the best wave in the whole of the region, outclassing Anchor Point and all other contenders. At other times it will be sectiony, rippy and frustrating. Killer Point is said to be named after the killer whales that are occasionally seen here.

Panorama's

A real Jekyll and Hyde wave, this point break can be a speeding hollow gem, a slow frustrating wall or a closeout, depending on the combination of swell, tide and sand banks. Catch it good and Panorama's can deliver some of the most exciting waves in the area. If Anchor Point is firing, Panorama's should be too, which helps keep crowds down. It's a low-tide break, where barrel after barrel spins off the point, but it's not for the faint-hearted. A rip pushes away from the take-off point by the apartments and a difficult, steep take-off leads into a fast, driving section.

after a wet winter and worth a visit at other times for its extraordinary limestone rock formations. This is an arid region and, generally, the water is used, more prosaically, for irrigation. To reach the foot of the waterfalls, located below the village, turn left in the main square (signposted) and descend for 4 km. There's a car park from where you can walk the five minutes through olive groves to the foot of the falls. The falls are popular for both sightseeing and swimming; there are pools where the water has gouged out deep holes into which daredevil divers plunge from rocks high above. Immouzer is also a good place for birdwatching and walking.

Coast north of Agadir → *Colour map 2, B2.*
The 175-km (2½ hours) journey on the N1 to Essaouira follows the coast for about the first 70 km before turning a little inland, often through hills covered with argan trees. Along this route are three of Morocco's finest natural sites: the bird reserve at Imzi, one of the last refuges of the bald ibis; Plage Tafadna; and Cap Sim, possibly the windiest beach in Morocco.

North of Taghazout, the road often stays close to the shoreline, which alternates between outcrops of rock and deserted sandy bays, with some picturesque views entering and leaving the small settlement of **Aghrod**. The most westerly outpost of the High Atlas drops over 360 m to the sea at the lighthouse and viewpoint at **Cap Rhir**, 40 km from Agadir. There are opportunities for birdwatching around a lagoon, as the road swings inland along the wide estuary valley of **Asif Aït Ameur**, past the banana plantations, to the small settlement of **Tamri**. The piste turn-off for the reserve at **Imzi** is around 8 km north of Tamri, marked by a sign to *Ministère des eaux et des forêts, site protégé*. Imzi is unique in that there are large sand dunes atop the cliffs, formed by eroded matter being blown back onto the land. At Km 89 there is a left turn to the resort and shrine at **Point Imessouane** and the clifftop viewpoint of **Point d'Igui-n-Tama**. Look, too, for the **Gouffre d'Agadir Imoucha** at Km 77, a ravine over 1 km long cutting into the plateau from the sea; you can find it by walking west across the fields. **Tamanar**, said to be the capital of the argan tree, is just beyond. There is a small hotel, **L'Étoile de Sud**, cafés, including **Café Argan**, shops, tagine stalls and petrol stations. From here the N1 soon descends to cross the two parts of the Oued Iguezoulen, passing a left turn to **Plage Tafadna**, sometimes marked on maps as Cap Tafelney, and then climbs through many bends around the side of Jbel Amsittene (905 m) to the village of **Smimou** (cafés and petrol). Here, a road leading east by the side of Jbel Amardma to **Souk el Tnine** and **Sebt des Aït Daoud** offers an interesting detour into the mountains of the Haha region. After a further 24 km, a turning to the left leads you 12 km to the **Marabout of Sidi Kaouki** on the coast. **Cap Sim** is just to the north. With its regular, strong swell, it is one of Morocco's best surf spots. To reach Essaouira, the best route is via the N1 and N8 roads.

Tizi Maachou pass → *Colour map 2, B/C2.*
The A7, a new Agadir–Marrakech–Casablanca motorway, was completed in 2010, cutting the journey time between Agadir and Marrakech to around 2½ hours and replacing what had been one of the country's most dangerous roads. It cuts through striking country, climbing from Agadir to begin the long journey across the western High Atlas. This is the northernmost region in which the argan tree survives, and browsing goats are common, but north of the village of Argana these trees are replaced by juniper. The Tizi Maachou pass (1700 m), while not as spectacular as those further east, has the advantage of being open to traffic all year when the others are closed due to snow.

South of Agadir → *For listings, see pages 236-241.*

Inezgane → *Colour map 2, C2.*

Busy Inezgane, 13 km south of Agadir, is now almost a part of Agadir. The streets get choked with traffic, there are sheep on the road, goats graze, and everything seemingly revolves around the bus station. Inezgane is above all a transport hub, which is why you will probably have to deal with it if you are travelling in the southwest. There are numerous coach, bus and *grand taxi* connections, and it may also be handy as a stopover, if you do not want to go into Agadir. At the end of the main street is the square, with the local bus stands. Off to the right of the square is a relaxed covered market, with the main day on Tuesday.

About 5 km west of Inezgane, past a couple of golf courses, is the **mouth of the Oued Souss**, an important place for birdwatchers. The best visiting times are February to April and September to November, when many varieties of gulls and terns are in residence. The surrounding area has more colourful birds, including the black-headed bush shrike, the great grey shrike, brown-throated sand martin and De Moussier's redstart.

Agadir to Tafraoute → *Colour map 2, C2.*

The R105 runs for 160 km from Agadir to Tafraoute (see page 250). Morning buses cover this route. **El Kolea**, a dusty settlement is popular with Moroccans from Agadir. Water from the central fountain apparently has curative properties and is taken home by visitors. Further on, **Biougra** is neat and clean with trees set into the tiled pavement along the central dual carriageway. Between the two settlements, the busy road winds across an almost level plain. After Biougra, the land rises. Workings in the huge limestone quarry on the left throw white clouds across the landscape. Beyond Imi Mgourn are the first foothills and the road rises up with good views towards Aït Baha. Driving here requires concentration, as stretches of the narrow winding road need repair after damage by heavy rain. **Aït Baha**, 92 km from Tafraoute, has a basic hotel and a souk on Wednesday. There are one or two small villages, such as Hadz Aït Mezzal, and abandoned houses high up the slopes. As the road swings over the cols, there are good views. The landscape grows increasingly other-wordly, with the strata of the hills and mountains waving across the landscape. Around 110 km from Agadir the R105 passes the extraordinary **Kasbah Tizourgane**, which is well worth a visit; see page 252. After the **Tizi-n-Taraktine pass** (1500 m) you sweep down into the **Ameln Valley** (page 251).

Oued Massa Nature Reserve

ⓘ *Off the Tiznit road from Agadir, take the right turn marked to Sidi Rbat. The road surface stops very suddenly, turning into sandy track over open farmland. Depending on your vehicle, you may have to cover the last few km to the reserve on foot. Ignore any faux guides at the entrance to the park telling you that you have to pay a fee. At Issoh you may find fishermen in the caves who will cook you up some of their catch.*

Held back by large sandbanks, the waters of the Oued Massa have formed a lagoon. The vast reed beds, the massive fringing dunes to the southwest, sandbanks at the mouth of the river, the water course itself and the mud banks to the north provide a home to both birds and mammals. Visit between February and April, or between September and November when there are over-wintering birds. The estuary can be home to crane, avocet, spoonbill, great flamingo, osprey, and night, squacco and purple heron. One of the few surviving groups of the endangered bald ibis live here; the other main site is north of Agadir at Tidzi. Several kinds of raptor are attracted by the populations of other birds, including small groups of ospreys.

For sleeping and eating price codes and other relevant information, see pages 22-28.

⦿ Where to stay

Agadir *p228, map p229*

A couple of boutique options have opened in recent years on the outskirts of town, and there is a small handful of good mid-range places in the city centre. Otherwise, despite the huge numbers of hotels, there are few choices between the huge 5-star beachside enclaves and the rather seedy budget options in the Talborjt area, away from the beach. Street-facing rooms on the 2 main avenues can suffer from traffic noise.

€€€€ **Atlantic Palace**, Secteur balnéaire et touristique, T0528-824146, www.atlantic palaceresort.com. One of Agadir's huge 5-star hotels, the **Atlantic Palace** has over 300 rooms and is an enclave that few of its guests leave. Refurbished, the rooms have dark-wood furniture, white walls and flat-screen TVs and all have terraces or balconies. There's a private beach, a large heated pool, a kids' pool, a bar with a view of the whole bay, and tennis courts.

€€€€ **Royal Atlas**, Av 20 Aout, T0528-294040, www.hotelsatlas.com. One of Agadir's most recently built 5-star resort-hotels, this place has a big pool area with palm trees and is close to the beach. There's a spa, and rooms are smart and spacious without ever being exactly stylish. Most of its customers are package holidaymakers.

€€€€ **Riad Atlas Kasbah Ecolodge**, Tighanimine El Baz, 15 km inland from the centre of Agadir, www.atlaskasbah.com. Sound ecological principles, a beautifully designed traditional building and a great location in the hills east of Agadir make this a romantic place to stay. The 8 rooms and 3 suites are kitted out in riad style, with ochre tones and traditional fabrics. Activities such as cooking classes and an astronomy night are available on request. Homecooked food but no alcohol licence; it's fine to bring your own drinks.

€€€ **Riad Villa Blanche**, Baie des Palmiers, T0528-211313, www.riadvillablanche.com. Sleek, contemporary Moroccan style and a managable size (there are 28 rooms) set this place apart from the super-hotel competition. There are 2 good pools, a large spa, a library, a restaurant and a bar at the southern end of Agadir's bay. It's a fair walk to the centre but you may not want to leave that much.

€€ **Atlantic**, Av Hassan II, T0528-843661, www.atlantichotelagadir.com. Competing with the nearby **Kamal** to be Agadir's best-value accommodation, the **Atlantic** is set back from the road with immaculate, comfortable rooms, a good (if rather cold in winter) pool and some Moroccan touches that give the place an element of style, lifting it above the average concrete Agadir block. Service is friendly and it's bang in the centre of town, albeit a 10-min walk from the beach. Price includes a reasonable buffet breakfast. Check their website for occasional discounts.

€€ **Kamal**, Av Hassan II, T0528-842817, www.hotel-kamal.com. An excellent mid-priced hotel in the centre of the city. It's large, with 128 rooms, but the welcome is friendly and there's a sparkling pool at the rear. The pastel decor has a slight 1980s feel but everything is spotlessly clean and there's a bar and restaurant.

€€ **Sindibad**, Pl Lahcen Tamri, T0528-823477, sinhot@menara.ma. Good-sized rooms and a tiny but secluded rooftop pool make this the smartest option overlooking Talborjt's popular square. Quiet, cool and clean, it's a little dated these days.

€ **Canaria**, Pl Lahcen Tamri, T0528-846727. A popular budget option on the square in Talborjit. Simple, fairly clean rooms, some with balconies overlooking the square. Good value but rather unfriendly.

€ **El Bahia**, Rue El Mahdi Bin Toummert, T0528-822724. Just off the square in

Talborjt, **El Bahia** is a quiet, clean and fairly contemporary option, with pine furniture and a good terrace. Some rooms have en-suite bathrooms.

€ Hotel Massa, Pl Lahcen Tamri, T0528-822409. Simple rooms face inwards to an open terrace with shared showers and toilets. Very cheap but not the cleanest hotel.

€ Petite Suede, Av Hassan II, T0528-840779, www.petitesuede.com. A friendly place with plain but well-priced and comfortable rooms not far from the beach. The hotel is in a quiet part of the centre but some rooms still suffer from street noise; choose a room at the back if you can.

Taghazout *p232*

Surf Maroc, Moroccan Surf Adventures, Surf Berbere and Dfrost are among the Taghazout outfits offering organized surfing with accommodation included. All encourage package stays of a week or more together with lessons but they also accept bookings for shorter stays, and there's no obligation to surf. It's a competitive market and you get much more for your money than in Agadir, plus a friendly, international and communal vibe. All the above companies also have, or can organize, good apartments for rent. Some surfers rent rooms from local families; you can get good prices, but don't expect too much in the way of facilities and check on security.

€€€ Villa Amouar, surfmaroc.com. Still being built at the time of writing, this promises to take the successful, British-run Surf Maroc model and elevate it, with more space and a boutique feel. Recycled vintage furniture mixed with contemporary touches and abstract art should create a posh surf vibe. All rooms will have big en suite bathrooms and most will come with sea views and private terraces. There's a great pool looking out onto the sea with a sunken bar next door. Touches, such as outdoor showers attached to the trees, will up the cool quotient and it promises to become a seriously chic place to stay.

€€ Dfrost Surf House Villa, T0528-200522, www.dfrostsurfmorocco.nl. A friendly, Dutch-run, surf-centred operation near Hash Point, at Taghazout's northern end. The villa's great terrace has a hot tub and good views of the surf. The 7 rooms range from shared dorms to "premium double". There's a good breakfast and optional home-cooked evening meals too, plus a big cinema screen and daily roof terrace yoga classes. A barbecue is served every Sun night. The company also has various apartments for rent nearby. The website has some of the best information on the surfing conditions in the Taghazout area. Minimum 3-night stay; weekly deals available.

€€ Surf Camp, Tamraght, T0528-314874, www.morocsurf.com. Moroccan Surf Adventures's purpose-built accommodation is in Tamraght, 2 km down the coast from Taghazout. There's a new terrace, complete with hammock, a restaurant and simple, clean, comfortable rooms.

€€ Taghazout Surf Camp, T0528-200290, www.surfberbere.com. The Surf Berbere team emphasize local culture and organize trips for flat days. Their surf camp is on 4 levels at Hash Point, right next to the sea with a big roof terrace and sunset yoga.

€€ Taghazout Villa, www.surfmaroc.co.uk. The 2 communal terraces both have great views straight out to sea and along the coast to Anchors. There's a very friendly communal vibe, and a slightly more upmarket feel than at the **Auberge**. Rooms are simple but comfortable and attractively decorated, with a combination of dorms and doubles. Evening meals are taken all together on wooden tables after homemade dips are served. There's Wi-Fi, a constant supply of fruit, and an honesty fridge for drinks and chocolate. For the surfing, Surf Maroc offer plenty of serious expertise and kit.

€€ Villa Mandala, www.surfmaroc.co.uk. Yoga and surf make good bedfellows in this spacious villa in a quiet (if a little isolated) spot near the sea in Aouir, run by Surf Maroc. There's plenty of communal space, a small pool, a hammam and everyone eats together in a beautifully decorated and sunny room. There's a more homely, feminine vibe than in the **Taghazout Villa**, with bougainvillea and rooms beautifully decorated with splashes of colour and plenty of Moroccan touches: fabrics, cushions, rugs and mirrors. Free Wi-Fi and a spectacular yoga space on the roof with views of Banana Beach.

€ Auberge, www.surfmaroc.co.uk. Right in the heart of Taghazout, on the town's beach, this friendly and great-value place is the nearest thing around to a conventional hotel. Above the ground-floor restaurant and café are 11 compact but nicely decorated rooms in colourful seaside tones with photos on the walls and blue slatted shutters. There's a great traveller atmosphere and terraces that overlook the fishing boats and the sea below. On Thu guests from all **Surf Maroc**'s accommodation gather for a barbecue.

Camping

Atlantica Parc, T0528-820805, www.atlanticaparc.com. A modern campsite with a pool, bungalows, "equipped tents" and chalets and mobile homes to rent (from around 600dh per day). There's drinking water throughout. Camping from 90dh per day for 2 people and a van. The beach is a 5-min stroll away. Although English is spoken, a better reception may be received if you use French.

Immouzer des Ida Outanane *p232*
€€ Hotel des Cascades, T0528-826016. A slightly dated hotel in an extraordinary location, with 27 en-suite rooms, with terraces or balconies. There's good French-Moroccan food in the restaurant, a bar, a tennis court, a pool lined with pomegranate and pear trees, and a beautiful tiered garden of fruit and olive trees located above the seasonal waterfalls. Lunch on the shaded terrace with wonderful views of the mountains is a popular option.

Camping is possible near the **Café de Miel** near the foot of the cascades.

Inezgane *p235*
Unless you're splashing out for the **Riad des Golfs**, transport connections are likely to be the main reason for staying overnight in Inezgane. Buses make most hotels noisy; most cheap hotels are near the *gare routière* and around the Pl el Massira.

€€€€ Riad des Golfs, Ben Sergao, T0661-237161, www.riaddesgolfs.com. Plush luxury between the golf courses of Inezgane, south of Agadir. Rooms have elements of traditional Moroccan style, with rugs, rose petals and handmade metal basins, and there's a pool and beautiful gardens. The out-of-town location means you'll probably need your own transport. The mouth of the Oued Sous is not far away.

€€ Hotel-Restaurant la Pergola, T0528-833100, www.lapergola.ma. Along the road to Agadir. Bungalows are set around a verdant garden, and there's a bar and a restaurant serving French food.

€ Hotel Hagounia, 9 Av Mokhtar Soussi, T0528-830783. A decent cheap option near the bus station, convenient for onward travel. 48 rooms with shower and WC.

⊙ Restaurants

Agadir *p228, map p229*
The new marina area has some good upmarket restaurants; the city centre has some surprisingly authentic pizza joints. Stalls by the port have excellent fresh fish and good prices maintained through hectic competition. (Take a *petit taxi* there for 10dh, or bus No 1.) The Nouveau Talborjt area has a few options on the tree-shaded Pl Lahcen Tamri.

€€ La Madrague, La Marina d'Agadir, T0528-842424. A sophisticated marina restaurant, **La Madrague**'s white tablecloths, red leather seats, up-lit glass floor and grey *tadelakt* walls give it a striking appearance. Outside heaters mean you can sit and watch the boats all year round, and there's a menu of fish, seafood and meaty options.

€€ **Le Quai**, La Marina d'Agadir, T0661 605822. Contemporary and stylish, this restaurant has white chairs and low lighting and offers modern European food, with an emphasis on fish and seafood. There are tables inside and out, with patio heaters for cooler winter nights.

€€ **Les Blancs**, La Marina d'Agadir, T0528-828393, dir@gmail.com. A terrace restaurant and bar in a fantastic position at the north end of the beach near the new marina development, this lounge beach bar and restaurant shows little trace of Morocco. Comfy shaded sofas, laid-back tunes, strutting staff in faded jeans and black t-shirts. The menu has a Spanish flavour, with good tapas and cocktails. There's even an area of private beach reserved for customers.

€ **Daffy**, Rue des Orangers, T0528-820068. A friendly little place serving traditional Moroccan food: couscous and tagines for around 50dh. There are a few wooden tables and chairs outside on the quiet street set back from Hassan II.

€ **Little Italy**, Av Hassan II, T0528-820039. Next door to Agadir's other decent pizza restaurant, **Little Italy** makes a reasonable stab at pizzeria authenticity. There are wooden beams and various bits of Italiana hung between black-and-white photos of film stars. Usually busy, the atmosphere and the pizzas are the highlights. Grab one of the outside tables if the prospect of other diners smoking bothers you.

€ **Mille et Une Nuits**, Pl Lahcen. A popular, good-value place on the square in Nouveau Talborjt with good Moroccan fish dishes and tagines for around 30dh. There are tables outside, and they serve food all afternoon, though the waiters can be a little pushy.

€ **Via Veneto**, Av Hassan II, opposite the Vallée des Oiseaux, T0528-841467. A high-quality pizzeria with a real wood oven and alcohol licence. They also do other Italian and some Moroccan food. Fish tanks and candles decorate the place and Western

pop plays on the stereo. Book ahead in high season.

Cafés and pâtisseries

€€ **Café Metropole**, opposite the mosque. Popular with locals; tables on the street make it a good place to watch people go by.

€€ **La Maison du Pain**, 19 Av Hassan II, close to the **Hotel Petite Suède**. Cakes, fruit juice and ice cream. Fresh bread – good for picnics.

€€ **Yacout**, Av Fevrier 29, T0528-846588. A pâtisserie, bakery and café with a green and shady seating area: a good spot for coffee or breakfast, and makes excellent cakes and biscuits. There's also a branch inside the Marché Centrale.

€ **Venezia Ice**, La Marina d'Agadir. No cones but good quality ice cream for a cool accompaniment to a stroll around the marina. Alternatively, they have wicker chairs outside under parasols.

Taghazout p232

As well as the restaurants and cafés below, there are fried fish stalls in the market next to the buses at the southern end of town.

€ **Aftas**, Taghazout beach. Opposite the **Auberge**, down on the beach, this place has drinks and sandwiches and good Moroccan food. Stools outside on the street are good viewpoints from which to watch Taghazout go by.

€ **Auberge**, Taghazout beach. The buzzing restaurant of Taghazout's hotel is the heart of international traveller life in town, offering good post-surfing food and excellent banoffee pie. Managing to be both funky and romantic, it has a greenery-covered terrace and candles, with views of the beach, though outside it can also be distinctly smelly. Inside there's a colourful bar with a big screen. The food is an international mix of pizzas, curries, fried fish, burgers and tagines.

€ **Banana Beach**, Km 14 near Tamraght. This chilled beach café has a volleyball court and sun-loungers and serves beer; an excellent place to relax for an afternoon.

€ **Le New Port**, T0613-411845. The best
option along Taghazout's main street, this
French-owned (and English-speaking)
place offers a mix of European and
Moroccan food. The fried fish is good,
served with generous portions of beans
and rice, and there are tagines too. The
terrace gives good views of the street
and the mosque. Service can be slow.
€ **Le Spot**. Good pizzas and fast food on
the main street.
€ **Tamazirt**. Just up the hill from the
Auberge, this little café sells good
smoothies and granola.

Immouzer des Ida Outanane *p232*
The €€ **Hotel des Cascades** (see Where to
stay, above) has the town's best restaurant.
€ **La Belle Vallée**, Km 33.5, Rte de Miel,
T0670-379642. On a bend in the road to
Immouzer next to a tree-fringed stream,
this little café-restaurant knocks up great
food on request: delicious omelettes and
one of the best Moroccan salads you'll find
anywhere, served with warm bread. If you
fancy staying around here, the **Auberge Bab
Immouzer**, 3 km down the road, has a pool
and good views.

Inezgane *p235*
€ **Café-Restaurant Bateau de Marrakech**,
on the main square. Good and inexpensive.
€ **Café/restaurant**, adjacent to **Hotel
Hagounia**. Right in the centre for a view
of the activity.

⊕ Entertainment

Agadir *p228, map p229*
Several of the large hotels have nightclubs.
Huge Actors, in the Royal Atlas, and plush
So Fun in the Sofitel are the best. For
homesick Brits, the **Central English Pub**,
Blvd 20 Août, serves beer and baked beans
and shows Sky Sports.

⊙ Shopping

Agadir *p228, map p229*
Crafts
Agadir has no shortage of Moroccan crafts
for sale, notably from traders along the paths
and roads leading from the big hotels to the
beach, and near the museum, to the north
of Av Mohammed V.
Ensemble Artisanal, Rue du 29 Février.
A cooperative of leatherworkers,
metalworkers, jewellers and other local
craftspeople with fixed prices.

General
There are a number of good beer and wine
shops on Av Mohammed V, right from Av
du Général Kettani. European newspapers
can be bought from stalls outside the major
hotels and on Av Hassan II. There is also a
Marjane hypermarket on the main N1 road
between Agadir and the airport.
Uniprix, Av Hassan II. 0830-1230 and
1430-1930. Well-stocked supermarket,
also serving alcohol.

⦿ What to do

Agadir *p228, map p229*
Golf
Golf du Soleil d'Agadir, Chemin Oued Souss.
Golf Les Dunes, Route d'Inezgane. More
central than **Royal Golf d'Agadir**.
Royal Golf d'Agadir, 12 km from Agadir,
between Inezgane and Aït Melloul, T0528-
241278. Snack bar and play area for children,
weekends can be very busy.

Swimming
Apart from the sea, there is a pool by the
beachfront, off Av Mohammed V by the
Syndicat d'Initiative. Most of the larger
hotels also have their own pools.

Tennis
Royal Tennis Club d'Agadir, Av Hassan II.
Clay courts.

Taghazout *p232*
Surfing
See Taghazout, Where to stay, above, for
details of surf schools in the area, offering
both lessons and great places to stay.

Tour operators
Operators include **Comanav Voyages**,
5 bis Av Mohammed V, and **Menara Tours**,
341 Av Hassan II.
Sahara Tours International, 27-29
Complexe Agador Blvd du 20 Août, T0528-
840421, www.saharatoursinternational.
com. Organize a range of excursions outside
Agadir, including visits to Taroudant,
Marrakech, Tafraoute and Essaouira, usually
including at least one meal. Other agents
in the same building also organize trips to
Immouzer des Ida Outanane, Tata and Akka.

⊖ Transport

Agadir *p228, map p229*
Air
Agadir's airport has exchange facilities, an
ATM and car rental. Airlines operating from
Agadir include **EasyJet**, **Ryanair**, **Air France**
and **Royal Air Maroc**.

Bicycle/motorcycle hire
There are several individuals hiring bicycles,
mopeds and motorbikes on Blvd du 20 Août.

Bus
Services run to and from the *gare routière*,
outside the town. There are private services to
Marrakech (5 a day), **Casablanca/Rabat** and
Taroudant (4 a day), **Essaouira** and **Tiznit**,
Tata and **Tan-Tan** and **Akka**; also **Tafraoute**.
CTM, T0528-822077, SATAS, T0528-842470,
and **Pullman du Sud**, T0528-846040.
  Local buses to **Inezgane** (Nos 5 and 6)
and **Taghazout** (Nos 12 and 14), leave from
Pl Salam. From Blvd Mohammed Cheik

Saadi, Nos 5 and 6 go to **Inezgane**, bus No 1
goes to the port.

Car hire
Avis, Av Hassan II, T0528-841755, and
at the airport, T0528-840345. **Budget**,
Av Mohammed V, T0528-840762. **Hertz**,
Bungalow Marhaba, Av Mohammed V,
T0528-840939, and at the airport,
T0528-839071. **Inter-Rent Europcar**, Av
Mohammed V. **Lotus Cars**, Av Mohammed V.

Taxi
Plentiful *petits taxis* are useful. They can carry
3 passengers but cannot go outside town
limits. Journeys are metered but expect
to pay around 10dh and 15dh after 2000.
Grands taxis leave for various destinations,
particularly **Inezgane** and **Taroudant**, from
Pl Salam, to the south of the centre.

Inezgane *p235*
There are bus services to and from
Casablanca and **Essaouira**, **Marrakech**
and **Taroudant**, **Ouarzazate**, **Tiznit** and
Laâyoune, among other places. *Grands taxis*
(4dh a seat) or local buses (Nos 5 and 6) to
Agadir. The **airport** bus is No 22. Coming
from Taroudant, you may have to change
grands taxis at Ouled Teïma.

⊕ Directory

Agadir *p228, map p229*
Banks There are ATMs at BMCE and BMCI,
on Av du Général Kettani, on your right
as you head towards Blvd Mohammed
V and the sea. Try also **Wafa Bank** in this
area. **Medical services** Pharmacie,
Municipalité d'Agadir, next to the post
office, T0528-820349, open all night. **Useful
numbers** Ambulance: T15. **Fire**: T150.
Police: Rue du 18 Novembre, T190.

Taroudant and the Souss

Taroudant is famous for its red-brown crenellated walls. Variously called 'the grandmother of Marrakech', or 'the elder brother of Marrakech', in reality it is not much more than a half-cousin. But it does have some of the character of its more famous neighbour across the Tizi-n-Test pass, albeit on a far smaller and sleepier scale. The medina is enclosed by impressive pisé (rammed earth) ramparts. Inside are two largish squares, higgledy-piggledy streets and some souks (although much of the older building has been replaced by concrete structures). Taroudant makes a good overnight stop on an exploration of Southern Morocco: Agadir and the coast are a short hop westwards; further afield are the pre-Saharan oases of Tata and Akka, with rock carvings close by; there is a spectacular mountain route to Tafroute and, to the north, are the western High Atlas mountains, while eastwards are routes to Ouarzazate and the Draâ, Dadès and Ziz valleys. ▸▸ *For listings, see pages 248-250.*

Arriving in Taroudant → *Colour map 2, C3.*
Getting there Buses and taxis arrive at Bab Zorgane outside the city walls. ▸▸ *See page 250 for further details.*

Getting around The town centres on Place Assarag and Place Talmoklate. The sights, the ramparts and souk, can be done on foot. You might hire a bike from an outfit near Place Assarag to explore a bit more. From Taroudant, possible day trips include the old village of Freija, some 10 km from town, and the oasis of Tioute, which has an old kasbah. Pale-brown *petits taxis* do runs in the local area, and there are a few horse-drawn calèches, too.

Background
Located at the heart of the fertile Souss valley, Taroudant was always an important regional centre and even managed to achieve national prominence on a few occasions. Taken by the Almoravids in 1056, it achieved a certain level of independence under the Almohads. Temporary fame came in the 16th century with the rise of the Saâdians. From 1510, the first Saâdian leader, Mohammed el Qa'im, was based in Taroudant as the Emir of the Souss. Even after the Saâdians had gained control of the rest of Morocco, Taroudant remained their capital for a while. Later, in the 17th century, Taroudant supported Moulay Ismaïl's nephew in his rebellion. When the great sultan took the town in 1687, he took his revenge by slaughtering the population and destroying much of the area. Decline set in, continuing into the 18th and 19th centuries. In the early years of the French protectorate, Taroudant harboured the rebel Sultan el Hiba and was consequently sacked by colonial forces. Today, the town is a regional market. A handful of riads have sprung up in recent years but many tourists are day trippers from Agadir or people overnighting on their way to other southern destinations. An inhabitant of Taroudant is called a Roudani.

Places in Taroudant

Walls
The terracotta-coloured 16th- and early 17th-century Saâdian *pisé* walls, crenellated and set here and there with chunky square towers, are Taroudant's best sight. You could follow the walls round the town, possibly in a calèche (horse-drawn carriage), generally available from outside the **Hotel Salam** for around 40dh per hour. There were originally only five

gates; running clockwise from the bus station they are Bab Zorgane, Bab Targhount, Bab Oulad Bounouna, Bab el Khemis and Bab el Kasbah. You can go up at least one of these for a look out over olive groves, orchards and building sites.

In the northeast corner of the medina is the kasbah, the most densely populated and poorest part of town. This was a fortress rebuilt by Moulay Ismaïl in the 17th century. Outside the walls, you can visit the tanneries by turning left from Bab el Khemis ('the Thursday gate'), where skins of a variety of animals are still cured using traditional methods.

Apart from its walls, Taroudant is not the most picturesque of places by day. Originally, part of the area within the walls was devoted to orchards and market gardening but much of this has now been built up, and the majority of the original low *pisé* buildings have long since been replaced by concrete housing. In the evening, however, Taroudant takes on a more interesting atmosphere, with men staying up late socializing in the cafés in the centre. It's also a relaxed place, where hassle is rare.

Souks

The souks of Taroudant are an easy, calm place to look around for souvenirs. Thursday and Sunday are busy days, with people coming in from the surrounding villages. Specialities of the town include jewellery and carvings in local limestone. The main souks are in the block to the north of Avenue Mohammed V, between the two squares. Some hotels have a useful map of the souks, detailing areas of specialities.

Taroudant

Where to stay	Palais Salam **4**	Saâdiens **6**
El Warda **10**	Riad Maia **3**	Taroudant **7**
La Gazelle d'Or **2**	Riad Maryam **9**	
Naturally Morocco	Riad Taroudant **8**	**Restaurants**
Guesthouse **1**	Roudana **5**	L'Agence **1**

The narrow, winding mountain route from Taroudant to Marrakech crosses the high Tizi-n-Test pass at 2082 m. For those with a good head for heights, Tizi-n-Test is a great drive, though its tight bends, lack of barriers and lorries mean that it's not recommended in the dark. Heading east out of Taroudant, take the N10 towards Ouarzazate. At Oulad Berrehil, where the road begins to leave the fertile Souss Valley, the road to the Tizi-n-Test branches north.

The other option is to continue east towards Ouarzazate (from where there's an alternative pass over the Atlas, the Tizi-n-Tichka) and the southern Atlas gorges. Aoulouz, on the N10 31 km east of the Tizi-n-Test junction, is a beautiful spot. There is easy access to the dammed Ouled Souss from here. The first notable town after this is Taliouine.

Taliouine → *Colour map 2, C4.*
Taliouine is said to produce the best saffron in Morocco and has a magnificent kasbah to the south of the road. It's also a good starting point for walking in the Jbel Siroua (see below). There is a petrol station at the eastern end of town beyond the triumphal arches and another in the centre, almost opposite the **Saffron Cooperative**.

Taliouine to Tazenakht → *Colour map 2, C4.*
From Taliouine there is a road south to Igherm and a minor road north to Askaoun. Between Taliouine and Tazenakht are two high passes, **Tizi-n-Taghatine** (1886 m) and **Tizi Ikhsane** (1650 m), with the small settlement of **Tinfat** and another imposing kasbah midway between. The highest pass, Tizi-n-Taghatine, incorporates some of the best scenery on this route: a mixture of landforms, terracing with small trees, views on all sides. Tizi n-Taghatin marks the end of the Souss basin and the beginning of the Draâ. Between the passes there is patchy shifting cultivation and little else.

Tazenakht and beyond → *Colour map 2, C4.*
Tazenakht is at an important junction, though much of the town stands to the northwest of the road. There's a market on Fridays and a number of carpet shops, displaying fine, geometrical wares produced by the local Ouzguita tribe. There are small shops and a mosque.

After Tazenakht, the N10 road climbs up to **Tizi-n-Bachkoum**, 1700 m. At the top there is a good view to the west and a place to pull off the road.

Jbel Siroua → *For listings, see pages 248-250.*

Rising to a twin-peak of 3305 m, the Jbel Siroua is an arid, isolated region forming a sort of volcanic bridge between the High Atlas of Toubkal to the north and the Anti-Atlas to the south. Compared with the busy, even prosperous, Imilchil region, there are few trekkers here, and communicating with locals can be a problem, unless you have fluent Tachelhit. Best trekked in autumn and spring, the Jbel Siroua is easily accessible from both Taroudant and Ouarzazate. From Marrakech, it is a long ride, nearly nine hours by the direct bus, with occasional breakdowns. The best starting point for Jbel Siroua treks is Taliouine.

Possible treks
From Taliouine, there are numerous possibilities for trekking up into the Siroua. Richard Knight in his excellent *Trekking in the Moroccan Atlas* (Trailblazer) gives an immense

amount of useful detail on a nine-day Jbel Siroua trek. If you have less time, the **Auberge Souktana** ⓘ *Taliouine, T0528-534075*, should be able to advise on short treks. Also try **Naturally Morocco Guesthouse** in Taroudant, as they have excellent contacts in the region. Another possibility would be to take a minibus from Taliouine up to **Akhfamane**, where many treks start. An irregular minibus service runs from the central garage in Taliouine up to Akhfamane, although it is possible to walk this in about five hours. At Akhfamane, there are a rooms available and mules for hire. A number of European-based travel companies run treks into the Jbel Siroua.

Taroudant to Tata via Igherm → *For listings, see pages 248-250.*

The wild landscapes on the route from Taroudant to Tata, via Igherm (distance 120 km), are among the most beautiful in southern Morocco. Allow plenty of time for photo-stops and, perhaps, a side-trip up to Tazegzaoute.

Near Taroudant: Feïja and Tioute → *Colour map 2, C3.*
Head east from Taroudant on the N10 and turn right onto the 7025 to reach the small village of **Feïja**. *Pisé* walls crumbling amid new buildings signal a rural community in full change. There are good views north over the orchards and fields of the Souss valley to the High Atlas. Returning to the 7025, a few kilometres further on is the next turn off for **Tioute** (souk on Wednesday), set in argan groves on the edge of the Souss plain, 33 km from Taroudant. Here the kasbah is easily reached by a more or less blacktop road. There are superb views over the plain. Below, in the village, you can see a strone threshing floor and the Zaouïa of Sidi Abd el Kader. Normally, someone will appear to volunteer donkey rides from the kasbah, around 30dh a head. As you arrive in Tioute, an argan oil co-operative is signposted.

Igherm and Tazegzaoute → *Colour map 2, C3.*
After Tioute, the 7025 winds upwards as the soft green of the Souss is left behind. **Igherm**, 88 km from Tata, is the first major settlement, a one-street town with shops and cafés. Look out for the **Restaurant Kratrit**, an eclectic little place. The route southwest (7038) from Igherm to Tafraoute is fully tarmacked and accessible to small hire cars. Look out for old granaries on the way. The piste running northeast to Taliouine is only for 4WD vehicles. South of Igherm, there are some very photogenic creases in the landscape in the region of **Souk Khémis d'Issafen**. Some 55 km south of Igherm, there is a turn off right (west) for the beautiful valley of Tazegzaoute. Well-equipped walkers with a guide could head over the hills for Tafraoute via Tazalrhite.

Tata → *Colour map 2, C4.*
The main town of the Jbel Beni region, built alongside an oasis, the rose-pink houses of Tata focus on an arcaded main street and dusty market square. The place has the feel of a desert garrison outpost. There are banks, an ATM, a post office and basic café-restaurants.

Within a couple of hours' drive of Tata are fascinating old villages and prehistoric rock art sites and the town, with a couple of decent hotels, makes a good base. Service stations at Akka and destinations east can run out of fuel, so try to fill up in Tata before heading onwards.

A good half-day side trip from Tata is to the impressively large *ksar* of **Tazaght**. Just before Addis, and after a big village on your left, turn left (east) off the 7084 to Akka. Tazaght is just visible across several kilometres of gravelly plain traversed by tracks. Follow the piste and park up near the new pink mosque and walk around the ridge to the right. The oldest part of the village, largely stone-built, sits atop a rocky crest, while other sections closer to the cultivated area crumble back into the earth. Look out for the original mosque which has a massive whitewashed simplicity recalling the Almoravid kouba in Marrakech. You can clamber round the semi-ruined houses and walk down to the oasis. There seems to be no trace of the once large Jewish community of the *ksar*.

Prehistoric rock art

The region southwest of Tata is rich in prehistoric rock art. You will see overlapping images of elegant gazelles, other beasts, spirals and human feet, carved on large flat stones in the unlikeliest of locations – witness to the civilization resident here in a time before the desert. A good selection of sites can be covered in a long day's exploring, if you have your own vehicle. For those dependent on public transport, the excellent site of **Adrar Metgourine** can be reached from Akka on foot. **Akka** is 70 km southwest of Tata. If you want to stay overnight here, there is one hotel, **Tamdoult** (€), on the main road, but it's pretty grotty. Akka also has cafés and shops, with souks on Thursday and Sunday.

The best guide to rock art in the area is **Mouloud Taâret**, T0662-291864 (mob). He lives in **Douar Touzounine**, a roadside settlement a few kilometres south of Akka, handy for the rock-art site of **Tamdoult**. He also has a base in **Oum el Aleg**, a village south of the main road a few kilometres east of Akka. A guide is essential if you want to find the best of the carvings. They tend to be on flatish boulders on low ridges which run parallel to the 7084 road. You may also see open-air sites where neolithic people worked flints. These tend to be more visible after winter rain. Watch out for snakes and wear good shoes.

Between Oum el Alek and Tata, there are two minor rock-art sites close to the 7084, **Oued Meskaou** (on your left, coming from Tata) and **Aman Ighriben** (on your right). The better of the two is Oued Meskaou. From the Tata direction, look out for the Akka 24 km post which is just a few metres after the turn-off for the site. As you come from Akka, look out for the Taroudant 234 km post, also a sign for Oued Meskaou and the Commune rurale de Tata. Turn off right between the concrete bollards. Park under the thorn trees near the gap between two ridges. The engravings are on the ridge tops, an interesting mix of smoothed and *piqueté* technique carvings, including some spirals. The chess-board designs, the so-called *bijoux berbères*, are probably recent nomad scratchings. Out in the distance, near a higher ridge line, is the oasis of **Ghans**, which has a *guelta* (pool) in rainy years.

Aman Ighriben is 12 km further on, 12.5 km from Akka. Turn off near the marker 259 km to Tiznit, 246 km to Taroudant. Coming from Tata, turn off right a couple of kilometres after the Guelmim 255 km marker, just before the white markers. You should park near the palm trees some 200 m from the road. The carvings are on a low (10 m high) stoney rise close to palms and thorn bushes. The site, probably because it is so accessible, is much deteriorated, although there are still some nice gazelles.

Lala Baït Allah

Past Tagadirt, there is evidence of the one-time importance of trans-Saharan gold, ivory and slave trade routes through the area in the form of the ruined Almohad minaret at Lala Baït Allah. Set in an oasis, the building comes as a real surprise. Adrar Metgourine, a low hill, which appears as a semicircle to the north, is a good 90 minutes' walk away. The prehistoric artists carefully executed their works in stones along the top of the hill, and their lines are highlighted to good effect by the setting sun. Even without the carvings, the site has its own special beauty.

Amtoudi (aka Id Aissa)

Amtoudi is well worth making the effort to reach (shared taxis are available from Taghjijt on the 7084), and is a good option for an overnight stay in order to do some walking. Because of the well-preserved *agadir* (fortified granary), Amtoudi is on the tourist safari circuit. Soon after you arrive, the key-holder will appear to accompany you up the mule track to the top (20 minutes' steep walk, mules occasionally available). The views are magnificent, and you can clamber round inside and look for the fitted stone beehives, the prehistoric carved feet at the highest point and the cisterns. The flat stone walls are superbly constructed to follow the line of the cliff. The *agadir* functioned as a guarded store for the villagers' harvest and was probably only inhabited in times of raids.

If you want to stay over, the campsite down below has French management, bunk room accommodation, hot showers and meals. Should there be any risk of a thunderstorm, avoid staying at the campsite, as it sits below the cliff at the meeting point of two canyons.

Exploring the agadirs of Amtoudi The campsite can set you up with a guide to take you walking in the area. There is an excellent short walk up to the *gueltas* through the palm groves further up the canyon (bring your picnic and swimming gear, as there's plenty of water and sun in winter). A day walk could start at the main agadir, then take you over the plateau to further ones, the best preserved of which is **Agadir Aglaoui**, an eagle's nest of a place. After this granary, there is a difficult descent down to the river and on to the pools. Another energetic scramble takes you 100 m up to the top again. Head across the plateau towards the red-and-white pylon to climb back down the gorge just above the campsite. Here is yet another ruined agadir and vertiginous drops. Barbary ground squirrels scamper among the rocks.

Taghjijt → *Colour map 4, A5.*

Back on the 7084, Taghjijt (Thursday market, interesting at date harvest time) is useful as a place to charter a *grand taxi* to take you up to Amtoudi. There is also a good breakfast café at the main junction and accommodation. As at Akka, there is no formal petrol station in Taghjijt.

Ifrane de l'Anti Atlas → *Colour map 4, A5.*

At the ribbon settlement of Timoulay Izder (petrol, pharmacy), you need to take the turn-off right onto the 7076 for Ifrane de l'Anti Atlas (aka Ifrane de l'Atlas Esseghir). There is a wide tarmacked main street and a Saturday market.

Try to find a local to guide you through the carefully tended olive groves and fields to the old **mellah**, or Jewish neighbourhood, which once held over 500 homes. A little restoration work has been undertaken on the whitewashed synagogue (*kenissat el yahoud*), which is kept locked, however.

For sleeping and eating price codes and other relevant information, see pages 22-28.

⊙ Where to stay

Taroudant *p242, map p243*

€€€€ Hotel La Gazelle d'Or, Rte d'Amezgou, T0528-852039/48, www. gazellador.com. A supremely elegant and supremely expensive hotel, 2 km outside Taroudant. Originally built by a Belgian aristocrat and generally closed in summer, it has 30 "cottages" and suites set in 80 ha of beautiful grounds with its own organic farm, pool, 2 clay tennis courts, a hammam, riding and a croquet lawn. Plushly stylish rooms and suites are decorated in traditional Moroccan style and have private dressing rooms and private gardens.

€€€ Dar Zitoune, T0528-551141. www.darzitoune.com. A very smart, Swiss-owned place with 20 suites and bungalows among flowers and fruit trees, 2 km outside the city walls. Rooms are individually decorated but all share a warm colour palette and sleek design. The best have their own sitting rooms with open fires. The pool is beautiful, as is the bar – the only plain aspect of the place is the restaurant, though the food is good. Wi-Fi, satellite TV. Half and full board also available.

€€€ Palais Salam, T0528-852312. Rambling and these days a little tired, the *Salam* is built into the ramparts around the kasbah district, in a building which was the local pacha's palace. Rooms are on 2 tiers around palm-filled courtyards: a great setting, though the shabby elements tend to overwhelm the palatial ones. 2 pools, including one in the shape of a Moroccan horseshoe arch that backs onto the city walls. 2 restaurants, a/c and satellite TV.

€€€ Riad Maia, 12 Tassoukt Ighezifen, T0641-037989, www.riad-maia-taroudant. com. A small, French-German run riad with a cute salon and beautiful antique *zellige*

tiles. The family room has a lovely turquoise sunken bathroom, and there's a multi-levelled roof terrace with sun loungers and views. Intimate and friendly.

€€€ Riad Taroudant, 243 Av Al Qods–Derb Jdid, T0528-852572, www.riad taroudant.com. Stylish and sophisticated, this riad is in an excellent position near the souk and has 16 rooms with *tadelakt* tiles, a courtyard pool and roof terrace with a cacti and sun loungers. There's also a brick-vaulted hammam which the French owner hopes to turn into a massage room.

€€ Hotel Saâdiens, Av du 20 Août, Borj Oumansour, T0528-852589. A reasonable mid-range place with a small pool and a restaurant.

€€ Naturally Morocco Guesthouse, 422 Derb Afferdou, T0661-236627, www.naturallymorocco.co.uk. Originally run from the UK, the ecological and exceptionally friendly guesthouse is now managed by local staff who know the region well. Rooms, mostly en suite, are large and comfortable, decorated in simple Moroccan style, and there's a roof terrace with views of both the Atlas and the Anti-Atlas. Vegetarian food is a speciality and their cookery lessons are highly recommended. The kitchen can be used by guests, and rooms can easily be made into apartments for families or small groups. Staff organize unusually well-informed cultural tours of the region, and the hotel has won awards for its community projects. Guests have free use of the pool at **Palais Salam**. If you get lost, ask for 'La Maison Anglaise', which is how the locals know it.

€€ Riad Maryam, 140 Derb Maalem Mohammed, T0666-127285, www.riad maryam.com. In a 140-year-old building well signposted off the south of Av Mohammed V, this little place doesn't have any of the decor chic of riads in Marrakech, but it does have a very friendly welcome from Habib and his wife, and Moroccan food

for which people come from far and wide.
Free internet, 4 rooms.

€ El Warda, 8 Pl Tamoklate, T0528-852763.
Absurdly cheap, especially for single
rooms and good value. Simple rooms have
comfortable beds, some with balconies
overlooking the stalls on Pl Tamoklate.
Don't be fooled by the promise of en suite
bathrooms though: you get a toilet and a
sink but the baths aren't plumbed in.

€ Hotel-Restaurant Taroudant, Pl Assarag,
T0528-852416. The best rooms here have
en suite bathrooms, though there are also
cheaper, more basic rooms. Inward facing
rooms can be noisy when the bar is in
action. A little basic, with its linoleum and air
of the 1950s. Could do with sprucing up.

€ Roudana, Blvd Sidi Mohammed 65, Rue
Tassoukt Ighezefen, T0528-550070. Popular,
very cheap and in a great spot on the main
square, though the dark pokey rooms with
wobbly beds don't match the place's initial
promise. There's a decent café-restaurant
downstairs though, and you will be at the
heart of the action.

East along the N10 *p244*

€€ Palais Riad Hida, Oulad Berrehil,
40 km out of Taroudant on the N10 road to
Aoulouz, T0528-531044, www.riadhida.com.
Built by a pacha in the 19th century and
restored by a Danish millionaire. Good
food, 10 rooms, verdant tropical gardens
and an excellent pool. Invaded by tour-
groups some lunchtimes.

Taliouine *p244*

€€ Ibn Toumert, T0528-534125,
www.hotelibntoumert.com. A pleasant
1970s hotel in lovely surroundings, with
100 rooms, some with a view of the kasbah.
A/c and heating, bar and pool. Has potential,
though the restaurant is impersonal, and it
is used by bus tours.

€ Auberge/Restaurant Souktana, T0528-
534075. On the north side of the road, west
of the road junction with **Hotel Ibn Toumert**
and east of the *oued*. Accommodation in

rooms, bungalows and tents surrounded by
a small, pleasant garden. Recommended for
good food, especially tagines. Good too for
guides, mules, tents for excursions up into
the Jbel Siroua.

Tioute *p245*

€ Auberge Tigmmi, T0528-850555,
aubergetigmmi.com. 10 simple but
comfortable en suite rooms, no a/c
but excellent home cooking. Highly
recommended for a quiet couple of
days' reading and walking.

Tata *p245*

€€ Dar Infiane, Douar Indfiane, T0661-
610170, www.darinfiane.com. A French-
owned converted kasbah with a small pool
and attractive terraces with great views.
Simple rooms manage to be both rustic
and stylish. Look out for the low ceilings.

Ifrane de l'Anti Atlas *p247*

€€ Tigmmi Alhana, at the northern end
of Ifrane, T0528-314768, www.addimaroc.
com. A *maison d'hôte*, with traditional
southern Moroccan rooms and terraces
with great views.

🍽 Restaurants

Taroudant *p242, map p243*

€€€ La Gazelle d'Or, Rte d'Amezgou,
T0528-852039. In the hotel of the same
name, this is high-class dining, with dishes
made mostly from produce grown on the
hotel's own organic farm. Dress up.

€ Hotel-Restaurant Taroudant (see Where
to stay, above). The restaurant has a simple
menu at 70dh, and an alcohol licence.

€ L'Agence, Av Sidi Mohammed, T0528-
558270. Taroudant's most popular restaurant
has sculpture, tablecloths and unusual
Moroccan dishes, such as *safa*, chicken
minced with almonds and cinnamon.
A friendly and atmospheric little place.

€ Riad Maryam (see Where to stay, above).
You'll need to give plenty of advance

warning but it's worth it. Tagines and *pastilla* specialities, and they'll proudly show you their dog-eared copies of French magazines in which their food has featured.

☼ What to do

Taroudant *p242, map p243*
Bike hire just west of Pl Assarag, opposite Hotel Taroudant. **Hammam**, near the Hotel Taroudant, also off Pl Assarag.

◉ Transport

Taroudant *p242, map p243*
Bus The journey to Agadir, only 80 km, can take up to 2 hrs by bus; it's probably better to take a *grand taxi*. For distant towns (**Casablanca**, **Marrakech** via the Tizi-n-Test, **Ouazarzate**, etc), buses leave early in the morning from the Bab Zorgane station. Regular buses to **Agadir** (4 per day), **Casablanca** (4 per day), **Inzegane** (on the hour), **Ouarzazate** (5 per day), **Tata** (3 per week). Early morning service to Marrakech

via Tizi-n-Test takes 9 hrs. Note that the buses can be very slow – the **CTM** from Marrakech on the easy Chichaoua route has been known to take 6 hrs for what is only a 223-km trip.

Car If driving to **Agadir**, you can take the main N10 (straightforward but boring), or (for an insight into rural Morocco) a poorly surfaced minor road along the northern side of the Oued Souss. This brings you onto the N8 from Chichaoua to the northeast of Agadir. For **Marrakech**, the quickest route is up the N8 to Chichaoua, then continue on the N8 eastwards.

Grands taxis For Agadir and **Inezgane** you sometimes need to change at Ouled Teïma.

❶ Directory

Taroudant *p242, map p243*
Banks ATMs at Banque populaire and Société générale (SGBM) on Pl Assarag and at the Crédit du Maroc, opposite the Hotel Taroudant; BMCI, Rue Bir Anzarane off Pl Talmoklate. **Medical clinic** T0528-852032.

Tafraoute and the Ameln Valley

Located 1200 m up in a natural Anti-Atlas amphitheatre near the Ameln Valley, Tafraoute is a rewarding town for climbers, walkers, mountain bikers and those who just want to chill in a spectacular mountain setting. Winter and early spring are good times to visit, when the almond trees are in blossom (usually late January and early February) and the pink and ochre boulders contrast with the sharp green of the early barley and palms in the small oases. To match the colour scheme, even the village houses are painted pink. There are rewarding and easily organized excursions to see canyons and prehistoric art, but it's the rocks that dominate – strangely beautiful and often awesomely large, they were shaped in the distant past to look like enormous Henry Moore sculptures. ▸▸ *For listings, see pages 252-254.*

Tafraoute → *Colour map 2, C2.*
With a population of about 4000, the village is the administrative centre for a large surrounding area. There is an almond festival here, the **Fête des Amandiers**, in January and February, with music and dance (see box, page 30), and a market on Wednesday, which brings in large numbers of people from the surrounding villages. There are stalls making and selling a variety of crafts, in particular *babouches* (traditional shoes), which are a local speciality – you'll find varieties here that are rare in Marrakech.

'The Valley of Almonds' is scattered with villages in between areas of irrigated agriculture, producing argan oil and almonds. The north side of the valley is walled off by an enormous expanse of rock, much loved by climbers (see What to do, page 253). The majority of the villages are precariously positioned on the south-facing slopes of Jbel el Kest. Older stone and *pisé* buildings, generally higher up above the agricultural land where springs emerge from the mountainside, are crumbling. Newer buildings are made using reinforced concrete, with dark red rendering picked out in white. The Vallée des Ameln is best explored on foot or mountain bike. PTT has mountain bikes for rent.

From Tafraoute, the valley makes an excellent day's walk. You can take a guide for this but, as long as you have a map, it shouldn't be necessary. Head northwest out of town between the cemetery and the campsite and you will find that paths converge over a col between two rocky outcrops. From here the path descends steeply into the valley below.

Once in the valley itself, paths to the north of the road connect the various villages. The best way back is southeast from **Azrou Ouadou**, over some dramatic high plateaus and along rocky paths. The paths coming back tend to peter out but, as long as you keep heading southeast, Tafraout will eventually come into view. Allow five or six hours for the walk.

Adaï, 3 km southwest on the Tiznit road, is particularly picturesque. The rock formations caused by weathering and reminiscent of onion rings are most unusual. Other villages, either on the road like **Taguenza** or high up to the left like **Annameur**, are also worth a visit. It is more interesting to walk the upper track (a distance of around 7 km) that connects these villages. **Oumesnate** is another popular stop, as there is a traditional house here open to visitors. The French-speaking blind owner does a guided tour.

Around Tafraoute

Napoleon's Hat and the painted rocks

To the south of Tafraoute, just 3 km on the new road to Tiznit, is **Agard Oudad**, an interesting village built below a rock referred to as *le chapeau de Napoléon*. From here you can walk or cycle west to see the local artistic landscape, *les pierres bleues*. These are rocks and mountainsides, painted in various colours by the Belgian landscape artist Jean Vérame, known for his massive-scale art projects. Now faded and a little shabby, it's questionable whether the rocks are an enhancement to the landscape, or an act of environmental vandalism.

Gorge Aït Mansour

About 15 km south of Tafraoute, the gorges of Aït Mansour have birdsong and palms, with glimpses of towering pink rocks through the branches. This is a great spot for a peaceful walk alongside the water, passing people collecting dates.

In **Tizght**, **Chez Massaoud** café (T0528-801245) makes a good resting point, and there is a fruit stall opposite. You can even stay overnight here if you wish.

Prehistoric carvings

Another 15 km or so south of the gorges, the landscape opens up into wide, dry, stony, flat-bottomed valleys, almost entirely empty but for the occasional nomadic encampment. There are some excellent prehistoric rock engravings at **Ukas**. You'll probably need a guide to find them, and a willingness to clamber up some rocks, but the beautiful animal and human figures are well worth the effort.

Kasbah Tizourgane

Around 50 km north from Tafroute on the Agadir road, the extraordinary **Kasbah Tizourgane** ⓘ *T0661-941350, www.tizourgane-kasbah.com, 20dh*, rises high out of the surrounding landscape like an intricately decorated cake. The kasbah has been lovingly restored and is open to visitors, with paved paths winding among the dusty pink buildings and opening out to give amazing views of the romantically bleak, undulating surroundings. A part of the kasbah operates as a simple hotel (see below). Be patient for someone to come and open the entrance gate for you.

⦿ Tafraoute and the Ameln Valley listings

For sleeping and eating price codes and other relevant information, see pages 22-28.

⬤ Where to stay

Tafraoute *p250*
It's best to phone ahead to reserve a room during winter and spring breaks.
€€ Les Amandiers, T0528-800088, www.hotel-lesamandiers.com. Once a very smart establishment, located on a rock above the town, the **Amandiers** has good views and a pool but is looking a little tired around the edges these days. There are 60 plain rooms with a/c and satellite TV and a large restaurant and bar. Tour groups occasionally invade, otherwise it's a calm spot, popular with climbers.
€€ Saint' Antoine, T0528-801497, www.hotelsaintantoine-tafraout.com. This fairly contemporary hotel, with a 1980s feel, has a pool, a lift, room service, internet access, restaurant and a/c.
€ Les Amis, Pl Moulay Rachid, T0527-543093. Bright, clean rooms in Berber style, with fleece blankets and a terrace overlooking the roundabout.
€ Redouane, T0528-800066. Close to the bridge, **Redouane** is pokey but has hot showers and a discount for students.
€ Salama, T0528-800026, www.hotel salama.com. Plum in the town centre, the large pink **Salama** has comfortable modern rooms with a/c, en suite bathrooms,

excellent showers and internet connections in rooms. They even do 24-hr room service, if occasionally reluctantly. The only possible downsides are the lack of heating for cold winter nights and the decidedly average café on the ground floor.
€ Tafraoute, Pl Moulay Rachid, T0528-800060. In the town centre near the petrol station. Hot water, simple rooms and friendly staff. Light and airy but on a noisy junction.
€ Tanger, T0528-800190. Opposite the **Redouane** and slightly cheaper, this place has 9 small rooms and a plain roof terrace with a washing line. It's a basic place with shared showers, but has friendly staff and good food.

Camping
Camping Les Trois Palmiers, 15 mins' walk out of town, along the Tiznit road, T0666-098403. A small site reasonably equipped, and with a café. Popular with motor caravaners. Also has a few rooms for rent.

Around Tafraoute *p251*
€€ Kasbah Tizourgane, T0661-941350, www.tizourgane-kasbah.com. A part of the restored kasbah operates as a simple hotel. Half- or full-board, it makes a stunning, if isolated place to stay.
€€ Kerdous, about 35 km out of town on the Tafraout–Tiznit road (54 km from Tiznit), T0528-862063, www.hotel-kerdous.com. This is in a spectacular spot with great views of the surrounding mountains. 39 rooms,

pool, a/c, telephone, TV, restaurant, 2 bars, panoramic terrace, shop, and secure parking.

🍴 Restaurants

Tafraoute *p250*
€€ **Chez Sabir**, Rue d'Amelne, T0528-800636. The chef who runs this atmospheric place is married to an English author and it closes in summer when they decamp to Cornwall. Worth seeking out for its superior Moroccan cuisine, using the best local ingredients.
€€ **Hotel Les Amandiers** (see Where to stay, above). This has a large restaurant and the only bar in town. The contrast of the white-jacketed waiters and the echoing school dinner hall atmosphere is striking but you'll get good traditional Moroccan food and there's wine too, should you wish. Functional rather than atmospheric.
€€ **La Kasbah**, Rte Agard Oudad, T0528-800536, T0672-303909. 5-mins' walk out of the centre, La Kasbah gets little passing traffic but deserves to be busier, with excellent quality Moroccan food. The tasty *kalia*, a spicy meat, tomato and onion dish with beaten egg on top, is a speciality. Wine available on request.
€ **Marrakech**. This popular local spot just up from the bus stop has few frills but does good traditional Moroccan food and makes a good lunch stop.
€ **Tanger**, downstairs from the hotel of the same name, see Where to stay, above. Basic bargain tagines (25-35dh).

Cafés and bakers
Café Étoile d'Agadir. With tables outside on one of the main squares, where it catches the morning sun, this is the town's best spot for breakfast. It also does a fine line in smoothies and juices. Lunch and dinner menus for 40dh and 75dh respectively.
Boulangerie Artisanal. Between the mock-Berber towers just over the bridge and past the market stalls, it would be easy to miss this subterranean baker who has built a traditional oven where the bread cooks on

hot pebbles. If you ask he'll let you go in and have a look. The crusty white loaves, with a subtle aniseed flavour are a good cut or two above the usual Moroccan fare.

🛍 Shopping

Tafraoute *p250*
Stalls in the small souk around the market square specialize in local *babouches* (Moroccan shoes), some of which are in styles not usually found in Marrakech.
Maison du Troc, 155 Rte Amiane, T0528-820536. Locally made carpets and rugs, this is also a good place to get information or guides for walks and climbing.

🎯 What to do

Tafraoute *p250*
Climbing
If you're interested in climbing, Claude Davies' Cicerone book, *Climbing in the Moroccan Anti-Atlas*, is highly recommended. The climbing scene in Tafraoute is still relatively young and you may be able to find some good undocumented routes.
Hotel les Amandiers (see Where to stay, above) has Davies' new routes log book.

Cycling
Said Oussid, opposite Maison Touareg, on the Hotel les Amandiers road, T0670-409384. Has a good selection of mountain bikes for hire. 50dh a day for basic models up to 100dh a day for specialized bikes.

Hammams
Tafraoute has a couple of hammams, both operating men's and women's sections.

Swimming
You can use the pool at the **Hotel les Amandiers** for a small fee.

Tour operators
Tafraout Aventure, T0528-801368, www.tafraout-aventure.com. Can arrange

4WD trips and trekking guides. They can also give you a map of the area if you want to strike out alone. A good day trip (300dh per person) goes to the Aït Mansour gorge for a walk and includes lunch before continuing to the prehistoric rock carvings in Ukas and returning via the Timguelchte gorges. Longer trips can also be arranged all the way to the coast or southeast into the desert.

Good local guides can be found at **Maison du Troc** (see Shopping, above), or ask for the well-connected, all-purpose fixer **Houssine Laroussi** (T0661-627921), who has a tiny shop, **Coin Nomade**, on the corner of the market square and can provide maps, advice and guidebooks from his piles on the floor.

Brahim Bahou, T0661-822677, brahim-izanzaran@hotmail.com. Brahim is an official Guide de Montagne. He speaks English and has a small office with maps and porters. Prices start at 300dh for a 4-hr trek.

⊖ Transport

Tafraoute *p250*
There are several buses a day to **Inezgane**, 3 to **Tiznit**, 2 for **Marrakech** and 1 to **Casablanca**. *Grands taxis*, often Landrovers, connect Tafraoute with **Tiznit**. Transport out to the villages is more difficult: there are 2 buses a day, or you can try hitching, or bargaining with *grand taxi* drivers.

South of Agadir: Tiznit to Tarfaya

Along the coast south of Agadir, Morocco's landscapes become increasingly barren, the hills and mountains of the interior subsiding into the desert. Tiznit, 90 km south of Agadir and a transport junction for routes south, has a seldom-visited walled centre and a jewellery souk. Out on the coast, Mirleft and Sidi Ifni have the added advantages of spectacular coastline. Sidi Ifni was an outpost of Spain until well into the 20th century; now its white colonial architecture is crumbling. Mirleft, by contrast, seems like a place of the future; championed by a handful of enthusiastic young French and British hotel and restaurant owners, it is a bastion of hip. And between and around the two towns are plenty of excellent beaches. Just inland, Goulimine is famous for its camel market. Further south, Tan Tan is a remote administrative centre and Tarfaya has been both English and Spanish at times in its past. ▸▸ For listings, see pages 260-265.

Tiznit and around → *For listings, see pages 260-265. Colour map 2, C2.*

Tiznit, seemingly ancient, and famed for its great red-ochre *pisé* walls, is, in fact, barely 100 years old. Although the town does not have much to offer in the way of sights, it's well worth a wander around after an overnight stop. The once-famed Source Bleue, the Blue Spring, close to the Great Mosque, is stagnant green today but the shopping is excellent: the quality of silverwork in the Souk des Bijoutiers is high and Rue Imzlin has some great shoe workshops. Tiznit is a laid-back and unexpectedly attractive town with very few tourists.

Arriving in Tiznit
Getting there Coming in from north or south by bus you get off near Place du Mechouar, the central square. Most *grands taxis* stop on nearby Boulevard Mohammed V, opposite the post office. Most of the cheap hotels are situated close by. ▸▸ *See Transport, page 264, for further details.*

Getting around Tiznit is a small place, easily explored on foot. You may, however, wish to go to the beach near Sidi Moussa d'Aglou, 17 km out of town, where there are some cave dwellings. *Grands taxis* from Avenue Hassan II run out to Aglou village, and the coast is a couple of kilometres further on. **Syndicat d'Initiative** ① *T0528-869199*.

Background

One theory is that Tiznit derives its name from Lalla Zninia, a woman of dubious morals, whose repentance here was supposedly rewarded by God creating the blue spring, or the Source Bleu de Lalla Tiznit. The main town was established in 1882 by the great reforming sultan Moulay Hassan (1873-1894), part of a general policy of strengthening the Alaouite Dynasty's authority in the south. He had a number of separate *ksar* enclosed within the 5 km of walls. There are 36 towers and, although there are eight gates in all, the three most important are Bab Ait Jarrar, Bab Jadid and Bab Laaouina – a later addition by the French.

It was at Tiznit that El Hiba had himself proclaimed sultan in 1912, challenging the French who were extending their power. In 1912, the French already controlled northeastern

Tiznit

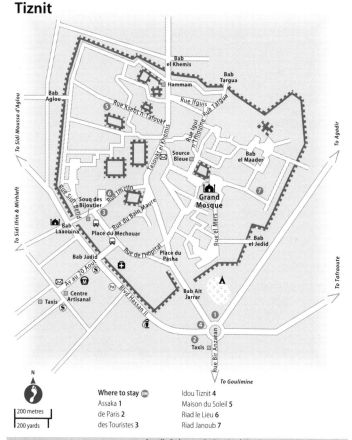

N

200 metres

200 yards

Where to stay ⬤	Idou Tiznit **4**
Assaka **1**	Maison du Soleil **5**
de Paris **2**	Riad le Lieu **6**
des Touristes **3**	Riad Janoub **7**

Morocco, the Chaouia and Casablanca. El Hiba, acting on the same basis of uniting the Muslims of Morocco to resist the infidel, organized southern resistance, declaring himself defender of the faith. A powerful confederacy seemed to be emerging, and El Hiba entered Marrakech in August 1912 unchallenged. The adventure ended in September, however, when French troops under Colonel Mangin stormed the city, outgunning El Hiba's forces.

Places in Tiznit

The open-air **souk** is on Bab Ait Jarrar, main days Thursday and Friday. Along Rue de l'Hôpital from the square is the **Grand Mosque**. The minaret has distinctive protruding wooden perches; the story is that these are to assist the dead as they climb to paradise; they probably also had a more prosaic function in the construction of the tower. Adjacent to the mosque is the **Source Bleue de Lalla Tiznit**, named after the town's saint, a reformed prostitute: where she died a spring appeared. Steps lead down to a large square pool but these days the water is a lurid shade of stagnant green. The town's walls are its other main attraction, and you can walk around the inside of most of the 3-km perimeter, along quiet dusty streets where children play football, men stand and chat and women scurry home with shopping. There are two religious **festivals** in Tiznit in August: the Moussem of Sidi Abderrahman, and the acrobat's Moussem of Sidi Ahmed ou Moussa, a village some 50 km away in the Tafraoute direction. On the Sidi Moussa/Sidi Ifni junction, the new **mosque**, buff with green tiles and a green cupola, is a distinctive landmark.

Around Tiznit

The nearest beaches (be careful bathing and aware of the Atlantic's strong undertow) are at **Sidi Moussa d'Aglou**, 17 km northwest of Tiznit. In winter, the beach is deserted apart from a few surfers and well organized people in camper vans. In summer, however, the place gets crowded, mainly with locals camping out. New homes are being built and there are some seasonal restaurants. From Aglou, you can take a track some 4 km along the beach to reach a fishing village, after which there is a small troglodyte community. The campsite opens only in summer. Exceptionally cheap, it is none too secure. As well as good food, the **Café-Restaurant Ouazize** has rooms.

The **Oued Massa nature reserve** (see page 235) is also easily accessible. Off the Sidi Ifni road, the **Domaine de Khenfouf** (T0661 657566, www.khenfouf.com) is an artisan, organic cooperative that opens to the public every Saturday and sells argan products and embroidery. If you're interested in exploring the local area, **Bab el Maader** is a great source of information and maps (see Where to stay, page 260).

Mirleft and around → *For listings, see pages 260-265. Colour map 2, C1.*

Until very recently Mirleft barely qualified as a one-horse village. Now, however, a stroll down its dusty street reveals a hive of activity as hip young Europeans create an enclave of laid-back bars and restaurants and cheap-yet-groovy hotels. Buoyed by the presence of surfers and paragliders, who come for the great beaches and the updrafts, and many others who come to hang out in the great year-round climate, Mirleft is very clearly a place on the up.

This was once the border between Morocco and Spanish Sidi Ifni. You can climb to old **fortifications** on the hill above the village, and longer walks are possible into the hills behind. There's also a Monday **market** and a handful of interesting shops but, otherwise, the attractions are the beaches and the waves.

The centre of Mirleft is set back 1 km or so from the coast, on the eastern side of the road but it just about joins up with **Les Amicales**, clustered on the clifftop overlooking

Imin Tourga beach, the best local spot for swimming. Due west of the centre of Mirleft (cross over the main road by the bus stop and head straight down the hill through the houses) is the small but beautiful **Aftas Plage**, with a cluster of new cafés and restaurants. Further south, but still just about within walking distance, are the larger bays of **Plage Sidi Mohamed Ben Abdallah** (also known as Marabou) and **Plage Sauvage**, and **Sidi Ouafi**, the latter being the best surfing spot. At 10 km before Sidi Ifni is the beach of **Legzira**, famous for its spectacular natural rock bridge that curves over the sand. Popular with surfers, it has a couple of beachside hotels and restaurants.

Sidi Ifni and around → *For listings, see pages 260-265. Colour map 2, C1.*

One of the most unlikely towns in Morocco, Sidi Ifni was, until 1969, Spanish territory and known principally to stamp collectors. Today, for much of the year, it is a quiet port town

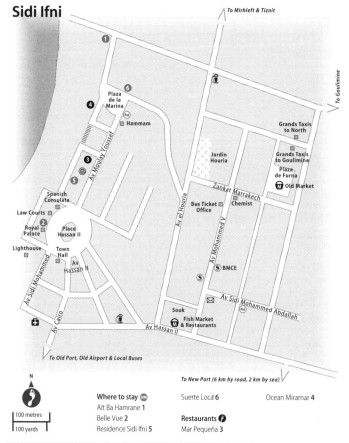

Sidi Ifni

To Mirhleft & Tiznit

To Goulimine

Plaza de la Marina

Hammam

Grands Taxis to North

Jardin Houria

Grands Taxis to Goulimine

Plaza de Furna

Old Market

Zankat Marrakech

Spanish Consulate

Law Courts

Royal Palace

Place Hassan II

Bus Ticket Office

Chemist

Av el Houria

Av Moulay Youssef

Lighthouse

Town Hall

Av Hassan II

Av Mohammed V

BMCE

Av Sidi Mohammed

Caïro

Av Sidi Mohammed Abdallah

Souk

Fish Market & Restaurants

Av Hassan II

To Old Port, Old Airport & Local Buses

To New Port (6 km by road, 2 km by sea)

N

100 metres
100 yards

Where to stay
Aït Ba Hamrane **1**
Belle Vue **2**
Residence Sidi Ifni **5**

Suerte Loca **6**

Ocean Miramar **4**

Restaurants
Mar Pequeña **3**

with a distinctive Iberian feel and some unusual buildings in the art deco/neo-kasbah vein, many of them beginning to crumble. Surfers have a number of spots nearby, while camper vans line the town beach in winter, escaping the cold weather further north. In July and August, Sidi Ifni fills up with returning migrant workers and occasional sea mist. Though it can feel like more of a ghost town than its upwardly mobile neighbour Mirleft, there are early signs of European money also arriving in Sidi Ifni, and there is an increasing choice of good places to stay and eat.

Background

Sidi Ifni was occupied by the Spanish from 1476 to 1524 and, again from 1860, as a consequence of the Treaty of Tetouan. The town was always an enclave, surrounded by Morocco from 1860 to 1912 and from 1956 to 1969, and between 1912 and 1956 by the French protectorate. The town had a port and an airstrip, and a role as a duty free zone. The economic survival of the town was based on the fact that the border was open to trade. In the 1960s Morocco grew tired of the continuing Spanish presence and forced Spain into negotiations from 1966. The enclave was returned in 1969.

Places in Sidi Ifni

Sidi Ifni is much bigger on atmosphere than sights. **Place Hassan II**, still commonly referred to as Plaza de España, is the centre of the town. Around it are buildings with a 1930s feel: running clockwise as you face the **Hotel Belle Vue** are the former church, now home to the law courts, the very faded Spanish consulate (open one day a month), the town hall, and the discreet Royal Palace. Past the palace and behind the police villa is an attractive lighthouse with neo-Moorish detailing. Past the hospital and campsite is a new housing development, with the aerodrome on your left. From here you can drop down to the beach and the port. Offshore, the massive concrete structure was once linked to the mainland by cable. Ships would moor here and everything would be hoisted ashore.

There's a **fish market** at the top of town, which quickly turns from soporific to lively once the catch comes in, usually around 1600-2000. The weekly **market** is held on Sunday on the old airfield. Sidi Ifni hosts a large **moussem** in June. At low tide it's possible to walk north along the shore to the local saint's **tomb** or *koubba*.

Goulimine (Guelmin) → *For listings, see pages 260-265. Colour map 4, A5.*

From the eighth century, Goulimine was an important trading post on a route swapping Saharan salt and West African gold but, by the 12th century, decline had set in. Back in the 1950s Goulimine was practically the last place accessible to the tourist. Beyond lay the desert. Nowadays, the nomad 'blue men' and the camel souk of Goulimine are really only there for tourist purposes. Apart from the market, most travellers move on swiftly. If you are visiting Sidi Ifni from Agadir, a loop back via Goulimine and Bou Izakarn provides some interesting variety. There is a **tourist office** ① *3 Residence Sahara, Blvd d'Agadir, T0528-872545.*

Goulimine is primarily a transit town. However, there are good side-trips to the hot springs in the little oasis of **Abbainou**, 15 km from Goulimine off the Sidi Ifni road, or to **Aït Bekou** (also known as Tighmart), another oasis 13 km away from Goulimine on the Asrir road. For these you will have to hire a *grand taxi* if you don't have your own transport. Around 60 km west of Goulimine is **Plage Blanche** but, given the state of the piste, sturdy transport is needed to get here.

Goulimine is a regular excursion from Agadir, thanks to its Saturday morning camel souk along the Tan Tan road. The **market** is nowadays geared mainly to tourist industry demands. Nomadic tribesmen ('blue men'), distinguished by their indigo boubou robes, dance dutiful attendance. More genuine, however, are the **religious festivals**, or *moussems*, held in June (at Asrir) and August. Look out for the ruined kasbah of **Caïd Dahman Takni**.

Around Goulimine

South and west of Goulimine, an enormous stretch of Atlantic coast is taken up by the **Plage Blanche** – tens of kilometres of flat, wide, sandy beach. It is also accessible from Sidi Ifni by the rough coastal piste.

South of Plage Blanche, the Oued Draâ reaches the sea. On isolated places along the Saharan coast, right down to Dakhla, there are still a few nomad fishing communities, the **Chnagala**, or Harpooners, who fish the coast with nets and harpoons. Traditionally, it was the Chnagala who collected valuable amber from whale corpses which washed up on the coast near the mouth of the Oued Draâ.

Tan Tan to Tarfaya → *For listings, see pages 260-265. Colour map 2, C1.*

Tan Tan used to be the southernmost town in Morocco, before the incorporation of the Spanish Sahara. The town is a rather dull administrative centre, with duty-free shops and a fishing port. The blue cloth worn by the formerly nomadic inhabitants of this area is sold in the souk. There is a beach 25 km away, with some good fish cafés. The **Venus of Tan-Tan**, a 6-cm stone carving found in a nearby river deposit in 1999, is claimed to be between 300,000 and 500,000 years old and the earliest representation of the human form.

There is not a lot to see in Tan Tan itself. However, it might be worth heading for **Tan Tan Plage**, 25 km away in the Tarfaya direction, and birdwatchers may also want to stop at **Oued Chebika**, some 30 km from Tan Tan, also in the Tarfaya direction. South of Tan Tan lies **Smara** (see page 268). There is not much of interest along this route; the settlement of **Abatteleh** is the best place for a coffee break.

Tarfaya → *Colour map 4, A3.*

Once a trading post owned by both the British and the French, as Villa Bens, Tarfaya became Spanish from 1916 and capital of the southern zone of the Spanish protectorate of Morocco from 1920 to 1958. These days it's a quiet place, with a few old sandblown Spanish colonial buildings and several wrecked ships. A Canaries–Tarfaya ferry crossing was injecting new life into the town until the boat was wrecked off the Moroccan coast. The line may start running again at some point.

The **post office** is the most prominent building in the centre. Tarfaya/Cap Juby was where the writer and pilot Antoine de St Exupéry (of *Little Prince* fame) was based for a few years in the late 1920s, responsible for the postal station where the planes would refuel and the pilots would rest up for a night. Flying over the desert was not easy in the primitive planes of the day, and there were frequent crash-landings in the desert, as well as encounters with unfriendly nomads, notably the fierce Rgueibet, who would take the aviators hostage. Of the flight down to Cap Juby, St Exupéry wrote that it gave, "an exact idea of nothingness".

The Aéropostale is now commemorated by a **monument** representing a Bréguet 14 biplane of the sort used in the 1930s, and the town now also has a **museum** dedicated to St Exupéry. The town's **market** is near the mosque.

⊙ South of Agadir: Tiznit to Tarfaya listings

For sleeping and eating price codes and other relevant information, see pages 22-28.

⊙ Where to stay

Tiznit *p254, map p255*
Budget travellers have a range of options near the Pl du Mechouar; a handful of smarter options have sprung up in the medina in recent years.

€€€ Idou Tiznit, Av Hassan II, T0528-600333, www.idoutiznit.com. A large, pastel-shaded, marble-clad modern hotel with 87 rooms, pool, restaurant and bar. Accordion music is piped throughout and the lobby is ludicrously overblown but rooms are comfortable and there's a good pool.

€€ Bab El Maader, 132 Rue El Haj Ali, T0673-907314, www.bab-el-maader.com. A homely guesthouse run by a French couple, Michèle and Yann, in a quiet part of town. All on the ground level, stylish rooms have plenty of carefully selected Moroccan details, and there's a courtyard with red ochre *tadelakt* seats. The owners are real enthusiasts for the area and a mine of good information and maps.

€€ Maison du Soleil, 470 Rue Tafoukt, T0676-360387, www.maison-du-soleil.com. Traditional Moroccan touches – fabrics, tiles, *tadelakt* – elevate this little guesthouse beyond the ordinary. Rooms at the top of the house are lighter, and there's a great roof terrace, where breakfast is served. The owners don't live here, however, and it doesn't feel as homely as the other riads in town.

€€ Riad Janoub, 193 Rue de la Grande Mosquée, T0679-005510, www.riadjanoub.com. Immaculately decorated, this is a new building constructed in traditional Moroccan style, albeit on a bigger scale than most. Large rooms on 2 floors around a pool are individually decorated, with pale walls and contrasting fabrics. They have their own water supply and solar heating. An extensive

top terrace has cushions and sunbeds, and there's a small Berber tent and a barrel-vaulted hammam and massage room.

€ Hotel Assaka, Av lalla Abla, T0528-602286, www.assakahotel.com. Ugly but good value, this 2-star has 35 modern, comfortable rooms.

€ Hotel de Paris, Av Mohammed V, T0528-862865. Complete with flashing Eiffel Tower, this hotel sits atop a male-dominated Moroccan café-bar outside the city walls. There are 20 basic rooms, on the noisy side.

€ Hotel des Touristes, T0528-862018. Clean and bright, with 12 small rooms and 24-hr hot showers. Probably the best budget bet in town.

€ Riad Le Lieu, 273 impasse Issaoui, T0528-600019, www.riad-le-lieu.com. Very good value, this riad, on a side-street off Rue Imzilin in the centre of Tiznit, also has a fantastic restaurant and a *salon du thé*. Elegant rooms are decorated in pale, romantic tones: white and silver predominate. There's free Wi-Fi and French newspapers. On the roof, the terrace has a Moroccan tent that can be used for dining or sleeping. 2 rooms have private terraces.

Mirleft and around *p256*
€€€ Kasbah Tabelkoukt, T0528-719395, T0661-582749 (mob), www.kasbah-tabelkoukt.com. 7 themed, spacious and elegant bedrooms, beautiful tiled bathrooms, sea views and an infinty pool are the highlights of this smart place 4 km south of Mirleft. Rooms are individually themed. Separate from the main building, stone houses give more independence and are a good mix of tradition and modernity.

€€€ Dar Najmat, Plage Sidi Mohammed Ben Abdallah, T0528-719056, www.dar najmat.com. 2 km south of Mirleft at Marabout Beach, this is a mellow spot where you'll hear little other than the crashing of the Atlantic waves. It has beautiful rooms and a pool that looks right onto the beach. Decorated in white, greys and sandy shades with dark wood, there are antique touches too, such as the spectacular front door. Restaurant, and half-board comes as standard.

€€€ **Les 3 Chameux**, T0528-719187, T0666-548579, www.3chameaux.com. Bringing the style of a French country house to the hill high above Mirleft, the **Three Camels** has 12 suites and 10 rooms of old-school colonial elegance. There's an international library, a swimming pool, with great views north over the hills, and ancient tiled floors. Airport transfer from Agadir 250dh.

€€ **Aftas Beach Guest House**, Aftas Beach, T0528-719540. A chilled little English-run place right on the beach at Aftas Plage, this has a great colourful salon, with a traveller/surf vibe, good beach café food and some fabulous quirky details. There's Wi-Fi too, and a hotel laptop. Rooms are comfortable but small and rather plain for the price.

€€ **Riad de l'Oasis**, T0528-719347, T0661-231677 (mob), www.mirleft-tourismir.com. Near the beach in Les Amicales, this riad has a turquoise pool surrounded by dusty pink walls and tiled rooms with draped beds. The roof terrace has an open grill as well as comfy seats. The owners have other properties, including 2 villas for rent.

€€ **Sally's B&B**, Les Amicales, T0528-719402, T0661-469888 (mob), www.sally mirleft.com. This high-quality English B&B is on the edge of the cliff in Les Amicales, Mirleft's coastal satellite. Sally herself is a friendly, talkative host, who will happily cook full English breakfasts. Beds are big and comfortable, and there are stunning, vertiginous views over the waves and the beach below. From the roof terrace the views are even better, and there's a stylish new, self-contained studio with its own terrace and a barbecue.

€€ **Un The Au Bout du Monde**, T0661-975742, www.untheauboutdumonde.com. 5 mins' drive up the coast north of Mirleft, this new place is beautifully put together,

if a little isolated. Rooms and apartments are in 5 separate low-rise buildings in immaculate gardens. There's a good pool and a well-regarded café-restaurant that uses home-grown produce in its French and Moroccan dishes. Sea views, though the place itself is set back from the coast.

€ **Abertih**, T0528-719304, www.abertih. com. Upstairs, there are 11 simple but very clean rooms. Only 5 have en suite bathrooms, but the shared facilities are excellent. Downstairs, there's a very laid-back bar and restaurant (evenings only), decorated in warm reds and yellows and with free Wi-Fi. There are rugs and black-and-white photographs, a good roof terrace with plants and candlesticks and occasional yoga sessions. The owner is a paragliding guide, and paragliding groups sometimes take the whole place over, usually in Nov and Mar.

€ **Atlas-Mirleft**, T0528-719309, www. atlas-mirleft.com. Pink walls, comfy chairs and atmospheric low lighting set the tone for this café-restaurant and hotel on Mirleft's main street. Ownership has changed twice in recent years but the model remains the same: 9 rooms are straightforward and carefully decorated with fabrics and complementary colours. There's a great roof terrace with a grill and a tent in summer. The restaurant serves good French food. Good-value rates include breakfast with unlimited drinks.

€ **Chez Abdoul** (Café Restaurant Legzira), Legzira, T0528-780457. 1 km down a dirt track from the main road, a cluster of hotels and cafés opens up right onto the beach. Simple, clean, cool double rooms (some en suite) here have wooden furniture and open onto a terrace facing the sea. The restaurant serves good, if slightly expensive, tagines and fish dishes, and there is a pet goat and turtles. Half or full board.

€ **Hotel du Sud**, T0528-719407, www. hotel-mirleft.fr. 18 simple, airy rooms and a good roof terrace. Showers and toilets are shared but good – tiled and spotlessly clean, and you can use the washing machine for 35dh. Downstairs in the chilled café, excellent French sorbets and ice creams are the order of the day.

Camping
Le Nomade, T0528-719228, www.nomade trip.com. Offers shared camping under large camel-skin tents.

Sidi Ifni and around *p257, map p257*
See ifniriad.com for villas that can be rented in and around Sidi Ifni.

€€ **Xanadu**, 5 Rue el Jadida, T0528-876718, www.maisonxanadu.com. Warm pink tones, cosy rooms and a roof terrace with views.

€ **Aït Ba Hamrane**, Rue de la Plage, T0528-780217. Right next to the sea. Recent, simple rooms with shower, no breakfast.

€ **Belle Vue**, 9 Pl Hassan II, T0528-875072. In an old building on the main square, the **Belle Vue** has sea views and a good terrace restaurant and bar. Wi-Fi in some areas and an alcohol licence.

€ **Residence Sidi Ifni**, 4 Av My Abdellah, T0528-876776. Above café-restaurant **La Barandilla** are spacious, cosy, en suite apartments, some with a sea view. The restaurant has a 70dh menu and there's a bar.

€ **Suerte Loca**, bottom of road leading from Pl Hassan II, T0528-875350. Multilingual, popular, friendly and overlooks the sea, though its rooms could do with some TLC. The café-restaurant has a pool table and excellent food in the evenings and at breakfast, when there are pancakes, juices and shakes on offer. Ask about small flats for rent.

The fishing village of **Sidi Ouarsik**, 17 km south of Sidi Ifni, is about 1 hr's drive from the town. There's cheap accommodation to rent – ask at **Hotel Suerte Loca**. You can get there by Landrover taxi from the *grand taxi* station in Sidi Ifni.

Camping
Camping Barco, beside the beach, just after the **Hotel Aït Ba Hamrane**. Popular

with motor-caravans. No shade, but almost always a breeze.

Goulimine (Guelmin) *p258*
€€€ **Fort Bou Jerif**, T0672-130017 (mob), www.fortboujerif.com. A French-run hotel-restaurant and campsite in a remote, crenellated ex-fort. Accommodation ranges from nomad tents to chalets and hotel rooms. From Goulimine, take the road towards Sidi Ifni and Plage Blanche; Fort Bou Jerif is signposted.

€€ **La Maison Saharaouie**, Oasis de Tighmart, T0528-870706, lamaison saharaouie.voila.net. A French-run, ecologically minded guesthouse, with *pisé* walls and 5 simple, attractive rooms.

€ **Hotel Salam**, junction of Rte de Tan Tan and Av Hassan II, T0528-872057. Friendly, 19 rooms, bar and restaurant. Sometimes block-booked, so phone ahead.

Tan Tan *p259*
€€ **Afra**, Av Bir Anzarane, T0528-765016, www.hotelafra.ma. A large white building with clean and modern, if not exactly characterful, rooms.

€ **Hotel Bir Anzarane**, Blvd Hassan II, on edge of town, T0528-877834. A bit of a trek, on the opposite side of the *oued* to the town centre.

Tarfaya *p259*
There are few facilities in Tarfaya, although there are basic cafés, which do snacks and harira, and a few shops.

€ **Hotel-Café Tarfaya**, at the end of the main street near the port. Clean, plain rooms.

🍴 Restaurants

Tiznit *p254, map p255*
€€ **Riad Le Lieu**, 273 impasse Issaoui, T0528 600019, www.riad-le-lieu.com. Daily lunch and dinner. Superbly good Moroccan-French food is served on lamp-lit tables in the courtyard of this central, 16th-century riad (see Where to stay). Flavour-filled dishes might include

sardine tagine and a tomato and 'cheese millefeuille. Lots of fresh herbs are used, and you might even get some live piano-playing from the owner. The only downside might be the lack of an alcohol licence. Good enough to justify a visit to Tiznit just to eat here.

€ **Hotel de Paris**, Av Mohammed V, T0528-862865. Tagines and couscous and alcohol are served on the ground floor of this hotel outside the city walls.

Mirleft and around p256

See Where to stay, above; most good places to eat in the centre of Mirleft (notably **Atlas** and **Abertih**) are also hotels.

€ **Atrim**, T0528-719352. A friendly, sophisticated family-run Italian restaurant in the middle of Mirleft, with candles, abstract art, black-and-white photos and a balcony overlooking the comings and going on the street below. The pasta is fresh and perfectly cooked; try the excellent ravioli with sage and butter. There's wine, too, and a very convivial, laid-back atmosphere.

€ **Café Aftas**, Aftas Beach, T0656-183762, cafeaftas.com. A popular German-run café-restaurant and surf school right on Aftas beach, with no electricity but plenty of candles. They'll cook up a tagine or couscous on demand and they can arrange accommodation too. Surf school **Chasseurs de Vagues** is also based here.

€ **Café des Pecheurs**, Aftas Beach. The only really Moroccan place at Aftas, and by far the longest standing ("since the hippies!"), offering good, simple dishes of fried fish.

€ **Said Surf Café**, Aftas Beach. As well as renting out boards and organizing trips to visit Said's mother's village in the hills, this little beach shack café does a good line in tagines, couscous and grilled fish. In the morning there are breakfasts too, with Moroccan crêpes and pancakes.

Sidi Ifni and around p257, map p257

In the market there are a cluster of cheap tagine stalls – depending on the catch, these may also offer grilled fish.

€ **Adou Art**, opposite the Hotel de Ville, just off the main square. A chilled little café with comfy seats, cinema posters and photos.

€ **Café Restaurant el Hourria**, Av Hourria, T0528-876343. Moroccan and European food and drink in a modern setting at the bottom of town. The garden, with trees and flowers, is a good place for a sandwich.

€ **Café Restaurant Mar Péquena**, 20 Av Elmowahidine. Excellent modern Moroccan food in a cosy little place near the seafront, with petal-scattered tables. Portions are huge; try the spicy octopus and vegetables.

€ **Ocean Miramar**, 3 Av Prince Moulay Abdellan, T0528-876637. Pizzas and good seafood served on a terrace overlooking the sea.

€ **Suerte Loca** (see Where to stay, above). Does excellent food and drinks all through the day.

O Shopping

Sidi Ifni and around p257, map p257

Miramar, next to the **Suerte Loca**. Little necklaces and skimpy tops in the bright tie-dye fabric used by local women for wraps.

O What to do

Mirleft and around p256
Horse riding

Ranch Les 2 Gazelles, Sidi Boulfdail, www.les2gazelles.com. A few kilometres up the coast, this ranch offers 3-, 5- and 8-day rides in the mountains as well as short lessons (from 150dh per hr). They have good, traditional-style accommodation on the ranch itself, too, where there are 15 horses and a donkey.

Paragliding

Mirleft is a centre for paragliders, who come from all over the world, especially in spring and autumn. At Nid d'Aigle (Eagle's Nest), 20 mins from Mirleft, a 5 km ridge just back from the coast creates unusually good thermal currents, enabling paragliders to stay up for several hours before landing on the beach. Find Nigel Smith at the **Arbertih Hotel** or contact him via www.paraglidemorocco.com for details of tandem or solo flights.

Quad biking
Anzid Quad Evasion, T0677-756548, www.anzidquadevasion.com. Quad bike trips into the countryside (€60 for a half-day).

Surfing
Chasseurs de Vagues, Café Atlas, on Aftas Beach (see above). Surf school.

Sidi Ifni and around *p257, map p257*
Guides
Hassan Jalloul, T0666-941555. A good local guide.

⊖ Transport

Tiznit *p254, map p255*
Bus
Most buses and *grands taxis* arrive at Pl du Mechouar. Several services a day go to **Tata**, **Agadir**, **Marrakech**, **Casablanca**, **Tafraoute**, **Sidi Ifni** and **Goulimine**, and on to **Laâyoune**. Buses to **Tafraoute** take 3 hrs. The early morning CTM bus leaves from Bab Ouled Jarrar for **Casablanca**, via **Agadir**, **Essaouira**, **Safi** and **El Jadida**.

Taxi
Grands taxis leave from Pl du Mechouar: **Sidi Moussa** beach (5dh), **Sidi Ifni** (20dh) and **Inezgane** (20dh).

Mirleft and around *p256*
Bus
To **Sidi Ifni** there are buses every hour and *grands taxis* too, though nothing that runs very late in the day.

Sidi Ifni and around *p257, map p257*
Bus
There are no direct buses south; head to **Tiznit** (2½ hrs), from where there are more

options. There's a daily bus to **Marrakech**, which leaves from halfway down Av Mohammed V in the early hours of the morning. You can buy your tickets from a man who sets up on the pavement the evening before. To **Goulimine**, 1½ hrs.

Taxi
There are regular *grands taxis* between Sidi Ifni and either **Tiznit** (18dh) or **Goulimine** (16dh), as well as daily buses, which leave from opposite Banque Populaire, to **Agadir** and **Tiznit** (16dh, 2½ hrs). From Sidi Ifni there is a rough piste southwards to **Foum Assaka**; this crosses 2 large *oueds*, neither of which can be forded after heavy rain.

Goulimine (Guelmin) *p258*
Goulimine is on the main road south to the Saharan provinces and there are bus and *grand taxi* connections from here both north and south. It's about 1 hr by road from Tiznit and Sidi Ifni, although note that the Sidi Ifni–Goulimine road is narrow.

Bus and taxi
The *grand taxi* stop is on Pl Bir Anzarane and by the café-restaurants on Pl Hassan II; nearby is the bus stop. There are express buses to **Marrakech**. Buses to **Sidi Ifni** (1½ hrs) or *grands taxis* (1 hr). Several buses a day to **Tiznit** (2½ hrs, 20dh) and **Tan Tan** (28dh). Bus to **Agadir** (4½ hrs) and Laâyoune (7 hrs, *grand taxi* 5 hrs). Note that most CTM and Supratours buses run from outside CTM office in the town centre. Other buses go from the *gare routière* on the Bou Izakarn road, 5 mins' walk from the town centre. One overnight bus (CTM) to **Casablanca**, via **Tiznit**.

Tan Tan *p259*
Air
There are flights from Aéroport Tan Tan, Pl Blanche, 9 km out of the town, T0528-877143/877164, to **Laâyoune**, **Smara** and **Casablanca** (1 a week). The Royal Air Maroc office is on Av de la Ligue Arabe, T0528-877259.

Bus

Several buses a day to **Goulimine** (25dh), **Tiznit** (40dh) and **Tarfaya/Laâyoune** (60dh, 4 hrs).

Taxi

There are *grands taxis* and Landrover taxis from Tan Tan to Tan Tan **port** (10dh), **Agadir** (6 hrs) and **Laâyoune** (3½ hrs).

Tarfaya *p259*

Tarfaya lies southwest of Tan Tan on a good road. *Grand taxi* to **Laâyoune** (117 km, some sand drifting onto road), 1½ hrs, 40dh.

ⓘ Directory

Tiznit *p254, map p255*

Banks Cash points on the main road outside the entrance to the square.

Mirleft and around *p256*

Banks Mirleft now has an ATM, on the main road near the bus stop.

Goulimine (Guelmin) *p258*

In the village there is a **bank** and **post office**. There is a **swimming pool** on the Asrir road, 10 mins from town centre.

Deep south

The would-be capital of Western Sahara, Laâyoune is an anomaly of action and urban life in the increasingly barren far south of the country. An extensive development programme has produced a city unrivalled south of Agadir and, attracted by all the activity, a population from elsewhere in Morocco has moved in. Beyond, there is sand and the sea. Inland, inhospitable Smara has some historic interest, while on the coast to the south, Dakhla is known for its fishing, and the wild Bay of Cintra has turtles and rare monk seals. Beyond that there is very little until you reach the Mauritanian border. Checkpoints in Western Sahara can be strict.
➤➤ *For listings, see pages 269-270.*

Laâyoune ➔ *For listings, see pages 269-270. Colour map 4, A3.*

Laâyoune, also spelt El Aïoun, was the capital of Spanish Sahara and continues to function as a provincial capital today. There is also a big military garrison here. Beyond the political curiosity of seeing a post-colonial boomtown, there is little to do. It is, however, a strangely calm place, and not unpleasant for a brief stay.

Arriving in Laâyoune

Getting there The **Hassan I Aéroport** is 2 km outside the town, T0528-893346/7. There are taxis into the town, although it may be necessary to wait a while. For the energetic, it is a manageable walk. The **CTM** buses arrive on Avenue de la Mecque, in the centre, the ONCF buses at the stadium a little further out. ➤➤ *For further details, see Transport, page 270.*

Getting around To get to Laâyoune Plage, you will have to hire a *grand taxi* from the taxi rank in the Colomina neighbourhood. You might even want to go to Laâyoune Port, for which there are *grands taxis* as well.

Tourist information **Tourist office** ⓘ *Av de l'Islam, BP 471, T0528-892233/75.*

Travelling in the deep south

Generally speaking, there are no particular problems for visitors to the far south of Morocco but it's worth checking the political situation before you leave (see www.fco.gov.uk). When setting out south of Tiznit, bear in mind that the Forces Armées Royales (FAR) are very present, so avoid photographing anything that could be taken for a military installation. (If you wish to film, you should first obtain a special authorization from the Ministère de la Communication in Rabat.) There are Gendarmerie royale checkpoints, who are always courteous and, on the whole, uninterested in foreigners driving hire cars. Although you can use mobile phones anywhere in the South, the military will take a very dim view of anyone in 4WDs using walkie-talkies.

Unleaded petrol is easier to come by than it used to be, though you may have problems if you're heading across the border into Mauritania. Alcohol is not on sale, apart from in a few rare hotels. Distances are huge, so fill up whenever possible and always travel with plenty of water and some food. In cases of breakdown, almost every tiny settlement has someone who can fix a basic vehicle. Payment is always in cash; nobody takes credit cards, and there are few cash dispensers.

Though the region is broadly speaking open to tourism, there are a couple of areas still off-limits. In the Jebl Ouarkziz, southeast of Goulimine, you can travel as far as Assa. From there to Zag is closed to ordinary traffic. This is the region of Morocco closest to the separatist Polisario camps, over the frontier at Tindouf in Algeria. Unfortunately, the handy frontier post with Mauritania near the Moroccan town of Gueltat-Zemmour is also closed.

Travelling on to Mauritania

To get to Mauritania by road you need to head south from Dakhla; you may be able to get a lift with some friendly 4WD drivers or in a truck. The road to the border is fairly good quality, with some drifting sand. Around the border (and especially between the two border posts) there are land mines. These are indicated by piles of stones at the edge of the road; drive carefully and don't stray off-road. Some 7 km from the border the road deteriorates. Get a visa in advance from the Mauritanian embassy in Rabat (Ambassade de Mauritanie au Maroc, 6 Rue Thami Lamdawar Suissi, Rabat, T0537-656678/79, €37, usually available the next day) as they are no longer available at the border. Make sure to ask for two weeks, otherwise you will be issued with a three-day visa. You can get an extension in Nouakchott, 444 km south of the border. Vehicle and customs procedures are generally fairly informal; a small gift of food or drink has been known to smooth the process. The border closes officially at 1800, though you may get lucky if you turn up slightly later. Formalities can be slow at the Mauritanian border post so allow two or three hours. Dirhams can be exchanged but the rates are poor. Beyond the border the road deteriorates into desert piste. The only settlement anywhere near the border is Nouadhibou, on the Mauritanian side. If you are pressed for time, it would be better to get a regular **RAM** flight from Casablanca to Nouakchott.

Background

Under the terms of a 1900 agreement, France and Spain agreed that the Sahara would be French – with the exception of Rio de Oro and Saquiet el Hamra. On atlases from the

1940s and earlier, Spain's former Saharan colonies are labelled Rio de Oro, literally 'River of Gold'. But the territories had neither water nor gold, and Spain paid scant attention to the windswept, arid expanses on the northwest coast of Africa, defined by ocean to the west and a zigzag frontier to the east.

Laâyoune was little more than a tiny settlement, where, according to the Odé guide (1952), "The Governor of Rio de Oro will show you 'his forest', composed of exactly four tamarisk trees, which, despite all his care, remain surprisingly stunted." Water was shipped in from the Canaries. Laâyoune became capital of Spanish Sahara in 1958, and the Spanish army developed a presence, including units of the Tercio, the Spanish foreign legion. Everything changed, however, when the potential of major phosphate deposits in the Boukraâ region, to the southeast of Laâyoune, was realized. The yellowish rock is rich in phosphorus thanks to the nitrogen-fixing action of seaweed – and hence useful as a fertilizer base. Although the resource had been spotted in 1947, it was not effectively exploited until the 1960s, when Spain began to invest in opencast mining and a 120 km long conveyor belt was built by Krupp to transport ore from the mines to the port 15 km south of Laâyoune. By 1974, the province was a major world producer – and the people of the Sahara and Morocco woke up to its importance.

Although Morocco retook Western Sahara in 1975, there was a long and tedious campaign against the separatist **Polisario** guerrilla movement, operating largely out of Algerian territory, fought in the early 1980s. Major public investment in urban infrastructure has turned Laâyoune into a significant town, with nearly 150,000 people from both the Saharan provinces and northern Morocco. The **Minurso** (www.minurso.unlb.org), the UN mission sent to observe the ceasefire and an eventual referendum on the Saharan provinces' future, continues to be a presence in the town – at a cost to the UN of around US$40 million per annum. The referendum, however, never seems to reach the point of actually happening, there being long protracted discussions over who is actually entitled to vote.

In 2000 the debate on the Sahara shifted slightly, with a new 'third way' being discussed, namely a more regional form of government for the Saharan provinces. (The first way would be full independence for some sort of Saharan statelet, the second way is maintenance of the status quo.) Considering that few countries actually recognize the Polisario movement, especially given Morocco's intensive diplomatic efforts in Africa and Latin America, the third way offers a chance for all concerned to resolve things. The regional solution also fits well with the move towards respecting regional government in Morocco as a whole, though not all are happy with it, and several people were killed in violent clashes between protestors and armed forces in Laâyoune in 2010.

Places in Laâyoune

In the main square, the Place du Mechouar, there are concrete canopies and an exhibition space commemorating the 1975 Green March (see page 434), plus the modern **Grand Mosque**. There is also a bird sanctuary, the **Colline des Oiseaux**, a calm place with some interesting species on Rue Okba Ibn Nafi, opposite the **Hotel Parador**. The Malhfa, on Boulevard Kairouan, off Avenue de la Mecque opposite the **Hotel Massira**, is the main **market** area. Below the town is the **lagoon**, a beautiful spot, but not for swimming in. ▶▶ See What to do, page 269, for trips and tours.

Laâyoune Plage and Port → Colour map 4, A3.

To get to Laâyoune Plage, it will probably be necessary to hire a whole grand taxi, as the regular services go to the port. However, the beach itself is not very clean. (It is possible to stay at the € **Maison des Pêcheurs**, no phone.) Laâyoune Port is a sand-swept phosphates port 25 km from Laâyoune (6dh by *grand taxi*), with a few café-restaurants but little else.

South into the Sahara

Smara → *Colour map 4, B4.*
The town of Smara lies east of Laâyoune, 240 km along the road to Tan Tan (daily bus services).

Smara is in one of the most inhospitable regions of southern Morocco. It was built by Sheikh Ma el Anin (The Blue Sultan – known for masterminding the resistance to the French and Spanish) in 1884-1885 and was on the great caravan route to Mauritania. It was a grandiose scheme, a town built from the local black granite on a rocky prominence some 6 m higher than the rest of the stone-strewn plateau. Here stood the larger kasbah with the mosque (never completed), which was based on the Mezquita in Córdoba. The circular cupola, arcades and some of the pillars survive today. There was also a library and a Koranic school (for Sheikh Ma el Anin was a scholar), grain silos, a hammam and living quarters. The isolated, smaller kasbah was some 100 m away.

It was from this region that Sheikh Ma el Anin launched his last stand against the French, hoping to save at least the Souss and the far South from Roumi domination. He led his nomad forces north towards Fès to overthrow the sultan. The clash with French forces took place on the Tadla plain in 1910, the fighting lasting for all of June and July, before the Saharan tribesmen were routed by superior French firepower. Exhausted, Ma el Anin fled south to Tiznit where he died in October. French vengeance was slow in coming, but terrible: Colonel Mouret led a raid of reprisal on Smara in 1912, destroying the town.

Today, as the Reguibet leave behind their nomad ways, Smara is becoming an important centre. Though gradually sanding up, the oasis planted by Ma el Anin in the late 1890s still survives, as do the Spanish barracks. There's petrol, banks, post office, hammam and half a dozen hotels, plus restaurants/cafés on the main street, Avenue Hassan II.

Boujdour and Dakhla → *Colour map 4, B2.*
Dakhla is over 1000 km south of Agadir and almost on the Tropic of Cancer. To continue along the coastal road, there are lorries making the journey to Dakhla, and an **ONCF** bus service leaving Laâyoune at 1200. **Boujdour**, 199 km south of Laâyoune, is capital of the new province of Tiris el Gharbia and has a fishing port and beach. Some 542 km south of Laâyoune, **Dakhla** is located on a spit with impressive beaches and cliffs. Under the Spanish, it was called Villa Cisneros. Today, it is a minor administrative centre and a military outpost. There is ocean fishing (sea bass) and surfing.

Bay of Cintra → *Colour map 4, C1.*
The Bay of Cintra, 120 km from Dakhla, is a wild and remote place, where ocean-going turtles and rare monk seals can still be found. The shy seals, or 'sea wolves', were much hunted by the Portuguese back in the 15th century. Their meat was also highly appreciated by the local tribes. Today, the monk seal is almost extinct in the Mediterranean; here on the Moroccan Atlantic, they have a last quiet refuge at the foot of the cliffs of Cintra.

◉ Deep south listings

For sleeping and eating price codes and other relevant information, see pages 22-28.

◉ Where to stay

Laâyoune *p265*
Finding a place in one of the better hotels can be problematic at times, as they tend to be block-booked for official delegations. Ring ahead, otherwise you'll have to be content with a cheap hotel.

€€€ **Hotel Parador**, Rue Okba Ibn Nafih, BP 189, T0528-894500. The old Spanish hotel has 72 rooms with balconies, restaurant, popular bar, tennis and a good pool.

€€ **Hotel Al Massira**, 12 Av de la Mecque, BP 12, T0528-894225. Comfortable and modern with 26 rooms, restaurants, bar, nightclub, tennis and pool. Used by the UN.

€€ **Nagjir Ville**, Pl de la Resistance Dchira, T0528-894168. A 4-star hotel with 75 rooms, a bar, restaurant, nightclub.

€ **Hotel Lakouara**, Av Hassan II, near the market, T0528-893378. 40 rooms with en suite bathrooms in a sleepy, faded establishment with satellite TV and a café.

€ **Hotel Marhaba**, Av de la Marine, T0528-893249. 36 rooms, with wash basins, not very friendly but probably the best cheap option. Clean rooms, hot communal showers, roof terrace and a café.

Smara *p268*
€ **Al Maghrib Al Arbi**, Av Hassan II, T0528-899151. Shared bathrooms.

€ **Hotel Amine**, Av Ribat el Khair, T0528-887368. Modern and comfortable with some en-suite bathrooms.

Dakhla *p268*
€€€ **Calipau Sahara Dakhla**, T0661-191634, www.dakhla-hotel-sahara.com. A smart place with an infinity pool, hammam, dark wood furniture, crisp white bedding and sea views from the balconies.

€€€ **Sahara Regency**, Av el Walaa, T0528-931666, www.sahararegency.com. A large, modern hotel with a small pool, restaurant and bar.

€ **Hotel Doumss**, 49 Av al Wallaa. Clean, comfortable, bar, rooms with bath/WC.

€ **Sahara**, T0528-897773, near the souk, basic, communal facilities.

◉ Restaurants

Laâyoune *p265*
Le Poissonnier has a good reputation for its fish. There are other, cheaper options on Av Mohammed V, and at the end of Av de la Marine near **Hotel Marhaba**. **Snack Fès** on Av Hassan II also does reasonable food.

Dakhla *p268*
There are good restaurants at **La Maison du Thé**, Av Mohammed V, T0676-192437; and **Villa Dakhla**, Av Mohammed V, T0648-315818.

There are basic restaurants around the town, and small cafés/restaurants near the souk. The restaurant in **Hotel Sahara** does good, cheap, local food.

◉ What to do

Laâyoune *p265*
Hammam
There are a number of hammams in Laâyoune where you can remove the dust and grime of the desert. Try the **Hammam Samir** in Hay el Kacem.

Tour operators
Agence Massira Tours International, 20 Av de la Mecque, BP 85, T0528-894229. Organizes excursions to Tarfaya for fishing, to Laâyoune Plage and to Oasis Lemsid, and hires out Landrovers and drivers.

Dakhla *p268*
Tour operators
The tourist office, 1 Rue Tiris, T0528-898228, is also a travel agent. Or try Dakhla Tours, Av Mohammed V, T141.

⊖ Transport

Laâyoune *p265*
Air
Hassan I Aéroport has flights to **Casablanca**, **Agadir** (1 a day), **Dakhla** and **Las Palmas** in the Canaries.

Bus
CTM buses leave from Av de la Mecque, by Agence Massira Tours International, with services to **Boujdour/Dakhla** (9 hrs), **Smara/Tan Tan** and **Agadir/Marrakech** (12 hrs). ONCF services to **Agadir** and **Marrakech**, depart from near the stadium.

Taxi
Grands taxis from the roundabout at the end of Av Hassan II, by the market, go to **Agadir** and **Marrakech**. For *grands taxis* to **Tarfaya** and **Tan Tan**, go by *petit taxi* across the river to the police control on the road out to the north, and pick one up there.

Boujdour and Dakhla *p268*
Air
From Aéroport Dakhla, 5 km from the town, T0528-897049, direct flights to **Casablanca**, **Agadir** and **Las Palmas**. The RAM office is on Av des PTT, T0528-897050.

Bus
Bus to **Agadir** departs 1200 (18 hrs), reservation recommended. Convoys to **Mauritania** generally leave Tue and Fri.

Contents

Footprint features

Rabat, Casablanca & the Atlantic Coast

At a glance

⊖ **Getting around** Rabat is small enough to explore on foot. Casablanca is big – use *petits taxis* to go beyond the centre. The rest of the area is accessible by bus and train.

✪ **Time required** Rabat and Casablanca both deserve at least a day of your time. Then take a few days to explore the coast to the south.

☀ **Weather** The sea generally keeps day temperatures on the coast between 17°C and 27°C all through the year.

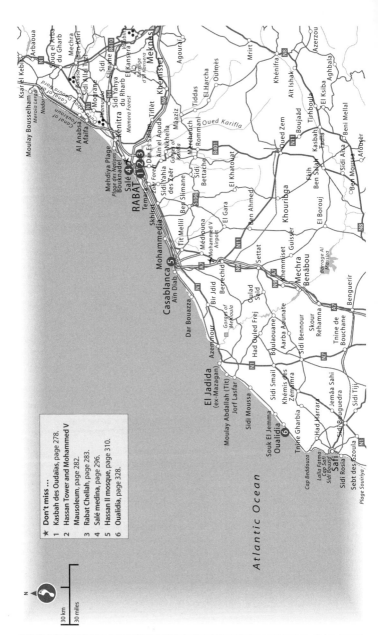

Don't miss ...

1 Kasbah des Oudaïas, page 278.
2 Hassan Tower and Mohammed V
  Mausoleum, page 282.
3 Rabat Chellah, page 283.
4 Salé medina, page 296.
5 Hassan II mosque, page 310.
6 Oualidia, page 328.

Atlantic Ocean

30 km
30 miles

N

Morocco's two most important cities are a mere half an hour apart, yet could hardly be more different. Rabat, the capital, is a city of diplomats and politicians, a relatively calm place for strolling, sipping coffee in street-side cafés and wandering through historic sites. South along the coast, brash Casablanca is a much bigger city, dominated by business and money, where the cars are faster and the lights are brighter. The huge Hassan II Mosque may be the city's biggest draw, but it can't mask the fact that Casablanca is built along an economic axis.

North of Casablanca, Mohammedia has a walled medina and a seaside promenade, while, to the south, lie the crumbling old Portuguese coastal bastions of El Jadida and Azemmour. These are easy day trips from Casablanca, as is the kasbah of Boulaouane. More distant are the beaches and stunning lagoon of Oualidia and a rougher, working town: phosphate-processing and pottery-producing Safi.

Rabat

Capital only since 1913, Rabat has a long history. Behind its work-a-day façade, Morocco's second city and the country's political nerve centre bears traces of numerous civilizations. It had Roman beginnings, as Colonia Sala Junonia, a prosperous settlement. Sala gave way to Berber Chellah, and then came the Almohads, who made Rabat el Fath, the Fortress of Victory, an imperial capital. (The unfinished Tour Hassan minaret dates from this time.) In the 17th century, Rabat was rebuilt by Andalucían refugees, for a short and vivid period becoming capital of a pirate republic. Under the first Alaouite ruler, Moulay Rachid, Rabat returned to central authority. The city's ville nouvelle *dates from the early 20th century, the land between the sultan's palace and the medina being developed as a pleasant plan of wide avenues and gardens.* ▸▸ *For listings, see pages 286-292.*

Arriving in Rabat → *Phone code: 0537. Colour map 1, B1. Population: 1,622,860*

Getting there

The small airport of **Rabat-Salé** ⓘ *T0537-808090*, has domestic flight arrivals, along with a few European flights (mostly from France). Take a taxi from here to Rabat, 120dh. Most international flights come into **Casablanca Mohammed V Airport** (see page 322). From here there's a shuttle train to Rabat (change at Casa-Voyageurs or Casa-Port stations, information on T0537-736060) or a *grand taxi* will set you back 400dh. When coming into Rabat by bus, the principal bus terminal, for both **CTM** and other buses, is at Place Zerktouni, 3 km out from the centre. For the city centre, catch a No 30 bus to Avenue Hassan II, or take a *petit taxi* for about 20dh. ▸▸ *See Transport, page 291, for further details.*

Getting around

The main sites of Rabat are close enough to each other to visit on foot. In 2011, the city opened the handy Rabat-Salé tramway, with trams every four to eight minutes on two lines and 31 stops. If time is limited, you may want to get one of the blue *petits taxis* between monuments, say from Chellah to the Kasbah des Oudaïas; this should cost around 10dh.

Tourist information National Tourist Office ⓘ *corner of Av al Abtal and Rue Oued Fès, T0537-775171.* **Office du Tourisme** ⓘ *22 Av d'Alger, T0537-730562.* **Syndicat d'Initiative** ⓘ *Av Patrice Lumumba, T0537-723272, not very useful.*

Background

Early origins

The first settlement of this area was probably outside the present city walls, on the site of the later Merinid mausoleum of Chellah. There may have been Phoenician and Carthaginian settlements, but it is with the Roman Sala Colonia that Rabat's proven urban history began. Awarded municipal privileges, Sala Colonia was the most southwesterly town of the Roman Empire for two centuries, a trading post on the Oued Bou Regreg (which has since changed course) and a defensive settlement close to the line of frontier outposts, which ran through the suburbs to the south of the present city.

Sala Colonia came under Amazigh rule from the eighth to the 10th century. However, the heretic Kharajite beliefs of the Imazighen represented a challenge to the orthodoxy of the inland Muslims. In the 10th century, the Zenata tribe built a fortified monastery, or *ribat*, on the site of the current Kasbah des Oudaïas. This functioned as a base from which to challenge the heretics on both sides of the river and their supporters, the powerful Berghouata tribe. Sala Colonia was thus eventually abandoned.

Rabat under the Almohads

The *ribat* was used by the Almoravid Dynasty, but it was the Almohad Sultan Abd al Mumin who redeveloped the settlement in 1150, transforming it into a permanent fortress town, with palaces, the main mosque which still stands, reservoirs, and houses for followers, and using it as an assembly point for the large Almohad army. However, it was his grandson Yacoub al Mansour who dreamed of making Rabat one of the great imperial capitals and who, from 1184, carried out the most ambitious programme of development. He ordered an enormous city, surrounded by walls, to be built. These walls were probably completed by 1197 and ran along two sides of the city, broken by four gates, most notably the Bab er Rouah. A grid of streets, residential quarters, a covered market, public baths, hotels,

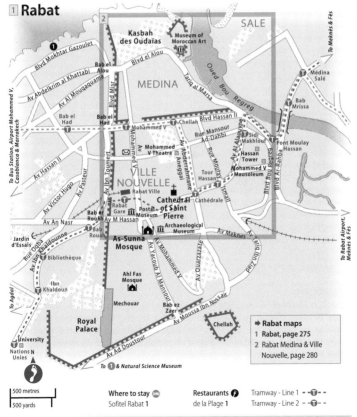

1 Rabat

Where to stay	Restaurants	
Sofitel Rabat 1	de la Plage 1	Tramway - Line 1
		Tramway - Line 2

➡ Rabat maps
1 Rabat, page 275
2 Rabat Medina & Ville Nouvelle, page 280

500 metres
500 yards

workshops and fountains were built, along with a new gateway to the medina. A bridge to Salé and its Grand Mosque, were also constructed. The most impressive monument from this period, the Hassan Mosque, was never completed, however. Projected as the largest mosque in western Islam, little more than pillars remain. The vast minaret never reached its full height and remains a stubby tower.

On Yacoub al Mansour's death in 1199 works were abandoned and Rabat then fell into decline. Parts of the city were destroyed in fighting between the Almohads and Merinids, to the point that Leo Africanus, visiting in 1500, found few inhabited neighbourhoods and very few shops. As Rabat declined under the Merinids, Salé prospered. The dynasty's most noteworthy contribution to Rabat was the funeral quarter on the Chellah site, with its impressive mausoleums, but even that eventually fell into neglect.

Piracy and Andalucíans

Rabat's fortunes revived in the 17th century. As maritime technology advanced and the Atlantic Ocean became important to international trade, corsairing, or piracy, boomed. For a time, Rabat was the centre, with the notorious 'Sallee Rovers' more likely to have been based here than in present day Salé. (Robinson Crusoe was a fictional captive of 'a Turkish rover of Sallee'.)

Rabat also benefited from the flow of Muslims leaving Spain during the Inquisition. First rejected by Salé, the Hornacheros settled in the Rabat kasbah in 1609, and the other Andalucíans in the Rabat medina in 1610. The medina they settled in was considerably smaller than the city Yacoub al Mansour had envisaged, as indicated by the 17th-century rampart, which, when built, demarcated the extent of the settlement, and now runs between the medina and the *ville nouvelle*. The area beyond this rampart was used for farming, and most of it remained undeveloped until the French arrived. In the medina, the Andalucían influence is visible, notably in the street plan.

Fierce rivalry existed between the Hornachero and the Andalucían communities, both setting up autonomous city-states, and the period between 1610 and 1666 was marked by intermittent strife between the three towns of the Bou Regreg estuary (Rabat, Salé and the Kasbah des Oudaïas). In 1627 the three were united under the control of the Hornacheros as the Republic of the Bou Regreg, a control against which the Andalucíans frequently rebelled, most notably in 1636. The Republic lost its independence in 1638. In 1641 the three cities were again united and, in 1666 when Moulay Rachid captured the estuary, they came under the authority of the Alaouite Sultanate.

The principal background to these conflicts was the struggle for control over the profits from piracy. Rabat was especially popular with corsairs, many of whom had Mediterranean origins, because, unlike several other ports, it had not been occupied by Europeans.

Alaouite Rabat

Under the Alaouites, Rabat changed considerably. Trade and piracy were taken over as official functions, the profits going to the sultanate. The port declined, being replaced by Mogador (Essaouira) in the 18th century. Moulay Rachid took over the kasbah, expelling its residents, and built the Qishla fortification to overlook and control the medina. However, Sultan Moulay Ismaïl, most closely associated with Meknès, ignored Rabat, and broke the power of the corsairs.

In the late 1760s, Mohammed Ibn Abdallah had a palace built in Rabat and, since then the Alaouite sultans have maintained a palace there, making the city one of their capitals. Increased trade with Europe in the 19th century temporarily revitalized Rabat's role as a port, but it was gradually supplanted, perhaps because of the shallow mouth of the Bou Regreg and the poor harbour facilities, but also because newer towns and cities, notably Casablanca, were more easily controlled by Europeans. In 1832 the rebellious Oudaïa tribe were settled in the abandoned kasbah, giving it its current name. The kasbah continued to be administered separately from the medina until the 20th century.

Modern Rabat, experiment in urban planning

In 1912, after complex diplomatic and military manoeuvrings, Morocco was split into two protectorates, with a large French central region and small Spanish zones in the north and the Sahara. Whereas the Moroccan sultanate had had no fixed capital, the power centre being where the sultan happened to be, the French decided that a capital was necessary for the new protectorate and Rabat was chosen in 1913. The first Resident-General, Hubert Lyautey, with his architect Henri Prost, planned and built the majority of the new capital, the *ville nouvelle*, both within and outside Yacoub al Mansour's walls, leaving the medina much as they found it, although the main thoroughfares were paved.

Efficiency and beauty were Lyautey's watchwords as he supervised the creation of the new Rabat. The European neighbourhoods were initally laid out in an area between the medina, to the northwest, and the *mechouar* or sultan's palace complex, to the southeast. A system of parks and gardens was created. The tree-lined street between the medina and the *ville nouvelle*, today's Boulevard Hassan II, a meeting place for Muslim and foreign communities, with municipal markets, bus and taxi stations and cafés.

The French planning of the new town reveals some interesting political undertones. It would have been possible, given the freedom that Lyautey had, to build the Residency General at a focal point on a new avenue, rather like Lutyens' House of the Viceroy in New Delhi. However, the new administrative buildings were built in a special area, close to the palace. With its luxuriant gardens, the Ministères neighbourhood recalls Anglo-American garden cities. The buildings, despite their importance to French rule, had simple whitewashed walls and green-tiled roofs and were linked by pergola walkways. They were kept unmonumental in scale (even the entrance to the Residency General had no obvious feature), hidden in vegetation. The French used such architectural devices to emphasize local culture, keeping the seats of power hidden in a mini garden suburb. More recent buildings, such as the new Ministry of Foreign Affairs, clash radically with this original principal. In short, in colonial Rabat, monumental buildings were only rarely used as a symbol of power. Today's Parliament Building, on the Avenue Mohammed V, is the exception, starting life as the Palais de Justice. Strongly symmetrical, with a massive colonnade, the building was probably designed to symbolize the equity and reason of French justice. Today, it is the centre of Moroccan political life.

After independence, Rabat continued to expand, its population swelled by the large number of civil servants required for the newly independent kingdom. Rabat's economy today is primarily based on its role as Morocco's administrative capital, with massive numbers of its inhabitants on the government payroll. The city has attracted large numbers of migrants from the countryside, and the formal housing market has been unable to keep up with the demand for accommodation, leading to the development of new self-built neighbourhoods like Douar Eddoum and Takaddoum. Rabat in many ways is a city of extremes, with streets of fine villas lying a stone's throw away from crowded slums (*bidonvilles*). South towards Casablanca, the new planned residential area of Hay Ryad is larger than the whole colonial city centre, while at Madinat el Irfane ('City of Knowledge'), Rabat has the country's largest concentration of faculties and university institutes. Neither

Almohad sultans nor Lyautey could have imagined that a city could grow so fast in just a couple of decades.

To try to ensure the city keeps up with the pace of change, a massive infrastructure overhaul has been implemented, in an attempt to try and solve Rabat's woeful road congestion. Project Bouregreg includes the building of the Hassan II Bridge across the river and a new tram link between Rabat and Salé, both of which were opened in 2011. The project, though, isn't without controversy. Many residents' whose homes were destroyed to make way for the tramway have complained of receiving unfair compensation, while other locals point out that the high cost of tram tickets can be prohibitive. Whether Rabat's new infrastructure ends up a help or a hindrance remains to be seen.

Places in Rabat

Walls and gates

Rabat has three sets of walls: the **Almohad wall** around the kasbah, the 5 km of **Almoravid wall** around much of the city centre dating from the 12th century, and the wall now separating the medina and the *ville nouvelle* built by the Andalucíans in the early 17th century. The walls are mainly built of *pisé* or *pisé*-cement and, though considerably repaired, strengthened and adapted, they are much as they were originally. There are four gates still standing in the Almoravid wall: Bab el Alou, Bab el Had, Bab er Rouah and Bab ez Zaer. **Bab er Rouah**, south of the train station, is the most important and impressive of these. **Bab el Had**, at the intersection of Avenue Hassan II and Avenue Ibn Toumert is also worth seeing. The substantially remodelled gate has a blind arch and is flanked by two five-sided stone towers.

The scale and beauty of **Bab er Rouah**, also known as the 'Gate of the Winds', at Place An Nasr, is best seen from outside the walled city. The gate is now used as an art gallery, and is only open when exhibitions are being held. The arch of the gate is framed by a rectangular band of Kufic inscription. Between the arch and the frame there is a floral motif, with the scallop symbol on either side. The arch itself, with an entrance restored by the Alaouites with small stones, is made up of three different patterns of great simplicity, producing the overall effect of a sunburst confined within a rectangle. The entrance passage inside follows a complex double elbow. This, combined with the two flanking bastions outside, indicate that the gate was defensive as well as ceremonial.

Kasbah des Oudaïas

The Kasbah des Oudaïas, originally a fortified ribat, later settled by Andalucíans, is both beautiful and peaceful, and well worth a visit. It can be reached along Rue de Consuls through the medina, Boulevard el Alou along the western side of the medina, or by Tarik al Marsa, which runs along the Oued Bou Regreg. There are a number of entrances to the kasbah, but the best is via the imposing **Bab al Kasbah** gateway at the top of the hill. (There's no need to use one of the unofficial guides who may present their services; the kasbah is small and easily explored without assistance. To avoid guides altogether, you can get to the kasbah up the steps from the esplanade, which runs along the beach below the cemetery.)

Bab al Kasbah was close to the Souk el Ghezel, the main medieval market, while the original palace was just inside. The gateway was built by Yacoub al Mansour in about 1195, inserting it into the earlier kasbah wall built by Abd al Mumin, and it did not have the same defensive role as the Bab er Rouah. The gate has a pointed horseshoe arch surrounded by a cusped, blind arch. Around this there is a wide band of geometric carving, the common *darj w ktaf*. The two corner areas between this band and the rectangular frame are composed

City tour

The following route takes in most of the main sites. Take a *petit taxi* for one of the longer hops, either from the kasbah to the Hassan Tower, or from the Chellah down to the far side of the medina. The three main sights in Rabat, namely the Kasbah des Oudaïas, the medina and the Chellah, have to be explored on foot.

Start at the kasbah then head for the Hassan Tower and the Mohammed V Mausoleum along Tarik al Marsa road, with its thundering lorries and buses. From the Tour Hassan, continue to skirt the city along Boulevard Bou Regreg, Avenue Tariq Ibn Ziad and Avenue Moussa Ibn Nossair to the fortified Chellah, clearly visible down on your left from the road. After the Chellah, head into the *ville nouvelle* by Bab ez Zaer to the As Sunna Mosque. Turn along Avenue Moulay Hassan and through Bab er Rouah to view it from the outside. Pass down Avenue Ibn Toumert, past Bab el Had to Bab el Alou, and right into the medina. Turn right down Boulevard Mohammed V and carry on through the medina to Boulevard Hassan II.

of floral decoration, with, as in the Bab er Rouah, a scallop or palmette in each. Above this are more palmettes, a band of Koranic lettering and, on top, a wide band of geometric motifs. The entrance to the kasbah is via stairs and through two rooms, a third room being closed to the public. The inside of the gate is also decorated, though more simply.

Inside the gate, the main street, Rue al Jamaâ, runs past the **Kasbah Mosque**, the oldest in Rabat, dating from 1150, the time of Abd al Mumin. As is the case with most city mosques in Morocco, it is hard to get any real idea of the size of this building, as homes are built all around it. The minaret, complete with elaborately decorative arches, was substantially rebuilt in the 18th century. Continue along Rue al Jamaâ and you come to the **semaphore platform**, where there is a carpet factory. This gives an excellent view over surfers in the sea below, the Oued Bou Regreg, with its natural sand-bar defence, and Salé. Steps down from the platform lead to a small fort built by an English renegade, known as Ahmed el Ingliz, and the popular Kasbah beach.

Coming back from the platform take Rue Bazo, the fourth street on the left. This narrow and cobbled street winds down through the whitewashed Andalucían-style houses to the bottom of the kasbah, directly into the **Café Maure** (see page 289), alongside which is a small but beautiful garden.

The **Andalucían Garden** is supposedly formal, but it is actually the semi-abandonment and the lack of formality that make it such a dreamy, engaging place – as long as you avoid occasional tour parties. The garden was built in the early 20th century by Prosper Ricard and the Traditional Arts Department. Nettles and wild poppies spill out of flowerbeds, and cats lounge among fallen leaves and oranges, accompanied by birdsong and the tinkling of fountains.

On the other side of the garden is the **Museum of Moroccan Art** ① *0900-1600, closed Tue, 10dh, T0537-731512*, exhibiting traditional dress and jewellery from many regions of Morocco. The opulent buildings are part of the 17th-century palace that Moulay Ismaïl once used as his Rabat residence. The central building now houses the main museum collection, with arms, instruments, jewellery, pottery, musical instruments and carpets. Unfortunately, labelling in a suitable array of languages is a bit lacking in the museum. If better managed, it could provide a fine introduction to Moroccan crafts and to life in an upper-class traditional home.

2 Rabat medina & Ville Nouvelle

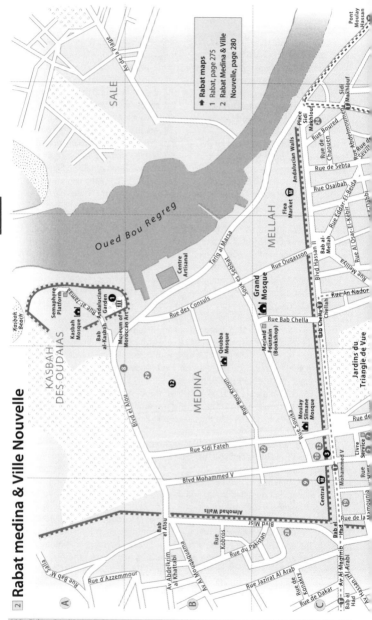

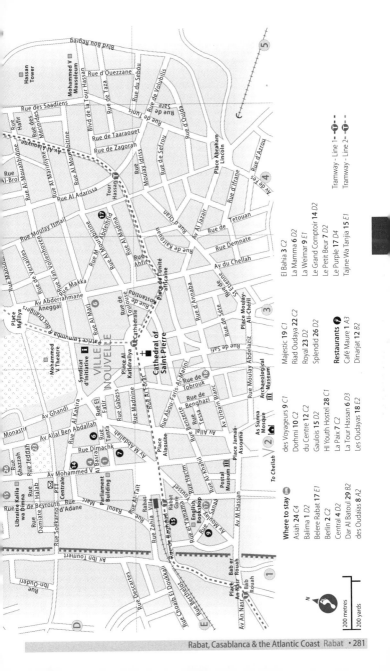

Tramway - Line 1
Tramway - Line 2

Where to stay
Asiah 24 C4
Balima 1 D2
Belere Rabat 17 E1
Berlin 2 C2
Central 4 D2
Dar Al Batoul 29 B2
des Oudaias 8 A2

des Voyageurs 9 C1
Dorhmi 10 C2
du Centre 12 C2
Gaulois 15 D2
HI Youth Hostel 28 C1
La Paix 7 C2
La Tour Hassan 6 D3
Les Oudayas 18 E2

Majestic 19 C1
Riad Oudaya 22 C2
Royal 23 D2
Splendid 26 D2

El Bahia 3 C2
La Mamma 6 D2
La Weimar 9 E1
Le Grand Comptoir 14 D2
Le Petit Beur 7 D2
Le Purple 17 D4
Tajine Wa Tanjia 15 E1

Restaurants
Café Maure 1 A3
Dinarjat 12 B2

200 metres
200 yards

Medina

Most of the buildings in the medina date from the arrival of the Andalucían Muslims in the 17th century, and this Andalucían character sets Rabat's medina apart from others, such as Marrakech. While the medina here is smaller and more limited in its range of markets, shops and buildings than Fès, Marrakech and Meknès, and less distinct in its way of life, its accessibility, size and the simplicity of its grid-like street pattern make it a good place to experience a Moroccan medina without getting lost. Physically close to the *ville nouvelle*, the medina is nevertheless very different in the design of its buildings and open space, and in the nature of its commerce and socialization. It is an interesting and safe place to wander, with little risk of getting lost or hassled. **Boulevard Mohammed V** is one of the major arteries.

As you enter from the *ville nouvelle*, the second right, Rue Souika, and its continuation Souk es Sebbat, are the main shopping streets, with an unusually wide range of shops and a number of traditional cafés for such a small area. **Souk es Sebbat**, originally where shoes were made, is easily recognized by its roof of woven straw and reeds. A great deal of leather work is on sale here, in particular worked leather for bags and the soft leather *babouches*. The mosque of **Moulay Slimane** at the junction of Rue Souika and Rue Sidi Fatah was constructed in 1812. The **Grand Mosque**, on Rue Souika, is a much restored Merinid building, the minaret of which is decorated with polychrome glazed earthenware tiles. Just opposite the Grand Mosque, on a side turning, is the interesting stone façade of a **fountain**, now a bookshop, but dating from the reign of the 14th-century Merinid Sultan Abu Faris Abd al Aziz.

Souk es Sebbat leads down to the river, past the mellah on the right. The **mellah** is the former Jewish area and still the poorest area of the medina, with its small, cramped houses and shops, and narrow streets. It was built in 1808 by Moulay Slimane. Originally there were 17 synagogues; those which remain today have become dwellings or storehouses. As in many Islamic cities, Jews were kept in one area, for both protection and control, and so that they would be easily accessible to the authorities when needed to carry out tasks that Muslims could not perform. There are few Jews left in the mellah, most having emigrated to Israel. There is, however, a moderately interesting *joutia*, or flea market – and some very striking poverty.

Turning left off Souk es Sebbat you can follow the **Rue des Consuls** to the kasbah. This road was where many European consuls and important merchants lived until 1912. Rue des Consuls is now lined with expensive shops selling silk embroidery, souvenirs, traditional Moroccan items in copper and leather, and carpets. The street has been enhanced by a range of roof features, including iron pillars and plexiglass vaults. There is a carpet market on the street on Tuesday and Thursday mornings. Turn right at the end of Rue des Consuls and you are in Tarik al Marsa (literally, Avenue of the Port). Here you may make a death-defying dash across the street to visit the kasbah and its traditional arts museum (see above). Also on the kasbah side of the street, to your right as you look at the kasbah, is the **Centre Artisanal**. All craft products sold here have fixed prices.

Hassan Tower and Mohammed V Mausoleum
ⓘ *Daily 0830-1830, free.*

The Almohad Hassan Tower dominates the skyline of Rabat, and, even unfinished, it is an impressive building, testimony to Yacoub al Mansour's unfulfilled vision of his imperial capital. It overlooks the Oued Bou Regreg and Salé, and can be reached most easily by Boulevard Bou Regreg, or by turning right at the end of Avenue Hassan II.

The building of the mosque was abandoned on Yacoub al Mansour's death in 1199, leaving most of the minaret, but just part of the columns and walls. All the portable parts –

tiles, bricks and the roofing material – have been taken for use in other buildings. The remains of the mosque were excavated and reconstructed by the French and Moroccans. The mosque would have followed a T-shape, with the main green-tiled roof section between the minaret and the modern mausoleum. The mihrab (prayer niche) would have been in the south *qibla* wall, where the mausoleum is, and therefore was not properly orientated towards Mecca. It is also unusual to find the minaret opposite the *qibla* wall.

The incomplete minaret of the Hassan Mosque stands at 45 m. When completed, it would have been 80 m, five times as high as it is wide, in keeping with the classic North African minaret style. It is decorated with geometric designs, the scale and clarity of which makes them clearly discernible from a distance. Each of the faces has a different composition, interweaving designs, arches and windows. The common Moroccan motif of *darj w ktaf*, resembling a tulip or a truncated fleur de lys, and formed by intersecting arcs with superimposed rectangles, is notable high on the north and south faces.

Adjacent to the Hassan Tower is the **Mohammed V Mausoleum**, dedicated to the first king of independent Morocco and grandfather of the current king. The building dates from 1971. The mausoleum is constructed on the site where Mohammed V, returning from his exile in 1955, gathered thousands of his people to thank God for giving independence to Morocco. The tomb chamber, but not the mausoleum's mosque, is open to non-Muslims, and features traditional Moroccan decorative motifs and techniques common in religious architecture, including a painted ceiling, the carved marble tomb, and the *zellige* (mosaic) tiles on the walls. Note the guards in their splendid uniforms.

Chellah
ⓘ *0830-1730, 10dh. Open to non-Muslims.*
The walled ruins of Chellah, a 14th-century Merinid citadel, are reached by going past the main As Sunna Mosque in the *ville nouvelle*, and on south down Avenue Yacoub al Mansour and through the **Bab ez Zaer**. It's an impressive place: granite fragments encrusted in orange lichen, the click-clacking of large numbers of nesting storks and thick beds of clover and brambles enveloping crumbling fragments of tiles and walls. Paved paths lead between trees down to the most intact ruins, in the far corner of the site.

There are five sides to the Chellah, all different lengths, and 20 towers. Chellah was built between 1310 and 1334, approximately on the site of the Roman town of Sala Colonia. The second Merinid Sultan, Abu Yusuf Yacoub, built a mosque, and Abul Hassan, the Black Sultan, then built the enclosure wall and the gate. The Roman ruins at the lower level of the Chellah enclosure have been excavated and include a forum, baths, shops and a temple. These are not open to the public.

Bab ez Zaer is smaller and less impressive than the Almohad Bab er Rouah. It is decorated with carving, and coloured marble and tiles, with an octagonal tower on either side above which is a square platform. The entrance is on the elbow pattern; you turn right through three chambers, before walking out into a wild and lush garden. To get to the mausoleum, take the wide path to the bottom, where it stands on the right, with the Roman ruins on the left. On the far right are the tombs of local saints, surrounding a pool.

The door into the Merinid **mausoleum** (look for the date carved above the doorway), facing the Roman ruins, opens into the **mosque** of Abu Yusuf Yacoub, which consists of a small courtyard, followed by a three-aisled sanctuary. The arched doorway on the left has the remains of floral and geometric *zellige* in five colours. Entering the sanctuary, the **mihrab** is straight ahead. A door to the right leads to an area including the remains of the mosque's minaret, and a pool. From this, one enters the area of tombs, including those of Abul Hassan

At the top

In public buildings, offices and shops all over Morocco you will see portraits of the country's Royals, members of the ruling Alaouite dynasty which has been on the throne since the mid-17th century. Sometimes there is a triptych: a photograph of the late King Hassan II (ruled 1961-1999), flanked by the two princes, the then crown prince Sidi Mohammed and his younger brother, Moulay Rachid. On the death of Hassan II in July 1999, the crown prince came to the throne as Mohammed VI. Increasingly, his portrait as a sober-suited young technocrat is replacing that of the late king on public display. (Trendy clothes shops may have the king in ski-gear complete with woolly *gnaoua* cap.) In Hassan II's reign, shop-owners picked portraits appropriate to place: in a sports shop, there would be a picture of the king playing golf or in hunting gear, while a *crémerie* would have a picture of the king alongside a Berber milkmaid; beauty salons favoured a picture of the king and one of his daughters fully made-up for her wedding day.

Hassan II had five children. Elegant Lalla Myriem, the eldest daughter, now in her forties, was married to the son of former prime minister Abdellatif Filali. She won much admiration for her courage in getting a divorce, apparently against her father's will. She is much involved in charity work, as are the younger sisters, Lalla Esma and Lalla Hasna.

Despite the ripples from the Arab Spring reaching Morocco, with protests throughout the country calling for political reform, for the moment, Morocco's royal family remain a popular lot. The July 2011 referendum on reforming the constitution saw Mohammed VI receive a landslide victory at the polls, further demonstrating the king's popular appeal. The king is seen by many as a modernizer – an adept jet-skier with a more Euro-centric outlook than his father. Mohammed VI's public image was enhanced by his marriage to a university-educated woman of a Fassi family, now Princess Salma. The couple's first child, Prince Hassan, was born in 2003; their second, Princess Lalla Khadija, in 2007. Although Mohammed VI has attracted growing criticism in recent years for Morocco's record on human rights and freedom of speech, his popularity has managed to endure, with the majority of Moroccans willing to put their trust in the king to introduce the much-needed reforms.

and his wife Shams al Dawha. The remaining area of the mausoleum is taken up with the *zaouïa*, or mosque-monastery, of Abul Hassan. This includes a minaret, and a ruined funerary chapel, with very intricate carving, notably on the exterior of the south wall. The main part of the *zaouïa* is a rectangular courtyard with a small mosque at one end, surrounded by small cells. It had a pool surrounded by a columned arcade, the bases of the columns still discernible. The mihrab has some intricate stucco carving. The tiles on the upper portion of the minaret are perhaps recent, but the effect would have been a bright tiled structure.

Ville nouvelle

The *ville nouvelle* contains some fine examples of French colonial architecture, which incorporate an element of local design tradition, particularly the main post office (**PTT Centrale**) and the **Bank al Maghrib**, both on **Avenue Mohammed V**. This main boulevard is wide and particularly impressive in the evening, when it is crowded with people out for a stroll. Off to the left, down a street opposite the railway station, is the Catholic **Cathedral of Saint Pierre**. Below the station is the Parliament building or **Majlis an Nuwwab**. Just past the **Hotel Terminus** is a small **postal museum** exhibiting stamps. The 18th-century (but much-restored) **As Sunna Mosque** dominates the view up Avenue Mohammed V.

The **Archaeological Museum** ① *23 Rue el Brihi, T0537-722231, Wed-Mon 0845-1630, 10dh, residents 5dh. Take the Rue Moulay Abdelaziz, opposite the As Sunna Mosque, and turn right on the Rue Brihi.* The museum houses the best archaeological collection in the country, and is worth an hour's visit. The section covering pre-history has human remains from 4000 BC. There are pieces of pottery, jewellery and metalwork from Mauritanian for bears, as well as some carved stones. Particularly fine is the Bronze Age Nkhila stela, with its concentric curves and humanoid figure.

The museum is best known, however, for its Roman pieces, displayed in the **Salle des Bronzes**, which may be closed, but should be opened on request. The Hellenistic bronzes, restored a few years ago with UNESCO assistance, are superb and include an exquisite head of Juba II (ruled 25 BC to AD 23) and a most realistic dog from Volubilis, Morocco's most spectacular Roman site (see page 166). Also from Volubilis is a portrait of Roman politician Cato the Younger (who was defeated by Julius Caesar in 46 BC at Utica, and who committed suicide by falling on his sword) and an *ephèbe* – a naked Graecian youth with ivy crown. The position of the left hand suggests that he is a doryphorous, a spear carrier. There is a fine athletic horserider, probably based on a Greek original by Polyclitus.

All around the Salle des Bronzes are a series of vitrines packed with archaeological finds. Most explanations are in French only, but you will be able to pick out candelabra, metal fittings from harnesses and furniture, a damascened trophy and a cuirass with lion and elephant heads. There are some small pieces of marble statuary, including some heads and a snoozing – or hungover – Silenus, with a jug from which water, or maybe wine, would have trickled. And there is some jewellery, brooches, odd bronze feet, minute acrobats, a gold feather and a tiny bracelet with crescent moon.

Among the most interesting pieces are those that tell something of life in the Roman garrison towns of Mauritania Tingitana. There is a display of builders' tools, including plumblines, compass and triangle from Banasa, and there is a bronze military diploma from Ceuta (Roman Ad Septem), conferring citizenship on a soldier who had completed his service in the area.

The **Postal Museum** was opened in 1970. It belongs to the PTT, which has brought together this small and interesting collection of instruments once used by their service. The items range from a post van to an envelope and between are telegraph machines, belinographs, which reproduced photographs over long distances, and the Baudot telegraph with printer. Among the postage stamps is Morocco's first official stamp from May 1912 but the collections of more recent stamps will catch the eye. Philately is a good export earner.

To the south of the As Sunna Mosque is the **palace complex** ① *not open to the public*, where the sovereign spends part of the year. It is not possible to go beyond this point up the central avenue of the complex. Construction of the Royal Palace began in 1864. It is surrounded by a wall cut by three gates. Inside the complex is an open space known as the *mechouar*. Here stands the **Ahl Fas Mosque** where the King leads prayers each Friday when he is in the capital.

Southwest of the *ville nouvelle* is the **Natural Science Museum** ① *Ministry of Energy and Mining, Quartier administratif, Agdal, T0537-688400, Mon-Fri 0800-1200 and 1430-1830, free,* is part of the Ministry of Energy and Mining. Here there is a reconstruction of a sauropod dinosaur. The skeleton of this creature, which is almost 15 m in length, was discovered in 1979 in the Azilal region of the High Atlas.

For sleeping and eating price codes and other relevant information, see pages 22-28.

◉ Where to stay

There are plenty of reasonably priced hotels in Rabat, although in summer hotels can fill up quickly, especially in the mid-price range. The cheapest hotels in the medina, for which prices can be very flexible, are best avoided (with a few exceptions). The centre of the *ville nouvelle* provides a wide range of good hotels. If not exactly catching up with Marrakech and Fès, Rabat now has a few pleasant guesthouses in the upper price bracket.

Medina *p282, map p280*
€€€ **Dar Al batoul**, 7 Derb Jirari, T0537-727250, www.riadbatoul.com. This atmospheric riad has bags of artistic style. Each of the 8 rooms is individually decorated with gorgeous tiling, traditional textiles, stained glass and quirky use of colour, and they open on to a peaceful interior patio. Evening meals available.
€€€ **Riad Kasbah**, 39 Rue Zirara, T0537-702392, www.riadrabat.com. Run by the same people as the **Riad Oudaya**, this is a less pricey option, with brick floors, colourful bathrooms and cosy, if narrow, rooms. It's a peaceful spot, with palms in the courtyard. Simple rather than overly chic but very well placed in the heart of the kasbah.
€€€ **Riad Oudaya**, 46 Rue Sidi Fateh, T0537-702392, www.riadoudaya.com. With just 4 rooms, this French-run riad is an intimate and thoroughly relaxing place. The quiet courtyard is filled with plants and birdsong, and the rooms are elegantly furnished with bright textiles and antiques. Evening meals are available.
€ **HI Youth Hostel**, 43 Rue Marassa, T0537-725769, auberge.jeunes.rbt@hotmail.fr. Well located for sights and almost opposite Bab el Had, Rabat's youth hostel is definitely showing its age. The dorm rooms (shared

facilities only) are basic but the courtyard garden is a good place to relax, and it's an easy walk to the sights.
€ **Hotel des Oudaïas**, 132 Blvd el Alou, near the kasbah, T0537-732371. On the far northern edge of the medina, the **Oudaïas** is convenient for sightseeing, though the rather tatty and none-too-quiet rooms don't match the promise of the palm and dark wood-filled reception. Nevertheless, it offers some of the best value in town.
€ **Hotel Dorhmi**, 313 Av Mohammed V, handily located just inside the medina on your right, T0537-723898. This is the best of the medina budget hotels, with rooms and reception all on the 1st floor up a flight of stairs. Spick-and-span rooms all face onto a central gallery, with white walls and pot plants. A great pick for the budget-conscious, though those who struggle with noise are best to look outside the medina.
€ **Hotel du Centre**, after you have crossed Av Hassan II into the medina, down an alley on your right, just before **Banque Populaire** and its café, T0537-708732. The clean rooms here open onto a long corridor; go for 14-23 which overlook the alley or 21-22 on the rooftop; the others get very hot in summer.

There is also a selection of very basic, budget hotels, most with double rooms for about 120dh and singles for about 80dh, down Souk Semara, in the alley on left after **Banque Populaire**, including: € **Hotel La Kasbah**, Rue Sidi Mohammed Ghazi, off Av Mohammed V, T0537-768537; € **Hotel Maghreb al Jedid**, T0537-732207; € **Hotel Marrakesh**, on Rue Sebbahi, right off Av Mohammed V, T0537-727703; € **Hotel National**, Rue Ben Rezouk, T0537-737671; € **Hotel des Voyageurs**, just behind the market, T0537-723720.

Ville nouvelle *p284, map p280*
€€€€ **La Tour Hassan**, 26 Av de Chellah, T0537-239 000, www.latourhassan.com. Traditionally decorated, using lashings of Moroccan-styling in the common areas,

this sprawling, sumptuous hotel has more than a glimmer of Arabian Nights to it. In a convenient city centre location, it boasts all the trimmings you'd expect: small pool, excellent restaurants, conference room, bar and free Wi-Fi.

€€€€ **Sofitel Rabat**, Aviation Souissi, T0537-675656, www.sofitel.com. This luxurious and recently completely revamped hotel is set in extensive gardens on the road out past the Chellah. Facilities are top-notch, and the spacious rooms feature fresh, modern interiors with a hint of arabesque. It's a fair way from the city centre but it's a peaceful haven to escape to after sightseeing.

€€€ **Hotel Asiah**, Pl Sidi Makhlouf, T0537-731091. Conveniently located at the end of Av Hassan II, overlooking the river and Salé, the Asiah is built around a courtyard in an approximation of a Moroccan palace. There's a pool and good facilities and services.

€€ **Hotel Balima**, 173 Av Mohammed V, BP 173, across from the station, T0537-707967, www.hotel-balima.net. Set back from Av Mohammed V, the best of the 71 rooms look right down the throat of the parliament opposite. Partly because of its position, the café-bar on the ground floor is very popular, though rooms, decorated in oranges and reds, are a little stale. Bathrooms are clean, modern and tiled but the whole is a little functional. Breakfast included.

€€ **Hotel Belere Rabat**, 33 Av Moulay Youssef Rabat Maroc T0537-703897, www.belerehotels.com. Despite the grim concrete exterior, the Belere is a business-orientated 3-star hotel with all the trimmings: beige and burgundy interior, marble tiles, a piano bar and rooms with free minibars, satellite TV and Wi-Fi. Rooms facing the street can be noisy.

€€ **Hotel Ennakhil**, 23 bis Av d'Alger, T0537-723355. Clean and quiet, located out towards the diplomatic quarter.

€€ **Hotel Ibis Moussafir**, across from the Agdal station, T0537-774919. This chain hotel is a solid choice with decent facilities, a pool and Wi-Fi. It's rather a long way from

the centre, but convenient if you're on business in the Agdal area.

€€ **Hotel Royal**, 1 Rue Amman, T0537-721171, www.mtds.com/royalhotel. This central, rather old-fashioned hotel has large, good-value rooms. If you don't fancy an early morning wake-up with the call to prayer, it's best to steer clear of the rooms facing the park. The café opposite the hotel is nice for breakfast.

€ **Hotel Berlin**, 261 Av Mohammed V, T0537-703435. Large but noisy rooms; ask for one not facing the street to avoid the worst of the traffic. A step up from the Hotel Central and Hotel Splendid.

€ **Hotel Central**, 2 Rue Al Basra, T0537-707356, hotel.central.rabat@gmail.com. Beside the **Balima**, just off Av Mohammed V, this is a well-run hotel with clean double rooms, some with shower, though toilets are all on the corridor. Rooms are large and light, with old wardrobes, sagging beds and orange curtains. Singles are not so good but it's one of the better cheap options.

€ **Hotel Gaulois**, corner Blvd Mohammed V and Zanket Hims, T0537-723022. A wooden staircase leads from a grand lobby up to more modest but freshly painted rooms. The 59 rooms go up in price as you add en suite and TV. Good-value single rooms (170dh). Private parking nearby.

€ **Hotel La Paix**, 2 Rue Ghazza, T0537-722926. This old-timer still displays wisps of a grander past, with its dusty chandeliers, solid wooden beds and hatstands. Grab a room with a balcony, as the rooms with smaller windows can be rather stuffy. Good-value single rooms (170dh).

€ **Hotel Majestic**, 121 Av Hassan II, T0537-722997, www.hotelmajestic.ma. A good-value choice at the upper-end of the budget price bracket. The **Majestic** has clean, pastel-toned rooms, boasting comfortable beds, balconies overlooking the medina and TV (no a/c). Double glazing keeps the noise levels down.

€ **Hotel Splendid**, 24 Rue Ghazza, T0537-7232 83. Beds are hard and pillows lumpy but the **Splendid** has a certain old-fashioned style: there are dial phones and ageing furniture in rooms and there's an ancient spiral staircase. Small balconies and a peaceful courtyard, with tiles, trees and metal animals, add to the good value, though the coffee is best avoided. Also good for solo travellers on a budget, with cheap single rooms (125dh).

Outside the centre

€€€€ Villa Mandarine,19 Rue Oulad Bousaa, Souissi, T0537-752077, www.villa mandarine.com. In the upmarket Souissi neighbourhood, close to the **Royal Golf Dar Es Salam**, this wonderfully peaceful small hotel is set among gardens and orange orchards. Antiques and local art abound throughout the communal areas, and the comfortable rooms all come with shady private terrace. Pool, bar, restaurant and spa.

🍴 Restaurants

Most higher-quality restaurants are within the *ville nouvelle*. Two areas have a good selection of mid-range restaurants: immediately behind the **Hotel Balima** and in the neighbourhood behind the train station. A range of fairly cheap restaurants is to be found throughout the city, but the budget options – small Moroccan canteens and café-restaurants doing set lunches, harira and brochettes – are in the medina, along Blvd Mohammed V, Rue Souika, Rue Sidi Fatah and adjacent streets. There are also plenty of *crémeries* doing juices, pâtisseries, snacks and sandwiches.

Medina *p282, map p280*

€€€ Dinarjat, 6 Rue Belgnaoui, close to the Kasbah des Oudaïas, T0537-704239, www.dinarjat.com. This upscale Moroccan restaurant is a dining experience of traditional costumed waiters, live Andalucían music and sumptuously restored architecture. After some fine dining on specialities, such as lamb and prune tagine or almond chicken, recline on your couch amid the tiling and carved arches (main dishes average 200dh).

€€€ Le Ziryab,10 Impasse Ennajar, T0537-733636, www.restaurantleziryab.com. Up a winding street in the medina, **Le Ziryab** hides a quality traditional Moroccan restaurant behind a heavy wooden door. More a gastronomic experience than just a meal, it only does a 5-course set menu which showcases Morocco's cuisine. Bring your appetitie.

€ La Maison des Grillades, just inside the walls of the medina to the west of Av Mohammed V. One of several cheap eateries on the edge of the medina, the popular **La Maison** offers tagine or chicken with chips and salad for 20dh. Seating indoors or out.

€ Restaurant el Bahia, Av Hassan II, in the wall near junction with Av Mohammed V. Moroccan food in a courtyard, good value, erratic service.

Ville nouvelle *p284, map p280*

€€€ Kanoun Grill, 6th floor, Helnan Chellah Hotel, 2 Rue d'Ifni, T0537-668300. A large menu of charcoal-grilled meat. Reservations recommended.

€€€ Le Grand Comptoir, 279 Av Mohammed V, T0537-201514, www.legrand comptoir.ma. This Parisian-style brasserie is the dining choice for Rabat's see and be seen crowd. An immaculately restored 1930s interior and live jazz add to the stylish ambience. The food is reliably excellent, with menu highlights including locally caught crayfish. Reservations recommended.

€€ Café Restaurant Saadi, 81 bis Av Allal Ben Abdallah, T0537-709903. A long-running restaurant serving up good Moroccan meals, as well as a large range of international dishes. Licensed.

€€ La Mamma, 6 Rue Zankat Tanta (ex-Paul Tirard), T0537-707329, behind **Hotel Balima**. This old stalwart of the Rabat eating scene has an eclectic interior of candles, dark wood beams, hanging plastic vegetables and illuminated photos. The atmosphere buzzes with everyone from politicians to policemen most nights. Unfortunately the food (Italian cuisine with a large pizza menu) can be hit and miss.

€€ **La Weimar**, Goethe Institut, 7 Rue Sanaâ, T0537-732650. Once you've got through the metal detector at the entrance, this is a great little place for pizzas, an unusually wide selection of salads and chocolate cake, handily located in the neighbourhood behind the train station. It's international rather than particularly German, and there's a young vibe; the clientele is a mix of students and be-suited diplomats.

€€ **Le Petit Beur (Dar Tajine)**, 8 Rue Damas, T0537-731322. One of the top places to sample the best of Moroccan cooking, Le Petit Beur is deservedly popular for its tasty tagines. It's a traditional restaurant, with tiles, low lighting and a rather formal ambience, so it's better for dinner rather than lunch.

€€ **Le Purple**, 14 Rue Mekka, T0537-733680. Advertizing itself as a 'resto lounge', Le Purple is aiming at a young hip audience. Colours are bright, and there's a chilli mosaic on the wall. Try the *bouquet de Aphrodite* (mixed seafood) for 50dh, or more substantial fish, meat or pasta dishes for 90-130dh.

€€ **Tajine Wa Tanjia**, 9 Rue Baghdad, T0537-729797. Closed Sun. A mix of traditional and contemporary, **Tajine Wa Tanjia**'s popularity stems from its offering great service, plus excellent tagines at good-value prices (68-86dh). This is the place to come and feast on a sumptuous banquet of Moroccan cuisine. A large mural fills one wall, and there's free Wi-Fi and live oud playing in the evenings. Licensed.

Outside the centre
€€€ **Restaurant de la Plage**, close to the Plage des Oudaïas, T0537-733148. Sea views and good, if expensive, seafood. Reservations recommended in summer.

Cafés, pâtisseries and cafés-glaciers
There are many good cafés, pâtisseries and *glaceries* on or near Av Mohammed V, including:
Au Délice–Pâtisserie Suisse, 285 Av Mohammed V, up from the **Balima**, opposite the Parliament. Looks as though it hasn't

changed since the late 1950s. Good cake and croissants.

Café Maure, at the bottom of Rue Bazo in the Kasbah des Oudaïas. Has a terrace overlooking the estuary. It's a standard stop on most tourist routes through the city but, if you can avoid the hordes, it's a good place to stop for a rest. It has good mint tea and specializes in *cornes de gazelle*, almond paste-filled pastries; someone will come round with a platter of these to tempt you.

La Génoise, Blvd Oued Akrech, opposite Dar Es Salam school. French cakes at reasonable prices.

Pâtisserie Gerber, 258 Av Mohammed V. Lovely Moroccan sweet cakes.

Salon de Thé Lina, 45 Av Allal Ben Abdallah, near the French consulate. This very French café has excellent pastries and is smoke-free.

🎵 Bars and clubs

Rabat *p274, maps p275 and p280*
Rabat has little of the nightlife one might expect in a capital city, particularly late at night. The rich kids tend to go over to Casablanca to the clubs on the Corniche or, in the summer, to seasonal places at one of the beach resorts between Rabat and Casablanca, or even up to Tangier.

Bars
Bar Americain, Hotel Balima, see page 287. A popular place for a beer or coffee, particularly during the evening promenade.
Lounge Bar, Hotel de la Tour Hassan, see page 286. Thoroughly swish, with comfy seating, low lighting and pricey cocktails.

Clubs
Amnesia, 18 Rue Monastir. Entry 100dh. City centre club frequented by more affluent Moroccans and Europeans. Doesn't really get going until 0200.
Fifth Avenue, Av Bin el Ouidane, Agdal. 60dh. Bar next door with pool tables. Take a *petit taxi* to get there; get out at the lively Pl Ibn Yassine.

Hotel Balima, see page 287. Has a small nightclub (access on street at back of hotel).
Le Pachanga, 2 doors up from **Café Hawaii** oppisite the main station. A piano bar with jazz in basement.
Le Puzzle, 79 Av Ibn Sina, T0537-670030. Chic bar, live music, Agdal quarter; take a *petit taxi* from city centre.

⊙ Entertainment

Rabat *p274, maps p275 and p280*
Keep an eye on the newspapers, including *Le Journal*, *La Vie économique*, *L'Économiste* or *Le Matin du Sahara* for cultural events and reviews.

Art galleries
The following all hold occasional exhibitions of varying quality: **Galerie Marsam**, 6 Rue Oskofiah; **Galerie Moulay Ismaïl**, 11 Av Bin El Ouidane; **Galerie Bab Rouah**, Av de la Victoire (set in an old city gate, turn right just before As Sunna Mosque at top of Av Mohammed V). Also check out the main gate to the Kasbah des Oudaïas, where occasional exhibitions are held.

Cinema
The 4 biggest cinemas are easily found, 3 in Av Mohammed V, and 1 at the junction of Av Allal Ben Abdallah and Rue al Mansour ad Dahbi, which has perhaps the best range of films. Most films are dubbed in French. You could also go to the **Dawliz** multi-screen complex over the River Bou Regreg, just outside Salé.

Cultural centres
France, Germany and Spain all maintain cultural centres which host events. **Alliance Franco-Marocaine**, Rue Benzerte, with instruction in Arabic and French. **British Council**, 11 Av Allal Ben Abdallah, T0537-218 130, www.britishcouncil.org. **Goethe Institut**, 7 Rue Sanaa, near the station, T0537-732650, www.goethe.de. **Institut Français**, 2 Rue Abou Inane, T0537-689650,

www.ifrabat.org. **Instituto Cervantes**, 5 Rue Madnine, T0537-708738, www.rabat.cervantes.es. Events are often held at the Theatre Mohammed V – see below.

Theatre and music
Theatre Mohammed V, Rue Al Kahira (du Caire), puts on a range of plays and concerts.

⊛ Festivals

Rabat *p274, maps p275 and p280*
Jun/early Jul Annual summer **arts festival**, with a mix of musical styles. Book accommodation in advance.

⊙ Shopping

Rabat *p274, maps p275 and p280*
Bookshops
American Language Centre, 4 Rue de Tangier. Small bookstall, with some books on Morocco in English, including books on crafts and birdlife.
Le Bouquiniste de Chellah, 34 Av du Chellah, opposite the Lycée Hassan II. Owner Abadallah el Ghouari will be able to help you find that elusive title; small stock of antiquarian books on Morocco.
Librairie Kalila Wa Dimna, 344 Av Mohammed V. Probably the best bookshop in Rabat, run by the people who own the **Carrefour du Livre** bookshop in Casablanca.
Livre Service, 40-46 Av Allal Ben Abdallah. Good postcards, wide selection of books in French; could be the place to buy a Moroccan art photography book.

Maps
Division de la Cartographie, a 20dh taxi ride out of the centre at Km 4, Av Hassan II. Sells official maps (*cartes d'état major*). Good for hiking maps. Most areas of the country, apart from those close to the Algerian border, are available, also some quite recent city maps. Allow a good 2 hrs for the whole operation, including travel time from the city centre.

Markets

Local markets are on Thu at Salé, Av du 11 Janvier, Fri at Bouznika, Sat at Temara, Sun at Bouknadel and Skhirat.

In Rabat medina the vegetable market is best on Sun, and carpets in Rue des Consuls on Tue and Thu morning. Although a little way away, Agdal Market, off Av des Dadès, to the west of the university, is noted for its fruit and vegetables. The Municipal Market, clearly marked off Av Hassan II after the gate into the mellah, also has good fruit and vegetables and a selection of fresh aromatic herbs. In the *ville nouvelle* there is an underground vegetable and fruit market at Pl Moulay al Hassan, with excellent flower sellers above ground outside. Supermarkets such as Makro (with items in large quantities) and Marjane are both on the road to the airport. There is also a huge new Marjane supermarket out in the plush Souissi residential area. Marjane stocks alcohol, as does a small shop behind the Hotel Balima, on your right as you go downhill.

Moroccan craftwork

Use the Centre Artisanal (Coopartim) in Tarik al Marsa to get an idea of the range, then bargain in the small boutiques in the medina, on or just off Av Mohammed V, Rue Souika, Souk es Sebbat and Rue des Consuls. There are many larger shops, in the *ville nouvelle*, on Av Mohammed V, or in the malls just off it, where the high prices may be negotiable.

Newspapers and magazines

There are places on Av Mohammed V stocking a full range of English-language, French and international press. The best is perhaps inside the main railway station.

☺ What to do

Rabat *p274, maps p275 and p280*
Golf
Royal Golf Dar Es Salam, 12 km from Rabat on Rue de Zaërs, T0537-755864, www.royalgolfdaressalam.com. The most

famous course in Morocco, with 45 holes, fees 500dh per day.

Horse riding and polo
Club Equestre Yquem, on the coast road 20 km south of Rabat, just across Oued Yquem, T0537-749197. Offers riding on the sands.
Royal Polo Equestrian Club, at Royal Golf Dar Es Salam, Rue de Zaërs, T0537-754692.

Swimming and surfing
The main beach in Rabat is the one below the kasbah, which is popular with surfers in winter. Look out for the jet-ski set, too. The beach at Salé is similar – be careful at both of dangerous currents from the river. For better beaches, you really need to go further afield, to the Plage des Nations (see page 297), Temara (see page 303) or Skhirat.

⊝ Transport

Rabat *p274, maps p275 and p280*
Air
To get to Mohammed V airport (Casablanca), take the train from Rabat to Casa-Port or Casa-Voyageurs, where you will need to change (page 305). There are trains every 30 mins to Casa-Port between 0630 and 2100. For information on Royal Air Maroc (RAM) flights, call T090-00800 or see www.royalairmaroc.com.

For Rabat-Salé airport, T0537-808090, take a taxi, or if you're driving, follow the N6 Salé–Meknès road. There are daily direct flights to Paris with Royal Air Maroc (www.royalairmaroc.com) and Jet4You (www.jet4you.com).

Airline offices
Royal Air Maroc, 2 agencies in downtown Rabat. Agence A is almost opposite the train station on Av Mohammed V, T0537-709766, central reservations on T0537-709710. Agence B, 9 Rue Abou Faris al Marini, T0537-709700, up the hill opposite the station. Air France is further down, after the Hotel Balima, T0537-707728. Iberia, 104 Av Mohammed V.

Bus

Local Buses run all over the city, many originating from Av Hassan II, near Bab el Had, or just past Parc du Triangle de Vue. Nos 6 and 12 go to **Salé**, 17 to **Temara**, 1, 2 and 4 for the **Chellah**, get off at Bab des Zaër.

The main bus terminal for all buses, T0537-795124, is at Pl Zerktouni, 3 km from the centre, to the west of the city in the direction of Casablanca. Catch a *petit taxi* there, or a No 30 bus from Av Hassan II. CTM has regular departures to **Casablanca** throughout the day (about every 30 mins 0345-2230, 1½ hrs). Other destinations include **Tangier** at 0730, 1230, 1600 and 1830 (4 hrs); **Meknès**, 9 daily (2½ hrs); and **Fès**, 10 a day (3½ hrs).

Car

Car hire Avis, 7 Rue Abou Faris el Marini, T0537-721818, also at Rabat-Salé Airport, T0537-831677, www.avis.com. **Budget**, Rabat-Ville Railway Station, T0537-767689, www.economybookings.com. **Europcar**, 25 bis Rue Patrice Lumumba, T0537-722328, also at Rabat-Salé Airport, T0537-724141, www.europcar.com. **Hertz**, 467 Av Mohammed V, T0537-707366, www.hertz.co.uk, also at Rabat-Salé Airport.

Taxi

Petit taxi In Rabat they are blue and some of the best in Morocco, nearly always metered and often shared. They can be picked up anywhere, most easily at the stand on Av Hassan II, close to the junction with Av Mohammed V. Alternatively, T0537-720518. Sample fare from Av Mohammed V to Hassan Tower, 10dh. A Rabat *petit taxi* cannot take you to Salé, which has its own taxis – take a *grand taxi* instead.

Grand taxi Shared between 6 passengers, these run from the stand on Av Hassan II, just past the Parc du Triangle de Vue, for local locations such as **Temara**, **Skhirat**, **Bouknadel** and **Salé**, and from the bus station for long-distance locations.

Train

Rabat Ville station, Av Mohammed V, T0537-767353, has departures for: **Casablanca**, regular services to both Casa-Port and Casa-Voyageurs stations; **Marrakech**, 9 daily 0315-1945; **El Jadida**, 18 daily 0315-1745; **Oued Zem**, at 1515 and 1545; **Meknès** and **Fès**, 18 daily 0600-2349; **Taza** and **Oujda**, at 0717, 1117, 1212 and 2347; **Tangier**, 8 daily 0647-0147.

Rabat Agdal station, Rue Abderrahman el Ghafiki, T0537-772385, has departures for: **Casablanca**, **Marrakech**, **El Jadida** and **Oued Zem**, as above, 4-6 mins later; and **Meknès**, **Fès**, **Oujda** and **Tangier**, as above 6-8 mins earlier.

Tram

Two local tram lines run between Rabat and **Salé**, providing a quick and reliable link across and between towns. Trams operate Mon-Fri 0700-2100 and Sat 0700-1300. **Rabat Gare tram station** on Line 1 is located beside Rabat Ville train station.

⊙ Directory

Rabat *p274, maps p275 and p280*
Banks Banque Marocaine de Commerce Extérieur (BMCE), 241 Av Mohammed V, is the best for exchange (cash, TCs and Visa/Mastercard) for which it has a separate door, Mon-Fri 0800-2000, Sat-Sun 1000-1200 and 1600-2000. **Emergency** Ambulance, T15. Fire, T15. Police, T19. **Medical** Hôpital Avicenne, Av Ibn Sina, T0537 77 31 94. SOS Médecins, Rabat and Salé, T0537-202020. Emergency private medical service. **Chemists**, Pharmacie du Chellah, Pl de Melilla, T0537-724723, and another on Rue Moulay Slimane. Pharmacie de la Préfecture, Av Moulay Slimane opposite town hall. If not open, look in any chemist's door for details or T0537-726150 for the name of the night chemist. **Police** Rue Soekarno, behind the PTT Centrale, T19.

Salé and excursions from Rabat

Historic Salé, on the north bank of the Bou Regreg estuary, was once a rival to Rabat in the days of piracy and Andalucían Muslims fleeing the expanding power of Catholic Spain. The medina of Salé has a fine medersa and a striking early Merinid gate, the Bab Mrisa. For those with enough time, Salé is worth a visit.

Outside the city, cork and eucalyptus forest, gardens and beaches stretch north along the Atlantic coast. Kénitra is an industrial and military port, while further north, Mehdiya attracts surfers to its sandy beach and other visitors to its overgrown kasbah overlooking the sea. This stretch of coast is rich in birdlife, particularly on the Lac de Sidi Bourhaba and the lagoon of Merdja Zerga. There are isolated Roman remains at Thamusida and Banasa. To the south of Rabat, spring flowers carpet the valleys of the Zaër Forest, an area of gorges and rolling hills.
➡️ *For listings, see pages 303-305.*

Arriving in Salé ➔ *Colour map 1, B1.*

Salé is most easily reached from Rabat by using the tram link. If you get off at **Gare Salé** tram station (beside the railway station) the city centre sights are within easy walking distance. You can also come by *grand taxi* (from the *grand taxi* rank just past the Parc du Triangle de Vue, on Avenue Hassan II) or by taking bus No 6 or 12 from Avenue Hassan II. Travellers coming in from the north can get off at Salé railway station.

Once in Salé it is possible to explore most of the centre on foot, though the tramline is also useful if you don't feel like walking and the city also has its own *petits taxis*. If you have your own transport, go along Tarik al Marsa, Avenue Hassan II or Boulevard du Bou Regreg and cross the bridge below the Hassan Tower. It is possible to walk this route in 30 minutes.

Background

Salé, Sala or Sla in Arabic, derives from the Roman Sala Colonia. Salé was founded in the 11th century, and its Great Mosque dates from 1163-1184. The town was embellished and fortified by the Merinids in the 13th century, becoming an important commercial centre. Great rivalry, even armed conflict, has existed between Rabat and Salé, although they were united in the Republic of the Bou Regreg. Up until the 17th century Salé enjoyed long periods as the more important of the two cities, being known for religious learning and piety. With the coming of Rabat's capital status, Salé gradually turned into a dormitory settlement for the city. New businesses and light industries, however, are gradually springing up on the road north out of Salé. While Rabat is known as the city of gardens, Salé is perhaps the city of sanctuaries. The 14th-century Medersa Abul el Hassan is well worth visiting.

Places in Salé

Salé medina is small and easy to explore. Walking in any direction you are likely to arrive at the souks, the Grand Mosque and Abul Hassan Medersa, or the city walls. As elsewhere, early 20th-century French planners at Salé preserved the historic city walls and left a wide space between the medina and land for new building. If you arrive by *grand taxi*, you will be dropped by the gardens adjacent to the Bab Mrisa gate, one of the most unusual city gates in Morocco.

Bab Mrisa

Bab Mrisa, or 'Gate of the Little Harbour', was originally the sea gate of the medina, as there was once a channel running to it from the River Bou Regreg. The gate is wide, and its 11-m high horseshoe arch would have allowed the sailing boats of the day to pass within the walls for repairs. (Since medieval times, the access canal has silted up.) Although Bab Mrisa was built by the Merinid Sultan Abu Yusuf in the 1260s, in style it is closer to the Almohad gates – the triangular space between the arch and the frame is covered with floral decoration centred on the palmette, with the use of the *darj w ktaf* motif down the sides. Originally it had a porch. Alongside the gate there are two tall defensive towers. It may be possible to get access to the top of the gate. You may be able to find a caretaker by a small door on the left, inside the gate, which gives access to a small garden leading to a round tower. From this tower walk back along the top of the rampart to the gate. There is another similar sea gate, the next gate around the wall to the left.

Abul Hassan Medersa

① *0800-1200, 1430-1800. Open to non-Muslims.*

This *medersa* (religious school) is the most important building in Salé and the only *medersa* in the region. It was built by the Merinid Sultan Abul Hassan, the Black Sultan, and was

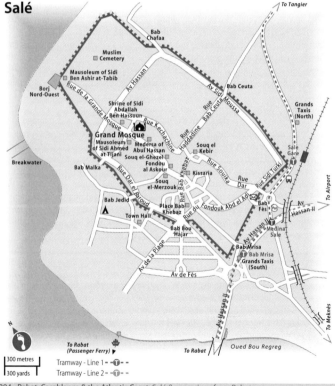

Salé

Medersa – place of education for Islam

"Learning is a city, one of whose gates is memory, the other is comprehension." (An Arab saying).

The *medersa* in North Africa is a college of higher education in which Islamic teachings lead the syllabus. The institution originated in Persia and developed in the Islamic West in the 13th century. The construction of places of advanced learning was a response by orthodox Sunni Islam to the growth of Shi'ite colleges, but they soon became important centres in their own right as bastions of orthodox Islamic beliefs. Subjects other than theology were taught at the *medersa*, but only in a limited form and in ways that made them adjuncts to Sunni teachings and acceptable to a very conservative religious hierarchy. Unfortunately, therefore, the *medersa* became associated with a rather uninspired and traditional academic routine in which enquiry and new concepts were often excluded. Knowledge and its transmission sadly fell into the hands of the least academic members of the theological establishment and the poor standards of science, politics, arts and ethics associated with the Arab world in the period since the 13th century has been put down to the lack of innovation and experiment in the *medersa* – a situation which has only very recently begun to break down in Sunni Islam.

The shortcomings of the *medersa* in creative teaching terms was in part compensated for by the development of the buildings themselves, however. They were mainly modelled on the Medersa Bou Inania at Fès (page 136), founded under Sultan Abu Inan (1348-1358), itself based on designs from Syria. The main courtyard *sahn* is surrounded by cloisters/galleries, separated from the *sahn* by ornate screens of wood. The mosque is to the east and the long *qibla* wall has a deeply set mihrab (see plan, page 440). The Merinids founded seven *medersa* in Fès during the 14th century.

"Let your eyelids enjoy my splendid beauty – you will find a marvellous virtue to chase away cares and sadness," reads one of the many carved inscriptions in the 16th-century Medersa Ben Youssef in Marrakech (see page 57), which is the largest *medersa* in North Africa and considered one of the finest. Originally a Merinid foundation but remodelled in the 16th century, it has an arcaded courtyard with intricate mosaic work, lace-like carved stucco, weathered to a faint rose-coloured patina, and finely worked cedar beams.

Moroccan *medersa* were, until quite recently, used for student accommodation and even for teaching, but the traditional life has now disappeared and the *medersa*, remain as intriguing monuments to an educational past where religious belief and education were tightly linked.

completed in 1342. To reach it follow the city walls around to the left from Bab Mrisa to a small square at Bab Bou Hajar, alongside a park. Just beyond this is an area where cars should be parked. Take the small lane off to the far right at the end of this area. Take the first left, then the first right. Some 200 m later, just after the lane passes under a house, turn left.

The particularly large **Grand Mosque** in front was built by the Almohad Sultan Abu Yusuf Yacoub in the late 12th century, although the minaret and door are both modern. Just beyond the mosque is the tomb of Salé's patron saint, **Sidi Abdallah Ben Hassoun**. The *medersa* is to the left of the mosque.

Before you pass through the beautiful Merinid doorway, note the intricate decorations below a green-tiled roof resting on cedar lintels. The *medersa* is quite small, with a courtyard surrounded by a gallery, its columns decorated with *zellige* mosaic tiling. The walls above the columns are decorated with geometric and floral motifs, while the ceilings of the ground floor have panelled wood in geometric patterns. Both the wood carving of the prayer hall ceiling and the stucco have been restored, but much of the decoration is original and in good condition. To reach the upper floors, return to the entrance and climb the stairs. These are the students' cells, which seem tiny and ill-lit, but give an insight into the nature of *medersa* life. From the roof is a view of Salé and, beyond it, Rabat.

Mausoleum of Sidi Ben Ashir at Tabib

The Mausoleum of Sidi Ben Ashir at Tabib is located close to the western wall of the cemetery that lies between the medina and the sea. This 14th-century Muslim saint was famous for curing people, and the sick still visit his tomb for its curative powers. This is a very striking building, quite tall, brilliant white in contrast to the blue sky and the background of ochre of the city walls. Adjacent, in the walls, cannon still point defensively out to sea.

Foundouk al Askour

The Foundouk al Askour is worth seeing for its portal. From Bab Bou Hajar follow Rue Bab al Khabbaz, and take the fourth lane on the left past the park, which is obstructed by three concrete posts. This leads to a textile souk. After 120 m the souk passes under an arch. On the right is the *foundouk* (merchants' hostel). It was originally built in about 1350 as a *medersa* by Abu Inan, son of Abul Hassan, and was later converted. The door is surrounded by a partially restored *zellige* mosaic of the *darj w ktaf* pattern. Above this is a panel of *zellige* with the traditional eight-pointed star motif and, above that, a row of nine niches carved into a plaster panel. Inside there is a courtyard with two storeys of arcades.

Souks

In this area there are some interesting souks, which are perhaps more traditional than those of Rabat, and worth exploring. The textile market is Souk el Merzouk, while Souk el Ghezel is the wool market. There are stonemasons and carpenters in Rue Kechachine, and blacksmiths and brassworkers in Rue Haddadine. The Souk el Merzouk is noted for its jewellery and embroidery. The medina of Salé is also noted for a procession of multicoloured candles, or thick poles bearing various representations, which occurs every year on the afternoon before the Prophet's birthday, Mouloud an Nabi. This proceeds through the town, culminating at the **Tomb of Sidi Abdallah Ben Hassoun**. He is the patron saint of Salé and this is the most venerable of the sanctuaries in the city. It is also the most picturesque, with a most curious dome and an exterior gallery decorated with polychrome tiles. The seafaring past of the city is particularly visible in this event, with the men in pirate costumes.

North of Rabat → *For listings, see pages 303-305.*

Mamora Forest

To the northeast of Rabat, the Mamora Forest is a peaceful area of cork and eucalyptus trees. Around half the cork oaks of Morocco are found here. The eucalyptus is also harvested for commercial purposes, and there are plantations of pine and acacia. More unusual is the Mamora wild pear, a tall tree, growing up to 15 m, which has white flowers in spring. There are *dayats* (shallow lakes) in the region and, in wetter years, these attract the white stork. The spotted flycatcher is a summer visitor, as is the magnificent blue roller. The turtle dove, visiting from the South, is declining in numbers as human hunting continues. Indeed, the whole area is under human pressure, as the neighbouring settlements expand and people use the forest as a source of charcoal and a place for grazing their livestock. Bissected in part by the main north–south *autoroute*, the forest can also be accessed off the Meknès road. Turn off left at Sidi Allal Bahroui. Return via the N1 and R405.

Jardins Exotiques
ⓘ *About 15 km north of Rabat, at Bouknadel on the N1, and the No 28 bus route, 0900-1830. 5dh, children 3dh.*

These 4 ha of garden were the work of French horticulturalist and Moroccophile, M François, in the 1950s. Originally, there were over 1500 species and varieties of plants from all over the world, laid out in a network of pools, bridges and summerhouses. There was a Japanese garden with bamboo bridges and flat-stone paths, a section of Brazilian rainforest, and an area of plants from Polynesia. Unfortunately, the Moroccan pavilion is in ruins, the Middle Atlas apes look miserable in their minute cages, and the general tendency is towards Barbary jungle. However, children with a taste for adventure could have a whale of a time exploring. There are some fine palm trees and flowering datura. Things horticultural apart, the Jardins Exotiques seem to function as a minor Garden of Eden where local couples discourse in the shade, safely out of the way of prying family eyes.

Plage des Nations
The Plage des Nations at Sidi Bouknadel, about 25 km northeast of Rabat, is very popular with the affluent, and more of a family beach than those of Rabat-Salé, although the currents can be dangerous. Take bus No 28 from Salé, and walk 1 km from the turning, or in summer share a *grand taxi* from Salé.

Dar Beghazi
ⓘ *T0537-822178, Mon-Sat, 40dh for main rooms, 100dh for whole collection.*

The Dar Beghazi is another sight close to Rabat, accessible for those with their own vehicle. Situated opposite the turn-off to the Plage des Nations, on the N1 road north of Salé, this home has been turned into a private museum to house the Beghazi family's collection of carpets, weapons and jewellery. Admission is expensive, but there is a lot to see, including a rather splendid coach.

Kénitra → *Colour map 1, B2.*
Kénitra is an industrial and military centre of importance within Morocco. It was a small military fort until 1913, when the French built a new town, as well as an artificial harbour used as a military port and to export citrus fruit and other products from the rich agricultural areas of the surrounding Gharb region. The port was developed to replace Larache, in the Spanish zone, and Tangier, in the International Zone. In 1933, Kénitra was renamed Port Lyautey by the French, after the first Resident-General of the Moroccan protectorate. US troops landed here in November 1942 as part of Operation Torch and experienced heavy casualties under fire from the port at Mehdiya. In 1947 the US returned to establish an important naval base, which they used until 1977. After independence, Port Lyautey was renamed Kénitra and it remains important as a military centre and port. It lies on the N1 from Rabat to Tangier. For the first-time visitor to Morocco, the attraction

of Kénitra (beyond some early 20th-century architecture) is its potential as a base for trips to the nearby Roman site of Thamusida and to Mehdiya, with its fine kasbah, on the coast.

Mehdiya → *Colour map 1, B2.*

Mehdiya (also spelt Mehdia and Mahdia) Plage is Kénitra's one-horse beach resort, noted for windsurfing but more interesting to visit for its kasbah (some way from the town's seafront) and the nearby nature reserve around Lac de Sidi Bourhaba.

Arriving in Mehdiya Bus No 9 from Kénitra has its terminus just opposite the kasbah entrance. If you are driving from Rabat, turn left off the N1 for Mehdiya Plage as you head north at a complicated junction with the Café Bustan and petrol. The road winds over heathland to drop down to Mehdiya Plage (where there are lots of new villas). For the kasbah, head through the town. You'll note a crumbling flight of steps up to the kasbah on your right (east). Parking may be awkward. Otherwise, follow the road round and up the hillside (estuary on your left), turn right (new housing area on your right), eucalyptus wood on your left. The entrance gate to the kasbah soon comes into view.

Background Historians think that a Carthaginian trading post was established here in the sixth century BC. Around the 10th century, the site was occupied by the Berbers. Naval shipyards were established here by the Almohads. By the 16th century, a small and active commercial port visited by European merchants, Al Mamora had grown up close to the site of present day Mehdiya. The Portuguese, then expanding along the African coast after taking Ceuta in the 15th century, became interested in the area, and thus it was that King Manuel of Portugal sent out an expeditionary force, which took the little town in June 1515, renaming it São João da Mamora. The Portuguese were quickly defeated, however, and the port became a lair for pirate adventurers. By the early 17th century, along with Salé and Algiers, it was one of the leading pirate ports in North Africa and a source of irritation to the European trading nations. Like Salé (Sila in Arabic), home of a band of renegades known as the Sallee Rovers, it functioned as a sort of autonomous republic. For a while Mamora was ruled by the English adventurer Henry Mainwaring, who later continued his career in the Royal Navy before becoming a member of the English parliament (1620-1623). And it was also at Mamora that another adventurer, Saint Mandrier, was captured by Moroccan forces; this enterprising Frenchman was later to become technical adviser to the sultan on fortifications and cannon foundries.

The pirate republics of Morocco harmed European trade with the Indies. In 1614, Spanish forces took Mamora and, on a hillside overlooking the river, a new fortress was constructed. Named San Miguel de Ultramar, it forms the basis of most of the kasbah still surviving today. In May 1681, this fortress in turn fell to the advancing armies of the Alaouite Sultan Moulay Ismaïl. The victory marked the end of the Spanish *presidios*: Larache and Tangier were subsequently evacuated.

The newly taken fort was renamed El Mehdiya, 'the citadel delivered'. (Henceforth the name Mamora was to be used for the vast cork oak forests to the northeast of Salé.) Moulay Ismaïl installed a garrison, strengthened the walls and began work on a new port at the mouth of the River Sebou, ultimately abandoned in the late 18th century.

Under the French, the fortress was occupied and was the scene of clashes between US and French forces during the American Expeditionary Force landings of November 1942.

Mehdiya kasbah Uninhabited apart from a few cows, the kasbah of Mehdiya is definitely worth a visit if you are in town. There is no entrance fee, although there may be a man sitting at the gate who should be given a small tip. Within the walls, the small mosque with its whitewashed minaret is still used by local people. The smaller of the two entrance gates, **Bab el Aïn**, is of Spanish origin, while the other gate, the grander **Bab Jedid** (New Gate), flanked by two massive rectangular towers, was erected by Moulay Ismaïl. From the roof terraces there is a magnificent panorama of the river and ocean to the northwest, and over to the Sidi Bourhaba lagoon, a protected area to the south. The northwest bastion, **Borj Bab el Aïn**, is well preserved with seven cannons still in place. Below, next to the estuary, is a labyrinth of extensive storerooms, well protected by a sea wall.

The most important building, however, is the governor's house, the **Dar el Makhzen**, which, with its great mosaic patio, must have been an extremely fine residence in its day, with extensive outbuildings – close to the main entrance are the remains of a hammam and a *foundouk* (merchants' hostel). A flight of brick steps leads up to dusty overgrown terraces. Today, however, the bustle of traders and soldiers in the fortress overlooking the Sebou belongs very much to the past: goats graze on the weeds growing out of the paving, fig trees sprout from the walls, and there is no foreign army to menace the great bastions and moats. Despite the neglect, the cobbling and some other features indicate that this kasbah was restored and used under the French. Birdwatchers will find finches flitting between the crab-apple and tamarisk bushes.

The southern section of the Lac de Sidi Bourhaba and adjacent marshes are the focus of the nature reserve, popular for birdwatching. The koubba has a festival in August. The northern section of the lake is a pleasant area for picnicking, either by the water's edge, which can be marshy, or in the surrounding woodlands. Overwintering waterbirds are the main interest (literally thousands of ducks) and, in April, you can see spring migrants. African marsh owls are frequently reported. There is a keeper's residence on the east side.

Ancient Thamusida → *Colour map 1, B2.*

The remains of the ancient Roman town of Thamusida can make an interesting excursion from Kénitra, though the ruins are only really feasible if you have your own transport or a lot of time. Ideally, go by car and try to cover Thamusida along with Mehdiya, the Roman site at Banasa and the stone circle at Mzoura in a long day trip.

Getting there The remains are in open agricultural land near Sidi Ali Ben Ahmed, on the left bank of the Oued Sebou, 18 km from the *oued* mouth. To get there, take the N1 for some 10 km north of Kénitra. At the major roundabout, take the turn-off signposted Tangier 222 km, Tetouan 249 km. After passing under a railway bridge, continue northwards. The turn-off left is easily missed: look out for a pink café, some 25 m before a small Total petrol station and a mosque. Turn left at the café, and a sandy track will take you past small houses and market gardens to a sort of crossroads (go straight on, not left for another small mosque). Crossing the fields, eventually you approach the riverbank, where the track follows round to the left. Markers to look out for are the distinctive white dome, or *koubba*, of Sidi Ali Ben Ahmed, a stand of trees and, on the river, the boatmen. In the far distance, the hill of the Mehdiya kasbah is just visible.

Note that access in wet weather is problematic in a small hire car. If coming down the N1 from the north, you should look out for the roadside houses of the village of Ouled Slama, and on the right of the road, the cream-painted administrative building of the commune rurale. The Total garage and pink café are about 100 m further on.

The site Thamusida was built in an excellent position, protected from flooding (being on a flattish hillock about 12 m above sea level) but accessible from the sea by good-size boats making use of the tidal flow. The site of Roman Thamusida had been settled on and off since prehistoric times but its first recorded mention is by Ptolemy. The Roman garrison was established here under the Flavians, and monuments have been found dating from that period. So far, discoveries include the remains of a temple with three shrines beside the *oued*, the baths and some dwellings; one named the House of the Stone Floor. This **Maison du Dallage** to the east of the complex has the traditional open central courtyard with the triclinium (dining room) at the eastern end. The baths, close to the *oued*, have been altered and extended a number of times, finally covering an area of around 3000 sq m – the ground plan showing a division into separate sections for men and women. Evidence also points to the existence of fish-salting works, an iron works and shops.

The large camp to the southwest of the site was constructed by order of Marcus Aurelius. It measures 166 m by 139 m and is considered to have been large enough to house a substantial military presence. The walls of the fort had four gates, one more or less central in each wall, and 14 towers which project inwards. In the centre is the praetorium, a rectangular porticoed courtyard 45 m by 30 m with rooms on three sides. In the southwest side, one of the rooms, built on a podium and reached by four steps, is larger. On the northwest side of the praetorium, projecting into the main courtyard, are the remains of a hall constructed in the time of Septimus Severus. A wall with a number of entrance gates encloses the town on the three land sides, the fourth side being protected by the *oued*. At intervals along the wall are semicircular towers which project outwards.

Excavations began in the early 1930s. On the basis of the finds, the settlement can be assumed to have been prosperous and quite active well into the third century AD. However, it is thought that the whole area was abandoned quite suddenly between AD 274 and 280. Excavation continues sporadically, and Thamusida remains a sleepy place, the croaking of frogs and drone of irrigation pumps occasionally disturbed by flights out of the Kénitra airbase.

Souk el Arba du Gharb → *Colour map 1, B2.*

Souk el Arba du Gharb (Rharb), the 'Wednesday souk in the West', is an important market town. It is the focal point for the rich agricultural region of the Gharb, which extends as far north as Larache, and as far south as Kénitra. Once important for cereal production, the region later became a centre for citrus and vegetable production. It is from Souk el Arba du Gharb that you will turn westwards for Moulay Bousselham on the coast. There are regular trains to Tangier, Meknès, Fès, Oujda, Rabat, Casablanca and to Marrakech, as well as regular buses and *grands taxis* to Ouezzane and Moulay Bousselham.

Moulay Bousselham → *Colour map 1, A2.*

The small beach resort of Moulay Bousselham is a relaxed summery place, increasingly popular with Fassis and others who have built second homes there. There is a fine stretch of coast but Moulay Bousselham is best known for its lagoon, Merdja Zerga ('the blue lagoon'), an important wintering site for migrating birds. Although easily reached from Souk el Arba du Gharb, only 44 km along the S216, Moulay Bousselham is bypassed by most tourists.

Background Moulay Bousselham, 'the man of the cape', is named after a 10th-century saint and mystic, who supposedly came from Egypt and converted the Atlantic coast of Morocco to Islam. The memory of Moulay Bousselham is commemorated in a *moussem* (religious festival), in July , and in a nearby *koubba* (tomb). The beach is spectacular but dangerous for swimming, although not bad for fishing. If you have a car, you could take in the nearish Roman sites of Banasa, near Souk Tlata du Gharb, and Thamusida, near Kénitra, on the way south to Rabat.

The lagoon and birdlife   The lagoon, Merdja Zerga, is one of Morocco's largest, covering over 30 sq km. This and the surrounding wetlands are a designated reserve offering protection for migrating and overwintering waterbirds.

By car it is possible to approach the reserve from the south. Proceed from Souk el Arba du Gharb and, after 34 km, turn left on the 2301. After crossing the Nador Channel (Canal de Daoura), turn sharp right and park in the village, Daoura Oulad Mesbah. Access to the reserve from Moulay Bousselham is across the Oued Drade, which flows to the south of the village. Arrange a lift or hire a rowing boat (bargain firmly) and arrange for a return trip with the fisherman who ferries you across. The track down the west side of the lagoon goes through Daoura Roissia to the minor coast road, but provides ample opportunity for peaceful observation. It is estimated that half of the ducks and small waders wintering in Morocco north of latitude 30°N are found here. It will be impossible to miss the greater flamingos and spoonbills and the familiar wigeon, mallard, shoveler, shelduck and teal. Sighting a slender-billed curlew is less likely.

Ancient Banasa → *Colour map 1, B2.*
If you need to prioritize, Banasa is the most important (in terms of visible ruins) of the ancient sites reached from the Rabat–Tangier N1 road. Like Thamusida, it is located south of the Oued Sebou, probably bridged here in ancient times. Unlike Thamusida, access is by metalled road. Banasa is awkward to get to without your own transport.

Getting there   Travelling north from Rabat on the N1, you need to turn right at a minor junction south of Souk Tlata du Gharb ('Tuesday Souk in the Gharb'): look out for some abandoned farm buildings just before the turn and an avenue of eucalyptus trees on the main road. Big road signs near the turn (showing Rabat 100 km and Tangier 173 km) are parallel to the N1 and so are not easily visible. After the turn, follow the narrow road to the bridge. Here the road is being widened and follows the river to your left. At a T-junction, go left and, after about 2 km, you will find a rusty sign telling you to turn off left for Banasa. The track runs across the fields and the site is easily located by a mosque and the domed shrine of Sidi Ali Boujnoun.

The site   Excavation at Banasa was not easy, as remains were buried beneath many layers of alluvium deposited by the flooding *oued*. The earliest settlement recorded here was third century BC, but the main colony was founded at the end of the first century BC by Roman Emperor Augustus. Remains include traces of houses (some indicating wealthy owners), five baths and shops. A wealth of distinctive pottery, mosaics and inscriptions has also been discovered. The alignment of the streets on a northeast-southwest grid can be seen, with a forum marking the centre of the town. Unfortunately, most of the better building material was removed and 'recycled'. The discovery here of a number of bronze inscriptions, legal texts, military diplomas and decrees of patronage, some of which are now visible in the Rabat Archaeological Museum, make this an important site.

There are also a few mosaics at the site. They include an ornamental design with the head of the ocean in the centre from one of the excavated baths; one containing fighting cocks and a bag of money; and a number with marine scenes. In one of the baths, traces of painted stucco and a very faint mural in a niche can just about be distinguished.

Arbaoua → *Colour map 1, A2.*

Arbaoua is signed to the west of the N1, and with its shady trees is a popular stopping place for Moroccan families making the journey back from Europe by car. (Note that the mosquitoes can be a nuisance.) The old frontier post between the Spanish and French zones of protectoral Morocco is at Kedhadhra, marked by a fine reinforced concrete building and lots of stalls selling pottery and wicker furniture. North of here, the first major town is Ksar el Kebir.

Ksar el Kebir (formerly Alcazarquivir) → *Colour map 1, A2.*

Kasar el Kebir means the 'Great Fortress' and probably stands on the site of the Roman colony Oppidum Novum, 'new town'. Off the main N1 road, it is only a must if you have an interest in neo-Moorish Spanish colonial architecture.

The exact location of the Roman town is uncertain. Two funerary inscriptions were found here, one in Greek and one in Latin. In its favour, Ksar el Kebir is close to other ancient settlements and, if the Romans had wanted a strongpoint to guard a crossing of the Oued Loukkos, where better than here? An 11th-century settlement here was expanded and fortified by Yacoub al Mansour in the late 12th century.

But Ksar el Kebir's chief claim to fame is that it lies near the site of a great battle. Nearby, in 1578, the famous Battle of the Three Kings was fought, in which King Sebastian of Portugal, Saâdian Sultan Abd al Malek and a claimant to the throne, former Sultan el Mutawakkil, all died. The flower of Portuguese chivalry was wiped out, leading to the end of Portugal as an independent nation for some 100 years. Moulay Ismaïl destroyed much of the town in the 17th century.

The Spanish occupied Ksar el Kebir in 1911, rebuilding it, renaming it Alcazarquivir, and developing it as a military centre. There are a number of Spanish buildings in various stages of decay. Particularly fine is the Alhambra-style decoration of the former officers' mess, now housing local Ministry of Education offices. The women who work there may allow you to have a look in. In the same area, there is a flag factory with weavers using handlooms to make red cloth for flags for official buildings. The regional market is held on Sunday outside the station. There is also a much transformed Grand Mosque (an Almohad foundation) near to a Merinid *medersa*.

South of Rabat

Zaër Forest → *Colour map 1, B1.*

The region to the south of Rabat, inland from the bustle of the coast roads, is known as the Zaër Forest, with valleys, the Karifla Gorges and rolling hills clothed with cork oak, juniper and acacia. It is impossible to explore this area without a car. A possible circuit leaves Rabat on the R401, follows the side of the *oued* and passes through the small village of Aïn el Aouda at Km 28. Turn right after a further 11 km towards Merchouch, almost immediately crossing the Oued Karifla. At Merchouch turn west along the S106 and across the Karifla Gorges, to the ancient rest site of Sidi Bettache on the old road from Rabat to Marrakech. Enjoy a steep descent and ascent on this winding route. Take time to admire the views. The S208 leads north to Sidi Yahia des Zaër and on to Temara. There are numerous small tracks into the forest and down to the streams.

One of the best times to do this tour is the spring: if the winter has been rainy, the dayats will have water, and there will be abundant wild flowers. There are numerous larks, warblers and shrikes in the open fields. The road between Sidi Bettache and Sidi Yahia des Zaër is reported to offer the best chance of sighting a double-spurred francolin. The valleys, too, have their bird populations, in particular magnificent bee-eaters with their cliffside nests.

A second route into this area leaves from Ben Slimane, a market town on the edge of the Zaër forest. There are some interesting tracks through this area, suitable for cars. The route recommended in the forest leaves Ben Slimane on the S106 going east. Ignore the turn right to El Gara and, after 15 km, take the next right into the forest. After 16 km turn left to Bir el Kelb and El Khatouat. This is a climb up the side of Jbel Khatouat (830 m). At El Khatouat turn west. Subsequently, either the first turn right after 12 km or the second turn right after a further 10 km will take you back to Ben Slimane. The first is slower but more scenic.

Temara → *Colour map 1, B1.*

The town, 14 km from Rabat off the N1, and the ruins of a kasbah, built by Moulay Ismaïl, can be reached on bus No 17 from Avenue Hassan II in Rabat. The beach is 4 km to the west. It is a popular destination, as the beach is long, sandy and clean.

◉ Salé and excursions from Rabat listings

For sleeping and eating price codes and other relevant information, see pages 22-28.

◉ Where to stay

Salé *p293, map p294*
Very few travellers stay in Salé, as there are few hotels and the city is easily accessible from Rabat. It's also a sleepy sort of place, with little streetlife in the evening.

Plage des Nations *p297*
€€ **Hotel Firdaous**, T0537-780407. Simple, clean and friendly hotel purpose-built in the 1970s. Also has a bar, restaurant and pool that is open to all-comers for a small charge.

Kénitra *p297*
€€ **Hotel Jacaranda**, Pl Administrative, T0537-373030. Reliable but unexciting large business-orientated 3-star, with restaurant, bar, heated pool and sauna. Avoid rooms overlooking the service station.
€€ **Hotel Mamora**, T0537-371775. Clean, but uninspiring, business-style hotel with good restaurant, a bar and a decent-sized pool.
€ **Hotel de France**, Av Mohammed V. One of several cheap hotels here.

€ **Hotel de la Poste**, Av Mohammed Diouri. Perhaps the best of the cheap hotels. Showers in most rooms.

Mehdiya *p298*
Camping
Camping Mehdia, north of the town next to Oued Sebou. Open in the summer with pool, restaurant and shop, this 15-ha site is 100 m from the beach. Bar, snacks, showers, laundry, first aid, electricity for caravans, petrol at 20 km. There are cafés near the beach. Try the **Restaurant-Café Dauphine** for fish.

Moulay Bousselham *p300*
€€ **Villa Nora**, T0537-432017. This guesthouse has a wonderful location right beside the sea but has unfortunately seen better days. The food, though, is exceptional.
€ **La Maison des Oiseaux**, on your left as you approach the village, T0537-432543, T0661-301067 (mob), http://moulay. bousselham.free.fr. The 'house of the birds' is a pretty, whitewashed place, with a garden and quirky decoration, run by a Franco-Moroccan couple, Gentiane and Karim. As well as individual rooms, there is accommodation to suit families and groups.

From here you can also do trips on the lagoon to see the birds.

Camping

Camping Moulay Bousselham. This is a basic place, with many mosquitoes in summer. Site of 15 ha, with bar, snacks, restaurant, grocery shop, pool, showers, laundry, electricity for caravans, petrol at 100 m.

Arbaoua *p302*

€ **Hotel Route de France**, T0539-902668. Bath, mid-range meals.

Camping

There is a 4-ha campsite with showers, laundry, electricity for caravans.

Temara *p303*

€€ **Hotel La Felouque**, T0537-744388, www.lafelouque.com. 24 rooms, restaurant, bar, tennis, a good pool and grassy garden. Crowded at weekends.
€€ **Hotel Panorama des Sables**, T0537-744289. Terrace overlooking the beach.

Camping

Camping la Palmeraie, T0537-749251. A 3-ha site, 100 m to beach, bar, snacks, restaurant, groceries, showers, laundry, petrol 600 m, electricity for caravans.
Camping Rose Marie, Ech Chiahna, south of Temara Plage. 100 m from the beach, restaurant, showers, laundry, electricity for caravans.

❼ Restaurants

Salé *p293, map p294*
There are a number of small and cheap café-restaurants just inside both main gates and along Rue Kechachin.

Kénitra *p297*
There is no shortage of restaurants on Av Hassan II and Av Mohammed V. **Hotel Mamora** and **Hotel La Rotonde** are recommended as places to eat and drink.

Moulay Bousselham *p300*
Eat at L'Ocean or La Jeunesse, or at one of the restaurants down by the lagoon, where the fishermen's rowing boats are pulled up on the beach.

⦾ Shopping

Salé *p293, map p294*
The artisans of Salé are as talented as their neighbours in Rabat, and quality goods are available in the medina. Look at the pottery (some is very distinctive), tooled leatherware, ironware, carpets (although perhaps not the best place to buy these), fine embroidery, drapery and, for the beach, rush matting.

Complexe artisanal d'Oulja, some 3 km from the town. Easily accessible by *petit taxi* from Salé (say 10dh). There is a central exhibition space with café and small restaurant. A series of craft potters, basket makers and blacksmiths are based in purpose-built workshops with adjoining exhibition space. Although many of the items on sale (apart from the pottery) are a little bulky and heavy to take home by plane, the Oulja centre does give a good idea of the range of products available. The high-quality basket work is particularly good value. The *zellige* work table tops are also very reasonable in price – but extremely heavy. To get back to Rabat from Oulja, there are buses running from the nearby crossroads.

⊖ Transport

Salé *p293, map p294*
Gare Salé tram station and **Gare Salé** railway station are opposite each other on Av Hassan II. Trams run Mon-Fri 0700-2100 and Sat 0700-1300. Take Tram Line 1 south from Gare Salé (via Medina Salé and Bab Mrissa tram stops) to get to **Rabat**. Gare Salé railway station has frequent daily services to **Casablanca** (via Rabat) from 0617 to 2048.

Kénitra *p297*
Bus

The **CTM** bus station is on Blvd Mohammed V. There's 1 bus daily to **Rabat** (1 hr) and **Casablanca** (2½ hrs) at 1100. Bus No 9 goes to **Mehdiya** but *grands taxis* are easier.

Train

From the railway station, south of the town centre, trains leave regularly to **Asilah**, **Tangier**, **Meknès**, **Fès**, **Oujda** and **Marrakech**, and there are services almost every 30 mins to **Rabat** and **Casablanca** 0230-2100.

Mehdiya *p298*

Mehdiya is 11 km from Kénitra, with plentiful *grands taxis*. Bus No 9 goes to **Kénitra.**

Moulay Bousselham *p300*

The village is just off the northern autoroute, midway between Rabat and Tangier. It is 130 km from **Rabat**, an easy 1 hr 20 mins' drive. Grands taxi to nearby **Souk el Arba du Gharb** (25 mins). Buses to Souk el Arba can take much longer, depending on the number of stops.

Ancient Banasa *p301*

From Ksar el Kebir there are 9 trains a day to **Rabat** and **Casablanca**, with the last service at 2310; 10 per day to **Tangier**; 5 to **Meknès** and **Fès**; 2 to **Oujda**; and 7 to **Marrakech**.

Casablanca

In the 1930s, only two French achievements are said to have surprised the Americans: the First World War and Casablanca. A boom-town, nicknamed 'the African Marseilles', 'Casa' was a city where you could drive around at 130 kph and where the streets were filled with luxurious cars. The city grew from a small trading port at the end of the 19th century into one of Africa's biggest cities. With a centre planned by Henri Prost in the early 20th century, the city, with its wide avenues, elegant buildings and huge port, was held to be the finest achievement of French colonial urbanism. It has remained the economic capital of independent Morocco, the centre for trade and industry, finance and the stock exchange. Sprawling and dynamic and with a population of more than four million people, Casa is now a modern, noisy and chaotic metropolis with its fair share of urban problems, as well as some interesting neo-Moorish and art deco architecture, an enormous mosque and an enviable seafront location. ▸▸ *For listings, see pages 315-323.*

Arriving in Casablanca → *Colour map 2, A4.*

Getting there

You may well fly into Casablanca, in which case, from **Mohammed V airport**, either take a *grand taxi* (250dh, 300dh at night) to the city centre (where most of the hotels are) or the shuttle train (30dh) to either **Casa-Port** station (the terminus, again close to the central area where the hotels are) or to **Casa-Voyageurs**, where there are connections onward for all the other main cities. Casa-Port station is also 10-minutes' walk from the main **CTM bus station**, just off Avenue des FAR behind the Hotel Sheraton. From there, coaches depart for destinations across the country. There are car hire agencies, ATMs and banks at the airport.

Arriving by **train** at Casa-Voyageurs station, you will find that the taxi drivers do not want to take individual passengers. From Casa-Voyageurs to the city centre should not cost more than 15-20dh, depending on the traffic. Watch out for taxi drivers who will try various tricks to persuade you to go to hotels for which they are paid commission.
▸▸ *See Transport, page 322, for further details.*

Getting around

Casablanca is a big place. The central area, with most of the interesting architecture, between the medina/Casa-Port station and the Parc de la Ligue Arabe, is just about small enough to do on foot. Other sites which you may want to visit – the seafront, or Corniche, with its restaurants and beach clubs at Aïn Diab, the Hassan II Mosque or the Quartier des Habous, a sort of garden city for Muslim notables – are short hops from the centre in one of Casablanca's red taxis (10-20dh for the trip, have change ready). There are numerous public and private bus lines, but it's better to maximize time by taking taxis.

Tourist information **Office du Tourisme** ① *55 Rue Omar Slaoui, T0522-271177*. **Syndicat d'Initiative** ① *98 Av Mohammed V, T0522-221524*. The latter is perhaps the more helpful of the two. There are also information booths in the city centre – they are friendly and eager to help but have almost no information to impart.

Background

Bold Phoenician pilots founded a trading post close to the present site of Casablanca during the seventh century BC, and the discovery of a Roman galley indicates use, if not settlement, of the area in the first century BC. (The silver coins found on this vessel are on show at the **Banque National du Maroc** in Rabat.) In the seventh century AD the Berber tribe, the Barghawata, held this area. It was conquered by the Almohads in 1188, and developed by Sultan Abd el Moumen as a port. In the 14th century the Portuguese established a settlement here on the site of the village of Anfa, but when it became a pirates' base in 1468, they destroyed it, repeating this act in 1515. The Portuguese

① **Casablanca**

re-established themselves in the late 16th century, and stayed until 1755, when an earthquake destroyed the settlement. The town was resurrected in the mid-18th century for strategic reasons, under Sultan Mohammed Ben Abdallah. There are various stories about how the town acquired its name ('the white house', Dar el Baydha in Arabic). One version says that it was named after the Caïd's house, a large white building visible from a distance.

French colonization

In the 19th century, European traders settled at Casablanca and, at the beginning of the 20th century the French obtained permission from Sultan Abd al Aziz to construct an artificial harbour. This was the beginning of Casablanca's rapid expansion. The French occupied the city in 1907 (and the rest of Morocco in 1912). Adventurers of all kinds were attracted to the place with its Wild West frontier feel. This first wave of French immigration greatly displeased the aristocratic resident-general, Lyautey, who wrote that "The citizens were Frenchmen who had built, beside the Moroccan city, a town to their own liking, but of the same disorderly, speculative and soulless nature as the American boom towns."

The town grew quickly: in 1907, the population was 20,000, including 5000 Jews and 1000 Europeans; by 1912, the population was 59,000, of which there were 20,000 Europeans and 9000 Jews. Morocco's first factory was founded in 1908 in Casablanca, the first labour union was founded in 1910, and the first modern banks came with the protectorate. Land speculation was rampant, with both Muslims and Europeans involved.

Lyautey was highly suspicious of the European inhabitants of this boom town on the coast of 'traditional' Morocco. (When he decided that Rabat should be the capital in 1913, there were street protests in Casa.) However, it became imperative to do something for the

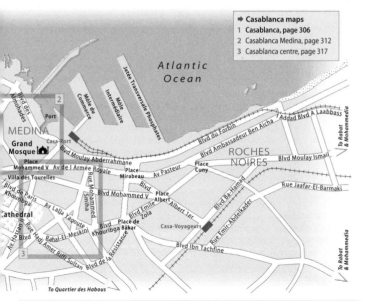

→ **Casablanca maps**
1 Casablanca, page 306
2 Casablanca Medina, page 312
3 Casablanca centre, page 317

city: in 1913, an observer described it as "an ocean of hovels, a sort of unstructured suburb to an as yet unbuilt metropolis."

Planning the new city

In 1915 Lyautey and his chief architect, Henri Prost, began work on planning the new city centre, creating a grid of wide boulevards, lined with fine stucco office and apartment buildings. Key state buildings (as in Rabat) were styled with detailing derived from Moroccan traditional architecture, a style known as Arabiasance. And, one of the first acts of the new city administration was to create a 4 km ring boulevard, considered far too wide at the time. But the city was to grow far more rapidly than anyone predicted.

Prost certainly had no easy task, given the settler interests at stake. His plan covered an area of 1000 ha. With a proposed density of 150 people per hectare, the city was designed for 150,000 people – which led to accusations of megalomania. Industrial areas were situated north and east of the centre, on rocky ground, while residential areas, on more fertile soil, were to the west and southwest. Between the two, Prost laid out a centre focusing on two large public squares, the Place de France, centre for commercial activity, and the Place Lyautey, site of the main administrative buildings. The walls of the medina were in part demolished. The Avenue du 4ème Zouaves, today's Avenue Houphouêt Boigny, led down to the railway station and the port. A fan-shaped system of roads and ring boulevards structured the new city – and it is a tribute to Prost's planning that the traffic runs as smoothly as it does today.

In terms of physical planning, colonial Casablanca was a relatively successful city – even though Prost's zoning was not always respected, and the suburbs subsequently sprawled far beyond the core, with vast planned projects and unplanned *bidonvilles* (the original *bidonville* or tin can city was in Casablanca). Between 1921 and 1951 the number of inhabitants grew by 85% due to an exodus from the Moroccan countryside and arrivals fleeing the wars of Europe. At the end of the Second World War Casablanca had a population of 700,000. With rising unrest in the expanding slums, it was essential to improve housing conditions. Planner Ecochard and the Atbat-Afrique team developed the concept of culturally adapted housing for the masses, that is to say inward-looking, multi-storey patio houses for the poor Muslim communities. However, as André Adam, chronicler of Casablanca's development, put it, "in her hanging patio, today's woman is like a bird in a cage".

After the war

In 1950, Casablanca was an exciting place to be, drawing in capitalists fleeing the socialist government in France, and where the focus of debates was Moroccan independence. A new building boom produced some modest skyscrapers and Casablanca-based trade unions were important in the nationalist struggle, notably in the riots of 1952 and insurrection from 1953 to 1955.

The city has continued to expand and has constructed a number of new architectural landmarks: the gigantic Hassan II Mosque, right on the Atlantic, and, on the Boulevard Zerktouni, the Twin Center, designed by Catalan architect Richard Bofill, dwarfing the Maârif neighbourhood.

Despite the increased building speculation at the expense of older property, it seems that Casablanca's architectural heritage is gaining recognition and there is increased official awareness that the city's architecture is potentially a draw for tourists. But Casablanca also has problems. The mix of ocean-humid air and diesel pollution makes an unpleasant cocktail. There are huge economic disparities between the wealthy villa quarters of Anfa Supérieur and Aïn Diab and extensive areas of sub-standard housing.

Laboratory of urban planning

For Resident-General Lyautey, Casablanca was to be the commercial nerve centre of the French protectorate. The decision was taken to build a vast new port at a site which many critics saw as totally impracticable. But the technical difficulties were overcome and, in 1921, the new port complex, with its kilometre-long **Delure Jetty**, was inaugurated, confirming Casablanca's world port status.

As for the rest of the city, the architecture of the early period of the protectorate was characterized by a variant of the neo-Moorish style, already used in Algeria and Tunisia. Lyautey wanted Morocco's official buildings to be simple and sobre in style, and some of the results can be seen in **Place Mohammed V**.

Later, in the interwar period, a local variant of art deco took root, using geometric motifs in low relief and wrought ironwork, and occasionally incorporating plaques of Moroccan *zellige* mosaic decoration. Set-back terraces on the top storeys and horizontal detailing gave the larger buildings a sculptural quality. The art deco aesthetic, strengthened by the success of the 1925 Paris Exhibition of Decorative Arts and Modern Industries, can be traced in buildings as diverse as the **Hotel de Ville** (by Marius Boyer, undoubtedly the leading architect of the city) and Paul Tournon's towering white **Cathédrale du Sacré Coeur**, occasionally used as a performance space.

One of the first cities to be planned using aerial photography and formal zoning regulations, Casablanca was also one of the first places to see the use of revolutionary construction techniques like concrete formwork. In the early 1930s, streamlining and speed stripes were all the fashion – hence the horizontal window bands of many

buildings – and the first mini-skyscrapers appeared, marking a break with the six-storey apartment buildings. Plot size and land prices (and the enterprising spirit of 'French California') allowed the construction of buildings difficult to envisage in the crowded cities of France. And, of course, there were numerous adaptations to local conditions: terraces and belvederes, granito floorings for the daily washing of floors, and separate servants' quarters. The year 1951 saw the completion of Morandi's **Immeuble Liberté** – 17 storeys high and in the finest ocean-liner style. (If you have time, take a look at the *Villa Souissi*, near the Espace Anfa, a private 1950s home transformed into a bakery and pâtisserie.)

With the arrival of the Allies in 1942 and the new US base at Nouasseur, American influence grew. American cinema and its capital Hollywood (with a similar climate to Casablanca), inspired the city's wealthy families. The new villas of the *zones de plaisance*, such as Anfa and Le Polo, were luxurious and functional according to the tenets of the modern movement. In a few decades, the city had acquired the most up-to-date facilities for work and leisure, and cinemas had a key place: the Rialto (1930) and the Vox (by Boyer, 1930, now demolished).

Casablanca was always more than just another colonial city and somehow it epitomized Jazz Age modernity. Today, the city has a great architectural heritage of which its inhabitants are increasingly aware. The demolition of the Boyer-designed **Villa el Mokri** in 1995 aroused widespread criticism and media interest, and the association **Casa Mémoire** (www.casamemoire.org) is now working for the preservation of the city's unique heritage of buildings.

There are still numerous *bidonville* areas. Some, like Beni Msick, have seen major rehousing projects, others huddle on odd strips of land next to railway lines and derelict factories.

Upstart city

Casablanca, grimy and frayed at the edges though it may be, also has a glitzy side. Alongside the imperial cities, it is an upstart. Its streets bear the names of rebel heroes, of French and Moroccan cities, and of trees and artists. If Rabat is a home-loving civil servant and Fès an austere imam, then Casablanca is a golden boy, often stressed-out but always on the move. Casablanca has a go-getting air, which builds glamorous careers for some – and leaves many in the gutter. The old Lusitanian port, destination for camel and mule trains coming up from plains and mountains far inland, is a very long way away. Casablanca is a place where an anonymity impossible in the traditional city can be found, where identities can sometimes break free of the old constraints. Although not the most attractive or hospitable of places to visitors, it is definitely the place where Morocco's future is made. Casablanca, stylish child of French colonial capitalism, has grown up. The vast city, made a household name by a Hollywood film, watches the world on satellite TV. Morocco-watchers observe its potentially turbulent suburbs and listen to the gossip in its villas and cafés to follow how things in the wider country are going.

The Casablanca suicide bombings of 2003, in which 45 people died, and the bomb of 2007, which killed a further five people, were carried out by young men from the shanty towns and poorest suburbs of the city. Since 2003, efforts have been made to help the poor of the city, with education and literacy programs and attempts to improve housing. Many Moroccans blame Algerian influences for the fundamentalist streaks in Casablancan society, but most of the contributory factors are probably nearer to home. These contributory factors of high unemployment and rising poverty were brought to the forefront in 2011 when Casablanca, like all of Morocco's big cities, experienced mass protest rallies as part of the Arab Spring. Whether these problems can be tackled sufficiently to appease critics, remains to be seen.

Places in Casablanca

When visiting Casablanca, you may notice changes in street names. The older French names in the central area are still in use, but on new plaques, the French 'rue' is written in Latin letters as 'zanka', while 'avenue' is 'chari'.

Hassan II Mosque

ⓘ *Blvd Sidi Mohammed Ben Abdallah, T0522-482886. Open to non-Muslims by 45-min guided tour only from the western side of the mosque 0900, 1000 and 1100, also at 1400 Sep-Jun, and 1400 and 1500 Jul-Aug. During Ramadan, tours are at 0900, 1000 and 1100, and on Fri at 0900 and 1400. 120dh.*

In many ways impeccably modern, with its traditional decorative detailing, including ceramic mosaic, carved plasterwork and painted wood, the Hassan II mosque is often also heralded as a symbol of the renaissance of Moroccan craftskills. Inaugurated in 1993, it is the world's fifth biggest mosque and took five years of intensive labour by over 30,000 workers and craftsmen to complete. Works were undertaken by French contractors Bouygues, also responsible for the huge Basilica of Yamasoukrou on the Côte d'Ivoire. The minaret, some 200 m high, was inspired by the minaret of the Koutoubia Mosque in Marrakech, and is Casablanca's chief landmark. Sometimes a laser beam, visible over 35 km away, indicating the direction of Mecca, probes the night sky. The mosque is huge: in terms

24 hours in Casablanca

Start the day with a coffee and pastry and a stroll around the central neighbourhood near the market on the **Avenue Mohammed V** and the **Rue du Prince Moulay Abdallah**. Take a *petit taxi* over to the **Grande Mosquée Hassan II**, right on the Atlantic shore, the westernmost mosque of the Islamic lands, for one of the morning guided tours. There will probably be time for a quick stroll along the seafront before lunch at the **Restaurant du Port de peche**, inside the port compound. Next, take a *petit taxi* over to the **Quartier des Habous**, a perfectly planned 1920s neighbourhood built for the notables of Fès to get them to settle in Casablanca. There are some good souvenir places here,

and have a look at the **Tribunal du Pacha**. Then take another *petit taxi* out to Maârif to visit the **Villa des Arts** and the nearby **Cathedral du Sacré Coeur**. Finally, in the early evening, those who like the crowds might want to explore the *medina* or the area round the **Parc de la Ligue arabe**. Evening activities could include a trip to a hammam, perhaps the **Bain Zaiani**, or one of the hammams near Boulevard Zerktouni and the Mosquée el Badr. Casablanca has plenty of good restaurants: try Taverne du Dauphin in the town centre or the expensive A Ma Bretagne out beyond Ain Diab. Casa nightlife centres on the **Corniche**, the beachfront, where there are bars and clubs to suit most tastes.

of covered area, it is the largest in the world and has space for 80,000 worshippers. There are upper prayer areas on a mezzanine floor that has space for 5000 female worshippers.

The mosque is built on a rocky isle, right next to the ocean, with the water practically lapping the bay windows of the prayer hall (which has a mobile roof allowing it to be opened to the sky and a partially glass floor so that certain VIP worshippers can kneel over the Atlantic as they pray). Visitors pass through the main prayer hall, the ablutions room (ritual ablutions are compulsory before prayer) and the two public baths, beautifully decorated but still closed. As one approaches the wide esplanade leading to the mosque, the buildings on either side were planned to house a *medersa*, a library and a museum of Islamic art but the necessary funding has yet to be found. The costly operation was all paid for by public subscription and, unusually for a mosque in the city, it is managed by the **Agence urbaine de Casablanca**.

The medina

The medina, site of the old city, is a ramshackle quarter, dating primarily from the 19th century (the fortifications are 18th century). Still densely populated, it can easily be explored in a couple of hours, entering from Place Mohammed V. There were three main sections: a bourgeois area with consuls, merchants, government officials and Europeans; a *mellah* or Jewish neighbourhood – which dominated the medina for much of the 20th century, and the *tnaker*, housing rural migrants (the term refers to a compound with a cactus hedge.) The **Grand Mosque** was built by Sultan Sidi Mohammed Ibn Abdallah at the end of the 18th century to celebrate the recapture of Anfa from the Portuguese.

The **koubba of Sidi Bou Smara** stands in the southwest corner of the medina near an old banyan tree. It is said that, in the 10th century, Sidi Bou Smara ('man of the nails') was passing through the town and asked for water to perform his ritual washing before praying. Insults and stones were thrown at him instead. Undaunted, he struck the ground with his staff and there issued from that place a spring which continued to flow. It seems that the inhabitants' earlier inclination to send him away changed to a reluctance to let him go, so he settled in the corner of the medina and planted a banyan tree which grew quickly and to an immense size. The tree is now studded with nails driven in by supplicants for the saint's assistance.

The **koubba of Sidi Beliout** (off-limits to non-Muslims) is the small complex of whitewashed buildings to your left on the Avenue Houphouët Boigny (ex-Avenue du 4ème Zouaves) as you walk towards the city from Casa-Port station. It used to be in the medina, until the demolitions created the boulevard linking station and city. Sidi Beliout is said to have blinded himself and gone to live with wild animals, finding them preferable to the human race. The animals cared for him, and a lion carried him to this resting place after his death. He is appealed to by those needing consolation. Near his shrine is a fountain. Those who drink the water will reputedly return to Casablanca. Sidi Beliout is now the name of the central district close to the shrine.

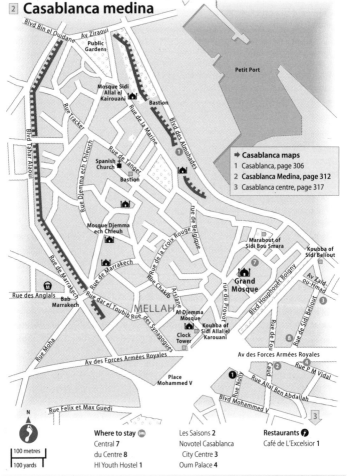

2 | Casablanca medina

➔ **Casablanca maps**
1 Casablanca, page 306
2 **Casablanca Medina, page 312**
3 Casablanca centre, page 317

Where to stay 🛏
Central **7**
du Centre **8**
HI Youth Hostel **1**

Les Saisons **2**
Novotel Casablanca
City Centre **3**
Oum Palace **4**

Restaurants 🍴
Café de L'Excelsior **1**

Modern medina

Resident-General Lyautey's respect for things Moroccan reached an apogee at the Quartier des Habous. Only too aware of the housing problems facing the Muslim population, Lyautey's planner Henri Prost proposed a new traditional town. The aim was to provide medium-cost housing for Muslims. Top families from Fès, wary of settling in 'impure' areas inhabited by Europeans, were to be attracted to a stylish mini-medina, close to the Sultan's new palace but a fair distance from the new city centre. The land was put forward by the Habous, a sort of religious property institution. (In Islam, land or other property can be held in mortmain to benefit descendants.) A Jewish merchant added a plot, but

as the Habous could not accept gifts from Jews, he gave the land to Sultan Moulay Youssef, who turned it over for development.

The task of designing the area was given to architect Albert Laprade, a great observer of traditional architectures in Europe. Too busy designing the residency in Rabat, however, he handed the project to Cadet and Brion, who produced a whole neo-traditional area with all the necessary modern infrastructure. There were all the facilities familiar to former residents of an old city: a market, public ovens, hammams, Koran schools, and mosques. Wealthy Fassis moved to the area, keen to be close to the heart of things while living in a traditional environment.

The remains of Sidi Allal el Kairouani and his daughter Lalla Beida are in a **mosque** on Rue Tnaker to the north of the medina. He was the patron of fishermen, and she was known as the White Princess due to the pale colour of her skin. One story goes that Dar el Baydha (House of the White Princess) was the name given to the town in 1770 when it was rebuilt, and that it only later took the Spanish translation Casa Blanca. The story recounts how Sidi Kairouani, travelling from Tunisia to Senegal, was shipwrecked off the coast here, but rescued by the locals. He sent for his motherless daughter who was not so fortunate. Her ship sank too but she drowned. Her body was carried to her grieving father who buried her facing the sea and left a place beside her for himself.

Outside the medina

Though rather abandoned, the **Cathédrale du Sacré Coeur** is a tall elegant white structure built in 1930 with nods to Moroccan as well as European architecture. Inside, the white space is pin-pricked by coloured glass and elevated by slender white columns. For 20dh the guardian will let you up the tower for good views over the city. Be warned, though, that you may have to fight your way past the pigeons, and it wouldn't pass any health and safety examinations. Look out for occasional events staged here.

Villa des Arts ⓘ *30 Blvd Brahim Roudani, T0522-295087, Tue-Sun 0930-1900, 10dh*, is a contemporary art gallery in a restored and whitewashed 1934 art deco building. Outside, fountains are embedded in the paving, while inside, polished wood floors and big white walls are a good setting for rotating displays of Moroccan and international art.

Notre Dame de Lourdes ⓘ *junction of Av du 2 Mars and the Rond-Point de l'Europe,* was built in the 1950s and is famous for its stained-glass windows by Gabriel Loire.

Quartier des Habous is 4 km southeast of the centre close to Mers Sultan train station, but it's better to take a *petit taxi* and ask for 'Derb el Habous'. An attempt to create a modern medina (see box, above), the Habous is a strangely artificial residential suburb – a

Sidi Abderrahman, the flautist

The story of Sidi Abderrahman – like that of so many saints – has been smudged over like an old manuscript. Sidi Abderrahman was a pious man or *wali salih*, who took refuge on an islet off the Atlantic coast to better contemplate the Almighty. But he was unable to pray. To serve the Lord, he played sweet music on a reed flute. Another *wali*, Sidi Bouchaïb Arradad, hearing of the piety of Sidi Abderrahman, came to see him and said that he should lay down his flute and that he would explain to him the intricacies of prayer. The two remained together for seven days and, on the eighth day, Sidi Bouchaïb spread his carpet on the sea and went away. Deep in prayer, Sidi Abderrahman didn't see him leave. When he realized that his guide had left, he called him back, then threw himself into

the sea to try to catch up. The waves drew back and an island appeared. Sidi Bouchaïb, seeing this miracle, cried out, "Oh Sidi Abderrahman, forget what I taught you and play your flute. Your *baraka* is greater than mine." And so Sidi Abderrahman stayed on his island to worship God until he passed away.

Of course there are many other legends explaining the past of Sidi Abderrahman. His tiny island retains a mystic fascination; it is a place where women may go to seek the saint's blessing, a cure for sterility, bad health and other maledictions. They come from all over Morocco, travel across to the island on makeshift 'boats', consult soothsayers in tiny damp rooms, visit the shrine, maybe organize a *lila* – a night-time ritual of dance and trance – and return home relieved of their cares.

surreally neat and tidy version of Morocco. The **Pasha's Courtrooms** (Mahkamat el Pacha), completed in the 1950s and rather Lutyens in style, make a focal point, but generally it's a place to wander and gawp. There are a number of shops selling *belgha* (leather slippers), Moroccan clothing and copperwork. Close to the Pasha's Courtrooms are a number of good bookshops, stocking mainly Arabic titles.

Beachfront
ⓘ *The ocean promenade, Blvd de la Corniche, west of the medina is easily reached by petit taxi or by local bus (No 9) from the junction of Blvd de Paris and Av des Forces Armées Royales.*
The beachfront, or Corniche, is most definitely a place to stroll and be seen. Along the ocean front, beach clubs with open-air pools have been built on the rocks. Beyond the beach clubs and hotels, the beach becomes public, and games of football take place on the big expanses of sand. Out on the coast road, you will come to the **shrine of Sidi Abderrahman**, built on a rocky islet (see box, above).

Mohammedia → *For listings, see pages 315-323. Colour map 2, A4.*

Mohammedia, known as 'Fedala' until 1960, when it was renamed after the present king's father, Mohammed V, is a curious, sleepy sort of town. It is home to the Samir Refinery, and is the second biggest port in the country. There is a small walled medina, a neighbourhood of fine, wide avenues lined with palm trees, and a park with a modern church – all somehow on a scale unsuited to such a quiet place. It is as though grandiose plans for city development in the 1920s never actually quite got off the ground. Beachside Mohammedia, with its promenade and cafés, comes alive in summer. A likeable little town, it could be the place to spend a last night at the end of a trip, perhaps if you have a late flight out of Casablanca the following day.

Arriving in Mohammedia Mohammedia is easily reached by the shuttle train running between Casablanca (10 minutes) and Rabat (25 minutes). Another option is to take a *grand taxi* from Boulevard Moulay Abderrahman in Casablanca (turn first left just before the Centre 2000 as you leave Casa-Port station). The town is easily explored on foot, although there are plenty of lime-green *petits taxis* if you need to get back to the station quickly. From in front of the kasbah gate, take the Avenue des FAR as far as the Rue de Fès. A left turn will take you to the Rue Farhat Hached, where the nicer restaurants are located. It's only about 1.5 km from the station to the main park area. **Tourist information** ① *14 Rue al Jahid, T0523-324299.* ▸▸ *See Transport, page 322, for further details.*

Background Just to the north of modern Casablanca, Mohammedia was a thriving port in the 14th and 15th centuries. Its trade with Europe expanded in the 17th and 18th centuries, notably with the export of horses, and the kasbah was built in 1773 to support this activity. A decline in trade left Mohammedia subordinate to adjacent Rabat. However, specializing in the handling of petroleum gave it a new lease of life, and the oil refinery, opened in 1961, raised its status to one of Morocco's major ports. Industrial activities are centred around a rock salt factory. Its 3 km of sandy beaches make it a popular recreational area for the people of Casablanca, both for weekend breaks and as a summer holiday haunt.

Places in Mohammedia The distinctive mosque, **Jamaâ Radouane**, was opened in 1991. There are three doors in arched apertures, approached by shallow steps across a gleaming white marble courtyard. More impressive is the wide open park but most come to Mohammedia solely for its beach

---

⊙ Casablanca listings

For sleeping and eating price codes and other relevant information, see pages 22-28.

⊙ Where to stay

Casablanca *p305, maps p306, p312 and p317*
Casablanca does not seem to have quite enough hotels, and mid-range hotels are often booked up early in the day. This is especially true when there is a major national event on in the city, and the authorities make block reservations.

City centre
€€€ **Hotel Les Saisions**, 19 Rue el Oraïbi Jilali, T0522-481898, www.hotelles saisionsmaroc.ma. The quiet rooms here host huge beds and old-fashioned dark furniture, including writing desks, while

old photos adorn the walls. **Cities** restaurant next door (page 319) is part of the same establishment.
€€€ **Novotel Casablanca City Centre**, Angle Bld Zaîd Ouhmad Sidi Belyout, T0522-466500, www.novotel.com. It may not have an inspiring name, but the **Novotel City Centre** is a surprisingly stylish hotel, with 281 rooms and a chic bar with colourful low lighting and billowing white drapes. Sleek modern rooms have prints on the walls, widescreen flat TVs, orange cushions and minibars.
€€€ **Oum Palace**, 12 Rue Kamal Mohammed, T0522-201500, www. oumpalace.com. Businesslike but also personable, the **Oum** is not quite palatial, but it does have huge beds, plasma screen TVs, marble tiles, immaculate shiny bathrooms and free Wi-Fi, which make

up for its lack of character. There are 2 restaurants, as well as a hammam and sauna.

€€€ Transatlantique, 79 Rue Chaouia, T0522-294551, www.transatcasa.com. Open since 1922, the **Transatlantique** claims to be the oldest hotel in Casablanca. Public areas have lots of carved wood and art deco details, though the rooms themselves are plainer. Each, as comfortable wooden furniture, a/c, and the best rooms have balconies over the street. There's a piano bar and nightclub downstairs; go for rooms higher up if you're worried about the noise.

€€ Hotel Guynemer, 2 Rue Mohammed Belloul, T0522-275764. Exceptionally friendly and helpful, the well-run **Guynemer** is no longer a secret and the 29 rooms here fill up fast. Clean, quiet and central, there is free internet in the lobby, as well as Wi-Fi. They can arrange airport transfer, run daily city tours and can sort out just about anything else you might want. Rooms are comfy, peach-coloured and modern. Quieter rooms overlook an ugly internal courtyard. Those at the front are lighter but noisier. Nice old pictures of Casablanca decorate the stairs.

€€ Hotel Maamoura, 59 Rue Ibn Batouta, T0522-452967, www.hotelmaamoura.com. A rare central hotel which has a modicum of traditional Moroccan style in its carved plaster ceilings and hanging lamps. Private parking, room service and Wi-Fi.

€€ Hotel Manar, 3 Rue Chaouia, T0522-452751, manarhotel@gmail.com. On the junction with Rue Allal Ben Abdallah, the **Manar** is a friendly spot with simple, modern rooms with baths, tiled floors and rugs. A little dated in places.

€€ Rio, 16 Av Houmman el Fetouaki, T0522-277896, hotelrio@menara.ma. On the corner of Rue Galli Ahmed, **Rio** has 60 rooms and rather dark corridors. The attempts at sultry style (red velvet-covered beds) are a bit much, but it's comfortable and there are good, fully tiled en suites, internet in the lobby and a bar and restaurant. Dated, but not at all bad.

€€ Volubilis, 20-22 Rue Abdelkrim Diouri, T0522-272771. www.volubiliscasa.com.

Decorated with a bit of originality, this is run by the same management as the Transatlantique (see above), onto which it backs. There's even a connecting door between them, and guests here can use the facilities of the Transatlantique. There's a pizzeria and bar, and the 45 rooms have floral bedspreads your granny would be proud of, plus good tiled bathrooms.

€€ Washington, 26 Blvd Rahal el Meskini, T0522-200377. A big place, on the expensive side for what it is, but with some compensation in the form of a low-lit bar, free internet in the lobby and swish marble staircases. Rooms are a little anonymous.

€ Gallia, 19 Rue Ibnou Batouta (corner of Blvd Homan el Fetouaki), T0522-481694, galia_19@hotmail.com. Frayed around the edges in places but clean and reliable, rooms in the **Gallia** have little balconies and basins. Toilets are shared though some rooms have private showers. There's a café, and free internet in the lobby.

€ HI Youth Hostel, 6 Pl Ahmed Al Bidaoui, T0522-220551. In a square in the medina off Blvd des Almohades, near the harbour. Both dorms (bed for 55dh) and doubles are kept very clean as long as you don't mind institutional flavour. Has a midnight curfew, so not for party people. The bus and train are nearby, and the whole place is well maintained. It can be noisy though.

€ Hotel Central, 20 Pl Ahmed el Bidaoui, T0522-262525. In the medina, the blue-shuttered Central has airy, light-filled rooms painted in traditional Moroccan styles and colours – lots of soft reds and purples – and windows that open onto the medina. It's very basic but you get clean sheets, en suites and, if you want to be in the medina, this is decent value.

€ Hotel du Centre, 1 Rue Sidi Beliout, T0522-446180. Opposite the **Royal Mansour**, this is a clean and convenient budget option. Rooms are plain and there are few added extras, but what you get is good: comfortable rooms and clean bathrooms. There's an ancient cage lift.

€ **Hotel de Paris**, Rue Prince Moulay Abdallah, T0522-273871. In the pedestrianized part of the centre of Casablanca, this is a friendly hotel whose staff really go the extra mile to help. The rooms are very decent for the price, with TV, a/c, nice balcony and extremely small bathroom. It can be noisy so pack your earplugs.

€ **Hotel de Seville**, 19 Rue Nationale, T0522-271311. The rooms at the front of this central hotel have good balconies overlooking the street. They are simple but clean and comfortable, with tiled floors and aged bedspreads. Good value.

€ **Hotel Lausanne**, 24 Rue Tata, T0522-268690. Popular central hotel which, like many places in the city, has seen better days. Plenty of hot water, and handy for some good breakfast cafés, including **La Loge**, just down the street.

3 Casablanca centre

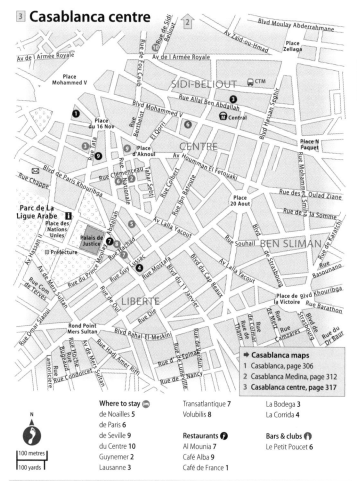

➡ **Casablanca maps**
1 Casablanca, page 306
2 Casablanca Medina, page 312
3 **Casablanca centre, page 317**

Where to stay
de Noailles **5**
de Paris **6**
de Seville **9**
du Centre **10**
Guynemer **2**
Lausanne **3**

Transatlantique **7**
Volubilis **8**

Restaurants
Al Mounia **7**
Café Alba **9**
Café de France **1**

La Bodega **3**
La Corrida **4**

Bars & clubs
Le Petit Poucet **6**

100 metres
100 yards

€ Hotel Negociants, 116 Rue Allal Ben Abdellah, T0522-314023. Clean, modern rooms, some of which have en suites, others just with in-room basins. It can be a bit noisy and there's no lift, but it's reasonable value, especially for its single rooms.

€ Hotel Noailles, 22 Blvd du 11 Janvier, just off Blvd Lalla Yacout, T0522-202554. Top-floor rooms here are the most desirable; they have balconies, with potted plants, and are furthest from the street noise below. Beds are newer and more comfortable than in most Casablanca budget hotels. There are baths, rugs and TVs, and rooms are shiny and clean, with comfy seats and even pouffes. Well looked after and good value.

Beachfront

€€€ Azur Hotel, 41 Blvd de la Corniche, T0522-797493, www.azurhotel.ma. There are some traditional Moroccan touches in this beachside hotel, and rooms have big balconies and flat-screen TVs but it's dreadfully overpriced for what you get. As usual along the seafront, the style is on the brash side.

€€€ Hotel Riad Salam, at start of Blvd de la Corniche, T0522-391313. A large hotel with very little of the riad style the name might suggest, but with a good pool from where you can hear the sounds of the sea. The best rooms are sleek and modern with natural tones, big beds and all mod cons, but there's better value to be had elsewhere.

Camping

Camping International Tamaris, 16 km out of Casablanca on the coast road to Azemmour, T0522-330060. Only 100 m from the beach (crowded in summer), 9-ha site, 10dh per person per night, snack restaurant, grocery shop, showers, laundry, first-aid post and electricity for caravans, noisy.

Mohammedia *p314*

€€ Hotel Hager, Rue Farhat Hached, T0523-325921, www.hagerhotel.ma. Probably the best address in Mohammedia.

Small, clean if rather ugly rooms with a vast amount of chintzy decor. Ocean view from some top-floor rooms.

€€ Hotel Sabah, 42 Av des FAR, T0523-321451. Mainly aimed at business travellers. Ugly furniture, 1st-floor rooms are noisy because of a nightclub. Poor value.

€ Hotel Ennasser, Av Abderrhamane Sarghini (as you stand in front of the kasbah entrance, it's on the left a few doors down the avenue). Cheap but very basic; most of the 11 rooms have no outside windows.

€ Hotel La Falaise, Rue Farhat Hached, T0523-324828. Close to the beach. Most rooms lack en suites but there's a good courtyard and a bar. Reservations necessary: it's popular and books up quickly.

Camping

Camping International Loran, T0523-322957. Pool, restaurant and shop, site of 4 ha, beach 100 m, bar, snacks, showers, laundry, first aid, electricity for caravans, petrol at 500 m.

Camping Mimosa, site of 0.5 ha, 3 km outside town. Clean site with shade. Beach 100 m, grocery, showers, laundry, electricity for caravans, petrol 5 km.

Camping Oubaha, at Mansouria, 10 km north up the coast, site of 3 ha. Beach 100 m, groceries, showers, laundry, first aid, electricity for caravans, petrol at 600 m.

🍴 Restaurants

Casablanca *p305, maps p306, p312 and p317*
Casablanca has a good range of restaurants, including cheap fried fish places, eateries that have survived from more cosmopolitan times and rather sleek lounge-bars with minimalist pretensions. You can eat good Moroccan food, too, and there are a number of popular Italian restaurants in the more prosperous neighbourhoods. Restaurants are typically open late, often until 0100, and some become drinking destinations later in the evening.

€€€ A Ma Bretagne, Sidi Abderrahman, Blvd de la Corniche beyond Aïn Diab,

T0522-397979. Mon-Sat. Excellent French restaurant with a good wine cellar. Classy without being stuffy and wonderful sea views as well as superior food. One of the best in Casablanca. It's pricey (mains 180-320dh) but recommended.

€€€ La Fibule, Blvd de la Corniche, T0522-360641. Smart and atmospheric Moroccan restaurant near the El Hank lighthouse, with an emphasis on seafood. The carved ceilings are impressive and there's an open fire for the winter. Sip one of the 11 Moroccan wines as you look down on the waves below.

€€€ Ostréa, just inside port compound on the right, T0522-441390. Daily 1100-2300, even in Ramadan. A smartly contemporary restaurant, where the oysters are the star attraction (an oyster farmer started the place) and the seafood is some of the best in town. Try to get a table by the window upstairs so you can look down on the bustle of the port below.

€€€ Rick's Cafe, 248 Rue Sour Jdid, T0522-274207/08. Taking its name from the eponymous café in the film, this is something of an institution among visitors to the city. There's atmosphere by the bucketloads, a piano player and, for film buffs, Casablanca is played every night. The food is good, if a bit pricey, but the ambience can't be beaten.

€€ Al Mounia, 95 Rue du Prince Moulay Abdallah, T0522-222669. One of the best places for traditional Moroccan food in Casablanca. There are tables outside under an enormous tree or you can eat inside in tiled and carved surrounds. All the usual Moroccan dishes – pastilla, tagines – are well executed and service is very good.

€€ Cities, 19 Rue Oraïbi Jilali, T0522-490928. Just of Av des FAR, this restaurant is attached to Les Saisons hotel, see above. There's an Italian-American theme, with pizzas and photos of the first Italian New Yorkers. The atmosphere is friendly, and there are also meat and fish dishes.

€€ La Bodega, 129 Rue Allal Ben Abdallah, T0522-541842. Open until 0100. A lively tapas bar, with Spanish cocktails upstairs

and a DJ and dancefloor downstairs. Fills up with Casablanca's beautiful people.

€€ La Corrida, 59 Rue Guy Lussac, T0522-278155. Closed Sun and Sep. Good Spanish food, faded decor tells of the days when Casablanca had a bullring. Grilled fish and tapas are specialities, as is the sangria. Outdoor seating.

€€ Matsuri, 21 Rue Zaïd Bnou Rifaâ, T0522-252563. A stylish conveyor-belt sushi restaurant, Matsuri has some nice touches, such as fresh lilies in alcoves on the walls and good use of bamboo. Norwegian salmon is brought in specially.

€€ Restaurant du Port de Pêche, close to the medina in the fishing port compound, T0522-318561. Excellent fish dishes in smart but simple atmosphere. It's a good lunchtime spot but service is on the slow side. Try to reserve. To get there, leave Casa-Port station on your right, go straight ahead and then turn left for port area.

€€ Sqala, Av des Almohades, T0522-260960. Tue-Sun. In the 18th-century fortified bastion at the edge of the medina, overlooking the fishing port, this is an excellent and popular spot for lunch on one of the outdoor tables among the fountains and cannons. Food is a combination of French and Moroccan, and there's a drinks licence too.

€€ Taverne du Dauphin, Blvd Houphouët Boigny, T0522-221200. Mon-Sat. One of Casablanca's best-known restaurants. Excellent seafood is served amid a colourful interior with stained glass accents.

€ Chez Brochette, Rue Tata. A good terrace and freshly made sandwiches and burgers make this a good quick lunch stop.

€ Euro Snack, 53 Rue Tata, T0522-472829. Casablanca's best burgers, served with a frenetic panache that McDonald's will never match. Between Rue Clemenceau and Blvd Driss Lahrizi.

Cafés and pâtisseries

Casablanca has a number of cafés-glaciers. If you are wandering up the Av Hassan II, try Oliveri for ice cream. Stella is another famous ice cream place, with enormous numbers of brightly coloured flavours and freshly made waffle cones.

Café Alba, 59-61 Rue Driss Lahrizi. Smart wicker chairs on the street and more comfortable soft chairs inside.

Café de France, on Pl Mohammed V. Has a slightly rakish air to it in the small hours, when nightclubbers come into town from the Corniche.

Café de l'Excelsior, Pl Mohammed V. Breakfast, handy for a kiosk with foreign papers.

Euro Jus, corner of Idris Lahrizi and Prince Moulay Abdullah. Excellent mixed juices for 10dh.

Pâtisserie Bennis, a little difficult to find at 2 Rue Fkih el Gabbas in the Derb el-Habous. The best place for good Moroccan pâtisserie.

Ramses, next door to **Café de France** (see above). More modern and gets a younger crowd.

Mohammedia *p314*

Most of the more expensive restaurants are on or around the Rue Farhat Hached end of town, close to the sea. Cheaper places with terraces can be found at the roundabout opposite the kasbah gate.

€€€ Restaurant Sans Pareil, Rue Farhat Hached, near **Hotel La Falaise**, T0523-320003. The Casablanca bourgeoisie pack the terrace for Sunday meals. Good seafood.

€€ Big Bamboo, Blvd Hassan II, T0523-324848, www.bigbamboo.ma. Thai and Asian cuisine in a smart setting, run by the same people as **Sqala** in Casablanca.

🍷 Bars and clubs

Casablanca *p305, maps p306, p312 and p317*
Bars
Bars in the city generally close at 2300, when the action moves on to the beachfront clubs.
La Bodega, 129 Rue Allal Ben Abdallah, T0522-541842. A chic tapas bar which makes a good spot for a cold beer or a cocktail.

La Petit Poucet, 86 Blvd Mohammed V. Staff will proudly show some old photos of the city centre and explain how aviator St-Exupéry would drink here when he stayed at the **Hotel Excelsior**.

Le Petit Rocher, on the Corniche, near the El Hank lighthouse, T0522-395748. Fine terrace, ocean view. Beers at 30dh, trendy mixed crowd. Recommended in summer.

Clubs
Most of the nightclubs are situated on the beachfront, liveliest in summer, and open around 2400-0400. Punters are an interesting mix of media people, expatriate kids, prostitutes, fashionistas, Saudis, hustlers and a handful of gay men. Allow around 200dh for entry, which will generally include your first drink. In order to procure a table, you'll usually be expected to buy a bottle of whisky for around 1300dh. Jeans are usually OK, but trainers are frowned upon.

Popular places include: **Pulp**, whose resident DJ, Sphinx, has a good reputation, and **Punjab**, a cabaret club with oriental music. **Armstrong** has live international bands and a lively atmosphere. **Village** is known for being gay-friendly. **Feriz** is a good late night sandwich spot.

In the city centre, tapas bar **La Bodega** (see above) has a downstairs dancefloor and stays open until 0100.

🎭 Entertainment

Casablanca *p305, maps p306, p312 and p317*
Cultural centres
Institut Français, 121 Blvd Zerktouni, T0522-779870, www.institut-francais-casablanca.ma. Shows films and hosts visiting theatre and dance groups. It also has a small cafeteria.

🛍 Shopping

Casablanca *p305, maps p306, p312 and p317*
Books and newspapers
Le Carrefour du Livre, in the Maârif neighbourhood (sometimes considered

Casablanca's equivalent of St Germain-des-Prés, a short taxi ride away. The city's best bookshop, established and up-and-coming Moroccan writers have their launches here. **Librairie de France**, 4 Rue Chenier, T0522-209077. A small selection of maps and guidebooks.

Clothes

Try the boutiques on central pedestrian street Rue Moulay Abdallah, or for something a little more upmarket, shops in the Maârif neighbourhood.

Food

There is a fine covered **market** on Av Mohammed V which stocks most fresh produce. If you're in need of some cheap presents, there are a number of stalls selling beautifully made basketry of various kinds. There are also a couple of souvenir stalls with fossils and miscellaneous pottery. At the **Twin Center**, there is Morocco's first urban hypermarket, **Marjane**, where you can find a big range of imported items.

Handicrafts

The best fixed-price shop, and a friendly place just to look, is the government-run **Coopartim in the Grande Arcade Complexe Commerciale**, just off Pl des Nations Unies, T0522-229444. There are smaller shops in the medina, close to Bab Marrakech, and along Blvd Houphouêt Boigny. There is also a large shop stocking everything from carpets to metal lamps in the **Centre 2000**, just next to Casa-Port station. Handicrafts and, in particular, traditional Moroccan clothing can be found in the Quartier des Habous.

⚙ What to do

Casablanca p305, maps p306, p312 and p317
Hammams
The men's hammam at Rue Imam el Ghazali in the Quartier des Habous is modelled on a traditional medina bath house. Closer to the city centre, try **Les Bains Zaini**, reputedly the only 'bain oriental' in Casablanca, at 59 Rue Abou Rakrak, www.hammamziani.ma, open 0700-2200, full package 250dh or cheaper for individual treatments. (Choose your masseur from the photo at the desk.)

There are 2 clean and popular hammams (men and women) in the Bourgogne neighbourhood, off Blvd Zerktouni, a short taxi ride from the city centre (ask for the Clinique Badr): **Hammam Beidaoua**, 3 Rue du Chevreuil/Rue Abou Kacem Kattabari, T0522-271063, open daily 0600-2200; **Hammam Idéal**, 9 Rue Ramée/Rue Annaba, has similar opening hours. Both are busy on Thu evenings and at weekends. A visit here might give you some insight into daily life in an ordinary residential part of Casablanca.

Swimming

Take out a day-ticket at one of the private beach clubs at Aïn Diab and mix it with Casablanca's young and trendy set. Both **Tahiti** and **Miami** offer day entrance for around 70dh, rising to 120dh at the weekend. Beyond the beach clubs the beach is free.

Tour operators

Comanav Voyages, 43 Av des FAR, T0522-310015, www.comanav-voyages.ma. For ferry reservations. Try also small travel agents left of CTM.
Discover Morocco, 62 Rue de Foucauld, T0522-273519.
Menara Tours, 19 Rue Chenier 19 (close to Pl du 16 Novembre and **Hotel Hyatt Regency**), T0522-225119.
Olive Branch Tours, 35 Rue El Oraibi Jalali, T0522-261416, www.olivebranchtours.com. A reliable agency that can set up trips almost anywhere in Morocco, with a focus on culture and activities such as trekking and horse riding. Also do excellent Casablanca city tours.

⊖ Transport

Casablanca *p305, maps p306, p312 and p317*

Air

Departures for foreign and internal destinations are from **Mohammed V Airport**, T0522-339100, south of the city at Nouasseur. Trains run to the airport from **Casablanca Voyageurs** and **Casa-Port** or you can take *grands taxis* from the bus station near the Hotel Hyatt Regency (200dh by day, 300dh at night). There are no bus services to the airport though.

Vendome Transport Touristique are friendly, efficient and English-speaking and will arrange airport pick-up for about the same price (250dh) as a *grand taxi* and will meet you at the airport and take you to your hotel. Arrange in advance by phone (T0522-277619) or email (vendome_tt@yahoo.com).

Among the many international flights, there are daily departures to **Brussels**, **Frankfurt**, **London** and **Paris** with Royal Air Maroc; BMI has regular departures to **London**; and EasyJet flies to **Lyon**, **Madrid**, **Milan** and **Paris**.

Royal Air Maroc Express operates many domestic flights, including regular scheduled departures to **Agadir**, **Al Hoceïma**, **Fès**, **Laâyoune**, **Marrakech**, **Ouarzazate**, **Oujda** and **Tangier**.

Bus

The CTM terminal is at 23 Rue Léon l'Africain, off Rue Colbert and Av des FAR, behind the Hotel Sheraton, T0522-541010. There are regular departures daily to **Essaouira** at 0700 and 1500 (7 hrs); **El Jadida** 7 per day (2 hrs); **Agadir** 9 per day (7 hrs); **Tiznit** 5 per day (10 hrs); **Beni Mellal** at 0900, 1300 and 1830 (4 hrs); **Marrakech** 14 per day (3½ hrs); **Fès** 12 per day (5 hrs); **Tangier** 5 per day (5½ hrs) and **Rabat** approximately every 30 mins 0415-2345 (1¼ hrs).

Private line buses leave from the new terminal, the Gare routière des Ouled Ziane, a hefty hike from the city centre (a *petit taxi* from the centre is around 15dh).

There are many touts in operation here to the point that the ticket windows don't always seem to function. All major Moroccan cities are served daily.

Car hire

All the main agencies are at the airport. After baggage reclaim, go left when you come through the frosted-glass doors into the main concourse.

Avis, 19 Av des FAR, T0522-312424, T0522-339072 (airport).

Hertz, 25 Rue de Foucauld, T0522-484710, T0522-539181 (airport).

Inter-Rent Europcar, Tour des Habous, Av des FAR, T0522-313737.

Train

From **Casa-Port** (T0522-223011), you can catch trains to **Rabat** every 30 mins 0630-2130. From Casa-Voyageurs there are hourly services to **Meknès** and **Fès** 0515-2245; 7 services daily to **Taza**, and 4 to **Oujda**. The mainline Tangier to **Marrakech** service also runs through Casablanca-Voyageurs.

There are trains every hour between Casa-Voyageurs and Mohammed V Airport on the Bidhaoui Service, starting at **Aïn Sebaâ** and calling at Casa-Voyageurs (departure at 7 mins past the hour), **Mers Sultan** and **Oasis**. Full details on www.oncf.ma, or T0522-220520.

Taxi

Grands taxis to **Mohammedia** and **Rabat** depart from the first street left as you leave Casa-Port rail terminal. For **El Jadida**, take a *petit taxi* to the Blvd Laouina. There are plenty of departures.

Mohammedia *p314*

There are frequent bus and *grand taxi* services into **Casablanca**. Trains from Mohammedia leave for **Casa-Port** 0713-2133; to **Casa-Voyageurs** 0403-2222; and to **Rabat** 0615-0108, as well as to all other major destinations.

Casablanca *p305, maps p306, p312 and p317*
Banks Handy central ATMs include the Wafa Bank, Av Hassan II just after the Ramsès restaurant, and BMCI, corner of Av Mohammed V and Pl des Nations-unies, just across from the Café de Paris. **Medical services** Any major hotel should be able to put you in

touch with a doctor, ask for the SAMU or a *médecin généraliste* (GP). **Emergency**: T15. **SAMU**, T0522-252525. **SOS Médecins**, T0522-444444. **Hospital**, T0522-271459. **Chemists**, Pharmacie de Nuit, Pl Mohammed V, T0522-22 94 91; and Blvd d'Anfa where it intersects with Pl Oued le Makhazine. **Useful addresses** Fire: Rue Poggi, T15. **Police**: Blvd Brahim Rodani, T19. **Traffic police**: T177.

South of Casablanca

South of Morocco's economic powerhouse, the coast takes on a comparatively neglected air, with old towns built by European powers slowly crumbling away. El Jadida's old Portuguese centre is a spectacular film set of a place and Azemmour also has its ancient ramparts. In places, notably Oualidia, blessed with an extraordinary natural lagoon, holiday development is starting to take hold but, for the most part, tourists are a rare sight. Low hills slope down to the coast and tomato growers line each side of the road with trailers piled high with produce.
▸▸ *For listings, see pages 329-332.*

Azemmour → *For listings, see pages 329-332. Colour map 2, A3.*

Perhaps the least visited of the old Portuguese coastal bastions, Azemmour has a backwater air. It is a town with a dual identity. There are the obvious attractions – the walk along the old ramparts, the stroll through the narrow streets of the medina, the view of the Oum er Rbia River – and then there is the walk up to the Zaouïa of Moulay Bouchaïb. Here you can see the whole gammut of stalls and actitivites that are so much a part of a pilgrimage centre: herbalists, apothecaries and fortune tellers, henna-tattoo ladies and candle sellers. And for a summer bathe, about 1 km from the town is Haouzia beach. Azemmour is an easy excursion from El Jadida, with plenty of *grands taxis* doing the 20-minute trip.

Arriving in Azemmour
The train station is a good 30-minute walk from the town. If you arrive by car, park near the ramparts, where there will be some sort of 'warden'. All the sights are in easy walking distance. A child may show you up to the ramparts, while the beach is about 30 minutes' walk away. The busy Rue Moulay Bouchaïb takes you up to the *zaouïa* of the same name.

Background
There was a trading post here called Azama in the Carthaginian period, but earlier marble columns, dating back to Punic times, and Roman coins have also been found in the area. In the 15th century Azemmour was an important trading port on the routes between Portugal and West Africa, trading horses, carpets, jallabah and haiks with Guinea, and cereals with Portugal. The Portuguese occupied Azemmour in 1513 as a base from which to attack Marrakech, but under opposition from the Saâdians had to withdraw in 1541. The town assumed regional importance under the Saâdians, but soon lost ground to the growth of its near neighbour, El Jadida. Azemmour is known for embroidery. The town is sometimes referred to as Moulay Bou Chaib, after its patron saint, who has a *zaouïa* above the town.

At the mouth of the Oued Oum er Rbia, the town was once noted for the widespread shad fishing throughout the cooler part of the year. The fish were caught as they went upstream to spawn. Water control barrages have drastically reduced their numbers.

Places in Azemmour

Azemmour is still partly surrounded by imposing ochre **ramparts**, with several attractively carved bastions often decorated with cannon. From the hill above the bridge on the east side of the river there is a striking view of the medina with its white, square-fronted, flat-roofed houses stretching along the top of the steep bank opposite. The **beach** is also one of the best, but the town attracts few visitors. The walls of the old **medina** can be explored by the rampart walk, also with excellent views of the town; the steps are at the northeast end of the walls. Enter via **Bab es Souk**, with its clear Portuguese architectural influences and impressive wooden doors, generally round-arched with carved keystones. Also visit the *kissaria*, or covered market, and the **Sanctuary of Moulay Abdallah Ben Ahmed**. The doors of this house have a particular Portuguese style. A passageway to the left leads to the **kasbah**, which also had a role as a *mellah*, or Jewish quarter. In the kasbah, visit the **Dar el Baroud** building, the house of the powder, built within the ramparts between the medina and the kasbah. It is dominated by a tower from which there are views back over the rooftops towards the *oued*. The 16th-century **kasbah gate** is a strikingly simple semicircular arch; climb its tower for a view of the town.

To get to the **Gorges de Méhéoula**, also known as the Gorges des Orangers, take the road south out of Azemmour, turning right just before the Oued Oum er Rbia, and left at the first junction to keep alongside the *oued*. About 9 km from here, there is a signed turning left (north), giving the best view of this gorge.

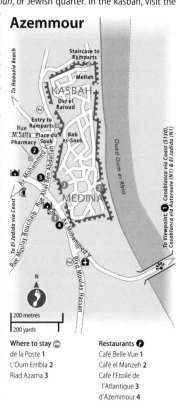

Azemmour

El Jadida (ex-Mazagan) → *For listings, see pages 329-332. Colour map 2, A3.*

Popular in summer with Casablancans, El Jadida hibernates out of season. With its avenues and araucaria trees, it has a faint elegance reminiscent of some forgotten Mediterranean resort, making it the sort of place where you might film a Moroccan remake of *Death in Venice*. El Jadida is best known, however, for its massive-walled citadel, the Cité Portugaise, its bastions and lookouts harking back to a time of armies equipped with pikestaffs and blunderbusses.

Where to stay 🛏
de la Poste **1**
L'Oum Erribia **2**
Riad Azama **3**

Restaurants 🍴
Café Belle Vue **1**
Café el Manzeh **2**
Café l'Etoile de
  l'Atlantique **3**
d'Azemmour **4**

Arriving in El Jadida

Getting there The bus station is south of the centre, along Avenue Mohammed V. From here it is a five- or 10-minute walk to Place Mohammed V, the focus of the town. The train station lies 3 km south of El Jadida, off to the west of the N1 (the Marrakech road), and is not well signposted from the centre of town. ▸▸ *See Transport, page 331, for further details.*

Getting around El Jadida is sufficiently small to do all the main sites on foot, and the reasonably priced hotels are all in the centre. The better beaches are a short taxi ride away; past the **Sidi Ouafi lighthouse** (Phare de Sidi Ouafi) is a beach popular with Moroccan families camping. The more distant **Sidi Bouzid beach** is also popular and has more facilities (take bus No 2 or a *grand taxi*). If you have your own transport, the coastal village of **Moulay Abdallah**, with its *zaouïa* complex, is 11 km southwards.

Tourist information Point Acceuil ⓘ *Av Mohammed VI, T0523-352507.* Actually the office of an estate agent, this is the best place to come for information – they produce a small printed guide to the town as well as a map; both are free. **Syndicat d'Initiative** ⓘ *Av Rafii opposite site of the Municipal Theatre, daily 0830-1200, 1430-1830.* Limited range of information available but helpful staff are happy to provide details of hotel accommodation, maps and tourist brochures of a general nature.

Background

El Jadida is short for 'El Medina El Jadida', the 'New Town'. Over its long history, however, the town has had at least four other names – El Breija, 'Little Fort', Mazagão for the Portuguese, El Mahdouma (The Destroyed) in the 18th century, and Mazagan under the French. The area was probably occupied by the Phoenicians and may well have been the trading post referred to as Rubisis by the ancient authors. Apparently a safe mooring and a strong defensive position, the site was occupied by the Almohads, who built a *ribat*, or fortress, later abandoned. In the 16th century, the Iberian powers were building their empires in the Indies and the Americas. With trade growing, Portugal was wealthy enough to establish strongpoints along the African coast, and the fortress town they founded and named Mazagão in 1515 was to become one of their most important bases, and one of the longest lived, holding out after the fall of their other enclaves in northwest Africa.

Sultan Mohammed Ben Abdallah retook the town in 1769. But the town had been mined by the defeated Portuguese who, according to legend, left someone behind to light the fuses; in the explosion, large numbers of celebrating Moroccan soldiers were killed. The old fortress town thus acquired a sinister reputation and the nickname El Mahdouma, 'The Demolished'. On the wild Atlantic coast, the massive defences left by the Portuguese were far too valuable remain left abandoned for long. Reconstruction works were launched in 1815 by Sultan Sidi Abd al Rahman. In 1844, after the Moroccan forces had been defeated by the French at Isly – and the sultan's authority duly weakened – the Doukkala tribes looted the town. However, European merchants were to settle and the town began to expand beyond the walls of the original Portuguese city. There was also an influx of Jews from neighbouring Azemmour in the 19th century, and the town was further developed by the French as the chief town of the Doukkala region, also handling much of the trade with Marrakech. Under the French protectorate, the usual new avenues, gardens, along with administrative and residential neighbourhoods, were carefully laid out.

Today, El Jadida is a sleepy sort of small town, home to provincial administration, a university and a busy port, much involved in sardine fishing. The summer influx of mainly

Moroccan tourists is short (mid-July to mid-September), after which hibernation sets in. The Portuguese have put some money into the citadel, and the Moroccan authorities' emphasis on promoting beach resort tourism may have spin-offs for the town.

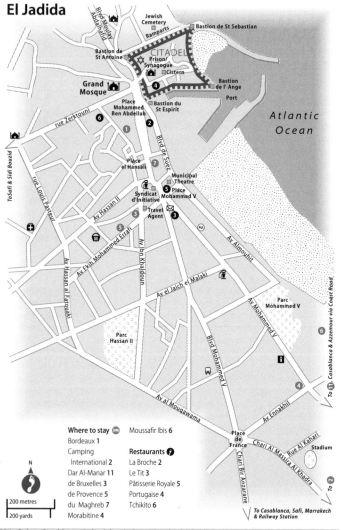

El Jadida

Jewish Cemetery

Bastion de St Sebastian

Ramparts

Blvd Moulay Abdelhafid

Bastion de St Antoine

CITADEL

Prison/Synagogue

Cistern

Bastion de l' Ange

Bastion du St Espirit

Port

Grand Mosque

Place Mohammed Ben Abdellah

rue Zerktouni

Atlantic Ocean

Blvd de Suez

Place el Hansali

Municipal Theatre

To Safi & Sidi Bouzid

rue Louis Pasteur

Syndicat d'Initiative

Travel Agent

Place Mohammed V

Av Hassan II

Av Fkih Mohammed Erraffi

Av Ibn Khaldoun

Pol

Av Almouhit

Av Hassan al Farouaki

Av el Jaich el Malaki

Parc Mohammed V

Blvd Mohammed V

Av Mohammed V

To Casablanca & Azzemour via Coast Road

Parc Hassan II

Av al Mouqawama

To Casablanca, Safi, Marrakech & Railway Station

Place de France

Chari Al Massira Al Khadra

Rue Al Kahari

Stadium

Chari Bir Anzarane

To ②

Where to stay 🛏
Bordeaux 1
Camping
 International 2
Dar Al-Manar 11
de Bruxelles 3
de Provence 5
du Maghreb 7
Morabitine 4
Moussafir Ibis 6

Restaurants 🍴
La Broche 2
Le Tit 3
Pâtisserie Royale 5
Portugaise 4
Tchikito 6

N

200 metres
200 yards

Cité Portuguese

A magical sun-bleached place of dusty crumbling corners, playing children and peeling paint, the **Citadel** was built by the Portuguese from 1513. Its distinctive character was maintained after their departure in 1769 by European and Jewish merchants, who settled here from 1815. The quarter is small and easily explored and contains attractive Portuguese and Jewish houses with decorated, arched doorways and wrought-iron balconies.

You can wander around the **ramparts**, parts of which have been repaved, from ramps to either side of the main entrances and also from the Porte de le Mer. These are surmounted by the escutcheons of the Portuguese kings and were completed in 1541.

The **Bastion du St Esprit** is located at the southwest corner and, from here, the walk along the ramparts follows a canal on the south side, which is all that remains of the old moat that once surrounded the citadel.

From the **Bastion de l'Ange** at the southeast corner there is a superb panoramic view of the citadel, the fishing harbour and beach. Looking north, the walls are broken on the coastal side by the **Porte de la Mer**, the old sea gate from where the Portuguese finally left in 1769; many of the other interesting features of the old walled city – including a chapel, hospital, prison, Governor's palace and a lighthouse converted into the Grand Mosque – can be seen from this vantage point. The **minaret**, built on the foundations of an old watchtower, has five sides making it unique in the Islamic world. The old prison was converted into a **synagogue**; this building dominates the skyline to the north and the Star of David can be seen clearly high up on the façade. It is possible to gain entry to the building if you are able to find the guardian with the key but there is little of note to see inside. Beyond the Porte de la Mer, the ramparts walk can be completed via the **Bastion de St Sébastian** and the **Bastion de St Antoine**. From this final section the old **Jewish cemetery** can be seen to the north outside the city walls.

Located between the entry gates and the Bastion du St Esprit is the **Church of Our Lady of the Assumption**, a Portuguese construction restored by the French in 1921, and later converted into a mosque.

In the centre of the citadel, the eerily beautiful and atmospheric underground **Cistern** ① *Rue Mohammed Ahehami Bahbai, 0900-1200, 1500-1800, 1500-1900 in summer, 10dh*, dates from the 16th century and was probably originally designed to store munitions. It served as a fencing school before being used, after completion of the town walls in 1541, as a tank to store water for times of shortage. When full, the Cistern reportedly held 4 million litres of water. The symmetrical construction has a vaulted roof supported by 25 circular and rectangular pillars, with just one central window in the ceiling, 3.5 m in diameter, producing a single shaft of light. Covering the flagstones is a shallow sheet of water, producing a shimmering reflection of the vaulted ceiling in the half-light. Orson Welles filmed scenes of his epic *Othello* in the Cistern. **Gallery Chaibia Tallal**, in the same block, has good exhibitions of contemporary art.

Outside the citadel, the other main focuses of interest are the **beach** and the area between **Place Mohammed V** and **Place Mohammed Ben Abdallah** and the immediately adjacent streets. The main shops, banks and restaurants are here, together with cinemas and the Municipal Theatre, and the pedestrianized **Place el Hansali** provides a pleasant alternative to the corniche for a relaxing drink on a café terrace.

Around El Jadida

The **beaches** south of El Jadida on the S121 are reached by bus No 2 and *grands taxis*. First is **Sidi Ouafi**, then the more developed (and polluted) **Sidi Bouzid**, with a bar, café-

Birds in paradise

After the industrial port of Jorf Lasfar, south of El Jadida, the coast starts to become of interest to birdwatchers. The range of habitats, including rocky coast, lagoons and salt flats, to dunes and scrub, makes for a variety of species. In addition, given its latitude, the area is important for over-wintering. All year there are flamingoes, cattle and little egrets, white storks and grey herons and even the tiny Sardinian warbler. Migrants include the collared pratincole and little tern, gulls and waders. The slender-billed curlew has also occasionally been spotted. Access is possible by bus, if you ask to be dropped off at a suitable place, but travel by car is far easier.

restaurants and a campsite. Here at Sidi Bouzid the gulls congregate in their hundreds between November and February each year.

Moulay Abdallah is a fishing village with an attached site of religious importance, lying 10 km from El Jadida. The minaret of Ismaïl Amghar dates from the Almoravid period and is almost intact. The shrine attracts up to 200,000 visitors to its annual *moussem* in August, one of the major festivals in the Moroccan calendar. Thousands of horsemen take part in the parades and displays, magnificent in their skill and their costumes.

Oualidia and around → For listings, see pages 329-332. Colour map 2, A3.

Almost midway between El Jadida and Safi, Oualidia has abundant natural beauty and is a restful sort of place, except in July and August when Moroccan tourists descend on it in their hordes. New holiday bungalows are beginning to cascade down the hillside but, for most of the year, it remains a chilled haven.

Named for the Saâdian Sultan el Oulalid, who built a kasbah there in the 1630s, the town is best known today for its oysters and its restaurants. There are caves, a lagoon, safe swimming – and ample amusement for birdwatchers, as the inlets and beaches are much appreciated by migrating birds in autumn and spring. It's also popular with surfers and, increasingly, kite-surfers, who ride the calmer waters in the lagoon.

Places in Oualidia

The village of Oualidia forms a crescent around a peaceful lagoon, entered by the sea through two breaches in a natural breakwater. Above the beach, the skyline on the wooded hillside is dominated by the **kasbah**, built in 1634 by a Saâdian sultan to defend the pleasant and potentially useful harbour (a track right off the S121 opposite the turning to Tnine Gharbia leads up to the building). Below it is the now disused royal villa built by Mohammed V as a summer palace.

The town has a **market** (Saturday) for local agricultural produce. The lagoon and beach provide an ideal sheltered location for sailing, kite-surfing, windsurfing and fishing. From late June to September, Oualidia is very busy. The beach gets crowded and the water is none too clean. Off-season, you have the beautiful surroundings almost to yourself.

At the far end of the beach to the south of the town, about a 10-minute walk, rocky outcrops are threaded with **caves**, some of which have been artificially enlarged over the years, especially during times of war, when they made useful hideaways and lookouts. If you walk down this way, Mustapha, who is often to be found fishing on the rocks here, may well offer to give you a guided tour.

The Oualidia **oyster beds** came into production in the late 1950s, and annual production is around 200 tonnes, mainly for local consumption. Early fruit and vegetables, in particular tomatoes, are produced here under plastic for local and European markets.

For a change of beach, you could head for **Lalla Fatna**, just 2 km outside the main village, signposted.

For those with a car, a possible side-excursion is to the **Kasbah Gharbia**, about 20 km to the southeast on the S1336. The kasbah is a huge enclosure, with a large white building in the centre.

⊚ South of Casablanca listings

For sleeping and eating price codes and other relevant information, see pages 22-28.

⊚ Where to stay

Azèmmour *p323, map p324*
€€€ L'Oum Erribia, 25 impasse Chtouka, T0523-347071, www.azemmour-hotel.com. This bright medina house has 5 spacious rooms, with big windows overlooking the river, and lots of contemporary art and modern style.
€€€ Riad Azama, 17 impasse Ben Tahar, Medina, T0523-347516. A stylish, whitewashed place with elegant columns, lamps and lots of carved plasterwork. The terracotta-tiled courtyard has plants around the traditional fountain. There are good views from the roof terrace, and rooms are cosy and romantic, with some nice old pieces of furniture.
€ Hotel de la Poste, next to the PTT, opposite the city walls, T0523-357702. Clean and basic.

El Jadida *p324, map p326*
El Jadida has a lack of good mid-range places to stay, and those at the top end cater more for business than tourism.
€€€ Dar al Manar, 7 km from El Jadida, just south of the golf course, T0523-351645, www.dar-al-manar.com. A cleverly designed modern building in traditional riad style. Wonderful artistic touches have created a unique and homely atmosphere in a peaceful, countryside setting. They also specialize in osteopathic massage.

€€ Hotel de Provence, 42 Av Fkih Errafi, T0523-342347. A popular and friendly choice but not especially good value. The carpets needed changing years ago, and bathrooms are small but the rooms are comfortable. Those at the back are quieter and the front ones have balconies. The bar and restaurant downstairs has a faded 1930s feel and isn't a bad place to spend part of your evening.
€€ Morabitine, corner of Av Mohammed VI & Av Ennakhil, T0523-379430, www. elmorabitine-hotel.com. A professional but somewhat anonymous hotel with 150 rooms, an international restaurant and a piano bar. There are pools, Wi-Fi in the lobby and bar and a strange grey, green and pastel pink colour scheme in the corridors. All the bright, modern rooms have balconies and a/c. Suites are overpriced and not that beautiful but do have 6 sofas.
€€ Moussafir Ibis, Pl Nour el Kamar Route Casablanca, T0523-379500. A big white and blue building at the end of the beach furthest from the Cité Portugaise. Modern and comfortable but you could be anywhere.
€ Hotel Bordeaux, 47 Rue Moulay Ahmed Tahiri, T0523-373921, hotelbordeaux.skyrock. com. 28 clean, tiled rooms around a central courtyard, with pine furniture and hot showers available. Well hidden in a largely residential part of town but well signposted, 150 m from **Restaurant Tchikito**, which anyone should be able to point you towards.
€ Hotel de Bruxelles, 40 Av Ibn Khaldoun, T0523-342072. There is an ant problem here, and en suite bathrooms come without toilet seats or paper. Nevertheless, this friendly

place, next door to the **Provence**, is actually one of El Jadida's better budget options; its 14 rooms are light and have balconies with wrought iron. There are old tiles in the rooms, the location is conveniently central, and there's parking.

€ **Hotel du Maghreb**, 16 Rue de Lescoul, just off Pl Mohammed V, T0523-342181. A little like an old mansion furnished with broken camping furniture, **Maghreb** is sagging, but sagging with a certain style. Marble staircase and peeling formica. Convenient, good low-budget option; it could be magnificent. Views from roof terrace.

Camping

Camping International, Av des Nations Unies, T0523-342755. At entrance to El Jadida, coming from Casablanca. Restaurant, shop and pool, site of 4 ha, only 500 m from beach, showers, laundry, electricity for caravans. Also has chalet accommodation for 260dh per night.
Camping Sidi Bou Zid, by beach, bus No 2, 5 km out of town.

Oualidia p328

Oualidia can get very crowded in high summer, when hotel reservations are essential. Prices drop in low season, Sep-Apr. Most restaurants are also places to stay.
€€€€ **La Sultana Oualidia**, T0524-388008, www.lasultanaoualidia.com. A sophisticated 5-star boutique hotel just to the north of town. Sandy pastel shades and a carved stone spa set the tone, and the restaurant goes big on lobster and oysters. There is painted furniture, lots of bare stone and wood and marble floors, which give this place a real air of elegance and exclusivity.
€€€ **Hotel Hippocampe**, Rte du Palais Oualidia, T0523-366108, hotelhippocampe@ hotmail.com. The location and amazing floral gardens, with a profusion of geraniums and nasturtiums set back from the lagoon, is the real drawcard here. The 23 bungalows are rather plainly furnished but the restaurant, serving fresh seafood, has patio

doors opening onto a terrace with great views and below this is the pool.
€€€ **Issa Blanca**, Beach Rd, T0523-366148. The 6 simple rooms at this family-run hotel have clean, tiled, black-and-white bathrooms and metal frame beds; one has a private terrace. There's an open kitchen in the French-style restaurant; try the salad Issa Blanca, with oysters, of course, and something from the good list of Moroccan wines.
€€€ **L'Initiale**, Oualidia Plage, T0523-366246. Opened in 2000, at the end of the road with 6 rooms near the ocean. If you can, get room 5 with its great sea view; you can sit up in bed and see the waves crashing on the sand about 70 m away. It's a comfortable, modern place that is very clean and charming. Great licensed restaurant with good Italian menu.
€€€ **Motel-Restaurant à l'Araigneé Gourmande**, T0523-366447. There are good views of the lagoon from some of the 15 rooms in 2 adjacent buildings, all of which have balconies. The rooms themselves are rather simple for the price but the popular restaurant offers seafood of just about every type imaginable. It's too large to have much atmosphere, and groups (everyone from old-aged bus tours to kitesurfers) come here but the food is excellent.
€€ **Le Relais**, at Sidi Abed, on the El Jadida–Oualidia road, T0523-345498. Restaurant open all year round (except Ramadan), accommodation in summer. A handy coffee stop if you're on a long drive.
€ **Villa La Brise**, El Jadida–Oualidia road, T0523-346917. With bar and good cooking.

Camping

Camping Municipal and **Camping International de Oualidia**, T0523-366160. Site of 30 ha, bar, snacks, restaurant, grocery shop, hot and cold showers, laundry, petrol at 1 km, electricity for caravans in summer only 10dh per night, other charges per night: caravan 30dh, tent 30dh, car 2dh, person 3dh.

🍴 Restaurants

Azemmour *p323, map p324*
Close to the medina the choice of cafés and restaurants includes: **Café l'Étoile de l'Atlantique**, a colourful place with a good terrace; and **Café el Manzeh**, Av Mohammed V, close to Pl du Souk. You might also try **Restaurant d'Azemmour**, for fresh fish, or **Café Belle Vue**, a good vantage point for a view of the town. Outside the town is the popular, fine sandy beach of Haouzia, a 30-min walk away, with cafés including **Restaurant La Perle**, T0523-347905, signposted from Pl du Souk (good in summer, a bit sad out of season).

El Jadida *p324, map p326*
€ **Restaurant La Broche**, Pl el Hansali. Small restaurant on 2 floors on a busy square, popular with locals, offering keenly priced choice of dishes and quick, friendly service. The menu is dominated by fish but you will also find couscous and chicken.
€ **Restaurant Portugaise**, Rue Mohammed Ali Bahbai, Cité Portugaise. Despite the name, this unlicensed little family-run restaurant is predominantly French. There are red-and-white checked tablecloths and good value omelettes and fish dishes as well as a *tagine du jour*. The waiter wears a bow tie, and everything is delightfully bijou.
€ **Tchikito**, Rue Mohammed Smiha. An El Jadida institution, Tchikito has sawdust on the floor, wipe-clean tablecloths and offers fresh fish dishes for 20-30dh.

Cafés and bars
Le Tit, 2 Av Al Jamia al Arabia. If you can suppress your smirks at the name, this is an OK, if rather rough-and-ready place for a drink.
Pâtisserie Royale. Best cakes in town and a good spot, just off the square, for breakfast or a coffee.

There is little to choose between the seafront cafés along Av Almouhit; they all make good spots from which to watch the games of football on the sand.

Oualidia *p328*
See also Where to stay above; just about all the hotels here also have good restaurants.
€€€ **Restaurant Ostréa II**, on your right as you come into Oualidia from the Casablanca direction. The sister of a restaurant in Casablanca, **Ostréa** is one of the best places to try the local oysters with a bottle of white wine and a great lagoon view.
€ **Restaurant Les Roches**. A small and friendly place opposite **L'Initiale**, painted white and blue and offering a menu of various seafood dishes.

🛍 Shopping

El Jadida *p324, map p326*
The main traditional shops and stalls are around **Rue Zerktouni**. El Jadida has a reputation for craftwork in brass, and you will find it on sale in **Pl Mohammed Ben Abdallah** and **Pl Moulay Youssef** at its junction with Rue Zerktouni close to the entrance to the Citadel. North of the ramparts, near the Bastion de St Antoine, there is an open-air **market**, providing cheap clothes and household goods to locals. A **souk** is held near the lighthouse on Wed; to find this, take the coastal route to Sidi Bouzid via Rue Zerktouni.

🚌 Transport

El Jadida *p324, map p326*
El Jadida is easily accessible by public transport. The town is a rather slow 1¾-hr drive from Casablanca, taking the coast road.

Bus
The bus station is in Av Mohammed V, approximately 1 km south of Pl Mohammed V. For **Safi** there are 9 buses daily (2½ hrs); plenty to **Essaouira** (a punishing 7-hr ride); to **Casablanca** 5 per day (2 hrs); **Marrakech** (4 hrs, depending on service); **Agadir**, 1 at 0900 (8 hrs); **Oualidia**, 1 bus at 1430 for most of the year, 2 buses in summer (1½ hrs); for **Taroudant** change at Agadir.

In summer, try to get your bus tickets to major destinations a day ahead.

Taxi
There are *grands taxis* that go up and down the coast: to **Oualidia** to the south (26dh, about 45 mins) and **Casablanca** to the north.

Train
The train service from **Casa/Rabat** has 7 daily services.

Oualidia *p328*
Oualidia is 78 km south of El Jadida, around 45 mins by *grand taxi*, and 66 km north of Safi. There is 1 bus a day (2 in summer) to **Casablanca**, via **El Jadida**, and 1 to **Safi**.

Directory

El Jadida *p324, map p326*
Medical services Chemists:
night pharmacies at **Sidi Daoui**, 14 Blvd Moulay Abdelhafid, T0523-353448, and **Pharmacy Ennour**, 77 Av Jamal Eddine el Afghani, T0523-351240.

Safi

Safi is the largest of the historic Atlantic coastal towns, with fortifications and other sights going back to a Lusitanian past, a good deal of industry and much poverty. Despite its medina and renown as a centre for fine, traditional pottery, it is probably for enthusiasts only. For those in search of architectural oddities, the medina contains a fragment of a cathedral in the Manueline Gothic style, all that the Portuguese had the time to build during their brief occupation in the 16th century. Unlike El Jadida to the north, Safi was an enclave where they stayed a mere 33 years.▸▸ *For listings, see pages 336-236.*

Arriving in Safi → *Colour map 2, A2.*

Getting there
The **train station** is south of the town centre; take a taxi to the medina. The **bus station** is southeast of the town centre, about 1.5 km from the medina. Bus No 7 takes you from main bus station into town centre, 2dh. Or you can walk: turn out of the bus station onto Avenue du Président Kennedy, past the **Hotel Abda**; at the first main junction, Place Idriss, bear right (north) and follow the road north for the Place de l'Indépendence and the medina. Parallel to this street, further west, Rue du Caïd Sidi Abderrahman, subsequently becoming Rue de R'bat, will also take you there.

Getting around
All the major sites in the old town are within walking distance of each other. Beaches are a different matter. South of the town, the coast is highly polluted by the chemical industry. Local buses (Nos 10 and 15) run up to **Lalla Fatna**, a sheltered beach 15 km north of the town.

Background

Safi is a port and industrial centre. Its harbour has been important since pre-Roman times, and it was one of the first areas of Morocco to receive Islam. Later it was the site of a *ribat* held by ascetic Muslim warriors.

The Almohads surrounded the city with ramparts and built the Zaouïa of Sheikh Mohammed Saleh. During their rule, Safi had an active intellectual and religious life. The first written mention of the town goes back to 11th-century geographer, El Bakri, who wrote that "the ships sail up along the coast from the Oued Souss to Marsa Amegdoul [today's Essaouira] … and then to Marsa Kouz [the mouth of the River Tensift], which is the port of Aghmat, and thence to Marsa Asafi." El Idrissi, writing in the mid-12th century, said that ships could load at Safi, "when the Ocean of Shadows was calm."

The Portuguese had had a trading centre at Safi since 1481 and took control of the town in 1508, building a citadel, repairing the kasbah and building the distinctive Dar el Bahr (Castle of the Sea) in 1523 to defend the northern entrance of the port and to be the official residence of the governor. Some of the cannon, cast in Spain and the Netherlands, remain today, 'protecting' the town. The Portuguese left in 1541. Under the Saâdians in the later 16th century, Safi developed a role as the port for the sugar produced at Chichaoua and for Souss copper, a strategic raw material much in demand in the foundries of Europe. The Saâdians also built the Grand Mosque in the medina.

In the 17th century, European countries had a significant trading presence in Safi, and Moulay Ismaïl was instrumental in developing the city in the early 18th century. Under Sidi Mohammed Ben Abdallah, trade intensified, with France, England, the Dutch Republic and Denmark all having agents. An indication of the effects of contact with Europe is given by

a Dr Lempriere, an English visitor in 1789: "During the time I spent in the town, I lodged in a Jewish house where I saw two Arabs who had been to London, and who spoke a few words of English. They thought to please me greatly when they proffered a chair and a small table. Since I had left Tangier, I had only seen this furniture, now completely indispensable to us, at the French consul's house in Rabat."

However, developments were cruel to Safi. Its position as the chief diplomatic port for the capital, Marrakech, was removed when Essaouira was rebuilt in the late 18th century. Between 1791 and 1883, no less than 18 natural catastrophes of various kinds hit the town. Nevertheless, not all was doom and gloom: in the mid-19th century, potters from Fès came to settle, bringing with them their craft skills. The Jewish community developed – it says much for the open-mindedness of Safi that there was never any walled-off *mellah* area – and a mixed Franco-Hispano-Portuguese commercial and fishing community gradually took root.

Safi was the base of a large sardine fishing fleet, which continues to this day, and, for many years, Safi was the biggest world sardine port. Large schools of sardines are present as a result of the currents of cold water bathing the coasts south of El Jadida in the summer, and more than 30,000 tonnes of fish now pass through the port annually, supplying an important processing and canning industry, which provides considerable employment for women.

Under the French, Safi was developed as a port for exporting phosphate rock, connecting it by rail to the mines around Youssoufia. In 1964 a new processing complex for Maroc-Chimie to the south of the town came on line, allowing the export of phosphate fertilizers, as well as unprocessed phosphates, and established Safi as one of Morocco's largest ports.

The development of Safi has been rapid, with the population rising from 40,000 in 1960 to over 400,000 today. The once bustling multinational sardine port has become a provincial city where a combination of factors has produced rather negative results. Chemical products poured into the sea have had a bad effect on the fish population. There are no useable town beaches, and scant respect has been paid to the town planning regulations. There is a huge sub-standard housing problem, especially in the medina. A few years ago, a large number of the urban poor of Agadir and Marrakech were apparently relocated to Safi, creating a climate of insecurity. Many former Safiots who grew up there in the 1950s and 1960s prefer not to go back. The town does have an interesting history and some sights, however, and, although it will never be a major destination, it would be a pity if Safi's tourist potential was totally neglected.

Places in Safi

The medina

The medina, with its ramparts and large towers, slopes westwards towards the sea and can be entered by the main gate, **Bab Chaaba**. The main thoroughfare which runs from Place de l'Indépendence to Bab Chaaba is **Rue du Socco**, around which are located the main souks. It is a busy, bustling area, with shops and street stalls selling all manner of food, jewellery, cheap toys and plastic goods. Close to the northern wall of the medina near Bab Chaaba is the **pottery souk**, a colourful alleyway and courtyard crammed with pots and plates displaying a wide variety of local designs. This leads on up some steps to an open courtyard with attractive archways housing some further pottery stalls. Just off the Rue du Socco is the **Grand Mosque**, with a notable minaret, and, behind it, a ruined Gothic church built by the Portuguese, and originally intended as part of a larger cathedral. There is also an interesting old *medersa*.

On the east flank of the medina is the Kechla, a large kasbah built by the Saâdians, clearly identifiable with its towers and green-tiled roofs. It offers some outstanding views over the medina and the potters' quarter at Bab Chaaba. The entrance opens out into the main courtyard, gardens and a terrace. It now houses the **National Ceramics Museum** ① T0524-463895, 0830-1200, 1400-1800, 10dh. Displays of ceramics here are divided into three sections: contemporary, local and ancient and, among these, are some very fine pieces of 20th-century Safi pottery. The visit might even inspire you to visit the local potters, where a cruder form of pottery is available and you can watch potters at work. On the right of its entrance is a large round tower built by the Portuguese and, within the Kechla, is the **Bahia Palace**, an 18th-century governor's residence flanked by gardens.

Dar el Bahar
① 0830-1200, 1430-1800. 10dh.
Just outside the medina ramparts, overlooking the sea, is the Dar el Bahar fort and prison built by the Portuguese in 1523. Used by them as the governor's residence, it was restored in the 1960s. Entry is under an archway, inscribed 'Château de Mer', opposite the **Hotel Majestic**. Just to the left of the pay kiosk is a hammam and to the right is the prison tower. You can see the dungeon area and climb the spiral staircase of the tower (narrow and dark

2 Safi centre

→ Safi maps
1 Safi, page 333
2 Safi centre, page 335

Where to stay
Assif 2
Atlantide 3
Majestic 7
Riad du Pecheur 1
Riad Safi 4

Restaurants
Café Oukaimeden 1
Café Sofia Ice 6
Chez Gegene 4
de Safi 2

in places) for views of the medina, Kechla and port from the top. Back at the foot of the tower, access to the **ramparts** on the seaward side of the fortress is via a ramp. Here you can see an impressive array of Dutch and Spanish cannon pointing out to sea; castings on two of these show 'Rotterdam 1619' and two others are marked 'Hague 1621'. From the top of the southwest bastion there is a further opportunity to enjoy a fine panorama, including the coast southwards towards Essaouira.

Town centre
Modern Safi has two main squares, the Place de l'Indépendence and Place Mohammed V. Located to the south of the junction of Avenue Moulay Youssef and Boulevard du Front de Mer, **Place de l'Indépendence** is a busy street with a central, tree-lined reservation, flanked by shops, banks, cafés and restaurants. There are also some markets here and in the Rue de R'bat to the south. Dar el Bahar sits at the northwest corner of the square. In contrast, on the hill high above the old town, **Place Mohammed V** is a grand, modern paved circular area lacking in character, a focal point for the seven streets converging on it. The town hall is the main building here, and the principal post office and the more expensive hotels are close by.

The Potters Quarters
These quarters at Bab Chaaba are well worth a visit; you can see all the stages of the pottery process happen in and around tiny workshops. From the port side of the old town, you can cut straight through to the potters' area, which centres on the marabout Sidi Abderrahman, Moula el Bibane, 'Protector of the city gates' and patron of the potters; the whole area was given official listing as being of historic importance in 1920.

Beaches
The best local beach is **Sidi Bouzid**, just north of the town and on the No 15 bus route, with cafés and the very good **Le Refuge** seafood restaurant. Further afield is the **Lalla Fatma** beach, just past Cap Safi. If they can, locals go further afield to **Plage Souiriya**, some 30 km to the south.

◉ Safi listings

For sleeping and eating price codes and other relevant information, see pages 22-28.

◉ Where to stay

Safi *p332, maps p333 and p335*
In Safi you can find hotels at a fraction of the price of those in Essaouira. The cheap hotels are all concentrated in the southwestern side of the medina, opposite the port, just below the long, sloping Pl de l'Indépendence (where there are some good cheap eateries). They are a 2-km walk from the bus station. If you can afford it, it's certainly worth the extra to stay in the **Riad du Pecheur**.

€€ Riad du Pecheur, Rue de la Crete, T0524-610291, www.ryaddupecheur.com. With its sun-drenched patio full of flowers and colourful simple rooms, this riad is by far Safi's friendliest and most relaxed accommodation option. It's a lovely place to spend a few days chilling out with staff that can't do enough to help. A great restaurant, and all the mod-cons of Wi-Fi and a/c are also provided.
€€ Riad Safi, Rue de l'eglise, T0614-050211 (mob), www.riadsafi.fr. The rooms here are a wonderfully eclectic merge of bright colours, local design and quirky decorating, with lots of traditional wrought iron-work,

textiles and tiling thrown in to create a really artistic feel.

€ **Hotel Assif**, Av de la Liberté, T0524-622940, www.hotel-assif.ma. Near Pl Mohammed, this is a large concrete block of a hotel beginning to look a little dog-eared but very friendly all the same. Rooms are simple but comfortable, and the balconies even have a few flowers growing in their window boxes.

€ **Hotel Atlantide**, Rue Chawki, T0524-462160, imsa-atlantide@menara.ma. Safi's best-value hotel in the higher budget end has a good pool plus a kids' pool, good views and comfortable rooms, with big beds, balconies and a/c. The place retains a pleasant 1920s air, and there is a bar and a grand piano. Breakfast not included.

€ **Hotel Majestic**, Pl de l'Indépendence (corner of Av Moulay Youssef), T0524-464011. Right on the Pl de l'Indépendence, opposite the castle, this is the best budget option in town; mattresses are thin but rooms are reasonably spacious and light.

Camping
Camping de Sidi Bouzid, 3 km north of Safi at Sidi Bouzid, T0524-462871. Site of 6 ha, bar/snacks, grocery shop, pool, showers, laundry, petrol 2 km, electricity for caravans.

❼ Restaurants

Safi *p332, maps p333 and p335*
Often, restaurants in Safi do not display menus outside, so check inside to be sure of prices and range of food on offer.

€€€ **Restaurant La Trattoria**, aka Chez Yvette, Rue Aouinate, on an uphill road leading south of the medina, T0524-620959. A large Italian restaurant serving salad and fish main course for 150dh, but also pizza, lasagne, osso bucco and, occasionally, tiramisu.

€€ **Chez Gegene**, 11 Rue de la Marine, T0524-463369. Specializing in fish and Italian dishes, this is just off the Pl de l'Indépendence near the Wafa Bank. The bar next door is run by the same people.

€€ **Restaurant de Safi**, 3 Rue de la Marine, just off the Pl de l'Indépendence, T0524-610472. This traditional Moroccan place with plastic tablecloths is easily identified by bright displays of vegetables and a basic Moroccan menu.

€€ **Restaurant La Corniche**, Rte de Sidi Bouzid, T0524-463584. Moroccan food and shellfish.

€€ **Restaurant Le Refuge**, Rte de Sidi Bouzid, out of Safi to the north (a *petit taxi* or car needed), T0524-464354. Closed Mon. Has a good reputation for French cuisine, particularly fish dishes.

Cafés
Café des Remparts, 1 Bir Anzarame. Well placed next to Bab Laasra, the gate to the medina just off Pl de l'Independence, Café des Remparts has a large terrace and makes a good spot for people-watching.

Café Oukaimeden, Av Zerktouni. Does good coffee and pastries and has seats outside on the street. A better option for breakfast than the hotel, if you're staying around here.

Cafe Sofia Ice, Blvd Idriss 1. A slick and modern place, with a big terrace, laid-back jazz and views down to the sea. Ice creams as well as drinks served.

Tartine, Av Elhourria. With its chocolate-coloured seats, pop music, candles, young staff and modern menu, this place largely succeeds in being more than just a café and pâtisserie. A good stop for a burger or a salad.

❶ What to do

Safi *p332, maps p333 and p335*
The beach at **Sidi Bouzid** is known for surfing. There is horse riding at **Club Equestre**, Rte de Sidi Ouassel.

⊖ Transport

Safi *p332, maps p333 and p335*

Bus

The bus terminal is on Av Président Kennedy to the south of the town. **CTM** has 7 services per day to **Casablanca** (4 hrs); 4 to **El Jadida** at 0615, 1000, 1130 and 1430 (2½ hrs); 2 to **Essaouira** at 1130 and 1945 (2¼ hrs), and 1 daily bus to **Agadir** at 11.30 (5¾ hrs). Try to reserve ticket day before. Other operators have services to **Marrakech** (2½ hrs), **Agadir**, **Casablanca**, **Rabat** and **Taroudant**.

Car

If driving, Safi is on the S121 coastal road from El Jadida and the R204 from Marrakech.

Approaching on the main N1 from Casablanca, turn along the R204 from Tleta de Sidi Bouguedra.

Taxi

Grands taxis run to **Oualidia** (1 hr, 25dh).

Train

The railway station is to the south of town, on Rue du Caïd Sidi Abderrahman, the continuation of Rue de R'bat, T0524-464993. There are 2 trains daily at 0545 and 1545 to **Benguerir** (1 hr), which connects with services to **Casablanca**, **Rabat**, **Kénitra**, **Meknès**, **Fès**, **Marrakech**, **Asilah** and **Tangier**.

Contents

Tangier & the North

At a glance

⊖ **Getting around** Tangier is small
enough to explore on foot, but
you'll probably want to get a taxi
from the station to the centre. The
rest of the area is served by buses
and *grands taxis*.

🕓 **Time required** Allow a couple
of days for Tangier, then spend a
week exploring the coast either
side and the Rif.

☼ **Weather** Winter in the north
can be cool and wet – in January
the average maximum temperature
in Tangier is 16°C – and in the hills
and mountains it can be downright
cold, especially at night. For most
of the year, however, the weather is
pleasant and cooler than the rest of
the country.

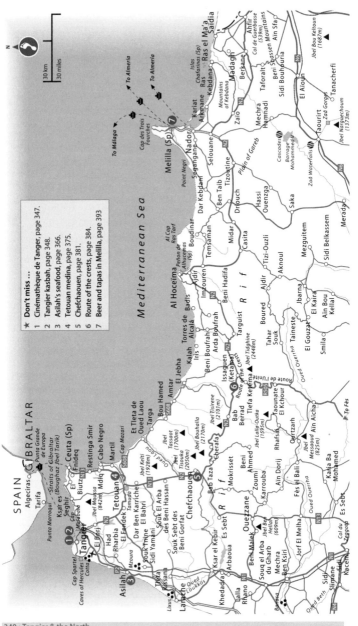

Don't miss ...

1 Cinémathèque de Tanger, page 347.
2 Tangier kasbah, page 348.
3 Asilah's seafood, page 366.
4 Tetouan medina, page 375.
5 Chefchaouen, page 381.
6 Route of the crests, page 384.
7 Beer and tapas in Melilla, page 393.

At the top of Morocco Africa is at its nearest to Europe, a short hop across the Straits of Gibraltar, yet a world away. It is this distance, rather than the closeness, that dominates northern Morocco, with the Spanish enclaves of Melilla and Ceuta as strange anomalies.

Tangier, one-time international city, is the most obvious example: despite its geographical closeness and ferry connections, it is a place characterized more by stasis than dynamic crossover; its most potent image is that of young African men standing for hours gazing across the sea at a hazy Spain. The city's seafront and kasbah are full of the decadent ghosts of writers, along with a great museum and people-watching cafés.

A short drive from Tangier is Ceuta, would-be Hong Kong of the Mediterranean and still a Spanish enclave. Inland from Tangier, Chefchaouen is a beautiful white- and blue-washed hill town, which, along with Ouezzane and Tetouan, reflects its links with Andalucía, long lost by the Moors. South of Ceuta is a string of small resorts: Restinga-Smir, Cabo Negro and Martil, along with many small fishing villages. Further east, Al Hoceïma, today a quiet Mediterranean resort, is a recent implant, a creation of the Spanish protectorate of the first half of the 20th century, and Melilla is another Spanish enclave, more easy-going than Ceuta. The Rif, inland, is a land of wild and beautiful mountains with a history of strong independence.

Tangier

Tangier is a product of its location: the gate to the Mediterranean Sea and the meeting point of Africa and Europe. The Phoenicians and Carthaginians established trading posts here. The Romans made it a capital city. It was invaded by the Vandals and Visigoths and occupied by the Arabs. The Portuguese took the town before the Spanish arrived. From 1923 to 1956, it was an international city, and its tax-free status and raffish reputation attracted European and American writers and artists. Tangier also had fame as a gay destination in the days when homosexuality attracted severe moral opprobrium in Europe. These days, Tangier is trying to bury these ghosts and reinvent itself as a modern city with a new port, stadium and business district. Arriving by sea, it may well be your first point of contact with Morocco and, despite a certain reputation for hassle, Tangier has remained popular with travellers. The kasbah, former residence of sultans, is particularly worth visiting, as is the medina, a dense maze of houses, shops and narrow, steep streets. A day is probably enough to see the main sights; two days would give you more time to take in the atmosphere and make a side trip to the Caves of Hercules on the Atlantic coast. ▸▸ *For listings, see pages 352-358.*

Arriving in Tangier → *Colour map 1, A3.*

Getting there

Tangier's **Ibn Battouta Airport** ① *T0539-393720*, is 15 km southwest of the city on the N1 road to Rabat. Entry formalities can be slow. Catch bus 17 or 70 from the terminal to the Grand Socco (Place du 19 Avril 1947), or take a *grand taxi* (160dh by day, 200dh after 2000, rates displayed on wall by customs).

The train no longer stops at Tangier Ville and Port. Rather, the terminal is at **Tangier Moghougha**, a 15dh *petit taxi* ride from the town centre, 20dh for the port, more at night; have change ready. Taxi drivers will want to fill up their vehicles so you may have to wait.

CTM buses arrive at the terminal in Avenue des FAR, adjacent to the port gates and the former Tangier Ville railway station. Private lines arrive at the terminal at the end of Rue de Fès. There are plenty of buses to Tangier from Casablanca, Fès, Meknès and Rabat, as well as from local places, such as Asilah, Larache and Tetouan. The bus station is a short (12dh) *petit taxi* ride from the city centre hotels.

If you are driving into the city in the summer from the south, expect slow traffic north of Asilah after the motorway ends. The A1 from Rabat brings the driver into Tangier along Rue de Fès. The N16 from Ceuta feeds into Av Mohammed V, as does the N2 from Tetouan.

There are car/passenger ferry services from Algeciras in Spain and Gibraltar. Within the port compound, there is a rank for both kinds of taxi. Hard negotiation over prices will probably be necessary. ▸▸ *See Transport, page 357, for further details.*

Getting around

Tangier is quite a small place but the bus station (*mahattat el kirane*) is a good way out. You will need to get a *petit taxi* (12dh), which ought to be metered, or a *grand taxi*. A trip within the city by *petit taxi* is 10dh. Taxis can be flagged down even when they have other passengers. If it is going in your direction, it will take you. A *grand taxi* ride will cost 10dh for a trip within the city. There are handy Boughaz minibuses and *grands taxis* from the Grand Socco to the bus station and the Atlantic coast sights.

Background

Perhaps the oldest city in Morocco, Tangier was active as early as 1600 BC. There was a Phoenician settlement here. Roman mythology ascribes its founding to the Greek giant Antaeus, son of Poseidon, god of the sea, and Gaia, goddess of the Earth. Antaeus challenged Hercules, but the hero killed the giant and had a child by his widow, Tingis. Hercules pulled apart Spain and Africa to give this son, Sophax, a city protected by the sea. Then, out of filial piety, King Sophax named his city Tingis.

Thanks to its location on the Straits of Gibraltar, Tangier has always been important. At one point, Rome made it capital of the empire's North African provinces, its people receiving Roman citizenship in AD 38. Rome controlled the city until AD 429. Later, the Vandals and Byzantines struggled to control the region, then the Muslim Arabs took the city in AD 706. It remained a point of conflict between major Arab and Berber dynasties, before achieving commercial importance in the Mediterranean during the 1300s.

Tangier was first conquered by the Portuguese in 1437 and subsequently reoccupied in 1471; it became Spanish in 1578 and Portuguese again in 1640. They built fine houses, Dominican and Franciscan chapels and a cathedral, and the city was part of the dowry brought by the Portuguese Catherine of Braganza when she married Charles II of England in 1661. The English succeeded in alienating the Portuguese population, forcing both religious orders and Jews out of the city, before finally departing themselves in 1684, destroying the kasbah as they left. Sultan Moulay Ismaïl rebuilt the town after they left.

In the 19th century Tangier became a popular base for European merchants, and housed a large European colony. It was also the focus of political competition between expansionist European powers. In 1923 the city became a tax-free International Zone controlled by a 30-member international committee. From then until the early 1960s, Tangier had its heyday as a hedonistic, decadent free port and the playground of an international demi-monde – thus reinforcing the truth of earlier descriptions of the city. St Francis had seen it as a centre of sin, while, in the 17th century, Samuel Pepys had described it as a latter-day Sodom.

Celebrity visitors

The streets of Tangier are full of artistic and literary memories. Among its illustrious visitors (other than Pepys and St Francis) are Camille Saint-Saëns (who drew on Issaoua trance music for his *Danse macabre*), film stars Marlene Dietrich and Errol Flynn, Oscar Wilde, author-translator Paul Bowles, Ian Fleming, Richard Hughes (*High Wind in Jamaica*) and James Leo Herlihy (*Midnight Cowboy*). Woolworth-heiress Barbara Hutton had a house here, as did the heiress to the Knoll furniture fortune, the crumbling York Castle, up in the kasbah. Winston Churchill, Ronnie Kray and the photographer Cecil Beaton all passed through. Painters who discovered light and the Orient in Tangier include Eugène Delacroix in 1832, Henri Matisse (1912), Kees Van Dongen and, more recently, Francis Bacon. The city's reputation as a haven of freedom for the likes of Tennessee Williams, Truman Capote, William Burroughs, Allen Ginsberg, Jack Kerouac, Brion Gysin and Joe Orton in the 1950s and 1960s continues to draw visitors. Today backpackers relive something of those heady days by visiting the **Tanger Inn**, Rue Magellan (see page 356), a surviving fragment of Burroughs' Interzone (see page 346).

1 Tangier

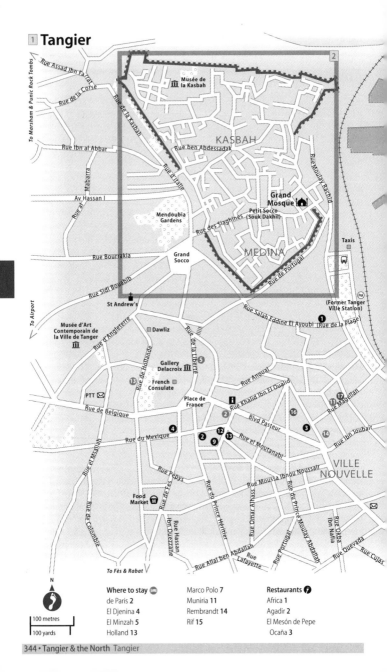

To Marsham & Punic Rock Tombs

Rue Assad Ibn Farrat
Rue de la Corse
Rue de la Kasbah
Rue Ibn al Abbar
Mabarra
Rue de l'Italie
Rue ben Abdessadak
Av Hassan I
Rue Bourrakia
Rue Sidi Bouabib
Rue Nouisy Rachid

Musée de la Kasbah

KASBAH

Mendoubia Gardens

Grand Socco

Grand Mosque

Petit Socco (Souk Dakhil)

Rue des Siaghines

MEDINA

Rue de Portugal

Taxis

(Former Tanger Ville Station)

St Andrew's

Rue Salah Eddine El Ayoubi (Rue de la Plage)

Musée d'Art Contemporain de la Ville de Tanger

To Airport

Rue d'Angleterre
Rue de Hollande
Rue de la Liberté
Rue de Belgique
Rue el Moutanabi
Rue du Mexique
Rue Pepys
Rue de Fès
Rue de Colombie
Rue el Madani
Ibn Ouezzane
Rue Hassan
Rue du Prince Héritier
Rue Moussa Ibnou Noussair
Rue Omar Athass
Rue Lafayette
Rue Attal ben Abdallah
Rue du Prince Moulay Abdallah
Rue Portugal
Rue Olfa Ibn Nafia
Rue Quevada
Rue Cujas

Dawliz

Gallery Delacroix

French Consulate

Place de France

Rue Khalid Ibn El Oualid

Rue Anoual

Blvd Pasteur

VILLE NOUVELLE

Rue Ibn Toubair

Rue Magellan

PTT

Food Market

To Fès & Rabat

N

100 metres
100 yards

Where to stay 🛏
de Paris **2**
El Djenina **4**
El Minzah **5**
Holland **13**

Marco Polo **7**
Muniria **11**
Rembrandt **14**
Rif **15**

Restaurants 🍴
Africa **1**
Agadir **2**
El Mesón de Pepe
Ocaña **3**

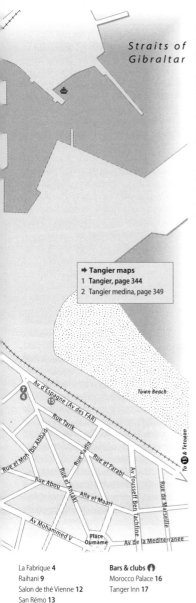

Straits of Gibraltar

➡ **Tangier maps**
1 Tangier, page 344
2 Tangier medina, page 349

Av d'Espagne (Av des FAR)

Town Beach

Rue Tarik

Rue el Moh Ibn Abbad

Rue Sidra

Rue el Farabi

Rue Abou

Alfa el Maari

Av Youssef Ben Tachfine

Rue de Marseille

Av Mohammed V

Place Oumame

Av de la Mediterranee

To 15 & Tetouan

La Fabrique **4**
Raihani **9**
Salon de thé Vienne **12**
San Rémo **13**

Bars & clubs 🎵
Morocco Palace **16**
Tanger Inn **17**

Though many of the city's literary sites were lost in the demolition-rebuilding of the 1990s, the romantic-minded can still find something of Tangier's artistic soul. There are plenty of decaying apartment buildings, restaurants and low-life bars. The **Grand-Hôtel Villa de France** still survives, home to Gertrude Stein and Matisse, as does the **Teatro Cervantes**. Down near the port, next to the **Hôtel Cecil** (a favourite with Roland Barthes), is the **Immeuble Renschaussen**, where Burroughs and Gysin did artistic cut-ups in one of the lofts. Up at the kasbah, the **Palais Menebhi** was home to Gysin's 1001 Nights bar. Further west on the Montagne at the **Villa Mimosa**, Bowles finished *Let it Come Down*, another tale of an American adrift in the mysterious East. West of the city, the **Plage Merkala** was the setting for tales by M'rabet, Charhadi and other members of Bowles' coterie. And the heavily revamped **Salon de thé Porte** still carries a hint of a literary yesteryear.

The end of cosmopolitan Tangier
Tangier as a centre of easy money and loose morals was not to last, however, and the free-port was reunited with Morocco in October 1956, although its tax-free status was maintained until 1960. Since Independence, Tangier has declined in international economic importance, and its tourism was soon overshadowed by the enormous development of the industry elsewhere in the Mediterranean. Today, the city functions essentially for the Moroccan tourist and travel market. In the summer, up to two million migrant workers and their families pass through the port, and Tangier is their first contact with their homeland. In the 1980s, the green cliff tops of La Montagne, west of the city, came to be favoured by Gulf emirs as the ideal place for a holiday home. Soon, vast palaces in the neo-Kuwaiti style appeared like UFOs in the pine and eucalyptus woods around the city.

With William Burroughs in Interzone

William Burroughs got interested in Tangier after reading a couple of Paul Bowles novels. In 1953, just after the publication of *Junkie*, he left New York for anywhere – and wound up in Tangier. Disappointment was quick to set in; the city's literary coterie was hostile and Burroughs wrote in a 1954 letter to Alan Ginsberg: "There is an end-of-the-world feeling in Tangier, with its glut of nylon shirts, Swiss watches, Scotch and sex and opiates sold across the counter. Something sinister in complete laissez-faire. And the new police chief up there on the hill accumulating dossiers. I suspect him of unspeakable fetishistic practices with his files." Paul Bowles proved hostile and manipulative, too. A moment of vengeance came, however, when the the city's senior writer was set upon by enraged baboons in the countryside and forced to flee for his life. Wrote Burroughs: "They got vicious purple-assed baboons in the mountains a few miles out of town … I intend to organize baboon sticks from motorcycles. A sport geared to modern times."

The exotic splendours of Tangier left Burroughs unmoved. As he put it in another letter to Ginsberg: "Don't ever fall of this inscrutable oriental shit like Bowles puts down." There was no adoration of the mysterious East here.

As Burroughs' life in the city gradually decayed into a drugged-up blur, he was dubbed the 'Invisible Man'. Rarely emerging from his hotel in the Petit Socco, he divided his time between writing, 'delicious afternoon sleeps in a darkened room', and the half-light of the Bar Mar Chica, whose denizens included fellow addicts and his lover Kiki. A cure at the Hôpital Benchimol produced meagre results, "the philosophic serenity conveyed by an empty scrotum" was not enough to break the opium habit. Eventually, Burroughs left for England for further treatment. He returned to take up residence at the Villa Mouniria and, in 1957, finished the manuscript which was to become *The Naked Lunch*. The 'International Zone of Tangier' features here as 'Interzone' (the book's first title), a place of shady deals and narcotic visions. Over time, however, Burroughs' idea of the city changed, and he came to find it had 'a wild beauty'.

For more on the Tangerine atmosphere of the 1950s, look out for the Bowles' novels *Let it come down* (1952) and *The Sheltering Sky* (1949), both republished in paperback. *The Letters of William S Burroughs* (1983) give a frank view of the writer's tribulations in Tangier.

Contemporary Tangier

Tangier has always been through highs and lows, and the 1990s were in many ways the trough of a low period. A building boom, in part financed by the profits of the kif trade, meant masses of new development as profits were recycled in. Many historic buildings were torn down, replaced by blocks of concrete-brutalist ugliness. And then came the late king's 'clean up public life' campaign. Corruption scandals and court cases hit the city, various local figures disappeared behind bars or overseas, all to the good many would say. But the big change came with Mohammed VI's accession to the throne in July 1999. The new king made the northwest the first region he visited outside the capital. Tangier was ecstatic. The long-ignored Palais Marshan was dusted down; there seemed to be some hope for a region too long forgotten by the powers that be.

A feisty local press have kept things moving along; associations have been set up to do something for street kids, to support the unemployed and illiterate, to save the kasbah and the Teatro Cervantes. The general environment has improved too, with new management for city services and an awareness that not everything old should be pulled down. Tangier's appeal for creative types has also remained intact; the **Cinema Rif** on the Grand Socco has been renovated and reborn as the **Cinémathèque de Tangier**, an important centre for the arts in the heart of the city.

The future of Tangier

With a population that has quadrupled from 250,000 in 1982 to a million, Tangier continues to sprawl ever further inland, its growth fuelled by rural in-migration and high unemployment. In times of pressure, the frustration of the deprived spills over in riots in the poor areas on the city edge. But things are better than they were, and many of the *bidonville* inhabitants are being rehoused. Work is expected to start soon on a rail tunnel between Spain and Morocco, though it is unlikely to be completed before 2025, and the city's future development will certainly be interesting to watch as Morocco moves closer to the European Union.

With its special history, Tangier is an endearing place, a town of past cosmopolitan glories. Some say it is best remembered from a vantage point, perhaps a cliff-top café, overlooking the Straits and the distant Iberian coast across the choppy sea, but no doubt it will remain a place of legend. As Mohammed Choukri put it, "In Tangier, any capable storyteller can invent a story and be sure to convince listeners of its truth."

Places in Tangier

Tangier is more of an atmosphere than a city with numerous unmissable sights. If you manage to avoid hasslers and hustlers, then it is a city for the flâneur, for strolling, with steep streets and stairways as well as boulevards. Yet there are minor galleries, out-of-the-way cafés and semi-sights for you to put together a wander with a purpose. The main attraction is the views: over the Straits to Spain, from *ville nouvelle* to the medina, down alleys which could twist on forever or end in a sticky situation.

Of the ancient city nothing remains. Descriptions are full of 'it is possible that' and 'probably be' and the few antique pieces that have been unearthed are disappointing from a dating and workmanship point of view. The limits of the city have been defined, using the position of necropolises. It extended west to Mendoubia, south to Bou Kachkach and northwest to Marshan Plateau, where there are Punic or maybe Roman tombs hollowed out of the rock, overlooking the Straits.

Grand Socco

The Grand Socco is where the medina begins. Tangier's answer to Jemaâ el Fna in Marrakech, the square has been spruced up, apparently on suggestion of the king, and it now has fountains and seats and tiled pedestrian areas. At the top of the square the **Cinémathèque de Tanger** ⓘ *T0539-934683, www.cinemathequedetanger.com*, has become one of Morocco's most significant arts venues, showing Moroccan and international arts films and documentaries. Formerly the Cinema Rif, it is the centrepoint of a cultural renaissance in the city and stages premieres, seasons and themed cycles and also has a good café with free Wi-Fi. Note the tiled minaret of the **Sidi Bou Abid Mosque** (1917) on the corner of the Grand Socco and Rue Sidi Bou Abid.

On Thursday and Sunday Rifi Berber women sell all sorts of wares in Rue de la Plage (Rue Salah Eddine el Ayoubi). Along Rue d'Angleterre they also sell woven blankets. On the Rue Bourrakia side of the Grand Socco, the arch with Arabic on it leads into the **Mendoubia Gardens**, a quiet, tree-filled place in the heart of Tangier. These gardens were formerly part of the residence of the Mendoub and contain 30 bronze cannons, remnants of old French and British warships. The Mendoubia Palace is the former residence of the sultan's representatives on the International Commission.

Kasbah

In Tangier, the kasbah is constructed on the highest point of the medina. It was fortified back in Roman days and it was the traditional residence in Tangier of the sultan and his harem. It was burnt to the ground by the English as they left in 1684. More recently, during the heyday of Tangier as an international city, the kasbah was considered a fashionable address for people such as the novelist Richard Hughes (who lived at 'Numéro Zero, La Kasbah, Tangier'). Today, parts of the kasbah are threatened by landslips: after particularly heavy rains, the locals hold their breath and wait to see whether a section of the cliffs will slither down towards the sea. Especially at risk is **York Castle**, 17th-century home of English governor, the Duke of York.

To get to the kasbah from the Grand Socco, head downhill across the square, aiming for the horseshoe-arched entrance gate and follow down Rue d'Italie and then up Rue de la Kasbah and enter by Bab el Kasbah. From the medina, follow Rue des Chrétiens from the Petit Socco, and then Rue Sidi Ben Rassouli to Bab el Assa.

Musée de la Kasbah ⓘ *T0539-932097, Sat-Mon, Wed and Thu 0900-1600, Fri 0900-1130, 1330-1600, 10dh*, is in the former palace of the kasbah, the Dar Al Makhzen, and includes Moroccan arts and antiquities. The palace was built by the Sultan Moulay Ismaïl in the 18th century, and was used as the Sultan's palace up until 1912, when Sultan Moulay Hafid, exiled to Tangier, lived there. The palace is itself worth seeing, with an impressive central courtyard. A museum since 1922, it has had a recent overhaul, with projections, video, large maps and music all illuminating the exhibits from Tangier and the surrounding region. The hub of the museum is seven rooms around a large central courtyard with pale marble columns. This is truly a magnificent setting for the displays. Exhibits range from prehistoric bone tools to decorated ostrich eggs. The collection of ceramics is especially strong and there is also a mosaic from Roman Volubilis. Pick up an explanatory leaflet in English on your way in.

The garden of the palace, a beautiful mature Andalucían arrangement with fragrant plants and a marble fountain, is also worth exploring. As you leave the palace, stop at **Café Le Detroit** – if it's open – for a drink and pastries. In front of the palace is the **Place de la Kasbah**, where criminals were once punished or executed. In the sea wall a gate leads out onto a belvedere with excellent views across to Spain. Nearby is **Villa Sidi Hosni**, former residence of Barbara Hutton, the American heiress who was famous for her parties, among other things (read all about it in Iain Finlayson's *Tangier, City of the Dream*).

Medina

Lying below the kasbah and running from the Grand Socco (Place de 19 Avril, 1947) down to the port, the medina is focused on the **Petit Socco**, and is full of narrow, twisting streets and old houses, many of which are now shops, hotels or restaurants catering for tourists. It is a quarter that has captured the imagination of numerous European and American writers, the stories of Paul Bowles being among the most evocative. Tangier medina has the advantage over many others of a slope, which aids one's sense of direction a little:

generally you go down to the Petit Socco and up to the kasbah. If you really don't have time to get lost, get an official guide, but avoid the advances of the unofficial ones.

Rue Siaghine, the old silversmiths' street, running from the Grand Socco to the Petit Socco, is still an important commercial area of the medina and the easiest route by which to enter the main area of the medina. To the right of Rue Siaghine, is the **mellah**, the Jewish quarter. You also pass the **Spanish Cathedral**, now boarded up.

The **Petit Socco**, the belly of the medina, was once bigger, but now seems strangely cramped. It is surrounded by a number of famous but primitive *pensiones* and the **Café Central**, formerly a café-bar attracting the likes of William Burroughs, Allen Ginsberg and Jack Kerouac. However, today, with no alcohol sold in the medina, it is a fairly ordinary café with a terrace from which to watch life pass by.

2 **Tangier medina**

➡ **Tangier maps**
1 Tangier, page 344
2 Tangier medina, page 349

Where to stay
Continental 1
Dar Nour 2
La Tangerina 4

Mamora 3
Nord-Pinus Tanger 6
Pensión Palace 5
Riad Tanja 9

Restaurants
Le Detroit 2

Below the Petit Socco, the **Grand Mosque** lies in between Rue de la Marine and Rue des Postes. This is built on the site of a Portuguese cathedral, although that had been predated by a mosque and, probably, a Roman temple. Opposite is a 14th-century *medersa*. Also on Rue des Postes (Rue Mokhtar Ahardan) is the **Pensión Palace**, where Bertolucci filmed scenes for *The Sheltering Sky*, based on the Paul Bowles novel.

The **Old American Legation** ① *8 Zankat Amerika, T0539-935317, www.legation.org, 0930-1200 and 1600-1830, free,* is America's oldest diplomatic property. It was given to the US by the Moroccan sultan in 1821 and used as a Consulate until 1961. It has the distinction of being the only historical monument to have remained in US possession since the birth of the American Nation. Now a museum and study centre, on display here is a letter from George Washington to Moulay Abdallah and a collection of mirrors, as well as a good collection of prints, including works by Lecouteux and Ben Ali Rbati, an early Moroccan naïve painter.

Ville nouvelle

Tangier's *ville nouvelle* is a veritable catalogue of late 19th and early 20th-century architectural styles. **Place de France** (Place de Faro) has a good view of the bay, with the famous **Café de France** alongside, where wartime agents met and made deals. Next to it is the **Terrasse des Paresseux**, where would-be emigrants can see across the Straits to Spain and shoe-shine boys and Polaroid-snappers harass the tourists. **Boulevard Pasteur** (becoming Avenue Mohammed V further down) is the main shopping and business street of the new town. Find time to explore the area behind here; look out for the 1940s cinemas, have tea at **Pâtisserie Porte**, then drop in at the Librairie des Colonnes back on the main boulevard. You could then wander medina-wards again down Rue de la Liberté, stopping off for contemporary art, photography and video art at the **Galerie Delacroix** ① *1100-1300, 1600-2030, free,* if there is an exhibition on.

Near the Grand Socco

At 50 Rue d'Angleterre, is the Anglican **Church of St Andrew's** consecrated in 1905. The churchyard gate is discreet, in a low white-washed wall, just left of some bird-sellers' stalls, at the top side of the Grand Socco. Inside, the church hides in luxuriant vegetation. The key is kept by the groundsman, who will unlock the church and give you a guided tour. Architecture and internal decoration are modelled on Moorish Granada. Note the Arabic inscriptions of the Lord's Prayer and Gloria at the altar end. Memorials and graves, both inside and outside, feature a number of important former residents of Morocco, including 19th-century British consul Sir John Drummond Hay, early 20th-century *Times* correspondent Walter Harris, Caïd Sir Harry McLean, Scottish adviser to Sultan Moulay Abd al Aziz, and Emily Keane, 19th-century wife of the Cherif of Ouezzane. Turn right out of the churchyard gate, follow the wall uphill and you will come to the former British Consulate, now the **Musée d'Art Contemporain de la Ville de Tanger** ① *52 Rue d'Angleterre, T0539-938436, 10dh.* Here there is a small but fine selection of late 20th-century Moroccan painters. There are a couple of wacky pictures by wild woman Chaïbia Tallal, plus early works by the likes of Farid Belkahia, founder of the Casablanca École des Beaux Arts, Saâd Hassani and others.

Marshan

Marshan is a neighbourhood of 20th-century villas up on the Marshan plateau, west of the kasbah. **Café Hafa**, the cliff-top café, lies down a narrow street near Rue Shakespeare. Crowded at weekends with local youth, it is the place for a sticky, Polo-mint tasting tea, flavoured in season with orange-blossom. The **Punic rock tombs**, little more than large coffin-sized shapes hollowed out of the soft rock, are nearby. The closest cliff-top viewing place near the poorer parts of the city, it is popular with local women and kids on weekend afternoons.

Beaches

Back in the centre, the town beach and the clubs alongside it (which still offer a range of drinking, eating and dancing opportunities) were previously an expat zone where anything was permissible and a good time easily available. In its heyday, this beach was said to be the third most beautiful in the world, after Rio de Janeiro and Miami. Jack Kerouac and Joe Orton were among the habitués. Roland Barthes enjoyed Las Tres Caravelas beach. More recently, Mario Testino photographed the local wildlife. During the day, the locals are out playing football. Work is continuing to clean it up, but it may still be wise to avoid the beach itself after dark. There are more relaxing, less crowded and cleaner beaches east along the coast – possibly on the stretch south of Ceuta. Nearer Tangier, there is bathing at **Playa Blanca** and **Sidi Kankouch**, also further on at **Plage Dahlia** (11 km after Ksar Es Seghir). Beaches west of Tangier such as **Plage Merkala** can be dangerous for swimming but have the advantage of being sunny until the early evening.

Atlantic coast west of Tangier

An excursion west is a rewarding experience, with a dramatic drive en route. The coast of Southern Spain can be easily seen on a clear day, and from the coast road to the north of the town, there is a special viewpoint. The options are to negotiate a round-trip price with a *grand taxi* driver in Rue d'Angleterre, take a Boughaz minibus from the port gates, or, in your own transport, follow Rue Sidi Bou Abid and Rue Sidi Amar on to the S701. This goes up into the **Montagne**, an exclusive suburb of royal palaces and villas, past discreet gates with plaques bearing names like Siddartha. In places, the road and woods would not be out of place in Devon (except for a few palm trees). You may see pines sculpted by the Chergui wind. After dense eucalyptus woods, the landscape opens up, with views of the ocean and fine stands of parasol pine.

Some 11 km from Tangier, the extreme northwestern corner of Africa is reached. Coming from Tangier, bear right for the **Cap Spartel lighthouse**, with its Café-Bar Sol. Going left, rocky coastline is followed by the wild Atlantic and **Robinson Beach**. This is a dramatic place, and swimmers should exercise caution (there are drownings every year and very little the coastguard can do). In spring, there are plenty of wild flowers, while in summer, tiny temporary cafés with cane awnings spring up among the rocks above the crashing surf.

South of Cap Spartel, the **Caves of Hercules** ⓘ *1000 to sunset, nominal charge*, are natural formations which were extended by quarries for millstones up to the 1920s. Later, prostitutes worked here and Tangier's rich and famous held parties. From a window shaped like Africa, which overlooks the sea, there is an impressive view.

After the Caves of Hercules take a rough farm track off the road to Roman **Cotta**, a small site centred around a factory for *garum* (anchovy paste) and the remains of a temple.

Coast east of Tangier

ⓘ *Bus 15 from Grand Socco, Tangier, serves this route, which is busy on a Sun and very busy in summer. Out of season many places are closed.*

From Tangier, 10 km east along the S704 road takes you around **Cap Malabata**, where tourist developments, including the **Hotel/Casino Mövenpick** complex, numerous cafés, as well as some excellent beaches, are used by the people from Tangier. Cap Malabata is where the Atlantic and the Mediterranean meet, and it is said the waters (with a little imagination) can be seen as two different colours. The views are certainly magnificent. The Victorian pile on the hill is the **Château Malabata**, a Gothic folly inhabited by a family.

Ksar es Seghir is a small seaside town 37 km east of Tangier, dominated by the ruined Portuguese castle. The town was named Ksar Masmuda under the Almohads and Ksar al Majaz under the Merinids, who added walls and gates in 1287. The Portuguese took the town in 1458. The floor of the town's hammam, the mosque and the intact sea gate arch should be noted. There are other cafés and restaurants, including the recommended **Restaurant Caribou**, **Café Dakhla** to the west of the town, **Café Dahlia** to the east and **Café Lachiri** on the bridge (seafood). There are possibilities for camping, and a splendid beach. Onwards, between Ksar es Seghir and Ceuta, is a string of beautiful and deserted beaches.

⊙ Tangier listings

For sleeping and eating price codes and other relevant information, see pages 22-28.

⊙ Where to stay

There are 3 main hotel areas: off the Petit Socco; near the port entrance (ask to be dropped near Hotel Marco Polo, for example); and around the Blvd Pasteur. For the budget traveller, the hotels near the seafront are easiest to find and deal with.

Medina *p348, map p349*

The best places to stay in the medina are mostly clustered at its northwestern tip, in or near the kasbah.

€€€€ Nord-Pinus Tanger, 11 Rue Riad Sultan, La Kasbah, T0661-228140, www.hotel-nord-pinus-tanger.com. Tangier's most sophisticated hotel, the attractive **Nord-Pinus** has an extraordinary position at the very top of the kasbah, looking over the sea to Spain, or down into the gardens of the palace. Opened in 2007, the hotel merges traditional Moroccan design elements (such as *zellige* tiles, embroidery and rugs) with strikingly bold contemporary artwork and decorative pieces managing to create a sense of timeless elegance and luxury. It's a wonderful place to stay and soak up the atmosphere of Tangier; sit on the terrace reading one of the many beautiful books lying around and listen to the birdsong in the palace gardens below. The restaurant (see page 354), serving high-quality French and Moroccan cuisine, is also open to non-guests; ring to reserve.

€€€ La Tangerina, 19 Rue Riad Sultan, La Kasbah, T0539-947731, www.latangerina.com. Lower key (and also lower in price) than the **Pinus** next door, this is still a very elegant place to stay. There are cosy communal areas with antique touches and a lovely outdoor terrace filled with pot-plants, shaded seating and hosting gorgeous seafront vistas. Rooms are stylish and contemporary and feature horseshoe arches. The best rooms have geranium-fringed private terraces with sea views. There's also a hammam.

€€€ Riad Tanja, Rue du Portugal, Escalier Américain, T0539-333538, www.riadtanja.com. Big, stylish bedrooms have ornate wooden furniture, red rugs, large pouffes and views over the market; the couple of smaller rooms without external windows are less desirable. The restaurant (see page 354) is a popular destination in its own right.

€€ Dar Nour, 20 Rue Gourna, La Kasbah, T0662-112724, www.darnour.com. Not for those partial to swinging cats, this is nevertheless a stylish, romantic place. The merging of several houses in the narrow backstreets of the kasbah has created lots of cosy nooks and crannies. If all this makes you feel a little claustrophobic, you can escape to the roof terrace, where there's a spectacular 360-degree view. It's a quiet spot too, away from the bustle of the medina. Old furniture and fresh flowers set off the Moroccan fabrics and lights to fine effect. Traditional Moroccan meals cooked to order. 10 rooms.

€€ **Hotel Continental**, 36 Rue Dar Baroud, T0539-931024, hcontinental@iam.net.ma. This old-timer hotel was used by Bertolucci in the film *The Sheltering Sky*. Faded glory in abundance, it has saggy furniture, beautiful old-but-chipped tiling, antique radios and timeworn rugs, perfect for those who revel in the atmosphere of a bygone era and don't mind a bit of down-at-heel shabbiness. Rooms are kept clean and some have fabulous views over the seafront. It's at the eastern end of the medina, directly above the port.

€ **Mamora Hotel**, 19 Rue des Postes (Rue Mokhtar Ahardan), T0539-934105. This clean and good-value hotel is right in the centre of the medina. The best rooms have big views over the green-tiled roofs of the mosque to the sea beyond. The morning call to prayer will almost certainly wake you, however.

€ **Pensión Palace**, 2 Rue des Postes (Rue Mokhtar Ahardan), T0539-936128. There's no chance of being treated like royalty here; in fact, you may not even be treated much like a paying guest. But reasonable rooms around a lovely, plant-filled square courtyard make up for the disinterested service.

Seafront and ville nouvelle
p350, map p344

There are cheap and basic *pensiones* on Rue de la Plage, past **Restaurant Africa**, up the hill from the port. Prices are around 80dh. They cater to those who need no more than a place to lie down before or after catching a ferry and many do not have showers. They include **Talavera**, **Madrid**, **Le Detroit**, **Playa** and **Atou**, the last being particularly cheap, while **Le Detroit** is about the best.

€€€€ **Dar Nilam**, 28 lotissement Tingis, T0539-301146, www.darnilam.com. Lots of ornate Moroccan decoration and antique style exude a sense of intimate luxury in this small hotel 2 km along the seafront from the town centre. The service here is warm, friendly and highly personalized.

€€€€ **Hotel el Minzah**, 85 Rue de la Liberté (Zankat el Houria), T0539-935885, www.elminzah.com. Big, central and luxurious, this place has 100 rooms. Dating from the 1930s, the hotel has beautiful gardens set around an Andalucían courtyard, 2 restaurants, wellness centre, wine bar, coffee bar, tea room, mini-golf, tennis and a pool. The place feels a little tired, however. Rooms are a little ordinary for the price, and even the pantalooned staff can't make it feel like value for money.

€€€ **Hotel Rif**, 152 Av des FAR (ex-Av d'Espagne), T0539-937870. A grand old landmark seafront hotel now refurbished and reopened with a pool, complete with waterfall, and soft red and blue furnishings. Business traveller centred.

€€ **Hotel de Paris**, 42 Blvd Pasteur, T0539-931877. Clean, central hotel with old tiled floors and ugly floral bedcovers. Street-facing rooms have no double glazing and can be noisy. Not bad value, especially if you can bargain them down a little.

€€ **Hotel el Djenina**, 8 Rue el Antaki (Rue Grotius), just off Av d'Espagne, T0539-942244, eldjenina@menara.ma. 40 well-renovated, airy rooms with en suite bathrooms. The hotel is clean and simple – not especially full of character or style but reliable and modern, which makes it stand out in Tangier.

€€ **Hotel Marco Polo**, Av d'Espagne, T0539-941124. Small comfortable hotel with a surreal cave in the reception. Modern, cool and tiled, rooms have satellite TV, minibars, sea views, comfy beds, traffic noise and terrible art. Big suites would be good for families.

€€ **Hotel Rembrandt**, Av Mohammed V, T0539-937870/2. Conveniently in the centre of the *ville nouvelle*, Rembrandt has a good pool, a restaurant and a popular, modern bar with views through buildings down to the sea. The 73 rooms lack much character but are double-glazed against the noise and some have good views.

€ **Hotel Holland**, 139 Rue de Hollande (up the hill on Av de Belgique from Pl de France, turn right, near the Dawliz multiplex), T0539-937838. A rambling, badly converted villa with fairly basic rooms and safe parking. Reservations essential in summer as it's used by Moroccans on the drive home.

€ **Hotel Muniria**, Rue Magellan, T0539-935337. A friendly, family-run little place with 8 rooms and a preponderance of blue, from the hand-painted wardrobes to the bedspreads. Former clients include William Burroughs, Kerouac and Ginsberg, though the hotel makes admirably little of the fact. Some sea views.

Camping

Campsites are not much cheaper than a budget hotel and rather far from the city. Camper vans should be secure enough.
Camping Miramonte, 3 km west from city centre, not far from Marshan district, very handy for Plage Merkala, T0539-937138. Well-kept site up on a hillside with lots of shade, bar/snacks, small pool, showers, laundry, petrol at 400 m.

Atlantic coast west of Tangier *p351*
€€€€ **Hotel-Club Le Mirage**, Cap Spartel, near the caverns, T0539-333332, www.lemirage-tanger.com. The discreetly rich rent one of the 25 'deluxe bungalow-suites' for the whole season. Excellent service, piano bar and 2 restaurants.

Camping

Camping Achakar, Cap Spartel, near the Caves of Hercules, 12 km west of town, T0539-333840.

🍴 Restaurants

Medina *p348, map p349*
If your stomach flora has adapted to Morocco, there are a number of cheap,

basic restaurants (€) in the medina, such as **Mauritania** and **Assalam** in Rue de la Marine, and a similar selection on Rue du Commerce.
€€€ **Nord-Pinus Tangier**, 11 Rue Riad Sultan, La Kasbah, T0661-228140. The views alone would make the cost of eating here worthwhile, but the food is also excellent and there's a Moroccan/French wine list too. High quality French and Moroccan cuisine, with an emphasis on seafood; ring to reserve.

€€€ **Riad Tanja**, Rue du Portugal, Escalier Américain, T0539-333538 (see Where to stay). With red rugs, brass candlesticks and dark wood tables, this cosy place is especially beautiful as the evening light streams in. Moroccan cuisine with a twist, with dishes such as monkfish *pastilla* and spicy couscous.

Seafront and ville nouvelle
p350, map p344

€€€ **El Khorsan**, Hotel el Minzah, 85 Rue de la Liberté, T0539-935885 (see Where to stay). Reservations recommended. Great views across the straits, and one of the country's best reputations for Moroccan cuisine.

€€€ **La Fabrique**, 7 Rue de Fès, T0539-374057. Tue-Sat. Tangier's top-spot for French dining, **La Fabrique** has a stylish, modern and light-filled dining room, excellent service and a fabulous menu of flavour-packed French favourites.

€€ **Anna e Paolo**, 77 Av Prince Héretier, T0539-944617. A bit of a schlep out of the centre, this is worth the effort for good Italian food such as *melanzane alla parmigiana*, as well as pizzas and pasta.

€€ **El Mesón de Pépé Ocaña**, 7 Rue Jabha el Ouatania. Easily missed, a popular and authentically dark and atmospheric tapas bar down a small street behind **Hotel Rembrandt**. Attracts a smart, though very male, crowd. Pull up a bar stool, order a drink and the tapas will flow.

€€ **L'Marsa**, 92 Av Mohammed VI. Good pizzas and pastas by the seafront, with a big outdoor seating area. It's large and modern – certainly not the most beautiful restaurant in town, but good for a quick eat. Also does salads and some traditional Moroccan food.

€€ **Populaire Saveur**, 2 Escalier Waller. Popular by both name and nature, this little fish place on the steps up from the market to Rue de le Liberté has good set menus in a homely atmosphere.

€€ **Raihani**, 10 Rue Ahmed Chaouki. Good Moroccan food as well as some French dishes, in the centre of the *ville nouvelle*.

€€ **San Rémo**, 15 Rue Ahmed Chaouki, T0539-938451. Tue-Sun. Fresh pasta and other European dishes in a pretty little bistro-style place with tablecloths and serious service.

€ **Agadir**, 21 Rue Prince Héretier. A tiny fragment of the 1950s near the Blvd Pasteur, this small and simple licensed place behind net curtains serves good, freshly cooked Moroccan and French food with a smile. Excellent tagines and *pastilla* as well as some seafood.

€ **Restaurant Africa**, 83 Rue de la Plage (Rue Salah Eddine el Ayoubi). At the bottom of the hill by the port, this is the first place many people come to, and though it's hardly an amazing first taste of Africa, it's not bad either for a light meal. Watch out for inaccuracies in the bill.

Cafés and pâtisseries
Café Central, in the Petit Socco. The former artistic rendezvous where William Burroughs and Tennessee Williams used to hang out. It's lost most of its magic but it's still a good place to watch the crowds go by.

Café de France, 1 Pl de France, has a history as a meeting place for artists and intellectuals. Mixed clientele of local notables, tourists and *passeurs* looking out for potential emigrants to hustle across the Straits.

Pâtisserie La Española, Rue de la Liberté. Posh pâtisserie and *salon du thé*.

Salon de thé/Restaurant le Detroit, Pl de la Kasbah. Pricey for food, but good for tea, coffee, pastries and a panoramic view of the Straits.

Salon de thé Vienne, corner of Rue du Mexique and Rue Moutanabi. Large and showy.

Zoco Chico, Petit Socco. A gringo-centric place, this is a contemporary little café with a few tiled tables right on the Petit Socco. It sells couscous, falafel and tabouleh, as well as good coffees.

Marshan p350
€€ **Casa d'Italia**, Palais des Institutions Italiennes, T0539-936348. In the one-time servants' quarters of the Palais Moulay Hafid, in this smart neighbourhood, this is an upmarket Italian place favoured by the expats who live around here. You might be able to sneak a look around the palace after your pasta.

Atlantic coast west of Tangier p351
€€€ **Le Mirage**, out at Cap Spartel, T0539-333331. International cuisine with a loyal following in a spectacular setting.

Bars and clubs

Tangier *p342, maps p344 and p349*
Tangier is not what it once was – most of the famously seedy bars of the past are gone. There is, however, a new generation of beach bars. See also the Restaurant section for tapas bars.

Caïd's Piano Bar, Hotel el Minzah, 85 Rue de la Liberté, T0539-333444 (see Where to stay). Moroccan decoration and expensive drinks in an atmospheric bar.

Morocco Palace, 11 Rue du Prince Moulay Abdallah, T0539-938614. An Oriental-disco with over-the-top decoration and a bizarre floorshow.

Pasarela, Av Mohammed VI, T0539-945246. Beachside complex with bars, a pool, and occasional live music.

The Pub, 4 Rue Sorolla, T0539-934789. Food, beer and other drinks in a pseudo-pub atmosphere.

Régine, 8 Rue Mansour Eddahbi, T0539-340238. A seriously out-dated club with music and decor that seems lost in an 80s timewarp.

Scotts, Rue Moutanabi. Gay-friendly club. The highlight is the paintings of Rif boys in Highland gear by local decorator, Stuart Church.

Tanger Inn, 1 Rue Magellan. Small bar popular with those reliving the Beat experience. The first stage on a long Tangerine night out.

⊕ Entertainment

Tangier *p342, maps p344 and p349*
Art galleries Galerie Delacroix, Rue de la Liberté. **Tanjah Flandria Art Gallery**, Rue Ibn Rochd, behind the Hotel Flandria, T0539-933000.
Cultural and language centres
Institut Français, Rue de la Liberté, easily identified by the Galerie Delacroix sign. Good temporary exhibitions.

⊛ Festivals

Tangier *p342, maps p344 and p349*
Sep The annual **Jazz Festival**, www. tanjazz.com, is popular so try to book accommodation in advance when it's on. There are street parades and free concerts on the Grand Socco and paying concerts in the Mendoubia gardens.

⊙ Shopping

Tangier *p342, maps p344 and p349*
Food
There is a market between Rue d'Angleterre and Rue Sidi Bou Abid and numerous fruit sellers along Rue de la Plage and its side streets. On Rue el Oualili, is another food market.

Handicrafts and antiques
Tangier is not the best place to buy handicrafts, for although shops have a

large selection, production tends to be in Marrakech and the pressure to buy in Tangier can be intense, with bazaarists and hawkers used to gullible day trippers from Spain. The cheapest shops and stalls, with the most flexible prices, will be found in the medina. Shops in the *ville nouvelle* may claim fixed prices but in most cases you will be able to bargain.

Coopartim Ensemble Artisanal, Rue de Belgique, T0539-931589. A government-controlled fixed-price craft centre with a number of workshops is a good place to start.

In the medina, try **Marrakech la Rouge**, 50 Rue es Siaghin. For crafts and antiques see **Galerie Tindouf**, 64 Rue de la Liberté, T0539-931525. For kitting out your villa on the Montagne with Indian antiques, try **Adolfo de Velasco**, down on Av Mohammed V on the opposite side to the Post Office. **Laure Welfling**, 3 Pl de la Kasbah, T0539-932083 is a cut above most of Tangiers' shops – aimed at the interior design set, it has good ceramics.

Newspapers and books
Foreign newspapers can be bought from shops in Rue de la Liberté or outside the post office in Av Mohammed V. For books in French, Spanish and a few in other languages, go to **Librairie des Colonnes**, 54 Blvd Pasteur, T0539-936955.

⊙ What to do

Tangier *p342, maps p344 and p349*
Bicycle and motorcycle hire
Mesbahi, 7 Rue Ibn Tachfine, just off Av des FAR, T0539-940974. Rents bicycles, 50cc and 125cc motorbikes, deposit required for 3 days or more.

Birdwatching
Without doubt, this is the best place in North Africa to watch the migrations to and from Europe. Over 250 different species have been counted crossing this narrow strip of water and, while the main movements are Mar-May and Aug-Oct, early and late movers

ensure that there are always some birds to observe. The stretch of coast from **Cap Spartel** in the west to **Punta Ceres** in the east and the advantage of height gained by Jbel Kebir and Jbel Moussa provide ample viewing spots. The massive migration of large raptors is very impressive. Flocks of white stork can be spotted too. Smaller birds, including warblers and wheatears, swallows, larks and finches, also take this route.

Tour operators
Holiday Service, 84 Av Mohammed V, T0539-933362; **Limadet Ferry**, Av du Prince Moulay Abdallah, T0539-932649; **Transtour Ferries**, 4 Rue el Jabha al Outania, T0539-934004.

⊖ Transport

Tangier *p342, maps p344 and p349*
Air
Tangier's **Ibn Batouta Airport**, T0539-393720, is 15 km southwest of the city on the N1 road to Rabat. Catch bus 17 or 70 from Grand Socco or a *grand taxi*. Arrive 1-2 hrs early. There are quite a few good international connections. **EasyJet** (www.easyjet.com) flies to **Madrid** and **Paris**. Royal Air Maroc flies to **Amsterdam**, **Barcelona**, **Brussels**, **London** and **Paris**. Ryanair has services to **Brussels** and **Madrid**.

There are domestic services to **Casablanca** with Royal Air Maroc.
Airline offices: Air France, 20 Blvd Pasteur. British Airways, 83 Rue de la Liberté, T0539-935877. Iberia, 35 Blvd Pasteur, T0539-936177. Royal Air Maroc, Pl de France, T0539-935501/2.

Boat
At the port avoid all touts selling embarkation cards – these are free from the officials. Ferries sail several times a day to Spain (**Algeciras** and **Tarifa**) and less regularly to France (**Sete**), **Gibraltar** and **Genoa**. Tickets can be bought online, at the ferry terminal or at travel agents in Tangier.

The travel agents on Blvd Pasteur all sell ferry tickets to Algeciras.

Trasmediterranea (www.trasmediterranea. es) runs a car and passenger ferry service to **Algeciras** 5 times a day at 1000, 1300, 1600, 1900 and 2300 (3 hrs), €17, child €11, with vehicle from €94. Check in at least 1 hr early to allow time to collect an embarkation card, complete a departure card and have your passport stamped.

To **Tarifa** there are departures at 1000, 1400, 1800 and 2200 (45 mins) with FRS (www.frs.es) on their passenger service, €34, child €18. From Tangier MED port (40 km east of Tangier) FRS also have regular ferries to **Algeciras** and **Gibraltar**.

For **Sete**, in the south of France, tickets can be bought from **Voyages Comanav** at 43 Rue Abou el Alaâ el Maâri, T0539-934096, (www.comanav-voyages.ma). There is a ferry every 2-4 days and services leave from **Tangier MED port** (40 km east of Tangier). Passenger tickets from €40, car and 2 passengers from €205.

Bus
The bus station is on Av Jami' al Duwal al Arabia, T0539-946682, information, T0539-932415. Tangier is fairly small and thus it is unlikely that you will want to use local buses. If you do, they can be picked up in the Grand Socco or in Av des FAR outside the port gates. **Boughaz** minibuses, from just outside the port gate, may be useful to get to the private bus station, or for excursions from Tangier westwards.

CTM buses depart from the ticket office near the entrance to the port in Av des FAR. Services include 5 departures daily to **Rabat** and **Casablanca** at 0515, 1100, 1430, 1615 and 2345 (5¼ hrs); 4 to **Meknès** at 1500, 1900, 2100 and 2345 (5 hrs); 6 to **Fès** (6 hrs); 1 to Agadir at 1615 (14 hrs); 3 daily to **Chefchaouen** at 1015, 1215 and 2000 (2½ hrs); 5 to **Larache** (1½ hrs) and 1 to **Tiznit** at 1615 (15 hrs).

Other buses, running from the terminal at the end of Rue de Fès, go to most destinations and are generally cheaper. There are services to **Tetouan** about every 15 mins and **Larache** every hour, as well as buses to **Asilah**, **Ceuta** and all destinations stated above. To get to the terminal take a *petit taxi*.

Car hire
Avis, 54 Blvd Pasteur, T0539-934646, and at the airport, T0539-393033. **Budget**, 7 Av du Prince Moulay Abdallah, T0539-937994, and at the airport. **Europcar**, 87 Av Mohammed V, T0539-938271. **Hertz**, 36 Av Mohammed V, T0539-322165, and at the airport, T0539-322210.

Taxi
Grands taxis Can be picked up from the Gare du Routier or in front of Tangier Ville railway station to destinations within or outside of the city. You will need to set a fare with the driver. To **Tetouan** and **Ceuta**, this is a quick, practical and not too expensive option. For excursions from Tangier to the **Caves of Hercules** or **Cap Malabata** negotiate for a *grand taxi* in Rue de Hollande.
Petits taxis Turquoise with yellow stripe, may be cheaper, although that will depend on your skill, as the meters are not always operated. For a taxi, call T0539-935517.

Train
The former port station on Av des FAR is firmly closed. Trains now arrive/depart from the suburban **Moughougha station**, a 20dh taxi ride out in the new suburbs. Departure times change. In general there are 9 trains a day to **Rabat**, **Casablanca** and **Marrakech**; while there are 5 to **Meknès** and **Fès** (the 0825 and 1040 services are straight through, on the later services you have to change at Sidi Kacem). The 1040 train also goes to **Oujda**. All trains stop at **Asilah**.

ⓘ Directory

Tangier *p342, maps p344 and p349*
Banks All the usual banks with ATMs are on Blvd Pasteur/Av Mohammed V. The **Crédit du Maroc**, on the ground floor of the Tanja Flandria Hotel, has a bureau de change, as does the **BMCI**, down the street opposite the Terrasse des paresseux, next to the Café de France. The **Wafa Bank** (ATM) is further down the slope, on your left just before the PTT. Banks are open 0830-1130 and 1430-1630. **American Express**: c/o Voyages Schwartz, 54 Blvd Pasteur, T0539-933459, Mon-Fri 0900-1230, 1500-1900, Sat 0900-1230. **Medical services** Ambulance: T15. Hospital emergencies: T0539-930856, also try T0539-934242. **Pharmacie de Garde**, 26 Rue de Fès, T0539-932616. **Useful addresses** Fire: T15. **Garage**: Tanjah Auto, 2 Av de Rabat. **Police**: (general) Rue Ibn Toumert, T19; (traffic) T177.

North Atlantic coast

With none of the hassle of Tangier, yet some of its European sophistication, it's not surprising that coastal Asilah has become a firm fixture on many tourists' itineraries. Beautifully whitewashed, its old fortified Portuguese centre makes a good spot for a peaceful couple of days by the sea. Further south, Larache is much less discovered but has some of the same architectural attractions in the winding streets of its medina and, across the estuary, some evocative ancient Roman remains at Lixus. ➤➤ *For listings, see pages 364-367.*

Asilah → *For listings, see pages 364-367. Colour map 1, A2.*

Asilah, 40 km south of Tangier (and also referred to as Arzila), is a striking fishing port and coastal town of white and blue houses, surrounded by ramparts and lying alongside an extensive beach. It is the northernmost of the former Portuguese outposts (the others include Azemmour, El Jadida and Safi). A small place with a Mediterranean feel, Asilah might provide a pleasant introduction to Morocco, in spite of the extent to which tourism dominates. If you turn up in August you'll coincide with the annual influx of people for the **International Festival of Asilah**, which usually includes jazz and Moroccan music, and exhibitions by contemporary Moroccan artists.

Arriving in Asilah
Asilah lies off the main N1 Tangier to Rabat road. The rail station is some 2 km north of the town, and there aren't very many taxis in Asilah. Buses and taxis stop at the Place Mohammed V, close to the old town. ➤➤ *See Transport, page 367, for further details.*

Background
Modern Asilah stands on the site of the Phoenician town of Silis, or perhaps Zilis. The area was subsequently settled by Romans in Anthony's reign and by the Byzantines. In 966, the town was rebuilt by El Hakim II, ruler of Córdoba. It was the last stronghold of the Idrissid dynasty. The Portuguese occupied Asilah from 1471 and built the town's fortifications and, in 1578, King Sebastian landed there on his way to defeat at what was to become known as the Battle of the Three Kings. This defeat led to the Spanish absorption of Portugal, and thus of Asilah, but the Portuguese influence on the town is still quite discernible.

The Moroccans recovered Asilah in 1691, under Moulay Ismaïl. In 1826 Austria bombarded Asilah, then a base of piracy, as did the Spanish in 1860. In the late 19th and early 20th century Ahmed al Rasouli, the bandit chief who terrorized much of northwestern Morocco, was based in the town, as described by his one-time hostage and later friend, Walter Harris, in *Morocco That Was*. Al Rasouli built his palace in the medina and from it exercised power over much of the region, being for a time its governor. The Spanish took Asilah in 1911, as part of their protectorate of northern Morocco.

In more recent years, Asilah has played host to an international summer arts festival. The old neighbourhoods are now squeaky clean and home to weekend retreats for wealthy Casablancans. The result is pretty and whitewashed, and there are some excellent restaurants.

Places in Asilah
The medina is the main place of interest of Asilah, a quarter of predominately white and blue buildings, reflecting in their design the influence of the Portuguese. Note the modern

murals on some of the houses in the medina, painted by artists during the festival. The ramparts were built by the Portuguese in the 15th century and are set with a number of important gates, including **Bab el Kasbah**, **Bab el Bahar** ('the sea gate'), **Bab lhoumar**, a structure topped with the eroded Portuguese coat of arms, as well as **Bab el Jbel** ('the mountain gate') and **Bab lhoumer**. At points it is possible to climb the fortifications for views of the town and along the coast. Within the medina, **Le Palais de la Culture** is a cultural centre converted from the former residence of the brigand Ahmed al Rasouli, built in 1909 right beside the sea. It is difficult to gain access except during the festival, but it is possible to visualize those who incurred al Rasouli's wrath being made to walk the plank from the palace windows over the cliff front.

The souk has a Thursday **market**, attracting farmers from the surrounding area. In addition to the sale of the usual fruit, spices and vegetables, handicrafts distinctive of the Rif region are also on display.

The **beach** is often windy (but at times can be beautifully calm) and is frequented by bathers, men touting camel rides and fishermen. It stretches beyond the building works to the north and south of the town.

Asilah

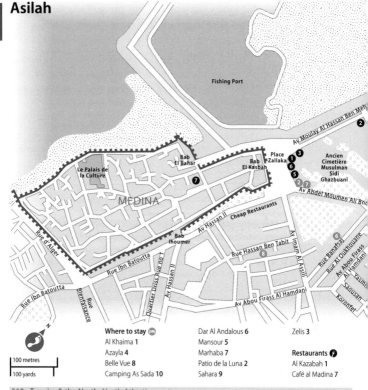

Where to stay		Dar Al Andalous 6	Zelis 3
Al Khaima 1		Mansour 5	
Azayla 4		Marhaba 7	**Restaurants**
Belle Vue 8		Patio de la Luna 2	Al Kazabah 1
Camping As Sada 10		Sahara 9	Café al Madina 7

El Utad, the stone circle at Mzoura → Colour map 1, A2.

The stone circle at Mzoura makes a good excursion from Rabat or Tangier for those with plenty of time and a car. Though there are numerous prehistoric rock art sites in the High Atlas and Djebel Beni, the barrow at Mzoura is the only one of its kind in the country. The best time to visit Mzoura is in late summer when the vegetation has died back. After a rainy winter, the countryside will be at its best. This is also a good trip for birdwatchers, giving them a focus point in a rolling landscape of open fields, stands of eucalyptus and occasional corrugated-iron roofed homesteads unspoiled by industrial agriculture. It also gives you a glimpse into the living conditions in the countryside.

The first trace of prehistoric occupation you meet are three great menhirs, lying on the ground. Look out for the scooped-out 'bowls' in one of the stones, referred to as 'cup and circle' by English archaeologists and testimony to some obscure cult after the stones had fallen. Further on, to your right, the stones of the circle once ringed a high barrow, heavily excavated by the Spanish. Most stones are only 1.5 m high and, within them, lies a sort of stone walkway – possibly the original base of the barrow. The most spectacular feature is a stone standing 4.5 m high. You can also locate a lintel in the circle, once the entrance to the barrow.

Getting there On the N1 north of Larache – a winding, busy road – there is a major roundabout near Sidi Tnine el Yamani where you should branch off for Tetouan (R417). Just under 4 km beyond the roundabout, turn left at the Somepi garage and head up the recently widened road for Sidi Yamani. After about 3 km, in the village, you reach a Y-junction, where you need to take the left-hand fork. About 6.5 km after the village, after passing a large abandoned Spanish building on your left, you should turn off right onto a sandy track that comes after a minor cutting, with the road running slightly downhill. (If in doubt, ask a local for 'el utad', the funerary monument.) Once you turn off, the track doubles back sharply, taking you the 2.5 km to the hamlet where the circle is located. When you get to the hamlet, keep left; the track to the circle runs between the bramble hedges of the farmsteads, eventually veering round to the left.

Casa Garcia **2**
El Espigon **4**
La Place **3**
La Symphonie des
  Douceurs II **6**
Le Pont **4**
Oceano Casa Pepe **5**

Bigger than Asilah, and rather less bijou, Larache is a relaxed, faded seaside town, with a good beach and not too many tourists. A halfway house between Spanish and Moroccan urban life, it is a sleepy sort of place, with views over the ocean and the Loukkos estuary, plus the evocatively named 16th-century Château de la Cigogne, the Fortress of the Stork. It was at Larache that Jean Genet was to find a haven, writing his last novel here.

Background

Larache (El Arayis in Arabic) is named for the vine arbours of the Beni Arous, a local tribe. The area has one of the longest histories of human occupation in Morocco, going back to

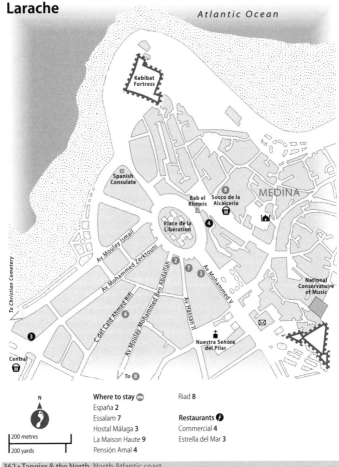

Larache

Atlantic Ocean

Kebibat Fortress

Spanish Consulate

MEDINA

Bab el Khemis

Socco de la Alcaiceria

Place de la Libération

Av Moulay Ismaïl

Av Mohammed Zerktouni

C del Caïd Ahmed Rifi

Av Moulay Mohammed Ben Abdallah

Av Hassan I

Av Mohammed V

To Christian Cemetery

National Conservatoire of Music

Nuestra Señora del Pilar

Central

To 8

N

200 metres
200 yards

Where to stay 🛏
España **2**
Essalam **7**
Hostal Málaga **3**
La Maison Haute **9**
Pensión Amal **4**

Riad **8**

Restaurants 🍴
Commercial **4**
Estrella del Mar **3**

Phoenician, Carthaginian and Roman times at the settlement of nearby Lixus. Larache was occupied by the Spanish from 1610 to 1689 and, as part of their protectorate, from 1911. At that time, the harbour was added and the new town was developed. Larache became the principal port of the Spanish northern zone. Today, the town draws its livelihood from the agro-food industry and fishing, although it has lost its status as a major port. Revenues from migrant workers and the building industry are important, too.

Places in Larache

On the very edge of the old town of Larache is a large piece of Renaissance military engineering, with the usual pointy bastions, dating from the 16th century. The isolated structure, now housing the local museum of antiquities, is the **Château de la Cigogne** ⓘ *T0539-912091, Wed-Sun 0900-1200, 1500-1730*. Also called Castillo de las Cigueñas or Al Fath, the museum contains a small amount of material from Lixus.

The Avenue Mohammed V is the main street of the new town. At the eastern end, heading for the central plaza, there are the fortifications and then the post office on the right and the **Iglesia de Nuestra Señora del Pilar** on the left. The circular **Place de la Libération**, with a fountain, is the heart of the town; the entrance to the medina, an arched gate, **Bab el Khemis**, is on the north side.

Exploring further, on the clifftop overlooking ocean and estuary, the 16th-century **Kebibat Fortress** was used by the Spanish as a hospital. Shamefully, it has been left to fall into ruin. The Spanish Consulate occupies a fine art deco building, and you will also easily locate the neo-Moorish central **market**, recognisable by its towers.

The medina is a poor quarter of steep and narrow streets and high walls best viewed from below or from the north side of the estuary. Just inside is the Spanish-built market square. There are a number of souks, notably **Socco de la Alcaiceria**, the cloth market.

The main beach is an extensive strip of fine (though littered, in season) sand with a number of cafés nearby. To get there, see Ancient Lixus, below.

One final port of call in Larache is the tomb of writer **Jean Genet** (1910-1986), out in the old Christian cemetery near the lighthouse and prison. The cemetery has been cleaned up as, part of the works currently being financed by the regional government of Andalucía. With the views over the ocean, Genet could hardly have chosen a better final resting place.

Ancient Lixus

ⓘ *The site is just over the Oued Loukkos, on a hillside to the west of the N1. Without a car, you may have to walk or take a petit taxi (30dh) and wait by the roadside for a grand taxi with a space in order to get back again. Best option is to get the bus No 2 (3dh), which runs from the port to the beach, Plage Rimmel. Open daylight hours. The east side of the site next to the N1 is fenced in by green railings. A small site map on a metal plaque can be found next to the locked entrance gate. After a recent incident of armed robbery here, you will be accompanied on your visit by a guard with a large wooden truncheon, which may or may not make you feel safer.*

Located on a spectacular site on the right bank of the Oued Loukkos about 4 km from the sea, Ancient Lixus is the second most important Roman site in Morocco after Volubilis. Heathland butterflies and the occasional raptor are added bonuses of a visit to the site.

Tchemich Hill, on which the town is located, 50 m above sea level, was obviously an excellent location for defensive reasons, and the views from here are beautiful, especially in the early evening, when the sun is going down over the meanders of the estuary. For some ancient writers Lixus was the location of the Garden of Hesperides, where Hercules harvested golden apples to gain his place on Mount Olympus. The first traces of settlement date from the seventh to sixth century BC, and in pre-Roman inscriptions the future Lixus is referred to as Semes. The oldest evidence of building goes back to the fourth century BC. There was a seventh-century Phoenician and later a Carthaginian settlement here. Rome annexed the town in 40 BC. Coins with Latin and neo-Punic inscriptions suggest the inhabitants had a dual culture, as was the case in so much of Roman North Africa. The town became a colony under the Emperor Claudius I, when salt, olives and fish were the main exports. Eventually reaching an area of 62 ha, Lixus prospered until the late third century AD, in part because of its strategic position on the road from Tingis (Tangier) to Sala Colonia (Rabat). It remained active and was occupied until the fifth century AD and, in Arabic historiography, re-emerges as Tohemmis. This remained a Muslim settlement until Larache was founded in the 14th century. Recent archaeological finds in the region will shed further light on the town's history.

Getting around the site The easiest way up into the site is via the track near the gate, generally closed, at the north end of the **garum** (fish salting) **basins** behind the railings on the N1 (just nip around the railings). Head uphill to find the **amphitheatre**, excavated in 1964 and, with its quality stonework, probably the most impressive ruin. Spectators would have been able to enjoy a play and superb views of the flood plain beyond at the same time. Just beyond the theatre is a small **bath complex**. There are some mosaics still in situ in the hall area, although the central mosaic of Neptune has been removed. In the circular caldarium are traces of painted plaster. Clear evidence of demolition/rebuild can be seen from the column drums inserted into a wall. After the amphitheatre, either follow the track uphill to discover the remains of **apsed temple** (crumbling half-tower) or cut across left (west) and scramble up to visit the **acropolis** area. Look out for the impressive vaulted cisterns. It is possible to make out an oratory, a small open space with a stubby column in the middle and twin semicircular niches. The layout of the colonnaded **forum** can also be seen. Dominating the highest point of the site is a rectangular, vaulted chamber some 4 m high, probably a **cistern** for feeding the nearby bath complex.

Beyond Lixus the road leads onto the **beach**, where there is a car park and camping areas. In summer, there are lifeguards and organized beach activities for the local children.

◉ North Atlantic coast listings

For sleeping and eating price codes and other relevant information, see pages 22-28.

◉ Where to stay

Asilah *p359, map p360*
Asilah is a good place to rent a private house. See the Spanish www.elbaraka.net.
€€€ **Dar Zuina**, Dchar el Hommar, T0661-243809, www.darzuina.com. 7 km outside Asilah, This colourful, peaceful guesthouse in the countryside is surrounded by attractive gardens. The rooms are simply but stylishly furnished with a rustic feel and some have a private terrace.

€€€ **Hotel Al Khaima**, Km 2 Rte de Tangier, BP 101, T0539-417428. A large hotel with 113 rooms by the beach, 2 km outside town. Reasonable sized rooms come with a decent amount of wear and tear and could do with a refit. Restaurant, disco, bar, tennis courts and pool. Can be noisy though, and you don't get any of the style of Asilah.
€€ **Dar Al Andalous**, 30 Rue Banafsaj, T0539-417840. If you can put up with the plastic plants and garish attempts at traditional Moroccan style, this is a clean and comfortable option along a street off the main square. Some rooms sleep 4.

€€ **Hotel Azayla**, 20 Av Ibn Rochd, T0539-416717, h.azayla@menara.ma. A modern hotel just outside the medina, **Azayla** is decorated with art and black-and-white photos, and the small rooms have wicker chairs, pine furniture, a/c and double glazing.

€€ **Hotel Mansour**, 49 Av Mohammed V, T0539-917390, www.hotelmansour.fr.fm. Decorated with faded photographs of scantily clad ladies in a forest with swans, this hotel doesn't go for minimalistic good taste. However the bedrooms are simple and clean. Much better value out of season.

€€ **Hotel Patio de la Luna**, 12 Pl Zelaka, T0539-416074, hotelpatiodelaluna@yahoo.es. Charming and whitewashed, this is Asilah's most attractive hotel. Spanish owned, it has blue shutters and a solar-powered water heater on the roof. There's a peaceful patio with candle lamps and views over the town from the little roof terrace. Comfortable and stylish rooms have good beds. Reservations essential in summer.

€€ **Hotel Zelis**, 10 Av Mansour Eddahabi, T0539-417069. With 61 rooms (3rd floor ones are best) and a pool, this place is modern in a 1980s sort of way. The bright red carpets might make your eyes water but there are sea views and minibars to compensate. Exercise machines on the roof terrace facing the sea.

€ **Hotel Belle Vue**, Rue Hassan Ben Tabit, T0539-417747. Sometimes referred to as the 'Belle Vue Zilis', this is not to be confused with the **Hotel Zelis**, above. There's some damp and certainly no *belle vue*, but it's a good deal for the price all the same. Reasonably big rooms, decent shared showers, a sunny rooftop terrace.

€ **Hotel Marhaba**, 9 Rue Zallaka. Overlooking a green space not far from the medina, red brick **Marhaba** has turquoise shutters and adequate rooms, the best of which have balconies at the front. Avoid the darker rooms, which are poor value. Showers are 5dh and are not always hot.

€ **Hotel Sahara**, 9 Rue Tarfaya, T0539-917185. With old tiled corridors and well-tended plants, the **Sahara** is a model budget hotel. Simple clean rooms have art and a lamp and a bed and nothing more. Some lack windows but the whole hotel is absolutely spotless and it's very friendly too. All the rooms face onto a central sunny tiled courtyard and the 5dh shared showers are good. At this price you'll struggle to find better accommodation in all Morocco.

Camping

There are numerous campsites just north of the town along the road to Asilah.

Camping Atlas, 100 m to beach, snacks, showers, laundry, grocery, first aid, electricity for caravans.

Camping International, site of 1 ha, 50 m to beach, showers, laundry, petrol 300 m, electricity for caravans.

El Camping As Sada, on the Tangier road, 300 m out of town, T0539-917317. Overlooks the ocean and also has some chalet-type accommodation. The wash-block isn't great.

Larache *p362, map p362*
Reserve in summer when the town is busy.

€€ **Hotel Riad**, Rue (or C or Zankat) Moulay Mohammed Ben Abdallah, signed from Av Mohammed V, T0539-912626. The converted former residence of the Duchess of Guise has 24 rooms with big tiles, coloured glass and worn, loose old carpet. There's a restaurant but no bar and a small pool. The place has some vaguely stylish wrought-iron furniture, but it could do with sprucing up. In summer, karaoke in the garden may keep you awake.

€€ **La Maison Haute**, 6 Derb ben Thami, www.lamaisonhaute.com. Stylish and colourful, this guesthouse has bags of character in a great spot in the medina, on the corner of Socco de Alcaiceria, just behind the Pl de la Libération. There are 6 simple rooms (some without en suite) ranging in price from €37 to €52, and a more expensive suite. The best rooms have good views, but all are light-filled and benefit from local textiles and homely touches. There is also a fantastic roof terrace to lounge on. Book in advance.

€ Hostal Málaga, Rue de Salé, T0539-911868. 25 rooms, many of which are small and a little stale, with tiny bathrooms. Larger rooms are lighter and some have balconies. Friendly.

€ Hotel Cervantes, 3 Rue Tarik Ibn Ziad, close to Pl de la Libération, T0539-910874, ali621@caramail.com. Bright, spacious rooms with sea views and some character. Bathrooms are none too clean but it's friendly.

€ Hotel España, 6 Av Hassan II, T0539-913195, hotelespana2@yahoo.fr. Once a grand place in an outpost of Spanish provincial life, this hotel had faded glory by the bucketful. It's now a little worn and the corridors are musty but large rooms are kept clean and bathrooms are modern. It's in an excellent central location and there are some views over the square or onto a colourful terrace with potted plants.

€ Hotel Essalam, 9 Av Hassan II, T0539-916822. Clean, central and bright, nice reception, all new bathrooms and big roof terrace.

€ Pensión Amal, 10 Rue Abdallah Ben Yassine, T0539-912788. The closest to bus and *grand taxi* stations. 14 rooms, clean, quiet and better than the other rock-bottom cheapies.

🍴 Restaurants

Asilah *p359, map p360*
Asilah has 2 main restaurant areas: near the old ramparts on Av Hassan II there are plenty of cheap places with seating areas under the walls, selling Moroccan food and pizzas. The more upmarket seafood restaurants are in Pl Zallaka and onto Av Moulay Al Hassan Ben Mehdi. In some of the more expensive restaurants, you will be shown a great dish of fresh fish to choose from. Your chosen fish is then weighed, and you are charged by the 100g. If this is the case, make sure you know how much you will be charged. In the cheaper restaurants, go for grilled rather

than fried fish, as the oil is sometimes used far more than it should be.

For the best value eating, wander along the line of restaurants along Av Hassan II and let the waiters tempt you in to the **Calairis**, which does pizzas, or **Rabie, Yalis**, or **Ali**. They're all similar and have good-value menus for 30dh.

€€ Al Kazaba, T0539-417012. This restaurant and *salon de thé* has a good reputation for seafood. It's smart, with white tablecloths and incongruous all-year tinsel. The menu includes French and Moroccan cuisine; if fish isn't your thing, try the brochettes.

€€ Casa Garcia, Av Moulay Al Hassan Ben Mehdi, T0539-417465. The most feted of Asilah's restaurants, **Casa Garcia** fills up quickly with well-off Europeans. There's nothing very Moroccan about it, but the food is good enough that at least 1 person regularly flies in from France for the day just to eat here. The decor, like the food, is fishy, with crabs and lobsters suspended in nets. Turn up early or reserve, especially for the outdoor tables.

€€ La Place, 7 Av Moulay Al Hassan Ben Mehdi, T0539-417326. Simpler than most of its neighbours, has a couple of tables outside, tagines for 50dh as well as fish dishes by weight.

€€ Le Pont, 24 Av Moulay Al Hassan Ben Mehdi. Straightforward Moroccan place, 4 plastic-covered tables facing the sea, serves seafood *pastilla*, couscous, tagines, and fish dishes, such as swordfish steak. An excellent place to try Asilah's seafood without any pretentions.

€€ Oceano Casa Pepe, Pl Zallaka, T0539-417395. Just outside the medina walls, this popular place has tables outside and smart white-jacketed waiters. Inside there are wooden beams and fake candle lamps. Good, varied seafood menu.

€€ Restaurant el Espigon, Av Moulay Hassan, T0539-417157. Famous for its paella, which must be ordered a day in advance. The roasted tomato and pepper salad is also recommended.

€ **Café al Madina**, just inside the medina.
A good place to sit, with seats facing the
square and walls. Coffee and pastries as
well as snacks and Moroccan standards.
€ **La Symphonie des Douceurs II**,
26 Pl Zallaka, T0539-416633. Long thin
café with 3D art and some pastries.
Ice cream is sometimes available.

Larache *p362, map p362*
Try the fish grills down by the port for
cheap fresh-out-of-the-sea seafood.
€€ **Restaurant Estrella del Mar**, 68 C
Mohammed Zerktouni, T0539-911052.
The town's best restaurant is opposite the
fish market and has a suitably fishy menu.
It's nicely decorated, with a carved ceiling,
tablecloths and a wooden boat. *Raciones*
downstairs, a bit smarter upstairs.
€€ **Restaurant Larache**, 18 Av Moulay
Mohammed Ben Abdallah, T0539-913641.
Tagines and fish – try the mixed fried
seafood – in a simple place with a blackboard.
€ **Restaurant Commercial**, Pl de la
Libération. Very cheap fish dishes served
under the arches, just to the right of the
gate into the medina.

✪ Festivals

Asilah *p359, map p360*
Aug The International Festival of Asilah is
a cultural festival which has taken place in
Asilah since 1978 and involves performers
and artists from all over the world. Events
throughout the town attract many spectators.

⊙ Transport

Asilah *p359, map p360*
Bus
The bus station is on Av de la Liberté,
T0539-987354. There are regular bus links
with **Tangier**, **Ouezzane**, **Tetouan**, **Meknès**,
Rabat and **Casablanca**. *Grands taxis*,
particularly convenient for **Tangier**, leave
from Pl Mohammed V.

Train
Asilah train station, T0539-987320, is a
pleasant 30-min walk outside the town
alongside the N1 to Tangier and can be
reached by local bus or by either *petit* or
grand taxi from Pl Mohammed V. There are
10 trains daily to **Tangier** (45 mins), 5 to
Meknès (3 hrs) and **Fès** (4 hrs), 2 of which
go on to **Oujda**. There are also 9 trains to
Rabat and **Casablanca**.

Larache *p362, map p362*
The town is easily reached by the N1 from
Tangier or Rabat. The bus station is just
off Av Hassan II. Buses to **Asilah** (1 hr),
Ksar el Kebir, **Rabat** (3½ hrs) and **Meknès**
(5½ hrs). There are *grands taxis* to **Rabat**,
Asilah and **Tangier**.

⊙ Directory

Asilah *p359, map p360*
Banks Banque populaire, Pl Mohammed
V, has ATMs. **Police** Av de la Liberté,
T19 or T0539-917089. **Post** PTT, Pl des
Nations Unies. **Medical services**
Chemist: Pharmacie Loukili, Av de la
Liberté, T0539-917278. **Hospital**: Av du
2 Mars, T0539-917318.

Ceuta

Ceuta is an odd sort of place, an enclave of provincial Spain, an African equivalent of Great Britain's Gibraltar. However, unlike Gibraltar, Ceuta has not established itself as a minor tourist attraction. Instead, it gives the impression that it would like to be a Mediterranean Hong Kong: it has the right sort of location, between two continents, developed Europe and upcoming Africa. But the Gibraltar-Spain frontier was opened in 1985, and in many ways Ceuta has been sidelined into becoming a passenger transit port. The chaotic Ceuta-Fnideq frontier may well be your first or last point of contact with Morocco. ▶▶ *For listings, see pages 372-373.*

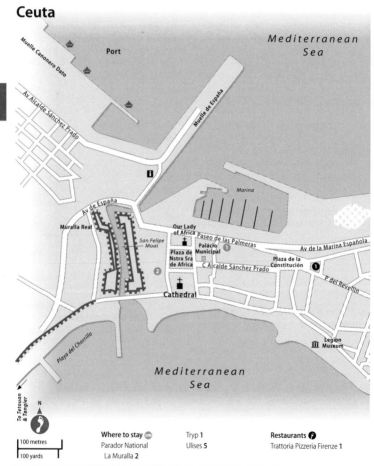

Ceuta

Mediterranean Sea

Port

Muelle Canonero Dato

Av Alcalde Sánchez Prado

Muelle de España

ⓘ

Marina

Av de España

Muralla Real

San Felipe Moat

Our Lady of Africa

Paseo de las Palmeras

Plaza de Nstra Sra de Africa

Palacio Municipal ❶

Av de la Marina Española

②

C Alcalde Sánchez Prado

Plaza de la Constitución ❶

P del Revellin

✝ **Cathedral**

Playa del Chorrillo

🏛 Legion Museum

Mediterranean Sea

To Tetouan & Tangier

N

100 metres	**Where to stay** 🛏	Tryp **1**	**Restaurants** 🍴
100 yards	Parador National	Ulises **5**	Trattoria Pizzeria Firenze **1**
	La Muralla **2**		

Getting there

There are frequent ferries from Algeciras to Ceuta, and the journey is rather quicker than Algeciras to Tangier, though the advantage of Tangier is that you are at the start of the Moroccan rail network. It's best to arrive early in Ceuta, so you have plenty of time to clear the frontier and move on to Tetouan or Tangier. Coming from Morocco, the Fnideq-Ceuta frontier is reached most easily from Tetouan by *grand taxi*. The taxis leave Tetouan from opposite the main bus station, expect to pay around 25dh a place. There are also occasional buses from Tetouan to Fnideq. Note that on the frontier formalities can be slow. Passports have to be checked and stamped by Moroccan officials both ways. Vehicles have to be registered and papers, including insurance, registration and licence, checked. Cash can be exchanged on the Moroccan side of the frontier at the Banque populaire booth. Driving up to Ceuta from Tetouan you can take the direct route or take the scenic route via Martil, which takes around 45 minutes.

▶▶ *See Transport, page 373, for further details.*

Getting around

Unless you intend to stay the night, you will need to get from the port to the Moroccan border at Fnideq, 3 km away. There is a bus from Ceuta city centre, leaving from Plaza de la Constitución. To get there, turn left as you leave the ferry terminal, and follow round along Paseo de las Palmeras (a 15-minute walk, maximum). You can spend both pesetas and dirhams in Ceuta in restaurants and shops. Like mainland Spain, the enclave has a long afternoon siesta with shops closed 1300-1600. Sunday is very much a day of rest.

Tourist information **Patronata Municipal de Turismo** ① *at the exit from the ferry port, Mon-Fri 0830-2030, Sat and Sun 1000-2000*, is helpful and has maps and leaflets. See also www.ceuta.es.

Background

Ceuta (Sebta in Arabic) is a Spanish enclave on the Moroccan coast, which since 1995 has had the status of 'autonomous town', putting it somewhere between the Spanish autonomous regions and the municipalities. Ceuta has an excellent strategic position on the Strait of Gibraltar and was occupied by the Carthaginians, Greeks and Romans. After being taken in the Arab conquest, the site was captured by the Portuguese in 1415 but, on the union of Spain and Portugal, was transferred to Spain in 1581, under whose control it has remained ever since as little more than a military prison. Its later fame arose from its importance as a supplying fortress for Spanish forces during a series of 19th-century sieges of the northern *presidios*. Fighting near Ceuta in 1859 nearly led to the total loss of the enclave. In 1860 a Spanish military force invaded Morocco from Ceuta. In the 20th century Spain once again became embroiled in a bloody war in northern Morocco in which it badly lost important battles at Anoual in 1921 and in the Chefchaouen-Tetouan campaign in late 1924. Ceuta ultimately survived this episode thanks largely to Abdelkarim's internal political difficulties and the improved Spanish generalship under Franco. And it was from Ceuta that the future *caudillo* launched his forces to impose his form of law and order on mainland Spain in 1936.

Ceuta and Melilla, to the east, remain potential friction points between Morocco and Spain. Morocco regards both as occupied territory and, in 2002, things came to a head when Moroccan soldiers occupied a tiny rocky islet, Isla Perejil, just northwest of Ceuta. Though the island was inhabited only by goats at the time, the action was called the first military invasion of Western European soil since the Second World War. Spain eventually reclaimed the island (though it's not entirely clear that anyone had actually taken enough notice of it before to know whether it was in fact part of Morocco or Spain), and relations between the two countries have since improved. Indeed, both would seem to have much more to lose by hostility than by a maintenance of the mutually advantageous status quo.

Places in Ceuta

Ceuta harbour lies tucked into a bay on the north of the peninsula, with the town largely packed onto a narrow isthmus lying between Monte Hacho (204 m) in the east and the Sierra Cimera hills adjacent to the frontier with Morocco in the west. The town is Spanish in character, with a heavy military presence – armed forces occupy most of the larger and older buildings including the fortress areas. The shopping streets, such as Paseo del Revellin and Calle Real, concentrate heavily on duty-free luxury goods and electronic equipment. To the east of the town is a tree-covered hill, which is a pleasant place for a stroll. At the far eastern edge is an old Portuguese fort, or stop off at the Ermitada de San Antonio, a convent rebuilt in the 1960s, from where there is a good view of the town.

Plaza de Africa

A visit to Ceuta should probably start on **Plaza de Africa**, home to two large Catholic places of worship. The **Cathedral Museum** ① *south of Plaza de Africa, open afternoons only*, is situated in the side wall of the cathedral itself, off Plaza de Africa, and has ecclesiastical items in its collection, including the highly decorated montage of the Virgen Capitana. The **Cathedral** stands on the site of a pre-Muslim church and a mosque from the Arab period. The present building dates principally from the 17th century, though there were large-scale renovations in 1949-1958.

The **Santuario de Nuestra Señora de África** (Church of Our Lady of Africa) dates from the 15th century with many later additions, the largest in the 18th century, and is also on the site of a former mosque. Long seen as important as a great Christian monument in Islamic North Africa, it has a spectacular baroque altarpiece. The **Palacio Municipal** (town hall) is an interesting modern building dating from 1926 and containing some fine

EU in Africa: immigration policies

It is estimated that in the year 2000, around 10,000 Africans tried illegally to cross the border into Ceuta. The reaction of the EU was to build a £200 million barrier along the border. It is made up of two 3-m razor wire fences with a patrol road between them. The fence is illuminated by spotlights, and cameras detect and record any movement. However, it has not been enough to deter some, who camp out in the hills on the Moroccan side of the border waiting for the chance to cut their way through, or to summon up the courage for the dangerous swim around the coast – one that claims the lives of many every year. Smoke from the camp fires of those wanting to cross drifts across the border post, which can have the feel of a war zone, albeit one that Europeans can stroll through unhindered.

panelling and frescoes by Bertucci. The centre of the Plaza de Africa is taken up with a large monument to those Spaniards who fell in the country's African wars (1859-60). Note the bronze reliefs of battle scenes by Susillo.

Museo de Ceuta (Archeology section)
ⓘ *30 Paseo del Revellin, Mon-Sat 1000-1400 and 1700-2000 (1000-1400 and 1900-2100 Jun-Sep), Sun 1000-1400, free.*
The Municipal Museum on Paseo del Revellin is well laid out and attractive. Rooms I and II have some fine Punic and Roman amphorae and display the activities of Ceuta and the sea, including the salt-making pans on the ancient site of what is now the Parador and the Plaza de Africa. Room III has items relating to underwater archaeology, with some well-preserved and decorated amphorae and pots, a corn-grinding wheel and a lead depth sounder. Other rooms (IV and V) display medieval crafts of Hispanic-Islamic origins. Rooms VII and VIII are given over to scenes, artefacts and written sources of the Spanish-Moroccan war (1859-1860). Nearby, the **Church of San Francisco** stands in Plaza de los Reyes, which reputedly contains the bones of the Portuguese King Sebastian.

Legion Museum
ⓘ *Av Dean Navarro Acuña 6, Mon-Sat 0900-1300, free.*
Celebrating the founding and activities of the Spanish Legion, there is a variety of armaments, uniforms and military memorabilia on display here.

City walls
Forming an impressive ring around the city, these Portuguese-built fortifications are at their best adjacent to the San Felipe moat and the Muralla Real. The exterior fortifications are also impressive – **Fort Desnarigado** and **Fortaleza del Hacho** (the latter, still occupied by the military, is closed to the public). Fortaleza del Hacho is probably Byzantine in origin but was strengthened under the Ommayyad dynasty. It was reconstructed by the Portuguese and redeveloped by the Spanish in the 18th and 19th centuries. In the west of the town above the Ramparts Pedro La Mata are the impressive **Merinid Walls**, a 14th-century construction on earlier buildings. Of the original 2 km of walls, there now remains only a 500-m section, interesting nevertheless, including the old **Fès Gate**. Adjacent to Plaza de la Paz on Paseo Marina are the ruins of the **Arab baths**, heavily reconstructed but accessible and a useful reminder of the high urban forms of the Arab period.

Museo de Ceuta (Fine Arts section)

ⓘ *Revellín de San Ignaciao courtyard, Mon-Sat 1000-1400 and 1700-2000 (Jun-Sep 1000-1400 and 1900-2100), Sun 1000-1400, free.*

Inside the city walls, the city museum's fine arts gallery is an excellent contemporary art space, with white angular walls and some interesting temporary exhibitions of Spanish art.

◉ Ceuta listings

For sleeping and eating price codes and other relevant information, see pages 22-28.

⬤ Where to stay

Ceuta *p368, map p368*

If you will arrive late in the day, make sure that you reserve your hotel room in advance.

€€€ Hotel Plaza Ruiz, 3 Pl Teniente Ruiz, T(+34) 956-516733, hostalesceuta@ hotmail.com. One of Ceuta's more desirable small hotels, it has 17 a/c rooms with small bathrooms and pine furniture on a little square just off the main street.

€€€ Hotel Ulises, T(+34) 956-514540, www.hotelulises.com. By far the swishest hotel in Ceuta. The 124 stylish rooms have dark wood furniture and floors, flat screen TVs and are decorated using lots of neutral tones, black-and-white photos and modern art. There's Wi-Fi on the 1st floor but the top-floor rooms have the best views. There's also a pool.

€€€ Parador Nacional Hotel la Muralla, Pl Virgen de Africa 15, opposite the Cathedral, T(+34) 956-514940. Pan pipes playing in the lobby further underline the 1970s feel of this large, business-centred hotel. There's a pool and plenty of modern facilities but they're not enough to make the place feel very inviting. May require a 2-night stay in high season.

€€€ Tryp, 3 Alcalde Sánchez Prados, T(+34) 956-511200, www.solmelia.com. A glass-fronted exterior opens up into the huge white lobby of this contemporary hotel. 121 sleek rooms in muted tones have designer lighting, a/c, minibar and Wi-Fi, and there's an open-air pool with comfy chairs.

€€ Bohemia, C Cameons, T(+34) 956-510615. A central place with a degree of old style, Bohemia has good rooms, 3 of which have balconies. Shared bathrooms, plants and lots of photos of Marilyn Monroe.

€€ Hostal Real, 1 C Real, T(+34) 956-511449, www.hostalreal.net. Bang in the centre of town, a good budget option, with clean if not overly bright rooms. Book ahead.

❼ Restaurants

Ceuta *p368, map p368*

The so-called **fisherman's village** (actually a modern area where nobody seems to live), just to the east of the marina, has several restaurants; try **Riad Ahlam**, **La Cantina** and **La Peña**.

€€ Gran Muralla, Pl de la Constitución, T(+34) 956-517625. A proper Chinese restaurant overlooking the square with views and an interior genuine enough to make it seem like a Chinese enclave in a Spanish enclave.

€€ La Marina, 4 Alférez Bayton, T(+34) 956-514 007. Posh but friendly, Marina does paella and a wide range of other fish dishes. Popular.

€€ Trattoria Pizzería Firenze, 3 Alférez Bayton, T(+34) 956-512088. Wed-Sun. Genuine Italian food; try the ravioli or tagliatelle with egg, spinach and porcini mushrooms or good pizzas.

€€ Ulises Café, next to the hotel of the same name (see above). A chic and bijou place for a fine glass of wine or a bar snack.

€ Café Central, 2 Millan Astray. Sophisticated café bar used by Ceuta's young professionals, with low lighting and hanging glass lamps.

€ **El Quijote**, 5 Pedro de Meneses. A small, friendly tapas bar on a pedestrian street.
€ **La Bodeguilla**, C Millán Astray. Buzzing tapas bar with a good range of *tostadas*.
€ **La Jota**, 6 Méndez Núñez, T(+34) 956-515365. Excellently priced and tasty meals, as well as snacks, sandwiches, cakes and ice cream in a real local-feel restaurant. A great place to hang out and it won't break the bank. They usually have a daily special for under €10.

⦿ Shopping

Ceuta *p368, map p368*
There are numerous shops selling duty-free electronic goods, though nothing seems cheaper than a web search would turn up in Europe. Spirits and fuel are cheaper here than in Morocco, or Spain, come to that, given Ceuta's tax status. If you've been in Morocco for a while, you might appreciate the European high street shops, including a massive branch of Zara. For travellers heading on to Morocco, stock up on Spanish cheese and wine from the local supermarkets as well as excellent fresh seafood.

⦿ What to do

Ceuta *p368, map p368*
The marina, T(+34) 956-513753, has capacity for 300 vessels. The waters around here are said to have the most interesting diving in the Mediterranean. Check www.ceutabuceo.com.

Tour operators
Most of the agencies are on Muelle Cañonero Dato. Try **Viajes Dato**, Marina Club, T(+34) 956-509582, or **Viajes Flandría**, C de la Independencia 1, T(+34) 956-512074.

⦿ Transport

Ceuta *p368, map p368*
Air
Transportes Aereos del Sur, T902-404704, www.aena.es, have helicopter flights from Ceuta to **Jerez** and **Málaga**.

Car hire
Africa Car, through Flandria Travel Agents, Independencia 1, T(+34) 956-512 074.

Taxi
T(+34) 956-515 406. Between the frontier and Fnideq there are *grands taxis*, 5dh.

Bus
There are some long-distance Spanish buses, from the bus station on the south coast road in Ceuta, to **Casablanca**, **Al Hoceïma** and **Nador**. Tetouan is a better option for finding bus services. There are bus and *grand taxi* services between Fnideq and **Tetouan**, and between Fnideq and **Tangier**. On the Spanish side, buses take euros only, though you can usually persuade taxi drivers to take dirhams (€3, or around 35dh).

Boat
The **Algeciras–Ceuta** high-speed ferries are cheaper and quicker than those between Algeciras and Tangier. **Trasmediterranea** (www.trasmediterranea.es) operates 8 departures to **Algeciras** (in Spain) daily at 0930, 1230, 1430, 1530, 1730, 1830, 2030 and 2230 (1 hr 20 mins), €26, child €15, car €70. Tickets can be bought in the port building, online or from the numerous travel agents around the town centre.

Tetouan

Set between the Rif and the Mediterranean Sea, Tetouan has a dramatic beauty, the white buildings of the medina contrasting with the backdrop of the mountains. There's some impressive colonial architecture in the Spanish town, and the medina has been made a UNESCO Heritage Site. The city is an interesting place to explore, albeit with more noise and hassle than Chefchaouen to the south. Tetouan's main sites can be covered in a rather rushed half day; a full day would give you time to explore the city pretty thoroughly. Between Ceuta and Tetouan, and also further round the coast, there are a number of resorts – some fashionable, others with a more downbeat appeal – which can be visited en route or as an excursion from the city. ►► *For listings, see pages 378-380.*

Arriving in Tetouan → *Colour map 1, A3.*

Getting there and around
Taxis from Tangier and Tetouan arrive in the new town, close to the bus station, about 10 minutes' walk from the medina. From the bus station, to get to the medina, head up Rue Sidi Mandri and turn third right down Avenue Mohammed V, which will bring you to Place Hassan II. ►► *See Transport, page 380, for further details.*

Note When visiting Tetouan watch out for the various seedy characters and con artists with a keen eye for tired backpackers stumbling off a late bus from Fès. If you are arriving by bus, you are at your most vulnerable at the main bus station. Pay attention to your belongings and avoid having any dealings with faux guides. The tourist office (below) can arrange for an official guide, should you want one, for 120dh for a half day.

Tourist information **Office du Tourisme (ONMT)** ① *30 Rue Mohammed V, T0539-961915, Mon-Fri 0830-1630.*

Background

Tetouan was founded in the third century BC as Tamuda, but was destroyed by the Romans in AD 42. The Merinid ruler Sultan Abou Thabit built a kasbah at Tetouan in 1307. Sacked by Henry III of Castille in 1399 to disperse the corsairs based there, Tetouan was neglected until it was taken over by Muslims expelled from Granada in 1484. They were to bring with them the distinctive forms and traditions of Andalucían Islamic architecture, still observable in the medinas of Granada and Córdoba. Many of the Andalucíans worked as corsairs, continuing the tradition. A Jewish community was established here in the 17th century, which gave the impetus to open up trade with Europe. Trade with the West continued to boom in the 18th century during the reign of Moulay Ismaïl. In 1913 Tetouan was chosen as the capital of the Spanish protectorate over northern Morocco. The Spanish created the new town, which has remained an important regional centre in independent Morocco.

Places in Tetouan

Ville nouvelle
Place Hassan II, the focal point of the city and a former market, is the best place for a stroll or a sit in a café terrace during the evening. It is dominated by the **Royal Palace**, with its

gleaming white walls and green tiled roof. Dating from the 17th-century, it was completely transformed under Hassan II. Looking onto the square is the **Pasha Mosque**, with its distinctive green door and green and brown tiled minaret. **Bab er Rouah**, to the southeast, has also had a facelift. The other major focus point in the *ville nouvelle* is **Place Moulay el Mehdi**, along Boulevard Mohammed V from Place Hassan II. Here there is an impressive golden-yellow **cathedral** and a large fountain in the middle. **Instituto Cervantes** ① *3 C Mohammed Torres, T0539-967056,* has good exhibitions and documentaries.

Medina

Bab er Rouah, in the corner of Place Hassan II, leads into the medina, where Andalucían influence is still apparent in the whitewashed walls and delicate wrought-iron decorations on the balconies. A typically confusing maze of streets and souks, it is well worth exploring, although, perhaps, with the assistance of an official guide. Look out for artefacts in the souks in Tetouan's favoured red colour. **Rue Terrafin** is a good route through the medina, and leads into Rue Torres and Rue Sidi el Yousti, and out at **Bab el Okla**. North of Rue Sidi el Yousti is an area with some of the larger and more impressive houses.

Souks Souk el Hout, with pottery, meat and fish, is to the left of Rue Terrafin behind the palace. Here there is a delightful leafy square; pleasant surroundings for admiring the wares. Behind the souk is a small 15th-century fortress, the **Alcazaba**, now taken over by a cooperative. Take the left hand of the two north-bound lanes from the Souk el Hout and on the right is **Guersa el Kebir**, a textile souk selling the striped, woven blankets worn by Rifi women. The red, white and blue of the fabric is particularly striking and it's sold by women dressed in the same colours. **El Foki** market can be found by following your nose – the smell of the traditional, flat, round loaves is impossible to miss. Look out too for the **L'Usaa Square**, with its white houses around a mosaic fountain and a rose garden.

Further on from this souk, leading up to Bab Sebta, are a number of specialist craft souks and shops. Running between Bab Sebta and Bab Fès is **Rue de Fès**, a more general commercial area, although with a number of souks around. From Bab Sebta the road out of the city passes through a large cemetery. Above the medina is the crumbling **kasbah** (closed to visitors), and nearby a vantage point providing stunning views over the city.

Jewish quarter On Place Hassan II, the first alleyway south of Bab er Rouah leads onto the main street of the mellah, the 19th-century Jewish quarter, where there are a number of abandoned synagogues. The original Jewish population has all but disappeared. The earliest mellah was near the Grand Mosque.

Archaeological Museum ① *Blvd Aljazaer, near Pl Hassan II, T0539-967103. Mon-Fri 0830-1630. 10dh.* Built in 1943, this museum contains a small archaeological collection from the prehistoric and pre-Islamic sites of the northern region of Morocco, plus some pieces from the once-Spanish Saharan provinces and a large library. Of most interest, however, are the Roman statues and mosaics found at ancient Lixus near Larache (see page 363). The most notable mosaic portrays the Three Graces of Roman mythology – there's been some modern conservation to fill in the gaps, but it's sensitively done. Other rooms display prehistoric tools, bronzes and pottery. Of note here is the Sumerian ex-voto statuette found close to Asilah. Most of the small figures date from the first century AD. Other highlights include a scale model of the stone circle of Mzoura (see page 361), 15th-century Portugese tiles and a Latin inscription from Tamuda telling of a Roman victory over the Berbers.

Musée d'Art Marocain/Musée Ethnographique ① *T0539-970505. Mon-Fri 0830-1200 and 1430-1730, Sat 0830-1200.* Housed in Bab el Okla and renovated in 2002, this small museum is definitely worth a visit. There are samples of local textiles and dress, weapons and musical instruments, plus a small Andalucían garden at the back. There is also a display of traditional tiles. Note that the technique for making tiles in Tetouan was different from the more mainstream Moroccan or Fassi *zellige* technique. The latter is a mosaic technique involving the assembling of thousands of tiny coloured ceramic pieces.

Tetouan

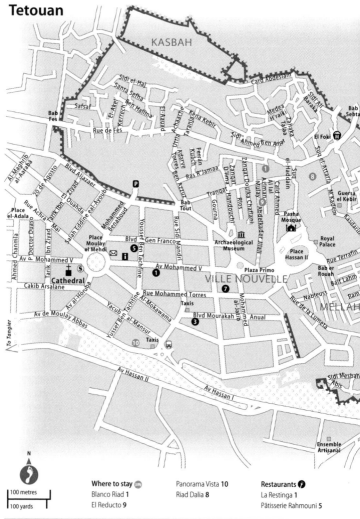

Where to stay 🛏
Blanco Riad **1**
El Reducto **9**

Panorama Vista **10**
Riad Dalia **8**

Restaurants 🍴
La Restinga **1**
Pâtisserie Rahmouni **5**

The artisans of Tetouan produced tiles imitating the *zellige* mosaics by using the *cuerda seca* ('dry cord') technique, by which the different coloured glazes were separated by a pattern of geometric lines.

École de Métiers Just outside the medina, across the road from Bab el Okla, is the École de Métiers (craft school), built by the Spanish. Here craftsmen and students work on tiles, leatherwork, carpentry and pottery. The school, generally closed for holidays in August, may be open to visitors.

To Ceuta

Cemetery

Bab Sfli

Bab Es Saidi

MEDINA

Grand Mosque

Alcazaba

Souk el Hout
Rue Torres

Musée d'Art Marocain/Musée Ethnographique

Bab el Okla

École de Métiers

Bab er Remuz

Av Massira

Buses to Martil, Cabo Negro & Mdiq

Pizzeria Roma **7**
Sandwich Ali Baba **3**

Tamuda

The remains of ancient Tamuda lie to the south of the N2 road running west out of Tetouan. It was founded in the third to second centuries BC. Later, during the Roman period, in the third century AD, the original settlement disappeared under a Roman camp. So far, only remains of dwellings have been excavated, no public buildings or religious buildings. Finds from Tamuda are in the Archaeological Museum in Tetouan.

Beach resorts around Tetouan
→ *For listings, see pages 378-380.*

Restinga Smir → *Colour map 1, A3.*
From Fnideq to Tetouan, the N13 passes through a flat strip of beaches and marshes, and a number of tourist developments. Restinga Smir, 22 km from Tetouan, has a long beach and a correspondingly long line of holiday complexes, hotels, bars, restaurants, bungalows and camping areas. Until recently it was still a small fishing village, frequented only by a small number of local visitors. Now it enjoys an international reputation. There is, however, sufficient space on the vast beaches for the activities on offer, which include horse riding, mini-golf, tennis, underwater fishing and windsurfing. There's also the small marina/pleasure port of Marina Smir.

Mdiq → *Colour map 1, A3.*
After Restinga Smir the road passes through Kabila, another beach and marina, to Mdiq, a small fishing port with some traditional boat construction. Mdiq shares the same

coastline (and clientele) as Cabo Negro (below) and there is a sense of competition between the two. Mdiq is a well-established resort offering a range of modern hotels and restaurants (mainly fish of course), nightclubs, swimming pools and the usual selection of watersports on the beach. This is certainly a popular family resort, which is spreading to the north.

Cabo Negro → Colour map 1, A3.
After Mdiq turn for Cabo Negro (also known as Taifor or Ras Tarf), which is 3.5 km off the N13. Here the beach is more rugged, with low hills, dotted with small houses, overlooking the sea. This is a slightly less commercialized region, though the number of discos and nightclubs is growing. Riding is very popular here, with horses for hire by the hour and day. The roads through the town follow the contours and rise at various levels up the hill.

Martil → Colour map 1, A3.
Martil, Tetouan's former port, and one-time pirate base, stands at the mouth of the Oued Martil. It is now a popular resort, with over 10 km of sandy beach. Once it was the resort of people from Tetouan who established holiday homes here on the coast but now Martil welcomes visitors from far afield.

Oued Laou and the coastal road south of Tetouan → Colour map 1, A3.
Oued Laou is 44 km southeast of Tetouan along the spectacular coastal road, the S608. It is a relaxed fishing village with an excellent beach but only basic facilities. The road continues from here along the coast through the villages of Targa, Steha, Bou Hamed, and Dar M'Ter. Possibly a more convenient place to stop is the fishing village of El Jebha (souk Tuesday), which is served by buses from Tetouan and Chefchaouen. A tortuous mountain road, the 8500, takes the intrepid traveller from El Jebha to meet the N2 west of Ketama.

⦿ Tetouan listings

For sleeping and eating price codes and other relevant information, see pages 22-28.

⊕ Where to stay

Tetouan *p374, map p376*
Budget hotels in and near the medina and Pl Hassan II are often primitive and unhygienic.
€€€ **Blanco Riad Hotel**, Zawya Kadiria 25, T0539-704202, www.blancoriad.com. All graceful arches and columns with lashings of Arabesque design, this riad is a special place to stay. With just 8 light-filled rooms, all individually decorated with intricate tiled floors, wood inlay, lanterns and *masharabeyya* details, Blanco Riad manages to ooze exclusivity without ever feeling stuffy. The roof terrace has incredible views over the town, and there is a lovely secluded inner courtyard. The house used

to belong to the Spanish consulate and has been lovingly restored but with a fresh, contemporary edge.
€€ **El Reducto**, Zanqat Zawya 38, T0539-968120, www.riadtetouan.com. This little riad, well signposted just off the Plaza at the end of Mohammed V, used to belong to the prime minister under the Spanish protectorate and has been given a thorough overhaul by its current Spanish owner, who may be able to get you a good guide to the medina. Set around a rectangular courtyard, the 4 rooms range from the fairly small to a huge space with spectacular carved wood and an enormous bath. All have luxurious fabrics, drapes and antique tiles. Price includes breakfast. Half-board also available.
€€ **Hotel Chams**, Av Abdelkhalak Torres, 2.5 km east towards Martil, T0539-990901. 76 rooms, 4 suites, all with bath and TV.

There's a small pool, a restaurant and a bar. Comfortable, if rather old-fashioned rooms.

€€ Panorama Vista, Av My el Abbas, T0539-964970. If you don't fancy staying in a riad, this is far and away Tetouan's best mid-range hotel option. The aptly (and tautologically) named **Panorama Vista** has enormous views across the valley to the Rif mountains. Rooms are modern and comfortable with TVs and good bathrooms. There's a popular café downstairs for breakfast, too.

€€ Riad Dalia, 25 Rue Ouessaa, Souika, T0539-964318, www.riad-dalia.com. At the heart of the medina (call when you arrive and they'll come and meet you), the **Dalia** offers a riad experience at bargain prices. The cheapest rooms are small, dark and without en suite but still atmospheric and, at €10-15 for a single and €20-25 for a double, are a snip. Other rooms (much grander and with en suite) range cost €30-60. There are stunning 360-degree views from the roof terrace. Popular with students and young Spaniards, who canoodle in dark corners and smoke the hookah pipes. The building was once the house of the Dutch consul, whose bedroom was in what is now the café on the top floor. The other guest rooms were apparently used by his several wives.

Camping

There are a number of campsites at the resorts along the coast (see below).

Restinga Smir *p377*

There are many good campsites, including **Al Fraia** and **Camping Andalus**.

€€ Hotel Karabo, T0539-977070. Has 117 rooms, bar, restaurant, pool, tennis and disco.

Mdiq *p377*

€€€ Hotel Golden Beach, T0539-975077. 87 rooms on the beachside opposite the bus station.

€€€ Kabila Hotel, T0539-975013. 96 rooms and a campsite.

Cabo Negro *p378*

€€ Hotel Petit Merou, T0539-978115/6. 22 rooms, restaurant, bar, disco.

Martil *p378*

There is also the **Hotel Nuzha** (**€**) on Rue Miramar.

€€ Hacienda, T0539-688668, www.haciendamartil.com. A good 3-star with modern rooms and a pool.

Camping

Camping Martil, by the river, or **Camping Oued La Malah**, signed further out of town. **Camping Tetouan**, site of 6 ha, beach only 200 m, bar/snacks, restaurant, shop, showers, laundry, electricity for caravans, petrol at 200 m.

Municipal Camping at Martil Beach, T0539-979435. Site of 3 ha, beach, showers, laundry, electricity for caravans, petrol at 600 m.

Oued Laou *p378*

€€ Hotel-Restaurant Oued Laou, T0539-670854. Also a campsite with a couple of chalets.

❼ Restaurants

Tetouan *p374, map p376*

€€ Blanco Riad, Zawya Kadiria 25, T0539-704202, www.blancoriad.com. Specializing in Moroccan dishes with a modern twist, **Blanco Riad** (see Where to stay, above) is a wonderful place to sample a contemporary version of the nation's cuisine. Eat outside on the patio on a balmy evening to top off a perfect day of sightseeing in Tetouan.

€€ El Reducto, Zanqat Zawya 38, T0539-968120. In a great setting (see Where to stay, above), **El Reducto** does very reasonable food, mainly traditional Moroccan, but with a few Spanish touches, such as a decent gazpacho. The quality of the food doesn't quite match that of the rarefied surroundings but there's some good wine.

€€ **La Restinga**, 21 Rue Mohammed V, T0539-963576. On the main street, this is a traditional place offering well-priced Moroccan food with good tagines. The restaurant has an alcohol licence.

€ **Pâtisserie Rahmouni**, 10 Rue Youssef Ben Tachfine. Whether you like your pastries creamy, nutty or flaky, you'll find an enormous selection here. There's a good savoury counter at the back, and they serve excellent coffee, too.

€ **Pizzeria Roma**, Rue Mohammed Torres. Decent pizzas with generous quantities of cheese. It's modern rather than atmospheric – entertainment comes courtesy of rock music and a TV – but a good spot for a quick lunch.

€ **Sandwich Ali Baba**, Rue Mourakah Anual. A popular place for cheap local food. Also try the places around Rue Luneta and Bab er Rouah.

⊖ Transport

Tetouan *p374, map p376*
Bus
The bus station, at the corner of Av Hassan I and Rue Sidi Mandri, T0539-966263, has both CTM and other services to most major destinations. With CTM there is 1 service daily to **Fnideq** (for **Ceuta**) at 0530 (30 mins); 6 buses a day to

Chefchaouen (1 hr); 4 to **Tangier** at 0500, 1500, 1700 and 2245 (1 hr); 1 to **Meknès** at 2245 (8 hrs); and 5 to **Fès** (6 hrs).

Supratours also operates a coach service to link up with the rail network at **Tnine Sidi Lyamani**. Through tickets can be bought from the office on Av 10 Mai (T0539-967579), where 2 coaches depart each day. Buses to **Martil**, **Cabo Negro** and **Mdiq** leave from near the old railway station on Av Massira (take Av Hassan II, to the right of the main bus station, which meets Av Massira after the Ensemble Artisanal on the right); those for **Oued Laou** leave from the main bus station.

Car hire
Amin Car, Av Mohammed V, T0539-964407. **Zeite**, Yacoub el Mansour.

Taxi
Grands taxis to **Tangier**, **Fnideq** (15dh, for **Ceuta**), **Chefchaouen** (30dh), the beaches and other places, leave from Blvd Maarakah Annoual or nearby.

⊙ Directory

Tetouan *p374, map p376*
Medical services Chemist: 24-hr, Rue al Wahda, T0539-966777. **Useful addresses Police**: Blvd General Franco, T19.

Chefchaouen, the Rif and Al Hoceïma

East of Tangier and Ceuta, along Morocco's northern coast, the Rif mountains rise steeply out of the Mediterranean, making access less easy and meaning that this is one of the country's less visited areas, despite its closeness to Europe. Chefchaouen is an exception to this rule – a popular traveller hangout, with good reason; it epitomizes the area's easy-going charms, not always disconnected from the region's kif (marijuana) production. ▶▶ *For listings, see pages 388-392.*

Chefchaouen → *For listings, see pages 388-392. Colour map 1, A3.*

The blue and whitewashed town of Chefchaouen, sometimes called Chaouen and even spelt Xaouen (the Spanish version), is an exceptionally photogenic Andalucían town in the Rif, 60 km south of Tetouan, set above the Oued Laou valley and just below the twin peaks of the Jbel ech Chefchaouen, the 'Horned Mountain'. The town itself could be explored in a day, but with a room in the right hotel, you might want to stay to relax in one of its many cafés or explore the surrounding countryside. At 600 m up in the hills, it makes a good centre for walking, and many who come for a quick visit end up staying much longer. The town also has many sanctuaries for pilgrims and, each year, thousands of visitors are attracted to pay homage to the memory of Sidi Ben Alil, Sidi Abdallah Habti and Sidi el Hadj Cherif.

Arriving in Chefchaouen
Getting there and around Chefchaouen's bus station is a 20-minute walk out of the town centre, or a short *petit taxi* journey. Coming in by *grand taxi*, you arrive close to the old town on Avenue Allal Ben Abdallah. Once you're in the old town, everything is accessible on foot. ▶▶ *See Transport, page 392, for further details.*

Tourist information **Chaouen Rural** ⓘ *Rue Machichi, T0539-987267, www.chaouen rural. org, daily 0900-1900,* is a Spanish-funded organization working with local communities and cooperatives. It organizes trips into the countryside around Chefchaouen and can also provide information on the town itself.

Note The selling of kif is big business here, the main production regions being to the east. Suitably persistent refusal should rid you of unwanted attentions, though these are almost always of the friendly-but-stoned variety, rather than aggressive (see also page 383).

Background
Set in the Djeballa region, Chefchaouen was founded in 1471 by Cherif Moulay Ali Ben Rachid, a follower of Moulay Abd es Salam Ben Mchich, the patron saint of the area, in order to halt the southwards expansion of the Spanish and Portuguese. The city's population was later supplemented by Muslims and Jews expelled from Spain, particularly from Granada, and, for a time, the rulers of Chefchaouen controlled much of northern Morocco. The town also grew in importance as a pilgrimage centre.

From 1576 Chefchaouen was in conflict with, and isolated from, the surrounding area, the gates being locked each night. Prior to 1920 only three Christians had braved its forbidding walls: the Vicomte de Foucauld disguised as a rabbi in 1883; Walter Harris, *Times* correspondent and author of *Morocco That Was*, in 1889; and the American William

Summers, poisoned in Chefchaouen in 1892. They found Jews still speaking 15th-century Andalucían Spanish. In 1920 the town was taken over by the Spanish as part of their protectorate. They were thrown out from 1924 to 1926, by Abd el Karim's Rif resistance movement but returned to stay until Independence in 1956.

Modern Chefchaouen has extended across the hillsides, and the old town is now ringed by a suburb of the usual three-storey family apartment buildings. Though it is now well established on tourist itineraries, both mainstream and backpacker, Chefchaouen manages to retain a village feel. Here you may have your first sighting of the distinctive garments of the women of the Rif, the red and white striped *fouta* or overskirt and the large conical straw hat with woollen bobbles.

Places in Chefchaouen

There are few major sites. The centre is Place Mohammed V, with its small Andalucían garden. Avenue Hassan II leads to Bab el Aïn and the medina. The market is down some steps from Avenue Hassan II, on Avenue Al Khattabi. Normally a food market, there is a local souk on Monday and Thursday.

Medina

The medina of Chefchaouen is an exceptionally photogenic place and rewarding to explore. Sufficiently small not to get lost in, it has intricate Andalucían architecture, arches,

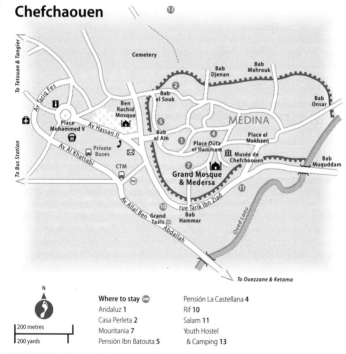

Chefchaouen

Where to stay
Andaluz 1
Casa Perleta 2
Mouritania 7
Pensión Ibn Batouta 5

Pensión La Castellana 4
Rif 10
Salam 11
Youth Hostel
& Camping 13

Reefer madness

The Northern Rif has long been an area of unrest and rebellion against central authorities, notably in the Rif rebellion of Abd el Karim against the Spanish from 1921 to 1926. More recently, bandits are said to have preyed on travellers and, today, although the situation has improved, the main dilemma is how to replace one of the major sources of income for local families – cannabis cultivation. (The term 'kif' refers to the dried and chopped leaves and flowers, not the resin, and the word 'reefer' probably derives from the word 'Rif'.) Government development programmes and pressure from the EU have had little impact, simply because the cannabis plant, especially if irrigated, grows very well on the region's hillsides. If you stop over in the area, you may be invited to see the process of turning the leaves into a ball of uncut, smokeable material, the understanding being that you will buy. Do not even think of smuggling cannabis out of the country. There are links between the police and vendors, who may try to blackmail you, and the European consuls in Tangier have enough would-be smugglers to visit in the local prisons already. The police are very likely to crack down on foreigners smoking in public, even though they may turn a blind eye to locals doing the same.

arcades and porches, white- or blue-washed houses, with ochre-tiled roofs, and clean, quiet cobbled streets. In the maze of these narrow streets you run into water points, small open squares with shops and the solid ramparts of the kasbah. If driving, park the car in **Place el Makhzen** and explore the rest on foot. Approaching the medina on foot, enter by **Bab el Aïn**. From Bab el Aïn a small road leads through to **Place Outa el Hammam**. This is the main square, lively at night, and surrounded by a number of stalls and café-restaurants, popular with kif smokers.

The square is dominated by the terracotta-coloured 15th-century kasbah, now the **Musée de Chefchaouen** ① *T0539-986761, Wed-Mon 0900-1300 and 1500-1830, 0900-1700 in Ramadan, 10dh*. As a prison it housed the Rifi leader Abd el Karim from 1926, and you can visit the suitably dark and forbidding dungeon. The museum itself is not that special – it has an exhibition of local costumes, some with very delicate embroidery, tools, musical instruments, pottery, weapons and a collection of decorated wooden caskets. More interesting is the building itself; you can climb to the top of the tower for a good view of the town from the roof. There is also a peaceful Andalucían-style courtyard garden, filled with flowers and birds.

The beautiful **Grand Mosque**, with its octagonal minaret, beside the kasbah, dates from the 15th century, but was restored in the 17th and 18th. Next door is a 16th-century *medersa*, unfortunately closed. Opposite the **Restaurant Kasbah**, at No 34, is an old **caravanserai**. Further on, **Place el Makhzen**, the second square, has stalls along the top side, the **Ensemble Artisanal** at the end.

Hill walking

Chefchaouen has some good hill walking, with spectacular scenery and plentiful animal and birdlife. Don't be too surprised, however, if you experience suspicious questioning from the military involved in cracking down on kif cultivation, and be prepared for a long and strenuous day. Taking a guide (could set you back around 100dh) is worth considering. Look out for the natural spring, **Ras el Maa**, 3 km out of town in the direction of **Jbel**

Tisouka (2050 m). You are within striking distance of the **Parc Naturel de Talassemtane**, still basically undiscovered by tourists. **El Malha**, **Beni Ahmed** and other isolated villages in this park are reached by landrover taxi from Bab Taza, 25 km to the southeast of Chefchaouen on the N2 road to Ketama (Issaguen).

Northern Rif → For listings, see pages 388-392. Colour map 1, A3.

The N2, the 'route of the crests' from Chefchaouen to Al Hoceïma, is one of Morocco's most dramatic journeys, a road running through a succession of small villages with stunning views over the remote valleys and towards the snow-capped Rif Mountains. Care must be taken on this narrow, hill-top road, which may be closed by snow in winter.

Ketama

Ketama (officially called Issaguen, but referred to by just about everyone as Ketama, confusingly also the name of the area) has long had a sulphurous reputation as Morocco's capital of cannabis, a reputation not entirely undeserved. Although much money is made from kif, it doesn't really seem to have found its way into this particular town, although there is, as everywhere in Morocco, some new building. Ketama could perhaps become a centre for summer hill walking, being at the heart of a region where the mountains are covered in cedar trees, but, for the moment, there is little infrastructure and few visitors stop here. The town can sometimes be snowbound in winter. The main point of interest in the area is the nearby Jbel Tidghine, the highest mountain in the Rif at 2448 m.

If you settle for a couple of minutes in a café in Ketama, someone is certain to approach you with an offer of cannabis. But the Gendarmerie royale are watching, so avoid making any purchases.

Climbing Jbel Tidghine (Tidiquin)

For Jbel Tidghine, you need to head for the village of **Azila**, about 5 km from Ketama. If driving, take the road south out of Ketama and turn left at the new, low angular building. Alternatively, take a local taxi from outside the **Hotel Saâda**. The houses of Azila are scattered around a valley below Jbel Tidghine. Follow the road through to the open 'football field', where the odd taxi parks up or, before this, turn off right by some trees on a dirt track to come out just above the mosque. With luck, a local kid will volunteer to show you the way across the valley. You will dip down through the village, over a rough plank bridge under the walnut trees. Then, passing some quite large, concrete houses, you reach the bracken and first cedars of Tidghine's lower slopes. For the climb, there are two options: either wind slowly up the old forestry department piste, or cut straight up to intersect with the forestry track further up – a good option if you're with a local. It is said that strong 4WDs can get to within 30 minutes of the summit. Climbing time should be about 2¼ hours, the descent 1¾ hours. Remember to bring a water bottle – there is a spring where you can refill it.

The forest is truly beautiful, with butterflies in late summer, but it's under threat from locals in need of more sources of income than livestock and barely profitable cannabis cultivation. To bring the great trees down, the practice is to light the needles under the trees in summer. The resinous trunks burn easily, weakening the whole tree, which is then easy to fell in winter when the forestry wardens are less likely to make tours of inspection.

The last stretch up the mountain is shaley scree, quite easy to deal with but slow going. At the top, the views are magnificent. There are two stone-built, corrugated-iron roofed huts where you could stay the night, if you have a warm sleeping bag.

Route de l'Unité

The R505 runs southwards from Ketama (Issaguen) to Taounate, Aïn Aicha and Fès, with views of deep valleys and forested slopes. This road, the Route de l'Unité, was built just after Independence by voluntary labour battalions to link the Spanish protectorate of the north with the former French areas. The whole region is untouched by tourism, despite its cedar woods and mountainous terrain. If driving in this region in summer, note that car accidents are frequent. Returning migrant workers out to impress in powerful cars may fail to appreciate the dangers of the winding roads.

Ouezzane and the Southern Rif → *For listings, see pages 388-392. Colour map 1, A3.*

Ouezzane is now a good sized town, rumoured to be the centre of cannabis-resin trading since the clean-up in Tangier in the late 1990s. It is also a centre for the production of olive oil and, because of its Thursday souk, is a draw for local farmers and tradesmen. For visitors, there is little to see, though perched on the north-facing slopes of Jbel Ben Hellal, it has a dramatic hillside location. A track from the town (3 km) leads up to the peak (609 m) and gives a splendid view across towards the Rif. Just 9 km north of the town is Azjem, burial place of an important Rabbi, Amram Ben Djouane, who came from Andalucía in the 18th century. Here, again, are impressive views of the rugged Rif Mountains and the verdant valleys between.

Arriving in Ouezzane

Getting there Ouezzane lies 60 km (1¼ hours) from Chefchaouen down the N13/N2 road (look out for the Pont de Loukkos, which used to mark the border between the two protectorates). There are *grands taxis* from Chefchaouen and Souk el Arba, as well as buses from Fès (five hours), Meknès (four hours) and Chefchaouen.

Getting around The bus and taxi terminals are close to Place de l'Indépendance, with budget hotels close by. Note that travelling on from Ouezzane can be awkward by bus, as a lot of buses are through services, which arrive full.

Background

Ouezzane, today an important regional centre with a population of 41,000, was founded in 1727 by Moulay Abdallah Cherif, founder of the Tabiya Islamic order. This brotherhood achieved great national prominence from the 18th century, when the *zaouïa* in Ouezzane became the focus of extensive pilgrimage activity. Ouezzane had close links with the sultan's court, which was often dependent on the *zaouïa* and its followers for support.

A mid 19th-century cherif of Ouezzane married an Englishwoman, Emily Keane, in 1877 in an Anglican service – they had met at the house of the American consul where Keane was governess – although she later separated from him to live out her dotage in Tangier, where she is now buried in the Anglican Church (see page 350).

Places in Ouezzane

Ouezzane's **medina** has some of the most interesting architecture in the Rif, with picturesque tiled-roof houses along winding cobbled streets. The focus of the town is the 18th-century **zaouïa**, on Rue de la Zaouïa, a distinctive green-tiled building with an octagonal minaret. Non-Muslims should not approach too close. Nearby are old lodgings for the pilgrims and the decaying cherifian palace.

Place de l'Indépendance, the centre of the medina, is busiest during the town souk on Thursday. To get to the craft souks, centred around **Place Bir Inzarane**, follow Rue Abdallah Ibn Lamlih up from Place de l'Indépendance. Ouezzane is known for woollen carpets woven in the weavers' souk at the top of the town. The blacksmiths' souk is along Rue Haddadine. There is a **Centre Artisanal** ⓘ *Place de l'Indépendance, 0800-1900*, and another on Avenue Hassan II.

Al Hoceïma → *For listings, see pages 388-392. Colour map 1, A4.*

Al Hoceïma has one of the most beautiful natural sites on the Moroccan Mediterranean coast. Although the town, a Spanish creation of the 1920s and 1950s, has no great monuments, there is compensation in the form of nearby beaches. Despite these coastal attractions and greenery of the surrounding hills, the difficulty of getting to Al Hoceïma by road reduces the flow of casual visitors. There is an airport, however, bringing in a few package tourists. In summer there are huge numbers of migrant workers and their families back from Europe, while the winter is very quiet. East of the town is a fertile plain enclosed on three sides by hills. And, off the Plage de Sfiha, also to the east of Al Hoceïma, is an intriguing group of islands, the **Peñon de Alhucemas**, Spanish territory since 1673, and once disputed by the French and English for their strategic position.

Arriving in Al Hoceïma

Getting there Al Hoceïma is possibly the most isolated resort town in Morocco. You can fly there from Casablanca (in summer) or, given the distances, take an early morning bus from Chefchaouen, Fès, Nador, Tangier or Taza. There are *grands taxis*, especially from Nador (three hours) and more rarely from Taza and Fès. ►► *See Transport, page 392, for further details.*

Getting around Al Hoceïma is not a big place. However, you might want to take a beige-and-blue *petit taxi* out to one of the beaches. The beaches at Torres de Alcalá and Kalah Iris, some 60 km away to the west, can also easily be reached by public transport. Ketama and Jbel Tidghine are a feasible day trip by *grand taxi* from Al Hoceïma.

Tourist information Délégation Régionale du Tourisme ⓘ *Immeuble Cabalo, Rue Tarik Ibn Ziad, off Pl de la Marche Verte, T0539-982830, 0830-1200 and 1400-1800.*

Background

The character of the town centre of modern Al Hoceïma is distinctly Spanish, reflecting the protectorate years. Established by the Spanish in 1926 as Villa Sanjurjo, it was built as a garrison to control the Beni Ouriaghel tribe, of which Abd el Karim was the chief, immediately after the Rif rebellion. (For those interested in colonial place names, the town was originally named Villa Sanjurjo, after one General Sanjurjo who led Spanish troops ashore here. The old part of town is still sometimes referred to by this name.) To the east of Al Hoceïma is the long and less busy beach of **Alhucemas bay**, while offshore is the Peñon de Alhucemas, a remarkable idiosyncrasy of history. This small island is owned and occupied by Spain and apparently used as a prison. It is completely dependent on Melilla for supplies and even water, and has no contact with the Moroccan mainland, off which it sits like a ship at anchor.

Today Al Hoceïma has a population of some 60,000. Off season, it has an isolated feel: Tangier lies 300 km away to the west, Melilla is 170 km to the east, Oujda some 250 km away. The image in the holiday brochures is of a villageish sort of place with low, whitewashed houses atop a cliff, surrounding a few colonial buildings. In fact, modern Al Hoceïma has streets and streets of three- and four-storey blocks, sprawling across the hillsides. This is where migrant workers put their savings. So, Al Hoceïma is turning into a big town, but one without any industry or major official functions.

Nador and Al Hoceïma are the key towns for the Ta'rifit-speaking region, and Arabic-speaking outsiders are not all that much appreciated here. Newsagents sell badges and stickers with the image of Abd el Karim, hero of the Rif War against the Spanish. Yet some cultural resistance aside, Al Hoceïma is very sleepy outside the summer season, when migrants from the Netherlands and Belgium pour in.

Places in Al Hoceïma
Buses and taxis pull into the neighbourhood of the Place du Rif. You should thread your way over to the Avenue Mohammed V (banks and cafés), which leads down to the wide expanse of **Place Mohammed VI**. The well-maintained colonial building at the bottom is the Spanish school. The cafés on your right as you head down are worth a pause, with their views over the horseshoe bay. At the **Hotel Mohammed V**, the road curves down to the main beach. The **port** is worth a look, if you have time, and there are a handful of restaurants here. A stroll round the town will reveal various other remnants of Spanish times.

Just before the **Hotel Mohammed V**, there is a steep flight of steps that leads down to the **Hotel Quemado** complex and the **beach**. This gets pretty crowded in summer, although the sand is cleaned and raked every morning. There are pedalos and rowing boats for hire and jet skis. There is a rock to swim out to, and lots of enthusiastic playing of beach tennis.

Beaches east of town
Kalah Bonita beach is just within the urban area (campsite, café-restaurant and crowds in summer, also sewage smells from the creek around the cliff). Further east are Isri, Sfiha, Souani and Tayda. The beach at **Isri** has gravelly sand and, being below a brick factory, receives a certain amount of rubble. The left turn-off for Isri beach, coming from town, is 50 m after the **Centre de visite technique**, a large white building. The gravelly beach also has the rock where Abd el Karim el Khattabi made a famous speech in 1926, urging his resistance fighters to give up their arms and accept a form of autonomous government under Spanish rule. The tribes rejected this proposal and subsequently took a pounding from the Spanish airforce. Note that city taxis do not run this far out.

The beach at **Souani** ('the orchards') is rather better. The turn-off left is signed. There is a 2-km drive down to the car park next to the beach. Take care on the looping road, and don't get distracted by the superb views over to Peñon de Alhucemas. (Without a car, Souani is accessible by *grand taxi*, 7dh a place; get out at Sfiha, then walk along the beach.) The sand is dark and fine, and there are few seasonal beach cafés, showers and the **Restaurant Yasmine**. In summer, for a modicum of quiet, you will need to walk along the beach towards the forest and **Tayda**, where there is an exclusive **Club Med**.

Around Al Hoceïma
There are some good day trips to the tiny fishing communities west of Al Hoceïma, namely Torres de Alcalá, Kalah Iris and rather remote Badis. Without your own transport, the

easiest approach is to take a *grand taxi* from Al Hoceïma to Beni Boufrah, via Imzouren. **Beni Boufrah** is a small rural community about 7 km from Torres. Here you change for a local share taxi. (There is also occasional transport from Beni Boufrah to Targuist.)

Torres de Alcalá has a pebbly beach and seasonal café. Just behind the beach is a campsite among the eucalyptus trees (practically no facilities). Up on the hill are the remains of the fortress, that gives the village its name: 'the towers of the citadel', Alcalá being a Spanish word derived from the Arabic for citadel.

More interesting than Torres is **Badis**, a tiny fishing settlement about 90 minutes' walk along a good piste to the east. The track starts just behind the two-storey houses of Torres village. You could drive (and there is another, more direct, piste off the Imzouren to Beni Boufrah road), but note that, in summer, Badis is off-limits to all outside vehicles as there is a royal campsite here. Princess Lalla Amina, Hassan II's sister, takes her annual holidays on the beach at Badis, which is unofficially off-limits to all but locals. The track runs along the clifftop and makes a good walk. You have to scramble down the last 100 m or so to reach the beach. Behind the beach, a wide valley runs inland. There is no accommodation. You can buy a few basic things at the tiny shop in the settlement about 300 m from the sea, behind the royal camping area. In summer, one of the royal security guards will probably come and have a chat.

You could make the long scramble up to what is said to be a ruined windmill high above the beach, and have a look at the tiny shrine to Abou Yacoub al Badis, born around 1260, hidden in the trees. As the Mediterranean port for Fès, Badis was once an important settlement. It was destroyed by earthquake in 1564. The Spanish-held **Peñón de Velez de la Gomera**, generally described in the press as an islet but in fact attached to the beach at Badis by a pebbly spit, may have some fortifications which go back to Merinid times.

Kalah Iris, 60 km west of Al Hoceïma and 9 km from Beni Boufrah, has an attractive beach. Sometimes fishermen can be persuaded to run trips out to see the impressive cliffs.

◉ Chefchaouen, the Rif and Al Hoceïma listings

For sleeping and eating price codes and other relevant information, see pages 22-28.

◉ Where to stay

Chefchaouen *p381, map p382*
Chefchaouen is a popular place for budget travellers, as it has a good supply of clean, cheap hotels. However, note that it gets pretty cold here in winter. Light sleepers will be awakened by the heavily amplified call to prayer from the numerous mosques.
€€€€ Atlas Chaouen, T0539-986265, www.achaouen@hotelsatlas.com. It's a big climb up the hill to the ugly and incongruous Atlas Chaouen: a modern building with 63 rooms that rather overshadows the town. Once you're there, the views are good and there's a small pool, a nightclub and a big

restaurant, but it feels out of keeping with the rest of Chefchaouen.
€€€ Casa Hassan, Rue Targui-Chaouen, T0539-986153, www.casahassan.com. A sophisticated place, with *tadelakt* bathrooms and big beds. Arches, painted wood ceilings, decorated chests and wood fires add interest, and there's the advantage of a/c. The place has an authentic feel, a big yellow and red hammam and a great roof terrace with views over the mountains.
€€ Barcelona, 12 Rue Al Andalous, T0539-988506. Rough wooden doors and good, simple rooms, 2 of which have a/c. Roof terrace with views and tables undercover. Coloured glass, old tiles, lots of blankets.
€€ Casa Perleta, Bab el Souk, T0539-988979, www.casaperleta.com. A highlight of Chefchaouen's riad-scene, Casa Perleta

manages to sum up the simple beauty of this region's architecture. The building has been restored lovingly with the whitewashed rooms hosting hand-painted wood details, blue-painted window frames and lots of regional fabrics and crafts. Some rooms have views of the mountains and others of the street, and there's a great shaded terrace to hang out on and soak up the atmosphere. Breakfast is included, the multi-lingual staff are ever-helpful, and there's Wi-Fi too.

€€ **Dar Mounir**, T0539-988253, www.hotel-darmounir.com. Opened in 2007, Dar Mounir has 11 rooms, most of which are big, and *tadelakt* bathrooms with horseshoe arches. Windows are high in the walls, which means there's not much of a view but it's all very comfortable, with good new beds, sofas and open fires.

€€ **Dar Rass el Mar**, Rue Rass el Maa, T0539-988080, www.chefchaouen.ch. A grand guesthouse, across the stream, under the mountain, overlooking the valley, **Rass el Mar** is good value for money. The garden is verdant, bedrooms are bright, bathrooms have colourful *tadelakt* and an excellent breakfast is served on the pretty terrace.

€€ **Hotel Madrid**, Av Hassan II, T0539-987496. A slightly old-fashioned but reliable hotel. Rooms have safes, TVs and showers.

€ **Andaluz**, 1 Rue Sidi Salem, T0539-986034. Simple rooms are arranged around an old tiled courtyard. Single beds are on the small side but there's a wood fire downstairs and a library. Showers included.

€ **Chaouen Youth Hostel**, T0539-986031, m.sarhan@hotmail.fr. 30 beds, meals available, kitchen, overnight fee 25dh, 20dh with a youth hostelling card. The dorms might be worth reserving for groups but otherwise you're better off in a cheap hotel.

€ **Cordoba**, Av Gharnata Qu Rif Andalousse. Simple rooms with small beds and views of kasbah walls. Rectangular courtyard with some slightly garish Moroccan fabrics. Some rooms good for 3-4 people.

€ **Dar Terrae**, Av Hassan I, T0539-987598, www.darterrae.com. Italian run, **Dar Terrae** is a riad with style at a very reasonable price. Rooms are quite small and not all have en suite bathrooms, but the beds are comfortable, and there is an excellent multi-levelled roof terrace where you can have breakfast or relax with a mint tea. Rooms have open fires for winter, and it's also one of the friendliest places in town.

€ **Hostel Gernika**, 49 Onsaar, T0539-987434. Immaculately decorated in riad style, with tiles and arches, **Gernika** is a cosy hotel with a wood-burning stove and a bright seating area. Rooms have plain white walls, white curtains, good wooden furniture and views. The rooms at the top of the building have no bathroom but open up onto the three-part roof terrace. Friendly and well run.

€ **Hotel Ahrazem**, 76 Av Sidi Abdelhamid, T0539-987384. 150dh with shower and loo. Friendly, blue-painted courtyard, with simple rooms just outside Bab el Souk.

€ **Hotel Koutoubia**, T0539-988433, hotel koutoubia@hotmail.fr. Opened in 2007, **Koutoubia** is a fresh place with warm orange and red fabrics in the bedrooms and modern blue and white bathrooms. Rooms are on the small side but have nice Moroccan touches. The view from the private terrace of the suite is great, as it is from the roof terrace, where you can have breakfast. Good English spoken.

€ **Hotel Rif**, 29 Rue Tarik Ibn Ziad, T0539-986982. Friendly hotel, bar and restaurant with good views from higher rooms over the valley. A good place to get information on walking and the local area. Traveller-friendly: drummers are encouraged, you can do your own laundry, and guests are welcome to drink on the roof terrace.

€ **Hotel Salam**, 38 Rue Tarik Ibn Ziad, T0539-986239. Just below the medina, **Salam** has 10 plain rooms and a bright salon. Rooms are clean but a little damp in places.

€ **Mouritania**, 15 C Kadi Alami, T0539-986184. The bedrooms are a bit dim but the beds are good and big with mirrors and clean white walls. Rooms without showers are even cheaper. If full, **Souika** next door is very similar.

€ **Pensión Ibn Batouta**, 31 Rue Abie Khancha, T0539-986044. Just off the road between Bab el Aïn and Pl Outa el Hammam, Ibn Batouta is clean and quiet with good-value, comfortable rooms. If you want to save even more pennies, you can sleep on the roof terrace for 20dh.

€ **Pensión La Castellana**, 4 C Sidi Ahmad el Bouhali, T0539-986295. Signposted just off the main square, La Castellana claims to be the oldest hotel in Chefchaouen. Good, hot, shared showers and bright rooms with blue walls and lots of beds. The roof terrace has good views of the medina and the hotel will happily look after bikes. Great for solo travellers watching their pennies; single rooms 75dh.

Camping

The campsite is next to **Chaouen Youth Hostel** (see above), 2 km from centre near the Hotel Atlas Chaouen. Follow the signs from the road in from Tetouan, or walk (carefully) through the cemetery above the medina.
Camping Municipal, T0539-986979. Small café, shop, simple toilets and showers, tents among the pine trees, good view of the valley. 20dh per person, 15-25dh per tent, or there are bungalows for 130dh.

Ketama *p384*

€ **Café-Hotel Saâda**, on the main drag and easily identified by its shaded terrace, about 100 m on from the **Hotel Tidghine**, T0539-813061. An acceptable option.

Ouezzane *p385*

Ouezzane is very limited for hotels and is perhaps best visited in passing or as an excursion from Chefchaouen. Budget hotels (**€**) include **Marhaba**, **Horloge** and **El Elam**, on Pl de l'Indépendance, or the more basic **Grand Hotel**, on Av Mohammed V, although none of these is an attractive option.

Al Hoceïma *p386*

Be aware that it can be difficult to get a quiet night's sleep in Al Hoceïma in summer and that practically no street names are shown.

€€€ **Hotel Mohammed V**, just off Pl Mohammed VI, above the beach, T0539-923314. All 30 rooms have sea views and balconies, as well as baths and tiled bathrooms. Quite plain for the money, but there is a bar and a restaurant.

€€ **Hotel Khouzama**, T0539-985669. Linking rooms for families, nice café. Yellow curtains and nasty art but not a bad choice. Same owner as Hotel Étoile du Rif.

€€ **National**, 23 Rue Tetouan, T0539-982141. Good-sized rooms with TVs and old carpets. Clean, modern bathrooms.

€ **Hotel du Rif**, 13 Rue Moulay Youssef, T0539-982268. Basic but OK. Rooms have basins; showers cost 10dh.

€ **Hotel Etoile du Rif**, 40 Pl du Rif (Sahat Rif), T0539-840847. A stylish pink and white Spanish building, once the town's casino, dominates the main square. Above a busy café-restaurant, it's friendly and clean and the best rooms overlook the square. Handy for bus station.

€ **Hotel Maghreb el Jadid**, 56 Av Mohammed V, T0539-982504. Has 42 good-sized rooms and a yellow and peach old-fashioned decor that will win no interior decoration prizes but it is nevertheless a decent option in the town centre. Traffic noise can be a problem.

€ **Hotel Nekor**, 20 Rue Tahnaoute, T0539-983065. Just off Place du Rif, Nekor has a café downstairs and is handily placed for making an early morning getaway in a *petit taxi*, though the regular cries of "Nador, Nador, Nador" may wake you.

Camping

Club Méditerranée, 10 km from Al Hoceïma, T0539-982222. Watersports and riding. Best booked through Club Med in your home country, but you could perhaps ring up.

El Jamil, also referred to as **Camping Cala Bonita**, T0539-982009. East of the town, crowded in summer as close to the beach. Awful wash-blocks.

🍴 Restaurants

Chefchaouen *p381, map p382*
€€ Casa Aladin/La Lampe Magique, 26 Rue Targui. Though it can't seem to quite make up its mind what it's called, this is a good restaurant, where the best tables overlook the end of the square. The covered roof terrace has geraniums, while downstairs it's cosier, with elaborate window frames and red curtains. The food is reliably good Moroccan fare

€€ Restaurant al Kasbah, just off the square. **Al Kasbah** has lots of carved wood and cushions. There's a wide choice of tagines and couscous.

€€ Tissemlal, 22 Rue Targui, T0539-986153. Part of **Casa Hassan** (see Where to stay, above), this is Chefchaouen's best restaurant, an atmospheric place offering warm bread, occasional free appetizers, great salads and excellent Moroccan main dishes in a peaceful and sophisticated courtyard setting. There are comfortable seats, candles, an open fire and big metal lamps.

€ Café Snack Mounir, at the end of the square. Mounir offers a range of light meals, including an unusually good vegetarian selection, as well as Chefchaouen's best coffee. A good spot to sit and watch the world go by, and better than the other options in the square.

€ Café Tunssi, Bab Ansar. Just outside the medina on the slope above the stream, **Café Tunssi** has good views across to Jemaâ Buzafar, the mosque on the opposite hill, from its three terraced levels.

€ Chez Fouad, Rue Adarve Chabu. Metal tables, blue and white tiles, tagines, fried fish, couscous and 'pizza'. Small and cheap.

€ Jardin Ziryab. Flowery gardens with tables above the far side of the stream from the centre of the town. Tea, live music and

snacks and, if you really like it here, you can even stay in one of the rooms here.

€ Restaurant Rincón Andaluz, just off Plaza Bab Souk. Couscous and fried fish for bargain prices at little tables on a blue-painted alleyway just outside Bab el Souk.

Ouezzane *p385*
Eat at the basic café-restaurants on Pl de l'Indépendence. If you are driving, **Café Africa**, 10 km north of the town, is a good place to stop for a drink.

Al Hoceïma *p386*
There aren't many good options in Al Hoceïma. Try any of the cafés off Pl Mohammed VI overlooking the Playa Quemado. **Café el Nejma** and **La Belle Vue**, next to each other at the end of Rue Mohammed V, both have far-end terraces with views out over the bay.

€€ Club Náutico, fishing port, T0539-981641. A down-to-earth licensed place in the port with lots of men sitting round plastic-covered tables watching football on TV. The food is probably Al Hoceïma's best, however; splash out on an excellent mixed plate of fried fish and don't miss the torchlit sale of the day's catch outside.

€€ La Dolce Pizza, Pl du Rif, opposite Hotel Étoile du Rif. Relatively speaking, a surprisingly atmospheric little restaurant serving up lasagne as well as pizzas.

€ Snack Maghreb el Jadied, Av Mohammed V. A friendly little snack bar next to the hotel of the same name that will rustle up brochettes or a sandwich at any hour of the day.

⚙ What to do

Chefchaouen *p381, map p382*
The manager of the **Casa Hassan** (see Where to stay, above) may be able to advise on mountain walking.

⊖ Transport

Chefchaouen *p381, map p382*
Bus
Try to reserve your bus seat in advance when you want to move on; as Chefchaouen is midway between central Moroccan towns and Tangier/Tetouan, buses often arrive full.

The bus station is down the hill out of town. **CTM** has 5 buses a day for **Ouezzane**, leaving at 0700, 1000, 1315, 1525 and 1810 (1¼ hrs). There are 4 for **Fès** at 1000, 1315, 1525 and 1810 (5½ hrs); 4 for **Tetouan** (45 mins) at 0530, 1215, 1510 and 1900 with the 0530 and 1510 service going on to **Tangier**. (2 hrs) To **Al Hoceïma** there are 2 CTM services daily at 0600 and 2300. **Meknès** is 5 hrs.

Grands taxis leave from the bus station on Av Allal Ben Abdallah to most of the above destinations.

Al Hoceïma *p386*
Air
The airport, **Aéroport Côte du Rif**, T0539-982005, is at Charif al Idrissi, 17 km southeast of Al Hoceïma on the Nador road, with flights to **Amsterdam**, **Brussels** and **Casablanca** in high season, operated by Royal Air Maroc.

Bus
Buses leave from Pl du Rif, which has ticket booths for the different companies. Most leave early in the morning. **CTM** runs 2 buses to **Nador** daily at 0515 and 1300 (5 hrs); 2 to **Chefchaouen** and **Tetouan** at 1230 and 2115 (7 hrs); 1 to **Tangier** at 2115; and 1 to **Rabat** at 2000. There are many private bus companies as well.

Taxi
Grands taxis for **Nador** and **Taza** leave from just off Pl du Rif. For destinations west of Al Hoceïma, they leave from C al Raya al Maghrebiya, off top of Av Mohammed V, between Mobil and Total garages and opposite the BMCI.

❶ Directory

Chefchaouen *p381, map p382*
Banks Banque populaire, Av Hassan II; BMCE, Av Hassan II; Crédit agricole, Pl Outa el Hammam. **Post** PTT, Av Hassan II. **Medical services** Chemist beside Hotel Magou.

Al Hoceïma *p386*
Banks All on or around Av Mohammed V, most have ATMs. **Internet** Cyberclub, Av Mohammed V, above the Méditel shop near the turn-off for Hotel Khozama. **Internet** Bades, Av Tarik Ibn Ziad, next to BCM, on left as you come from Pl de la Marche verte. **Medical services** Hôpital Mohammed V, Av Hassan II. Pharmacies on Av Mohammed V.

Eastern Mediterranean coast

Just beyond the headland of the Cap des Trois Fourches, the enclave of Melilla is a long way across the Mediterranean from its Spanish motherland. Similarly, Nador, a sort of Moroccan half-brother and neighbour to the Spanish town, seems isolated in Morocco. So the two exist side by side, in a strange symbiotic relationship, mutually dependent on each other. Indeed, Melilla seems less threatened by its Moroccan surroundings than Ceuta to the West; it is a place much more relaxed in its own skin, and its tapas bars and museums make it a pleasant place to arrive in or depart from Africa. Nador has less going for it, though, along the coast, there are fishing villages and some good Mediterranean beaches, all the way to the resort of Saïdia, snuggled up against the Algerian border. ➍ *For listings, see pages 400-404.*

Melilla ➍ *For listings, see pages 400-404. Colour map 1, A5.*

Melilla is the main town of a small Spanish enclave on the eastern stretch of Morocco's Mediterranean coast. It stands on the promontory, facing eastwards, 16 km south of Cap des Trois Fourches and 12 km north of Nador. A friendly and relaxed place, it seems more at ease with itself than Ceuta. The enclave is worth a day's visit for its good tapas bars, reasonable tax-free shopping, for the fortifications of Medina Sidonia and its modernist and art deco buildings. There is a relaxed, clean beach and a small archaeological museum.

Arriving in Melilla

From the border post at Beni Ansar, the town centre is a good 40 minutes' walk on foot, so take one of the buses, which run regularly from 0700 to 2200 (a 15-minute journey, €0.70) to Plaza de España. The ferry terminal is just off the old town. Stumbling into Melilla half-asleep off a night-boat, you are particularly vulnerable to pickpockets. Have your wallet and passport well stowed away under your clothing. The town centre is easily covered on foot.

Tourist information There is an **tourist information booth** ① *Plaza de Espana, Tue-Sun 1000-1400, Tue-Sat also 1700-2100 in summer, 1600-2000 in winter. See also www.melillaturismo.com.* They will be able to give you a map and other useful information about the town. The **Oficina de Turismo** ① *C Fortuny 21, T(+34) 95-2675444, Mon-Fri 0900-1400, 1700-2000,* is less conveniently located, in the conference centre behind the bull ring.

Background

Melilla started life as Phoenician Rusadir. The Greeks and Romans were here too. The Spanish captured the town from the Berbers in 1497. Occupied by the usual dynasties in the Middle Ages, Melilla was taken by the Merinids in 1272 and, along with Badis, was to become one of the ports for Fès and Taza, involved in trade with Genoa, Pisa, Marseille, Catalonia and Aragon.

The ancient citadel area is today called **Medina Sidonia**, after the Duke of Medina Sidonia, who was urged by Ferdinand of Aragon and Isabel of Castille to take the town. In 1497, Melilla fell to Don Pedro Estepiñan with a contingent of 700 men and a fleet later to participate in Columbus' second voyage to the Americas. Under the Spanish, the old fortified town on its huge rocky outcrop rising out of the sea was rebuilt, the first fortifications being completed in 1515, final touches were made in 1739.

From the late 15th century on, the history of Melilla was one of sieges and clashes. In 1774, Sidi Mohammed Ben Abdallah led 40,000 troops to take the town – but to no avail. In 1909, Spain appropriated large territories around the old fortress core, which then had barely 9000 inhabitants. In the early 1920s, however, Abd el Karim el Khattibi's Rif forces, fighting for an independent state, nearly put an end to this expansion of Spanish Melilla.

Spain had become interested in the town for economic reasons. A local potentate sold to a Spanish mining company one of the largest open-cast iron ore mines of the time, at Bou Ifrour. Spain built a railway line between the mine and Melilla, and the town's development was rapid. By 1925, the population was 25,000 – more than many Andalucían cities – and reached a high of 90,000 in 1950. However, when the rest of the

Melilla

Spanish protectorate was returned to Morocco in 1956, Melilla, along with Ceuta, became a somewhat sleepy symbol of Spanish pride on the coast.

Since the late 1960s, the bright entrepreneurs of Melilla have built themselves fortunes via the contraband trade with Morocco, based on a clientele in an area that stretches far beyond the immediate Rif region. Today the Spanish Christian population is around 30,000, and there are some 6000 Spanish Foreign Legion soldiers. The Muslim population also numbers around 30,000, many of whom once lived in the slum Cañada de la Muerte neighbourhood. They received Spanish papers in 1987, and Muslim areas, such as the Cañada and María Cristina, have been much improved. Morocco continues to demand the return of the city but the city's mixed Rif and Spanish population carries on plying its trade in foodstuffs, household goods and clothes regardless. Although lots of Nadori residents have the right to come into Melilla on a daily basis for work, the border has been tightened up considerably, as Spain fears mass influxes of Algerians and sub-Saharan Africans claiming refugee status. There were stormings of the border post during the Euro 2008 football championships, the would-be immigrants presumably hoping that the Spanish border guards would be more easily distracted.

La Pergola **15**
La Traviata **12**
Mar de Alborán **11**

Places in Melilla

Melilla has enough to keep you busy for a long half-day, longer if you take full advantage of its cafés and restaurants. Approaching from the frontier post to the south, Avenida General Astilleros takes you through an undistinguished suburb (barracks and army housing to the left). The main beach area is behind the buildings to your right. After the concrete bridge over the Río de Oro, a large modern mirror-glass construction, put up to celebrate the 500th anniversary of the discovery of the Americas, hoves into view, rather marring the vision of the old town, Medina Sidonia, just behind. The modern city, an example of late 19th- and early 20th-century planning, starts with the round **Plaza de España**, from which the twin main shopping streets, Ejército Español and Juan Carlos Rey, run. Plaza de España was something of an architectural showcase in its day and is still home to the **Banco de España**, the town hall building and the ferry office (also banks with ATMs).

Twentieth-century Melilla was laid out by Don Enrique Nieto, the money for its expansion coming from the export of iron ore mined in the hinterland. (The Edificio Quinto Centenario sits on what was the old ore loading quay or *cargadero*.) Take a look at the neo-Moorish or *historicista*-style mosque. There are a few gems along the streets named after Spanish generals and cultural heroes. Buildings in the *estilo ondulante* draw inspiration from natural forms; for the *estilo geométrico* see the **Edificio de la Asamblea** on the Plaza de España. If you have lots of time, walk up to the **Parador de Melilla**, for good views of the city. Below it, the **Parque Lobera** is pleasantly shady and has slides and an aviary.

The **Medina Sidonia** is a fine example of elaborate 16th-century fortifications and now a sleepy sort of place, where palm trees wave over stone façades decked with mustard-coloured classical detailing. In Melilla the Spanish picked one of the best defensive locations on the north Moroccan coast to construct an elaborate fortified settlement, divided into two parts by a moat and gates. The entrance to the main, earliest section (parking nearby) is below the walls at the end of Avenida General Macías. On foot, you head up a ramp and come out onto a small square with the Chapel of Santiago over to your left. You can then wander through the narrow streets in search of views across the Mediterranean, the Church of the Immaculate Conception and the town's museums.

A great deal of Medina Sidonia is still occupied by the military and is used as a prison, in the case of the San Fernando barracks. Now that the EU has funded a good deal of restoration work, it will be interesting to see if more cultural tourism develops – or whether the city's odd geopolitical position (and other factors) maintain its backwater status. Certainly, large sums need to be invested in the sub-standard housing, much of it occupied by families of Moroccan origin, which sprawls up the hillsides above the modern town.

The highest point of Medina Sidonia is occupied by a bastion, the **Baluarte de la Concepción**, a mixture of medieval and 18th-century building on the site of the first walled area. In the same area, the 17th-century **Iglesia de la Purísima Concepción** (Church of the Immaculate Conception) has some period carving and contains the statue of Nuestra Senora de la Victoria, the patroness of Melilla, who is celebrated on 17 September.

The ground floor of the small but well planned **Museo Amazigh** ① *T+34 952-699158, Tue-Sun 1000-1400, Tue-Sat also 1700-2100 in summer, 1600-2000 in winter, free*, is set aside for visiting exhibits. More interesting, on the first floor, the archaeological section has Carthaginian coins, amphorae, an exquisite Etruscan *oinochoé* and a pair of dove-shaped gold earrings beside the skull whose ears they once adorned. Look out for the model of a Punic burial with amphorae. The top floor has some good displays on the development of Melilla. There is access to a small walkway with views across the town. Through gaps in a defensive wall, cannons stand ready to bombard the Parador. There are plans to move the museum to a new location in the medina at some point in the future. Next to the museum, dedicated by the people of Melilla in 1970, stands a statue of a be-armoured Don Pedro de Estepiñan, waving his sword at 'the mainland'.

Underneath Medina Sidonia, the **Cuevas del Conventico** ① *Muralla de la Cruz, T+34 952-680929, museodemelilla@eresmas.com, visits by guided tour only, daily 1045, 1150, 1215, 1300, Mon-Sat also 1645, 1730, 1815 and 1900, free*, is a complex of caves on three levels that played a key role in the siege of the town in 1774. Enlarged by the town's inhabitants, they contained space for worship and ovens, as well as sleeping quarters. Damaged by earthquakes at the end of the 20th century, the caves have been spruced up and given new supports as well as an enormous parabolic arch and a winding path down to a beach at the bottom of the cliffs. The tours are informative but in Spanish only.

Close to the city, the **beaches** of Melilla are well equipped with ice cream kiosks, stands renting loungers, and showers. **Playa San Lorenzo** is nearest to the town and least attractive. **Playa de los Carabos** is fine; **Playa de la Hípica** is the furthest away, only walkable for the very energetic.

Nador → *For listings, see pages 400-404. Colour map 1, A5.*

By the salt lagoon of Sebkha Bou Areq, the provincial capital and port Nador (the name is Arabic for lighthouse) is a relaxed place with the atmosphere of a border town. Travellers will probably pass through en route to or from Melilla. With its steel plant and modern harbour, Nador was a flagship for Moroccan development after independence, when the new town was developed on a grid-iron pattern alongside a small Rif village. Today, it is a centre for the agri-food business, fish farming – and contraband with neighbouring Spanish-held Melilla. Politically, Nadoris are increasingly proud of their Amazigh origins. (Nador is the largest Ta'rifit-speaking city in Morocco.) Birdwatchers may want to use the town as a base for exploring the wetlands and coastal habitats to the east. Otherwise, there is little to detain you here for very long.

Arriving in Nador
Getting there There is an international airport. Buses and *grands taxis* arrive at a large and fairly confusing terminal at the lagoon end of Avenue des FAR. **CTM** and **SATAS** buses

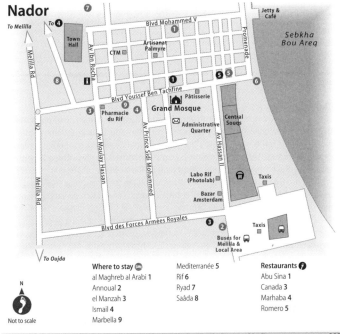

Nador

Where to stay		Mediterranée 5	Restaurants
al Maghreb al Arabi 1		Rif 6	Abu Sina 1
Annoual 2		Ryad 7	Canada 3
el Manzah 3		Saâda 8	Marhaba 4
Ismail 4			Romero 5
Marbella 9			

Not to scale

have a city centre terminus near the Hotel Ryad and the Municipality. ▸▸ *See Transport, page 403, for further details.*

Getting around One principal street, Boulevard Youssef Ben Tachfine (at right angles to the lagoon), cuts right through the centre, from the roundabout on the Melilla road to the Hotel Rif on the waterfront. The administrative quarter, post office and the modern Grand Mosque, with its unusually tall and slender minaret, are all located on this road. If you come in by public transport, turn right out of the bus/*grand taxi* terminus and walk into the centre along Avenue Hassan II to meet Boulevard Ben Tachfine. A couple of the better eateries are near here. The grid pattern of the town makes orientation straightforward, though street signs are notable by their almost total absence.

Places in Nador

Nador's attractions are limited. The original centre was developed on a grid-iron pattern by the Spanish in the 1920s and 1930s. After independence, the town mushroomed in size, the population reaching 100,000 in the late 1980s. When relations collapsed with Algeria, large numbers of Moroccans resident in that country settled in Nador. With Moroccans living abroad spending their money on homes for family left behind, Nador has become a magnet for the rural poor seeking work. In summer, the people-watching can be quite interesting, as the *fakansiya* – the MRE back for their holidays – parade up and down the small corniche in their new cars. The art deco pier building at the lagoon end of the Boulevard Mohammed V is good for a coffee in summer. Men meet their friends and watch TV under the palm trees on this street.

Nadoris have a somewhat sinister reputation among other Moroccans – they're held to be back-stabbing sorts. But you won't be hassled in Nador. In summer everyone is busy with their returned relations; in winter things are fairly comatose, apart from the cross-border trade with Melilla.

Around Nador

Kariat Arkmane

At the extremity of the lagoon, 20 km east of Nador, Kariat Arkmane (souk Wednesday) is a small settlement divided into three separate parts some distance away from each other. The main village, on the lagoon, is a bustling, rough-and-ready sort of place. There is a morning fish market behind the square. Beyond the modern residential area, about 1 km inland along the road, you will find the turning to **Kariat Plage**, which is itself a further 2 km further on, across a stretch of marshlands. Although the swimming is safe and clean here, the beach is litter-strewn and very crowded in high summer. There are no hotels, but family-sized apartments are available in the large block at the beach, next to well-known fish restaurant **Restaurante Arena de Oro**; ask around for other cheaper possibilities. For simpler fare, there are a couple of places by the beach. There's a **Crédit du Maroc**, in the main village by the taxi rank, and the **Pharmacie Centrale**, is next to the bank.

Ras Kebdana (Ras el Ma'a)

From Kariat Arkmane to Ras Kebdana is about 40 km; the N16 winds inland across attractive rolling farmlands and seasonal riverbeds eroded into the soft, red sandstone. On the right stand the jagged and wild Kebdana mountains and, on the left, the sea appears from time to time. It can be reached on foot by following one of the many dry *oued* beds for 2 or 3 km, although there is no beach, only low, muddy cliffs. The village of Ras Kebdana is entirely devoted to fishing and is dwarfed by its large modern harbour, beyond which there is a wonderful unspoilt **beach**, stretching for 6 km to the estuary of the Oued Molouya and, beyond that, to the resort of Saïdia. The view from the headland over the coast and the Spanish-held **Ja'farine Islands** is spectacular. From the breakwater at the far end of the harbour, a flight of steps leads up to the lighthouse, where a bored sentry may stop you out of curiosity. Take care walking along the crumbling cliff edge. It is possible to walk back along the crest of the headland to the road and down another flight of steps to the back of the village. The headland itself has been spoilt by military installations. Camping is possible on the large space behind the beach but there are no facilities as yet. There's a restaurant in the middle of the harbour, T0536-605972, serving huge portions of very fresh fish and prawns.

Cap des Trois Fourches
Jutting some 30 km into the Mediterranean, north of Nador, the Cap des Trois Fourches peninsula is rocky, wild and windswept. To get out to the peninsula you will need your own transport – or get a taxi from Beni Ensar or Farkhana as far as it will go, and then walk. The scenery on the way to the cape is very beautiful. For the adventurous, there are a couple of tiny beaches close to the lighthouse, accessible by a 14 km rough and hilly track from the village of **Taourirt**, north of the border post of Farkhana. Past Taourirt, there is a turning on the left to another tiny beach at **Cala Tramontana**, 4 km away. There are few settlements, just a couple of impoverished hamlets. Note that there are strong currents around the peninsula and swimming can be dangerous.

Saïdia → *For listings, see pages 400-404. Colour map 1, A6.*

Saïdia is a pleasant resort popular with Moroccans, not yet overly developed and, hence perhaps, lacking in some comforts. It has an old 17th-century fortress from the time of Moulay Ismaïl and a more recent 19th-century construction. It is packed in the summer, with no shortage of places to eat, but limited and expensive hotels, some of which are closed in winter, when the place is fairly deserted.

Places in Saïdia
The Saïdia region has orchards, vineyards and market gardening. Saïdia itself is located on the coastal plain of Triffa, with forested mountains not far to the south. There is an attractive sandy beach, which stretches for 12 km, and views of the Spanish **Islas Chafarinas** (Ja'farine Islands) and east to Algeria. Saïdia is easily explored, with a grid of brightly coloured houses, restaurants and hotels parallel to the beach.

In the low season, Saïdia feels like an empty film set, waiting for the big show, which in a sense it is; the **Saïdia Music Festival**, in August, marks the high point of the year, when virtually the entire populations of Oujda and Berkane to the south seem to migrate here to escape the heat. Unfortunately, the beach-cleaning services cannot always keep up with the invasion. The tiny, square 19th-century **kasbah**, with its intact walls and humble dwellings, was all that existed here prior to the 1930s. It was built by Hassan I to guard against the French, then occupying Algeria. The adjacent **market** enclosure, which holds a souk on Sunday, backs onto the Oued Kiss which marks the border with Algeria. From the kasbah, it is a short walk to the **beach** through a eucalyptus forest.

For sleeping and eating price codes and other relevant information, see pages 22-28.

⊜ Where to stay

Melilla *p393, map p394*
The city has a range of good accommodation. Reasonably priced hotels fill up early, so phone ahead. The **Parador** is better than the expensive hotels in Nador. The best of the cheaper hotels is the **Tuhami**, though you'll get more for your money in Nador.

If phoning from Morocco, dial 0034 (for Spain) before the 9-figure local number.
€€€ Melilla Puerto, Explanada de San Lorenzo, T(+34) 952-695525, www.hotel melillapuerto.com. A large 4-star hotel with conference facilities and lots of comfort but not much style.
€€€€ Parador de Melilla, Av de Cándido Lobera, T(+34) 952-684940, www.parador.es. 40 rooms and lots of facilities: telephone, TV, parking, lift, facilities for disabled, credit cards, exchange, a/c, heating, restaurant, coffee shop/bar and a small pool.
€€€ Rusadir, 5 Pablo Vallescá, T(+34) 952-681240, hotelrusadir@grupokm.com. A smart, business-like hotel, with shiny wooden floors and all modern facilities but lacking in character and expensive for what you get.
€€ Cazaza, 6 Jose Antonio Primo de Rivera, T(+34) 952-684648. A small place with 8 rooms and a café, next to **Hotel Nacional**.
€€ Hostal Tuhami, 13 General Margallo, T(+34) 952-68 60 45, hostaltuhami@hotmail.com. Big, modern rooms with TVs, solid furniture, three-quarter-sized bath, all super clean. Same management as the **Hotel Méditerranée** in Nador (see above).
€€ Hotel Anfora, 16 Pablo Vallescá, T(+34) 952-683340, www.hotel-anfora.com. A big hotel opposite the **Rusadir**, with 145 rooms, garage, lift, a/c, café, bar and restaurant. Free internet for guests in reception. All rooms have balcony and minibars. Ugly on the outside but good value.

€€ Nacional, 10 Jose Antonio Primo de Rivera, T(+34) 952-684540. Central hotel with 30 rooms. Telephone, bar/café. Modern, rather uninteresting but reliable rooms, and bathrooms with half baths. OK if you're very small or don't fancy stretching out. Take credit cards and exchange money.
€€ Pensión Rosa Blanca, 7 C Gran Capitan, T(+34) 952-682738. A friendly place, popular with travellers. Only one room has en suite bath but all rooms have TVs and a basin. A helpful owner and a warm welcome make this a good deal, especially if you manage to negotiate the price down a little.

Nador *p397, map p397*
There is a decent, if rather plain, selection of hotels. Best hotels fill up quickly in summer, as migrant workers return with their families. Try to reserve ahead.
€€ Hotel Rif, 1 Blvd Youssef Ben Tachfine, T0536-603635. A 1970s gem on the lagoon front, reopened in 2002. 62 a/c rooms, restaurant, murky pool and 2 earth tennis courts. Best upmarket option.
€€ Hotel Ryad, Blvd Mohammed V, BP60, T0536-607717. Has 41 rooms, 18 suites, lavish decor, restaurant, 2 bars, café and is used by returning emigrants keen to display their wealth. Entrance round the back.
€ Hotel al Maghreb al Arabi, on street of the same name just off Blvd Mohammed V in the best part of town. Very cheap, very simple, but clean.
€ Hotel al Mahatta, 38 Av Abbas Mohammed Akkad, T0536-602777. Large and cheap basic hotel with restaurant, to the left off Av des FAR, with sea and bus station behind you.
€ Hotel Annoual, overlooks bus station. Good value at the lower end of this price bracket. Check hot water works, rooms at front are very noisy, large ornate café.
€ Hotel el Manzah, corner of Blvd Youssef Ben Tachfine and Av Moulay Hassan, T0536-332578. Adequately comfortable with

private bathrooms. Centrally located, with a receptionist who speaks English and a guarded parking space.

€ Hotel Ismail, 34 Blvd Prince Sidi Mohammed, T0536-606280. Cheaper than Hotel Mediterranée and almost as good, clean and comfortable, pleasant staff, nice café but no restaurant. Recommended.

€ Hotel Marbella, 75-77 Blvd Youssef Ibn Tachfine, T0536-603900. Good mid-range place, café downstairs, clean modern rooms, all with (poorly laid out) en suite bathrooms and TVs. Good value at the higher end of this price bracket.

€ Hotel Mediterranée, 2/4 Blvd Youssef Ben Tachfine, opposite Hotel Rif, T0536-606495. Very clean, airy rooms, quiet-ish location near seafront, lift, restaurant, menu 80dh. Same management as **Pensión Tuhami** in Melilla (see below). Satellite TV, a/c, parking.

€ Hotel Saâda, 26 Rue Ibn Rochd, T0536-602881. A rambling hotel in a central location roughly behind the town hall. Fairly clean, large multi-bed rooms, showers on corridor.

Kariat Arkmane *p398*
Camping
Kariat Plage, at Kariat Arkmane, east end of salt lagoon. 2 ha, 20 m to beach, bar, snacks, restaurant, grocery shop, showers, laundry, electricity for caravans, petrol at 400 m.

Saïdia *p399*
For Jul and Aug, try to reserve. Apartments can be rented cheaply Sep-May if you bargain. Some hotels close for the winter months.

€€ Hotel Hannour, Pl 20 Août, T0536-625115. Centrally located, with a good restaurant and a bar.

€€ Titanic, Blvd Mohammed V, T0536-624071. Inauspiciously named but good modern rooms with sea views.

€ Hotel Paco, Blvd Hassan II, T0536-625110. Comfortable, friendly, family hotel close to the beach, 15 rooms, restaurant, open Jun-Oct.

Camping
In season, campsites get packed and services do not always keep up with the demand.

Camping Caravaning Al Mansour, Rue de Moulouya. Site of 6 ha.

Camping Centre Autonome, at Saïdia Plage. Site of 8 ha, beach only 200 m, bar/snack, grocery shop, pool, showers, laundry, petrol at 500 m, electricity for caravans.

Camping Essi, site of 2.5 ha, beach 200 m, groceries, showers, laundry, electricity for caravans, petrol 500 m.

⑦ Restaurants

Melilla p393, map p394

€€€ La Muralla, Florentina, 1 El Pueblo, T(+34) 952-681035. Only open 2100-2400 Thu and Fri. This is a smart restaurant in the corner of the medina, with barrel-vaulted ceilings and a menu that is half meat half fish.

€€€ La Traviata, 5 El Ejército Español, T(+34) 952-681925. A posh wine bar with chandeliers and bar stools, which also does light meals.

€€€ Mar de Alborán, 26 C Prim, T(+34) 627-440824. From outside you'd think it was closed, or not know it was a restaurant at all. But inside, it's buzzing. And the food is great and very good value. There's no menu, just speedily spoken Spanish. Don't leave without sampling a *crema catalana* – one of the best you're ever likely to taste, on any continent.

€€ Dragón de Oro, 10 C José Antonio Primo de Rivera, T(+34) 952-686116. Next to **Hotel Nacional**, a Chinese restaurant that also does a cheap Spanish menu.

€€ La Pergola, 12 Paseo Rafael Ginel, T(+34) 952-685628, www.melillacomercio.com/lapergola. €10 for a 3-course menu plus a drink. Seats and tables overlooking port or you can sit at stools around barrels. Stylish and right by the water's edge. Good for a coffee.

€ Bodega Madrid, 6 C de Castelas. A proper old-school, stand-up, big beers and blackboard tapas bar. Aproned men, discarded paper on the floor and plenty of Spanish attitude.

€ **Cafe con Libro**, 12 General Marina. A hip place with loud but laid-back tunes, art deco lights, old bar stools, a huge drinks selection and a Buddha behind the bar.

€ **Cafe Gallery**, Plaza Cdte Benítez. Modern, with jazz and photo exhibitions on the walls.

€ **Cafeteria los Arcos**, just off C del Ejército Español. Attractive old art deco building with covered seating area outside in a little plaza.

€ **Heladería La Ibense**, Plaza Héroes de España, T(+34) 952-681188 (also Paseo Marítimo, T(+34) 952-676013). Founded in 1912, they've spent the years well, perfecting some very good ice cream.

Nador *p397, map p397*

€€€ **Hotel Rif**, T0536-606535, and **Hotel Ryad**, T0536-607715, see Where to stay, above, both have international and Moroccan cuisine.

€€ **Marhaba**, 2 Rue Ibn Rochd, near **Hotel Ryad**, T0536-603311. Large establishment with a fast service aimed at Spanish day trippers, wide choice.

€€ **Restaurant Arrif**, 45 Rue Ibn Rochd, Opposite **Cinema Rif**. Dark, atmospheric little place, with tools on the walls. As the menu says, "fish, and meat, what you want".

€€ **Restaurant Romero**, 48-50 Blvd Youssef Ibn Tachfine, T0536-332777. Fishy main courses simply but well prepared.

€€ **Victoria**, 292 Blvd Hassan II, T0536-604511. More fish in a vaguely upmarket setting near the bus station.

€ **Abu Sina**, Rue Abu Sina, just off Blvd Youssef Ben Tachfine on right as you head towards Blvd Mohammed V. Busy, small restaurant open at lunchtime, wide selection including fish soup, grilled prawns and paella.

There are plenty of cheap eateries close to bus station, including **Canada**, Blvd des FAR. Try Blvd Mohammed V for cafés and ice cream. The mirador building jutting out into the lagoon at the end of this avenue is the nicest place for a coffee and cake.

Saïdia *p399*

€€ **Café/Restaurant al Nassim**, Rue Bir Anzarane, T0536-625008. Open all year, breezy panoramic salon, very fresh fish.

€ **Café/Restaurant Mexico**, Blvd Zerkatouni. In the centre, facing the beach, friendly proprietor who speaks English, very good value, open all year.

Several standard restaurants on Rue Sidi Mohammed, open all year, including **Café Restaurant Plus**. Try **Café Bleu**, Rue Laâyoune, for a relaxed and friendly atmosphere.

⊕ Entertainment

Melilla *p393, map p394*
Bull ring C Querol, T(+34) 952-699213.
Theatres Auditorium Carvajal, Parque Lobera. **Grand Teatro National**, 8 Cándido Lobera.

Nador *p397, map p397*
Despite the Spanish influence, Nador is practically a dry town, so head for nearby Melilla for café terraces with cold beer.

○ Shopping

Melilla *p393, map p394*
The main shopping streets are **Av Juan Carlos I Rey** including **Plaza de los Héroes de España** (crowded with shoppers and groups in the evening), **Ejército Español** and **C O'Donnell**. Duty-free shops offer a limited range of electrical goods. Moroccan craft goods can be found at fairly high, fixed prices so wait till you get to Morocco for the real thing. Best book shop is **Rafael Boix Sola**, 23 Av Juan Carlos I Rey. Books in Spanish on local history. Surf and windsurf equipment is sold at **Ultrafun**, 36 C General Polavieja.

◑ What to do

Melilla *p393, map p394*
Swimming
Municipal Swimming Pool, Av de la Juventud, covered pool.

Tour operators

Renfe, 113 C O'Donnell, T(+34) 952-683551, for rail/sea travel. See also Transport, below. Independent travel agents include: **Andalucía Travel**, 13 Av de la Democracia, T(+34) 952-670730, and **Viajes Melvia**, Pasaje Av, T(+34) 952-688526.

⊕ Transport

Melilla *p393, map p394*
Air
Air services by **Iberia**, 2 C Cándido Lobera, T(+34) 952-670386 (at airport, T(+34) 952-673123/673800), to **Almería**, **Barcelona**, **Granada**, **Málaga**, **Madrid** and **Palma de Mallorca**.

Also, **Panair**, 2 C Musico Granados, T(+34) 952-674211, run jets to **Madrid**, and **Trasmediterranea**, General Marina/Plaza España, T(+34) 952-681918, flies propeller-driven aircraft, to **Málaga** 8 flights per weekday (6 flights Sun) return service (30 mins). Flight frequencies can vary on a quarterly basis – check in Melilla with the appropriate agency.

Boat
Trasmediterranea runs a regular ferry service (6 times a week) to **Málaga** (7½ hrs) and **Almería** (6½ hrs) from the terminal just off the old town. Frequency of service varies with season, reserve ahead for summer months. Cheaper rates apply to ordinary deck/public cabin tickets but the margin against the air fare for a half hour flight is close. Info and tickets at Trasmediterranea, 1 General Marina/Plaza España, T(+34) 952-681918 in Melilla; Estación Maritima, El Puerto, T(+34) 95-2224391 in Málaga; Parque Nicolàs Salmeron 19, T(+34) 95-0236155 in Almería. The UK agent is **Southern Ferries**, T020-7491 4968.

Bus
There are cheap bus services within Melilla, most calling at Plaza de España. For travel to the border take the regular bus from Plaza de España (every 15-30 mins, 0700-2200).

Car hire
Available at the airport and from agencies in the town such as **Rent-a-car La Mezquita**, who have agencies in Oujda and Nador, too, ring T0661-363396 (mob) or T0536-349389 for the Beni Ansar border office.

Taxi
Comparatively cheap, pay on the meter. For services ring T(+34) 952-683623 or 2683621. Taxis to/from the airport take 10 mins.

Nador *p397, map p397*
Apart from Melilla, Nador is a fair distance from other major towns: 175 km from Oujda, 120 km from Al Hoceïma on an often tortuous though beautiful road, 275 km from Taza, 400 km from Fès.

There are 3 main departure points for public road transport: the busy, grotty main bus station, shared with *grands taxis*, at the junction of Av des FAR and Hassan II; **CTM** and the better private lines depart from Av Ibn Rochd near the Municipalité; and *grands taxis* for Melilla from behind the town hall. The **CTM** departures for Al Hoceïma leave from the Av des FAR terminus.

Air
Flights to Nadar Airport are irregular. **Royal Air Maroc** (24 Blvd Mohammed V, T0536-606478) flies to **Amsterdam**, **Brussels**, **Casablanca** and **Frankfurt**. For Spanish connections, head to nearby Melilla Airport.

Boat
There is a **Comanav** car and passenger ferry service from Nador to **Sète** in France, every 4 days Jun-Sep, tickets and information from **Comanav Passages**, Immeuble Lazaar Beni Enzar, BP 89, T0536-608538, or from the same company in Casablanca, 43 Blvd des FAR, T0522-310015/6. The ferry service between Nador and **Almería**, which is operated by **Ferrimaroc** (www.ferrimaroc. com), runs up to 5 times a day in summer, less often in winter, arriving in **Almería** 8 hrs later. Cost is €47, cabins from €93.

Bus

CTM buses run to **Tangier** at 1815 and 1900 (8 hrs). There are 3 buses daily to **Fès** (4½ hrs) and **Meknès** (6 hrs) at 1045, 1900 and 2100; the 1045 and 1900 services go on to **Rabat** (8 hrs) and **Casablanca** (9½ hrs). Buses to **Al Hoceïma** leave at 0945 and 1815.

For **Melilla**, take a private line bus to **Beni Enzar** (frequent departures). If you want a seat be sure to board the bus at the terminal as it fills up rapidly along the way (journey time 30 mins). Other private line destinations include: **Er Rachidia** (8 hrs via Missour/Midelt), **Figuig** (9 hrs via Oujda), **Kariat Arkmane, Ras el Ma'a/Ras Kebdana, Taza** (several departures, including early morning), **Casablanca, Guercif, Oujda** (numerous during day), **Chefchaouen, Tetouan** and **Tangier** (take early morning bus to see mountainous route), **Targuist, Al Hoceïma, Rabat, Taourirt** and **Berkane.**

Taxi

Grands taxis leave from beside the bus station, with numerous destinations including **Ahfir** (over 1 hr) and from there to **Saïdia**, to the border with **Melilla** (5dh, 20 mins), to **Al Hoceïma** (50dh), **Meknès** and **Fès**.

Taxis for **Beni Enzar** (border) and other points north depart from the main road near **Hotel Ryad.**

Train

There are 3 trains daily to **Taourirt** and **Fès** at 0843, 1248 and 1803.

Kariat Arkmane *p398*

Buses for **Nador** leave near hourly in the morning and at 1600. For **Ras Kebdana/ Ras el Ma'a**, at 1130 and 1400. All depart from the main village where there are also frequent *grands taxis*.

Ras Kebdana *p398*

Buses to **Nador**, 0830, 1500; **Berkane**, 1230, 1530. *Grands taxis* run from time to time to **Kariat Arkmane** and **Berkane.**

Saïdia *p399*

Buses depart from Rue Laâyoune to **Ahfir/ Oujda**, more frequently in summer. *Grands taxis* leave from Rue Laâyoune or from the tree-lined road behind and parallel to Rue Sidi Mohammed to **Ahfir** (20 mins), and on to **Oujda, Berkane** and **Nador**. *Grands taxis* also depart from the taxi rank by the kasbah.

⊙ Directory

Melilla *p393, map p394*
Banks Money changers operate outside the Trasmediterranea office on Plaza de España. **Medical services Hospitals:** Hospital Comarcal, Remonta, T(+34) 952-670000; Red Cross Hospital, Av Duquesa Victoria, T(+34) 952-684743. **Useful addresses** Ambulance: T(+34) 952-674400. Fire service: T080. Guardia Civil: T(+34) 952-671300/2671400. Police: (Local) T092 (emergencies), also T(+34) 952-674000 (National) T091. Red Cross Ambulance: T(+34) 952-672222.

Nador *p397, map p397*
Banks There is no shortage of banks to process money sent home by migrant workers. **Wafa Bank**, on your right on Blvd Ben Tachfine as you head uphill, not far from Hotel el Menzah. Other ATMs are on or near this street. **Medical services Chemists:** Pharmacie du Rif, corner of Blvd Ben Tachfine and Av Moulay Hassan; **Pharmacie Ibn Sina**, top end of Blvd Ben Tachfine under the arches.

Saïdia *p399*
Banks Nearest are in Ahfir, 20 km away. In high summer, a mobile branch service operates in Pl du 20 Août. **Medical services** Pharmacie Nouvelle, Blvd Hassan II.

Contents

At a glance

⊖ **Getting around** The area is served by buses.

🕐 **Time required** Allow a day for Oujda and a couple of days exploring further south.

☀ **Weather** The further south you go the hotter it is. Spring is the best time to visit.

✖ **When not to go** A dry and hot region, covering eastern Morocco's long distances becomes especially arduous in summer.

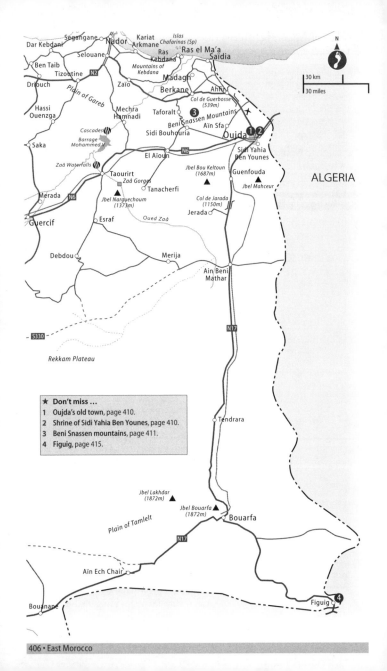

★ **Don't miss ...**
1 Oujda's old town, page 410.
2 Shrine of Sidi Yahia Ben Younes, page 410.
3 Beni Snassen mountains, page 411.
4 Figuig, page 415.

The sleepy, isolated eastern edge of Morocco has been on the way to nowhere since the Algerian border was closed in 1994. With the ceasing of official border traffic, there has been a corresponding downturn in the area's tourism industry, and both Oujda and Figuig are, for the moment, border towns without a border. To a certain extent, the situation is eased by a lively trade in contraband, as petrol, which costs half as much in Algeria, flows fairly freely across the long and porous border, while chickens, apparently, head the other way. The area has little of the geographic excitement of further west, with date palms and sub-Saharan scrubland descending slowly into desert, but it does have an open and welcoming society, and lacks the hassle you may experience in other parts of the country.

Oujda and around

Founded in the late 10th century and capital of the Zenata tribe for nearly a century, Oujda then largely disappeared from the history books until the 19th century, when it was twice occupied by the French. In the 20th century, Oujda was developed by the French as the capital of Maroc Oriental. The city has a distinctive feel to it, more relaxed than the Rif towns to the west, and with a university and some light industry. Until the border with Algeria was closed, Oujda used to have a flourishing hotel trade. Although there have been moves to reopen the border in recent times, few people expect it to happen soon. Oujda has few sights, but it makes a convenient stop before moving on to Spanish Melilla, or travelling south to Figuig, in the Sahara. ▶▶ *For listings, see pages 411-414.*

Arriving in Oujda → *Colour map 1, B6.*

Getting there and around
Aéroport Oujda-Les Angads ⓘ *T0536-683636*, is 15 km north of the city, a *grand taxi* ride away. From most destinations, if you arrive by bus or *grand taxi*, it's a fair 15-minute walk (or a cheap 5dh *petit taxi* ride) from the Oued Nachef terminal to the hotels on Boulevard Zerktouni, which runs to the city centre from the train station. Leave the bus station and head for the busy roundabout with a Petrom station. Turn left, keeping Petrom on your right, and a long tree-lined avenue brings you to the rail station roundabout. Some **CTM** buses, however, arrive in the centre, on Place du 16 Août, behind the central clock tower and mosque. *Grands taxis* from Nador, Berkane and Ahfir terminate near Place du Maroc in the town centre. The train station is not far from the town centre. Oujda is easily covered on foot. ▶▶ *See Transport, page 413, for further details.*

Tourist information   **Délégation Régionale du Tourisme** ⓘ *Pl du 16-Août, BP 424, T0536-685631, open 0800-1200 and 1430-1830.*

Background

Although Roman ruins have been found at Marnia, Zenata Berbers founded Oujda in AD 944, on the main route from Rabat and Meknès to Algeria. Traditionally, the town was fought over by the rulers of Fès, in Morocco, and Tlemcen, in Algeria. Captured by Sultan Youssef Ben Tachfine in 1206, it was a major centre for the Almohads who added to the fortifications. The Merinid ruler Abou Youssef rebuilt the city in 1297, constructing new walls and a kasbah, a mosque and a palace. Later the Ottoman Regency of Algiers gained control of the city, but Moulay Ismaïl regained it in 1687, subsequently doing much to develop the city. Though acknowledged as part of Morocco by international treaties, the city was occupied by French forces in 1844, after the decisive Battle of Isly, fought 8 km west of the city, and again in 1859. In 1903 Oujda was the centre of the uprising led by Bou Hamra, and was again taken by French forces from Algeria in 1907.

Oujda is now the most significant city in northeastern Morocco. Because it was occupied by the French several decades before the rest of Morocco, modern education was available earlier here than elsewhere in the country. Thus, Oujda's inhabitants consider themselves rather more sophisticated than many of their co-nationals. Indeed, a large number of Oujdis were active in the national independence movement. Contact with neighbouring

Algeria also gives Oujda a less provincial feel than you might expect. Sadly, after the border was closed in 1995, the sharp fall in visitors crossing from Algeria hit the local economy badly. Revenues from migrant workers do something to compensate, however, and the king has visited several times, with a number of regional development initiatives promised.

Oujda

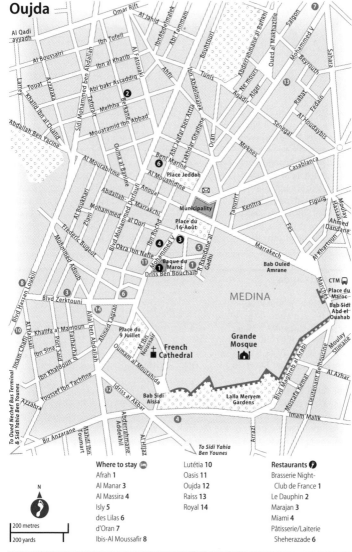

Where to stay 🛏
Afrah 1
Al Manar 3
Al Massira 4
Isly 5
des Lilas 6
d'Oran 7
Ibis-Al Moussafir 8

Lutétia 10
Oasis 11
Oujda 12
Raiss 13
Royal 14

Restaurants 🍴
Brasserie Night-
Club de France 1
Le Dauphin 2
Marajan 3
Miami 4
Pâtisserie/Laiterie
Sheherazade 6

Places in Oujda

Ville nouvelle

In its heyday in the mid-20th century, Oujda must have been a prosperous place. The town centres on a 1930s municipal **clock tower**, on Place du 16 Août, and the central section of **Boulevard Mohammed·V**, home to the best cafés and setting for the evening promenade. Close to the 1970s **Hotel Oujda** is the French **Cathedral**.

Medina

Oujda's heavily rebuilt small medina is surrounded by the *ville nouvelle*. There are no notable sights, as such, but there are some interesting and authentic souks used every day by the town's inhabitants. On the southeastern side of the medina is a short section of *pisé* Merinid ramparts; continuing along the line of the walls, you come to the most animated part of the old town, the area around the **Bab Sidi Abd el Ouahab** at the end of Avenue du Marché, where you will find the fish, meat and vegetable markets.

Just outside the Bab Sidi Abd el Ouahab is a large area where street entertainers used to perform for the evening crowds. Sadly, the square has now been turned into a parking lot but some of the former atmosphere can be enjoyed on the far side of Place Bab Sidi Abd el Ouahab, where there is also a junk market. Inside the gate is a fresh produce market with a confusing layout. Nearby, there is an extensive *kissaria* (covered market), with all sorts of cloth and clothing on sale. Past the vegetable stalls, try to find Place Al Attarine, with the *koubba* of **Sidi Abd el Ouahab**, as well as the heavily restored 13th-century Merinid **Grand Mosque** (one of the city's finest buildings) and **medersa**, built by Sultan Abu Ya'qub. Still in this area, ask for the **Hammam du Jardin**, a public bath built in the early 20th century that will give you a good introduction to the arts of the Moroccan bath.

Around Oujda

There are a handful of things to do from Oujda, the most obvious being a trip to the shrine of Sidi Yahia (see below). On the way, the **Lalla Aïcha Park** is popular with locals. In summer, the beach at **Saïdia** (see page 399) is a huge draw. The gorges of the **Beni Snassen Mountains** to the northwest are in easy day-trip distance. Another side-trip option, some 25 km south of Oujda, is the plateau-like **Jbel Mahceur** on the Touissite road. Taking the Berkane/Nador road, **Ras el Ma'a** and its long beach is another option for a day out.

Sidi Yahia Ben Younes

On summer evenings, the Shrine of Sidi Yahia Ben Younes, located in the oasis of the same name, is popular with Oujdans seeking fresh air and room to let kids run around. Set in a pleasant if slightly scruffy park of tamarisk and eucalyptus trees, the shrine is thought by some to be the tomb of St John the Baptist. It has been revered by Jews, Christians and Muslims alike. A series of small stalls selling pilgrims' needs, sandwiches and drinks precedes the shrine. You might be invited into the shrine, to sit in the cool on the carpets and contemplate the green silk-covered tomb. There are two annual *moussems* (religious festivals) in honour of Sidi Yahia, in August and September. To get there, take a town bus from Bab Sidi Abd el Ouahab; they run every 10 minutes and the ride takes 20 minutes, or a *petit taxi* to here from the city centre (12dh).

Berkane → *Colour map 1, B6.*

Berkane is a bustling modern agricultural centre with little of historical or cultural interest. It is, however, a convenient base for excursions to the nearby mountains, and there is a comfortable hotel with a good restaurant. A sharp contrast exists between the leafy, well-to-do end of town, close to the administrative and military buildings on the Oujda Road, and the busy crowded dusty streets which characterize the rest. Most facilities are on the main Boulevard Mohammed V, the Nador to Oujda main road. At the western end of this road, before the bridge over the *oued*, is a large open space with the main mosque, several cafés and a large weekly market each Tuesday. The town is also a centre for the Boutchitchiya soufi brotherhood.

Beni Snassen Mountains → *Colour map 1, B6.*

In geological terms, the Beni Snassen mountains are a continuation of the Rif. The hillsides are covered with Mediterranean vegetation – almond and orange, lavender and oleander, olive, juniper and pine – and the rockscapes are dramatic. Well-tended orchards cling to the lower slopes. In the **Gorges du Zegzel**, terraced cultivation is necessary, striping the scenery with changing bands and blocks. Certain caves here have fine formations of redeposited calcium and shapes formed by water erosion of the limestone. In the **Plombo caves** there are rare prehistoric drawings. The highlights are the Gorges du Zegzel and the **Grotte du Chameau**, where it is possible to camp. A warm stream flows out of the main entrance of the cave and joins the nearby Oued Zegzel. Inside the cave there are stalactites and an extensive warren of unlit passageways. Both sites are accessible, even walkable, from Berkane.

Getting there and around A circular route from Berkane takes in the gorges and the caves in two to four hours, either by taxi or by using a combination of taxis, walking and lifts (lifts are easy to come by in this area, but you should always offer to pay). Taxis from Berkane don't normally pass via the gorges, so you may have to charter one. Make sure the price you agree on is for a return trip, including stop-offs. A cheaper option is to do the circuit anti-clockwise by taking a shared taxi heading for Taforalt (20 km) along the S403, and getting off at the pass shortly before the village. From here, there is a signposted road winding 9 km to the caves along a very attractive valley of fruit trees and tiny hamlets. From the Grotte du Chameau you can return to Berkane, a further 10 km downhill, via the Zegzel Gorges.

◉ Oujda and around listings

For sleeping and eating price codes and other relevant information, see pages 22-28.

◖ Where to stay

Oujda *p408, map p409*
Since the closure of the Algerian border, times have been hard for hotels in Oujda. The benefit of this state of affairs for the traveller is the fact that in some of the more expensive hotels in town you can often get a good deal.

Ville nouvelle
€€€ Atlas Terminus and Spa, Blvd Zerktouni, Pl de la Gare, T0536-711010, www.hotel-atlas-terminus-oujda.com. Smart, modern hotel built around a pool, conveniently placed for the train station. There's a gym too, and free Wi-Fi.
€€ Al Massira, Blvd Maghreb al Arabi, T0536-710797, el.massira@wanadoo.net.ma. A large place with 102 rooms, tennis courts and a noisy band on summer nights. There's also a pool though it can be a little murky.

€€ **Hotel Oujda**, Blvd Mohammed V, T0536-684093. A big block of a hotel for those nostalgic for the 1970s. TV, a/c, small clean pool.

€€ **Hotel Royal**, 13 Blvd Zerkatouni, on your right heading away from the station, T0536-682284. This hotel has seen better days but has 51 good rooms. It's worth bargaining hard to get a good deal and insisting on towels and soap. The street-side rooms can be noisy.

€€ **Ibis Al Moussafir**, corner of Blvd Abdallah Chefchaouani and Pl de la Gâre, T0536-688202. A sparklingly white place, with 74 good rooms with a/c, TV, shower, telephone, bureau de change, restaurant, parking. The pool is also used by locals.

€ **Hotel d'Oran**, Blvd Mohammed V, Rte d'Alger, T0536-701001. Tastefully decorated, comfortable and friendly family-run hotel with a restaurant. Very clean, efficient, reliable hot water and heating. All rooms have a bath and TV.

€ **Hotel Raiss**, Blvd Mohammed V, Rte d'Alger, T0536-703058. A modern and elegant hotel, all the rooms have a bath, and are comfortable and very clean. Enthusiastic staff, lift, café, TV, garage.

Medina

€ **Hotel Afrah**, 15 Rue de Tafna, T0536-682328. Central position, clean and good value. Near CTM and cheap eateries. Inward-facing rooms are quieter. Views from the roof terrace.

€ **Hotel Tlemcen**, 26 Rue Ramdane el Gadhi, down a side street just off Pl du 16 Août 1953, T0536-700384. A basic, friendly, clean hotel, probably the best of the cheapies.

Youth hostel, 11 Blvd Allal ben Abdallah, T0536-680788. 45 beds, kitchen, meals available, bus 100 m, train 500 m, overnight fee 20dh.

Berkane *p411*

€€ **Hotel Zaki**, 27 Rte Principale d'Oujda, opposite the municipality building, T0536-613743. This is a stylish

little hotel with a/c in the rooms as well as having an excellent restaurant.

€ **Hotel Ennajah**, Blvd Moulay Youssef, T0536-612914. Simple hotel with clean rooms, street noise can be annoying in the early morning, and there's no hot water but there is a café/restaurant below.

€ **Hotel Mounir**, just off Blvd Mohammed V on Rue Cheraâ, T0536-611867. A popular, efficiently run hotel with a friendly and helpful owner, self catering possible.

🍴 Restaurants

Oujda *p408, map p409*

€€€ **Brasserie Night-Club de France**, 87/89 Blvd Mohammed V. Rather formal licensed restaurant and club serving international cuisine.

€€€ **Ibis Al Moussafir**, Pl de la Gare, T0536-688202. International and Moroccan food, good service, adequate set menu. See also Where to stay.

€€ **Comme chez soi**, Rue Sijilmassa, left up a side street off Av Mohammed V near the Pl du 16 Août 1953, T0536-686079. Alcohol, mixed Moroccan and European menu.

€€ **Restaurant Le Dauphin**, 38 Rue de Berkane, T0536-686145. Smart but homely fish restaurant, nice ambience.

€ **Marajan**, 9 Rue Tafna. Moroccan food, speciality is tagine.

€ **Miami**, 67 Blvd Mohammed V. Good for standard Moroccan cuisine.

€ **Restaurant National**, 17 Blvd Allal Ben Abdallah, near the railway station. Good cheap tagines and brochettes.

€ **Sandwich Sindibad**, 95 Blvd Derfoufi. Sandwiches, fruit juices, popular, fast service.

Cafés and pâtisseries

The best cafés in Oujda are in and around the central section of Blvd Mohammed V. The smartest is **Le Royal**, handy for the neighbouring **Cinéma de Paris**, on your right down Blvd Allal Ben Abdallah as you come from the station. **La Défense**, opposite the Wilaya building, is also good. For cakes, try Pâtisserie/Laiterie Sheherazade, on Rue Ben Attia, off Pl Jeddah. The local speciality, *karane*, essentially chickpeas in a sandwich, can be found on stalls on the Av du Marché.

Berkane *p411*
€€ **Restaurant des Orangers**, in Hotel Zaki, T0536-613743. Excellent little restaurant.
€ **Sandwich Venisia**, 144 Rue Sultan Moulay Mohammed. Good for basic snacks.
€ **Wine cellar**, 21 Blvd Mohammed V opposite the post office. A cheerful drink and snack with the locals can be sampled in this tiny place with probably the best evening entertainment in town.

O Shopping

Oujda *p408, map p409*
The central souks are packed in summer with returning migrant workers' families buying clothes and electric goods to kit out newly married couples. While the atmosphere is interesting, there are few if any crafts on offer.

O What to do

Oujda *p408, map p409*
Hammam Hammam du Jardin, on the Bab Sidi Aissa and **Hotel Massira** side of town, was built shortly after the French occupied Oujda in the early 1900s. Large and clean and architecturally more interesting than your average neighbourhood hammam.

Berkane *p411*
Oriental Voyages, 94 Blvd Mohammed V, T0536-613918. A friendly and helpful tour operator.

O Transport

Oujda *p408, map p409*
Air
Aéroport Oujda-Les Angads is 15 km from the city, off the N2, T0536-683636. To get

there take a *grand taxi* from Pl du Maroc. There are flights to **Marrakech**, **Casablanca** (daily), **Amsterdam**, **Brussels**, **Dusseldorf**, **Frankfurt**, **Marseille** and **Paris**. Flights are more frequent in the summer season. **Royal Air Maroc** has an office at the Hotel Oujda, Av Mohammed V, T0536-683963, as does **Air France**. Ryanair flies to Brussels and Marseille.

Bus
There are 2 bus departure points, the Oued Nachaf bus station, T0536-682262, a 15-min walk from the centre, and the central **CTM** office, 12 Rue Sidi Brahim, behind the central clock tower and mosque, just off Pl du 16 Août, T0536-682047. Services to **Fès**, **Nador** and **Casablanca** (evening). Oued Nachaf *gare routière* has private line services to **Casablanca** (Express Tassaout), **Fès**, **Meknès**, **Taza**, **Midelt**, **Figuig** (get the early morning service to avoid the heat), **Bouarfa**, **Nador** (lots of services), **Al Hoceïma**, **Berkane**, **Saïdia**, and **Ahfir**.

Car hire
Demand for hire cars is heavy in the summer. **Avis**, 110 Av Allal ben Abdallah, T0536-683993, and at the airport. **Budget Cars**, on left just as you leave the railway station, T0536-681011. **Hertz**, 2 Immeuble el Baraka, Blvd Mohammed V, T0536-683802, and at the airport.
If driving, Oujda is a long haul over the N6 to **Casablanca** (nearly 12 hrs) and **Fès** (6½ hrs). **Figuig** is a hard 7-hr drive across the bare expanses of eastern Morocco. The N2 leads from Oujda to **Melilla** and **Nador** (2½ hrs) and Ahfir.

Taxi
Grands taxis to **Berkane**, **Ahfir** and the **border** leave from just off Pl du Maroc. For **Saïdia** change at Berkane or, preferably, Ahfir. To **Taza**, **Figuig** and **Bouarfa** leave from the bus station. There are regular *grands taxis* for **Nador**.
Petits taxis are red. Watch out for unofficial red vehicles without signs.

Train

The train station is on Pl de l'Unité africaine, T0536-683133. Check departures when you arrive. The line runs west via **Taza**, **Fès** and **Meknès** to meet the main north–south, Tangier to Marrakech line at Sidi Kacem, north of Kénitra/Rabat. Journey times are long and you may have to change at Sidi Kacem. Expect to do Oujda to **Tangier** in 12 hrs, Oujda to **Marrakech** in not much less. In summer, there are 4 trains a day to **Casablanca** (10 hrs) on the Oujda–Casa Voyageurs run.

Berkane p411

Bus

The **CTM** offices are located midway along Blvd Mohammed V next to the **Café des Jardins**. There is a bus to **Oujda** and one to **Fès/Casablanca** from here. Most other bus services depart from Blvd Moulay Youssef opposite Café des Jardins. From here there are hourly departures for **Ahfir** and **Oujda**. Buses for **Nador** stop to pick up every hour on the hour (roughly) by the Grand Mosque. There is normally only 1 bus for **Saïdia** at 1400 departing from the same place as the taxis.

Taxi

Grands taxis for **Nador**, **Taforalt**, **El Aioun** and **Taourirt** leave from the parking space under the tall trees by the Grand Mosque. For **Saïdia**, the taxis leave from the Saïdia road at the opposite end of town (bear left at the roundabout with the emblem in the middle). All other *grands taxis* depart from the main bus stop in Blvd Moulay Youssef.

Directory

Oujda p408, map p409

Banks Most banks are on Blvd Mohammed V where both the **Wafabank** and **Crédit de Maroc** have ATM machines. Closest ATM to rail station is the **BCM**, almost opposite Hotel Manar. Outside normal banking hours, the main branch of the **BMCE** is open on Sat. There is also the **Hotel Al Moussafir** bureau de change. **Medical services** Chemist: all night on Rue de Marrakech, T0536-683490. As you arrive by train, there is a handy pharmacy almost in front of the station on your right. Also try the pharmacy opposite Café Royal. **Useful addresses** Fire: T15. Police: T19.

Berkane p411
Medical services Chemist: Pharmacie de la Mosquée, Pl de la Grand Mosquée.

South to Figuig

The journey south by road is long, monotonous, and very hot and is to be avoided, if possible, in summer. Only the initial part of the road, climbing up towards the Col de Guerbouss and the mining district of Jerada is green and varied. The rest of the route crosses the eastern edge of the vast Rekkam Plateau, which extends across into the high plateaux of Algeria. A low carpet of esparto grass and wormwood stretches to the horizon. Travel by bus is punctuated by frequent stops to pick up and set down shepherds who somehow survive in this scorched, windswept emptiness. The only towns along the route are Guenfouda, Ain Beni Mathar, Tendrara and Bouarfa, none of which holds much interest other than their remoteness and an opportunity to stretch the legs and buy basic provisions. ▶▶ *For listings, see page 417.*

Bouarfa → *Colour map 1, B6 & C6.*

The administrative and garrison town of Bouarfa serves as transport hub for the southeastern corner of Morocco. A stop here is unavoidable for those travelling to/from Er Rachidia (see page 192). The town is well provided with shops and services. The Saturday market is held in the large enclosure off to the right below the bus station. It is a major event, attracting shepherds and traders from the whole southeastern region.

Figuig → *For listings, see page 417.* *Colour map 3, B6.*

The 100-km route from Bouarfa to Figuig (pronounced Fg'eeg) is mesmerizing in its isolation and in the quality of the light, particularly along the final stretch, where the valley narrows. Although the first 60 km or so out of Bouarfa are difficult, the road is being improved, with the last 40 km now widened. Figuig itself is tucked away in a remote

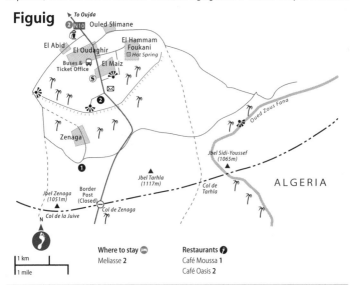

Figuig

Where to stay
Meliasse 2

Restaurants
Café Moussa 1
Café Oasis 2

southeastern corner of Morocco, 400 km south of Oujda and right next to the Algerian border. It is a town of around 13,000 people on the edge of a huge date palm oasis and surrounded by mountains. Few overlanders make the trek this far east, so the oasis and desert environment is a largely peaceful one. The charms of Figuig are not instantly apparent in its new administrative centre, but a trip is still worthwhile.

Background

Figuig's frontier location has given it a strategic significance, and it has often been fought over by the Moroccan sultanate and the powers to the east. Most recently, in 1963 and 1975, there were clashes between the armies of Morocco and Algeria. The closed border has resulted in even fewer visitors to this least-frequented of the southern oases. Work for its inhabitants is limited to small-scale farming and the date harvest.

Places in Figuig

Figuig comprises seven distinct villages on two levels: the upper level **Ksar el Oudaghir**, which straddles the main road where most shops and facilities are located, as well as the adjacent villages of El Maiz, El Abid, Ouled Slimane, and El Hammam Foukani and the lower plain, or 'Baghdad' as it is known here, consisting of a large area of palm groves connected by a network of alleyways, with **Zenaga**, the largest of the *ksar*, in the middle. The two levels are separated by an escarpment, the Jorf.

Until recently, each of the *ksar* of Figuig was independent, and their history was one of continuous feuding with each other, mainly over the issue of water. Centuries of management and protection of this precious resource have moulded the appearance of each *ksar*, with their watchtowers, high walls and winding irrigation channels. Reached by turning between the hotels **Sahara** and **Meliasse**, **Ksar el Oudaghir** has springs and an interesting round stone minaret, which it may be possible to climb. See if a local will take you to one of the *ksar*'s underground hammams. **Ksar el Maiz**, with its vaulted streets and arcaded square, is close to the main road and easily accessible. **Ksar el Hammam Foukani** ('Ksar of the Upper Hammam') is so called because of its underground hammam, fed by hot springs and reached by a slippery flight of steps. Of all the *ksar*, perhaps **Ksar Zenaga** has the most to offer, being the largest, most distinctive and also furthest from the administrative centre. Zenaga has a pleasant square with a café and a mosque from where several alleys radiate into the palmery. A platform with excellent views over the lower half of Figuig can be reached by turning right at the bottom of the main street, through the small market enclosure (Friday souk), and following a narrow path across fields. On the horizon is a gap between two mountains which marks the Moroccan/Algerian frontier. A good panorama of the Figuig ensemble can be obtained in the evening (for the best light) from the rocky pass situated on the road that encircles Figuig to the west.

Possible trips, for some fine views, include the **Oued Zousfana Valley** and the **Taghla Pass**, 4 km to the southeast of the administrative centre. To avoid any unnecessary arousing of border guards' suspicions, you are advised to notify the police station if visiting the Zousfana Valley and surrounding hills.

South to Figuig listings

For sleeping and eating price codes and other relevant information, see pages 22-28.

Where to stay

Bouarfa *p415*

€€ Climat du Maroc, T0536-796382, www.climatdumaroc.com. A large pink hotel with a pool and a tennis court. Trips into the sub-Saharan surroundings organized.

€ Hotel des Hauts Plateaux, above the bus station by the mosque (no phone), a panoramic location at the foot of the Jbel Bouarfa.

€ Hotel Tamalt, on high street below the bus station, above a café, T0536-798799. Clean, well-ventilated rooms with attractive tiling.

Figuig *p415, map p415*

€ Hotel Figuig, T0536-899309. There are only 6 rooms, so try to reserve, though there is also some cheaper dormitory-type accommodation, and you can camp too. Pool and restaurant. Good views south into Algeria.

€ Hotel Meliasse, Blvd Hassan II, T0536-899062. A basic place next to the petrol station at the entrance to the town. No comforts, cold on winter nights.

Restaurants

Figuig *p415, map p415*

Figuig is hardly a gastronomic destination, although dew-fed mushrooms are picked by the local shepherds and sometimes sold in the market. There are no real restaurants, but the following 2 places do simple meals (eg omelette, tagine). **Hotel Figuig** will also cook for you on request.

€ Café Moussa, down in Zenaga new town (take 2nd turning signposted for Zenaga after Hotel/Camping). Garden at rear with a stage, where concerts are sometimes held.

€ Café Oasis, situated in the municipal gardens at the end of the main street, Av Hassan II.

What to do

Figuig *p415, map p415*

Abderrahmane Sassi, Ksar el Hammam el Foukani, T0536-899493. Hot sand therapy where you are partly buried in holes in the sand. The treatment is said to be very effective against rheumatism, though watch out for overcooking. From early Jun to mid-Sep only.

Transport

Bouarfa *p415*

Buses from **Oujda** to **Figuig** pass through Bouarfa. 2 buses a day to **Er Rachidia**.

Figuig *p415, map p415*

Buses leave from Av Hassan II, in front of the **Hotel Sahara**, which operates as the ticket office. There are 4 buses a day to **Oujda**. For **Er Rachidia**, you will probably have to take a bus for Oujda and change at Bouarfa. In summer, get the early bus to avoid the afternoon heat.

If **driving**, there will be a close check on your papers by the **Gendarmerie royale** a few kilometres from Figuig.

Directory

Bouarfa *p415*

Medical services 2 pharmacies on the main street.

Figuig *p415, map p415*

Medical services Chemist: on the main street or in Zenaga. **Hospital**: near the barracks. There is usually at least a nurse present. The doctor lives next door.

Contents

Background

History of Morocco

Morocco's location has always been a central factor in shaping the country's history. The westernmost country in the Muslim world, for centuries it was *El Maghreb el Aqsa*, 'the Land of the Farthest West', to the Arabs. Despite being the closest Arab land to Europe, Morocco was the last to come under European domination.

Moroccans are highly aware of the particularities of their location, and are convinced that their history has given them a civilization combining the virtues of the Arabs, Berbers, Andalucíans, Jews and Christians who converted to Islam.

Conventionally, Moroccan history is divided into two major periods: the distant pre-Islamic past, marked by the Phoenicians and Romans, and the better-documented times of the Islamic dynasties, at their most brilliant during a period roughly equivalent to the European Middle Ages. From the 16th century onwards the rulers of Morocco were constantly fighting back the expansionist Iberian states and, later, France, under whose rule the majority of the Cherifian Empire (as it was called by the colonizers) came from 1912 to 1956. The last areas under colonial rule, the former Spanish Sahara, were retaken in the 1970s. The later 20th century saw the formation of the modern Moroccan State.

Pre-Islamic times

Human settlement in Morocco goes back millennia. Rock carvings in the High Atlas and Sahara, and objects in stone, copper and bronze have survived from early times. Nomadic pastoralism is thought to have existed in North Africa from around 4000 BC, among a population today referred to by historians as Libyco-Berber, probably part of the wider Hamito-Semitic group that eventually sub-divided into the Egyptians in eastern North Africa and the Berbers to the west.

The enterprising Phoenicians traded along North Africa's coast. Utica in Tunisia is thought to have been their first port in North Africa. Carthage (also in modern Tunisia) was founded in 814 BC and was to develop an extensive network of trading posts along the Mediterranean and African coasts. Archaeological excavations at Russadir (Melilla) on the Mediterranean and at Larache and Essaouira on the Atlantic coast have shown that these towns started life as Phoenician settlements. Daring Carthaginian seafarers also undertook journeys far to the south, along the West African coast.

Lost in the mists of ancient times is the history of the Imazighen, the Berber peoples of inland Morocco, referred to by the Romans as the Maures – hence the Latin name 'Mauretania' for the kingdom that seems to have taken shape in the fourth century BC over part of what is now Morocco. This early state may have had its capital at Volubilis, near modern Meknès and no doubt traded with the maritime Carthaginian empire.

After the defeat and destruction of Carthage in 146 BC, and the establishment of the Roman province of Africa, it was only natural that the empire of the Caesars develop an interest in the lands of the Maures – always a potential source of trouble. Roman forces had had considerable problems in putting down the revolts of the Berber kingdoms, the most difficult campaigns being in the eastern Maghreb against Jugurtha, 109-105 BC. To establish stable rule in northwestern Africa, Augustus entrusted Mauritania to Juba II, son of Juba I, an enemy of Julius Caesar, who had committed suicide after Pompey's defeat in the civil war between Caesar and Pompey.

Chronology: ancient Morocco

6000-3000 BC Neolithic era. Tumulus (burial mounds) of Mzoura, near Larache, dates from this time.

3000 BC onwards Proto-historic period. Bronze tools manufactured in Morocco, to judge from evidence of rock-carvings.

7th century BC First confirmed Phoenician presence in the form of trading posts in Morocco, notably near the sites of modern Essaouira and Larache.

5th century BC Carthage establishes trading posts on the coast.

4th-3rd centuries BC Kingdom of the Maures established.

146 BC Fall of Carthage to Rome. Northwest Africa (or Mauretania, as it is referred to by the Latin authors) comes under Roman influence.

33 BC King Bocchus II leaves the Kingdom of the Maures to Rome.

24 BC Juba II comes to the Mauretanian throne. Augustus rules in Rome.

AD 40 Ptolomy, son of Juba II and Cleopatra Selene, is assassinated on the orders of Emperor Caligula.

AD 42 Northwestern Morocco becomes a Roman province as Mauretania Tingitana, with its capital at Tingis, modern Tangier.

3rd century Christianity appears in Morocco. Rome abandons the province south of the Oued Loukkos.

4th century The elephant becomes extinct in northwestern Africa.

AD 429 The Vandals invade north Africa, but fail to establish a lasting presence in Mauretania Tingitana.

AD 533 During the reign of Justinian, the Byzantine Empire re-establishes control of the coastal cities of Ceuta and Tangier.

A cultured monarch, Juba II married Cleopatra Selene, daughter of Cleopatra and Mark Anthony. From 25 BC, he reigned over much of what is now Morocco. Fluent in Amazigh, Greek, Latin and Punic, he was interested in the arts, sciences and medicine. His portrait in the form of a fine bronze bust was discovered during the excavation of the ancient city of Volubilis near Meknès.

An independent-minded Mauretanian monarchy was too much for Rome. The last king, Ptolomy, grandson of Anthony and Cleopatra, was put to death by the Roman emperor Caligula, and the client kingdom was transformed into a Roman colony. Roman northwestern Africa was reorganized as two provinces, with capitals at Iol-Caesarea (Cherchell in Algeria) and Tingis, today's Tangier.

Roman administration and Latin culture were grafted onto Punic and Berber peoples. The army was an important influence: until 19 BC there was fighting in North Africa, and the army continued to extend its influence. A major Berber revolt, led by one Tacfarinas, took seven years to suppress. Such tensions were probably aggravated by Roman centurions settling to farm wheat and olives on lands once grazed by the nomads' flocks. The towns had all the trappings of Romanized urban life and flourished until the third century AD.

The third to eighth centuries AD are a hazy time in northwest Africa's history. The Amazigh rebelled frequently, while Romanized populations protested against the low prices of wheat, wine and olive oil supplied to the metropolis. Although Christianity became Rome's official religion in AD 313, it proved insufficient glue to hold the Empire together against the Germanic invasions. The Vandals swept down from Spain and across into the eastern Maghreb in the fifth century. Although the Byzantine Empire was to take back certain territories in the sixth century, its unity was undermined by struggles within the Church. Mauretania Tingitana was never effectively ruled again by a Roman administration.

Arrival of Islam

The key event in shaping Morocco's history was the conquest by the Muslim Arabs in the eighth century AD. Islam, the religion of the Prophet Mohammed, was born in the oases of Arabia in the seventh century AD. It gave the warring Arab tribes and oasis communities – formerly pagan, Jewish and maybe Christian – the necessary cohesion to push back the Byzantine and Sassanian Empires, exhausted by years of warfare.

In eighth-century North Africa, Islam was welcomed by the slaves – who freed themselves by becoming Muslims – and by Christian heretics, who saw the new religion as simpler and more tolerant than Byzantine Christianity. In 711, therefore, it was an Islamized Amazigh army that crossed the Straits of Gibraltar under Tariq Ibn Ziyad, conquering the larger part of the Iberian peninsula. Along with North Africa, the southern regions of the peninsula, referred to as Al Andalus (whence Andalucía), formed a unified socio-cultural area until the 15th century.

Islam, which vaunts a spirit of brotherhood within a vast community of believers and condemns petty clan interests and local loyalties, was to prove an effective base for new states based on dynastic rule, with central governments drawing their legitimacy from their respect for the precepts of the Koran and the Hadith, the codified practice of the Prophet Mohammed.

From the moment that Islam arrived, Morocco's history became that of the rise and fall of dynasties, often ruling areas far wider than that of the contemporary nation state. Simplifying heavily, these dynasties were the Idrissids (ninth century), the Almoravids (11th century), the Almohads (12th-13th centuries), the Merinids (13th-15th centuries), the Wattasids (15th-16th centuries), the Saâdians (16th century) and, finally, the Alaouites, rulers of Morocco from the 17th century to the present. Almost all these dynasties arose from politico-religious movements.

To return to the early centuries of Islamic rule in North Africa, the new religion took hold fairly slowly, as struggles between rival dynasties in the Middle East – the Ummayads and the Abbasids – divided the Islamic heartlands. The Islamic ideal was certainly not the only interest of the Arab governors sent out by the caliphs. Power was often exercised despotically, with repression leading to a major revolt against the Arab rulers (740-780) in the name of Islam. The revolt was of Kharijite inspiration – the Kharijites considering that they practised the most pure and egalitarian form of Islam. They rejected the split between Sunni and Shi'a Muslims and refused to submit to the authority of the caliphs of Damascus and Baghdad. Even at the end of the struggle between Umayyads and Abbasids, in 750, and the victory of the latter, central Islamic power was slow to reassert itself in the northwestern extremities of Africa, which remained, along with the northern Sahara, independent as the Berber Kharijite Kingdom of Tahert. Then, in the mid-eighth century, an Ummayad descendant of the Prophet, fleeing the Middle East, founded the first great Muslim dynasty in 788. Idriss I founded Fès in 789. A further refugee Umayyad prince was to build a kingdom in Al Andalus, centred on Córdoba.

The ninth and 10th centuries saw the development of the trans-Saharan caravan trade, notably in gold. There were routes leading up into what is now Tunisia and Libya, and other, longer routes across the western regions of the Sahara. The shorter, western route finished in the Drâa Valley and the southern slopes of the Atlas. Sijilmassa, close to today's eastern Moroccan town of Rissani, was to be the capital of this trade, the mustering place from which the caravans headed onwards to the Middle East and the Mediterranean ports. Sijilmassa was to be taken by a Shi'ite group who, thanks to their control of the

Chronology: medieval and early modern Morocco

622 Prophet Mohammed is forced to leave Mecca for Medina. His *hijra* ('emigration') on account of his beliefs is the start of the Muslim era.

703 Moussa Ibn Nusayr conquers Morocco and begins the conversion of Berbers to Islam.

704 Tangier falls to the Muslim armies with the help of Count Julian.

711 Tariq Ibn Ziyad crosses the straits which today bear his name (Jabal Tariq) to begin the conquest of Iberia, which lasts until 732.

740 Berber revolt against central authorities in Damascus. Their heretic, Kharijite brand of Islam leads to a political break with the Arab Near East.

786 Idriss I, descendant of caliph Ali and the Prophet's daughter Fatima, reaches Morocco, fleeing the Abbasids of Baghdad.

788 Idriss becomes religious leader of the Berber tribes of the Middle Atlas.

789 Foundation of Fès.

791 Idriss I poisoned at orders of Haroun Errachid.

803 Idriss II on the throne.

809 Fès re-founded by Idriss II.

817-818 Hundreds of Jewish and Muslim families move to Fès from Córdoba and Kairouan.

1048 Abdallah Ibn Yassin, a religious reformer from Sijilmassa, creates a fortified settlement or ribat, home to warriors (*murabitoun*) – hence the name of the dynasty he founded, the Almoravids.

1062 Youssouf Ibn Tachfine founds Marrakech.

1086 The minor kings of southern Spain appeal for help to the Almoravids, who go on to beat Alfonso VI at the Battle of Sagrajas.

1125 Ibn Toumert declares himself mahdi, 'the rightly guided one', at Tin Mal in the High Atlas. The purist Almohad movement is launched.

1126 The Almohad Abd el Mu'min Ibn Ali (ruled 1130-63) takes the title of caliph. Goes on to conquer North Africa and Iberia up to the Guadalquivir.

1143-1147 Collapse of the Almoravid Empire.

1148-1197 Construction of major mosques, including the Koutoubia in Marrakech, the Tour Hassan in Rabat and the Giralda, Seville.

1244-1269 Almohad Empire falls apart, having lasted barely 100 years.

1248 Fès falls to the Merinids. They begin the construction of Fès el Jedid.

1269 Fall of Marrakech marks the beginning of the Merinid era.

1300s Merinid rule is at its height.

1400s Internal anarchy in Morocco. Merinid collapse in 1465.

1492 Fall of Granada to the Catholic monarchs, Ferdinand and Isabella.

1509 Spain takes Oran.

1525-1659 Saâdian rule.

1578 Battle of the Three Kings ends Portuguese threat to sultanate.

1578-1607 Reign of Ahmed el Mansour ed Dahabi.

1664 Alaouite rule established at Fès under Moulay Rachid.

1672-1727 Moulay Ismaïl rules with an iron hand.

1757-1790 Sidi Mohammed Ben Abdallah rules a stable country.

1817 Corsairing is banned.

gold trade, were able to found the Fatimid dynasty – named after Fatima, daughter of the Prophet and wife of Ali, considered by the Shi'ites as the legitimate caliph or successor of the Prophet Mohammed.

Tribal dynasties and religious causes: Almoravids and Almohads

The Saharan gold trade in the 11th century was to be dominated by a nomad Berber group based in fortified religious settlements (*ribats*), hence their name, *el murabitoun*, which transposes as Almoravid. Based in the northern Sahara, they founded a capital at Marrakech in 1062. Their empire expanded to include much of Spain and present-day Algeria.

In the 12th century, the Almoravids were overthrown by the Almohads, *el muwahhidoun* or 'unitarians', whose power base lay in the Berber tribal groupings of the High Atlas. United by their common religious cause, the Almohads took Sijilmassa, the 'gold port', and their empire expanded to include the whole of present day Morocco, Algeria and Tunisia, along with Andalucía. This political unity lasted from about 1160 to 1260. Towns expanded, distinctive mosques were built (along the lines of the Koutoubia at Marrakech), trade grew with southern European merchant cities and Arabic took root as the language of the urban areas.

The Almohad dynasty disintegrated towards the end of the 13th century. The ruling tribal elite lost its sense of cohesion and the feudal Christian rulers of Spain reacted quickly: Seville fell to the Christians in 1248 and Granada became a protectorate. The Almohad Empire split into three separate kingdoms, roughly corresponding to the independent states of today. Ifrikiya (Tunisia) was ruled by the Hafsids, who initially ruled in the name of the Almohads; the Abdelwadids ruled from Tlemcen in modern Algeria; in Morocco, the Merinids established their capital in Fès.

Merinids: from tribal to urban dynastic rule

The Beni Merini, rulers of Morocco from the mid-13th to mid-15th centuries, were not champions of any particular religious doctrine. Nomads from the Figuig region, they appear in Moroccan history in the late 12th century and grow in influence during the early 13th century.

In the 1250s, the Merinid forces took the main cities under Abou Yahya el Merini, and Abou Youssef Yacoub (1258-1286) consolidated their rule. The 14th and 15th centuries saw the Merinids build a state centred on Fès – but they were more or less constantly involved in struggles with mountain tribes and neighbouring dynasties: the Tlemcen-based Zayyanids, the Hafsids further to the east, and the Nasrids to the north in Granada.

Home to the Merinid court and administration, Fès grew as a centre of religious learning, too. Having conquered power in a land where political authority depended closely on religious credentials the Merinids tried to build legitimacy by sponsoring theological education. *Medersas*, operating rather like the colleges of some early European universities, were founded at Fès and in other cities, providing teaching reflecting the urban elite's piety. Students, however, came from both town and country. In attempting to build an educated group with formal theological and legal training, the Merinids sought to counter the influence of Sufi leaders in rural areas.

Merinid power, unlike that of previous dynasties, was not based on a single tribe – probably because large settled communities of merchants and artisans were emerging. Subsequent dynasties, although they had to use tribal support initially, never maintained a single tribal affiliation. The European threat which emerged in the 15th century (Ceuta was occupied by the Portuguese in 1415) led to a resistance based on religious ideals, with leaders referred to as *cherifs*, descendants of the Prophet Mohammed. When the Merinids proved ineffective in fighting back the Europeans, alternative local leaderships appeared, suitable symbols around which unity could be built due to cherifian descent. The Saâdians exemplify this trend.

Morocco and marauding Europe

The routes of the gold caravans linking sub-Saharan Africa to North Africa meant that any Moroccan dynasty had importance. However, as of the 14th century, new routes opened up, reducing the significance of northwest Africa. The Mamlouks in Egypt fought back the Christian kingdoms of Nubia; Spain and Portugal began the quest for sea routes to the 'gold coasts' and the epoch of the great discoveries began, as the Portuguese explored the Atlantic coast of Africa. In 1492, Granada, the last Muslim stronghold in Andalucía, fell to Ferdinand and Isabella, and Columbus sailed for America. The era of European imperialism had begun, and the Maghreb was first in the firing line as the Catholic monarchs continued the Reconquista into Africa. The two Iberian powers occupied strong-points along the Atlantic and Mediterranean coasts (the Spanish garrison towns of Ceuta and Melilla date from this time). However, under Iberian powers, resources were soon taken up with the commercially more important development of far-flung empires in the Indies and Americas. And the people of North Africa put up solid resistance.

In 1453, the last bastion of eastern Christianity, Constantinople, fell to the Ottoman Empire. Muslim resistance to the Christian powers in the western Mediterranean was led by corsairs, who called on the Ottoman sultan in Istanbul for support. By the end of the 16th century, the eastern part of the Maghreb had been divided into three Ottoman *ilayet* or regencies: Algiers, Tunis and Tripoli. Morocco, however, remained independent, ruled by dynasties of cherifian origin. The Saâdians (late 15th-16th century) sprang from the Souss region (Taroudant) and, under Ahmed el Mansour (1578-1603), destroyed an invading Portuguese army, re-established (for a short while) the gold trade, developed sugar cane plantations in the Souss and re-founded Marrakech.

Alaouites and the foundations of the cherifian state

After the decay of Saâdian power, a second cherifian dynasty, the Alaouites, originally from the oases of the Tafilalet (southeastern Morocco), came to power. The first sovereigns, Moulay Rachid (1666-1672) and Moulay Ismaïl (1672-1727), a tireless builder, restored order. As Fès and Marrakech had risen against him, he created a vast new capital at Meknès; with a large palace and four mosques, he transformed a provincial town into a regal city.

There seems to have been major political and strategic motives behind the decision to centre Alaouite authority on Meknès. It enabled the sultan to avoid identifying himself too closely with the interests of either Fès or Marrakech. Meknès was also very central, and better situated for campaigning against the Middle Atlas Berbers and it was more distant than Fès from Turkish-dominated lands further east.

Moulay Ismaïl's authority depended on a special corps of black slave troops, the Abid Bukhari. By the end of his long reign, Moulay Ismaïl had a loyal force of some 150,000 men, ever ready to deal with Ottoman encroachments or Sanhaja Berber rebellion. By 1686, the sultan's authority was complete, with only remote mountain areas outside his control. Such a security force required considerable resources, which meant resorting to rather un-Islamic forms of taxation. Repressive taxation produced resentment in the already defiant cities, notably Fès.

After a period of chaos in the 1730s, the work of Moulay Ismaïl continued under Mohammed Ben Abdallah (1757-1790). Stability was restored and the influence of Moulay Ismaïl's Abid army was ended. Many of the *presidios* were re-taken, including Mazagan (today's El Jadida), while Essaouira was fortified. In 1760, the port of Anfa (today's

Casablanca) was fortified, and Christian merchants were exempted from customs duties as an incentive to settle. Morocco came to be respected by the European powers.

Mohammed Ben Abdallah was the first Alaouite sultan who was keen to gain the real support of the urban religious elite, the *ulema*. While previous sultans – and especially Moulay Ismaïl – had relied on their cherifian lineage as an ideological prop for their rule, Mohammed Ben Abdallah sought *ulema* support for his policies. He won them over because of his piety and scholarly interests. Thus the Moroccan State, although dependent on tribal soldiery, began to become identified with the interests of Morocco's city dwellers. This trend continued under Mohammed Ben Abdallah's successor, Moulay Suleyman (1792-1827).

The 19th century: colonialism held at bay

In 1798, Napoleon Bonaparte led an expedition to Egypt. The lands of Islam became aware of the newly acquired technological power of European armies. Modernization was essential, despite the high financial costs, if colonial rule was to be avioded. The European peace of 1815 established conditions favourable to colonialism, and France, anxious to re-establish lost prestige, looked towards North Africa. Algiers was taken in 1830, and French colonial expansion continued throughout the 19th century, with a settler population of largely Mediterranean origin putting down roots. European farming grew, thanks to the redistribution of land confiscated after revolts and modern land registration. New European-style cities were constructed. Although Algiers fell with little resistance, the central Maghreb was occupied at a terrible price to the local population.

Because of the development of French Algeria, Morocco increasingly found itself isolated from the rest of the Islamic world and subject to severe pressure from the European powers who were steadily growing in confidence. France attacked Morocco for providing shelter to the Algerian leader, the Emir Abdelkader, defeating the Moroccan army at the Battle of Isly in 1844. Great Britain forced Morocco to sign a preferential trade treaty in 1856, while, in 1860, a Spanish expeditionary force took the key northern city of Tetouan. Sultan Aberrahman was forced to accept unfavourable peace terms, with customs coming under foreign control by way of an indemnity; an ill-defined Saharan territory, was ceded to Spain. The departure of Spanish troops in 1862 left Morocco considerably weakened.

A reform policy had been launched, however, under a series of bright, dynamic sultans: Abderrahman (1822-1859), Mohammed IV (1859-1873) and Hassan I (1873-1894). Despite the latter's efforts to expand his power base with the support of the High Atlas tribes, further treaties were imposed by Great Britain, Spain and France. The country ran into increasing debt problems with foreign banks. The situation continued to worsen under the weak rulers who succeeded Hassan I.

In 1906, the Conference of Algeciras brought 12 nations together to discuss the Moroccan debt. France and Spain emerged as key contenders for occupation. In 1907, following the killing of some Europeans during unrest, France occupied Casablanca. A new sultan, Moulay Hafidh (great-uncle of the present king), was proclaimed the same year. In 1911, with Fès surrounded by insurgent tribes, he called in Algerian-based French forces to end the state of siege.

The last act came in 1912, when the Treaty of Fès, signed by France and Moulay Hafidh for Morocco, established the French protectorate over the Cherifian Empire. A subsequent Franco-Spanish treaty split the country into a northern zone, under Spanish control, a vast central area under French rule, and a southern zone, also assigned to Spain.

Chronology: modern Morocco

1844 Battle of Isly. Moroccan sultan's forces defeated by the French near Oujda.
1880 Conference of Madrid, while recognizing Morocco as an independent kingdom, confirms the major European powers' trade interests.
1905 Kaiser William II visits Tangier and makes a speech proclaiming himself 'defender of Islam'.
1907 France uses major riots in Casablanca as a pretext for sending in troops.

1912 30 March. Proclamation of a French protectorate over central Morocco.
1942 Allied landings at Casablanca (8 November).
1943 Allied conference at Anfa, Casablanca.
1947 Sultan Mohammed V calls for independence.
1953 Mohammed V deposed and sent into exile, replaced by puppet ruler Mohammed Ben Arafa.
1956 Moroccan independence.

The protectorate: separate development and exploitation

The full occupation of Morocco was an arduous affair, with tribes putting up resistance and an area of the Rif (northern Morocco), establishing itself as an independent republic for a short period in the 1920s, threatening the protectorate system's stability.

The protectorate bore the firm imprint of the first French resident-general, Maréchal Lyautey – and the work accomplished during his 12-year rule was to leave a long-lasting mark on the country. Lyautey, a Roman Catholic aristocrat who had seen service in Algeria, Indochina and Madagascar – and witnessed at first hand what he considered to be the errors of the colonial system – was fascinated by Morocco; as something of a monarchist, he had respect for the sultanate, and was not disposed to intervene in the new protectorate's traditional life.

Thus, the first period of French rule saw local institutions consolidated, alongside the gradual occupation of the main cities and the coastal plains. The sultan remained ruler, although executive and legislative powers were shared with the French resident-general. To govern the vast southern regions, the French relied on local Berber chiefs – Marrakech and its region was ruled by co-opting a local potentate, T'hami el Glaoui, for example. This meant that large-scale forces did not have to be committed at a time when they were needed elsewhere. Exploitation of Morocco's natural wealth turned out to be a capitalist venture, rather than a settler one. French private banks financed public and private building works and exploited mineral concessions through the Compagnie Générale Marocaine and the Omnium Nord Africain. Infrastructure development was impressive: 1600 km of railway lines were created, a major new port was constructed at Casablanca. Rabat was chosen as the capital, and other new towns were planned using the most up-to-date techniques. Working closely with the planner Léon-Henri Prost, Lyautey ensured that Morocco's traditional cities were preserved and carefully separated from the elegant new European quarters.

It was quickly realized, too, that the lands controlled by the sultan's government, the *bilad el makhzen* (the coastal plains, along with the Fès, Meknès and Oujda regions), were the most fertile – hence the term *le Maroc utile*, 'useful Morocco'. An increasingly dynamic European community undertook to develop the country's resources to its own advantage, helped by tax concessions. By 1951, the European population had reached 325,000.

But for Lyautey, Morocco was not to be a settler colony, like neighbouring Algeria, where the French had shattered local society. Efforts were made to understand Moroccan

Monarchs, battles and freedom fighters

Moroccan city streets tend to draw on the same selection of names. The biggest avenue in any town will be named after **Mohammed V** (1909-1961). Third son of Sultan Moulay Youssef, the young Mohammed was chosen by the French to be sultan because he was thought to be more malleable. In the event, he ruled Morocco from 1927 to 1961, seeing the country to independence in 1956. His son, **Hassan II**, who ruled 1961-1999, also has many streets named after him, as does **Prince Moulay Abdallah**, the late king's younger brother. There are also streets named for dynasties (avenue des **Almoravides**, des **Almohades**, des **Saâdiens**, des **Alaouites**) and for major monarchs (ninth-century founder of Fès, **Idriss II**, 16th-century **Mansour Eddahbi**, 'the victorious and golden').

In any self-respecting town, central streets also bear the names of freedom fighters and the battles of the resistance. **Oued el Makhzen** was the battle in 1578 near modern Larache, where Mansour Eddahbi wiped out the invading Portuguese. The **Amir Abdelkader** fought the French in Algeria in the 19th century, while **Abdelkarim el Khattabi** was the leader of the Rif rebellion that set up an independent republic in northern Morocco in the 1920s. At the Battle of **Anoual** in 1921, he won a famous victory over Spanish forces. In the 1950s, **Mohammed Zerktouni** lobbed a bomb into a market much frequented by French shoppers in Marrakech, thus ensuring his commemoration on numerous major boulevards. (Imprisoned, he took his own life to avoid torture.)

society – the rural areas were administered by the specially trained *officiers des affaires indigènes*, and special government departments were created to catalogue and restore Morocco's heritage of historic buildings and crafts.

Lyautey may have been too 'pro-Moroccan' to satisfy a growing settler lobby. The fatal moment came in 1925. The Rif uprising, led by the enterprising Abdelkrim el Khattabi, imperilled the two protectorates. In July 1921, the Rif armies had captured or killed around 15,000 Spanish soldiers at the Battle of Anoual. Lyautey was recalled to France, replaced by Maréchal Pétain at the head of a large army which finally defeated the Rifans in 1926 in co-operation with Spain. Fighting to defeat tribes resisting colonial incursions elsewhere in Morocco continued into the early 1930s.

Hardly had Morocco been 'pacified' than a nationalist movement arose. A focal point for nationalist resentment was the so-called Berber *dahir* (decree) of 1933, an attempt to replace Muslim law with Berber customary law in the main Berber-speaking regions. French colonial ethnography, which had provided the reasoning behind this project, had made a fundamental miscalculation: Morocco could not be divided into Berbers versus Arabs. The educated urban bourgeoisie demanded a reform programme in 1934 and, with the Second World War, the international situation clearly shifted to favour independence. The urban elite formed the Istiqlal (Independence) Party in 1944, with the goodwill of Sultan Mohammed V. Although closely watched by the French, the Alaouite sultan came to be seen as an instrument of French policy.

Tension grew in the early 1950s; under the Pacha of Marrakech, contingents of tribal horsemen converged on Rabat to demand the deposition of the sultan. In 1953 the resident-general, in violation of the protectorate treaty, deposed Mohammed V and replaced him with a relative. The royal family found themselves in exile in Madagascar, which gave the nationalist movement another point of leverage. The sultan's return from exile was a key nationalist demand.

The situation elsewhere in the French Empire was to ensure a fast settlement of the Moroccan question. France had been defeated in Indochina in 1954, and there was a major uprising in Algeria, considered an integral part of France by Paris. The La Celle-St Cloud agreements of November 1955 ensured a triumphal return from exile for the royal family, and independence was achieved in March 1956, with Spain renouncing its protectorate over northern Morocco at the same time. The issue of the southern desert provinces under Spanish rule, like Río de Oro, was left to one side.

Thus, Morocco's independence was achieved under the leadership of the country's traditional ruler. The Istiqlal Party had fostered political consciousness in the Moroccan middle classes, and a confrontation between a colonial regime and the people had developed into a conflict between colonial rulers and the Muslim ruler. The sultanate under foreign protection became an independent kingdom, with a unique position in the Arab and Mediterranean worlds.

Modern Morocco

Morocco today is a complex and rapidly changing country. In political terms, the country is one of the most interesting Arab states, with a degree of media freedom and debate (within certain limits), rare in Northern Africa and the Middle East.

Recent political history

After independence, the national pact was increasingly criticized by the urban elite, who thought to push the monarchy aside – rather as had happened in Egypt, Tunisia and Iraq – and rule the country under a one-party system supported by the educated middle classes. The Istiqlal and socialist parties jockeyed for leadership; a revolt in the Rif was put down. The monarchy proved to be durable, however. After the death of his father, Mohammed V, in 1961, the new king, Hassan II turned out to be an able political player. An alliance with conservative rural leaders ensured the success of the constitutional referendum of December 1962. After the Casablanca riots of 1965, the army was called in to guarantee order. The Left lost its leader, Mehdi Ben Barka, assassinated in Paris in November 1965. As of July 1965, Hassan II was to rule without parliament.

The 1970s and 1980s
Such a centralized system was fraught with risk, as was realized following two attempts on the King's life: the Skhirat Palace attempted coup in 1971 (see box) and the attempt to shoot down the royal plane in 1972. So the King sought to rebuild a political system which would end the monarchy's relative isolation on the political scene and leave considerable room for manoeuvre. The 'Moroccanization' of the remaining firms still (mainly) in French hands, launched in 1973, was part of the strategy, winning the support of the middle classes. Spanish Río de Oro and Saquiet el Hamza were regained in the mid-1970s; the army was to be kept busy in these new Saharan provinces, fighting the Polisario, often at bonus pay rates. A number of key players emerged to second the King on the political scene. Foremost among them from the early 1980s was Driss Basri, Minister of the Interior. The dialogue between the King and Abderrahim Bouabid, head of the left wing UNFP in

Pilgrimage

In the 1980s, 'Tazmamart' was a taboo word. Mentioning this name was enough to send shivers down the spines of those who knew. For Tazmamart, a nothing sort of place in the southeastern Moroccan outback, was home to cruelty. The officers involved in an attempted palace coup in the early 1970s were imprisoned here in a specially built goulag.

Rewind to 9 July 1971. Army cadets broke loose in the palace at Skhirat near Rabat, where King Hassan II was having his annual birthday bash. Poorly managed, the putsch failed. The king emerged from a hiding place to find tens of guests and soldiers dead. Vengeance was swift to follow. Several hundred officers were put on trial for treason; 58 of them were transferred to Tazmamart to live out their sentences in conditions of unimagined horror. There were two buildings of 30 cells. Each cell, 3 m long and 2.5 m wide, had a cement platform for a bed and a hole in the floor for toilet waste. A tiny panel in the door and 18 holes in the wall provided ventilation. Each prisoner had a plate, a plastic jug and a five-litre water container. For the first three years, the prisoners wore the clothes they had arrived in. The food was bread, weak coffee and chickpea gruel. Fortunately, the guards changed rarely and a sort of complicity between the two sides grew, allowing a few items – medicines, a transistor radio, the occasional letter – to be smuggled in.

In the late 1970s, news of Tazmamart filtered to the outside world. Pressure from human rights groups abroad grew. In the late 1980s, the fax changed everything: people sent the latest French press reports to friends and family back in Morocco. For the country's international reputation, Tazmamart prison camp had to go. In October 1991, the survivors of this most inhumane of gaols, 28 in all, were released from their cement cages. By mutual support and a dose of religious mysticism, they had survived the cold and scorpions, madness, hunger and fear.

In October 2000, Tazmamart became a place of pilgrimage. Former prisoners returned to the place of their suffering on the anniversary of their release. With them came the families of those who died there, human rights activists and journalists. The message was that in the new Morocco of Mohammed VI, the horror of Tazmamart must never happen again. Things seem to be moving in the right direction. The fact that the pilgrimage was able to go ahead to the site of a prison whose very existence was denied until 10 years ago is a sure sign of change, an indication that Morocco is beginning to look the sinister aspects of its recent past in the face. Such was the interest aroused that Ahmed Marzouki's moving account of his time in the prison, *Tazmamart Cellule 10* (Gallimard, 2001), has sold thousands of copies.

---

the mid-1970s, was to give the opposition a chance to express itself and represented a return to the methods used by Mohammed V after independence. In the 1990s, Parliament came to be dominated by the ruling conservative Wifak grouping and the opposition bloc, the Koutla. The early 1990s saw the King actively working to bring the opposition into government. Finally, in November 1997, elections produced a parliament with an opposition majority, led by the USFP (Union socialiste des forces populaires).

The 1990s: l'alternance or bringing the opposition to power

It is clear that Hassan II was trying to leave Morocco in good running order for his son, Crown Prince Sidi Mohammed. By the late 1980s, the Palace was aware that the political elite born of the independence struggle was running out of steam and that the opposition criticism of the inequalities in living standards (*la fracture sociale*, in Moroccan political parlance) had good grounds. World Bank 'remedies', strenuously applied in the 1980s and early 1990s, only helped to impoverish a large section of the population. Drought and poor harvests accelerated the rural exodus, rendering the split between poor and wealthy all the more visible in the cities. The first opposition government of 1998 thus had a very clear remit to 'do something' – and quickly – for the poorest in Moroccan society.

Underlying the opposition's coming to power was a fear that a large part of the *bidonville* (shanty town) population might be tempted by radical Islam. The middle classes have everything to lose should the country head towards an Algerian-type scenario, where thousands died in the 1990s.

July 1999: a new reign
The equation changed on the death of Hassan II on 23 July 1999. His eldest son, crown prince Sidi Mohammed, came to the throne as Mohammed VI. The battle against social inequality soon figured at the top of the royal agenda. And, for the first time in decades, areas of the country never visited by the reigning monarch received a royal visit. In long-ignored Tangier and the north, crowds turned out in the rain to welcome the king. In the palace, a new cohort of reform-minded counsellors joined the royal cabinet.

The new king moved quickly to improve the human rights situation. Former political prisoners and the families of those who 'disappeared' during the repression of the 1970s and 1980s received compensation payments; the house arrest of a leader of Islamist movement El Adl wal Ihsane, the ageing Cheikh Yassine, was ended. In early 2001, the International Federation of Human Rights held its annual conference in Casablanca.

The 2000s: slow, gradual reform
The Youssoufi government was much criticized for its inability to deal with deeply entrenched networks of economic cronyism. There were no spectacular reforms. Gentle but constant improvement was felt to be the best way – and, given the shortage of competent personnel, probably the only one. Most Moroccans realized that the habits of decades could not be changed overnight. Reform continued in the civil service, the security forces and justice; dynamic young ministers were appointed to the key portfolios of communications, housing and regional development, tourism and transport.

2003 and 2011: Islamist urban bomb attacks
In early May 2003, Morocco celebrated the birth of Crown Prince Hassan. Shortly after, on 16 May, tragedy struck. The country was dumbstruck by suicide bomb attacks in the centre of Casablanca. Targets included a Jewish social club and a downtown hotel. Over 40 people were killed, all Moroccans, and many were injured. The bombers were members of the Salafiya-Jihadiya purist Islamist movement. Several hundred arrests in Islamist circles swiftly followed.

Morocco's tourist capital was the target for a more recent terrorist attack, on 28 April 2011, when a bomb exploded in a café overlooking the Jemaâ el-Fna square in Marrakech, killing 17, most of whom were foreign tourists. Though initially blamed for the attack, Al Qaeda denied responsibility. In October, Adel al-Olthmani was sentenced to death for his role in the attack and seven others received prison sentences for their part. For the Moroccans, the bombings were shocking: undermining an assumption that unprovoked urban slaughter of this kind could only happen elsewhere – notably in neighbouring Algeria.

2011 and beyond

Morocco did not escape the effects of the Arab Spring, which began in neighbouring Tunisia in December 2010. On 20 February 2011, tens of thousands took part in demonstrations calling for political reforms, including further devolved powers from the king to parliament and a more independent judicial system. A group called the 20 February Movement was formed, which, like other protest movements around the Arab world, was led by young people and created through social networking. On 11 March, the king promised 'comprehensive constitutional reform' but, despite these guarantees, the demonstrations continued, led by the 20 February Movement. This prompted the televised announcement by the king of a series of reforms to be put to a national referendum on 1 July. Again, the protest movement rallied against the proposed reforms, arguing that they did not go far enough.

The referendum went ahead and, following a resounding vote in favour of the reforms (98% voted 'yes' with an estimated turnout of 73%), the new constitution enshrined the following changes: the new prime minister is selected from the party that receives most votes in an election rather than chosen by the king; the prime minister is able to appoint goverment officials and is also able to dissolve parliament. The king does retain significant powers, however he is the key power-broker in matters of security, religion and the military, and continues to chair the Council of Ministers and the Supreme Security Council.

Pro-democracy protests continued, with the 20 February Movement taking to the streets on 3 July to reject the new constitution. Following these demonstrations, early elections for the National Assembly of Representatives were held on 25 November 2011. The moderate Islamist Jusive and Development Party (PJD) became the largest party, more than doubling their number of seats from 46 in 2007 to 107, though this was still short of an overall majority. Abdelilah Benkirane, leader of the PJD, was appointed prime minister and formed a coalition goverment with the centre Independence Party (who won 60 seats out of total of 395) and the Popular Movement (who won 32 seats).

Challenges for the 21st century

Things have moved forward considerably since the 1970s and, on the whole, the situation in the early 21st century looks positive. While Morocco, with (for the moment) no oil resources, suffers from rising oil prices, the country's proximity to Europe and an expanding internal market has made it an ideal base for relocating manufacturing industry. The question, however, remains how to reduce poverty and social inequality and so avoid the bloodshed of the Arab Spring or the Algerian-type fundamentalist destabilization and strife. The 20 February Movement announced its readiess to enter into dialogue with the new government – in exchange for the release of political prisoners, press freedom and more civil liberties – thus confirming a strong national desire for consensus. This, in itself, should allow much to be achieved.

Issues and pressures

Arab Spring-influenced liberals and Islamists, now all clearly a part of the political equation, are not the only sources of political pressure in Morocco. Other issues include future of the Saharan provinces (several people were killed in 2010 during clashes between protesters and security forces near the Western Saharan capital of Laâyoune), and relations with the EU, the other North African states and international lenders. Businesses, farmers, a vocal middle class and unemployed graduates, Amazigh communities and shanty-town dwellers all have their agenda. The Moroccan print media constantly monitors how far the government is managing to satisfy such disparate groups' expectations.

Demands and expectations

The *Confédération générale des entreprises marocaines* (CGEM), the Moroccan employers' organization, wants corruption tackled head on and a reform of the civil service, which it sees as slow and inefficient. The liberal middle classes want radical Islam kept in check. Unemployed graduates, including many with post-graduate qualifications, want jobs suited to their qualifications – and demonstrate vigorously for this. The farming community, including modern, mechanized agro-business, wants to preserve its subsidies. The Amazigh agenda is mainly cultural. Based in the North, the High Atlas and the Souss, Amazigh activists, the so-called Berberistes, want wider recognition of their language in the education system and public life. The most pressing issue is poverty, however. The shanty-town dwellers and the rural poor want access to education, health care and decent housing. But in essence, it is only by reducing the terrible deprivation to which a high percentage of the population is condemned that the country can hope to avoid political instability fuelled by fundamentalist influence.

Islamist pressures

The question of Islamic revivalist movements (*les Islamistes*) is a complex one. The King of Morocco, as a descendant of the Prophet Mohammed and Commander of the Faithful, undoubtedly occupies the religious high ground. Religious legitimacy has always formed an important part of the monarchy's power base. In Morocco, the *ulema* (experts on religious matters) have maintained their influence: their councils authorize new mosque building; religious studies graduates are trained at the Kénitra School to take up jobs in the Ministry of the Interior. Under Hassan II, the monarchy's religious profile was maintained by projects such as the Great Mosque at Casablanca (cost over 4 billion dirhams). While maintaining the public face of an Islamic monarch, Mohammed VI is much more concerned with the practical aspects of reducing poverty – hence his nickname, *le roi des pauvres*. The symbolic dimension is maintained, however. In 2006, the ceremonies surrounding the circumcision of Crown Prince Hassan took place in Fès, the country's religious capital.

There are four main strands to the Islamist movements of Morocco. Originally of Pakistani inspiration, the Tabligh wa Da'oua type of Islamist is an ascetic, taking the true faith to rural markets and shanty towns. Tablighis may move on to join the more urban Adl wal Ihsane, whose main figure, Abdallah Yassine, is more a writer producing 'intellectual propaganda' than a charismatic figure. El Adl is active in poor areas, assisting families in difficulty. In parliament, the PJD is a force arguing for a more 'moral' type of government. Both El Adl and the PJD have been effective in organizing mass demonstrations in Casablanca. Finally, there is a shadowy, purist brand of Islamism out there, the Salafiya-Jihadiya movement. Until May 2003, the Salafists had avoided large-scale terrorist violence of the kind which proved so counter-productive in Algeria. Close links with Al Qaeda are unproven, and there does not appear to be a centralized national command structure. Nevertheless, extremist groups frequently reach the headlines on account of cruel and sometimes violent incidents involving the 'punishment' of individuals who fail to live up to their exacting standards of what it means to be a 'true' Muslim. Managing the Islamist movements will be a delicate task for Morocco's governments. A pious people, the Moroccans have a strong sense of the injustice of the current Middle Eastern political order. The American occupation of Iraq exacerbated this feeling of injustice.

The Saharan provinces

After independence from France and Spain in 1956, a number of pieces of Moroccan territory remained under Spanish rule: some enclaves in the north, notably Ceuta and Melilla (Spanish since the 15th century), Sidi Ifni (retaken by Morocco in 1969), and Río de Oro, a large chunk of Saharan territory fronting onto the Atlantic. In 1974, as General Franco ailed in Madrid, the Moroccans launched their claims to the Spanish Sahara once more. On Franco's death in 1975, Morocco and Mauritania moved into the Sahara and, in November 1975, the Green March (Al Massira Al Khadhra) took place, with 350,000 Moroccans marching southwards into the former Spanish colony. Underlying the issue was the question of resources – the Atlantic waters off the Saharan provinces are excellent fishing grounds and there are phosphates. There was also the additional fear that neighbouring Algeria might possibly sponsor a dummy Socialist republic.

In the event, Algeria was to provide a rear base for the Polisario, an armed liberation group fighting for an independent 'Saharan' state. However, by 1987, the Moroccan army had completed seven earth ramparts to protect the Saharan provinces from armed incursion from across the frontier. In 1988, Algeria began to change its line on the Sahara issue. (In 1984, Libya had withdrawn financial help to the Polisario and, as of 1986, petrol revenues began to fall.) The Islamists had begun to appear as a major threat to the powers in Algiers. In February 1989, the Union du Maghreb Arabe treaty was signed at Marrakech, with North African leaders clearly agreed on the need to focus on the Islamist menace. Morocco continued to invest heavily in the Sahara, developing Laâyoune and other towns. The Polisario ran out of steam and Morocco agreed to a UN-sponsored referendum, originally to be held in 1992, on the future of the provinces.

The urgency of any referendum disappeared in the 1990s as Algeria grappled with its civil war. Agreement has never been reached on who should actually be allowed to vote in a Sahara referendum – or indeed on the object of the referendum. With the vast growth of Laâyoune through migration from the north, the original Sahraoui component of the population is in a minority. Although the USA would like to see a referendum-based 'settlement', the provinces seem set to remain part of Morocco.

Union du Maghreb Arabe (UMA)

A United Arab Maghreb, free of outside domination, was a dream back in colonial days. In February 1947 the Committee for the Liberation of the Maghreb was set up. Just over 40 years later, a united Maghreb seemed to be on the way to becoming reality. At Marrakech, the leaders of the five states, King Hassan II of Morocco, President Chedli Bendjedid of Algeria, President Ben Ali of Tunisia, Colonel Muammar Gaddafi of Libya and President Ould Sidi Ahmad Al Taya of Mauritania, signed the founding act of the Union du Maghreb Arabe, whose acronym, UMA, recalls the Arabic word *umma* (community). The new union was to be presided over by each nation in turn for six-month periods.

Very quickly, however, the UMA faced problems. With Bendjedid removed from power in Algeria, there was a cooling of Algero-Moroccan relations. Libya proved to be a difficult member of the team, and neither Morocco nor Tunisia were keen on weather-vane diplomacy à la Gaddafi. The security situation deteriorated rapidly in Algeria, with guerrilla warfare and appalling massacres in certain regions. Thousands of Algerians began looking to emigrate. In 1994, after a terrorist attack on a Marrakech hotel, Morocco sought to limit any risk of Islamic fundamentalist contagion and introduced a visa for Algerians – thereby depriving itself of over a million foreign visitors each year. Algeria replied by closing the frontier. In response, Morocco put its activities in the UMA on hold.

The events of December 2010 in Tunisia and the beginning of the Arab Spring, followed by the civil war in Libya and overthrow of Gaddafi, have put any hopes for the future of UMA further into cold storage. However, if it is to succeed, any relaunch of the UMA will have to be based on the settlement of Algero-Moroccan differences over the latter's Saharan provinces. Broadly speaking for Morocco, commercial relations with the European Union are more crucial than a perilous project for North African political unity. And Algeria continues to export large quantities of natural gas to Europe via Morocco.

Morocco and the European Union

As of the late 1980s, Morocco opted to intensify its ties with Europe and, in 1987, the country requested membership of the EEC, perhaps more as a symbolic gesture than anything else. Although relations have soured with Spain on occasion over the question of fishing rights and illegal migration, Europe and Morocco have too much in common for the two sides not to work together. Algerian gas transits over Moroccan territory on its way to the Iberian peninsula, and European companies – notably French and Spanish ones – are always on the starting blocks for major public works contracts in Morocco. Morocco's credentials as a stable country, close to Europe, with a certain democratic openness, will doubtless continue to make it favourable terrain for business relocation.

Early 2000s: technocratic pragmatism

In the early 2000s, finance was a difficult issue. The IMF recommended a devaluation of the dirham, while Morocco wanted help servicing its debt. For the moment, widening the tax base does not seem to be a viable option, and the government has raised money through privatizations to finance its social programmes. The Jettou government found itself with a tightrope to tread: foreign investors had to be reassured that the liberalist rigour imposed by the IMF and the EU would be respected, while the local constituency needed jobs and social services. With foreign debt repayments absorbing up to a third of the budget, there is little room for manoeuvre for any government, whatever its political colour.

Despite the financial constraints, predictions of serious social unrest and the morose international climate, the prospects for Morocco in the early 2000s were by no means black. Tourism and remittances from Moroccans abroad were growing. The poverty of the shanty towns of Casablanca was not as harsh as it had been in the 1960s, and there were numerous social housing projects underway. It's hard not to notice the huge amount of new building in Morocco. The Arab Spring seems to have given fresh impetus to this building boom, partly because of a widespread belief that bureaucratic processes and regulations will be relaxed.

In the final analysis, a new version of the old national pact seems to be being worked out. It could be that a form of social democracy, possibly with PJD 'Muslim democrat' participation, will facilitate the move towards a more limited role for the monarchy. Europe is seen as the principal foreign partner in this venture – and the Moroccans feel that help and understanding should be forthcoming from the economic giant to the north.

Future directions

In the late 1990s institutions were being modernized, industry upgraded, the civil service reformed. Human rights were openly discussed, a critical press emerged and flourished. After periods of political repression, Moroccans were proud of the changes taking place. Much is still to be done, however. Though parliamentary elections are free, open and multi-party, there are abuses. Though factories are getting their ISO 9000 certification, workers' salaries are rock bottom. Though there is a growing freedom of expression and civil liberties are respected, there are appalling and surprising exceptions. Moroccan society is in a period of change – and it can be difficult for Moroccans to explain to outsiders the factors, historical and social, which have led the country to where it is today.

The urban/rural divide

Morocco's population is moving towards a two-thirds/one-third urban/rural divide. The land no longer provides the living it used to, expectations are higher, parents want their children to have some chance of an education and this is most easily available in the towns. In the country, life is often hard, with women obliged to carry water, firewood and animal fodder over long distances. But getting by is not easy either in the *bidonvilles* (shanty towns) around Morocco's cities. When it rains, the streets fill with water. Urban life, however, offers more opportunities. There are plenty of people with money to buy from a street stall selling cigarettes and biscuits, chewing-gum and fruit; there is occasional work on building sites and in factories. There are also chances of better housing, as government projects 'restructure' the *bidonvilles*, bringing in water and electricity.

For the middle classes, opportunities have improved considerably, even though recruitment into government service has been cut back. There are, however, jobs in multinational companies, the banking sector and the new service economy. Compared with other Arab countries, there is a freedom in Morocco's cities. The streets, though increasingly traffic ridden, are pleasant; there are cafés, bookshops and cinemas. For those with salaries, there are car and home loans. Domestic help is available for two-career families, and there is a wide range of consumer goods. For the bright and energetic, the prospects are good – although family connections do help.

Outside the cities, life is improving, too. Mobile phones are making life easier, and electricity is arriving in isolated mountain valleys. The ONEP has undertaken major infrastructure projects to improve drinking water provision. The ERACs (social housing authorities) are active in all major cities, putting up huge social housing schemes. Even in quite out-of-the-way places, much new building is in evidence, an indication that there is money in circulation and that there is a lot of work for unskilled and semi-skilled male labour. Though the official economic figures are often disappointing, Morocco's informal sector is undoubtedly extremely dynamic.

The Moroccan countryside is likely to see further depopulation. The countryside has changed hugely. In the 1960s, the *caïds* ran affairs, with quasi-feudal authority over sharecroppers, shepherds and harvesters. By the 1990s, the *caïds'* descendants had become entrepreneurs, running mechanized farms. Seasonal workers had to get by on tiny smallholdings, or perhaps travel to cities to work as unskilled labour. Private landowners are doing well, especially in irrigated areas. However, it is increasingly difficult for the poorer parts of the countryside – most notably the Rif – to export its surplus labour to Europe.

Economy and development

In terms of the economy, Morocco has been heading in the right direction, despite the global recession. The adventurous financial policies of the 1970s are a thing of the past, though the budget deficit has increased to 5.6% of GDP in 2011 from 4.5% in 2010. (It had been at 12-14% in 1982.) Growth was down from 5.5% in 2007 to 4.2% in 2010, and though the new goverment has forecast a return to pre-2008 levels of around 5%, the country faces major difficulties: for sale of agricultural products, Morocco has stiff competition from Spain and Portugal; there are still large numbers of graduates coming onto the job market for whom there is no employment; and, in 1998, Morocco only came 125th out of 179 countries in the UNDP human development index, a fair way behind neighbours, Algeria and Tunisia.

Morocco culture and customs

What makes Morocco so different from, say, Spain? In the travel brochures, it is a land peopled by men in flowing robes, its cities full of winding streets, garden courtyards and banquets. It is an Islamic country – but the women (who do not feature in the brochures) are not, on the whole, veiled. Standing back from the bright postcards and garden courtyards, the Arab-Amazigh dichotomy, the clichés about tolerance and eternal Moroccan civilization, what sort of a culture is this? What are its main architectural and material features? And, first of all, who are the Moroccans?

Moroccan people

The population of Morocco was estimated in 2011 at 32 million. Although the crude birth rate has fallen sharply in recent years to 28 per 1000 of population, potential fertility is high. Better medical facilities and mass vaccination campaigns since the mid-1990s have improved the child-survival rate. At the same time, death rates are also down to five per 1000 and life expectancy, now 71.5 years on average, will no doubt improve to swell the total population. The population is fairly young on average. Around 28% are under 14; only 6% are over 65.

Population distribution
Half the population now lives in cities, the great concentrations being in Casablanca (3.2 million), Rabat-Salé (1.8 million), Fès (1 million) and Marrakech (909,000) and Meknès (985,000). Areas of heavily settled land with 60 to 95 people per sq km are found round the Mediterranean (Tangier's population is 768,000) and northern Atlantic coastal areas, notably in the Rif, Jebala, the Gharb plain and the southern Souss valley. Densities fall off rapidly as you go inland. Other than the great cities of Marrakech, Meknès and Fès, the inland regions have low population densities, averaging between 20 to 60 per sq km. The arid southern and eastern regions are sparsely settled with less than 20 people per sq km.

The typical Moroccan
The population of contemporary Morocco is the result of a long history, during which various settlers came to the country. The earliest populations of northwestern Africa, the ancestors of today's Imazighen (Berbers) were probably of Hamitic stock (ie descendants of Biblical Ham, brother of Shem and Japeth). Since the arrival of the Imazighen, there have been numerous other inputs, including Phoenicians and Romans and, in particular, the Arabs, who first occupied the region in the eighth century AD. Until the mid-20th century, there was an important Jewish community, originally part of the rural Amazigh population. After the 15th-century *Reconquista*, Iberian Jews settled in Morocco. However, the vast majority of Jews left Morocco in the two decades following the establishment of the State of Israel in 1948. Many of the rest headed for France and Canada. As of the late 18th century, a European population of mainly French and Spanish origin settled in the coastal towns and was particularly numerous in the mid-20th century. There is also a sub-Saharan African ethnic component to Morocco's population, originally the result of the slave trade and the preference of 17th-century ruler Moulay Ismaïl for an all-black royal guard.

There are, therefore, certain noticeable regional physical differences. The inhabitants of cities like Fès, Meknès and Rabat tend to be pale-skinned and slightly built, and have a distinctly Iberian look. There are certain faces that, to the insider, look very Fassi, and others that are distinctly Amazigh. The older generation of Moroccans, particularly the mountain people, are shorter than their European counterparts. Lifestyle for the urban middle classes differs little from that of southern Europeans. The rural regions, however, are vastly different, and there are still areas without electricity and other basic infrastructure, and in these regions life expectancy is lower.

Language and education

Morocco not only has an ethnic mix, it is also a multilingual country. Arabic is the national language. However, the written form, called *fusha* or literary Arabic, is very different from *darija*, the Moroccan Arabic of everyday life. A significant proportion of Morocco's population, around 40%, has an Amazigh (Berber) language as their mother tongue. School textbooks are in a version of the Arabic of the Koran; the grammar is similar to that of the great Arabic literary texts, while the vocabulary has been expanded constantly since the 19th century. This means that children with an Amazigh (Berber) language as their mother tongue are faced with a foreign language at school. Children with Moroccan Arabic as a mother tongue have to learn a new range of verb and adjectival forms, rather like an English-speaking child having to learn to use Old English verbs with modern English vocabulary. This is basically manageable, although given translation problems, there is a severe shortage of reading material in Arabic.

A further problem comes at university. All subjects are in French, bar family and criminal law, Arabic literature and some of the humanities. Hence, parents with means put their children into bilingual primary schools with greater resources and more modern teaching methods. At secondary school level, the children with a bilingual background have much better chances of passing the baccalauréat. And, after secondary school, private institutes providing training in secretarial skills, IT, management and accounting function exclusively in French.

The school system is criticized for perpetuating Morocco's social divide, the gap between the bilingual middle classes, with their access to knowledge and wealth production, and the illiterate masses, using spoken Arabic and/or Berber in daily life. Moroccans are a linguistically mobile lot, however, and used to the idea of learning languages. In the coastal cities, a lot of people have some French or, particularly in the north, Spanish.

A development of the 21st century is the expanded public presence of the Amazigh languages. There are three of these in Morocco: Ta'rifit spoken in the Rif mountains of the north; Tamazight, spoken in the Middle Atlas and finally, Tachelhit, the language of the High Atlas and the Souss Valley. While Tachelhit and Tamazight are fairly mutually comprehensible, Ta'rifit is very different. All have a rich heritage of oral literature, now transmitted on film and by a new wave of popular music. And, since 2004, Amazigh languages feature in the primary school curriculum.

Cultural focus

Moroccans differ greatly from north Europeans in the way their lives are focused. The family is of primary importance and determines a person's life chances to a great degree. Family loyalty is of great importance, with the father seemingly the dominant figure – although, very often, wives rule the roost. Islam is a strong force, laying down the limits of what can and cannot be done. Also important to Moroccan culture is the notion of *qa'ada* (tradition). The home is a private place – but strangers, when a friendship forms, are readily invited in. On the whole, however, men meet their friends in cafés, while women socialize in each others' homes.

A changing society

As society changes, Moroccan cultural attitudes are changing too. Though not yet a nation of city-dwellers, Morocco's urban population is now over 50%. Morocco's old families and the brightest and best-connected of the university-educated elite have done very well for themselves since Independence from France in 1956. (Some would say too well, arguing that the Moroccan upper-middle class behaves in a colonial fashion in its own country.) The second-generation urban populations have new aspirations, however, and expect some part of the national cake. And, with urbanization and growing affluence come changes. Women work, gain economic power and become ready to stand up to macho tradition. However, since the late 1990s, purist brands of Muslim religious practice, which often imply considerable bigotry, have extended their influence. In short, Moroccan society is subject to considerable stresses and tensions.

Architecture

Morocco has a wealth of characteristic buildings and craft forms. Though in certain areas traditional architecture is giving way to less aesthetic building forms, there is much of architectural interest.

Prehistory

The earliest traces of human settlement in Morocco go back to 800,000 BC. Towards 5000 BC, new nomadic pastoralist groups, probably the ancestors of today's Berbers, are thought to have arrived. Morocco has numerous rock carvings left behind by these nomads. Concentrations of prehistoric art can be found in the High Atlas (Yagour Plateau, and at Oukaïmeden) and in the Anti-Atlas, near Tafraoute, as well as in the oases of Akka and Foum Hassan. A stone circle survives at Mzoura, southeast of Asilah near Souk Tnine de Sidi el Yamami, in northwestern Morocco. The Archeological Museum in Rabat has the finest collection of objects from ancient times, see page 285.

Roman times

When Rome was founded in 753 BC, the coast of Morocco was on the trade routes of Phoenician merchants. Inland areas were inhabited by a people called the Maures by the Romans – hence the name Mauretania for the Roman province covering part of what is now Morocco. No doubt the land was divided into Berber Kingdoms. From 25 BC to AD 23, Juba II ruled Mauretania from Volubilis, today Morocco's best-preserved Roman site, close to Meknès. Some of the finest Hellenistic and Roman bronzes extant from this site can be seen today at the Archaeological Museum (see page 285), along with pottery and other objects from Roman times. Other visitable Roman sites, all in northwestern Morocco, include Thamusida (near Kénitra), Banasa (near Souk el Arba du Gharb) and Lixus (near Larache).

Buildings of Islam

In 682, the Arab general Uqba Ibn Nafi and his army crossed the Maghreb, bringing with them a new revealed religion, Islam. This religion was to engender new architectural forms, shaped by the requirements of prayer and the Muslim urban lifestyle. The key building of Islam is, of course, the mosque, which evolved considerably from its humble beginnings as a sort of enclosure with an adjoining low platform from which the call to prayer could be made. Mosques became spectacular buildings demonstrating the power

Inside the mosque

In all Muslim countries, mosques are built orientated towards Mecca, as the believers must pray in the direction of

Kasbah Mosque

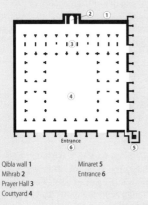

Qibla wall **1**
Mihrab **2**
Prayer Hall **3**
Courtyard **4**

Minaret **5**
Entrance **6**

their holy city. In Morocco's case, this means that the orientation is east-south-east. A large mosque has four main areas: prayer halls, courtyard and colonnade, minaret and, in all likelihood, attached ablutions facility and hammam. Most mosques will have: the **qibla wall** (1), facing east-southeast, with a decorated niche or **mihrab** (2) in the middle, towards which the believers pray; a colonnaded **prayer hall** (3) and a large **courtyard** (4), often with a fountain; a **minaret** or *midhana* (5) from which the call to prayer is made five times a day; an **entrance** (6), through which the non-Muslim visitor may glimpse the courtyard if there is no wooden lattice-work screen.

On Fridays, there will often be so many people for the weekly midday prayers and accompanying sermon that latecomers, equipped with their rugs, will have to pray outside in the street.

of ruling dynasties, centring on colonnaded prayer halls and vast courtyards. Originally inspired by the church towers of Syria, elegant minarets gave beauty to the skylines of the great Muslim cities.

Mosques cannot generally be visited in Morocco by the non-Muslim visitor, with some notable exceptions, including the Grand Mosque Hassan II in Casablanca, the ruined mosque of the Chellah necropolis in Rabat and the restored Almohad mosque at Tin Mal in the High Atlas. Minarets, visible from afar, are not always easy to photograph close up, being surrounded by narrow streets and densely built-up areas.

Minarets As an essential feature of the mosque, the minaret probably developed in the late seventh century. Islam had adopted a call to prayer or *idhan* rather than bells to summon the faithful. (Bilal, an Abyssinian slave, was the first muezzin.) Moroccan minarets are generally a simple square tower, with a small 'lantern' feature on the top, from which the muezzin makes the call to prayer. Older minarets tend to have blind horseshoe arches and a small dome on the topmost 'lantern' room. On top of the dome is an ornamental feature resembling three metal spheres on a pole, topped by a crescent. This is the *jammour*, and tourist guides have a number of entertaining explanations for this, for example, that the spheres represent the basic ingredients of bread (flour, water and salt). There are unusual exceptions to the square minaret, however, including the octagonal minaret of the Kasbah Mosque in Tangier. The great Almohad mosques – the Grand Mosque at Taza, Koutoubia at Marrakech and the partially completed Tour Hassan in Rabat – are characterized by an interlinked lozenge pattern, executed in stone on their façades. One school of art history sees the proportions, arcades and decorative motifs of these buildings as setting a stylistic trend that was reproduced and eventually transformed in European Gothic architecture.

Layout and decoration Mosques tend to have large covered prayer halls, comprising a series of narrow transepts, created by lines of arches supporting pitched roofs, generally covered with green tiles. There will be a main 'aisle' leading towards the mihrab (prayer niche), which indicates the direction of Mecca for prayer. The main nave in the traditional Moroccan mosque does not, however, have the same dimensions as the main nave of a Christian cathedral. Islam also does not favour representation of the human form, hence the use of highly elaborate geometric decorative motifs executed in ceramic *zellige* (mosaic) and on wood and plaster. There is no religious pictorial art. The same geometric motifs can be found in domestic architecture, too. A mosque will also have an open courtyard, sometimes with a decorative fountain. Although all the usual decorative techniques can be seen, the 1990s Grande Mosquée Hassan II is an exception in layout, having just one major aisle, flanked by two narrower secondary naves.

Schools of religious science The non-Muslim visitor can get a very good idea of Muslim sacred architecture by visiting one of the *medersas*, the colleges which were an essential part of the Moroccan Muslim education system from medieval times onward. One of the largest is the Medersa Ben Youssef in Marrakech, a 14th-century foundation entirely rebuilt in the 16th century. Like all *medersas*, it is essentially a hollowed-out cube, the blockiness of the architecture being relieved by mesemerizingly decorative detail on every flat surface: ceramic mosaic, and densely carved stucco and cedar wood. The austere students' rooms come as something of a shock after the elaborate decoration of the courtyard. Other *medersas* can be seen in Salé, Meknès and Fès.

Medinas

Visitors to Morocco quickly have to learn to navigate through the narrow streets of the medina or old towns. In much 19th-century European writing, the medina of the Maghreb – and of the Arab world in general – were seen as chaotic places, which although harbouring exotically clothed populations, were also home to disease and ignorance. The medina was taken as a metaphor for the backwardness of the *indigène* or native. In fact, the tangled streets of the average Moroccan medina are no more disorganized than many a European medieval town. Today's visitor will immediately be struck by the external ramparts in *pisé* (sundried clay, gravel and lime mix). Disorientation due to narrow alleys and high walls sets in later, perhaps after leaving the main souks.

Logic of the medina The medinas of Morocco do, however, obey a logic, satisfying architectural requirements arising from climatic and religious factors. The climate is hot in summer, but often very cold in winter. In the coastal towns, damp ocean mists roll in, while, inland, there are hot summer winds from the south. The city therefore has to provide protection from this climate, and networks of narrow streets are the ideal solution. Streets could be narrow as there was no wheeled transport, there being plenty of pack animals for carrying goods around. And narrow streets also ensured that precious building land within the city walls was not wasted.

For housing the Muslim family, the courtyard house was the ideal solution. This, of course, is an architectural model that goes back to Mesopotamia, Greece and Rome. For Islamic family life, with its insistence on gender separation in the public domain, the courtyard house provides a high level of family privacy. In densely built-up cities, the roof terraces also provided a place for women to perform household tasks – and to share news and gossip. The biggest houses would have several patios, the main one having arcades on two levels. Thus extended families could be accommodated in dwellings with large open areas. Old Moroccan courtyard homes are generally not easily visited, except in Marrakech and Fès, where there are houses that have been restored and altered to function as upmarket restaurants and riads. In Marrakech you can also discover a superb concentration of Moroccan craftwork in a lovingly restored patrician house, the Maison Tiskiwine, close to the Bahia Palace (see page 61). If you are invited into an ordinary home, however, you may see fridges and pressure cookers used alongside traditional *braseros* in the main courtyard.

Earthen architectures

The courtyard home is the most characteristic building in Morocco's cities, discreet and anonymous to all but a neighbourhood's inhabitants from the outside, spectacularly decorated in its patrician form on the inside. There are other, more rustic, building traditions in use, however, the best known being the kasbahs and *ksars* of the areas south of the High Atlas, in the valleys of the Dadès, the Draâ and the Ziz. Much of this traditional building in the south is in compacted earth and gravel.

Kasbahs The word kasbah probably derives from the Turkish *kasabe*, meaning small town. In contemporary North Africa, it is generally used to refer to the fortified strong point in a city. Morocco also has numerous kasbahs scattered across its territory, many erected by energetic 17th-century builder-ruler Moulay Ismaïl. (See, for example, the kasbah at Boulaouane, near Settat, and the derelict Kasbah Tadla, near Beni Mellal.) In the southern reaches of Morocco, the term kasbah is used to denote often vast fortified villages, with spectacular tower houses often several storeys high. Good examples can be found near Ouarzazate, at Aït Ben Haddou (as used in part of Orson Welles' *Sodom and Gomorrah*) and up in the High Atlas at Telouet, where a vast crumbling kasbah testifies to the power of T'hami el Glaoui, ruler of Marrakech in the early part of the 20th century. There are a fair number of Glaoui kasbahs scattered across the southern valleys, and they tend to have decorative features of more urban inspiration than the kasbahs of the old Berber communities. There are good examples at Tamnougalt, south of Agdz in the Draâ Valley, and in the Skoura oasis (the Kasbah Amerhidl), Dadès Valley.

Ksars *Ksar* country is really the Ziz Valley (main towns Er Rachidia and Erfoud). *Ksars* sit surrounded by palm groves and walled market gardens. They house the families of the oasis dwellers and, like the kasbahs, are defensive structures. Their smooth high walls, fortified with corner towers, and narrow windows enabled the inhabitants to protect their harvests. Back west again, in the mountains, the *tighremt* or *agadir*, the fortified grain store, held the same function. The ground floor was used for the animals, the first floor as a food store and the top floor for family living space. For fine *agadirs*, see Amtoudi in the Anti-Atlas.

Spectacular though they often are, the kasbahs and *ksars* are under threat. This form of earth building is vulnerable to the weather and, despite its excellent qualities in terms of temperature regulation, it needs maintenance. Reinforced concrete building, perceived as 'modern', is now popular. However, in the southern regions, there is a new wave of mock kasbah architecture. The crenellations, window slits and tapering towers of the ancient earthen buildings can be found on official buildings, hotels and electricity sub-stations.

The tourist industry may yet fuel some sort of return to traditional – and more ecological – building types. Kasbahs are being recycled as hotels at Skoura, Tineghir and Nkob.

Fortified ports

On the coasts of Morocco is another form of defensive architecture, the military port of early modern European inspiration. During the 15th century, both the Atlantic and the Mediterranean coastlines were targets for the expanding Iberian powers. Ports such as Agadir, Safi, Asilah and Tangier were occupied, all the better to control the lucrative trade routes to Asia and the Americas. In the early 16th century, Portugal was still at the height of its glory as an imperial power, and elaborate fortifications were erected at Azemmour, Mazagan (today's El Jadida), Safi, Mogador (today's Essaouira) and Agadir, each equipped with monumental gateways, cannons, watchtowers and round bastions.

Citadel of El Jadida   The most spectacular example of this military architecture is the Citadel of El Jadida, held by the Portuguese until 1769. The citadel was built in 1516 on the model of the most advanced Italian military building technology of the day. Five arrow-shaped bastions jut into the ocean, to pre-empt attack from all possible angles. The thick walls would have necessitated enormous firepower to reduce them – a firepower beyond the reach of Moroccan rulers until the 18th century. The citadel as seen today was rebuilt at the beginning of the 19th century. The same ruler who took El Jadida in 1769, Sidi Mohammed Ben Abdallah, understood the importance of European military architecture. In 1764, he employed a French engineer, one Théodore Cornut, to lay out the new fortifications at Essaouira. This was to be the first example of modern urban planning on Moroccan soil.

Modern cities

The contemporary Moroccan city is very much an early 20th-century achievement, the work of two far-sighted people, Hubert Lyautey and urban planner Henri Prost. France's first resident general in Morocco had been much impressed by Prost's plans for the redesign of Antwerp in Belgium and was willing to give such schemes a chance in the new French protectorate. Prost's Antwerp plan included features that seemed particularly adaptable to the Moroccan context. Old walls were not demolished and reused as development land, but were kept as part of a buffer zone between old and new. The new areas had large open spaces planted with regular rows of trees, while a system of avenues within the city enhanced existing monumental buildings and linked into a system of highways leading in and out of the city. The crucial point on which Prost focused was the preservation of the aesthetic face of the city, without totally cutting it off from new forms of transport and infrastructure.

Prost, like Lyautey, was all for technological innovation. However, this position was balanced with a strong dose of social conservatism: existing hierarchies were to be kept. In Morocco, 'respect for difference' was the justification for the strict zoning between old and new quarters, rich and poor.

In Morocco, Lyautey and his experts found themselves in an enviable position. They were able to appropriate land, levy taxes and develop a land-use policy with a freedom unthinkable in France. As they drew up plans for the *villes nouvelles*, their task was made all the easier by the fact that the watchwords of the French republic – liberty, equality and fraternity – were not applied in Morocco. Equality was out of the question. Although some lip-service was paid to fraternity, liberty to participate in decisions on the country's future was reserved for the technocratic elite around the Residency General – after a show of consultation with the sultan.

Uses of urbanism

Lyautey in Morocco wanted to apply the modern principles of 'the science of urbanism', and attempted to attract as many new architects as possible. With Algeria as the negative example of how the French had behaved abroad, Lyautey set out to promote a new system, the theatre of which would be the city. The crises of French and Algerian cities were to be avoided and the new urbanism was to be the showcase for the benefits of French rule. As Lyautey is reputed to have said in a famous dictum, 'a construction site means I can avoid using a battalion.'

The Moroccan notables in many cases wanted cleaner neighbourhoods with modern infrastructure, but separate from the new, impure Christian population. (Spatial segregation by religion had been a feature in many of the older Moroccan towns.) However, the new European neighbourhoods were built close enough for there to be social contact. Where British colonialism had been based essentially on a structure of police intelligence, the French *villes nouvelles* of Morocco were to allow social meeting – or so the theory went. The urban planners faced a problem of how to integrate these social requirements into development plans: the Meknès plan, in particular, was criticized for the distance between the two communities. Speculation and building styles were to be strictly controlled, while new rail systems were planned and embedded into the city's structure.

Another French creation was the Fine Arts Department to ensure the protection of the main historic monuments. Sites for protection were selected, and the ground was prepared for tourism and a new historic awareness. Both Lyautey and Prost detested the kitsch of modern Algerian neo-Moorish architecture and the banality of French suburban building. New construction was thus to follow principles valued by Lyautey and Prost, essentially simplicity of form and a high degree of functionality. Public buildings were to have simple lines, taking on the contours of traditional Arab building. Craft techniques were used for detailing, giving a 'Moroccan style' to otherwise modern buildings. Geometric public spaces made great use of fountains and vegetation.

The Prost plans laid the basis for the development of Morocco's cities for the 20th century, creating spacious urban centres which are still agreeable today, despite vehicle pollution. Most importantly, a tradition of planning and architectural innovation, along with respect for architectural heritage, was established. New official building across Morocco incorporates features of traditional architecture – green-tiled roofs, stone detailing, mosaic work – in a style referred to as Neo-Makhzen. Other building is often symbolically ambitious – take, for example, the Twin Center in Casablanca, designed by Catalan architect Bofill.

Arts and crafts

Contemporary painting

Morocco has proved a considerable bed of talent, perhaps surprisingly for a country that had no tradition of representing human and animal form. Painting soon took root after the arrival of the French protectorate. (A stay in Morocco had already been a popular source of inspiration for numerous European painters, for whom the kingdom was all exotic street scenes, cavalcades in movement, and sharp, often violent colour contrast.) European artists settled in Morocco, among them Jacques Majorelle, best known for his scenes of the High Atlas, Edouard Edy-Legrand and Marianne Bertuchi. In the 1940s, self-taught Moroccan painters emerged, sometimes directly imitating European styles – others, such as Moulay Ahmed Drissi, illustrating the rich heritage of oral literature.

Pottery and belief

Until perhaps the 1960s, old-fashioned heavy pottery plates and dishes were in general use in Fassi homes. A study on Fassi ceramics quotes an elderly housewife recounting how her father, back in the 1930s, was insistent on eating from Fassi pottery. Said the patriarch, member of a Soufi group: "I want to eat from *fakhar* (traditionally made) dishes, made from the *trab* (clay) of Morocco, because such plates and vessels have been made with a prayer, in accordance with religion. Any foreign vessel is *haram* (sinful)."

For great family occasions, the poorer families would rent large dishes called *tabaq* or *mtirda*. The great families did not use *mokhfia* dishes, but other shapes and forms. Today, these traditional forms are often recycled in less hard-wearing pottery for the tourist market, often decorated with metal or bone insets.

Pottery also accompanied the Muslim in the cemetery. A *ghorraf* or *zlafa* of water was left on top of tombs, the idea being that birds would come to drink and sing to the dead. Maybe some believed the birds to be God's messengers – and it was seen as a very worthy charitable action to leave them water to drink. Pigeons and doves were particularly appreciated, nicknamed *deker Allah*, as their cooing was said to sound like the words for 'remember Allah'.

But old-style pottery was also delicate. Oil and butter penetrated the surface, rendering the glaze fragile. Large plates were expensive, and would be repaired, sometimes with metal patches or occasionally staples. Sometimes a small piece of pot was cemented in to replace a missing piece. This attachment to pottery shows the material value of tableware in times gone by. But it also indicates a sentimental, maybe even religious value. After all, the members of a family would have sat round a large communal dish to eat together hundreds of times, saying the words *bismillah*, 'in the name of God', at the start of each meal. The *hadith*, or saying of the Prophet, runs that anything you do starting with the *bismillah* will go well.

After independence in 1956, a generation of Moroccan painters came to the fore, working in varied registers – abstract, naïve, calligraphic. Some had training at the fine arts schools set up in Tetouan in 1945 and Casablanca in 1950. Major abstract painters of this era include Ahmed Cherkaoui, Jilali Gharbaoui, Saâd Hassani, Mohammed Kacimi and Fouad Belamine. Mehdi Qotbi produces vast expanses of calligraphic signs, while Farid Belkahia works with wood, animal skins and natural pigments to produce objects and canvasses, using ancestral symbols and archetypes.

Naïve painting has an important place in the Moroccan art scene. The Galerie Frédéric Damgaard in Essaouira has enabled many local artists to exhibit and live from their work, and an 'Essaouira school' of painting has emerged, filled with movement and joyful figures. Leading figures include Abdallah el Atrach and Rashid Amerhouch. Of Morocco's self-taught naïve painters, the best known is Chaïbia, creator of raw and colourful scenes of daily life.

Urban and rural crafts

Morocco has long had a reputation as a country with a vivid and imaginative craft industry. Collections of traditional arts and crafts from recent centuries are held at the Musée Dar Saïd in Marrakech, the Musée Dar Jamaï in Meknès and the Dar Batha in Fès. The souks of the historic cities are full of vivid pottery and carpets, the delicate tracery of wrought iron, polished thuya wood and beautifully worked leather. The traditional arts divide into two categories, rural and urban. Urban crafts are generally taken to be more refined, displaying an Andalucían influence. Rural crafts, generally from the Berber-speaking regions, have provided a rich source of inspiration for contemporary designers.

But rural and urban crafts are in many ways very different. Rural craft items – carpets and woven items, such as saddle bags and tent strips, pottery, jewellery – were, and still are to a great extent, produced in very different conditions to urban items. Rural craftwork is solid, practical, made to stand up to long years of use under a harsh climate. Carpets and pottery are made by women, jewellery and metal utensils by men. The signs and symbols used to decorate these items are generally geometric, arranged in simple, repetitive combinations to pleasing effect. Lines, dots and dashes, lozenges and squares are combined to cover surfaces made from clay, metal and wool. Sometimes these decorative forms are linked to the tribal marks tattooed on women's faces and arms. The isolation of rural communities meant that people of different areas could develop very individual styles of craftwork. This is apparent in weaving, clothing and women's accessories. But, given the fact that craft-made items were in heavy use, few pieces can be safely said to be more than a hundred years old.

Striking colour and form are often features of rural crafts. Made from thick wool, the carpets of the Middle Atlas, used both as mattresses and blankets, may have striking red and deep brown backgrounds. Carpets from the Haouz Plain (Marrakech region) also have strong orange-red backgrounds. Jewellery in southern Berber communities is always silver; necklaces include silver tubes and spheres, along with tozra, oversized orange copal beads. *Serdal*, silk headbands hung with silver coins and coral beads, and *khalkhal* ankle bracelets are also worn. Simple enamel *cloisonné* work is another feature of southern jewellery. Pottery varies greatly from region to region, each area having very individual forms. With the spread of cheap plastic and enameled utensils, many of the local forms have disappeared.

In contrast, urban craft items are generally produced by men, often working in structured corporations. While the women folk of nomad tribes produced for their own use, men in towns were working to sell their produce. They did not, however, build up sufficient capital to develop production on a large scale. City craftsmen produced carpets, jewellery, pottery, leather items and metal ustensils. They worked the raw materials for their production. Urban jewellery is in gold, set with precious stones, and very finely worked. Pottery was enamelled and decorated with designs flowing and floral, as well as geometric. The leather workers produced footwear (*belgha*) and high-quality bindings for the sacred texts. Traditional copper work included chandeliers, lamps, kettles, trays and perfume sprinklers. Wooden items were often very elaborate – and still are: witness the workshops near the Kasbah des Oudayas, Rabat. There was a vogue for mosaic-type marquetry, with wooden furniture and other objects being inset with coloured woods and precious materials, such as mother-of-pearl and ivory. There was, however, one area of craft production (excluding the art of cooking) in which city women were highly active: embroidery. Azemmour, Fès and Salé were particularly well known for this.

It is perhaps in dress that urban crafts have best resisted change. Although most Moroccans, both women and men, dress in Western style in the cities, traditional dress is alive and well. A full-blown wedding requires the bride to be displayed to guests in various costumes – the most expensive and elaborate being rented. It is deemed more fitting for Moroccan men to wear a long, hooded garment to the mosque over their ordinary clothes. A stylish *caftan*, a long and elegant long-sleeved gown, generally decorated with brocade motifs, is essential in a woman's wardrobe. The *jellaba* is the most common woman's garment. In the 1930s, Moroccan city women began to abandon the *haïk*, the traditional

The jeweller's craft

Jewellers must be masters of many crafts. Those in Morocco certainly are. The many types of metal and insets used, call for great skill on the part of the jeweller.

Engraved jewellery is popular. The craftsperson prepares their silvered plates and moulds them to shapes. They then smear them with 'jeweller's black', a preparation made from oil. When this is dry they remove, with a dry tip, the lines they intend to work on, and eventually the pattern emerges. They set up their metal on a tripod called a *h'mar el aoued*, or 'wooden donkey', and carefully chisel where they have previously drawn. This three-dimensional work is very skilful, particularly where the work is fine and the ornament small.

Jewellers must also be masters of the art of gilding. In earlier days this process was done with veneers of thin gold leaves or powdered gold, mixed with fish glue which was then baked in a small wood-fired oven. Today the gilding is done with an amalgam of powdered gold and a mercury base. This is brushed on to the base metal and then heated, leaving a small film of gold. This process is repeated many times until the desired thickness of gold has been deposited.

Enamelled jewellery is very popular. The shape for the decoration is scraped out of the metal and the liquid enamel poured in. An alternative method is to place the powder in the desired shape and use fire to vitrify the enamel. In the southwest of the country and in the Meknès region, jewellers still prepare their insets in the traditional way. Small enclosures are constructed with silver wires by welding them to the surface of the ornament. These circular and geometric spaces are filled with a dough of enamel paste which is then exposed to heat, care being taken not to melt the silver surround. Colours are obtained from copper (green), lead (yellow) and cobalt (blue).

wrap, too constraining for the new ways of living. They adopted the *jellaba*, a man's tunic with hood, as a garment that respected the need for modesty and was practical. Today the *jellaba* is worn everywhere, in bright colours and synthetic fabrics, with fantasy embroidery. Things have changed since 1939, when the bourgeoisie of Fès petitioned the pasha to outlaw the wearing of the *jellaba* by women.

Within living memory, Morocco's cities had very locally specific forms of craft production. Today, certain items are mass-produced for the tourist market and very fine production it is too. However, older items can often be found in the antique shops of Marrakech and Casablanca, where they go for very high prices. The aesthetic qualities of Moroccan craftwork are much appreciated by collectors. Unlike the rest of the Maghreb, and Egypt and the Levant, for that matter, Morocco was never occupied by the Ottomans. Craft production hence retained a certain artistic independence, evolving in great isolation in the case of the mountain areas. As in building, a sureness in aesthetic touch is the hallmark of the best craftwork, be it a Zaïane carpet, a pair of *babouches* with khanjar motif, or a simple blue and white bowl from Fès.

Music

Morocco's linguistic diversity is no barrier to music appreciation. A glance at any pavement CD stall will show that tastes are very eclectic indeed and pirated music is very cheap. Top-selling CDs are by Arab singers, including Iraqi crooner Kazem Essaher, the sensuous

Robi and the scandalous Haifa Wahbi. The latest videos and interviews are to be seen on satellite TV – *Star Academy Arab World* is hugely popular. Algerian *raï* music is popular too; top stars include Khaled, Mami and Cheb Hosni, Nasro, Bilal and Faudel. Local *chaâbi* music had gone out of fashion by the late 1990s, with only a few of the best known singers, such as Stati and Jadwane, and groups like Tagada still popular. The 'politically committed' sound of the leading 1970s and 1980s groups still has its fans. You may want to buy albums by Jil Jilala, Nass el Ghiwane or Lmachaheb. Other popular Moroccan sounds include Gnaoua Jazz (listen out for Saha Koyo) and the Casablanca movida (Hoba-Hoba Spirit and H-Kayen). Western music (*el gharbi*) is popular too. You'll certainly hear some Bob Marley in Morocco, and probably a lot of Dire Straits and The Eagles. French rappers and Quebec's Céline Dion also have quite a following.

An Andalucían taste: classical city music

There is, of course, a more classical taste in music. Moroccan urban music divides into a number of strands: *gharnati*, *el alat el andulsi* and *malhoun*. The latter is perhaps the most accessible form to the ear attuned to European sounds. In top bookshops you may find CD collections of these musical styles. Malhoun artists to look out for include the deceased Houcine Toulali from Meknès, Saïd Guennoun (Fès) and Mohammed Berrahal. In the late 1990s, writer Touria Hadraoui was the first woman to sing *malhoun*, and has produced a CD. In the evening, during Ramadan, Moroccan television broadcasts music by the classical Andalucían-style orchestras.

Middle Eastern divas and tenors

Still popular in Morocco – as elsewhere in the Arab world – are the great Egyptian and Syro-Lebanese singers who had their heyday in the 1950s and 1960s. Um Kalthoum, a peasant girl from the Nile Delta who became a diva of the Arab world, is popular everywhere. Her songs have probably done more for promoting classical Arabic poetry than any schoolbook. Other great names from this period include Druze princess Asmahane, Mohammed Abdewahab, Farid el Atrach, the Lebanese divas Fayrouz and Sabah, Najet Es Saghira and the brown nightingale, Abdel Halim Hafez.

Entertainment

Music is definitely at the heart of Moroccan good times. Traditional women's groups, the *chikhate*, play to appreciative all-male audiences during Ramadan nights, while a small but lively minority likes a night out clubbing. Marrakech clubs feature international DJs and Tangier gets lively in summer with returning immigrant families. Casablanca has year-round clubs for all tastes: after the Western hits, *musique orientale* and old Arabic hits remixed always fill the dancefloor.

Weddings

The vast majority of young Moroccans never get near a nightclub or a rock concert. But they like to have a good time, as is evident if you happen to get invited to a wedding party. At their most elaborate, weddings involve several days of festivities, and large sums are spent on ensuring that fun is had by all (and that family status is maintained). There will be a henna party at which the bride will have elaborate patterns printed on her hands and feet by a relative or (preferably) an expert *nakkacha*. During the actual wedding party, bride and groom sit upon twin thrones before the assembled guests and receive their best wishes. Custom has it that the bride will appear in seven different costumes. The general logistics of this are handled by a *neggafa*.

Religious holidays

Also important as they create opportunities for gatherings of family and friends are the big religious holidays of the Muslim year. There is the Mouloud (celebration of the Prophet Mohammed's birthday), Aïd el Fitr, marking the end of Ramadan, and Aïd el Kebir, aka Aïd el Adha, 'the Festival of the Sacrifice', two months later, when all right-minded families sacrifice a lamb to commemorate Ibrahim's near-sacrifice of his son, who was saved at the last minute when Allah sent a sheep as replacement. No matter how poor they are, the sheep-sacrifice is vital to Muslims. Of more pagan origin is the annual celebration of Achoura, a sort of Muslim Guy Fawkes. Banging on small clay-pot drums, children run round the streets collecting small change to light bonfires (*el afiya*) in the street. Cheap and cheerful toys and especially firecrackers are on sale everywhere. On the actual morning of Achoura, you have licence to throw water at anyone you feel like.

Amusements ordinary and extraordinary

Outside high days and holidays, Moroccans' free time is spent in ways not dissimilar to those of their Spanish neighbours. In summer, in cities and towns, a *paseo* (stroll) of some kind is the thing. In the early evening, people throng public gardens and central streets, happy to be out of crowded homes.

Access to leisure pursuits depends very much on social and economic status. The children of the wealthy – the *aoulad Lyautey*, schooled in prestigious French lycées – may enjoy horse riding and tennis, jetskiing and even occasional skiing at Ifrane or abroad. Their fathers will probably be golfers, their mothers may nip over to France for a spot of shopping – or down to Essaouira for *thalassothérapie*.

With limited financial resources, the average student or employee has simpler tastes. For a young couple, a big night out will be the cinema. Cheaper cinemas are men-only affairs, showing kung-fu epics and Hindi extravaganzas. Adolescents enjoy cards, pool and, video games.

For most women, social life focuses on the visiting each other in the home, the hairdressers and the weekly outing to the hammam. Women in nightclubs will either be wealthy or confident professional women in Casa-Rabat or sex workers.

For the very poorest, entertainment is limited. Making an early departure from a big Moroccan city, you soon become aware of the street children. You see them sleeping out under arcades or gazing into nothing, a piece of cloth held to the nose. These are the *chemkara*, the glue-sniffers, those who have fallen completely through the social net. Nabil Ayyouche's 2001 film *Ali Zaoua* is a moving portrait of street-kid life. Aware of the inequalities, others with the wherewithal to survive clutch the minimal salvation offered by fundamentalist-managed mosques.

Sport

Morocco's sporting heroes are footballers and runners. The country has been particularly successful in international athletics. In 1984, Saïd Aouita won the 5000 m at the Los Angeles Olympics and went on to set five world records, ranging from the 1500 m to the 5000 m. Other Moroccan athletes went on to imitate his success, including Brahim Boutayeb, Khalid Skah and Hichem Guerouj. Women's sport is catching up. At the 1984 Olympics, Nawal

Moutawakil unexpectedly won the 400 m hurdles, the first major title won by an Arab woman in an international competition – and is now a cabinet member. Like Aouita and Guerouj, Moutawakil provides a model for aspiring Moroccan athletes to look up to. Events like the Marrakech marathon attract numerous participants and much media coverage.

But football (*koura*) remains the number one spectator sport. At age six or seven, boys are out in the street or on a piece of rough ground, kicking a football around. Their heroes are the Lions of the Atlas, the national team. A match between the two big Casa sides, El Wydad and Raja, empties streets across the country. As does El Classico in Spain, widely broadcast. Morocco has hopes of organizing the World Cup one day, and a new 45,000-seater stadium, the Stade de Marakech, capable of one day holding such matches, was completed in 2011.

Religion

The people of Morocco follow Islam in the main, a montheistic religion similar to Judaism and Christianity in its philosophical content. Muslims recognize that these three revealed religions have a common basis, and Jews and Christians are referred to as Ahl al kitab, 'people of the book'. Even so, there are considerable differences in ritual, public observance of religious customs and the role of religion in daily life, and when travelling in Morocco it is as well to be aware of this.

Islam is an Arabic word literally meaning 'submission to God'. As Muslims often point out, it is not just a religion, but a way of life. The main Islamic scripture is the Koran, an Arabic term meaning 'the recitation'. Islam appeared in the desert oases of western Arabia in the early seventh century AD. The isolated communities of this region were Jewish, Christian or animist, and existed on oasis cultivation and the trade in beasts of burden against a backdrop of inter-tribal warfare. It was in this context that Islam was to emerge. Its prophet Mohammed, born in AD 570, was a member of the aristocratic Meccan tribe of Quraysh.

The Koran

The Koran divides into 114 *souras* or chapters, placed in order of length running from the longest to the shortest. Muslim and western scholars disagree on the nature of the Koran. For the true Muslim, it is the word of God, revealed to humankind via the Prophet Mohammed. The Koran appeared in this way in segments, some in Mecca, some after the Prophet was forced to leave Mecca for Medina in 622. The later *souras* tend to have a more practical content, and relate to family and inheritance law, for during the period in Medina, an embryonic Muslim community was taking shape. Western scholars have opened up more critical approaches to the Koranic text and the way it was assembled. During the Prophet's lifetime, nothing was written down. After his death, fragments of the text, noted in simple script on parchment or flat bones, were assembled at the order of Abu Bakr, Mohammed's successor or *khalifa*. In fact, the Arabic script was not fully codified at the time. The language of the Koran was eventually to become the base reference point for the Arabic language. For most Muslim Arabs, the written classical form of the language can never escape this divine influence.

The Hadith

The Koran does not cover all aspects of the Muslim's life – and it became apparent to early Islamic rulers that they would need another source. The *hadith*, short statements which recount what the Prophet is supposed to have said about various issues, were assembled and codified in the early days, providing crucial supplements to the main scripture.

Five pillars of Islam

The practice of Islam is based on five central points, the Pillars of Islam, namely the *shahada* or profession of faith, *salat* or prayer, *sawm* or fasting during the month of Ramadan, *zakat* or giving charity, and the *hajj* or pilgrimage to Mecca, which every Muslim is supposed to accomplish at least once. The mosque is the centre of religious activity. There is no clergy in Islam, although major mosques will have an imam to lead prayers. In principle, the *mesjed*, a small local prayer-room, will have someone chosen from the neighbourhood with enough religious knowledge to conduct prayers correctly.

The *shahada* involves reciting the statement, "There is no god but God, and Mohammed is the Messenger of God." A Muslim will do this at *salat*, the prayer ritual performed five times a day, including at sunrise, midday and sunset. There are also the important Friday noon prayers, which include a sermon or *khutba*. When praying, Muslims bow and then kneel down and prostrate themselves in the direction of Mecca, indicated in a mosque by a door-sized niche in the wall called the *qibla*. A muslim must be ritually pure to worship. This involves washing in a ritual manner, either at the hammam (local bathhouse) or the *midha*, the ablutions area of the mosque.

A third essential part of Islam is the giving of *zakat* or alms. A Muslim was supposed to give surplus revenues to the community. With time, the practice of *zakat* was codified. Today, however, *zakat* has largely disappeared to be replaced by modern taxation systems. The practice of *zakat al fitr*, giving alms at Aïd el Fitr, the Muslim holiday which marks the end of Ramadan, is still current, however.

The daytime month-long fast (*sawm*) of Ramadan is a time of contemplation, worship and piety. Muslims are expected to read one thirtieth of the Koran each night. Muslims who are ill or on a journey, as well as women breastfeeding are exempt from fasting. Otherwise, eating, drinking and sexual activity is only permitted at night, until "so much of the dawn appears that a white thread can be distinguished from a black one."

The *hajj* or pilgrimage to the holy city of Mecca is required of all physically able Muslims at least once in their life time and should take place during the month of Dhu al Hijja. The 'lesser pilgrimage' to the holy places of Islam is referred to as the *umra*, and can be performed at any time of year. Needless to say, the journey to Mecca is not within every Muslim's financial grasp – fortunately, perhaps, as the mosques would probably be unable to cope with the millions involved, despite the extension works of recent years.

Muslim revivalists lay stress on a sixth element in their faith: *jihad*, which literally means struggle. The term was originally used to refer to the taking of Islam into the *dar al harb*, 'the house of war', ie the lands outside the *dar al islam*. (The fundamentalist Muslim world view is a bipolar one.) Early Islam expanded rapidly through the mobilization of thousands of tribal warriors in *jihad*, taking the new religion out into Mesopotamia, Persia and the Mediterranean world.

On prophets and revelation

Islam is a revealed religion, and God chose certain men to be prophets, his true representatives on Earth. In Arabic, a prophet is a *nabi*, while Mohammed is the messenger of God, *rasoul Allah*. The first prophet in Islam was Adam and the last was Mohammed, 'seal of the prophets'. Major prophets are Sidna Nouh (Noah), Sidna Ibrahim (Abraham), Dawoud (David), Mousa (Moses) and 'Issa (Jesus). Yaqoub (Jacob), Youssef (Joseph) and

Ayyoub (Job) are all mentioned in the Koran. Prophets were recognized by their miracles, apart from Mohammed, who was to be the instrument via which the Koran was transmitted to humankind. Nevertheless, Mohammed's *mi'raj* or ascent to heaven on the winged horse, *Al Buraq*, may be considered as a sort of miracle. The miracles performed by the prophets are not detailed in the Koran. 'Issa (Jesus) is pictured in a particularly favourable light but, while the virgin birth is mentioned in the Koran, Issa is definitely not the son of God in Islam.

Sunna (standard Islamic practice)

The Koran and the *hadith* also lay down a number of other practices and customs, some of which are close to the practices of Judaism. Sex, provided it is within marriage, is seen as positive, and marriage is forbidden to no one. Sensuality and seduction between the married couple are encouraged. Eating pork is prohibited, as is drinking alcohol and gambling. In the matter of dress, habits have changed hugely in recent years. Except in certain rural areas, young women no longer automatically veil their faces and Moroccan Islam is a long way from the more extreme forms practised in Saudi Arabia, where women are all but invisible in the public sphere. While in traditional families the women's domain is most definitely the home, Islam does not stop Moroccan women getting themselves educated and into jobs once thought of as being exclusively for men.

Fundamentalist interpretations

Literalist interpretations of the Koran would, however, lead to women being pushed out of positions of responsibility in public life, although they would no doubt continue to operate in professions where they could work in women-only institutions (hospitals, schools). Muslim fundamentalists, including the Moroccan Salafiya, claim to have the absolute monopoly on applying the letter of the Koran, in understanding the words of a book 'written' in the seventh century AD as a programme for social organization applicable in every time and every place. But as a reading of the text will show, Mohammed had no political programme: he was the vessel for the transmission of the divine word.

Improving women's status

Women's status in Morocco achieved a major step forward in 2004 with the reform of the country's personal status code, the Moudawana. Under the original terms of the code, first drafted after Independence and timidly reformed in 1993, women were essentially eternal minors, unable even to initiate divorce proceedings. While it does not actually go so far as to abolish polygamy, the new code advances women's rights considerably. The unilateral repudiation of a wife is abolished and the taking of a second wife subject to the first wife's approval. Women can now take custody of their children. Hailed as a major achievement, the new Moudawana is facing problems in application. The norms of married life vary enormously between social classes and regional groups. Paradoxically, perhaps, in poorer areas women often seem to be the most vigilant guardians of the status quo.

Nevertheless, in traditional society, women very definitely had space of their own, if not direct authority. All was not repression – far from it. While weddings are fairly often a matter of alliances between families, loving marriages certainly developed in the traditional context. Increasingly, women are present in Morocco's economic and professional life and spearhead the dynamic NGO movement. The reform of the Moudawana thus recognizes women's changing status in society – and corresponds to the image that the country wishes to project to the outside world. Women's quest for full rights is clearly inseparable from the changing identity of the Moroccan nation-state.

Morocco land and environment

The present-day Moroccan kingdom occupies the northwestern section of Africa. It is the African country closest to Europe, separated from Spain by the Straits of Gibraltar. The third largest country in the Maghreb (area: 703,000 sq km; Algeria and Libya are bigger), Morocco has beautiful, diverse landscapes, from arid desert to cedar forest, snow-topped mountains and spectacular gorges, oases and olive groves.

Geography

There are 10 main regions in Morocco: the Rif mountains in the north, the agriculturally rich Atlantic plains (from north to south, the Gharb, Chaouia and Abda-Doukkala), Fès/Meknès and surrounding plains, the Middle Atlas, the Haouz region of Marrakech, the High Atlas, the Souss Valley east of Agadir, the Anti-Atlas, the Tafilalet desert areas of eastern Morocco, and the southern desert fronting the Atlantic. Tribal loyalties, language, history and landscape give these regions distinctive flavours.

Borders
Morocco has a 1835-km coastline, from Saïdia on the Algerian frontier to La Gouera on the border with Mauritania, of which a fifth lies on the Mediterranean, the rest facing the Atlantic. Main ports include Nador, Tangier, Kénitra, Mohammedia, Casablanca, El Jadida, Safi, Essaouira, Agadir, Tan Tan, Laâyoune and Dakhla. Morocco has long-standing claims to the Spanish enclave cities of Melilla and Ceuta on the Mediterranean coast. Tension with neighbouring Algeria in 1994 led to the closure of the eastern frontier. The Mauritanian frontier is generally open, although those wishing to take the land route into Mauritania are advised to check before heading for the deep south, and also check whether the journey back is possible.

Mountains and plateaux
The average altitude for Morocco as a whole is 800 m above sea level, making the country the most mountainous in North Africa. Huge mountain chains running northeast to southwest dominate the relief. Around 100,000 sq km of the country's surface area is above 2000 m in altitude. The High Atlas alone has over a dozen summits exceeding 4000 m.

The limestone crescent of the Rif mountains rises sheer from the Mediterranean, few areas lying below 1500 m. The highest peak at 2492 m is Jbel Tidghine, not far from Issaguene. Together with the outlying Jebala range, these mountains all but seal off the rest of Morocco from the Mediterranean coast. This is the best-watered range in the country and despite much human pressure, cedars still cover the sides of the remoter mountains and pines and holm oaks cover the crests. There are even heather and ferns on the moorlands on the wetter north-facing slopes. To the south lie the Atlas Mountains in three great chains – the Middle Atlas, the High Atlas and, farthest south of the three, the Anti-Atlas.

In parts forested and fertile, the Middle Atlas divides into two main regions. Best known is the limestone Plateau des cèdres, east of Khenifra. Here oaks and great stands of cedar survive on gently undulating terrain scattered with small lakes. In winter, snow blocks many routes. The eastern Middle Atlas, higher and more rugged, rises to 3343 m at Jbel Bou Naceur.

The great mass of the High Atlas extends for more than 650 km with 400 peaks over 3000 m. The range acts as a huge barrier, dividing the better-watered Atlantic and central inland plains from the extensive desert regions. The western part of the range, south of Marrakech, called the High Atlas of Toubkal after its highest peak, Jbel Toubkal (4167 m), is popular with walkers. Further east, south of Beni Mellal, northeast of Ouarzazate, lies the High Atlas of Azilal, a limestone massif rising to 4071 m on the long shoulder of the Ighil Mgoun. Here there are deep, spectacular gorges and valleys, while some rivers have been dammed to form large lakes. Rain-fed slopes have a cover of pine and juniper, reduced by grazing and cutting for firewood. Further east again is the High Atlas of Imilchil, a region of more arid mountains and chalky plateau between Imilchil and Midelt (highest peak: Jbel Ayyachi, 3737 m).

Travellers should plan to travel over the main High Atlas passes, such as the Tizi-n-Test (Marrakech–Taroudant) and Tizi-n-Tichka (Marrakech–Ouarzazate), in daylight to see a maximum of scenery. Heavy snows and landslides can disrupt transport through these passes from time to time in the winter and early spring. In most years, the mountain snows have melted away by June.

The Anti-Atlas is another impressive range. It extends for 400 km. The highest peak, directly east of Irherm, is Adrar-n-Aklim reaching 2531 m. There is an eastern extension, Jbel Saghro, with the high summits Amalou n'Mansour (2712 m) and Fengour (2516 m). The Atlantic Ocean lies at the western extremity of the range. Minimal mountain vegetation is compensated for by fertile oases valleys, of which the most spectacular is probably the lower reaches of the Oued Ziz, south of Er Rachidia.

The Jbel Siroua (pronounced Sirwa), a vast volcanic outcrop, is the connection between the High and Anti-Atlas ranges. The ancient black basaltic lava produces a rugged landscape, with deeply carved valleys radiating from the central point of 3304 m.

The country's richest agricultural areas are the plain of the Gharb, hinterland of Kénitra, and the inland basins around Fès and Oujda. The coastal region, aligned along the Atlantic between Rabat and Essaouira and limited to the east by the High and Middle Atlas, forms a broken plateau of 210 m average height. To the east of the High Atlas and south of the Middle Atlas is the western fringe of the High Plateau, which runs in fuller form through Algeria. To the south of the Anti-Atlas is the western part of the Sahara Desert.

Rivers

Morocco's rivers run from the high mountain zone to the sea. In the northeast, the Oued Moulouya originates in the Middle Atlas and collects the streams of the eastern Rif, before reaching the Mediterranean at Saïdia. The Rif proper is drained by a series of fast-flowing streams to the Mediterranean, such as the Oued Bou Frah and the Oued M'Ter, but to the south, surface water runs to the Sebou and its tributary the Ouerrha, and thence to the Atlantic near Kénitra. The Jebala region, south of Tangier, is drained by the Loukkos and its tributaries to the Atlantic coast at Larache. Coming down from the Middle Atlas, the Oum Er Rbia drains the Tadla plain before running across the Plateau des phosphates and the coastal plain to the Atlantic. The Oued Tensift drains the Haouz plain around Marrakech. In southern Morocco, two important rivers, the Souss and the Draâ, run from sources in the High Atlas towards the Atlantic. On the southeastern side of the High Atlas, 'rivers' like the Ghéris and the Guir run southwards in occasional flood to lose themselves in the desert.

Even in the northern rivers, there are considerable variations in flow. The larger streams drawing their sources in the higher mountain areas run for most of the year, fed by snow-melt persisting as late as July. Many *oueds* elsewhere are short-lived.

Climate

Morocco's climatic zones are varied. While the northern coastal region is in the Mediterranean zone, the proximity of the Atlantic effects the classic Mediterranean pattern of mild, wet winters and warm, dry summers: depressions move across northern Morocco from the ocean, bringing heavier and more reliable rainfall than in much of the rest of the Mediterranean basin. The Atlantic coast in the south feels the moderating influence of the ocean even in summer, thanks to the cold Canaries current.

Away from the coasts, high altitudes and the influence of the Sahara produce a complex set of micro-climates. The further south and east you go, the more you feel the influence of the desert, including higher daytime and lower night temperatures, together with greater aridity. Increasing altitude in the Atlas reduces temperatures and also means very cold nights in exposed areas, and higher risks of rain and snow between November and March. Winters can be bitterly cold and wet throughout the Middle and High Atlas. Marrakech averages only 16°C in January, but 33°C in June. Rabat on the coast has temperatures in January of 19°C against 25°C in June.

With so many people dependent on farming for a living, the rains make the difference between a good and bad year for the Moroccan economy. Periods of extreme drought are disastrous for rural areas. Rabat on the Atlantic coast receives an average of 530 mm of rain, while Marrakech, further south and in the foothills of the High Atlas, receives only 230 mm. In the southeast, arid desert conditions prevail. Rain often comes in heavy showers, sometimes with intense thunder and lightning. In the north, this can occur at any time of year. During storms there is a high risk of flash floods, with *oued* beds carrying violent spates for short periods. Be very wary of venturing into an *oued* in your four-wheel drive vehicle at such times. If you are going to be travelling to Morocco in the winter, it is as well to have waterproofs with you, as well as good shoes or boots, as it really can bucket down.

The prevailing winds are from the Atlantic Ocean and invariably westerly. Occasional winds from the desert to the south, known as the *chergui*, bring high temperatures, very low relative humidity and dust storm conditions, a miserable combination. In the Tangier area and the Strait of Gibraltar, a 'levanter' east wind brings cool mists at almost any time of the year.

Wildlife and vegetation

All these regional variations in climate, vegetation and relief have given Morocco a diverse and interesting flora and fauna. Although the country is too densely settled to have many large mammals, birdwatchers will find much to twitch about, and the spring flowers can be wonderful, particularly in the north.

Arid lands
Semi-desert scrub is widespread and gives a green hue to wide expanses after the spring rains. In regions even less likely to receive precipitation, the vivid desert flowers appear at very infrequent intervals. On the eastern steppes, clumps of alfalfa grass help to stabilize the fragile soils and sage bushes appear here too, an ungainly plant but able to withstand the wind, the cold and the drought. The soft pink flowering tamarisks hold back the sand, while handsome oleanders flower white and red in the *oueds*. Though attractive, the leaves are highly poisonous to animals.

Forests

Morocco's woodlands are both natural and human-made, ranging from the mountain cedar forests of the Rif in the north to the great palm forest of the Ziz canyon south of Er Rachidia. On the plain north of Rabat lies the Mamora cork oak forest, much overgrazed by cattle but just about surviving. Nearby are monotonous expanses of industrially farmed eucalyptus. Natural forest is densest in the Rif – where it comprises holm oaks, juniper and great stands of cedar. On the northern, better-watered slopes of the High Atlas, thick trunked junipers and bushy thuya are the main trees, surviving best where they are too far from human habitation to be cut for fire wood. Walnuts and poplar are the trees of the valleys, while Aleppo pine survives in protected areas. In February, in the valleys south of the Atlas, the wild almond, which ought to be the national tree, produces its own breathtaking version of 'snow'.

Cedar forest

Morocco's cedar forest has much receded under human pressure. Maybe 130,000 ha of cedar forest survive, of which 74,000 ha is in the Middle Atlas. A cedar tree may grow over 50 m in height and live for several hundred years. The cedar forest is a unique natural environment – where leopards are said to survive.

Arganeraies, the rarest woodland

Central Atlantic Morocco, from Essaouira down to Sidi Ifni, is home to the rare argan groves, until recently the most threatened of Morocco's trees. A survivor of a remote time when the region had a tropical climate, the arganier requires a unique climatic cocktail of aridity tempered by ocean mists to survive. Looking for all the world like a wild and wooly version of the olive, the arganier grows over some 650,000 ha, some of which is human-planted in groves. Goats climb into the trees to graze. Most importantly, the oil produced from the soft white heart of the argan 'almond', now internationally recognized for its therapeutic value, is one of the costliest nut oils on the market. And in the production process, no part of the fruit is wasted: the flesh can be fed to pack animals, while the hard shell can be used to fuel a brasero.

Recognizing the arganier's importance, UNESCO has declared the Essaouira-Agadir region a specially protected biosphere. In the same zone grow the caroubier, the red juniper and the Barbary thuya, whose large underground roots are much used in the Essaouira craft and carpentry industry.

Oases

The date palm is the miracle tree of the arid desert expanses of southern Morocco. Wherever there is a good supply of water, oases have sprung up. Although the oasis was originally a wholly natural environment, given the pressure on the scarce resources of the desert, it has been 'domesticated' for centuries now. Black haratine populations and Berbers kept cultivation going under the protection of nomad tribes. Special *khettara*, underground 'canals', were created to bring melt water from the foothills to the oases. Under the protective canopy of the date palms, the ideal oasis has different layers of cultivation, including the pomegranate, and crops like wheat, barley, oats and coriander. Today, the palm trees in many Moroccan oases suffer from the bayoud fungus. Increasingly, the production of food for local consumption is abandoned and the cultivators focus solely on date production. Oases can also be rewarding areas for birdwatchers.

Birdlife

Home to 460 species, Morocco has the greatest diversity of birdlife north of the Sahara. The untrained eye will spot bright-coloured bee-eaters and blue rollers, storks nesting on ramparts and minarets, pink flamingos and the striped hoopoes. Swifts soar and dip over Fès before settling to roost in the ramparts, while many a riad garden has a resident pair of dowdy bulbuls, 'oasis nightingales'. The trill of a *moknine* (goldfinch) can be heard coming out of shops in the souk. Of the raptors, lesser kestrels and owls are often taken for use in obscure magic preparations.

Top destinations for birdwatchers include coastal marsh and lagoon sites, including Kariet Arkmane and the Oued Moulouya (Nador), the lagoon of Moulay Bouselham north of Rabat, Oualidia and Essaouira. The reserve at Tidzi, south of Essaouira, and the Oued Massa National Park (Agadir) are home to Morocco's rarest resident bird, the bald ibis. Once widespread in Central Europe, this bird nests alongside the gulls and lanner falcons at Oued Massa.

Another top birdwatching location is the Jbel Moussa, near Tangier, from where the spring and autumn migrations from and to Europe can be observed. Migratory birds making use of this route to cross the narrow Strait of Gibraltar include storks and vultures, and smaller (by comparison) buzzards and eagles. Such large birds depend on soaring in the thermal currents rising from the land and, hence, they opt for the shortest sea crossing possible. Smaller birds tend to migrate on a broad front, often being able to cross both the desert and the Mediterranean without stopping.

Reptiles

Morocco's reptilian fauna is among the richest in the Mediterranean region. While Europe has 60 species of reptiles, Morocco has over 90. You will, however, see few lizards and even fewer snakes, as many are nocturnal and most shun areas inhabited by humankind. In tiny shops in the souks, sad chameleons (*bouiya* in Arabic) may be seen clambering in tiny cages – or dried on skewers, ready for pounding into powder to complete a special incense.

Mammals

Morocco's mammals include genets, jackals, striped hyena, wild cats, fennecs, gerbils and jerboas, as well as the famed Barbary apes of the Middle Atlas. Wild boar are still common in the Rif and the endangered Dorcas gazelle can be found in desert regions. The forests of the Middle Atlas also harbour a few elusive leopards. With their nocturnal habits, most of these animals are sufficiently elusive to evade casual visitors. You will, however, see a selection of animal pelts and horns at apothecaries' stalls in the medinas.

The most easily observed of all the large mammals are the Barbary apes (*magot* or *macaque de Barbarie*), which are to be found in the Azrou area of the Middle Atlas and at the Cascades d'Ouzoud near Demnate, east of Marrakech. The Barbary ape can live for as long as 20 years. It forages on the ground for food (leaves, roots, small insects) and has been known to enjoy the yoghurt, bread, occasional Flag beer and other tidbits thoughtfully contributed by passing picknickers.

Another observable mammal is the *anzid* or *sibsib*, known as the Barbary squirrel in English, chiefly found in the Anti-Atlas. In the Tafraoute area, you may see children at the roadside offering hapless rodents for sale. In Islam, animals have to be ritually slaughtered with the head turned towards Mecca. As the *sibsib* is said to have medicinal properties, it is licit and makes a delicious tagine.

Insects

Insects are much more easily observed than large mammals. As pesticides are far beyond the means of most farmers, there are beautiful butterflies and a multitude of moths, both in evidence when the spring flowers are in bloom. There are flies both large and small, bees, wasps and mosquitoes; these are not elusive and can at times be too attentive. Scorpions are to be found in arid areas. If camping out, make sure you check your boots in the morning.

National parks

The most important of Morocco's national parks is the Oued Massa National Park. In addition to being the haunt of the endangered bald ibis and a wide selection of water and wetland birds, it also has an interesting reptile and mammalian fauna because of its geographical position, which combines tropical, Mediterranean and Saharan features. Toads, frogs, terrapins, skinks and lizards abound. The Egyptian cobra is reported in the vicinity. The National Park Authority has reintroduced the oryx, ostrich and various types of gazelle, most of which are doing quite well. There are ground squirrels and foxes too. A favourite with visitors, however, is often the Egyptian mongoose with its tufted tail.

Wildlife under threat

Most Moroccan mammals manage to evade all but the keenest visitor. Some animals are not elusive enough, however, and you will see shops offering stuffed varans, tortoises – both live and converted into banjo-like instruments – snake-skin bags, and the furs of fennecs, genets and wild cats. (Leopard and lion skins are likely to have been brought up from Mali.) Widely held beliefs about the efficiency of various animal parts in traditional medicine are borne out by even the most cursory glance at a medicine stall in the souk. With modern medicine out of people's ken, due to poor education and cost, traditional lotions, potions and spells find a ready market, putting heavy pressure on the population of crows, owls, chameleons and other lizards. The snakes suffer even more. For the entertainments of Jemaâ el Fna, the Egyptian cobra is much favoured, as is the puff adder. In some cases, their mouths are sewn up to ensure no one gets a nasty bite. The ecological consequence of snake collection from the wild is a rapid growth in the rodent population, the snakes' natural snack. Saddest of all are the Barbary macaques. For the first few years of their lives as tools of the tourist trade, they are amusing and seem to enjoy life with their keepers. But on reaching early adulthood, they want to assume a position in the troop, turning aggressive and potentially dangerous in their bid to win top-place in the hierarchy. Happily, however, there are signs that Morocco is waking up to the fact that its wild species and their denizens can be maintained hand-in-hand with the development of sustainable forms of tourism.

Books on Morocco

In Morocco, bibliophiles should look in at bookshops in central Rabat (**Kalila wa Dimna, Le Livre Service**) and in Maârif, Casablanca (**Le Carrefour du Livre**). Try also **Librairie Chater**, Av Mohammed V in Guéliz, Marrakech. **The Maghreb Bookshop** in Bloomsbury (45 Burton St, London WC1, T020-7388 1840, www.maghrebbookshop.com) has a range of Morocco-related literature.

Arts, architecture and crafts

Huet, K and Lamazou, T *Sous les toits de terre* Casablanca: Belvisi/Publication (1988).

Superb portrait in coloured line drawings and text of life in the Vallée des Aït Bougmez.

Ouazzani, T'hami *La colline des potiers* Casablanca: Editions LAK International (1993). Introduction to the pottery of Safi. A superbly produced book.

Pochy, Y and Triki, Hamid *Médersa de Marrakech* Paris: EPA (1990). Magnificent photograph album of the Medersa Ben Youssef in Marrakech.

Ethnography

Bennani-Chraïbi, Mounia *Soumis et rebelles, les jeunes au Maroc* Casablanca: Editions Le Fennec (1994). Good, readable account based on interviews on what it feels to be young and aspiring in Morocco today.

Crapanzano, Vincent *Tuhami, story of a Moroccan* Chicago University Press (1980). Life and times of an illiterate Moroccan tilemaker – and a great storyteller.

Dwyer, K *Moroccan Dialogues: Anthropology in Question* Baltimore: John Hopkins University Press (1982). A classic of anthropology writing.

Mernissi, F *Beyond the Veil: Male/Female Dynamics in Modern Muslim Society*, London: Al Saq (1994). The grand title suggests a lot more than you get.

History

Abun-Nasr, J M *History of the Maghreb in the Islamic Period* Cambridge: CUP (1987). Densely written scholarly account of the Islamic history of North Africa.

Bovill, E W *The Golden Trade of the Moors* Oxford: OUP (1968).

Novels

There is a growing amount of contemporary fiction in Arabic and French. The most translated writers include Tahar Ben Jelloun, Mohammed Choukri and Driss Chraïbi. The latter's *Le Passé simple* is an outstanding autobiographical piece of writing. You will probably easily find Paul Bowles' translations of stories by Mohammed Mrabet and Driss Ben Hamed Charhadi. Also translated are Brick Ousaïd and Abdelhak Serhane. If you read French, look out for Lotif Akalay (*Les nuits d'Azed*), Mahi Binebine and Fouad Laroui. Rachid O, (*L'enfant ébloui, Plusieurs vies*) and Paul Smaïl (*Vivre me tue*) are both published in France, but written with a vigorous spoken-language style. In Arabic, Mohammed Berrada and Mohammed Zezaf are highly regarded.

European writers working in a Moroccan background or on North African themes include the following:

Busi, Aldo *Sodomies in Elevenpoint* London: Faber and Faber (1992). The title sets the tone. Adventures of an Italian novelist in Agadir and Taroudant.

Goytisolo, Juan *Makbara* London: Serpent's Tail (1993). Surreal tale shifting between Morocco and Paris by Spain's leading writer – who resides partly in Marrakech.

Johnson, Jane *The Tenth Gift*. A meticulously researched romantic tale of white slavery that follows the story of a Cornish girl kidnapped by Moroccan pirates, Johnson's tale entwines a modern storyline with a historical counterpart to exciting effect.

Hughes, R *In the Lap of the Atlas* London: Chatto & Windus (1979).

Travel writing

Canetti, Elias *The Voices of Marrakech* (1982). Thin and readable but also wry and sharply observed, the Nobel Prize winner's travel observations have gathered little dust in the 40 years since the book was first published.

Freud, Esther *Hideous Kinky* London: Penguin (1992). A child's view of travels with a hippy mother in search of primal religious experience. Made into a film.

Kennedy, Sylvia *See Ouarzazate* and *Die* London: Abacus Travel (1992). Journeys with a jaded former EFL teacher. A travelogue in which the kif sellers are always swarthy, the German blondes spaced out and looking for a cause for tears and confrontation.

Maxwell, Gavin *Lords of the Atlas* London (1966).

Mayne, Peter *A Year in Marrakesh*. This is the account of an Englishman who, in the 1950s, moved to the city to write a novel. Though the novel itself did not survive, his travel journals have become something of a minor classic. He tells of life on the Moroccan streets as both an insider and an outsider, becoming at once part of the world he inhabits and yet keeping a critical distance.

Meakin, B *The Land of the Moors* London (1901).

Ogrizek, Doré *L'Afrique du Nord* Paris: Editions Odé (1952).

Potocki, Jean *Voyage en Turquie et en Egypte, en Hollande at au Maroc* Paris: Fayard (1980).

Potocki, Jean *Voyage dans l'Empire du Maroc fait en l'année 1791* Paris: Dédale (1997).

Secret, Dr Edmond *Les sept printemps de Fès* Privately published (1990). Memoirs of one of the first French doctors to work in Fès.

Vieuchange, M *Smara: The Forbidden City* New York: Ecco Press (1987, reprint). A heart-breaking account of a painful and fatal journey.

Wharton, Edith *In Morocco* London: Macmillan (1920).

Trekking

Dickinson, M *Long Distance Walks in North Africa* Crowood Press (1991).

Fougerolles, A *Le Haut Atlas central*. Guide alpin with many good diagrams and maps.

Peyron, M *La grande traversée de l'Atlas marocain* (also apparently available in an English version). Describes trekking in the Toubkal region and beyond.

Shah, Tahir *The Caliph's House*. Shah paints a colourful and affectionate picture of the characters and the frustrations involved in doing up an old building on the edge of the Casablancan slums.

Smith, Karl *The Atlas Mountains, a walkers' guide* Milnthorpe: Cicerone (1989).

Wildlife

Bergiers, P and Bergier, F *A Birdwatcher's Guide to Morocco* Perry: Prion Ltd. This is a slim but useful guide to the best localities in Morocco for bird observation. Good site maps and fairly comprehensive species list.

Blamey, M and Grey-Wilson, C *Mediterranean Wild Flowers* London: Harper Collins (1993). Beautifully illustrated and comprehensive guide to the flowers of this region. Biased towards coastal areas and not particularly easy for the non-specialist to use. Many Moroccan endemics are not described. Highly recommended nonetheless.

Cremona, J and Chote R *The Alternative Holiday Guide to Exploring Nature in North Africa* Ashford. Difficult to obtain, but a very good general introduction to the flora and fauna of North Africa. Insufficiently detailed for the specialist but good coverage of Moroccan wildlife, including the desert regions.

Road maps

The early 2000s saw a spate of road improvement schemes across Morocco, and road map publishers have found it hard to keep pace.

Michelin 959 is probably the most accurate. **Geo Center World Map**, 1:800,000 scale, is another option. The heading 'other minor roads' can include both tarmac surfaced road and difficult piste. Maps identify roads by letters and numbers (P = parcours, ie main road, S = route secondaire, generally tarmac-surface). Road signs, bilingual in Arabic and Latin letters, rarely show route numbers at all. Note that Morocco does not use the Arabic numerals in use in the Middle East. If you need more detailed maps, try the **Institut géographique national** (IGN), 107 Rue de la Boétie, Paris 75008, which may supply 1:100,000 scale maps with latitude and longitude, useful if you are working with a GPS system.

Contents

Footnotes

Language in Morocco

Moroccan Arabic

For the English speaker, some of the sounds of Moroccan Arabic are totally alien. There is a strong glottal stop (as in the word 'bottle' when pronounced in Cockney English), generally represented by an apostrophe, and a rasping sound written here as 'kh', rather like the 'ch' of the Scots 'loch' or the Greek 'drachma'. And there is a glottal 'k' sound, which luckily often gets pronounced as the English hard 'g', and a very strongly aspirated 'h' in addition to the weak 'h'. The French 'r' sound is generally transcribed as 'gh'. Anyway, worry ye not. Moroccan acquaintances will have a fun time correcting your attempts at pronouncing Arabic. And for those with a little French and/or Spanish, the word lists after the Arabic section will be a handy reminder.

The language section here divides into three parts: Moroccan Arabic, a short section of Tachelhit Berber for the mountains (useful for reading topographic names), and a final section of French and Spanish. For Arabic and Tachelhit, the symbol 'í' is used to represent the English 'ee' sound. An apostrophe represents the glottal stop, as in the word *sa'a* (hour), for example. As mentioned above, Arabic has two sorts of 'h', and a capital H is used to represent the strongly aspirated sort.

Polite requests and saying thank you
excuse me, please – *'afek* (for calling attention politely) – عفاك
please – *min fadhlek* – من فضلك
one minute, please – *billatí* – بلاتي
(to call the the waiter) – *esh-sherif* or *ya ma'alem* – الشريف / يامعلم
thank you – *teberkallah alík/Allah yekhallík* – تبرك الله عليك
thank you – *shukran* – شكرا

Saying hello (and goodbye)
Good morning – *sabaH el-khír* – صباح الخير
How's things? – *kí yedirkí dayir?* – كي داير ؟ كي يدير
Everything's fine – *el Hamdou lillah* (lit Praise be to God) – الحمد لله
Everything's fine – *kull shay la bas* – كل شيئ لاباس
Congratulations – *mabrouk* – مبروك
Goodbye – *bisslema* – بسلامة
Goodbye – *Allah ya'wnek* – الله يعاونك

Handy adjectives and adverbs
Like French, Moroccan Arabic has adjectives (and nouns) with feminine and masculine forms. To get the masculine form, simply knock off the final 'a'.
good – *mezyena* – مزيان
happy – *farhana* – فرحانة
beautiful – *jmíla, zwína* – جميلة
new – *jdída* – جديدة
old – *qdíma* – قديمة
cheap – *rkhíssa* – رخيسة
clean – *naqía* – نقية

full – 'amra – عامرة
in a hurry – zarbana – زربانة
quickly – dghiya dghiya – دغية دغية
it doesn't matter – belesh – بلاش

Quantities
a lot – bezaf – بزاف
a little – shwíya – شوية
half – nesf – نصف

Numerals

one – wahed	twenty – 'ashrine
two – zouj or tnine	twenty-one – wahed ou 'ashrine
three – tlata	twenty-two – tnine ou 'ashrine
four – arba'	twenty-three – tlata ou 'ashrine
five – khamsa	twenty-four – 'arba ou 'ashrine
six – setta	thirty – tlatine
seven – saba'	forty – 'arba'ine
eight – tmaniya	fifty – khamsine
nine – ts'oud	sixty – sittine
ten – ashra	seventy – saba'ine
eleven – hedash	eighty – temenine
twelve – t'nash	ninety – t'issine
thirteen – t'latash	one hundred – miya
fourteen – rb'atash	two hundred – miyatayn
fifteen – kh'msatash	three hundred – tlata miya
sixteen – settash	thousand – alf
seventeen – sb'atash	two thousand – alfayn
eighteen – t'mentash	three thousand – tlat alaf
nineteen – ts'atash	one hundred thousand – miyat alf

Days of the week
Monday – nhar el itnayn – نهار الاثنين
Tuesday – nhar ettlata – نهار الثلاثاء
Wednesday – nhar el arba – نهار الاربعاء
Thursday – nhar el khemís – نهار الخميس
Friday – nhar el jema' – نهار الجمعة
Saturday – nhar essebt – نهار السبت
Sunday – nhar el had – نهار الحد

A few expressions of time
today – el yawm – اليومة
yesterday – el-bareh – البارح
tomorrow – ghedda – غدة
day after tomorrow – ba'da ghedda – بعد غدة
day – nhar – النهار
morning – sbah – الصباح
midday – letnash – لاتناش

evening – *ashíya* – العشية

tonight/night – *el-líla/líl* – الليلة / الليل

hour – *sa'a* – ساعة

half an hour – *nes sa'a* – نصف ساعة

Miscellaneous expressions

Watch out! (as a mule comes careering down the street) – *balak! balak!*

No problem – *ma ka'in mushkil*

How much? – *bayshhal? aysh-hal ettaman?*

Free (of charge) – *fabor*

Look – *shouf* (pl *shoufou*)

OK, that's fine – *wakha*

Good luck! – *fursa sa'ída*

At the café

tea – *ettay* – التاي

weak milky coffee – *un crème* – قهوة بالحليب

half espresso, half milk – *nes nes* – نص نص

a small bottle – *gara' sghíra* – قرعة صغيرة

a large bottle – *gara' kbíra* – قرعة كبيرة

a bottle of still mineral water – *gara' Sidi Ali/Sidi Harazem* – قرعة سيدي علي

a bottle of fizzy mineral water – *gara' Oulmes/Bonacqua* – قرعة اولماس

ashtray – *dfeya, cendrier* – طفاية

do you have change? – *'indak sarf/vous avez de la monnaie?* – عندك الصرف

At the restaurant

bill – *l'hseb* – لحساب

fork – *foursheta, lamtíqa* – فورشتة / لمتيقة

knife – *mous, mis* – موس

spoon – *mu'allaka* – معلقة / عاشق

glass – *ka's* (pl *kísan*) – كاس / كيسان

bowl – *zellafa* – زلافة

plate – *tobsil* – تبصيل

could you bring us some more bread – *afak tzídna khubz* – عفاك تزيدنا الخبز

Food and drink

bananas – *mouz* – موز

beef – *lham bagri* – لحم بقري

butter – *zebda* – زبدة

bread – *khobz* – خبز

chicken – *djaj* – دجاج

chips – *btata maklya, frites* – بطاطة مقلية

egg – *bíd* (sing *bída*) – بيض / بيضة

fruit – *fekiha* – فواكه

mandarins – *tchína* – تشينة

mutton – *lham ghenmí* – لحم غنمي

milk – *hlíb* – حليب

olive oil – *zít zítoun* – زيت زيتون

oranges – *límoun* – ليمون

rice – *rouz* – روز

tomatoes – *ma'tísha* – مطيشة

vegetables – *khudra* – خضرة

water – *ma* – ماء

At the hotel

room – *el-bít/la chambre* – البيت

bed – *tliq, farsh* – تليق / فراش

mattress – *talmíta* – طلميتة

shower – *douche* – دوش

without shower – *bila douche, sans douche* – بلا دوش

key – *es sarrout/la clef* – السروت

blanket – *ghta'/couverture* – غطاء

sheet – *izar/le drap* – أزار

corridor – *couloir* – كولوار

noise – *sda'* – صداع

At the hotel – a few requests and complaints

Can I see the room, please? – *Afak, mumkin nshouf el bít* – عفاك ممكن نشوف البيت

The water's off – *El ma maktou'a* – الماء مقطوع

There's no hot water – *El-ma skhoun ma ka'insh* – الماء سخون ماكاينش

Excuse me, are there any towels? – *Afak ka'in foutet* – عفاك كاين فوطاط

Could you bring us some towels? – *Mumkin tjíbilna foutet* – ممكن تجيب النا فوطاط

The washbasin's blocked – *El lavabo makhnouk* – الاڤابو مخنوقة

The window doesn't close – *Esh sherajim ma yetsidoush* – الشراجم مايتسدوش

Can you change the light bulb? – *Mumkin tebedil el bawla* – ممكن تبدل البولة

The toilet flush doesn't work – *La chasse ma tekhdemsh* – لاشاس ماخدامش

There's a lot of noise – *Ka'in sda' bezef* – كاين صداع بزاف

Can I change rooms? – *Mumkin nebedil el bít* – ممكن نبدل البيت

On the road

Where is the bus station? – *Fayn kayin maHata diyal kíran?* – فين كاين المحطة ديال الكران

Where is the *CTM* bus station? – *Fayn kayin mHata diyal Saytayem?* –
فين كاين المحطة ديال الستيام

road – *tríq* – طريق

street – *zanqa* – زنقة

neighbourhood, also street – *derb* – درب

bridge – *qantra* – قنطرة

straight ahead – *níshan* – نيشان

to the right/left – *ila l-yemin/sh-shimal* – الى اليمن / الى اليسر

turn at the corner – *dour fil-qent* – دور في القنت

wheel – *rwída* – رويدة

Public transport

aeroplane – *tayyara* – الطيارة

bus – *tobís, Hafila* – طوبيس / حافلة

inter-city bus – *kar* (pl *kíran*) – كار / كيران

customs – *díwana* – ديوانة

express service – *sarí', mosta'jal, rapide* – سريع

luggage – *Hwayaj, baqaj* – حوايج

porter – *Hamal* – حمال

ticket – *bitaqa*, also *warqa* (lit 'paper') – ورقة

train – *qitar* – قطار

How much is the ticket? – *Aysh Hal taman diyal warqa?* – ابش حال الثمن ديال ورقة ؟

I didn't understand – *Ma fehimtiksh* – مافهمتكش

Speak slowly please – *Tekellem bishweyya min fedlek* – تكلم بشوية من فضلك

Could you write that down please? – *'Afak, uktebhu liya* – عفاك اكتب لي

Tachelhit

A few handy expressions to help you function in a village in the High Atlas, plus some topographic words to help you understand the maps. Note that Arabic and French words for numbers are generally understood.

Greetings and things

How are you? (woman/man) – *La bes darim? La bes darik?*

Fine thanks – *La bes*

Please – *Allah yarhum el welidín/'afek /mardi el welidín*

Thank you – *Barak Allaw fík*

Thanks (responding to congratulations) – *el agoub alík*

Yes / No – *ayer, wakha / oho*

Travelling around

Is Aremd near here? – *Aremd iqarreb zeghí?*

near/far – *iqarreb/yagoug*

It's on the right/on the left – *foufessí/fozlemad*

On your right/on your left – *foufessínek/fozelmadnek*

Go straight ahead – *Zayid goud/níshen*

On foot – *Fudár*

How far is it on foot? – *Mishta nugharas aylen fudár?*

How long will it take me to get there on foot? – *Mishta el waqt ayikhsen afade adrouHagh fudár?*

30 mins/one hour/two hours – *nus sa'a/sa'a/sa'atayn*

Where is Mohammed the guide's house? – *Mani eghtilla teguemí en Mhamid le guide?*

Can you take me to Mohammed's house? – *Izd imkin aystitmellet?*

mule – *asserdoun* (m), *tasserdount* (f)

How much is it to rent a mule? – *Mishta izkar lekra nesserdoun?*

When does the minibus leave for Marrakech? – *Melouqt arrifough minibus ne Maraksh?*

In an hour? In two hours? – *Zeghík yan sa'a? Zeghík sa'atayn?*

How long does it take? – *Mishta fra naruh?*

In the village

Can we camp here? – *Izd imkin enkhayim ghí?*

Can we find a room to rent here? – *Izd imkin anaf kra la chambre ghí?*

How much for the night? – *Mishta iyad?*

In the shop

Please, do you have – *'afek, íz daroun*
Do you have – *kre (particle to make question)*
Can we buy – *'afek, íz imkin edsagh*
Please give me – *'afek, fkíyí*
bread – *aghroum*
eggs – *tiglay*
Sidi Ali bottled water – *amen Sidi Ali*
salt – *tisent*
meat – *tifiyí*
onions – *azelim*
potatoes – *betata*
tomatoes – *ma'tísha*
almonds – *louz*
walnuts – *guirga'a*
a little – *ímík*
a lot – *agoudí*

Expressions of time

today – *ghassa*
dawn – *zíg sbaH*
tomorrow – *azga*
day after tomorrow – *nefouzga*
next week – *símana yedísoudan*
yesterday – *idgam*

Some numbers

one – *yen*	eight – *tem*
two – *sín*	nine – *tza*
three – *krad*	ten – *mrawet*
four – *koz*	eleven – *yen de mrawet*
five – *smous*	twelve – *sín de mrawet*
six – *sddes*	twenty – *ashrínt*
seven – *sa*	one hundred – *míya*

Landscape words

Tachelhit is given first to help you identify the meanings of the terms found on the maps

adrar – mountain
afella – summit
agdal, aguedal – grazing land (also a garden in Marrakech)
agharas – path, track
aghbalou (pl *ighboula*) – spring (*taghbalout* – small spring)
aghoulid – steep slope
agrour – enclosure
aguelmane – lake
aït – lit 'the people of'
ahir (pl *iheren*) – slow flowing spring
almou – pasture

amen – water
aourir – hill
aserdoun – mule
asif – river which dries up in summer
azaghar – plateau (pl *izghwar*)
azib – shepherd's shelter
azrou – rock
douar – village
ifri – cave
ighil – arm, by extension long mountain
ighir – shoulder, rocky shoulder of mountain
ighzer – ravine
imi – mouth, hole
kerkour – cairn
moussem – annual festival
taddart – house
tagadirt – fortified granary
talat – ravine
tamda – lake
targa – irrigation channel
tighermt – fortified house
tiguimine – house
timzguida – mosque
tizi – moutain pass
taourirt – (pron tawrirt) hill
taslit – fiancée
unzar – rain
And finally, some words for beautiful: *ifulkí* (m) *tfulkí* (f)

French and Spanish

English	French	Spanish
hello	salut	hola
good morning	bonjour	buenos días
good afternoon/evening/night	bonsoir/bonne nuit	buenas tardes/noches
goodbye	au revoir/ciao	adiós/chao
see you later	à tout à l'heure	hasta luego
Pleased to meet you	enchanté(e)	encantado/a
how are you?	comment allez-vous?	¿qué tal?
fine, thankyou	très bien, merci	muy bien, gracias
yes	oui	sí
no	non	no
please	s'il vous plaît	por favor
excuse me	s'il vous plaît/excusez-moi	con permiso
I do not understand	je ne comprends pas	no entiendo
Speak slowly please	parlez lentement s'il vous plaît	hable despacio por favor

English	French	Spanish
Do you speak English?	Parlez-vous anglais	¿Habla usted inglés?
What is your name?	Comment vous appellez-vous?	¿Cómo se llama?
How do you say ...?	Comment est-ce qu'on dit ...?	¿Cómo se dice ...?
What is this called?	Comment ça s'appelle?	¿Cómo se llama esto?

Some basic vocabulary and phrases

toilet/bathroom	les toilettes/la salle de bain	los servicios/el baño
where are the toilets?	où sont les toilettes?	¿dónde están los servicios/está el baño?
police/policeman	la police	la policía
hotel	hôtel, auberge	el hotel, la pensión
youth hostel	auberge de jeunesse	albergue turístico juvenil
restaurant/fast food	le restaurant/le snack	el restaurante
post office	les PTT, la poste	los correos
stamps	des timbres poste	los sellos
corner grocery	l'épicerie	la tienda
market	le marché	el mercado
bank	la banque	el banco
ATM machine	GAB guichet automatique	el cajero automático
bureau de change	le bureau de change	la casa de cambio
notes	les billets de banque	los billetes
coins	les pièces de monnaie	las monedas
do you have change?	est-ce que vous avez de la monnaie?	¿tiene cambio?
cash	du cash/du liquide	el efectivo

Meals

breakfast	petit déjeuner	el desayuno
lunch	le déjeuner	el almuerzo
dinner	le dîner	la cena
meal	le repas	la comida
without meat	sans viande	sin carne
drink	la boisson	la bebida
mineral water	l'eau minérale	el agua mineral
fizzy drink	une boisson gazeuse	la gaseosa/el refresco
wine	le vin	el vino
beer	la bière	la cerveza
dessert	le dessert	el postre
without sugar	sans sucre	sin azúcar

Some useful adjectives

French and Spanish adjectives have masculine and feminine forms, which correspond to noun genders.

English	French	Spanish
far	loin	lejos
hot	chaud/chaude	caliente (liquid)
		hace calor (temperature)
cold	froid/froide	frío/fría
that's great	c'est super	¡qué maravilla!
beautiful	beau/belle	hermoso/hermosa

Travelling around

on the left/right	à gauche/à droite	a la izquierda/a la derecha
straight on	tout droit	derecho/todo recto
first/second street	la première/deuxième rue	la primera/segunda
on the right	à droite	calle a la derecha
to walk	marcher	caminar/andar
bus station	la gare routière	la terminal
town bus/inter city coach	le bus/le car	el bus/el autobus
city bus stop	l'arrêt (des buses)	la parada
ticket office	le guichet	la taquilla
train station	la gare (de l'ONCF)	la estación de
(Moroccan railways)		ferrocarril
train	le train	el tren
airport	l'aéroport	el aeropuerto
airplane	l'avion	el avión
first/second class	première/deuxième classe	primera/segunda clase
ticket (return)	le billet (aller-retour)	el billete (de ida y vuelta)
ferry/boat	le ferry/le navire	el ferry/el barco
a hire car	une voiture de location	un coche alquilado

Accommodation

room	une chambre	el cuarto, la habitación
I'd like to see the room	J'aimerais voir la chambre	Me gustaría ver el cuarto
with two beds	avec deux petits lits	con dos camas
with private bathroom	avec salle de bain	con baño
hot/cold water	de l'eau chaude/froide	agua caliente/fría
there's no hot water	il n'y a pas d'eau chaude	no hay agua caliente
noisy	bruyant	ruidoso
(there's a lot of noise)	(il y a beaucoup de bruit)	(hay mucho ruido)
to make up/clean the room	arranger/nettoyer	limpiar el cuarto/
	la chambre	la habitación
sheets/pillows	des draps/des oreillers	las sábanas/la almohadas
blankets	des couvertures	las mantas/cobijas
clean/dirty towels	des serviettes propres/sales	toallas limpias/sucias
loo paper	le papier hygiénique	el papel higiénico

Health

chemist/all night chemist	la pharmacie/	la farmacia
	pharmacie de garde	
doctor	le médecin	el médico

English	French	Spanish
Do you have the number of a doctor ?	Avez-vous le numéro de téléphone d'un médecin?	¿Tiene el número de teléfono de un médico?
emergency medical services	la SAMU	las urgencias
stomach	l'estomac	el estómago
fever/sweat	la fièvre/la sueur	la fiebre/el sudor
diarrohea	la diarrhée	la diarrea
blood	le sang	la sangre
headache	un mal de tête	un dolor de cabeza
condoms	les préservatifs	los condones
contraceptive pill	la pillule	la píldora anticonceptiva
period/towels	la règle/serviette hygiénique	la regla/las toallas sanitarias
contact lenses	les lentilles de contact	los lentes de contacto

Numbers

one	un	uno
two	deux	dos
three	trois	tres
four	quatre	cuatro
five	cinq	cinco
six	six	seis
seven	sept	siete
eight	huit	ocho
nine	neuf	nueve
ten	dix	diez

Days of the week

Monday	lundi	lunes
Tuesday	mardi	martes
Wednesday	mercredi	miércoles
Thursday	jeudi	jueves
Friday	vendredi	viernes
Saturday	samedi	sábado
Sunday	dimanche	domingo

Expressions of time

today	aujourd'hui	hoy
yesterday	hier	ayer
tomorrow	demain	mañana
day	le jour	el día
morning	le matin	la mañana
midday	midi	mediodía
evening	le soir	la tarde
night/tonight	la nuit/ce soir	la noche/esta noche
hour	une heure	una hora
in half an hour	dans une demie heure	en una media hora
later	plus tard	más tarde

Food and cooking glossary

A
Amlou Runny 'butter' from argan kernels
Arganier Tree producing an almond-like nut. The kernel of the nut produces the highly valued argan oil

B
Beghir Thick pancakes often served for breakfast
Bestila Elaborate sweet and sour pie. made of alternating layers of filo-pastry and egg, pigeon, and crushed almonds. Speciality of Fès
Bissara Bean and pea soup, workingman's breakfast
Briouet Filo pastry envelopes, filled with crushed nuts and basted in olive oil, then dipped in honey
Brochettes Kebabs made with tiny pieces of liver, meat and fat

C
Chermoula Marinade sauce
Couscous Steamed semolina made from durum wheat, heaped with meat and vegetables. Couscous may also be served with nuts, dates, raisins, sugar and milk for dessert. In the countryside, couscous is made from barley

F
Fliou Peppermint, also used in tea preparations

H
Harcha Thick round unleavened 'bread', popular for breakfast
Harira Chickpea and mutton soup, especially popular when breaking the fast in Ramadhan

K
Kaâb el-ghizal Gazelles' horns. Traditional marzipan-filled pastry
Kahoua Coffee
Kefta Minced meat

Khliaâ Preserved meat (dried, boiled). Fr 'viande boucanée')

L
Likama Mint
Luiza Verbena herbal tea

M
Mahchi (or **mo'ammar**) Stuffed (chicken, vegetables, etc)
Mechoui Barbecued meat
Mqali Meat dishes simmered with sauce reduced rapidly on high flame at end
Mouhallabiya Milk pudding

N
Na'na Mint, essential for preparing tea, also called 'likama' The best mint is produced in Meknès

O
Orz bil-bahiya Paella

Q
Qa'ida Tradition – vital to any meal prepared for guests in a Moroccan home

R
Ra's el Hanout (lit. 'master of the shop') Special spice mix
Roumi (lit. 'from Rome). Adjective designating things foreign or modern, especially with regard to food and recipes. Used in opposition to things 'bildi' (qv), indigenous and traditional

S
Seksou (Amz) Couscous, qv

T
Tajine Moroccan stew traditionally cooked slowly in a clay pot on a brasero
Tajine barkouk Sweet and sour prune and mutton stew

Z
Zitoun Olives
Zit el oud Olive oil

Index → Entries in **bold** *refer to maps*

Advertisers' index

Credits

Footprint credits
Project Editor: Jo Williams
Layout and production: Emma Bryers
Cover and colour section: Pepi Bluck
Maps: Kevin Feeney

Managing Director: Andy Riddle
Content Director: Patrick Dawson
Publisher: Alan Murphy
Publishing Managers: Felicity Laughton,
Jo Williams, Nicola Gibbs
Marketing and Partnerships Director:
Liz Harper
Marketing Executive: Liz Eyles
Trade Product Manager: Diane McEntee
Account Managers: Paul Bew, Tania Ross
Advertising: Renu Sibal, Elizabeth Taylor
Finance: Phil Walsh

Photography credits
Front cover: Julian Love / awl-images.com
Back cover: Romain Cintract / hemis.fr

Colour section
Page i: Julius Honnor
Page ii: Julius Honnor
Page vi: Julius Honnor,
xNstAbLe / Shutterstock.com
Page vii: Julius Honnor
Page viii: Libor Píška / Shutterstock.com
Page iv: Julian Love / awl-images.com
Page v: Wigbert Röth / imagebroker / Alamy,
Galyna Andrushko

Printed in India by Replika Press Pvt Ltd

Publishing information
Footprint Morocco
6th edition
© Footprint Handbooks Ltd
May 2012

ISBN: 978 1 907263 31 6
CIP DATA: A catalogue record for this book
is available from the British Library

® Footprint Handbooks and the Footprint
mark are a registered trademark of
Footprint Handbooks Ltd

Published by Footprint
6 Riverside Court
Lower Bristol Road
Bath BA2 3DZ, UK
T +44 (0)1225 469141
F +44 (0)1225 469461
footprinttravelguides.com

Distributed in the USA by Globe Pequot
Press, Guilford, Connecticut

Footprint Mini Atlas
Morocco

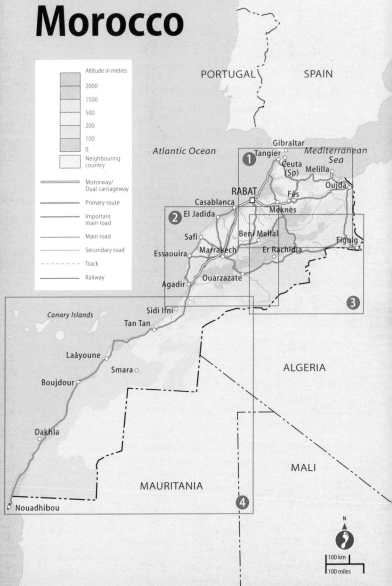

PORTUGAL

SPAIN

Altitude in metres

2000
1500
500
200
100
0

Neighbouring country

Motorway/ Dual carriageway

Primary route

Important main road

Main road

Secondary road

Track

Railway

Atlantic Ocean

Gibraltar

Tangier

Mediterranean Sea

Ceuta (Sp)

Melilla

RABAT

Oujda

Casablanca

Fès

El Jadida

Meknès

Safi

Beni Mellal

Essaouira

Marrakech

Er Rachidia

Figuig

Agadir

Ouarzazate

Sidi Ifni

Canary Islands

Tan Tan

Laâyoune

Smara

ALGERIA

Boujdour

Dakhla

MALI

MAURITANIA

Nouadhibou

N

100 km

100 miles

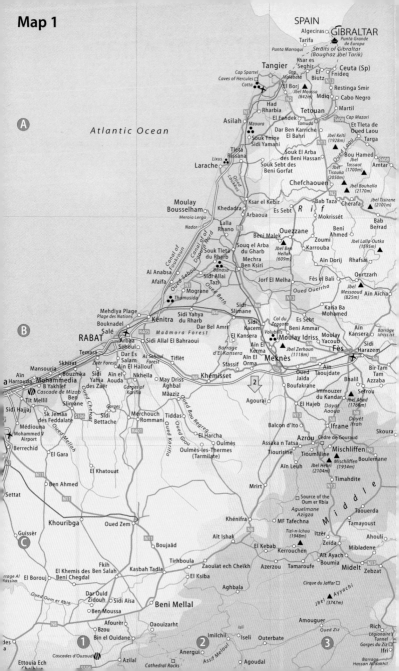

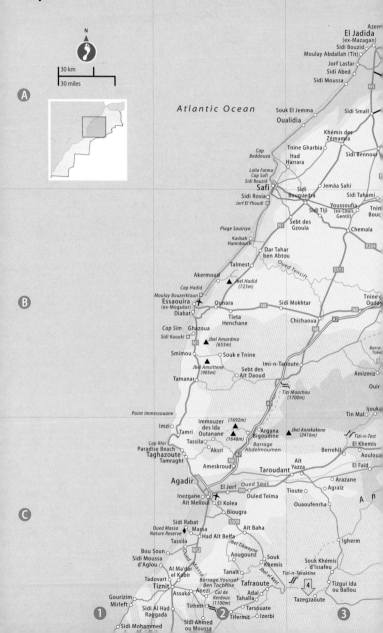

Map 2

N

30 km
30 miles

Atlantic Ocean

El Jadida
(ex-Mazagan)   Azem
Sidi Bouzid
Moulay Abdallah (Tit)
Jorf Lasfar
Sidi Abed
Sidi Moussa

Souk El Jemma   Sidi Smail
Oualidia

Khémis des
Zémamra
Tnine Gharbia
Cap   Had   Sidi Bennour
Beddouza   Harrara

Lalla Fatma   Jemâa Sahi
Cap Safi   Sidi
Sidi Bouzid   Bouguedra
Safi   Sidi Tahami
Sidi Rosia   Youssoufia
Jorf El Yhoudi □   Sidi Tiji   (ex-Louis   Tnin
Gentil)   Bouc
Sebt des
Gzoula   Chemaïa
Plage Souiriya
Kasbah   R204
Hamidouch
Dar Tahar
ben Abtou   *Oued Tensift*   S511
Talmest
Akermoud   ▲ *Jbel Hadid*
Cap Hadid   (725m)   Tnine
Moulay Bouzerktoun □   Sidi Mokhtar   Ouda
Essaouira   Ounara   N8
(ex-Mogador) ✈
Diabat   Tleta   Chichaoua   A7
Henchane   N8
Cap Sim   Ghazoua
Sidi Kaouki □   ▲ *Jbel Amardma*   Imi-n-Tanoute   Amizmiz
(655m)   Ouir
Smimou   Souk e Tnine
▲ *Jbel Amsittene*   Sebt des   *Barra*
(905m)   Aït Daoud   *Take*
Tamanar
Tizi Maachou   Ijouka
(1700m)   Tin Mal
Point Immessouane
Imzi   Immouzer *(1692m)*   *Tizi-n-Test*
des Ida   ▲ *Jbel Anrekakene*
Tamri   Outanane   (2410m)   El Khemis
▲ *(1648m)* ○ Argana
Tassila   Bigoudine   Aoulou
Cap Rhir   Aksri   *Barrage*   Berrehil   El Faïd
Paradise Beach   *Abdelmoumen*
Taghazoute   Ameskroud   Aït   Arazane
Tamraght   **Taroudant** Yazza
Agadir   El Jorf *Oued Sous* N9   Agraïz
Inezgane ✈   Ouled Teïma   Tioute
Aït Melloul □ El Kolea   Ouaoufenrha   A n
Biougra
Sidi Rabat   Aït Baha
Oued Massa ♦ Massa   S509
Nature Reserve Had Aït Belfa   Igherm
Tassila   *Jbel Tikwayne*
Bou Soun   Aougounz   Souk
Sidi Moussa   Khemis
d'Aglou   Tanalt   Souk Khémis
Al Ma'dar   d'Issafeu
el Kabir   *Barrage Youssef*   *Tizi-n-Taraktine*
Tadovart   *Ben Tachfine*   Adai   Tizgui Ida
Tiznit Assaka Anezi *Col de* Tahalla ↓ 4   ou Ballou
Kerdous   Tarsouate
Gourizim   Tirhmi *(1100m)*   Izerbi   Tazegzaoûte
Mirleft
Sidi Al Had   Tifernit
Raggada   Sidi Ahmed
ou Moussa
Sidi Mohammed

1   2   3

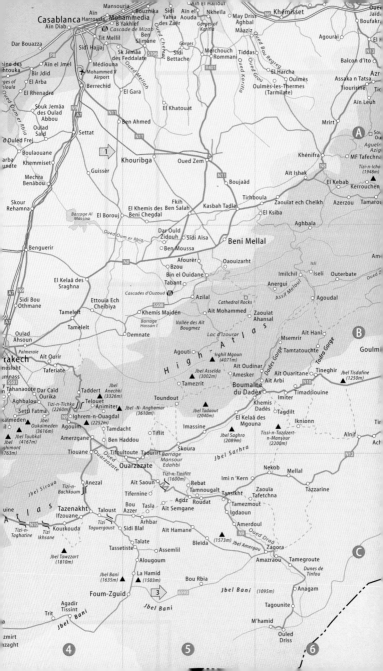

Map 4

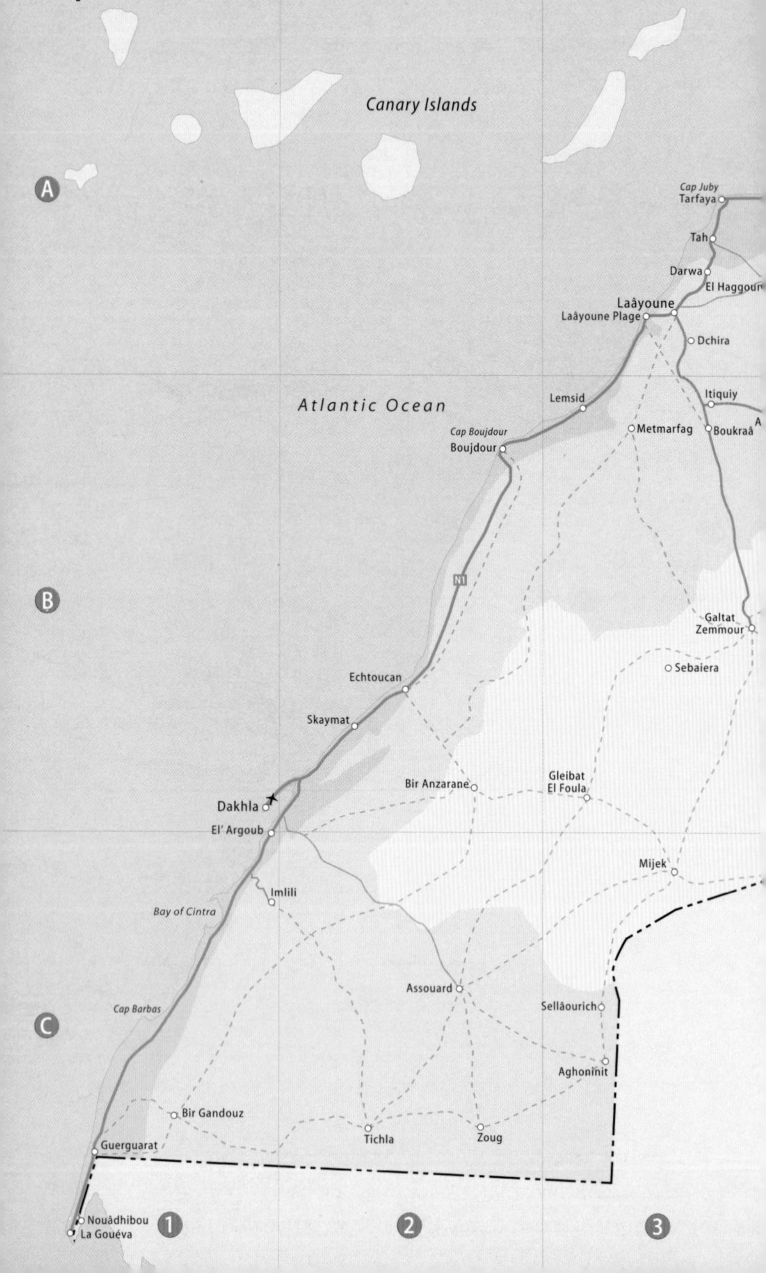

Canary Islands

Atlantic Ocean

Cap Juby
Tarfaya
Tah
Darwa
El Haggour
Laâyoune
Laâyoune Plage
Dchira
Itiquiy
Lemsid
Metmarfag
Boukraâ
A
Cap Boujdour
Boujdour
Galtat
Zemmour
Sebaiera
N1
Echtoucan
Skaymat
Bir Anzarane
Gleibat
El Foula
Mijek
Dakhla
El' Argoub
Imlili
Bay of Cintra
Assouard
Sellâourich
Cap Barbas
Aghoniînit
Bir Gandouz
Tichla
Zoug
Guerguarat
Nouâdhibou
La Gouéva

A

B

C

1

2

3

Index